SCRIPTURES AND SECTARIANISM

Scriptures and Sectarianism

Essays on the Dead Sea Scrolls

John J. Collins

WILLIAM B. EERDMANS PUBLISHING COMPANY
GRAND RAPIDS, MICHIGAN

William B. Eerdmans Publishing Company
2140 Oak Industrial Dr. NE, Grand Rapids, Michigan 49505
www.eerdmans.com

© 2014 Mohr Siebeck, Tübingen, Germany
All rights reserved
This edition published 2016 by
Wm. B. Eerdmans Publishing Company

ISBN 978-0-8028-7314-9

Library of Congress Cataloging-in-Publication Data

Names: Collins, John J. (John Joseph), 1946–   author.
Title: Scriptures and sectarianism : essays on the Dead Sea Scrolls / John J. Collins.
Description: Grand Rapids : Eerdmans Publishing Co., 2016. | Originally published: Tübingen :
   Mohr Siebeck, 2014. | Includes bibliographical references and index.
Identifiers: LCCN 2016041302 | ISBN 9780802873149 (pbk. : alk. paper)
Subjects: LCSH: Dead Sea scrolls. | Bible. Old Testament—Criticism, interpretation, etc. |
   Dead Sea scrolls—Relation to the New Testament. | Dead Sea scrolls—Criticism,
   interpretation, etc. | Messiah—Biblical teaching. | Eschatology, Jewish. | Judaism—Doctrines.
Classification: LCC BM487 .C5713 2016 | DDC 296.1/55—dc23
   LC record available at https://lccn.loc.gov/2016041302

Contents

Preface	x
Acknowledgments	xi

1. Introduction. What Have We Learned from the Dead Sea Scrolls? 1
  The origin of the collection 1
  The Scrolls and the Bible 4
  The phenomenon of rewritten scriptures 5
  A biblical canon? 6
  The Scrolls and Judaism 8
  The Scrolls and Christianity 12
  Conclusion 16

Part One
Scripture and Interpretation

2. The Transformation of the Torah in Second Temple Judaism 19
  The transformation of Torah 21
  Ancestral law in the Hellenistic period 25
  Antiochus Epiphanes 28
  The *Temple Scroll* and *Jubilees* 31
  Halakah and Sectarianism 34

3. Changing Scripture 35
  The case of Deuteronomy 35
  The second century BCE 40
  Rewritten scriptures 42
  Jubilees 44
  The *Temple Scroll* 47
  The question of fraud 50

4. Tradition and Innovation in the Dead Sea Scrolls 51
  The nature of the Scrolls collection 52
  The sectarian ideology 55

Pseudepigrapha in the Scrolls	56
The Torah rewritten	59
The sectarian view of revelation	60
The role of the Teacher	61
An oral tradition?	62
A distinctive view of tradition	65
Scripture and interpretation	66
Conclusion	68
5. The Interpretation of Genesis in the Dead Sea Scrolls	**70**
The earliest interpretations	71
Ben Sira	73
Wisdom texts in the Scrolls	77
4QInstruction	78
The *Instruction on the Two Spirits*	83
Conclusion	84
6. The Interpretation of Psalm 2	**87**
The relation between 2 Samuel 7 and Psalm 2 in 4Q174	89
The messianic interpretation of Psalm 2	90
Psalm 2 in the Pseudepigrapha	92
The *Psalms of Solomon*	93
The *Similitudes of Enoch*	95
4 Ezra 13	97
The Scrolls	99
The *Florilegium* again	101
7. The Book of Daniel and the Dead Sea Scrolls	**102**
Explicit citations	102
Allusions to Daniel in sectarian literature	104
Texts related to Daniel	106
The *Prayer of Nabonidus* (4QPrNab)	107
The Pseudo-Daniel texts	109
The *Aramaic Apocalypse*	111
The *Four Kingdoms Text*	112
Conclusion	114

Part Two
History and Sectarianism

8. Historiography in the Dead Sea Scrolls — 119
   Apocalyptic historiography — 120
   The *Pesharim* — 123
   Historiographical texts among the Scrolls — 126
   The so-called "annalistic lists" — 128
   Conclusion — 132

9. Reading for History in the Dead Sea Scrolls — 133
   The *Damascus Document* — 136
   The *Hodayot* — 140
   The *Pesharim* — 141
   Conclusion — 148

10. "Enochic Judaism" and the Sect of the Dead Sea Scrolls — 150
   The Essenes — 151
   The Hasidim — 152
   A split in the emerging movement — 154
   "The Qumran community" — 158
   The Essenes revisited — 159
   Enochic Judaism and the Scrolls — 160
   Conclusion — 163

11. Sectarian Consciousness in the Dead Sea Scrolls — 164
   The *yahad* — 166
   Creation and election — 170
   4QInstruction — 171

Part Three
The Sectarian Worldview

12. Covenant and Dualism in the Dead Sea Scrolls — 179
   Covenantal nomism — 179
   A sectarian covenant? — 180
   The Two Spirits — 182
   Persian dualism — 186
   The provenance of the *Instruction* — 188
   Covenant and dualism — 189

13. The Angelic Life — 195
Angelic afterlife — 195
Angelic afterlife in the Scrolls — 197
Fellowship with the angels in this life — 199
The *yahad* — 200
The *Songs of the Sabbath Sacrifice* — 202
Personal transformation — 204
Permanent or temporary transformation — 208
Resurrection and transformation — 209

14. The Essenes and the Afterlife — 212
Josephus and Hippolytus — 212
Essene eschatology according to Josephus — 217
Does Josephus reflect a Semitic belief? — 219
The evidence of the rule books — 220
Hippolytus and the Scrolls — 222
Conclusion — 226

15. Prayer and the Meaning of Ritual in the Dead Sea Scrolls — 227
The meaninglessness of ritual? — 227
Prayer in Dead Sea Scrolls — 230
Discourse and ritual in covenant renewal — 233
Confession and ablution — 234
Conclusion — 239

16. The Eschatologizing of Wisdom in the Dead Sea Scrolls — 241
The eschatology of *4QInstruction* — 242
Engraved is the ordinance — 244
An inheritance of glory — 246
Wisdom and eschatology — 248
The derivation of eschatological wisdom — 250
4QInstruction and the Dead Sea sect — 252

Epilogue

17. The Dead Sea Scrolls and the New Testament. The Case of the Suffering Servant — 257
The Essenes and the New Testament — 258
A foretaste of Christianity? — 259

Debate renewed in the 1990's	261
The "suffering servant"	263
The servant in the *Hodayot*	264
The *Self-Exaltation Hymn*	267
4Q541	267
Servant and messiah?	268
The Servant and Jesus	268
A common scripture	270
Bibliography	273
Index of Ancient Names and Sobriquets	307
Index of Modern Authors	309
Index of Scripture and Other Ancient Sources	317

Preface

The essays in this volume were written over a decade, roughly 2003 to 2013. The introductory essay, "What have we learned from the Dead Sea Scrolls?" has not been published in this form before. The essays are grouped in three clusters. The first deals with the authority of Scripture and the various ways in which it is interpreted. The second deals with historiography, the emergence of the sect and its relation to the Enochic writings and *4QInstruction*. The third cluster deals with aspects of the sectarian worldview: covenant and dualism, the angelic world, the afterlife, prayer and ritual, and wisdom. Finally, an epilogue consisting of one essay illustrates the relevance of the Scrolls for early Christianity by discussing the case of the Suffering Servant.

These essays are intended to complement my other writings on the Dead Sea Scrolls: *Apocalypticism in the Dead Sea Scrolls* (London: Routledge, 1997); *The Scepter and the Star. Messianism in Light of the Dead Sea Scrolls* (2nd ed.; Grand Rapids: Eerdmans, 2010); *Beyond the Qumran Community. The Sectarian Movement of the Dead Sea Scrolls* (Grand Rapids: Eerdmans, 2010); and *The Dead Sea Scrolls. A Biography* (Princeton: Princeton University Press, 2012). I have not included in this collection essays that are reworked in one or other of those books, but some occasional overlap is inevitable.

I would like to thank Jörg Frey, with whom I have co-chaired a seminar at SNTS on the Scrolls and the New Testament for five years, for accepting the volume for publication in WUNT, Mark Lester for preparing the bibliography and James Nati for compiling the indices.

Acknowledgments

My thanks are due to **E. J. Brill of Leiden** for permission to republish the following essays:

"The Transformation of the Torah in Second Temple Judaism," *Journal for the Study of Judaism* 43 (2012) 455–74.

"Tradition and Innovation in the Dead Sea Scrolls," in Sarianna Metso, Hindy Najman, and Eileen Schuller, eds., *The Dead Sea Scrolls. Transmission of Traditions and Production of Texts* (STDJ 92; Leiden: Brill, 2010) 1–23.

"Sectarian Consciousness in the Dead Sea Scrolls," in Lynn LiDonnici and Andrea Lieber, eds., *Heavenly Tablets. Interpretation, Identity and Tradition in Ancient Judaism* (JSJSup 119; Leiden: Brill, 2007) 177–92.

"'Enochic Judaism' and the Sect of the Dead Sea Scrolls," in Gabriele Boccaccini and John J. Collins, eds., *The Early Enoch Literature* (JSJSup 121; Leiden: Brill, 2007) 283–99.

"The Interpretation of Psalm 2," in Florentino García Martínez, ed., *Echoes from the Caves: Qumran and the New Testament* (STDJ 85; Leiden: Brill, 2009) 49–66.

"Prayer and the Meaning of Ritual in the Dead Sea Scrolls," in Jeremy Penner, Ken M. Penner and Cecilia Wassen, eds., *Prayer and Poetry in the Dead Sea Scrolls and Related Literature* (STDJ 98; Leiden: Brill, 2011) 69–85.

"Reading for History in the Dead Sea Scrolls," *Dead Sea Discoveries* 18 (2011) 295–315.

"Historiography in the Dead Sea Scrolls," *Dead Sea Discoveries* 19 (2012) 159–76.

"The Essenes and the Afterlife," in Florentino García Martínez, Annette Steudel and Eibert Tigchelaar, eds., *From 4QMMT to Resurrection. Mélanges qumraniens en homage à Émile Puech* (STDJ 61; Leiden: Brill, 2006) 35–53.

"The Interpretation of Genesis in the Dead Sea Scrolls," in Akio Moriya and Gohei Hata, eds., *Pentateuchal Traditions in the Late Second Temple Period. Proceedings of the International Workshop in Tokyo, August 28–31, 2007)* (JSJSup 158; Leiden: Brill, 2012) 157–75.

"The Eschatologizing of Wisdom in the Dead Sea Scrolls," in J. J. Collins, G.E. Sterling and Ruth Clements, eds., *Sapiential Perspectives. Wisdom Literature in Light of the Dead Sea Scrolls* (Leiden: Brill, 2004) 49–66.

To **Walter de Gruyter, Berlin**, for permission to republish the following:

"Changing Scripture," in Hanne von Weissenberg, Juha Pakkala and Marko Marttila, ed., *Changes in Scripture. Rewriting and Interpreting Authoritative Traditions in the Second Temple Period* (BZAW 419; Berlin: de Gruyter, 2011) 23–45.

"The Angelic Life," in Turid Karlsen Seim and Jorunn Økland, eds., *Metamorphoses. Resurrection, Body and Transformative Practices in Early Christianity* (Ekstasis 1; Berlin: de Gruyter, 2009) 291–310.

To **Vandenhoeck & Ruprecht of Göttingen** for permission to republish

"The Book of Daniel and the Dead Sea Scrolls," in Nóra Dávid, Armin Lange, Kristin De Troyer, and Shani Tzoref, eds., *The Hebrew Bible in Light of the Dead Sea Scrolls* (FRLANT 239; Göttingen: Vandenhoeck & Ruprecht, 2011) 203–17.

And to **The Society of Biblical Literature, Atlanta**, for permission to republish

"The Dead Sea Scrolls and the New Testament. The Case of the Suffering Servant," in Andrew B. McGowan and Kent H. Richards, eds., *Method and Meaning. Essays on New Testament Interpretation in Honor of Harold W. Attridge* (Atlanta: SBL, 2011) 279–95.

The essay "Covenant and Dualism in the Dead Sea Scrolls" was presented at an Orion Seminar at the Hebrew University in Jerusalem in May, 2013.

CHAPTER ONE

Introduction.
What Have We Learned from the Dead Sea Scrolls?

It is probably fair to say that the Dead Sea Scrolls have commanded more attention in the last sixty years or so than any other body of literature related to the Bible. Not all of that attention has been salutary. The Scrolls have been sensationalized and misrepresented; Vatican plots have been alleged; they have been the occasion of bitter controversy over the rights of editors and the obligation to publish primary sources, and they have given rise to at least two lawsuits. Exhibitions of the Scrolls continue reliably to draw thousands of visitors (and letters of complaint from the dissident scholar Norman Golb).[1] It is not unreasonable to ask whether all the fuss is justified, and whether the Scrolls have had an impact on our knowledge of the Bible and its *Umwelt* that is commensurate with the controversies they have generated. Now that the entire corpus is finally in the public domain, the time seems ripe to take stock and assess the significance of what has been called the greatest archeological discovery of the twentieth century.

The origin of the collection

At the outset, it may be well to recall some basic facts about the corpus. Fragments of approximately 930 manuscripts were recovered from the caves around Qumran. 750 of these are in Hebrew, 150 in Aramaic and 27 in Greek.[2] Their dates have been estimated, on the basis of paleography, to range from the third century BCE to the first century CE. They include all the books we know from the Hebrew Bible with the exception of Esther, but a huge range of literature besides. Nearly all the texts recovered from the caves are literary, as opposed to documentary, texts. Before the discovery of the Scrolls we had no surviving literature in Hebrew or Aramaic from the land of Israel between the mid-second century BCE and the mid-second century CE. The Scrolls, then, have the potential to shed unprecedented light on Judaism around the turn of the era.

---

[1] On the reception of the Scrolls and the controversies they have engendered see my book *The Dead Sea Scrolls. A Biography* (Princeton: Princeton University Press, 2012) especially 213–42.

[2] For a comprehensive inventory see Emanuel Tov et al., *The Texts from the Judaean Desert. Indices and An Introduction to the Discoveries in the Judaean Desert Series* (DJD 39; Oxford: Clarendon, 2002).

But how far are these Scrolls representative of the Judaism of their time? Since the initial batch of scrolls included a rule for a sectarian religious community, the immediate assumption was that the scrolls had been the property of that community, and were hidden for safekeeping in time of upheaval. This assumption appeared to be confirmed by the excavation at Qumran and the discovery of Cave 4, a mere stone's throw from the site. While no manuscripts were actually found in the ruins, the archeologists found pottery identical to the "scroll-jars" that had been found in Cave 1. Consequently, the corpus of texts recovered from the caves became known as "the library of Qumran," a designation popularized by Frank Moore Cross in his classic account of the scrolls in 1958.[3]

But the idea of a library of this size by the shores of the Dead Sea is anomalous. Libraries were rare in antiquity, although they became somewhat more common in the Hellenistic period. The great palace library of the Assyrian king Asshurbanipal and the famous library of Alexandria were exceptional, and Qumran was a far cry from Alexandria. Libraries were often associated with temples, but these were usually of modest size. The largest known Mesopotamian temple library had about 800 tablets. At the other end of the spectrum, a temple at Edfu in Hellenistic Egypt had a catalogue with merely 35 titles. If indeed the site of Qumran housed a community such as the one described in the *"Manual of Discipline"* or *Community Rule* (1QS), then we should expect that there was some library at the site, since the members were supposed to devote a part of their nights to study (1QS 6:6–7). But it is difficult to believe that a community at this remote location had a library equal to that of the largest Mesopotamian temples.

In the early 1960's, a German scholar, Karl-Heinrich Rengstorff, suggested that the scrolls were the library of the Jerusalem temple.[4] He supposed that the library had been taken out of Jerusalem and hidden in the wilderness in 68 CE, when the priests realized that Jerusalem was doomed. This idea has been defended energetically by Norman Golb.[5] But many of the scrolls are clearly sectarian in character, and are highly critical of the Jerusalem temple and the High Priesthood. There are eleven copies of the sectarian *Community Rule*, seven copies of the Damascus Rule, and six copies of an avowedly separatist *halakhic* document known as 4QMMT, "Some of the Works of the Torah" which sets out the issues on which this sect disagreed with other Jews. The archenemy of the Teacher in the *Pesharim*, or biblical commentaries, is the Wicked Priest, who is universally understood to have been a High Priest. In contrast, only one text, 4Q448, which has been interpreted as a prayer for "Jonathan the King" (probably the Hasmonean king Alexander Jannaeus),

---

[3] Frank Moore Cross, *The Ancient Library of Qumran and Modern Biblical Studies* (Garden City, NY: Doubleday, 1958; 3rd ed.: Sheffield: Sheffield Academic Press, 1995).

[4] K. H. Rengstorff, *Ḥirbet Qumran and the Problem of the Dead Sea Cave Scrolls* (Leiden: Brill, 1963).

[5] Norman Golb, *Who Wrote the Dead Scrolls? The Search for the Secret of Qumran* (New York: Scribner, 1995).

can be construed as positive to the Hasmonean priest-kings, and even that is disputed. It is incomprehensible that the Jerusalem temple would have contained such an archive of sectarian writings, critical of the temple. This problem is not relieved by supposing that the manuscripts came from various libraries in Jerusalem.

My own suggestion on the provenance of the scrolls is bound up with my understanding of the sectarian movement attested in the rule books.[6] Too often, "the Qumran Community" has been regarded by scholars as an isolated, self-sufficient community, cut off from the outside world. But both the *Community Rule* and the *Damascus Document* envision multiple settlements within the same broad movement. The *Community Rule* speaks of a quorum of ten members for an assembly (1QS 6:3,6). The *Damascus Document* speaks of people who live in "camps" according to the order of the land (CD 7:6). The movement is commonly identified with the Essenes, and these too are said to have been spread throughout the land.[7]

The corpus of scrolls found near Qumran has a sectarian character, but is too large and diverse to have been the library of a single settlement. I suggest that these scrolls represent many libraries, but sectarian libraries; the libraries of many settlements of the sect or movement. At the time of the war against Rome, members of the sect from various communities fled to the wilderness, and sought refuge with their brethren, either because of the remoteness of the area or because Qumran was a "motherhouse" as some have proposed.[8] They would have brought their scrolls with them. Hence the multiplicity of rules with minor variations, and the great variety of scribes attested by the handwriting. On this scenario, the scrolls would include the library of the people who lived at Qumran, but also the libraries of many *sectarian* communities that lived elsewhere. Both the sectarian character of the corpus and its internal variety can thus be acknowledged.

To say that the collection has a sectarian character is not to say that all these texts were composed at Qumran. Many of them were copied before the site of Qumran was settled at all. It is not even to say that all of them were composed by members of the sectarian movement, which is still most plausibly identified as the Essenes. As Carol Newsom pointed out twenty years ago, many of the scrolls lack "sectually explicit language" and were shared with other Judeans who were not members of this movement.[9] The Book of Tobit is a case in point. We must reckon then with the

---

[6] John J. Collins, *Beyond the Qumran Community. The Sectarian Movement of the Dead Sea Scrolls* (Grand Rapids: Eerdmans, 2010); "Beyond the Qumran Community: Social Organization in the Dead Sea Scrolls," *DSD* 16 (2009) 351–69.

[7] Philo, *Quod omnis probus liber sit* 75–6; *Apologia pro Iudaeis* (= *Hypothetica*) 1–2 (in Eusebius *PE* 8.6–7); Josephus, *JW* 2.124.

[8] It is also possible that some of the scrolls had been brought to Qumran earlier, at the time of the disturbances after the death of Herod. See Daniel Stökl Ben Ezra, "Old Caves and Young Caves: A Statistical Reevaluation of a Qumran Consensus," *DSD* 14 (2007) 313–33.

[9] Carol A. Newsom, "'Sectually Explicit' Literature from Qumran," in W. H. Propp, B. Halpern and D. N. Freedman, eds., *The Hebrew Bible and Its Interpreters* (Winona Lake, IN: Eisenbrauns, 1990) 167–87.

fact that some of this literature is peculiar to a sect, but also that much of it is not peculiarly sectarian, but part of the literary heritage of Judaism at large.

The Scrolls and the Bible

Perhaps the most obvious area where the Scrolls shed light on Judaism at large concerns the development of the Hebrew Bible.[10] Already in the 1950's William F. Albright and Frank Moore Cross pointed out the existence of different textual traditions.[11] A manuscript of Exodus (4QpaleoExod^m) dated to the middle of the first century BCE (on the basis of paleography) consistently preserves the expansions beyond the Masoretic Text that are known from the Samaritan Pentateuch. It does not, however, appear to have the specifically Samaritan commandment, to build an altar at Mt. Gerizim. A manuscript of the book of Numbers, 4QNum^b, is similar. It also included expansions found in the SP but not in the MT, but it does not contain specifically Samaritan readings. Again, a form of the text that was essentially the same as the Samaritan, but without the special references to Mt. Gerizim, seems to have been circulating in Judea in the first century BCE.

The Scrolls also yielded Hebrew texts of some books that correspond to the Septuagint rather than to the MT, and so might be labeled "proto-LXX." The text of Samuel found in three scrolls from Cave 4 consistently agrees with the Greek where the latter disagrees with the MT. One manuscript (4QSam^a) contains a paragraph that is not found in either the MT or the LXX, but is reflected in the paraphrase of the biblical account by the historian Josephus (*Ant* 6.68–9). An interesting case is provided by the Book of Jeremiah. The Greek text is shorter than the MT by about one eighth. Before the discovery of the Scrolls, it was often thought that the translators had simply abbreviated the book. Two small fragmentary manuscripts, however, attest to a Hebrew form of the "short" text underlying the Greek. Both of these manuscripts (4QJer^b and 4QJer^d) are relatively early, dating from the second century BCE. Two other manuscripts of Jeremiah, however, including one early one (4QJer^a, from the early second century BCE), have the long form of the text known from the MT.

The Scrolls have provided plenty of evidence that the traditional text of the Hebrew Bible, the MT, or rather the proto-MT, was well known already in the last centuries BCE. But it was not the only form of the text. Different editions circulated side by side, much as different English translations of the Bible circulate in the modern world.[12] (The textual differences in the Scrolls, however, are considerably more

---

[10] See especially James C. VanderKam, *The Dead Sea Scrolls and the Bible* (Grand Rapids: Eerdmans, 2012).

[11] Cross, *The Ancient Library of Qumran* (3rd ed.), 121–42.

[12] The existence of variant editions is emphasized especially by Eugene C. Ulrich, *The Dead Sea Scrolls and the Origin of the Bible* (Grand Rapids: Eerdmans, 1999).

substantial than the differences between modern translations, at least in some cases.) The Book of Exodus was part of the Torah of Moses, and was certainly regarded as authoritative. But it was the book that was authoritative, rather than a particular form of the text, just as in a modern context the authority of the book does not depend on the wording of any one translation. For Christians brought up to believe in verbal inspiration, this may come as something of a shock. The actual words of the Bible, even the words of the Pentateuch or Torah, were not definitively fixed in the time of Christ.

The phenomenon of rewritten scriptures

The fluidity of the biblical text is related to another phenomenon that figures prominently in the Dead Sea Scrolls. Beginning about the late third or second century BCE, it became popular to write paraphrases of biblical books, often introducing new ideas in the process.[13] These rewritings could serve various purposes. The Aramaic *Genesis Apocryphon*, one of the initial scrolls found in Qumran Cave 1, is an entertaining account of some episodes of Genesis that includes an expanded description of the beauty of Sarah, wife of Abraham. In other cases, the rewritten scriptures lay claim to the status of revelation, and their relation to the traditional scriptures becomes problematic.

A particularly clear case of rewritten scripture is provided by the *Book of Jubilees*. This text was preserved in full in Ethiopic, and was regarded as scripture in the Ethiopian church. Fragments of the Hebrew original were found at Qumran. It is believed to date from the second century BCE. It is a paraphrase of Genesis and the first part of Exodus, with a definite theological message. The laws of Moses were already observed by the patriarchs in Genesis, and the true calendar was the solar one, with 364 days. *Jubilees*, however, sometimes refers to what had been revealed in "the first Torah," and so it clearly was not trying to replace the traditional Torah, only to supplement and interpret it.[14] Nonetheless, it is cited as an authoritative text in the *Damascus Document*, and it later became canonical in the Ethiopian church.

The situation was different with the *Temple Scroll*. This too was a rewriting of a part of the Torah, but in this case there was no acknowledgement of "the first Torah," and the reformulated laws were presented as divine revelation.[15] The *Temple Scroll*

---

[13] For overviews see Daniel L. Falk, *The Parabiblical Texts. Strategies for Extending the Scriptures* (London and New York: Clark, 2007); Sidnie White Crawford, *Rewriting Scripture in Second Temple Times* (Grand Rapids: Eerdmans, 2008); Molly M. Zahn, "Rewritten Scripture," in Timothy H. Lim and John J. Collins, eds., *The Oxford Handbook of the Dead Sea Scrolls* (Oxford: Oxford University Press, 2010) 323–36.

[14] James C. VanderKam, "Moses Trumping Moses: Making the Book of Jubilees," in S. Metso, H. Najman and E. Schuller, eds., *The Dead Sea Scrolls. Transmission of Traditions and Production of Texts* (Leiden: Brill, 2010) 25–44.

[15] For a recent study of the compositional technique of the *Temple Scroll* see Bernard M. Lev-

does not repeat everything that is found in the laws of the Pentateuch. It does not, for example, include the ten commandments. But for the matters it does address (largely matters relating to the purity of the Temple, but also some laws from Deuteronomy), it claims the highest imaginable authority. When it was first published, some scholars thought that this was "the Torah of Qumran," the special sectarian edition of the Law. In fact, however, citations of the Torah in the Scrolls generally conform to the traditional text, not to the *Temple Scroll*. If the authors of the *Temple Scroll* wanted it to be accepted as the official Torah, they failed. Nonetheless, several copies of it were preserved among the Scrolls.

An even more problematic case is that of a text known as *4QReworked Pentateuch*.[16] This title refers to a set of five fragmentary manuscripts, that were originally thought to pertain to the same text. They are now regarded as five separate compositions. Compared with the MT, all five show major expansions. For example, the "song of Miriam" in Exod 15:21 was filled out in a way that has no parallel in the MT. Material is also rearranged in some cases. There is no indication, however, that this material records a new revelation. The differences over against the MT are typical of the proto-Samaritan tradition. Increasingly, scholars have come to regard these fragments not as "Reworked Pentateuch" or "Rewritten Bible," but simply as a variant edition of the Book of Exodus. Here again it seems that scribes were not bound by any official, standard, form of the text in the last centuries before the turn of the era.

A biblical canon?

Strictly speaking, it is anachronistic to speak of a Bible at Qumran or in the Dead Sea Scrolls. The Bible as we know it had not yet taken its final shape. That did not happen until the late first century CE, or possibly later. Nonetheless, there existed by the first century BCE a corpus of authoritative Scriptures, shared across sectarian lines, even though its extent had not been decided definitively.[17]

Most important in this regard is the testimony of 4QMMT. When a sectarian leader appealed to the High Priest to acknowledge the sectarian interpretation of certain laws, he wrote:

---

inson, *A More Perfect Torah. At the Intersection of Philology and Hermeneutics in Deuteronomy and the Temple Scroll* (Winona Lake: Eisenbrauns, 2013).

[16] Molly M. Zahn, *Rethinking Rewritten Scripture: Composition and Exegesis in the 4QReworked Pentateuch Manuscripts* (Leiden: Brill, 2011).

[17] On the question of the canon see now Timothy H. Lim, *The Formation of the Jewish Canon* (Anchor Yale Bible Reference Library; New Haven: Yale, 2013); idem, "Authoritative Scriptures in the Dead Sea Scrolls," in Lim and Collins, eds., *The Oxford Handbook of the Dead Sea Scrolls*, 303–22.

A biblical canon?

We have written to you that you may study the book of Moses and the books of the Prophets and David ...[18]

"David" here means the Book of Psalms, which was often read as a prophetic text.[19] This passage in 4QMMT shows that the sectarians accepted the same basic scriptures as the High Priest, and even as their opponents, the Pharisees. The Law and the Prophets, or the Law, the Prophets and David, were the scriptures shared by all Judeans in the first century BCE.

The traditional Hebrew Bible contains a third category besides the Law and the Prophets – the Writings or Kethuvim. The earliest evidence for this division is found in the Greek translation of the Book of Ben Sira, by his grandson, in the late second century BCE. In the prologue to the translation the grandson says:

So my grandfather Jesus, who had devoted himself especially to the reading of the Law and the Prophets and the other books of our ancestors ... was himself also led to write something pertaining to wisdom and instruction.

This passage has often been taken as evidence that the three-part canon of scripture was already established by the end of the second century BCE. In fact, it indicates that the Law and the Prophets were well-established categories. "The other books," however, was an open-ended category of edifying literature. Ben Sira fancied that he himself could contribute to it.

When 4QMMT was published, some scholars thought it provided evidence for a three part canon: the Law, the Prophets, and David. A fragmentary mention of "generations" was sometimes read as a reference to the books of Chronicles, and thought to imply that the whole Hebrew canon as we know it was included. This is not convincing, however. It is clear that both the sect and its opponents regarded the Torah, the Prophets and Psalms, in some form, as authoritative, but that was the extent of the shared scriptures in the early first century BCE.

The word "canon" means measuring-stick. It was applied to the scriptures by the Christian Church Fathers. There was no such term in Hebrew, but the idea of a corpus of authoritative scriptures was certainly present by the time of the Dead Sea Scrolls. It has often been pointed out that every book of the Hebrew Bible except the Book of Esther has been found at Qumran, with the implication that they were all recognized as authoritative scriptures. But the situation is somewhat more complicated than this.

A huge corpus of supposedly revelatory texts was found at Qumran. It is difficult to know how these texts were regarded by the people who read them. Some texts (such as the *Books of Enoch*) that did not become part of the traditional Hebrew canon were preserved in multiple copies. Some books that did become canonical,

---

[18] 4QMMT C 10. Elisha Qimron and John Strugnell, *Qumran Cave 4. V. Miqsat Ma'ase Ha-Torah* (DJD 10; Oxford: Clarendon, 1994) 58–9.

[19] Lim, *The Formation of the Jewish Canon*, 127, argues that the reference is to "the deeds of David" rather than to the Psalms.

such as Chronicles, are barely represented. If we judge by the number of copies preserved, such books as *1 Enoch* and *Jubilees* were more important to the sectarians than Proverbs or Qoheleth.

In short, the Dead Sea Scrolls attest to a collection of authoritative scriptures that overlaps to a great degree with the later Bible of the rabbis. It was substantially the same in the Torah and the Prophets, although the status of some works, such as the *Temple Scroll* and *Jubilees* is unclear. The Essenes may have had a larger collection of prophets and other writings than the authorities in the Jerusalem Temple or the Pharisees; they did not have a smaller one. The whole category of "Writings" was ill-defined. It is clear that the sectarians valued many writings that claimed to be revelatory, but that were not included in the rabbinic Bible. Only in the period after 70 CE, in the writings of the historian Josephus and in *4 Ezra*, an apocalypse written about 100 CE, do we find authoritative sacred writings limited to a specific number. Josephus says that 22 books were properly accredited (*Against Apion*, 1.39). *4 Ezra* gives the number as 24 (probably the same books counted differently), but it also refers to 70 hidden books which contained even greater wisdom. It may be that Josephus's list of 22 books had been defined before 70, either by the Pharisees or by the Temple authorities, but there is no evidence of such a limitation in the Scrolls, and it was evidently not universally accepted.

The Scrolls and Judaism

Prior to the discovery of the Scrolls, our knowledge of Judaism in the land of Israel between the Maccabees and the Mishnah was heavily dependent on the Apocrypha and Pseudepigrapha. While some of these texts were composed in Hebrew or Aramaic, they only survived in translations, transmitted in the Christian churches. Consequently there was always some question as to their validity as expressions of Second Temple Judaism. George Foot Moore chided Wilhelm Bousset and R. H. Charles for their focus on texts that were not accepted as authoritative by the Jewish tradition. Bousset argued, with some justification, that his critics' concerns were theological rather than historical.[20]

The Dead Sea Scrolls went some way towards resolving this controversy. The discovery of fragments of *1 Enoch* in Aramaic and of *Jubilees* in Hebrew showed beyond doubt that these were indeed Jewish, pre-Christian, works, and that suspicion of authenticity because of Christian transmission was unfounded. Moreover, they brought to light a host of related apocalyptic works (*Pseudo-Daniel, Pseu-*

---

[20] See my essay, "Early Judaism in Modern Scholarship," in John J. Collins and Daniel C. Harlow, eds., *Early Judaism. A Comprehensive Overview* (Grand Rapids: Eerdmans, 2012) 1–29. George Foot Moore, "Christian Writers on Judaism," *HTR* 14 (1921) 197–254; Wilhelm Bousset, *Volksfrömmigkeit und Schriftgelehrtentum: Antwort auf Herrn Perles' Kritik meiner 'Religion des Judentums im N. T. Zeitalter'* (Berlin: Reuther und Reichard, 1903).

do-*Ezekiel*, *Pseudo-Jeremiah* etc.) that showed that apocalyptic literature was not as marginal a phenomenon as some had assumed. (Since many of these works are very fragmentary, their significance has not yet been fully appreciated.) Indeed, the initial impression created by the Scrolls, on the basis of the *Instruction on the Two Spirits* in 1QS and the *War Scroll*, was of an extreme form of apocalyptic dualism, that went beyond anything known from the Hebrew Bible. This dualism of Light and Darkness remains something of an anomaly, since it is clearly related to Persian dualism and is confined to a small number of texts in the Scrolls.[21] But it gave substance to the claim of Frank Cross that the Essenes were the bearers and in no small part the creators of apocalyptic tradition. That claim was somewhat over-stated. The Essenes were not the only creators or transmitters of apocalyptic traditions. But the Scrolls provide ample evidence that the kind of apocalyptic and eschatological speculations found in apocalyptic literature, and cherished by early Christians, were at home in Judaism around the turn of the era.

This picture was complicated, however, by the ongoing publication of the Scrolls. The single text that has done most to change scholarly views of pre-Christian Judaism is 4QMMT (*Miqsat Ma'ase Ha-Torah*, "Some of the Works of the Law") also known as the Halakic Letter (or letter about religious law). The text is not actually in the form of a letter, but it seems to be a treatise addressed to a leader of Israel, presumably a High Priest, urging him to accept the writer's interpretation of the Law rather than that of a third party. It concludes by telling him that if he does this, it "will be counted as a virtuous deed of yours, since you will be doing what is righteous and good in His eyes, for your own welfare and for the welfare of Israel." It was presented at the first International Conference on Biblical Archaeology, in Jerusalem, in April 1984, by John Strugnell and Elisha Qimron.[22] In the view of Strugnell and Qimron, this text was "a letter from the Teacher of Righteousness to the Wicked Priest," and it outlined the fundamental issues between the sect and the authorities in Jerusalem. One passage stated explicitly: "we have separated ourselves from the multitude of the people ... and from being involved with these matters and from participating with [them] in all these things."

Part of the text dealt with the religious calendar. (There is some dispute as to whether this part of the text is a separate document.) The importance of the calendar for the sect had been recognized early on. In the commentary on Habakkuk, we are told that the Wicked Priest confronted the Teacher on "the Day of Atonement, his Sabbath of rest." Since it is unlikely that the (wicked) High Priest would have staged this confrontation on the day when he himself was celebrating the Day of Atonement (Yom Kippur), it was evident that the two figures observed different cultic calendars. The Scrolls generally attest to a solar calendar of 364 days, whereas the

---

[21] See my discussion in *The Dead Sea Scrolls. A Biography*, 147–60.
[22] For a colorful account of the presentation see Lawrence H. Schiffman, *Reclaiming the Dead Sea Scrolls* (Philadelphia: Jewish Publication Society, 1994) xvii–xviii.

traditional calendar observed in the Temple was a lunar calendar of 354 days. Most scholars agree that calendrical difference was a major reason why the sect had to withdraw from the Temple. The solar calendar is found already in the *Temple Scroll* and in *Jubilees*, both of which are likely to have been written before the sect actually broke off. Differences could simmer for a time, but eventually they led to action.

The main body of 4QMMT, however, deals with some 20 issues bearing on holiness and purity, sacrifice and tithing, forbidden sexual unions, and the like. In each case, the view of the author's group ("we") is contrasted with that of another group ("they"). For example:

concerning liquid streams: we are of the opinion that they are not pure, and that these streams do not act as a separative between impure and pure. For the liquid of the streams and that of the vessel which receives them are alike, (being) a single liquid.

So a stream of liquid that is being poured into an unclean vessel is itself impure. From the viewpoint of Christian scholars, and indeed of many modern Jews, many of these issues seem trivial, but for the author and his opponents these matters determined whether the Law was being properly observed.

Several of the issues discussed in 4QMMT appear again in rabbinic literature. The views of the opponents (the "they" group) generally correspond to those of the rabbis, and consequently were those of the rabbis' predecessors, the Pharisees. In some cases, the views espoused in the Scroll correspond to those of the Sadducees.[23] This does not necessarily prove that the author and his group were Sadducees, but that they had a similar approach to the Law. In all cases, the views of the "we" group are stricter than those of their opponents. While 4QMMT does not explain how the author arrived at his positions, the issue was evidently the correct interpretation of the Torah of Moses. The author appeals to the addressee to study the book of Moses and the books of the Prophets and the writings of David. It may well be that the sectarians believed that the true interpretation of the Law had been revealed to them, but if so the revelation came in the course of their study.

There are other indications in the Scrolls that the sect, presumably the Essenes, was at odds with the Pharisees, whom they called "seekers after smooth things." What became clear from 4QMMT was that these disputes about religious law were the primary factor in the separation of the sect, not only from the Pharisees but from the rest of society. In fact, this might already have been inferred from the *Damascus Document*, which says that God had revealed to the sect the hidden things in which Israel had gone astray. These "hidden things" included the cultic calendar, but also "the three nets of Belial" (CD 4): fornication, riches, and profanation of the Temple. On each of these matters, the sect held a different interpretation of the Law from that of the authorities who controlled the Temple. Again in CD 6 we are told that the members of the new covenant

---

[23] Y. Sussmann, "Appendix 1: The History of the Halakha and the Dead Sea Scrolls," in Qimron and Strugnell, *Qumran Cave 4. V* (DJD 10) 179–200.

shall take care to act according to the exact interpretation of the Law during the age of wickedness ... They shall distinguish between clean and unclean, and shall proclaim the difference between holy and profane. They shall keep the Sabbath day according to its exact interpretation, and the feasts and the Day of Fasting according to the finding of the members of the New Covenant in the land of Damascus. They shall set aside the holy things according to the exact teaching concerning them.

It is clear from such passages as this that the exact interpretation of the Law was the *raison d'être* of the sect. Only when 4QMMT became known, however, was this fact fully appreciated.

4QMMT may also give us a better idea of when this sect broke off from the rest of Judaism. When would a sectarian leader have been likely to appeal to the High Priest to adopt his group's rulings rather than those of the Pharisees? The Pharisees were embroiled in conflicts especially in the early first century BCE. They clashed especially with Alexander Jannaeus, the Hasmonean king who ruled from 103 to 76 BCE. At one point the Pharisees led a revolt against him, on the grounds that he was not fit to be High Priest, and he responded by having some 6,000 people killed. He later crucified some 800 of his opponents. On his deathbed, however, he advised his queen Salome Alexandra to make peace with the Pharisees. She did so, and entrusted them with the government. According to Josephus

she permitted the Pharisees to do as they liked in all matters, and also commanded the people to obey them; and whatever regulations, introduced by the Pharisees in accordance with the tradition of their fathers, had been abolished by her father-in-law Hyrcanus, these she again restored. And so, while she had the title of sovereign, the Pharisees had the power (*Ant* 13. 408–9).

She appointed Hyrcanus II High Priest and he served in that capacity until 67 BCE. He later had a second term from 63–40. We should not be surprised if the reversal of royal attitude towards the Pharisees and their rulings provoked a protest from the other sects. This is perhaps the time in Hasmonean history when a High Priest was most likely to take action against people who were contesting the Pharisaic interpretation of the Torah. Josephus says that the Pharisees tried to persuade the queen to kill those who had urged Alexander to put the eight hundred to death, and that they themselves assassinated some of them. We are told in a commentary on Psalms found at Qumran that the Wicked (High) Priest tried to kill the Teacher. This struggle for sectarian hegemony provides a plausible context for the conflict about the Pharisaic interpretation of the Law, when both sides would have sought the endorsement and support of the High Priest.[24] In fact, the great bulk of the historical references in the Scrolls refer to people and events in the first half of the first century BCE.[25] In contrast, there is no evidence of sectarian conflict in the middle of the

---

[24] Collins, *Beyond the Qumran Community*, 88–121.
[25] Michael O. Wise, "Dating the Teacher of Righteousness and the *Floruit* of His Movement," *JBL* 122 (2003) 53–87.

second century BCE (the time of Jonathan Maccabee), which had been, and in some circles still is, presumed to be the time of the Teacher and the Wicked Priest.[26]

The sect described in the Scrolls did not come into being because it believed in the coming of the messiah or the final battle between the sons of Light and the sons of Darkness. It came into being because of disagreements with other Jews on the exact interpretation of the Law, the proper cultic calendar and the state of the Temple cult. The fact that it had so many irreconcilable differences with other Jews, however, called for explanation. One way of explaining the situation was to suppose that God had hardened the hearts of their opponents, for his own mysterious purposes, and assigned them to the lot of the Spirit of Darkness. It could not be that God would allow error to triumph indefinitely. He must bring an end to it, and soon. Not only must the other Jews who were children of darkness be overthrown, but also the Romans, the Kittim, who were desecrating the land. Hence the need for a final battle in which God would eliminate the forces of evil.

It would not be enough that truth and justice prevail in the public order. Individuals must also be punished or rewarded for their deeds. The fact that a judgment is expected, however, does not in itself tell one what conduct is approved. In the case of the Scrolls, right conduct depended on right interpretation of the Law. Early Christianity would have a view of the world that was largely similar, insofar as this world was passing away and would be subject to judgment, but the criteria for the judgment would be quite different, and reflect a different evaluation of the Law, especially its ritual aspects.

The Scrolls and Christianity

I turn finally to the relevance of the Scrolls for Christian origins. This is the area of scholarship that has suffered most from wild speculation. In the 1950's André Dupont-Sommer claimed that the Teacher of Righteousness had been crucified and rose from the dead, and so prefigured Jesus.[27] This claim was further sensationalized by John Allegro in the 1950's,[28] and revived by the British authors Baigent and Leigh in the 1990's.[29] Variants of this attempt to find a "messiah before Jesus" were put forward a little more than a decade ago by Michael Wise and Israel Knohl.[30]

---

[26] E.g. Hanan Eshel, *The Dead Sea Scrolls and the Hasmonean State* (Grand Rapids: Eerdmans, 2008) 29–61; James C. VanderKam, *The Dead Sea Scrolls Today* (2nd ed.; Grand Rapids: Eerdmans, 2010) 132.

[27] A. Dupont-Sommer, *Aperçus préliminaires sur les manuscrits de la Mer Morte* (Paris: Maisonneuve, 1950).

[28] Judith Ann Brown, *John Marco Allegro, The Maverick of the Dead Sea Scrolls* (Grand Rapids: Eerdmans, 2005) 77.

[29] Michael Baigent and Richard Leigh, *The Dead Sea Scrolls Deception* (London: Jonathan Cape, 1991).

[30] Michael O. Wise, *The First Messiah* (San Francisco: HarperSanFrancisco, 1999); Israel M.

Wise's theory to be sure was far less sensational than that of Allegro. He pointed out, correctly, that the speaker in some of the Thanksgiving Hymns, or Hodayot, seemed to model himself on the Suffering Servant of Isaiah. Wise construed this as a messianic claim, which is doubtful, but at least the allusions to the Suffering Servant were well founded. Knohl's thesis was more far-fetched, and was based on a fanciful interpretation of a fragmentary text in which the speaker claims to have a throne in heaven, later supported by the *Vision of Gabriel*, a controversial text written in stone, of uncertain provenance.[31] Knohl argued that these texts attested a belief in a messianic figure who died and rose again, a few decades before Jesus. His reading of these texts, however, has found little support.[32]

The attempt to find an exact prototype for Jesus in the Dead Sea Scrolls has fascinated people repeatedly for more than 60 years. The fascination of this mirage is obviously theological or ideological, but its implications are not at all clear: if Knohl were right, would this undermine the credibility of Christianity? Or enhance it by showing that such ideas were grounded in Judaism? Would it redound to the glory of Judaism, by showing the Jewish origin of influential ideas? Or would it tarnish that glory by showing that some of the more "mythological" aspects of Christianity were at home in Judaism too? Or should it have any bearing on our judgments about Judaism or Christianity at all? What is clear is that the desire to prove, or disprove, claims that are thought to be fraught with theological significance, can only distort the work of the historian.

In fact, messianic expectation is one of the areas where the Scrolls have shed some light on early Christianity. Two examples may suffice. One is the so-called *Aramaic Apocalypse*, or *Son of God text*, 4Q246, which speaks of a figure of whom it is said: "Son of God he shall be called, and they will name him Son of the Most High."[33] This text immediately brings to mind the story of the Annunciation in the Gospel of Luke. There the angel Gabriel tells Mary:

And now you will conceive in your womb and bear a son, and you will name him Jesus. He will be great, and will be called the Son of the Most High, and the Lord God will give to him the throne of his ancestor David ... the child to be born will be holy; he will be called Son of God.

Both texts also use the phrase "will be great" and speak of everlasting dominion.

Knohl, *The Messiah before Jesus: The Suffering Servant of the Dead Sea Scrolls* (Berkeley, CA: University of California Press, 2000).

[31] On the *Vision of Gabriel*, see Matthias Henze, ed., *Hazon Gabriel. New Readings of the Gabriel Revelation* (Atlanta: SBL, 2011).

[32] See my essays, "A Messiah Before Jesus," and "An Essene Messiah? Comments on Israel Knohl, The Messiah Before Jesus" in John J. Collins and Craig A. Evans, eds., *Christian Beginnings and the Dead Sea Scrolls* (Grand Rapids: Baker, 2006) 15–35 and 37–44 respectively.

[33] John J. Collins, *The Scepter and the Star. Messianism in Light of the Dead Sea Scrolls* (2nd ed.; Grand Rapids: Eerdmans, 2010) 171–90.

The interpretation of this text has been controversial. J. T. Milik argued that the figure who is called Son of God was not a Jewish messiah, but rather a Syrian king, probably Alexander Balas, a second century BCE ruler who referred to himself on his coins as *theopator*, divinely begotten. That interpretation was not well received when Milik proposed it in a lecture at Harvard in 1972, but it subsequently won a following, although its proponents usually favor a different pagan ruler. By far the closest parallel, however, is found in the passage in Luke, where these titles are explicitly messianic. Scholars have been strangely reluctant to acknowledge this parallel, because it is found in the New Testament. I would not want to suggest that resistance to recognizing this figure as the messiah is entirely due to theological considerations, specifically a desire to protect the uniqueness of Jesus as the messianic Son of God, but such theological considerations have not been entirely absent.[34]

Another intriguing parallel to the New Testament is provided by a larger Hebrew fragment designated 4Q521 and sometimes dubbed "the messianic apocalypse," which begins: "heaven and earth will obey his messiah."[35] The passage goes on to say:

The glorious things that have not taken place the Lord will do as he s[aid] for he will heal the wounded, give life to the dead and preach good news to the poor...

This text brings to mind a passage in the Gospel of Matthew 11:

When John heard in prison what the Messiah was doing, he sent word by his disciples and said to him, "Are you the one who is to come, or are we to wait for another?" Jesus answered them, "Go and tell John what you hear and see: the blind receive their sight, the lame walk, the lepers are cleansed, the deaf hear, the dead are raised, and the poor have good news brought to them."

Both the Qumran text and the Gospel draw on Isaiah 61:1, where the prophet says:

The spirit of the Lord God is upon me, because the Lord has anointed me; he has sent me to bring good news to the oppressed, to bind up the brokenhearted, to proclaim liberty to the captives and release to the prisoners...

(This text is famously read by Jesus in the Capernaum synagogue, in Luke 4:18.) The Isaianic text does not mention raising the dead, and this suggests that the Gospel and the Qumran text had at least a further tradition in common.

In the Qumran text, it is God who is said to heal the wounded, give life to the dead and preach good news to the poor. It is very odd, however, to have God preaching the good news: that was the work of a prophet or herald. Moreover, neither Isaiah 61 nor Matthew 11 has God as the subject. In Isaiah, the agent is an anointed prophet. The suspicion arises, then, that God is also thought to act through an agent in 4Q521, specifically, the "messiah" or anointed one whom heaven and earth obey. This messiah, however, is not a warrior king, but rather a prophetic "messiah" whose actions

---

[34] See further my comments in *The Dead Sea Scrolls. A Biography*, 114.
[35] Collins, *The Scepter and the Star*, 131–41.

resemble those of Elijah and Elisha, both of whom were said to have raised dead people to life. If this is correct, then this Qumran text throws some genuine light on the career of Jesus, who certainly resembled Elijah more than a warrior king.

The Scrolls have filled out to a great degree our knowledge of messianic expectation in the Second Temple period. Such expectation was almost entirely lacking in the apocalypses of the Maccabean period (Enoch and Daniel) where we might have expected to find it. It revived in the Hasmonean period, first in reaction to the Hasmonean appropriation of the monarchy, which some Jews regarded as illegitimate, and then in reaction to Roman rule. The Scrolls show that more than one kind of messiah was expected. The most widespread hope was for a kingly warrior who would drive out the Romans and restore the kingdom of David, but there were also hopes for a priestly messiah and for a messianic prophet. One of the enigmas of the New Testament is how Jesus of Nazareth came to be identified as the militant kingly messiah. The (admittedly rare) attestation of a prophetic messiah in the Scrolls raises the intriguing possibility that he may originally have been identified as a different kind of messiah, as a wonder-working prophet.

Messianism, of course, is only one of many areas where the Scrolls shed light on the New Testament. The Scrolls provide a context for debates about such matters as divorce and Sabbath observance, which were of concern to all Jews at the time. Sapiential texts found at Qumran contrast flesh and spirit in ways similar to what we find in the Pauline letters. Another wisdom text contains a list of Beatitudes, which are similar at least in form to the Sermon on the Mount, although the details are quite different. 4QMMT, the treatise on "some of the works of the Law" that sets out the points on which the sect differed from other Jews, has been invoked as a parallel for what Paul means by "works of the Law." A document about a heavenly figure named Melchizedek provides a possible background for enigmatic references to Melchizedek in the Epistle to the Hebrews. Examples could be multiplied. Very seldom is it possible to argue that a New Testament writer was influenced by a specific text found at Qumran. The point is rather that both movements drew on the same cultural and religious tradition, and often understood their sacred texts in similar ways, or raised similar questions about them.

If we look at the *Gestalt* of the two movements, however, the differences are at least as striking as the similarities. Both movements expected the coming (or second coming) of a messiah (or messiahs) and believed that actions in this life would determine salvation or damnation in the next. The scenario envisioned in the War Scroll is not so far removed from that of the Book of Revelation. Both envisage a violent confrontation between the forces of good and those of evil, and the eventual destruction of the latter. But the kind of conduct that is thought to lead to salvation in the two movements is fundamentally different. In the Scrolls, the emphasis is on attaining and maintaining a state of purity, and this is achieved by separating from "the men of the pit," which is to say from the rest of society. Jesus, and even more so Paul, in contrast, downplayed the importance of the ritual laws. According to Jesus, it is not what goes into a man that makes him unclean, but what comes out of his mouth. So far from separating from the world of impurity, Paul launched a mission to the Gentiles. Essenism and Christianity were different movements, with different values, even though they arose in essentially the same environment.

Conclusion

The extraordinary historical importance of the Scrolls lies in the fact that they provide a previously unknown corpus of literature in Hebrew or Aramaic from Judea in the period between the Maccabees and the Mishnah. They fill out our knowledge of Judaism in this period in countless ways. Despite the sectarian ideology of much of the corpus, it also includes much material that is reflective of the common Judaism of the time. Much of the debate about the Essene hypothesis has been fuelled by conflicting desires to see the Scrolls as marginal and negligible, on the one hand, or as representative of mainline Judaism on the other. Neither of these categorizations can be sustained in isolation. The sectarian movement reflected in the Scrolls was marginal, insofar as it was a movement that died out and had no discernible influence on later Jewish tradition. But it was not completely isolated, and the writings found in the caves are illuminating in many ways for the Judaism of the time.

As scholars have increasingly recognized in the last quarter century, the Scrolls are documents of ancient Judaism. Despite sensationalist claims, they are not Christian, and do not witness directly to Jesus of Nazareth and his followers. Nonetheless, they illuminate the context in which Jesus lived, and in which earliest Christianity took shape. While the Scrolls sometimes provide parallels to particular ideas in the New Testament, more often they provide a foil. The ways of the Teacher of Righteousness and of Jesus were alternative paths in the context of ancient Judaism, different ways in which the Jewish tradition might be appropriated and different interpretations of its scriptures.

Part One
Scripture and Interpretation

CHAPTER TWO

The Transformation of the Torah in Second Temple Judaism

The Dead Sea Scrolls have provided ample confirmation, if any were needed, of the centrality of the Torah in late Second Temple Judaism. The Torah was the well dug by the "penitents of Israel" in CD 6:4, from which the Interpreter of the Law derived the statutes by which they should live. The command in Isaiah to go to the desert to prepare the way of the Lord is interpreted in 1QS 8:15 as referring to "the study of the Torah, which he commanded through the hand of Moses." Moreover, the Scrolls show that concern for the correct interpretation of the Torah was not just a preoccupation of this sect. The publication of 4QMMT made clear that the basic reason why this sect separated from the rest of Judaism was the conflict of interpretations, especially with the Pharisees, that raged in the Hasmonean era (and not the Hasmonean usurpation of the High Priesthood as earlier scholarship had supposed).[1] This should have already been clear from the Damascus Document, which specifies some of the issues in dispute: "But with those who remained steadfast in God's precepts, with those who were left from among them, God established his covenant with Israel for ever, revealing to them hidden matters in which all Israel had gone astray: his holy Sabbaths and his glorious feasts, his just stipulations and his truthful paths and the wishes of his will which a man must do in order to live by them" (CD 3:12–16). The sectarians claimed new revelation, but the subject of the revelation was the interpretation of the Torah. When they appealed to the ruler of Israel, probably the High Priest, in 4QMMT, the appeal was that he study the books of Moses and the Prophets and David, and appreciate that the interpretations proposed by the sectarians were correct.[2]

Halakhic interest, however, does not characterize the entire corpus of Dead Sea Scrolls. It is notably lacking in the corpus of Aramaic texts found at Qumran.[3] These texts are often thought to be pre-sectarian, and most of them surely are, though not necessarily all. They are part of the literary heritage of the third and early second

---

[1] Elisha Qimron and John Strugnell, *Qumran Cave 4. V. Miqsat Ma'ase Ha-Torah* (DJD X; Oxford: Clarendon, 1994). The text was first brought to public attention in a paper by Qimron and Strugnell at the first International Conference on Biblical Archaeology in April, 1984.

[2] 4QMMT Composite Text C 10.

[3] Katell Berthelot and Daniel Stökl Ben Ezra, eds., *Aramaica Qumranica. Proceedings of the Conference on the Aramaic Texts from Qumran in Aix-en-Provence, 30 June – 2 July 2008* (STDJ 94; Leiden: Brill, 2010), especially Devorah Dimant, "Themes and Genres in the Aramaic Texts from Qumran," *ibid.*, 15–45.

centuries BCE. These texts do not lack familiarity with the Torah, but they typically develop its narrative themes, or treat it as a source of wisdom, but not of legal rulings. So, for example, the *Book of the Watchers* in *1 Enoch* takes its departure from the story of the sons of God in Genesis 6, but makes no mention of the Mosaic covenant. This omission might be explained by the pre-diluvian time-frame of that book, but there is a notable contrast with the Hebrew *Book of Jubilees*, which has no inhibition about reading the provisions of the Torah into the primeval history. Even the *Animal Apocalypse*, which gives an account of the ascent of Mt. Sinai, does not mention the giving of the Law.[4] As George Nickelsburg has written:

> This use of material from the Pentateuch (and the Hebrew Bible more generally) notwithstanding, to judge from what the Enochic authors have written, and not written, the Sinaitic covenant and the Mosaic Torah were not of central importance to them.[5]

Likewise, the wisdom literature from Qumran, which is written in Hebrew rather than Aramaic, does not treat the Torah as a source of legal rulings. Ben Sira identifies wisdom with "the book of the covenant of the Most High God, the law that Moses commanded us" (Sir 24:23). But he reads the Torah as a source of wisdom and insight, not of prescriptive law.[6] The same is true for *4QInstruction*, which draws heavily on Genesis in its account of the human situation, but does not thematize law as such.[7] Even works that do thematize law, such as Psalm 119 and 4Q525, speak of the Torah in general terms as a guide to life, something on which the righteous should meditate (compare Psalm 1). Psalm 119 refers repeatedly to statutes and ordinances, but its main concern is with wisdom and understanding: "make me understand the ways of your precepts, and I will meditate on your wondrous works" (Psalm 119:27). The psalmist prays that God open his eyes so that he may behold the wondrous things contained in the Law. What we do not find in the psalm is a concern with specific legal rulings. It attests to a kind of Torah piety, but it is not halakhic. One may argue that the difference between the wisdom texts and the more halakhic texts from Qumran is a matter of genre, and to some degree this is also true

---

[4] George W. E. Nickelsburg, *1 Enoch 1. A Commentary on the Book of 1 Enoch, Chapters 1–36; 81–108* (Hermeneia; Minneapolis: Fortress, 2001) 380. There is mention of "a law for all generations" in the *Apocalypse of Weeks* (*1 Enoch* 93:6) but it is not discussed further.

[5] George W. E. Nickelsburg, "Enochic Wisdom and the Mosaic Torah," in Gabriele Boccaccini and John J. Collins, eds., *The Early Enoch Literature* (JSJSup 121; Leiden: Brill, 2007) 81–94. See also Andreas Bedenbender, "The Place of the Torah in the Early Enoch Literature," *ibid.*, 65–79, and John J. Collins, "Enochic Judaism. An Assessment," in Adolfo D. Roitman, Lawrence H. Schiffman and Shani Tzoref, eds., *The Dead Sea Scrolls and Contemporary Culture. Proceedings of the International Conference held at the Israel Museum, Jerusalem (July 6–8, 2008)* (STDJ 93; Leiden: Brill, 2011) 219–34.

[6] See my discussion in *Jewish Wisdom in the Hellenistic Age* (Louisville: Westminster, 1997) 42–61.

[7] See my essay "The Interpretation of Genesis in the Dead Sea Scrolls," in Akio Moriya and Gohei Hata, eds., *Pentateuchal Traditions in the Late Second Temple Period. Proceedings of the International Workshop in Tokyo, August 28–31, 2007* (JSJSup 158; Leiden: Brill, 2012) 157–75 (reprinted as chapter 5 in this volume).

of the narrative texts preserved in Aramaic. But it is remarkable that no halakhic works are preserved in Aramaic. Neither, I would argue, have we any works devoted primarily to halakah that date clearly to the time before the Maccabean revolt. Undoubtedly, halakhic exegesis went on from early times, and is often implicit in the Bible itself.[8] Halakhic concerns are sometimes implicit in the wisdom texts from Qumran.[9] There seems, however, to have been a great upsurge in interest in *halakhic* issues in the Hasmonean period, and they assume much greater prominence in the literature of that time.

The transformation of Torah

The question of the origin of *halakhic* exegesis intersects with another debate about the transformation in the understanding of Torah. It is widely agreed that the great law codes of the ancient Near East were not prescriptive in nature. They did not provide the basis for the practice of law. They are variously viewed as literary exercises, royal apologia or juridical treatises.[10] In ancient Israel too, the practice of law was not based on the written law codes.[11] Written laws served various purposes. They might serve didactic purposes, or be used for ritual reading.[12] This is not to suggest that they were entirely irrelevant to the practice of law, but they did not serve as the basis of law in the manner of a modern law code. In the age of the monarchy, the king rather than a law code was the ultimate authority.

At some point, however, biblical law came to be understood in a prescriptive sense. Scholars disagree as to whether that shift should be located at the time of Josiah's reform, of Ezra's reform, or in the Hellenistic period.

For Dale Patrick,

A shift in the understanding of God's law can be detected in the literature bearing the stamp of the Deuteronomic school and sustaining the impact of Josiah's reform. The new under-

---

[8] See especially Michael Fishbane, *Biblical Interpretation in Ancient Israel* (Oxford: Clarendon, 1985) 91–277.

[9] Lawrence H. Schiffman, "Halakhic Elements in the Sapiential Texts from Qumran," in John J. Collins, Gregory E. Sterling and Ruth A. Clements, eds., *Sapiential Perspectives: Wisdom Literature in Light of the Dead Sea Scrolls* (STDJ 51; Leiden: Brill, 2004) 89–100.

[10] Michael LeFebvre, *Collections, Codes, and Torah. The Re-Characterization of Israel's Written Law* (New York and London: T & T Clark, 2006) 8–18; Raymond Westbrook, "The Character of Ancient Near Eastern Law," in idem, ed., *A History of Ancient Near Eastern Law* (2 vols.; Leiden: Brill, 2003) 1.12–24.

[11] LeFebvre, *Collections, Codes, and Torah*, 31–54. See also Anne Fitzpatrick McKinley, *The Transformation of Torah from Scribal Advice to Law* (JSOTSup 287; Sheffield: Sheffield Academic Press, 1999) 81–112.

[12] B. S. Jackson, *Studies in the Semiotics of Biblical Law* (JSOTSup 314; Sheffield: Sheffield Academic Press, 2000) 121–41; LeFebvre, *Collections, Codes, and Torah*, 32–39. Jackson also distinguishes archival and monumental uses of law.

standing comes to expression in statements exhorting the addressee to adhere strictly to the words of the legal text and praising persons for doing so.[13]

Yet when Josiah hears the words of the book of the law, he promptly consults the prophetess Huldah. In the words of Michael LeFebvre, "It is Huldah (not the book) who reveals heaven's ruling."[14] Her response is not an interpretation of the book, but a direct word from the Lord. It is evident that Josiah accepted the authenticity of the book, but needed an oracle to determine its application in the specific case. Moreover, as J. G. McConville observes, "Deuteronomy's king is nothing like King Josiah."[15] Deuteronomy denies the king any role in the cult, but Josiah is firmly in control. The Law of the King may be a later addition to Deuteronomy, but it does not appear that Josiah subordinates his authority to that of the Law. The discovery of the book seems to be used primarily to authorize Josiah's cultic reform. While Josiah's reform was certainly a milestone in the development of the Torah as Law, his lawbook was not yet a statutory law for Judah.

A stronger claim can be made that the shift in the perception of the Torah took place in the time of Ezra.[16] Westbrook, who sees the beginnings of legislative thinking in Deuteronomy, finds the full bloom of statutory law in Ezra and Nehemiah. Ezra, a 'scribe skilled in the torah of Moses,'

may be credited with laying the jurisprudential foundations of Jewish Law as we understand it today. For he and his fellow priests read 'from the book, from the torah of God, with interpretation' before the assembled people (Neh 8:1–8). Thus the legal system became based upon the idea of a written code of law interpreted and applied by religious authorities.[17]

Bernard Jackson similarly looks to Nehemiah 8 as a pivotal moment: "It is in this context," he writes, "that we should locate the transformation of the biblical legal collections into 'statutory' texts, binding upon the courts and subject to verbal interpretation."[18] Jackson appeals to Peter Frei's theory of imperial authorization of law in the Persian period.[19] In Ezra 7:26, the Torah is called both "the law of your God" and "the law of the king." Many scholars infer that the Torah acquired the status of statutory law in virtue of its royal authorization. Against this, however, the objec-

---

[13] Dale Patrick, *Old Testament Law* (London: SCM, 1986) 200.

[14] LeFebvre, *Collections, Codes, and Torah*, 59.

[15] J. G. McConville, *Deuteronomy* (Leicester: Apollos, 2002) 33.

[16] The Book of Ezra poses significant problems from an historical point of view. See Lester L. Grabbe, *Ezra-Nehemiah* (London: Routledge, 1998) 125–53; idem, *A History of Jews and Judaism in the Second Temple Period Vol. 1. Yehud: A History of the Persian Province of Judah* (New York and London: T & T Clark, 2004) 324–31. For the present, we are only concerned with what is claimed in the book, without pressing its historical accuracy.

[17] Westbrook, "Biblical Law," 3–4.

[18] Jackson, *Studies*, 141–2.

[19] Peter Frei and Klaus Koch, *Reichsidee und Reichsorganisation im Perserreich* (OBO 55; Fribourg: Universitätsverlag, 1984); Frei, "Persian Imperial Authorization: A Summary," in James W. Watts, ed., *Persia and Torah: The Theory of Imperial Authorization of the Pentateuch* (SBLSymS 17; Atlanta: SBL, 2001) 5–40.

tion has been raised that Persia did not itself have a written law code, so it is unlikely that it would have instituted one in Judah.[20] Ezra's lawbook appears to have been something close to our Pentateuch, even if not in its final form. (It included the Priestly laws as well as Deuteronomy.) Ezra presumably required Persian permission in order to give his lawbook any authority at all, but it is noteworthy that the Torah was not translated into Aramaic, and so the Persians could not read it without a translator.[21] James Watts infers that "the Persians may have designated the Pentateuch as the 'official' law of the Jerusalem community simply as a token of favor, with little or no attention to that law's form or content."[22] Kyong-Jin Lee sees the Persian authorization as an act of royal propaganda. By equating the law of Ezra's God and the law of the king, the king announced himself as the divinely authorized champion of law, and reaffirmed his legitimacy as the ruler of the land.[23]

In fact, the actions of Ezra and Nehemiah are not a simple implementation of Pentateuchal Law. Lefebvre lists several cases where there are discrepancies with the Torah as we have received it.[24] For example the Davidic temple courses were said to conform to "the book of Moses." Stipulations regarding the Feast of Booths "according to the Law" (Neh 8:13–18) are different from what we find in the Torah. The prohibitions against intermarriage go beyond Deuteronomy (Neh 10:31), and making purchases on the Sabbath is not actually prohibited in the Pentateuch (Neh 10:32). The institution of an annual temple tax and of a wood offering (also in Nehemiah 10) lack scriptural support. Conversely, Nehemiah does not appeal to scriptural authority when he could have done so, in his lawsuit in Nehemiah 5. Michael Fishbane has argued that the innovations may have been derived exegetically,[25] but there is no account of exegetical activity in Ezra-Nehemiah. The interpretation that accompanies the reading of the law in Nehemiah 8 is more plausibly taken to be a matter of translation, for those who did not know Hebrew, or know it well, than of exegesis.[26]

Fishbane has argued that Ezra-Nehemiah attest to "the axial transformations that mark the onset of classical Judaism. This involves making the movement from a culture based on direct divine revelations to one based on their study and reinterpretation."[27] Ezra is introduced as "a scribe skilled in the law of Moses that the Lord the

[20] LeFebvre, *Collections, Codes, and Torah*, 98–99.
[21] See Kyong-Jin Lee, *The Authority and Authorization of Torah in the Persian Period* (Leuven: Peeters, 2011) 213–53.
[22] Watts, *Persia and Torah*, 3.
[23] Lee, *The Authority and Authorization*, 249.
[24] LeFebvre, *Collections, Codes, and Torah*, 103–31. Compare Judson R. Shaver, *Torah and the Chronicler's History Work: An Inquiry into the Chronicler's References to Laws, Festivals, and Cultic Institutions in Relationship to Pentateuchal Legislation* (BJS 196; Atlanta: Scholars Press, 1989) 100–3.
[25] Fishbane, *Biblical Interpretation*, 107–34.
[26] LeFebvre, *Collections, Codes, and Torah*, 129–30.
[27] Fishbane, "From Scribalism to Rabbinism," in John G. Gammie, ed., *The Sage in Israel and the Ancient Near East* (Winona Lake, IN: Eisenbrauns, 1990) 439–56, here 440.

God of Israel had given" (Ezra 7:6). Further, he "had set his heart to study the law of the Lord, and to do it, and to teach the statutes and ordinances in Israel" (7:10). "This," says Fishbane, "is no mere depiction of a routine priestly function of ritual instruction ... It is, rather, an extension and virtual transformation of this role." The word *darash* had been used in earlier times for consulting an oracle (e.g. 1 Kgs 22:8). "Since Ezra's textual task is to seek from the Torah new divine teachings (or explication of older ones) for the present, there is a sense in which exegetical praxis has functionally co-opted older mantic techniques of divine inquiry."[28]

There is no doubt that Ezra's use of the Torah marks a new development in the history of Judaism. Prior to Ezra, there was scarcely a Torah to be studied. It is also indisputable that Ezra and Nehemiah invoke the authority of the Torah for new rulings (even in cases where the Torah that has come down to us does not support them). But we are very far here from the kind of systematic scrutiny of scriptural law that we find in the Dead Sea Scrolls. In fact, the reforms of Ezra are quite limited. They concern primarily mixed marriages (Ezra 9) and the festival calendar (Nehemiah 8), and there are discrepancies with the biblical text in both cases. Nehemiah also addresses social and cultural issues. In the matter of the mixed marriages, the people defer to the authority of Ezra, and ask that things be done "according to the Law" (10:3). In Nehemiah 8, he reads to the people from the book, and afterwards "the heads of ancestral houses of all the people, with the priests and the Levites, came together with the scribe Ezra in order to study the words of the law" (Neh 10:13). In a society where few people could read, however, study was heavily dependent on the word of the scribe. But as Kyong-Jin Lee has observed: "There is no record that Ezra launched a massive educational campaign to inform the people of the content of the Torah."[29] Neither does it seem that he undertook a systematic examination of all the Torah. Rather, he seems to have focused on a few issues of great symbolic importance, primarily the matter of mixed marriages and the festivals.

Consequently, even though the Torah as Law acquired new importance in the Persian period, I agree with LeFebvre that the "axial shift" described in the Book of Ezra was less dramatic than Fishbane claims. The Torah was enshrined as the official statement of the Jewish way of life, but this did not necessarily mean that it would henceforth be scrutinized in great detail. Its importance was largely symbolic, and a few issues had metonymic significance for the way of life as a whole.[30] If Ezra's Law was substantially the Pentateuch that has come down to us, it was far from a consistent document. Later scribes and rabbis would labor to resolve the inconsistencies, but there is much to be said for LeFebvre's argument that it was originally compiled "as a collection of historic descriptions, not as a prescriptive code."[31] It does take on prescriptive force in the Book of Ezra, but its prescriptive use re-

---

[28] *Ibid.*, 441.
[29] Lee, *The Authority and Authorization*, 246.
[30] This, I would argue, is still the case for conservative Christians in contemporary America.
[31] LeFebvre, *Collections, Codes, and Torah*, 141.

mains sporadic and selective, and not closely based on the literal wording of the text (at least if that text corresponded to the Pentateuch as we know it).

Ancestral law in the Hellenistic period

Whether or not the Law brought to Jerusalem by Ezra had official authorization from the Persians, Judah was certainly thought to have its own ancestral law in the Hellenistic period. Josephus claims that Alexander the Great visited Jerusalem, and that "when the High Priest asked whether they might observe the ancestral laws and in the seventh year be exempt from tribute, he granted all this."[32] This whole narrative is highly legendary; it is unlikely that Alexander went to Jerusalem in person. As Erich Gruen has put it, "Alexander's visit to Jerusalem is outright fabrication."[33] The idea that the conquering king, however, would affirm the right of the conquered city to observe its ancestral laws is quintessentially Hellenistic. We find references to ancestral laws already in Thucydides.[34] When Andokides was on trial for impiety, he cited an earlier decree of Teisamenos which stated that "The Athenians shall conduct their affairs in the traditional manner" (*kata ta patria*).[35] Elias Bickerman demonstrated that "the first favor bestowed by a Hellenistic king on a conquered city – and the basis of all other favors – was the re-establishment of the municipal statutes. In virtue of the conquest, the subjugated city was no longer entitled to its institutions and laws, and it regained these only by means of an act promulgated by its new master."[36] There are plentiful examples. When Philip V of Macedon gained control of the island of Nisyros in 201 BCE, he proclaimed to the inhabitants that "The king has re-established among us the use of the ancestral laws which are currently in force."[37] When Antiochus III conquered Jerusalem he issued a proclamation that "All who belong to the people are to be governed in accordance with their ancestral laws" (*Ant* 12.142). "Ancestral laws" usually meant "laws hitherto in effect."[38]

---

[32] Josephus, *Ant* 11.338.

[33] Erich Gruen, *Heritage and Hellenism. The Reinvention of Jewish Tradition* (Cambridge, MA: Harvard, 1998) 195.

[34] Thucydides 8.76.6, in the context of a debate between democratic and anti-democratic parties on Samos. Robert Doran, "The Persecution of Judeans by Antiochus Epiphanes. The Significance of 'Ancestral Laws,'" in Daniel C. Harlow, Karina Martin Hogan, Matthew Goff and Joel Kaminsky, eds., *The 'Other' in Second Temple Judaism* (Grand Rapids: Eerdmans, 2011) 427.

[35] Andokides 1.83. Doran, *ibid.*

[36] Elias J. Bickerman, "The Seleucid Charter for Jerusalem," in idem, *Studies on Jewish and Christian History* (Leiden: Brill, 2011) 1.340. Compare John Ma, *Antiochus III and the Cities of Western Asia Minor* (Oxford: Oxford University Press, 2000) 112–3.

[37] Bickerman, *Studies*, 1.342, other examples on 340; Doran, "The Persecution of Judeans," 427.

[38] Alexander Fuks, *The Ancestral Constitution: Four Studies in Athenian Party Politics at the End of the Fifth Century B.C.* (London: Routledge and Kegan Paul, 1953) 40.

In the case of Judea, writes Bickerman, "the ancestral laws meant the law of Moses. What was 'the book of the Jewish laws' (*Ps. Aristeas* 30), if not the Pentateuch?"[39] Moses was famous as lawgiver of the Jews in the Hellenistic world.[40] Our earliest witness in this regard is Hecataeus of Abdera, who says that "at the end of their laws there is even appended the statement: These are the words that Moses heard from God and declares unto the Jews."[41] The book of the Jewish law was so well known that Ptolemy was supposed to have sought a copy for his library in Alexandria. We should not necessarily assume, however, that reference to the ancestral laws brought to mind the full Pentateuch in all its details.

In fact, the decree of Antiochus is reminiscent of Ezra in its selective focus. Most of his provisions have to do with the upkeep of the temple. Josephus tells us that "out of reverence for the temple he also published a proclamation throughout the entire kingdom of which the contents were as follows: 'It is unlawful for any foreigner to enter the enclosure of the temple which is forbidden to the Jews, except to those of them who are accustomed to enter after purifying themselves in accordance with the law of the country. Nor shall anyone bring into the city the flesh of horses or of mules or of wild or tame asses, or of leopards, foxes or hares, or, in general, of any animals forbidden to the Jews. Nor is it lawful to bring in their skins or even to breed any of these animals in the city. But only the sacrificial animals known to their ancestors and necessary for the propitiation of God shall they be permitted to use.'" (*Ant* 12.145–6).

There are plentiful parallels for conquering monarchs showing concern for temples in the Hellenistic world. Early in the Persian period the Egyptian Udjahorresnet, who had become a courtier to the Persian conqueror of Egypt, Cambyses, reports:

I made a petition to the majesty of the King of Upper and Lower Egypt, Cambyses, about all the foreigners who dwelled in the temple of Neith, in order to have them expelled from it, so as to let the temple of Neith be in all its splendor, as it had been before. His majesty commanded to expel all the foreigners [who] dwelled in the temple of Neith, to demolish all their houses and all their unclean things that were in this temple. When they had carried [all their] personal [belongings] outside the wall of the temple, his majesty commanded to cleanse the temple of Neith, and to return all its personnel to it.[42]

In Egypt, temples were off-limits to all but the priests except for festivals, "because one may enter only in a state of purity, after observing numerous abstinences."[43] As

---

[39] Bickerman, *Studies,* 1.342.

[40] John G. Gager, *Moses in Greco-Roman Paganism* (SBLMS 16; Nashville: Abingdon, 1972) 25–79.

[41] Hecataeus, in Diodorus Siculus 40.3 (6); Menahem Stern, *Greek and Latin Authors on Jews and Judaism. I. From Herodotus to Plutarch* (Jerusalem: Israel Academy of Sciences, 1976) 26–29.

[42] Miriam Lichtheim, *Ancient Egyptian Literature. Volume III: The Late Period* (Berkeley, CA: University of California, 1980) 38.

[43] Chaeremon in Porphyry, *De abstinentia* 4.6. E. J. Bickerman, "A Seleucid Proclamation concerning the Temple in Jerusalem," in *Studies,* 1.360.

Bickerman noted, there is no precept excluding foreigners from the temple in the Law of Moses.[44] He supposed that it was probably deduced from the rule in Exod 30:20 that purification is necessary before making an offering. A more probable source is Ezek 44:9: "No foreigner, uncircumcised in heart and flesh, of all the foreigners who are among the people of Israel, shall enter my sanctuary." The exclusion does not only apply to those who would offer sacrifice. The ancestral law includes more than was explicit in the Torah of Moses.

Neither is the prohibition of the flesh or hides of certain animals explicit in the Torah. To Bickerman, "the choice of animals in the ordinance seems bizarre: why do we find the panther, but not the pig?"[45] He suggests that the ordinance had Gentiles rather than Jews in mind, and that it singles out animals that visitors might actually have brought to Jerusalem. He attributes the mention of the panther to the fact that a panther hunt is depicted in the decorations on a tomb at Maresha. Tobias the Ammonite is said, in the Zenon papyri, to have sent Ptolemy II a gift consisting of horses, dogs, and colts of wild asses. But in any case, the list of excluded animals is not based on the Torah. Interestingly, the prohibition of certain hides appears again in 4QMMT B 21–22, which also prohibits dogs in "the holy camp" (B 58).[46] The prohibition is quite probably based on reflection on the discussion of unclean carcasses in Leviticus 11. We should note, however, the narrow focus of this reflection: it concerns only what is brought into the temple. Moreover, we should note that dogs were prohibited on Delos, and a sacred law of Ialysos from the beginning of the second century BCE decrees that "The horse, the ass, the male mule, the little mule, and any other animal whose tail is furnished with long hairs may not enter the sacred enclosure of Alectrone."[47]

LeFebvre claims that the decree of Antiochus is "the first indication of Israel expecting to prescribe its legal institutions from Torah."[48] The decree is a slender basis for such a far-reaching conclusion. There is something to be said for the view that the idea that each people should have its ancestral laws was a by-product of the Hellenistic age. This observation in itself, however, does not explain the explosion of interest in *halakhic* issues in Jewish texts of the Hasmonean period and later.

Antiochus, interestingly enough, does not say anything about the written form of the ancestral laws. In the cases of both Ezra and Antiochus there are some discrepancies between the written laws that have come down to us and the ancestral laws observed in antiquity. I would suggest that the written laws had mainly an iconic role. The ancestral law was known from tradition and custom, and it was presumed to correspond to the written law. Neither in the case of Ezra nor in the case of the Seleucid take-over of Jerusalem, however, was there great interest in checking to

---

[44] Bickerman, "A Seleucid Proclamation," 363.
[45] Bickerman, *ibid.*, 364.
[46] Qimron and Strugnell, DJD X, 155.
[47] Bickerman, "A Seleucid Proclamation," 366.
[48] LeFebvre, *Collections, Codes, and Torah*, 181.

see whether traditional custom corresponded to the written law. That situation changed, however, in the second century BCE.

Antiochus Epiphanes

The traditional Jewish way of life came under threat in the time of Antiochus IV Epiphanes. According to 2 Maccabees, when Jason made his bid for the High Priesthood he also sought permission to establish a gymnasium, and

> to enroll the men of Jerusalem as citizens of Antioch. When the king assented and Jason came to office, he at once shifted his countrymen over to the Greek way of life. He set aside the existing royal concessions to the Jews, secured through John, the father of Eupolemus ... and he destroyed the lawful ways of living and introduced new customs contrary to the law" (2 Macc 4:9–11).

Bickerman argued that Jason in effect set up a *politeuma* around the gymnasium, which was exempt from the traditional laws.[49] But it seems clear that the changes affected the whole city. The view that Jason was reconstituting the city as a *polis*, "Antioch-at-Jerusalem," now draws support from a parallel in an inscription in which the Attalid king Eumenes II (197–60) granted the Phrygian community of Tyriaion permission to become a *polis*.[50] Danny Schwartz argues plausibly that "it is doubtful that all Jerusalemites were forced to become citizens of the new city and to participate in its institutions; those who wanted to go on observing the ancestral ways were certainly allowed to do so."[51] But the reorganization probably had the effect of marginalizing traditional observance.

A more direct threat was posed by the actions of Antiochus Epiphanes a few years later. At the time of Epiphanes' second invasion of Egypt, which ended with his humiliation by the Roman legate Popilius Laenas on "the day of Eleusis," civil war broke out in Jerusalem, when Jason tried to recover the High Priesthood from Menelaus, who had procured it by offering to increase the tribute to the king. As 2 Maccabees tells it, "when news of what had happened reached the king, he took it to mean that Judea was in revolt. So, raging inwardly, he left Egypt and took the city by storm" (5:11). Not long afterwards, he sent "Geron the Athenian to compel the Jews to forsake the laws of their fathers and cease to live by the laws of God" (6:1).[52] The reasons for this measure have been endlessly debated. At the least, as Robert Doran has shown, 2 Maccabees provides a coherent account that is plausible in the Seleucid context: "Thinking the city was in revolt, Antiochus IV took it by storm

---

[49] E. J. Bickerman, *The God of the Maccabees*, in *Studies*, 2.1072–76.
[50] Daniel R. Schwartz, *2 Maccabees* (CEJL; Berlin: de Gruyter, 2008) 530–2. For the inscription see L. Jonnes, *The Inscriptions of the Sultan Dagi, I* (Inschriften griechischer Städter aus Kleinasien 62; Bonn: Habelt, 2002) 85–9, no. 393.
[51] Schwartz, *2 Maccabees*, 220.
[52] So Schwartz, *2 Maccabees*, 275. Alternatively, he sent "an Athenian elder."

and abrogated the gift of allowing the city to live by its ancestral laws, as his father had done formerly to Apollonia at Rhyndacos."[53] Instead, he imposed new laws that included cultic celebration of the king's birthday, sacrifices to Zeus, and processions in honor of Dionysus. The enforced observances were cultic in nature, and it was the disruption of the cult that provoked the Maccabean revolt.[54]

Our present concern, however, is not so much with the causes of Epiphanes' action as with what we can glean from the episode about the understanding of ancestral law in Judea in the early second century BCE. Doran summarizes:

> The ancestral laws abrogated included circumcision, Sabbath observance and kosher regulations. It appears that these were attacked not because Antiochus IV was persecuting the Jewish religion, but because circumcision affected citizenship, Sabbath observance affected the civic economy, and kosher regulations affected cultic meals.[55]

Antiochus, no doubt, did not have a concept of "Jewish religion." What he wanted to break down was the ancestral law of Judea and thereby the distinctive identity of the rebellious people.[56] One might equally well argue that these practices were singled out because of their symbolic value. For the same reason, it was forbidden to have copies of the Torah, the iconic representation of the Judean way of life (1 Macc 1:56). These were the practices most widely associated with Judaism. In addition to practices like circumcision and Sabbath observance, the king also struck at the temple cult, the most prominent public expression of the Jewish way of life, both by forbidding the traditional offerings and requiring sacrifices to foreign gods. Conversely, we may infer that the practices forbidden by Epiphanes were protected and authorized by the decree of Antiochus III some thirty years earlier.

The rallying cry of the Maccabees was the defense of the ancestral laws. 1 Maccabees has Mattathias cry out: "Let everyone who is zealous for the law and supports the covenant come out with me!" (1 Macc 2:27). They were not necessarily bound by the letter of the law. They famously made an exception for fighting on the Sabbath: "If we do as our brethren have done and refuse to fight with the Gentiles for our lives and our ordinances, they will quickly destroy us from the earth" (2:40–41). Yet they attempted not only to defend but to impose, "the Jewish way of life" within the territory they controlled. According to 1 Maccabees, they

---

[53] Doran, "The Persecution of Judeans," 432. His commentary on 2 Maccabees for the Hermeneia series is in press at the time of writing.

[54] See my essay, "Cult and Culture: The Limits of Hellenization in Judea," in my book *Jewish Cult and Hellenistic Culture* (JSJSup 100; Leiden: Brill, 2005) 21–43. Compare Peter Franz Mittag, *Antiochos IV. Epiphanes. Eine politische Biographie* (Klio NF 11; Berlin: Akademie Verlag, 2006) 245.

[55] Doran, "The Persecution of Judeans," 432.

[56] See Anathea Portier-Young, *Apocalypse Against Empire. Theologies of Resistance in Early Judaism* (Grand Rapids: Eerdmans, 2011) 140–210, on the logic of the Seleucid repression. For an attempt to explain the king's actions in political terms see Mittag, *Antiochus IV*, 279–81. His attempt to shift responsibility to the king's advisers cannot relieve the king of ultimate responsibility.

struck down sinners in their anger and lawless men in their wrath; the survivors fled to the Gentiles for safety. And Mattathias and his friends went about and tore down the altars; they forcibly circumcised all the uncircumcised boys that they found within the borders of Israel ... They rescued the law out of the hands of the Gentiles and kings. (1 Macc 2:44–47; compare Josephus *Ant* 12.278)

Josephus tells us that when John Hyrcanus was negotiating with Antiochus Sidetes, he sent envoys with the request that he restore to Judea its ancestral form of government (*politeia*) (*Ant* 13.245). When he conquered the Idumeans "he permitted them to remain in their country so long as they had themselves circumcised and were willing to observe the laws of the Jews. And so, out of attachment to the land of their fathers, they submitted to circumcision and to making their manner of life conform in all other respects to that of the Jews. And from that time on they have continued to be Jews" (*Ant* 13.257–8). Also Aristobulus I, when he conquered the Itureans, "compelled the inhabitants, if they wished to remain in their country, to be circumcised and to live in accordance with the laws of the Jews" (*Ant* 13.318–9). We do not read that the Hasmoneans required these subject peoples to be instructed in the details of the Torah. Rather they were required to observe key practices such as circumcision. We might expect that they were also expected to observe the Sabbath, and the other practices that had been suppressed in the time of Antiochus Epiphanes.

Josephus's accounts are not always confirmed by archaeology. There is no material record of the conquest of the Itureans or Galilee by Aristobulus, but it is clear that the northern regions were under Judean control by the end of the reign of Alexander Jannaeus.[57] From the archaeological perspective, the expanding Jewish presence is shown by material remains that indicate a greater concern for ritual purity. These include *miqvaot*, or immersion pools, and the use of stone vessels, which begin to proliferate in the later Hasmonean period.[58] Josephus says that Alexander Jannaeus on his deathbed advised his widow to yield a certain amount of power to the Pharisees (*Ant* 13.400). After his death,

she permitted the Pharisees to do as they liked in all matters, and also commanded the people to obey them; and whatever regulations, introduced by the Pharisees in accordance with the tradition of their fathers, had been abolished by her father-in-law Hyrcanus, these she again restored. And so, while she had the title of sovereign, the Pharisees had the power. (*Ant* 13.408–9)

---

[57] Eric M. Meyers and Mark A. Chancey, *Archaeology of the Land of the Bible. From Cyrus to Constantine* (AYBRL; New Haven: Yale, 2013) chapter 3.

[58] For overviews and bibliography see the articles by Byron McCane, "Miqva'ot," in *DEJ* 954–6 and Mark A. Chancey, "Stone Vessels," *ibid.*, 1256–7. According to Chancey, "Exactly when usage of stone vessels began is uncertain, but it clearly increased in the late first century B.C.E. when Herod's renovation of the Jerusalem Temple resulted in increased quarrying of limestone." Jodi Magness, *The Archaeology of Qumran and the Dead Sea Scrolls* (Grand Rapids: Eerdmans, 2002) 142, following Ronny Reich, notes that stepped pools are widespread in Judea during the first century BCE and the first century CE.

We might expect an intensification of Torah observance when the Pharisees held sway. So, while the Hasmoneans were not noted for their piety, by professing adherence to the Law they opened the way for stricter *halakhic* debate and observance.

The *Temple Scroll* and *Jubilees*

The oldest extant works that show sustained engagement with *halakhic* issues are the *Temple Scroll* and *Jubilees*. Neither of these works is thought to be a product of the "new covenant" or the יחד. Both are thought to have originated in the kind of priestly circles from which the sect emerged. Neither of these works is presented as exegesis, but both are clearly reworkings of older scriptures. The *Temple Scroll* is presented as revelation from God, addressed to Moses on Mt. Sinai. It begins with renewal of the covenant of Exodus 34 and continues with the instructions for building the sanctuary. It systematically integrates the laws about the temple in Exodus, Leviticus and Numbers, dealing with the construction of the temple, the festivals, sacrifices and purity. The latter part of the Scroll is a rewriting of Deut 12–23, with a noteworthy treatment of "the law of the king" of Deuteronomy 17.[59] Throughout, it practices "a distinct form of harmonistic exegesis," mainly on legal materials.[60] *Jubilees* retells the story of Genesis and Exodus through Exodus 19. While *Jubilees* makes occasional reference to "the first law" (Jub 6:20–22; 30:12), it too is presented as a revelation, delivered to Moses by the angel of the presence. Its relation to the "first law" has been aptly described by James VanderKam as "Moses trumping Moses," insofar as it claims to supersede the older scripture at some points, without rejecting its general validity.[61] Here again, the new material is derived exegetically, even if the exegesis is not explicit.[62] Michael Segal has argued persuasively, in my opinion, for a distinct *halakhic* redaction, that juxtaposes laws known from the legal corpora of the Pentateuch with stories of the patriarchal period.[63] The *Temple Scroll* and *Jubilees* were not the first exercises in "rewritten scripture." That process can be found as early as the books of Chronicles. The novelty of these texts lies in the halakhic focus of their rewriting. The novelty of *Jubilees* can be appreciated by

---

[59] See the description of the contents by Florentino García Martínez, "Temple Scroll," *EDSS*, 929.

[60] Lawrence H. Schiffman, *Reclaiming the Dead Sea Scrolls* (Philadelphia: Jewish Publication Society, 1994) 260.

[61] James VanderKam, "Moses Trumping Moses," in Sarianna Metso, Hindy Najman and Eileen Schuller, eds., *The Dead Sea Scrolls. Transmission of Traditions and Production of Texts* (STDJ 92; Leiden: Brill, 2010) 25–44.

[62] See especially James L. Kugel, *A Walk through Jubilees. Studies in the Book of Jubilees and the World of its Creation* (JSJSup 156; Leiden: Brill, 2012) 18–205.

[63] Michael Segal, *The Book of Jubilees. Rewritten Bible, Redaction, Ideology and Theology* (JSJSup 117; Leiden: Brill, 2007) 45–82. Kugel also sees a redactional hand at work in Jubilees (*A Walk through Jubilees*, 227–96).

contrasting its treatment of the Watcher story with that of the *Book of the Watchers* in *1 Enoch*. As Michael Segal has shown, the purpose of the story in *Jubilees* is no longer to explain the origin of evil in the world. Instead it functions as a paradigm for the observance of the commandments, and emphasizes the punishment awaiting anyone who does not follow them.[64] While the *Book of the Watchers* took no note of the Sinai covenant, *Jubilees* is a thoroughly Mosaic work, which integrates the perspective of the Mosaic law even into the primeval period.[65]

Hartmut Stegemann claimed that the *Temple Scroll* was written as early as 400 BCE, but there is no specific evidence for such an early dating. The question is complicated by the fact that the scroll as found in 11Q19 was compiled from sources.[66] Arguments for dating based on specific passages may only reflect the date of the source from which the passage was taken. Since our present concern is with the rise of halakhic exegesis, however, the date of the sources is significant.

4Q524 is variously taken as the oldest copy of the *Temple Scroll*, as a possible source or early edition, or simply as a closely related text.[67] It contains close parallels to TS cols 59–66, but also significant discrepancies. The text is very fragmentary, but it clearly parallels the "law of the king" and also some of the levitical laws. It evidently contained reworking of passages from both Deuteronomy and Leviticus. Puech dates the script to 150–125 BCE, and takes it to be a copy of an even earlier manuscript.[68] Others allow for a slightly later date, but "no later than the last quarter of the second century BCE."[69] The law of the king in the *Temple Scroll*, however, is often thought to be a polemic against the Hasmonean rulers, because it proposes "a king subject to the priesthood and free from all cultic activities."[70] As Florentino García Martínez put it: " The need for reformulating the biblical data with respect to royalty seemed more pressing once the Maccabees attained national independence than had been the case during the Persian period or under Ptolemaic or Seleucid dominion."[71] Whether this requires a date after the Hasmoneans formally proclaimed themselves king is less certain. García Martínez pushes the date of the pu-

---

[64] Segal, *The Book of Jubilees*, 143.

[65] The contrast between *Enoch* and *Jubilees* in this regard sets the agenda for the essays in Gabriele Boccaccini and Giovanni Ibba, eds., *Enoch and the Mosaic Torah. The Evidence of Jubilees* (Grand Rapids: Eerdmans, 2009). See the Preface by Gabriele Boccaccini, xiv.

[66] Michael Owen Wise, *A Critical Study of the Temple Scroll from Qumran Cave 11* (Studies in Ancient Oriental Civilization 49; Chicago: Oriental Institute, 1990).

[67] See the overview of the discussion by James H. Charlesworth, with Andrew de la Ronde van Kirk, "Temple Scroll Source or Earlier Edition (4Q524[4QT^b])," in Lawrence H. Schiffman, Andrew D. Gross, and Michael C. Rand, eds., *Temple Scroll and Related Documents* (The Dead Sea Scrolls. Hebrew, Aramaic, and Greek Texts with English Translations 7; Tübingen: Mohr Siebeck/ Louisville: Westminster, 2011) 249–51.

[68] Émile Puech, *Qumrân Grotte 4. XVIII. Textes Hébreux (4Q521–4Q528, 4Q576–4Q579)* (DJD 25; Oxford: Clarendon, 1998) 87.

[69] Schiffman, *Temple Scroll*, 4.

[70] Florentino García Martínez, "Temple Scroll," in *EDSS*, 931.

[71] *Ibid.*

rity laws back to the Maccabean era, and suggests that the "midrash on Deuteronomy" containing the Law of the King may have been prompted by the discussions leading to the investiture of Simon. All this is very tentative, however. Schiffman argues that "we must see the composition of the Law of the King as taking place no earlier than the second half of the reign of John Hyrcanus. He is the first of the Hasmoneans to have consolidated a stable empire."[72] The dating of this and other key Scrolls has been influenced on occasion by the assumption that the sect originated in a dispute over the High Priesthood when the Hasmoneans assumed that office. That assumption, however, is unfounded. The disputes that are cited in CD and 4QMMT as generative of sectarian separation are all *halakhic* issues, and the high priestly succession is not among them. There is no need, then, to push a "pre-sectarian" text such as the *Temple Scroll* back to the middle of the second century BCE. The Law of the King is likely to presuppose a certain development of Hasmonean power and is not likely to be earlier than the reign of John Hyrcanus.

Jubilees also is likely to have originated in the Hasmonean era, in the second century BCE. In an influential study, James VanderKam dated the composition between 161 and 140 BCE, with a preference for the first half of that period.[73] His argument rested in large part on supposed references to the Maccabean wars in *Jubilees*, but this would at most provide a *terminus a quo*. The oldest copy of *Jubilees*, 4Q216, dates from the last quarter of the second century. A number of scholars have tried to date the book on the basis of 23:9–32. Nickelsburg takes this as polemic against the Hellenizers before the Maccabean revolt.[74] Menahem Kister argues to the contrary that the revolt is not mentioned because it was already long past.[75] Doron Mendels argued for a date in the 120's, arguing that *Jubilees* 38, which refers to the subjection of the Edomites, must presuppose the final conquest of Idumea by John Hyrcanus.[76] None of these considerations can be considered decisive.[77] The question is complicated further if we accept that the work is the product of more than one hand, as Segal and Kugel have argued. Nonetheless, it seems safe to say that *Jubilees* is a product of the Hasmonean period, roughly contemporary with the

---

[72] Schiffman, *Temple Scroll*, 5.

[73] James C. VanderKam, *Textual and Historical Studies on the Book of Jubilees* (HSM 14; Missoula: Scholars Press, 1977) 207–85.

[74] G. W. E. Nickelsburg, "The Bible Rewritten and Expanded," in Michael E. Stone, ed., *Jewish Writings of the Second Temple Period* (CRINT 2/2; Philadelphia: Fortress/Assen: van Gorcum, 1984) 103.

[75] Menahem Kister, "Concerning the History of the Essenes: A Study of the *Animal Apocalypse*, the *Book of Jubilees*, and the Damascus Covenant," *Tarbiz* 56 (1986) 1–18 (Heb). See Segal, *The Book of Jubilees*, 35–41.

[76] Doron Mendels, *The Land of Israel as a Political Concept in Hasmonean Literature* (Tübingen: Mohr Siebeck, 1987) 80.

[77] See the cautionary comments of Robert Doran, "The Non-dating of Jubilees. Jub 34–38; 23:14–32 in Narrative Context," *JSJ* 20 (1989) 1–11.

Temple Scroll. The fact that the two works have much in common is widely recognized.[78]

The kind of halakhic analysis that we find in the *Temple Scroll* and *Jubilees* cannot have developed overnight. Undoubtedly, these issues were being discussed for some decades before these books were written, certainly before they attained their final shape. Halakhic issues must have exercised priests already in the biblical period. The fact that the surviving writings that reflect halakhic debates date from the Hasmonean era, however, suggests that they enjoyed new prominence in Jewish society at this time, and this accords with the appearance of stone vessels and *miqvaot* in the archaeological record. The attempt to displace the traditional Torah in the time of Antiochus Epiphanes had the contrary effect of making the Torah, construed specifically as law, the touchstone for Jewish observance. While the Hasmoneans were not especially known for their piety, they accorded the Law a pivotal place in forming Judean national identity, and thereby created the context in which *halakhic* discussion, and controversy, flourished.

Halakah and Sectarianism

The Hasmoneans may have hoped that the Torah as ancestral law would unify the newly independent nation, and in a sense it did, but it would also be the source of bitter divisions. In his study of the rise of Jewish sectarianism, Albert Baumgarten noted several contributing factors.[79] These included urbanization, increased literacy, and disappointment with the native dynasty when independence was achieved. Most relevant to our present discussion is the maxim formulated by Morton Smith in 1960: "But touch the Law, and the sect will split."[80] Jews could tolerate a range of opinions on belief – one or two messiahs, the role of supernatural forces in human sin, etc. But the range of tolerance on legal issues, among people who took seriously the call to be zealous for the Law, was narrow. Moreover, the received laws were ambiguous and elliptic, and so disagreement was inevitable. The increased focus on the Torah as Law in the Hasmonean period had, perhaps, its inevitable outcome in 4QMMT, which posited the conflict of legal interpretation as the primary cause of sectarian division. The light shed on that conflict is one of the great contributions of the Dead Sea Scrolls to our understanding of late Second Temple Judaism.

---

[78] James C. VanderKam, "The *Temple Scroll* and the *Book of Jubilees*," in George J. Brooke, ed., *Temple Scroll Studies* (JSPSup 7; Sheffield: Sheffield Academic Press, 1989) 211–36; Lawrence H. Schiffman, "The *Book of Jubilees* and the *Temple Scroll*," in Boccaccini and Ibba, eds., *Enoch and the Mosaic Torah*, 99–115.

[79] Albert I. Baumgarten, *The Flourishing of Jewish Sects in the Maccabean Era: An Interpretation* (JSJSup 55; Leiden: Brill, 1997).

[80] Morton Smith, "The Dead Sea Sect in Relation to Ancient Judaism," *NTS* 7 (1960) 347–60 (here 360). See Baumgarten, *The Flourishing*, 76.

CHAPTER THREE

Changing Scripture

"How can you say, 'We are wise, and the law of the Lord is with us,' when in fact, the false pen of the scribes has made it into a lie?" (Jer 8:8)

We do not know precisely what Jeremiah had in mind in his scathing denunciation of scribal activity on the Torah. Many scholars think that the prophet was opposed to any written Torah.[1] He was certainly concerned that the authority of the prophet to speak for God was being usurped by the scribes, as indeed it was. But it is also established beyond doubt that scribes frequently changed the supposedly revealed texts that they transmitted. Ironically, the book of Jeremiah is itself a prime example of scribal composition, where the original oracles of the prophet are now overshadowed by the accretions, often ideological, of scribal transmission.[2] Of course, Jeremiah's judgment on such accretions reflects a particular perspective, which is not inevitable. Religious traditions sometimes value the contributions of the editors, who gave the material its canonical shape, more than those of the prophets. It is often assumed that these editors were attempting to preserve and explicate the true meaning of their sources, and undoubtedly this was often so. But Jeremiah's outburst should warn us that a "hermeneutic of suspicion" towards the ideological underpinnings of scribal activity is not entirely anachronistic. Claims to speak with divine authority were especially fraught with implications for power in ancient society, and were inevitably, and properly, contested.

The case of Deuteronomy

The role of scribes not only in the transmission of the biblical tradition but also in its development has received renewed attention in recent years.[3] Michael Fishbane's

---

[1] For a summary of the discussion see William L. Holladay, *Jeremiah 1* (Hermeneia; Philadelphia: Fortress, 1986) 281. It has been suggested that the verse summarizes Jeremiah's view of Josiah's reform, but most scholars reject that view as exaggerated.

[2] See e.g. Christl Maier, *Jeremia als Lehrer der Tora: Soziale Gebote des Deuteronomiums in Fortschreibungen des Jeremiabuches* (Göttingen: Vandenhoeck & Ruprecht, 2002); Carolyn Sharp, *Prophecy and Ideology in Jeremiah: struggles for authority in Deutero-Jeremianic prose* (London/New York: T & T Clark, 2003).

[3] William M. Schniedewind, *How the Bible Became a Book: The Textualization of Ancient Israel* (Cambridge: Cambridge University Press, 2004); David M. Carr, *Writing on the Tablet of the*

classic study of inner-biblical exegesis was a pioneering work in this regard.⁴ Fishbane's student, Bernard Levinson, built on this foundation in his influential study of the hermeneutics of legal innovation in Deuteronomy. But, wrote Levinson,

> in the end, however, inner biblical exegesis does not provide a satisfactory model to describe the achievements of the authors of Deuteronomy. The concern of the authors of Deuteronomy was not to explicate older texts but to transform them. Neither 'interpretation' nor 'exegesis' adequately suggests the extent to which Deuteronomy radically transforms literary and legal history in order to forge a new vision of religion and the state.⁵

Rather than the continuity of tradition, Levinson sought to emphasize

> the extent to which exegesis may make itself independent of the source text, challenging and even attempting to reverse or abrogate its substantive content, all the while under the hermeneutical mantle of consistency with or dependency upon its source.⁶

So, he concludes,

> Deuteronomy's use of precedent subverts it. The old saw of Deuteronomy as a pious fraud may thus be profitably inverted. Is there not something of an impious fraud – of *pecca fortiter*! – in the literary accomplishment of the text's authors?⁷

Levinson's view of the matter has not gone unchallenged. Hindy Najman accuses him of assuming "a contemporary conception of fraudulence, and a contemporary conception of piety towards tradition."⁸ Ideas of authorship in antiquity were very different from their modern counterparts.⁹ Anonymity was often the norm, but the attribution of texts to specific figures was also a significant practice, not least as a way of claiming authority for a text.¹⁰ Karel van der Toorn distinguishes between

---

Heart (New York: Oxford, 2005); Karel van der Toorn, *Scribal Culture and the Making of the Hebrew Bible* (Cambridge, MA: Harvard University Press, 2007).

⁴ Michael Fishbane, *Biblical Interpretation in Ancient Israel* (Oxford: Clarendon, 1985).

⁵ Bernard Levinson, *Deuteronomy and the Hermeneutics of Legal Innovation* (New York: Oxford, 1997) 15.

⁶ Ibid.

⁷ Ibid., 150.

⁸ Hindy Najman, *Seconding Sinai. The Development of Mosaic Discourse in Second Temple Judaism* (JSJSup 77; Leiden: Brill, 2004) 5.

⁹ Karel van der Toorn, "Authorship in Antiquity," in idem, *Scribal Culture*, 27–49; Leo G. Perdue, "Pseudonymity and Graeco-Roman Rhetoric," in Jörg Frey, Jens Herzer, Martina Janssen and Clare K. Rothschild, eds., *Pseudepigraphie und Verfasserfiktion in frühchristlichen Briefen* (WUNT 246; Tübingen: Mohr Siebeck, 2009) 27–59, especially 28–39 ("Authorship in Antiquity"), Jed Wyrick, *The Ascension of Authorship: Attribution and Canon Formation in Jewish, Hellenistic, and Christian Traditions* (Cambridge: Harvard University Press, 2004).

¹⁰ Perdue, "Pseudonymity," 29: "while in the ANE authorship may at times have been viewed as collective, i.e. texts were produced by the scribal communities, attribution to individuals was a significant practice especially among the composers of the wisdom corpora." Philip R. Davies, "Spurious Attribution in the Hebrew Bible," in James R. Lewis and Olav Hammer, *The Invention of Sacred Tradition* (Cambridge: Cambridge University Press, 2007) 258–75 (259), says that scribal communities in the ancient Near East considered authorship to be unimportant, but does not reconcile this with the phenomenon of pseudonymous attribution, which he also notes.

"honorary authorship," whereby a work was attributed to a patron, often in the interests of political propaganda (e.g. the Laws of Hammurabi) and pseudepigraphy, whereby authors attribute their work to a (fictive) author from remote times in order to present their work as a legacy from the venerable past.[11] Pseudepigraphy was very widespread in the ancient world, and was motivated in various ways.[12] To regard it simply as fraud or deception in all cases would obviously be simplistic. Even when works were denounced as forgeries in antiquity, the issue was not necessarily authorship in the modern sense. Tertullian famously denounced *The Acts of Paul and Thecla*, because it served "as a licence for women's teaching and baptizing."[13] But the same Tertullian wrote that Luke's gospel ought to be ascribed to Paul and Mark's to Peter, because "that which disciples publish should be regarded as their master's work."[14]

Najman suggests that works like Deuteronomy, that reformulate the revelation given to Moses on Mt. Sinai, should be compared to modern *discourses that are inextricably linked to their founders*, such as Marxism or Freudianism.

> When someone proclaims 'Back to Marx!' or 'Back to Freud!' she claims to represent the authentic doctrine of Marx or Freud, although she may express it in different words ... In some ancient cultures, the way to continue or return to the founder's discourse was precisely to ascribe what one said or wrote, not to oneself, but rather to the founder.[15]

There is some precedent for this in antiquity, in the Greek philosophical schools. The Neo-Pythagoreans thought it most honorable and praiseworthy to publish one's philosophical treatises in the name of Pythagoras himself.[16] Najman does not suggest that there was a "Mosaic school," but suggests an analogy nonetheless. So, to rework an earlier formulation of the law of Moses is not to claim that the rewritten text represents the words of the historical Moses but "to update, interpret and develop the content of that text in a way that one claims to be an authentic expression of the law already accepted as authoritatively Mosaic."[17]

Levinson's argument that Deuteronomy is a deliberate subversion of the older Covenant Code is based in large part on its reworking of key terms from the older text. So, for example, the Deuteronomic writers rework the key terms in the altar law of Exodus

> in such a way as finally to make it prohibit what it originally sanctioned (multiple altar sites as legitimate) and command the two innovations it could never have contemplated: cultic

---

[11] Van der Toorn, *Scribal Culture*, 34.
[12] The literature is vast. See Wolfgang Speyer, *Die literarische Fälschung im Altertum* (Munich: Beck, 1971); Bruce M. Metzger, "Literary Forgeries and Canonical Pseudepigrapha," *JBL* 91 (1972) 3–24; and the essays in Frey et al., eds., *Pseudepigraphie und Verfasserfiktion*.
[13] Tertullian, *De Baptismo*, 17.
[14] Tertullian, *Adversus Marcionem* 6.5.
[15] *Seconding Sinai*, 12.
[16] Iamblichus, *De Vita Pythagorica*, 198.
[17] Najman, *Seconding Sinai*, 13.

centralization and local, secular slaughter... The antithetical reworking of the original text suggests an extraordinary ambivalence on the part of the authors of Deuteronomy, who retain the old altar law only to transform it and who thereby subvert the very textual authority that they invoke.[18]

Najman counters:

If one *intends* to replace an earlier code, why should one exert so much effort to incorporate and preserve its wording? Why should one constantly remind the reader of the earlier text, already accepted as authoritative, which one wishes to supplant?[19]

In her view, the ambivalence that Levinson perceives arises from his assumption that Deuteronomy was intended to replace an older authoritative law. Najman argues that there is no reason to think that the Deuteronomic writers wanted to suppress the older law: "Instead, there is good reason to think that they intended the Covenant Code to be preserved alongside the Deuteronomic Code, with the latter serving as the authentic exposition of certain laws in the former."[20] Approximately two thirds of the laws in the Covenant Code are not repeated in Deuteronomy, and are presumably not annulled. Moreover, both the Covenant Code and Deuteronomy were eventually acknowledged as Holy Scripture. The acceptance of Deuteronomy did not require the suppression of the laws in Exodus.

Levinson's analysis assumes that the Book of the Covenant was an authoritative text when Deuteronomy was written: "The authors of Deuteronomy sought to locate their innovative vision in prior textual authority by tendentiously appropriating texts like the Covenant Code ..."[21] This is a reasonable assumption. The Covenant Code would hardly have survived as authoritative scripture if it had not already enjoyed that status, at least in some circles, before the Deuteronomic revision. But in fact we have no explicit evidence as to what status the Book of the Covenant enjoyed in the seventh century BCE. Neither do we have any explicit evidence as to whether the authors of Deuteronomy intended that the older writing be preserved. *Pace* Najman, it does not seem to me that the reuse of language from an older text argues against replacement: revisions and new editions normally reuse the language of the original, but seek to supersede it nonetheless.[22] The Covenant Code echoes the Laws of Hammurabi at many points,[23] but surely did not regard the Mesopotamian code as authoritative. The fact that Deuteronomy does not repeat or revise all the

---

[18] Levinson, *Deuteronomy*, 46.
[19] Najman, *Seconding Sinai*, 22–23.
[20] *Ibid.*, 24.
[21] Levinson, *Deuteronomy*, 16.
[22] The new edition of Emil Schürer's *History of the Jewish People in the Age of Jesus Christ*, edited by Geza Vermes et al. (3 vols.; Edinburgh: Clark, 1973–1987) was intended not only to update the classic original but also to subvert its view of Judaism in some respects. Yet large portions of the original were repeated verbatim. The revision attested to the authoritative status of the original, but it unambiguously sought to replace it.
[23] David Wright, *Inventing God's Law. How the Covenant Code of the Bible Used and Revised the Laws of Hammurabi* (New York: Oxford, 2009) 9.

laws of the Exodus code is a stronger argument that the older text was expected to be still available.

But in fact, framing the question in terms of whether or not one code was meant to replace the other may reflect an anachronistic understanding of the function of law codes in ancient Judah. Many scholars have argued that early law codes were descriptive rather than prescriptive.[24] They recorded representative rulings, and had some value as precedents, but ultimately law depended on the decision of the king or the judge. Some scholars argue that this situation changed with Deuteronomy, with its emphasis on the book of the Law.[25] Others place the transition later, in the Persian era.[26] Michael LeFebvre argues that the Torah did not become a legislative text before the Hellenistic era.[27] In any case, it is unlikely that the Book of the Covenant was used as prescriptive law before Josiah's reform.[28] Neither, of course, was it part of a "canon," in the sense of an exclusive collection of authoritative texts. The authors of Deuteronomy surely intended to supersede the older code on the topics that they addressed. But ultimately, law was decided by the king, or by the competent authorities in the community after the demise of the kingship. It was not necessary to suppress the Covenant Code, which contained much material with which the Deuteronomic authors had no quarrel. The important thing was that the rulers should know which formulation offered the better guidance. In fact, even when law is understood prescriptively, its exercise always requires a competent authority to interpret it.

Two other aspects of Deuteronomy should be noted. First, the book is not presented as a transcription of the revelation at Mount Sinai/Horeb. It is a secondary account of the revelation, a recapitulation by Moses on the plains of Moab – hence the name, Deuteronomy, the second law. Najman's designation of it as "Mosaic discourse" is fully justified. It contains a prohibition (probably vain)[29] against adding or subtracting anything from its formulation (Deut 13:1), but it does not preclude the existence of other accounts. But, second, it does not acknowledge the existence of any prior "book of the covenant," despite its well-documented dependence on the laws of Exodus. The source of its authority is not its relationship to an earlier book but its claim to give the substance of the revelation at Sinai, and the credibility of Moses as narrator. Echoes of other formulations that might be known

---

[24] Michael LeFebvre, *Collections, Codes, and Torah. The Re-characterization of Israel's Written Law* (New York and London: T & T Clark, 2006) 1–30.

[25] Dale Patrick, *Old Testament Law* (London: SCM, 1986) 189–204; Raymond Westbrook, "Cuneiform Law Codes and the Origins of Legislation," *ZA* 79 (1989) 201–22.

[26] Anne Fitzpatrick-McKinley, *The Transformation of Torah from Scribal Advice to Law* (JSOTSup 287; Sheffield: Sheffield Academic Press, 1999).

[27] LeFebvre, *Collections, Codes, and Torah*, 258.

[28] Wright, *Inventing God's Law*, 4, suggests that the Covenant Code is to be viewed as "an academic abstraction rather than a digest of laws practiced by Israelites and Judeans over the course of centuries."

[29] We do not know at what point this prohibition was inserted.

to those who read or heard these laws may have added to their credibility, by evoking associations, but it is not from the earlier formulations that Deuteronomy derives its authority.

The second century BCE

It is generally agreed that the authority of the Torah had been clarified and solidified considerably by the second century BCE. "Considerably," however, is not "absolutely." One of the revelations of the Dead Sea Scrolls has concerned the extent of textual variation in the Hebrew scriptures, down to the turn of the era. It is now clear that textual traditions known to us from the Samaritan Pentateuch and the Septuagint were current in Hebrew in the land of Israel, as well as the precursors of the Masoretic text, and there were other variations besides.[30] Variant editions of several biblical books were in circulation (Exodus, Jeremiah, Psalms).[31] This in itself presents an interesting problem, as it shows that authority resided in a book rather than in a particular textual form of that book. Scribal variation was not necessarily perceived as problematic. The variants include scribal errors, but also intentional changes. Some of these consist of additions, rearrangements and paraphrases, sometimes intended to clarify the text, and sometimes tendentious.[32] There is a movement towards standardization of the text in the first century CE, as can be seen from the revisions of the Greek translation of the Minor Prophets and from the prevalence of proto-Masoretic texts at Masada, but there is still considerable evidence of textual variation in the New Testament and in Josephus.

Prior to the discovery of the Dead Sea Scrolls, it was easy enough to distinguish between a biblical text that was at variance with the MT (e.g. the Samaritan Pentateuch) and a book like *Jubilees* that retold the story of Genesis and part of Exodus but was clearly an independent composition. The distinction is blurred, however, in the text (or texts) known as *4QReworked Pentateuch* (4Q158, 4Q364–7). This title refers to a group of five fragmentary manuscripts, which were originally thought to

---

[30] For a concise summary see Armin Lange, "'Nobody dared to add to them, to take from them, or to make changes' (Josephus, *Ag.Ap.* 1.42). The Textual Standardization of Jewish Scriptures in Light of the Dead Sea Scrolls," in Anthony Hilhorst, Émile Puech and Eibert Tigchelaar, eds., *Flores Florentino. Dead Sea Scrolls and Other Early Jewish Studies in Honour of Florentino García Martínez* (JSJSup 122; Leiden: Brill, 2007) 105–26, especially 107–10; idem, *Handbuch der Textfunde vom Toten Meer. Bd. 1: Die Handschriften biblischer Bücher von Qumran und den anderen Fundorten* (Tübingen: Mohr Siebeck, 2009).

[31] Eugene C. Ulrich, *The Dead Sea Scrolls and the Origin of the Bible* (Grand Rapids: Eerdmans, 1999) 17–50; 99–120.

[32] Michael Segal, "Between Bible and Rewritten Bible," in Matthias Henze, ed., *Biblical Interpretation at Qumran* (Grand Rapids: Eerdmans, 2005) 12. See the discussion of the Samaritan Pentateuch by Magnar Kartveit, *The Origin of the Samaritans* (VTSup 128; Leiden: Brill, 2009) 279–312.

make up a single, independent composition.[33] Since there are no significant overlaps, however, they are now increasingly viewed as distinct but related compositions.[34] All five manuscripts reflect Pentateuchal texts, with variations, including rearrangements and additions (notably the "Song of Miriam"). In the words of Sidnie White Crawford, "these texts are the product of scribal interpretation, still marked mainly by harmonistic editing, but with one important addition: the insertion of outside material into the text, material not found in other parts of what we now recognize as the Pentateuch."[35] But many fragments correspond to the traditional text with minimal variation. The extant fragments do not suggest any changes of speaker or setting over against other forms of these texts. Consequently, they are increasingly viewed not as distinct compositions but as expansionistic variants of the text known from our Bible.[36] If this is so, it suggests that the there was still great freedom in copying the scriptural texts as late as the first century BCE.[37] How far these texts were accepted as authentic scriptures, we do not know. They survive in single, fragmentary copies. It has been suggested that *Jubilees* relied on 4Q364, frag. 3 (Isaac/Rebekah) and that the *Temple Scroll* relied on 4Q365, frag. 23 (the New Oil/Wood festival), but the evidence is not conclusive.[38] White Crawford believes that "we can say with almost complete certainty that 4Q364 and 4Q365 were meant by the scribes who prepared them to be read as regular pentateuchal texts."[39] Given the tolerance of textual variation that we find at Qumran, this does not mean that these scribes would have made any attempt to suppress other forms of these texts. Most of their variations can be viewed as exegetical, and taken as attempts to clarify the received text and bring out its fuller significance.

---

[33] Emanuel Tov and Sidnie White Crawford, "Reworked Pentateuch," in Harold Attridge et al., *Qumran Cave 4, VIII* (DJD 13; Oxford: Clarendon, 1994) 187–351.

[34] Michael Segal, "4QReworked Pentateuch or 4QPentateuch?" in L. Schiffman, E. Tov, and J. VanderKam, eds., *The Dead Sea Scrolls: Fifty Years after Their Discovery* (Jerusalem: Israel Exploration Society/Shrine of the Book, Israel Museum, 2000) 391–99; George Brooke, "4Q158: Reworked Pentateuch[a] or Reworked Pentateuch A?" *DSD* 8 (2001) 219–41; Sidnie White Crawford, *Rewriting Scripture in Second Temple Times* (Grand Rapids: Eerdmans, 2008) 39; Molly M. Zahn, *Rethinking Rewritten Scripture: Composition and Exegesis in the 4QReworked Pentateuch Manuscripts* (Leiden: Brill, 2011).

[35] White Crawford, *Rewriting Scripture*, 39–40.

[36] For a list of scholars who hold this view, including now Emanuel Tov, see White Crawford, *Rewriting Scripture*, 56. See the discussion by Molly M. Zahn, "The Problem of Characterizing the 4QReworked Pentateuch Manuscripts: Bible, Rewritten Bible, or None of the Above?" *DSD* 15 (2008) 315–39; eadem, "Rewritten Scriptures," in Timothy H. Lim and John J. Collins, eds., *The Oxford Handbook of the Dead Sea Scrolls* (Oxford: Oxford University Press, 2010) and her book, *Rethinking Rewritten Scripture*.

[37] The manuscripts date from the late Hasmonean period. White Crawford, *Rewriting Scripture*, 40.

[38] White Crawford, *Rewriting Scripture*, 59.

[39] *Ibid.*, 56.

Rewritten scriptures

There are other texts, however, which are closely based on the traditional text of the Torah, but are generally recognized as distinct compositions in their own right. These texts are often categorized as "Rewritten Bible," a label introduced by Geza Vermes, to describe such works as *Jubilees*, the *Genesis Apocryphon*, the *Biblical Antiquities* of Pseudo-Philo and the *Antiquities* of Josephus.[40] The designation is problematic, since that which is rewritten was not yet "Bible," and so scholars increasingly refer to them as "rewritten scriptures."[41] The rewriting has much in common with what we find in expansionistic texts like *4QReworked Pentateuch*. It involves harmonizing, rearranging and expansion. Some scholars see a spectrum, which ranges from minor editorial changes in the received text, to changes so extensive that they are deemed to constitute independent works.[42] But, as Michael Segal has pointed out, the difference between "Bible" and "Rewritten Bible" is not simply quantitative.[43] If it were, the variant editions of Jeremiah that underlie the MT and LXX would be considered different compositions.

More important are differences in the literary frame, the authorial voice, and the scope of the composition.

There has been extensive debate about the extent and definition of this category of writing.[44] It is not strictly a literary genre.[45] Individual compositions tend to follow the genre of the prototype.[46] A great amount of Jewish literature from the late

---

[40] Geza Vermes, *Scripture and Tradition in Judaism: Haggadic Studies* (SPB 4; Leiden: Brill, 1973, first edition 1961) 67–126.

[41] See e.g. Anders Klostergaard Petersen, "Rewritten Bible as a Borderline Phenomenon – Genre, Textual Strategy or Canonical Anachronism?" in Hilhorst et al., eds., *Flores Florentino*, 284–306. Jonathan G. Campbell, "'Rewritten Bible' and 'Parabiblical Texts': A Terminological and Ideological Critique," in idem et al., eds., *New Directions in Qumran Studies: Proceedings of the Bristol Colloquium on the Dead Sea Scrolls, 8–10 September 2003* (London: T & T Clark, 2005) 43–68, also objects to "rewritten scriptures." He suggests terminology along the lines of "scripture" and "parascripture."

[42] So White Crawford, *Rewriting Scripture*, 14.

[43] Segal, "Between Bible and Rewritten Bible," 16. See also Zahn, "Rewritten Scriptures."

[44] In addition to works already cited see Moshe Bernstein, "'Rewritten Bible': A Generic Category Which Has Outlived Its Usefulness?" *Textus* 22 (2005) 169–96; George J. Brooke, "Rewritten Bible," in L. H. Schiffman and J. C. VanderKam, eds., *The Encyclopedia of the Dead Sea Scrolls* (New York: Oxford, 2000) 2.777–81; idem, "The Rewritten Law, Prophets and Psalms: Issues for Understanding the Text of the Bible," in E. D. Herbert and Emanuel Tov, eds., *The Bible as Book: The Hebrew Bible and the Judaean Desert Discoveries* (London: British Library, 2002) 31–40; Antti Laato and Jacques van Ruiten, eds., *Rewritten Bible Reconsidered* (Winona Lake, IN: Eisenbrauns, 2008).

[45] Philip S. Alexander, "Retelling the Old Testament," in D. A. Carson and H. G. M. Williamson, eds., *It Is Written: Scripture Citing Scripture* (Cambridge: Cambridge University Press, 1988) 99–121, argues that the texts so classified by Vermes, *Jubilees*, the *Genesis Apocryphon*, the *Antiquities* of Josephus and the *Biblical Antiquities* of Pseudo-Philo, do constitute a literary genre. These are all narrative texts, and do not include such compositions as the Temple Scroll.

[46] Compare Brooke, "Rewritten Bible," 780: "Rewritten Bible texts come in almost as many genres as can be found in the biblical books themselves."

Second Temple period is based on older scriptures in one way or another. For example, the fragments of Hellenistic Jewish literature preserve re-tellings of stories about the patriarchs and the exodus not only in narrative form, but also in epic poetry and even in the form of a tragedy.[47] There is no question in these writings of replacing the original scriptures: they simply present (and often embellish) these stories in ways that render them more interesting for a Hellenized audience, and use them to reshape Jewish identity in a Diaspora setting. They treat the scriptures as sources for their literary imagination. This is also true of Josephus' great re-telling of biblical history in his *Antiquities*, which was one of the works originally categorized as "Rewritten Bible" by Vermes. These works may have an exegetical dimension, insofar as they sometimes try to resolve problems in the scriptures, but they are not primarily works of exegesis. They are new compositions that draw their source material from the traditional scriptures. The same is arguably true of the Aramaic *Genesis Apocryphon* and *Aramaic Levi Document*. The fact that so much of Jewish literature in this period draws its source material from the Pentateuch is powerful testimony to the authoritative status of the narrative parts of the Torah. Authority in these cases means primarily literary authority. Genesis and Exodus are classic texts that are infinitely adaptable to new circumstances, just as the epics of Homer were classic texts for the Greeks.

In the case of legal texts, however, the issues were somewhat different. We know from the Dead Sea Scrolls that halakhic disputation was common in the first century BCE, and contributed to the division between sects, probably as early as the reign of John Hyrcanus. 4QMMT provides a classic example of the halakhic mentality, which unambiguously reads the laws of scripture as prescriptive. Halakhic disputation did not immediately lead to textual standardization, as we might expect from a modern perspective, but it meant that variation in legal texts became fraught with significance. If we seek an analogy to the revision of the Covenant Code in Deuteronomy, our concern is primarily with texts that rewrite the laws of the Torah, or rewrite the narratives with a halakhic focus.

Two such texts have attracted great attention in recent years. The *Book of Jubilees* was one of the prototypical texts adduced by Vermes. It retells the narrative of Genesis and part of Exodus, but it supplies a new literary frame: the narrative is dictated to Moses by an angel on Mt. Sinai. In this case, the re-writing is far more tendentious than anything we find in the fragments of *4QReworked Pentateuch*. Much of it is concerned with a strict interpretation of halakhic issues, including a 364-day calendar, which is injected into the retold narrative. The *Temple Scroll* is also presented as a revelation on Mt. Sinai, but in this case God speaks directly to Moses. In contrast to *Jubilees*, it is entirely concerned with the legal texts of the Pentateuch. In that

---

[47] See further John J. Collins, *Between Athens and Jerusalem. Jewish Identity in the Hellenistic Diaspora* (2nd ed.; Grand Rapids: Eerdmans, 2000) 29–63; Martin Goodman, "Jewish Literature Composed in Greek," in Geza Vermes, Fergus Millar and Martin Goodman, *The History of the Jewish People in the Age of Jesus Christ* III.1 (Edinburgh: Clark, 1986) 509–66.

sense, the two books complement each other, although Ben Zion Wacholder's suggestion that the two were parts of a single composition is universally rejected.[48] Both *Jubilees* and the *Temple Scroll* are likely to date from the second century BCE.[49] Neither text engages in the kind of pesher-style exegesis, which carefully distinguishes the scriptural lemma from its interpretation, that we find in the sectarian texts from Qumran, which probably date to the first half of the first century BCE.

As with Deuteronomy, there has been debate as to whether these books are intended to replace or supplement the traditional Torah. Najman has argued vigorously that they

> seek to provide the interpretive context within which scriptural traditions already acknowledged as authoritative can be properly understood. This is neither a fraudulent attempt at replacement, nor an act of impiety. It is rather, we may charitably assume, a pious effort to convey what is taken to be the essence of earlier traditions, an essence that the rewriters think is in danger of being missed.[50]

Moreover, she claims, "they claimed for their interpretations of authoritative texts, the already established authority of the texts themselves."[51] Their goal is to solve interpretive problems in the older texts, and to appropriate the authority of the Torah for their interpretations. So, argues Najman, while they do not replace the existing Torah, they do claim the status of Torah for themselves. Najman is aware that there are significant differences between the two compositions.[52] I would suggest that these differences are important for the kind of authority claimed in each text, and for the way in which their relationship to the older scriptures is conceived.

Jubilees

In the case of *Jubilees*, we are fortunate that the beginning of the work has been preserved. Both the short prologue and the opening chapter are attested in the fragments of 4Q216 and preserved in full in Ethiopic. From allusions to Exod 24:12–18, it appears that the setting is Moses' first forty-day sojourn on Mt. Sinai.[53] Moses is told to write down

---

[48] Ben Zion Wacholder, "The Relationship Between 11Q Torah (the Temple Scroll) and the Book of Jubilees, One Single or Two Independent Compositions," in K. H. Richards, ed., *Society of Biblical Literature Seminar Papers* (Atlanta: Scholars Press, 1985) 205–16.

[49] On the date of Jubilees, James C. VanderKam, *The Book of Jubilees* (Sheffield: Sheffield Academic Press, 2001) 17–21; for the *Temple Scroll*, see Sidnie White Crawford, *The Temple Scroll and Related Texts* (Sheffield: Sheffield Academic Press, 2000) 24–26. VanderKam and White Crawford both favor dates before the middle of the second century BCE for their respective works.

[50] Najman, *Seconding Sinai*, 46.

[51] *Ibid.*, 45.

[52] *Ibid.*, 59.

[53] See James C. VanderKam, "Moses Trumping Moses," in Sarianna Metso et al., eds., *The Dead Sea Scrolls. Transmission of Traditions and Production of Texts* (Leiden: Brill, 2010) 25–44.

everything I tell you on this mountain, the first things and the last things that shall come to pass in all the divisions of the days, in the law and in the testimony, and in the weeks of the *Jubilees* till eternity, till I descend and dwell with them through all eternity (*Jub* 1:26).

The actual dictation is performed not by the Deity but by the angel of the presence, who in turn derives the information from the heavenly tablets.[54]

Jubilees evidently presupposes that the story of the revelation on Sinai is familiar to readers, and so it can dispense with the narrative of the arrival at Sinai. It also clearly presupposes the existence, and authority, of "the first law." The most explicit reference is in *Jub* 6:20–22, with reference to the laws of Shavuoth: "for I have written in the book of the first law, which I have written for you, that you should celebrate it at its proper time . . ." Again in *Jub* 30:12, à propos of Dinah and the Shechemites: "I have written for you in the words of the law all the details of what the Shechemites did to Dinah . . ." But in addition to the Torah, there was also the "testimony" תעודה, which, as VanderKam argues persuasively, should be identified with the contents of the book of *Jubilees* itself, although they may not exhaust the testimony contained in the heavenly tablets.[55]

Insofar as *Jubilees* claims to transmit revelation given to Moses on Mt. Sinai, it may reasonably be described as Mosaic discourse, but only in a qualified sense. Moses is not the speaker in *Jubilees*. His authority here is not that of a founder (although he was commonly so perceived in the Hellenistic world), but only that of a mediator. More properly, *Jubilees* is angelic discourse, or even mediated divine discourse. The authority claimed for it is not ultimately that of Moses, as in Deuteronomy or the *Testament of Moses*, but that of divine revelation. Moses is important as guarantor of its transmission, but he is not its source. Again, the discourse may reasonably be said to be "seconding Sinai," since it supplements and provides an interpretive context for "the first Torah." VanderKam points out that *Jubilees* claims to be the only revelation that survives from Moses' first sojourn on the mountain, since the tablets with "the first law" were smashed and had to be replaced. He therefore says that "he was not seconding Sinai; he was initiating it."[56] The point about precedence may be a quibble, however. Presumably the tablets that were destroyed were accurately replaced. The fact that the traditional Torah is called "the first law" would seem to grant it priority, in a sense. But the "testimony" is also revealed on Mt. Sinai, so for all practical purposes *Jubilees* and the "first law" are coeval and complementary.[57]

---

[54] Hindy Najman, "Interpretation as Primordial Writing: *Jubilees* and its Authority Conferring Strategies," in eadem, *Past Renewals. Interpretative Authority, Renewed Revelation and the Quest for Perfection in Jewish Antiquity* (JSJSup 53; Leiden: Brill, 2010) 39–71. This article was originally published in *JSJ* 30 (1999) 379–410.

[55] VanderKam, "Moses Trumping Moses." Cana Werman, "'The תורה and the תעודה Engraved on the Tablets," *DSD* 9 (2002) 75–103 thinks that the "testimony" is "the preordained march of history."

[56] VanderKam, "Moses Trumping Moses."

[57] Compare Werman, "'The הרות and the הדועת,'" 95: "Moses came down from Mount Sinai

The body of *Jubilees* is made up of a rewritten narrative of Genesis and Exodus. Much of the re-writing can be explained as an exegetical attempt to resolve problems in the traditional text of the Torah, although some other traditions are also introduced, notably the Enochic story of the fallen angels.[58] But *Jubilees* is not presented as an exegetical text, and there is no acknowledgement that its authority derives in any way from other scriptures.[59] Its authority does depend on the setting at Sinai, and the reader's acceptance that a foundational revelatory event occurred there. Verbal echoes of the older scriptures would probably have facilitated acceptance of *Jubilees* as a credible account of Sinaitic revelation. But this is not quite the same thing as appropriating the authority of the existing scriptures. *Jubilees* is presented as a distinct revelation. It is not intended to replace "the first law," but it does supersede it in some respects. Where it differs from or adds to the traditional Torah, there is no doubt in *Jubilees* as to which formulation has the higher authority.[60]

In view of the divine and angelic authority claimed for *Jubilees*, the appeal to the heavenly tablets may seem superfluous. For VanderKam, they simply add another layer of assurance of the reliability of the revelation: "these tablets are a written unchangeable, permanent depository of information under God's control."[61] James Kugel, in contrast, argues that the passages that refer to the heavenly tablets are in-

---

carrying two Torahs." Similarly Martha Himmelfarb, *A Kingdom of Priests. Ancestry and Merit in Ancient Judaism* (Philadelphia: University of Pennsylvania, 2006) 54–5: "*Jubilees* does not attempt to nudge the Torah out of its niche and replace it, but rather embraces the authority of the Torah even as it seeks to place itself alongside it." See also Himmelfarb, "Torah, Testimony, and Heavenly Tablets: The Claim to Authority in the *Book of Jubilees*," in Benjamin G. Wright, ed., *A Multiform Heritage: Studies on Early Judaism and Christianity in Honor of Robert A. Kraft* (Atlanta: Scholars Press, 1999) 22–8.

[58] Michael Segal, *The Book of Jubilees. Rewritten Bible, Redaction, Ideology and Theology* (JSJSup 117; Leiden: Brill, 2007) 103–43. Gabriele Boccaccini, "From a Movement of Dissent to a Distinct Form of Judaism: The Heavenly Tablets in *Jubilees* as the Foundation of a Competing Halakah," in Gabriele Boccaccini and Giovanni Ibba, eds., *Enoch and the Mosaic Torah. The Evidence of Jubilees* (Grand Rapids: Eerdmans, 2009) 193–210 construes the use of Enochic tradition in *Jubilees* as an attempt to merge two forms of Judaism. This construal entails assumptions about the social history of Second Temple Judaism that are not widely shared. See also John S. Bergsma, "The Relationship between Jubilees and the Early Enochic Books," in Boccaccini and Ibba, eds., *Enoch and the Mosaic Torah*, 36–51, who notes that the influence of the early Enoch material in Jubilees is limited to the period from Enoch to Noah, and does not come close to rivaling the importance of Moses.

[59] Najman, "Interpretation as Primordial Writing," in eadem, *Past Renewals*, 40, says: "Jubilees claims that its teachings are the true interpretation of the Torah" and "derive their authority from that of the Torah." But while the teachings of Jubilees are largely interpretations of the Torah, that is not how *Jubilees* presents itself.

[60] Ben Zion Wacholder, "Jubilees as the Super Canon," in M. Bernstein, F. García Martínez and J. Kampen, eds., *Legal Texts and Legal Issues* (STDJ 23; Leiden: Brill, 1997) 195–211, is correct that *Jubilees* trumps the traditional Torah in many places, even if it does not deny the Torah's authority.

[61] VanderKam, "Moses Trumping Moses." Similarly Najman, "Interpretation as Primordial Writing," 50–62.

terpolations, which stand in tension with the rest of the text in various ways.[62] The argument rests on perceived contradictions between these passages and the rest of the text, and some are more persuasive than others.[63] If Kugel is correct, however, this would explain why the interpolator has to trump even the angel of the presence by appealing to a still higher authority.

In any case, the heavenly tablets appear as a source of truth to which both the Torah and the Testimony are subordinate. Moreover, Enoch also "wrote his testimony and left it as a testimony on the earth for all the sons of men for every generation" (*Jub* 4:19), and Noah is also cited as an author.[64] The testimony of Enoch and Noah is not explicitly associated with the heavenly tablets, but they are further evidence that revelation is not confined to the traditional Torah. As Martha Himmelfarb has observed: "This approach not only exalts *Jubilees* but also, less obviously, demotes the Torah, which must share its authoritative status with another text even as both are subordinated to the heavenly tablets."[65]

VanderKam and Kugel agree, however, that the author of *Jubilees* could not just insert his new ideas into the received text of the Torah. For Kugel, this is why the interpolator made his insertions into *Jubilees* rather than into the Torah itself: "By the mid-second century BCE, any major, sectarian tampering with the Pentateuch would surely have been a controversial undertaking; its text was simply too widely known, and its study too well entrenched, across the spectrum of Jewish groups."[66] Whether this was already the case by the mid-second century BCE may be open to question, but at least the author of *Jubilees* chose not to change the text. He did not, however, subordinate his re-writing to the existing text by presenting it in the form of a commentary. Rather, he seems to have claimed for his "testimony" a status equal, at least, to that of the first Torah.

The *Temple Scroll*

In the case of the *Temple Scroll*, we do not have the opening column, and so there is some uncertainty as to how its revelation is presented. There is a passing reference to "Aaron your brother" in TS 44:5, and another to "those things which I tell you on this mountain" in TS 51:6. From these references, many infer that the discourse is

---

[62] James Kugel, "On the Interpolations in the Book of Jubilees," *RevQ* 24 (2009) 215–72. Kugel is building on the work of Segal, *The Book of Jubilees*.

[63] A persuasive example is the contrasting roles of Mastema in *Jubilees* 48–9.

[64] *Jub* 8:11; 10:13; 21:10. Himmelfarb, "Torah, Testimony, and the Heavenly Tablets," 27.

[65] Himmelfarb, *A Kingdom of Priests*, 55; cf. Himmelfarb, "Torah, Testimony, and the Heavenly Tablets," 27–28. Note also Najman, *Past Renewals*, 71: "Jubilees' insistence on the pre-Sinaitic origin of its heavenly tradition could be seen to undermine the special authority that had been accorded to the Mosaic Torah," and Boccaccini, "From a Movement of Dissent," 193–6.

[66] Kugel, "On the Interpolations," 271.

addressed to Moses on Mt. Sinai,[67] but these are the only nods to Moses in a lengthy text, and he is never mentioned by name. Najman argues that "by means of the second person singular pronoun, the reader is placed in the position of Moses, as the addressee of divine revelation on Mount Sinai."[68] But she also recognizes that the *Temple Scroll* is not about Moses: "Moses is nothing but the implicit, initial addressee and the implicit teacher of a Torah whose authority rests primarily on its direct revelation from God."[69] Schiffman entertains the possibility that the allusions to Moses are mere lapses, where the author had not fully revised his sources, and that he did not intend to acknowledge the role of Moses at all.[70] Without the opening column of the Scroll, it is impossible to know for sure whether Moses had more than the incidental role he appears to have in the extant fragments.

There is no doubt, however, that the speaking voice in the *Temple Scroll* is that of God. Consequently, Schiffman is correct that this is a "divine" rather than a "Mosaic" pseudepigraphon. It is only "Mosaic discourse" insofar as its content resembles the discourse of Moses in Deuteronomy. It is actually presented as "divine discourse." As such, its claim to authority would seem to be unambiguous. It would be anachronistic to say that the *Temple Scroll* is "canonical," but it claims to be a direct revelation of divine law. It is true that large portions of the *Temple Scroll* follow the same kinds of procedures that we find in expansionistic "biblical" texts – rearranging passages and harmonizing them, to smooth out the tensions between them. But unlike *Jubilees*, the *Temple Scroll* does not acknowledge any "first law." If the revelation is indeed set on Mount Sinai, then it would seem to be prior at least to Deuteronomy, perhaps even prior to the laws of Leviticus which were allegedly given to Moses at the Tent of Meeting. Also unlike *Jubilees*, there is no appeal to the Angel of the Presence or to the heavenly tablets. No further authority is needed than the voice of God.

The claim to authority of the *Temple Scroll* is as strong as any we find in the Torah and stronger than many. There can be no doubt that it claims the status of Torah: several passages demand that the Israelites observe "the regulation of this law" (50:5–9, 17) and it refers to itself as "this Torah" (56:20–1, the law of the king; cf. 57:1, the law of the priests, 59:7–10).[71] The fact that it uses language familiar from the traditional Torah would probably make it easier to accept as the authentic revelation on Sinai. Moreover, TS 54:5–7 appropriates the stricture of Deut 13:1: "all the

---

[67] So White Crawford, *Rewriting*, 86; eadem, *The Temple Scroll and Related Texts*, 18.
[68] Najman, *Seconding Sinai*, 68.
[69] Ibid.
[70] Lawrence H. Schiffman, "The Temple Scroll and the Halakhic Pseudepigrapha of the Second Temple Period," in E. Chazon and M. E. Stone, eds., *Pseudepigraphic Perspectives: The Apocrypha and Pseudepigrapha in Light of the Dead Sea Scrolls* (STDJ 31; Leiden: Brill, 1999) 121–31. See also Baruch A. Levine, "The Temple Scroll: Aspects of its Historical Provenance and Literary Character," *BASOR* 232 (1978) 17–21, who argued that the Temple Scroll follows Priestly understanding of revelation, according to which all commandments are attributed directly to God.
[71] Najman, *Seconding Sinai*, 52.

things which I order you today, take care to carry them out; you shall not add to them nor shall you remove anything from them." This could well be taken as a claim to exclusive authority. The strongest argument that the *Temple Scroll* presupposes the continued authority of other scriptures is that there are so many basic issues that it does not address. But even the traditional Torah does not address all aspects of the law – for example, there is no law regulating divorce, although the custom is clearly acknowledged in Deuteronomy 24. *De facto*, by the time the *Temple Scroll* was written many laws, such as the ten commandments, must have been so familiar that they could be taken for granted. It would have been unrealistic, in any case, to seek to suppress books that were current and enjoyed authority. The whole biblical tradition is full of examples of material that corrects older scripture but does not erase it. It may be that "the *Temple Scroll* is meant to stand alongside the Torah, to supplement and explain it," like the *Book of Jubilees*,[72] although it is then surprising that it does not explicitly acknowledge the existence of the older scripture. But there can be little doubt that the authors of the *Temple Scroll* intended that this law would be decisive on the matters it addressed.

The author of *Jubilees* may not have felt free to change the traditional text of scripture. The author of the *Temple Scroll* appears to have had no such inhibition. *Jubilees* may be a work based closely on traditional scripture; the *Temple Scroll* is more properly scripture rewritten. The date of its composition is controversial. Some scholars have dated it as early as the Persian period, others as late as the early first century BCE.[73] One fragmentary manuscript (*4QRouleau du Temple*, or 4QRP), which parallels 11Q Temple cols. 35 and 50–66, is dated by its editor to approximately 150–125 BCE.[74] If 4QRP is an actual manuscript of the *Temple Scroll*, rather than a source, this would require a date of composition in the mid-second century BCE, and there is nothing that requires an earlier date than this. In this case, it was roughly contemporary with *Jubilees*. If the author of *Jubilees*, then, felt he had to acknowledge the "first law" as authoritative, this attitude was not universal. In the mid-second century BCE it was still possible to rewrite the Torah radically, and present it as the Torah revealed by God on Mount Sinai.

This is not to say that such a rewritten Torah would necessarily be accepted. If the authors aimed to produce a normative text, there is little evidence that they succeeded. Unlike *Jubilees*, the *Temple Scroll* does not seem to have been translated into any other language. It survives in only a few copies – two that can be identified with certainty, a possible third and a manuscript that seems to contain a different, older form of the text (4QRP).[75] The fact that it was copied at all, at no small expense, suggests that some people accepted its claim to be divine revelation, but it is never

---

[72] White Crawford, *Rewriting*, 87.
[73] White Crawford, *The Temple Scroll*, 24–6.
[74] Émile Puech, "4QRouleau du Temple," in idem, *Qumrân Grotte 4, XVIII: Textes hébreux (4Q521–528, 4Q576–579)* (DJD 25; Oxford: Clarendon, 1998) 87.
[75] White Crawford, *Rewriting*, 85.

clearly cited as an authority. To say that the authors did not succeed in having their work accepted, except by few, is not to say that this was not their intention.

The question of fraud

The people who copied and preserved the *Temple Scroll* presumably accepted it as an authentic formulation of the revelation at Sinai, which was an event, prior to any written record of it. We may also, with Najman, charitably assume that the authors of the Scroll wrote in good faith, although we can only guess at what they thought they were doing. To charge these authors with fraud, however, is not entirely anachronistic. Whether or not any person or group would have regarded the *Temple Scroll* as a fraud would depend on whether they accepted its interpretation of the divine law, and many Jews of the time did not. The author of some of the *Hodayot*, often thought to be the Teacher of Righteousness, complains bitterly about the "men of deception" who "said of the vision of knowledge, it is not certain, and of the path of your heart, 'it is not that'" (1QH 12:18). The Damascus Document complains about the "man of the lie" (CD 20:15) who "spread over Israel the waters of lies" (1:15). There are also charges of false teaching and deception in the *Pesharim*.[76] There is no reason to think that these "deceivers" promulgated rewritten texts of scripture; most probably they interpreted the traditional scriptures in ways that the members of the "new covenant" considered false. But feelings between members of different sects were probably mutual. It is not unlikely that Pharisees or Sadducees would have considered *Jubilees* and the *Temple Scroll* fraudulent. Of course, their reasons for doing so would have been quite different from those of modern skeptics. They would have been based on the content of the alleged revelations rather than on the scribal activity by which they were produced. But Jews of other sectarian persuasion would not have been immediately seduced by "Mosaic discourse" or by the evocation of Sinai. Revelation was a contentious matter, even in antiquity. Indeed, if it had not been there would have been little incentive to rewrite scripture to begin with.

---

[76] Lloyd K. Pietersen, "'False Teaching, Lying Tongues and Deceitful Lips' (4Q169 FRGS 3–4 2.8): The *Pesharim* and the Sociology of Deviance," in Campbell et al., eds., *New Directions in Qumran Studies*, 166–81.

CHAPTER FOUR

Tradition and Innovation in the Dead Sea Scrolls

In the introduction to the classic study of *The Invention of Tradition*, Eric Hobsbawm defined tradition as "a set of practices, normally governed by overtly or tacitly accepted rules and of a ritual or symbolic nature, which seek to inculcate certain values and norms of behaviour by repetition, which automatically implies continuity with the past."[1] The definition admits of refinement.[2] Traditions of thought and belief are no less important than practices in shaping values and norms. Tradition, by its nature, develops, and consequently changes, but it nevertheless presupposes a certain degree of continuity over time. This continuity is essential to the sense of identity that tradition confers. It provides a sense of order and stability, and it also provides a framework within which innovation can occur. In the words of Karl Popper, "traditions have the important double function that they not only create a certain order or something like a social structure, but that they also give us something upon which we can operate: something we can criticize and change."[3]

In the case of ancient Judaism, one of the ways in which tradition was articulated was in a corpus of writings that was accorded authoritative status. One of the many ways in which the Dead Sea Scrolls have contributed to our understanding of ancient Judaism is by providing a snapshot of this process, as it developed in the last centuries before the turn of the era. It is now generally agreed that it is anachronistic to speak of a canon in this period. But it is also generally agreed that the Torah of Moses, or the Pentateuch, and also the books of the prophets, enjoyed a special status, at least by the time the Scrolls were written in the last two centuries BCE. Exactly what that status entailed, however, is not always clear. In fact, the Scrolls document several different ways in which these authoritative writings could be construed. As George Brooke has noted,

---

[1] Eric Hobsbawm, "Introduction: Inventing Traditions," in Eric Hobsbawm and Terence Ranger, eds., *The Invention of Tradition* (Cambridge: Cambridge University Press, 1983) 1–14. The definition is on p. 1.

[2] Marcel Sarot, "Counterfactuals and the Invention of Religious Tradition," in Jan Willem van Henten and Anton Houtepen, eds., *Religious Identity and the Invention of Tradition* (Assen: van Gorcum, 2001) 21–40, especially 22–28. Sarot compares Hobsbawm's view of tradition with that of Karl Popper, "Towards a Rational Theory of Tradition," in *The Rationalist Annual* 66 (1949) 36–55, reprinted in Popper, *Conjectures and Refutations: The Growth of Scientific Knowledge* (3rd ed.; London: Routledge and Kegan Paul, 1972) 120–35.

[3] Popper, "Towards a Rational Theory of Tradition," 50; Sarot, "Counterfactuals," 25.

It is no longer possible to argue that tradition is passed from one generation to another along single trajectories. Intelligent readings of the evidence ... demand that the pluralities of early Jewish tradition are taken seriously. No longer is it possible, even if it ever was, to read back interpretative norms in a direct way from one age to another.[4]

The nature of the Scrolls collection

At the outset, it may be well to clarify our understanding of the Dead Sea Scrolls as a collection. It has long been customary to refer to the corpus as "the Qumran library," and Hartmut Stegemann, in particular, has argued that the Scrolls belonged to "the central library of the Qumran settlement."[5] Libraries were rare in antiquity, but became more common in the Hellenistic period.[6] The great palace library of Asshurbanipal and the famous library of Alexandria were exceptional. In the Near East, libraries were often associated with temples. These were usually of modest size. The largest known Mesopotamian temple library had about 800 tablets.[7] The temple library at Edfu in Egypt had a catalogue with 35 titles.[8] It is generally assumed that there was a library in the Jerusalem temple. 2 Maccabees (2:13–16) claims that such a library was established by Nehemiah and restored by Judas Maccabee. The reliability of this account is open to question, especially with regard to Nehemiah, but it may be taken as evidence that there was some collection of books in the Jerusalem temple. Other evidence for a temple library in Jerusalem is scant indeed.[9] There are scattered references in Josephus to books laid up in the temple,[10] and he claims that the records of the Jewish people were assigned to chief priests and prophets.[11] But he also says that the number of "justly accredited books" was only

---

[4] George J. Brooke, "The Formation and Renewal of Scriptural Tradition," in Charlotte Hempel and Judith M. Lieu, eds., *Biblical Traditions in Transmission. Essays in Honour of Michael A. Knibb* (JSJSup 111; Leiden: Brill, 2006) 39–59, here 47.

[5] Hartmut Stegemann, *The Library of Qumran. On the Essenes, Qumran, John the Baptist, and Jesus* (Grand Rapids: Eerdmans, 1998) 80–5.

[6] Armin Lange, "2 Maccabees 2:13–15: Library or Canon?" in Géza G. Xeravits and József Zsengellér, eds., *The Books of the Maccabees. History, Theology, Ideology* (JSJSup 118; Leiden: Brill, 2007) 156–64.

[7] Karel van der Toorn, *Scribal Culture and the Making of the Hebrew Bible* (Cambridge, MA: Harvard, 2007) 240. On Mesopotamian libraries see Olof Pedersén, *Archives and Libraries in the Ancient Near East 1500–300 B.C.* (Bethesda, MD: CDL Press, 1998).

[8] Van der Toorn, *ibid.* Vilmos Wessetzky, "Die Bücherliste des Tempels von Edfu und Imhotep," *Göttinger Miszellen* 83 (1984) 85–9.

[9] Yaacov Shavit, "The 'Qumran Library' in the Light of the Attitude towards Books and Libraries in the Second Temple Period," in Michael O. Wise et al., eds., *Methods of Investigation of the Dead Sea Scrolls and the Khirbet Qumran Site. Present Realities and Future Prospects* (Annals of the New York Academy of Sciences 722; New York: The New York Academy of Sciences, 1994) 299–315, here 303.

[10] *Ant* 3.1.7 (38); 5.1.7 (61). Roger T. Beckwith, *The Old Testament Canon of the New Testament Church* (Grand Rapids: Eerdmans, 1985) 84.

[11] *Ag Ap* 1.29.

twenty-two.¹² The spoils when the temple was captured included a copy of the Jewish Law (*JW* 7.150), which was laid up in Rome in the Temple of Peace (*JW* 7.162). Josephus claims that Titus allowed him to take some sacred books when the temple was destroyed (*Life*, 418). All of this would suggest that the temple library in Jerusalem was very modest in size.

The existence of a major library in a place like Qumran would be surprising, but then the discovery of the Scrolls was surprising in any case. One could perhaps explain the library by the priestly character of the *yahad*, which seems to have viewed the community as a substitute temple,¹³ or suppose that the priestly members brought their manuscripts with them. But the size of the supposed library in the wilderness is anomalous enough that we should consider possible alternative explanations.

It is generally acknowledged that the texts found in the Scrolls cannot all have been authored at Qumran. The collection includes many texts, including those we know as biblical, that were composed before the site was occupied in the Hellenistic period, and before the sectarian movement originated, on any reckoning. It is also recognized that not all the non-biblical texts are necessarily sectarian compositions. Moreover, it is remarkable that "among the Qumran manuscripts very few individual scribes can be identified as having copied more than one manuscript."¹⁴ The idea that locus 30 at Qumran was a scriptorium, proposed by de Vaux,¹⁵ now seems doubtful to many scholars.¹⁶ Emanuel Tov has identified a group of 167 nonbiblical and biblical texts which reflect an idiosyncratic scribal practice, including distinctive orthography and morphology.¹⁷ He argues that this group includes virtually all commonly agreed upon sectarian writings and so refers to it as "the Qumran scribal practice." But there are exceptions and anomalies: he acknowledges seven or eight sectarian texts (including two manuscripts of the *Serek*, some *Pesharim* and one manuscript of 4QMMT) that do not follow this practice, while some that do, such as 4QQohᵃ, predate the settlement at Qumran.¹⁸ He also grants that "the texts written in the Qumran scribal practice could have been penned anywhere in Palestine," al-

---

¹² *Ag Ap* 1.31.

¹³ So David Carr, *Writing on the Tablet of the Heart. Origins of Scripture and Literature* (New York: Oxford, 2005) 217–20, who regards Qumran as an extension of priestly book-culture. So also Lange, "2 Macc 2:13–15," 160–61, who argues that "the Qumran library resembles ancient Near Eastern temple libraries because of the particular character of the Qumran community as a spiritual temple."

¹⁴ Emanuel Tov, *Scribal Practices and Approaches Reflected in the Texts Found in the Judean Desert* (STDJ 54; Leiden: Brill, 2004) 22. Compare M. O. Wise, "Accidents and Accidence: A Scribal View of Linguistic Dating of the Aramaic Scrolls from Qumran," in idem, *Thunder in Gemini* (JSPSup 15; Sheffield: Sheffield Academic Press, 1994) 103–51, here 124.

¹⁵ Roland de Vaux, *Archaeology and the Dead Sea Scrolls* (The Schweich Lectures; London: Oxford, 1973) 29–33.

¹⁶ See Tov, *Scribal Practices*, 15.

¹⁷ Tov, *Scribal Practices*, 261–88.

¹⁸ *Ibid.*, 262. See also Dong-Hyuk Kim, "Free Orthography in a Strict Society: Reconsidering Tov's 'Qumran Orthography'," *DSD* 11 (2004) 72–81, and Tov's "Reply to Dong-Hyuk Kim's Paper on 'Tov's Qumran Orthography'," *DSD* 11 (2004) 359–60.

though he claims that "they were probably written mainly at Qumran."[19] The latter claim is unfounded, even if one were to grant that the scribal practice was peculiar to the *yahad*. Moreover, the number of texts following the supposed Qumran scribal practice is less than one fifth of the entire corpus. Tov then supposes that the corpus includes many texts "which were presumably taken there from elsewhere."[20]

The provenance of the Scrolls is a separate issue from the question whether they constituted a library. Most libraries are made up of books composed elsewhere. There is another possibility, however, that deserves consideration. Many of the Scrolls may have been brought from elsewhere to be hidden in the wilderness and preserved from destruction in time of war. The obvious occasion is the great revolt of 66 CE. It is possible that some Scrolls were also hidden in the caves earlier, around the turn of the era, as Daniel Stökl Ben Ezra has suggested.[21] I would still argue that the collection as a whole has a sectarian character, since it conspicuously lacks anything that could be considered Pharisaic, and contains very little that could be pro-Hasmonean, with the possible but controversial exception of the "Prayer for King Jonathan."[22] But if the Scrolls were brought to Qumran from various settlements of the *yahad*, this might explain the presence in the collection of different, even contradictory, copies of the *Serek* or *Community Rule*.[23] Rather than suppose that different editions of the Rule were preserved simultaneously in a single community, we might suppose that not all communities had the latest or fullest edition of the text.

Even if many scrolls were brought from elsewhere, Qumran must have had some library, if indeed it was a settlement of the *yahad* at all, and I assume that it was. Study of the Torah was a significant factor in the *raison d'être* of the sect, and a community that was devoted to study probably had some other texts as well. But it is now apparent that the Dead Sea Scrolls cannot be viewed only as the library of an isolated settlement. Many of these texts circulated more widely. They may not constitute a random sampling of Judean literature around the turn of the era, but they are representative of a broader segment of the population than the inhabitants of Qumran.

---

[19] *Ibid.*

[20] *Ibid.*, 261.

[21] Daniel Stökl Ben Ezra, "Old Caves and Young Caves. A Statistical Reevaluation of a Qumran Consensus," *DSD* 14/3 (2007) 313–33.

[22] On the Prayer for King Jonathan, see my discussion in *Beyond the Qumran Community* (Grand Rapids: Eerdmans, 2010) 118–20.

[23] Alison Schofield, *From Qumran to the Yahad. A New Paradigm of Textual Development for the Community Rule* (STDJ 77; Leiden: Brill, 2009) especially 183–90.

The sectarian ideology

The sectarian movement reflected in the Scrolls, both the "new covenant" of the Damascus Rule and the *yahad* of the *Community Rule*, had as its *raison d'être* the proper observance of the Torah of Moses. The person who wished to join the new covenant in the *Damascus Document* "must impose upon himself to return to the law of Moses with all his heart and soul" (15:12). He must also impose the oath of the covenant on his son, when he reaches the age of enrollment (15:5–6). Equally, in the *Serek* or *Community Rule*:

whoever enters the council of the community ... shall swear with a binding oath to revert to the Law of Moses, according to all that he commanded, with whole heart and soul, in compliance with all that has been revealed of it to the sons of Zadok, the priests who keep the covenant and interpret his will and to the multitude of the men of their covenant ... (1QS 5:7–9).

This centrality of the Torah was not a peculiarity of the Damascus Covenant, or of the *yahad*. The attempt to make the Torah central to the tradition goes back to Deuteronomy and Josiah's reform. Ezra is said to have attempted to impose it in the Persian era, and Nehemiah to have instituted a renewed covenant based on it.[24] In the Hellenistic age its centrality was recognized by Gentile observers such as Hecataeus.[25] When the Seleucids conquered Jerusalem in 198 BCE, the "ancestral laws" recognized by Antiochus III were probably some form of the Mosaic Torah.[26] By the first century BCE, it is clear that even opposing parties agreed on the centrality of the Torah, even as they disagreed on its interpretation. This is apparent in 4QMMT, which is apparently addressed to a leader of Israel. Even if we lay aside the controversial supposed reference to a tri-partite canon,[27] the whole treatise presupposes that both the author and the addressee accept the authority of the Torah. There is also a third party, which also accepts its authority, but interprets it differently. I accept the view that the "they" of MMT is most probably the Pharisees.[28] There is, in

---

[24] Michael Duggan, *Covenant Renewal in Ezra-Nehemiah (Neh 7:72b-10:40): An Exegetical, Literary and Theological Study* (Atlanta: Society of Biblical Literature, 2001).

[25] Hecataeus of Abdera, apud Diodorus Siculus, *Bibliotheca Historica* 40.3; Menahem Stern, *Greek and Latin Authors on Jews and Judaism* (Jerusalem: The Israel Academy of Sciences, 1976) 1.20–35.

[26] Josephus, *Ant* 12.142; Victor Tcherikover, *Hellenistic Civilization and the Jews* (Peabody, MA: Hendrickson, 1999, originally published by the Jewish Publication Society in 1959) 83.

[27] Elisha Qimron and John Strugnell, *Qumran Cave 4. V. Miqsat Ma'ase Ha-Torah* (DJD 10; Oxford: Clarendon, 1994) 58–9; Composite text C 10. The reconstruction is questioned by Eugene Ulrich, "The Non-attestation of a Tripartite Canon in 4QMMT," *CBQ* 65 (2003) 202–14. Ulrich proposes as "a cautiously reconstructed text": "we have [written] to you so that you may study in the book of m[... pr]ophets and in d[..." A reference to "generation and generation" in the following line has sometimes been read as a reference to Chronicles, but this is gratuitous. See also Hanne von Weissenberg, *4QMMT: Reevaluating the Text, the Function and the Meaning of the Epilogue* (STDJ 82; Leiden: Brill, 2009) 204–6.

[28] Eyal Regev, *Sectarianism in Qumran. A Cross-Cultural Perspective* (Berlin: de Gruyter, 2007) 98.

any case, no doubt that the Pharisees, no less than the "new covenant," accorded central importance to the Torah. The importance accorded to it in the Scrolls, then, might seem to be unremarkable.

But in fact the focus on the Torah as law in the sectarian Scrolls, while it was not without precedent, was to some degree a departure from tradition. Not all of Jewish tradition was Torah-centric. When Ben Sira, in the early second century BCE, equated wisdom with the Torah of Moses, he was departing from the tradition of Proverbs and Qoheleth, which do not refer to the Torah explicitly at all. Even *4QInstruction*, the major wisdom text found at Qumran, which alludes to the Torah in various ways, does not thematize it, or refer to it as the ultimate source of wisdom.[29] More significantly for our topic, the Scrolls themselves include a corpus of literature, most of it in Aramaic, which deals with the stories and traditions that we now find in the Pentateuch but does not have the legal, halakhic, focus that we find in the Scrolls.[30] This literature is generally, but not necessarily always, older than the clearly sectarian texts, which are all in Hebrew.

Pseudepigrapha in the Scrolls

Among the texts that clearly were not composed at Qumran, or by members of the *yahad*, are texts such as the *Books of Enoch, Aramaic Levi,* and *Jubilees*, some of which were known before the discovery of the Scrolls. Many of these texts are in Aramaic, and they are representative of the tradition, or traditions, inherited by the sectarian movement known from the Scrolls. Many of the Aramaic works found at Qumran deal with primeval history and the patriarchs; others like the Daniel pseudepigrapha and the tales from the Persian court are set in the Diaspora. These books do NOT typically deal with Moses, the history of Israel or the Prophets (unless Daniel or Enoch be so categorized). Moreover, many of the Aramaic scrolls are dated early. Some of the fragments of the *Testament of Amram* date to the second century BCE, and Puech argues that the composition must be prior to *Jubilees*.[31] The extant Aramaic sections of *1 Enoch* and the *Book of the Giants* are plausibly dated before the Maccabean revolt. Not all the Aramaic literature is necessarily so early.

---

[29] See the recent review of this issue by M. J. Goff, "Recent Trends in the Study of Early Jewish Wisdom Literature: The Contribution of *4QInstruction* and Other Qumran Texts," *Currents in Biblical Research* 7 (2009) 377–416, specifically 393–5. For the evident use of Torah in 4QInstruction see Lawrence H. Schiffman, "Halakhic Elements in the Sapiential Texts from Qumran," in J. J. Collins, G. E. Sterling and R. A. Clements, eds., *Sapiential Perspectives: Wisdom Literature in Light of the Dead Sea Scrolls* (STDJ 51; Leiden: Brill, 2004) 89–100.

[30] See Katell Berthelot and Daniel Stökl Ben Ezra, eds., *Aramaica Qumranica. Proceedings of the Conference on the Aramaic Texts from Qumran in Aix-en-Provence, 30 June – 2 July 2008* (STDJ 94; Leiden: Brill, 2010).

[31] É. Puech, *Qumrân Grotte IV. 22. Textes Araméens. Première Partie 4Q529–549* (DJD 31; Oxford: Clarendon, 2001) 285–7.

4Q245 provides a list of High Priests that extends into the Hasmonean era, at least as far as Simon, possibly as far as Aristobulus I.[32] But the fact remains that much of the Aramaic literature found at Qumran comes from a time before the formation of the sectarian movement known from the Scrolls.

Two features of this early literature are noteworthy. One is the use of pseudepigraphy – the appeal to the authority of figures such as Enoch or Levi. The second is the lack of focus on the law of Moses. The latter feature is especially conspicuous in light of the centrality of the Torah in the main sectarian texts.

The attribution of books to venerable figures from ancient times is evidently a strategy to enhance the authority of their contents. The phenomenon was common in the ancient Near East. The standard version of the Epic of Gilgamesh presents it as an autobiographical account of Gilgamesh, and there are similar pseudo-autobiographical accounts of Naram-Sin and Sargon.[33] There was a tradition of pseudepigraphy in Egyptian wisdom literature. Pseudepigraphy can be viewed as a way of inventing tradition, to borrow Hobsbawn's terminology.[34] The contents of the early Enoch literature may have been quite novel in the Hellenistic period, but they were presented as dating from before the Flood. This is not to deny that the authors of these works drew on traditional materials. The *Book of the Watchers*, for example, surely displays familiarity with materials known to us as biblical, and probably incorporates some older stories about Asael and Shemihaza, but we do not know at what point those stories originated. But as far as rhetorical strategy was concerned, the authors of the books of Enoch did not wish to claim novelty at all. Rather, they wanted to claim great antiquity, and the prestige attendant thereto.

Where these authors made use of older traditions, did they regard these traditions as authoritative? Not necessarily. Armin Lange distinguishes here between literature and scripture. In his view, the paradigm shift takes place in the second century BCE, after the Hellenistic reform and the Maccabean revolt.[35] The author of Daniel chapter 4 surely knew some form of the tradition preserved in the *Prayer of Nabonidus*. He found this story useful and malleable for his purpose, but it is not apparent that he accorded any authority to it. Texts such as the *Book of Giants* may use the Book of Genesis as a jumping off point, but the relationship is tangential. Even the *Genesis Apocryphon*, which follows the biblical story to a greater extent, uses it freely, and does not attend to the details of the text. The Aramaic texts from Qumran

---

[32] So Michael O. Wise, "4Q245 and the High Priesthood of Judas Maccabaeus," *DSD* 12 (2005) 313–62 (344). The so-called 'Son of God' text, 4Q246, must also, in my view, be assigned to the post-Maccabean period, probably to the first century BCE, in view of its probable dependence on the Book of Daniel and its espousal of royal messianism. The manuscripts of 4Q540–541 have been dated around 100 BCE, and the composition need not be much older.

[33] Van der Toorn, *Scribal Culture*, 34.

[34] Compare the comments of Brooke, "The Formation and Renewal of Scriptural Tradition," 51–3, on "inventing the past" in apocalyptic literature.

[35] Lange, "Hebrew Scriptures," 103–6. See also Eugene Ulrich, "From Literature to Scripture: Reflections on the Growth of a Text's Authoritativeness," *DSD* 10 (2003) 3–25.

seldom if ever appeal to older literature as normative. Even the book of Tobit, which refers respectfully to "the law of Moses," uses this phrase broadly to refer to traditional custom rather than to specific laws or a specific book.[36] All the Aramaic texts presuppose traditions about figures who are mentioned in what became the Hebrew Bible (although the Daniel mentioned in the Book of Ezekiel bears little resemblance to the hero of the Aramaic writings). But they treat the inherited tradition with considerable freedom.

The Aramaic texts from Qumran certainly allude to traditions now found in the Hebrew Bible and draw on them in various ways, but they are not Torah-centric. There has been some debate recently as to the status of the Torah in the early Enoch literature, as reflected in the Astronomical Book and the *Book of the Watchers*. As George Nickelsburg has written:

the heart of the religion of *1 Enoch* juxtaposes election, revealed wisdom, the right and wrong ways to respond to this wisdom, and God's rewards and punishments for this conduct. Although all the components of 'covenantal nomism' are present in this scheme, the word *covenant* rarely appears and Enoch takes the place of Moses as the mediator of revelation. In addition, the presentation of this religion is dominated by a notion of revelation – the claim that the books of Enoch are the embodiment of God's wisdom, which was received in primordial times and is being revealed in the eschaton to God's chosen ones.[37]

It is not that the authors were not familiar with what we call the books of Moses. Several of the works relating to primeval and patriarchal history are para-biblical, in the sense that they paraphrase and elaborate stories known to us from the Bible.[38] But this literature also testifies to a form of religion that is less centralized, less exclusively focused on Moses, than what emerged in later centuries.

This is not to deny that some circles in Judaism were Torah-centric in the period before the Maccabean revolt. While Ben Sira was a wisdom teacher rather than an exegete, his deference towards the Torah is eloquent testimony to its cultural importance.[39] But that importance seems to have attained a new level in the period after the Maccabean revolt. The revolt itself is presented in 1 Maccabees as a defence of the Torah against those who wished to abrogate it. In the words attributed to Mattathias, "Far be it from us to desert the law and the ordinances" (1 Macc 2:21). (The

---

[36] See my essay, "The Judaism of the Book of Tobit," in Géza G. Xeravits and József Zsengellér, eds., *The Book of Tobit. Text, Tradition, Theology* (JSJSup 98; Leiden: Brill, 2005) 23–40.

[37] George W. Nickelsburg, "Enochic Wisdom: An Alternative to the Mosaic Torah?" in Jodi Magness and Seymour Gitin, eds., *Hesed Ve-Emet. Studies in Honor of Ernest S. Frerichs* (BJS 320; Atlanta: Scholars Press, 1998) 123–32 (129).

[38] Philip S. Alexander, "The Enochic Literature and the Bible," in Edward D. Herbert and Emanuel Tov, eds., *The Bible as Book. The Hebrew Bible and the Judaean Desert Discoveries* (London: The British Library and Oak Knoll Press, 2002) 57–69, takes the *Book of the Watchers* in *1 Enoch* as an example of "rewritten Bible," and argues that it implies that Genesis was "in some sense authoritative" (65). The nature of the authority, however, is debatable, and the focus on Genesis, as distinct from the Moses traditions, is significant.

[39] See my discussion in my book, *Jewish Wisdom in the Hellenistic Age* (Louisville: Westminster John Knox, 1997) 42–61.

actual motivations of the rebels were undoubtedly more complex, but that need not detain us here.) When the Hasmoneans came to power, they at least paid lip-service to the Torah, and sectarian disputes about the correct interpretation impinged directly on affairs of state, as can be seen from the fluctuating relations of the Hasmoneans with the Pharisees in the early first century BCE.

The focus on the Torah in the sectarian Scrolls, then, is more innovative than it might at first appear. It is not a peculiarity of the sect. It was a focus shared with other sectarian movements, and even with the Hasmonean rulers. But if the pseudepigraphic books of Enoch and Levi are at all representative of circles from which the early sectarians came, there was a break with what we might call the proto-sectarian tradition. The break should not be exaggerated. The older literature was still preserved and copied, and does not seem to have been repudiated. But the sectarians no longer produced "revelations" in the name of Enoch or Levi. What we find in the new covenant and in the *yahad* is not Enochic Judaism, but very decidedly Mosaic Judaism.

The Torah rewritten

The ascendancy of the Torah as law is reflected in such works as *Jubilees* and the *Temple Scroll*, both of which are widely believed to pre-date the formation of the new covenant. *Jubilees* purports to give the revelation dictated to Moses by the angel of the presence (*Jub* 1:27; 2:1). It is a rewriting of Genesis and part of Exodus that retrojects the observance of the Torah into the primeval and patriarchal periods. The *Temple Scroll* is presented as the words of God to Moses, and is in large part a harmonization of the Priestly and Deuteronomic laws. Like the pseudepigraphic writings, these works were exercises in the invention of tradition, while at the same time affecting deference and conformity. In the words of Hindy Najman:

> On the one hand, they retold biblical stories in ways that resolved apparent inconsistencies or solved puzzles for their readers. On the other hand, they wove their own versions of law, temple ritual, calendrical system and covenant, along with the very words of already authoritative traditions, into a single seamless whole. Thus they claimed, for their interpretations of authoritative texts, the already established authority of the texts themselves.[40]

Both these texts appeal to the revelation at Sinai, unlike the early Enoch literature, but *Jubilees* also acknowledges pre-Sinaitic revelations, and refers to the heavenly tablets as the ultimate deposit of truth.[41] Both *Jubilees* and the *Temple Scroll*, how-

---

[40] Hindy Najman, *Seconding Sinai. The Development of Mosaic Discourse in Second Temple Judaism* (JSJSup 77; Leiden: Brill, 2003) 45.

[41] Hindy Najman, "Interpretation as Primordial Writing: Jubilees and its Authority Conferring Strategies," *JSJ* 30 (1999) 379–410. See also Florentino García Martínez, "The Heavenly Tablets in the Book of Jubilees," in M. Albani, J. Frey and A. Lange, eds., *Studies in the Book of Jubilees* (Tübingen: Mohr Siebeck, 1997) 243–60, and especially James L. Kugel, "On the Interpolations in

ever, claim to present a higher revelation, which is surely meant to provide an authoritative guide to the interpretation of the Torah, even if it is not intended to replace it.[42] *Jubilees* makes a clear distinction between Torah and "testimony," often the "testimony of the heavenly tablets" (the distinctive interpretation advanced in *Jubilees*?),[43] but there is no such distinction in the *Temple Scroll*, which is presented simply as divine revelation. Not even *Jubilees*, however, makes the kind of distinction between text and interpretation that we will find in the sectarian writings from Qumran.

The sectarian view of revelation

The sectarian texts from Qumran neither appeal to the authority of an ancient patriarch nor attempt to reformulate the Sinai revelation. Instead they claim to have a new revelation as to how the Sinai revelation should be interpreted. This alleged revelation is a factor in the origin of the sectarian movement. According to the *Damascus Document*:

But with those who remained steadfast to God's precepts, with those who were left from among them, God established his covenant with Israel forever, revealing to them hidden matters in which all Israel had gone astray: his holy Sabbaths and his glorious feasts, his just stipulations and his truthful paths, and the wishes of his will, which man must do in order to live by them. (CD 3:12–15)

Even though the recipients of this revelation had remained steadfast, they did not know all that they needed to know from tradition. As Larry Schiffman especially has argued,

The sect divided the law into two categories – the *nigleh*, "revealed," and the *nistar*, "hidden." The revealed laws were known to all Israel, for they were manifest in Scripture, but the hidden laws were known only to the sect and were revealed solely through sectarian exegesis.[44]

There was, then, a common tradition, the *nigleh*. But this alone was not sufficient. It should be noted here that the sectarians do not claim to have a superior chain of tradition, or indeed that the *nistar* could be known from tradition at all, although it may now become a new tradition in sectarian circles. Equally, they do not claim

---

the Book of Jubilees," *RevQ* 24 (2009) 215–72, who argues that the heavenly tablets are only found in passages that are interpolated.

[42] On this issue see Najman, *Seconding Sinai*, 41–69.

[43] See James C. VanderKam, "Moses Trumping Moses: Making the Book of Jubilees," in S. Metso, H. Najman and E. Schuller, eds., *The Dead Sea Scrolls. Transmission of Traditions and Production of Texts* (STDJ 92; Leiden: Brill, 2010) 25–44. See also Michael Segal, *The Book of Jubilees. Rewritten Bible, Redaction, Ideology and Theology* (JSJSup 117; Leiden: Brill, 2007) 282–91, especially 290.

[44] L. H. Schiffman, *Reclaiming the Dead Sea Scrolls* (Philadelphia and Jerusalem: The Jewish Publication Society, 1994) 247.

that the true understanding was revealed to some ancient figure whose writings they now, miraculously, possessed, or even to Moses himself, as in *Jubilees*. Rather, the inadequacy of tradition is acknowledged, or at least it is viewed as a broken chain.

The role of the Teacher

In some sectarian writings, the Teacher of Righteousness had a crucial role in mediating the new revelation. According to CD 1, God "raised up for them a Teacher of Righteousness, in order to direct them in the path of his heart." The Teacher is most probably identical with the figure called "the Interpreter of the Law" in the exposition of Numbers 21:18 in CD 6:3–10:

The well is the law, and those who dug it are the converts of Israel, who left the land of Judah and lived in the land of Damascus ... and the staff is the Interpreter of the Law ... And the nobles of the people are those who come to dig the well with the staves that the staff decreed ... until there arises one who teaches justice at the end of days. (CD 6:3–10)

The figure elsewhere known as the Teacher of Righteousness, and who is clearly a figure of the past in the *Damascus Document*, should be identified with the Interpreter of the Law in this passage, rather than with the figure who was still to come at the end of days.[45]

From this it would seem that the Teacher is regarded as the source and authority for the halakah of the Damascus covenant. Again, in CD 20:31–32 those who abide by the "first ordinances" are said to "lend their ears to the voice of the Teacher of Righteousness." Moreover, in the *Pesharim* the Teacher is credited with knowledge of the mysteries of the end-time. God told Habakkuk to write down the things that were to come upon the last generation, but he did not make known to him the fulfillment of the end-time. The phrase "that he who reads it may run" is applied to the Teacher, "to whom God has made known all the mysteries of the words of his servants the prophets."[46] The same *pesher* refers to those who

---

[45] P. R. Davies, *The Damascus Covenant* (JSOTSup 25; Sheffield: JSOT, 1983) 124; idem, "The Teacher of Righteousness at the End of Days," *RevQ* 13 (1988) 313–17, argued that the reference is to an earlier figure, and that the Teacher is the figure referred to as "one who teaches justice at the end of days" in CD 6:11. See my critique of this position in "Teacher and Messiah? The One Who Will Teach Righteousness at the End of Days," in Eugene Ulrich and James VanderKam, eds., *The Community of the Renewed Covenant* (Notre Dame, IN: University of Notre Dame, 1994) 193–210; also Michael Knibb, "The Teacher of Righteousness – A Messianic Title?" in P. R. Davies and R. T. White, eds., *A Tribute to Geza Vermes: Essays on Jewish and Christian Literature and History* (JSOTSup 100; Sheffield: Sheffield Academic Press, 1990) 51–65.

[46] 1QpHab 7:1–5.

do not believe when they hear all the things that [are to come] upon the last generation from the mouth of the priest in whose [heart] God put [understand]ing that he might interpret all the words of His servants the prophets, through [whom] God foretold all the things that are to come upon his people ...[47]

In light of these passages I have in the past suggested that the reason for the absence of pseudepigraphy in the sectarian texts was that the authority of the Teacher rendered appeal to primeval and patriarchal authorities unnecessary.[48] Steven Fraade has objected that

not a single Qumran sectarian scroll is explicitly attributed to the authorship of the Teacher, nor is the Teacher mentioned all that often in those scrolls, notwithstanding the enormous industry of modern scholars to intuit his identity and role from them.[49]

It is indeed remarkable that all the major sectarian scrolls are anonymous, including the section of the *Hodayot* that is often, and plausibly, designated as Teacher Hymns.

An oral tradition?

Samuel Byrskog argues that it is

likely that there were channels besides the written records by which the Qumranites could recognize the traditions from the Teacher. They did not think of the Teacher as merely a wisdom teacher uttering anonymous sayings. Their interpretative activity and their salvation depended on hearing his voice ... There were presumably oral means of communicating the traditions' attachment to the Teacher.[50]

In fact, the sectarian Scrolls are remarkable for their emphasis on *written* transmission, an emphasis that has also been noted in the book of *Jubilees*.[51] But however the sectarian traditions were transmitted, it is clear that that they were more extensive than what we now possess in written form.

The centrality of Torah study is emphasized again and again in the rule books. The famous passage in 1QS 8 that cites Isa 40:3, about going into the wilderness to prepare the way of the Lord, adds

---

[47] 1QpHab 2:7–10.

[48] J. J. Collins, "Pseudepigraphy and Group Formation in Second Temple Judaism," in E. Chazon and M. E. Stone, eds., *Pseudepigraphic Perspectives: The Apocrypha and Pseudepigrapha in Light of the Dead Sea Scrolls* (STDJ 31; Leiden: Brill, 1999) 43–58 (56–7).

[49] Steven Fraade, "Interpretive Authority at Qumran," *JJS* 44 (1993) 46–69, here 49.

[50] Samuel Byrskog, *Jesus the Only Teacher. Didactic Authority and Transmission in Ancient Israel, Ancient Judaism and the Matthean Community* (Con Bib, NT series 24; Stockholm: Almqvist & Wiksell, 1994) 151–2.

[51] Najman, "Interpretation as Primordial Writing," 381–88.

An oral tradition?   63

this is the study of the Torah which he commanded through Moses, that they should act in accordance with all that has been revealed from time to time and in accordance with what the prophets revealed by His holy spirit.[52]

It is apparent that members needed to study more than the text of the Torah. On admission, the new member had to swear an oath to abide not only by the Torah of Moses but also by "all that has been revealed from it to the Sons of Zadok, the priests, who are the keepers of the covenant and interpret his will and to the multitude of the men of the community."[53] He must also be instructed in all the rules of the community (1QS 6:13–15). According to the *Damascus Document*, a person whose deeds did not conform to "the explanation of the law in which the men of perfect holiness walked" should be shunned by the community, "for all the holy ones of the Most High have cursed him."[54] Shemaryahu Talmon claims that "the Covenanters routinely committed to writing their own extrapolations of biblical laws, as well as entirely new *Yahad* statutes, such as Sabbath observances and purity injunctions,"[55] but we probably have to reckon with some oral tradition too. We are not told, however, that this tradition consisted of the teachings of the Teacher.[56] At most, the Teacher may have inaugurated the tradition.

The main description of the study carried on in the *yahad* is found in 1QS 6:6–7:

And in the place in which the ten assemble there should not be missing a man to interpret the law day and night, always, one relieving another. And the Many shall be on watch together for a third of each night of the year in order to read the book, explain the regulation, and bless together.

The relation between the two statements in this passage has been the subject of some debate. Several scholars read the two statements disjunctively, as relating to different settings.[57] A.R.C. Leaney argued that the second statement "serves as a link between the regulations for small dispersed communities and similar regulations for the larger community at Qumran,"[58] and Sarianna Metso has taken a similar posi-

---

[52] 1QS 8:12–16.
[53] 1QS 5:8–10. There is no reference to the Sons of Zadok is 4QS b and d.
[54] CD 20:6–7.
[55] Shemaryahu Talmon, "Oral and Written Transmission in Judaism," in Henry Wansbrough, ed., *Jesus and the Oral Gospel Tradition* (JSNTSup 64; Sheffield: Sheffield Academic Press, 1991) 121–58, here 146.
[56] Talmon, "Oral and Written Transmission," 157–8, entertains the possibility that the parenetic speeches at the beginning of the *Damascus Document* derive from the Teacher, but adds: "if these speeches can indeed be ascribed to the Teacher, we may assume with much confidence that they were submitted to writing almost simultaneously with their oral delivery, or after a minimal lapse of time."
[57] See the discussion of this passage by Martin Jaffee, *Torah in the Mouth. Writing and Oral Tradition in Palestinian Judaism, 200 BCE – 400 CE* (New York: Oxford University Press, 1991) 32–33; Charlotte Hempel, "Interpretative Authority in the Community Rule Tradition," *DSD* 10 (2003) 59–80, especially 61–5.
[58] A. R. C. Leaney, *The Rule of Qumran and Its Meaning* (London: SCM, 1966) 185–6.

tion.⁵⁹ Charlotte Hempel has argued that the two statements reflect different stages in the development of the community:

> Speaking very broadly the impression gained is that interpretative authority originated as a shared grassroots commodity that characterized the community from its earliest days in small groups. Over time the texts seem to testify to a restriction of access to the correct interpretation of the law by referring to individuals and groups with privileged access and special revelations.⁶⁰

It seems to me, however, that it is easier to read the two statements as complementary.⁶¹ The nightly watch by the "Many" is in no way incompatible with a special role for an interpreter. The idea that "interpretative authority originated as a shared grassroots commodity" seems unlikely, since the passage in CD 6 clearly asserts the primacy of the original "Interpreter of the Law," who is presumably to be identified with the Teacher of Righteousness.⁶² The very fact that an expert was needed in a group of ten strongly suggests that not every member of the sect would be able to interpret; not all members were necessarily able to read. We might imagine a scene where a literate member of the group read the text aloud, and all joined in the discussion. This is not just one official, since there must be at least one in each group of ten, and probably more, so that they can relieve each other. The parallel in CD 13:2–3 ("and in a place of ten, a priest learned in the book of HAGY should not be lacking; and by his authority all shall be governed") suggests, even if it does not require, that this role would be filled by a priest.⁶³ The "Many," then, are required to study the law, but there also seems to be a special role for an interpreter.

As Fraade also notes, the role of this "interpreter" brings to mind the "Interpreter of the Law" in CD 6, who is identified as the "staff" of Num 21:18. This figure is usually, and plausibly, identified with the Teacher. The passage in CD 6 continues: "the nobles of the people are those who come to dig the well with the ordinances (מחוקקות) that the 'staff' (מחוקק) ordained (חקק) for them." The implication seems to be that the original Interpreter of the Law established some principles of interpre-

---

⁵⁹ Sarianna Metso, *The Textual Development of the Qumran Community Rule* (STDJ 21; Leiden: Brill, 1997) 133–5. Metso regards the regulations for groups of ten as anomalous in the Community Rule "which seems to mirror the circumstances of a larger Essene settlement" (135).

⁶⁰ Hempel, "Interpretative Authority," 79–80. Her interpretation of the passage is in line with her broader views on the development of the sect. The idea of a priestly, Zadokite, takeover at Qumran seems to me very dubious. "Sons of Zadok" is more likely to be an honorific title for the community than a reference to a specific group (cf. CD 4:3–4, and Collins, *Beyond the Qumran Community*, 60–5).

⁶¹ So also Fraade, "Interpretative Authority," 67.

⁶² If, as Davies proposed, the Interpreter belonged to the "parent community" before the advent of the Teacher, this would argue even more strongly against the idea that interpretative authority was originally a grassroots phenomenon.

⁶³ So also J. Maier, "Early Jewish Biblical Interpretation in the Qumran Literature," in M. Saebø, ed., *Hebrew Bible/Old Testament: The History of Its Interpretation, vol. 1. From the Beginnings to the Middle Ages (until 1300)* (Göttingen: Vandenhoeck & Ruprecht, 1996) 108–29, especially 115.

tation, which were then applied by the community. If we may assume continuity between the "new covenant" of the *Damascus Document* and the *yahad* of the *Serek*, then it would seem that each "interpreter of the law" in the various settlements or cell communities played the role of the original Interpreter, and also, incidentally, anticipated the role of the one who would teach righteousness at the end of days (CD 6:11).

Fraade has argued that in 1QS 6

the Qumran sectaries are to accompany their reading of 'the book' with their study of *mishpat*, the latter most likely denoting the esoteric laws of the community. Even as the latter most likely derive by inspired exegesis from the former, they constitute a distinct component of the nightly curriculum.[64]

If this is correct, there must have been an ancillary tradition of interpretation that was passed along in the nightly study sessions. While these sessions were communal, they were not entirely democratic; there was still a hierarchy, as there was in all aspects of life in the *yahad*. It also seems to me that the interpretive authority of the individual "interpreters of the law" still derived from that of the original Teacher, even if the latter was not credited as the author of any written compositions. But the focus in the Scrolls is on the Torah and its interpretation, not on the personal teaching of the Teacher.

A distinctive view of tradition

In this respect, the view of tradition and its transmission found in the sectarian scrolls contrasts sharply not only with the older (and later) pseudepigrapha, but also with that of the Pharisees and the later rabbinic sages. The rabbis claimed an unbroken chain of tradition all the way back to Moses: "Moses received Torah from Sinai and delivered it to Joshua, and Joshua to the Elders, and the Elders to the Prophets, and the Prophets delivered it to the men of the Great Synagogue" (Aboth 1:1). Thereafter, the succession of sages is attested by names. While the Talmudic formulation of the Oral Torah may be relatively late, both the New Testament and Josephus attest to the importance the Pharisees attached to "the traditions of the fathers."[65] So, for example, we read in the Gospels that the Pharisees and scribes questioned Jesus as to why his disciples did not abide by "the tradition of the elders" (Mark 7:5), and Josephus tells us that "the Pharisees passed on to the people certain ordinances from a succession of fathers, which are not written down in the laws of Moses."[66] Whether the Pharisees necessarily relied on *oral* transmission is disputed, although no

---

[64] Fraade, "Interpretive Authority," 57.
[65] Jacob Neusner, "Oral Torah and Tradition," in idem, *Method and Meaning* (BJS 10; Atlanta: Scholars Press, 1979) 59–75, especially 69–70; Jaffee, *Torah in the Mouth*, 39–61.
[66] *Ant* 13.297–8. See Jaffee, *Torah in the Mouth*, 51.

verifiably Pharisaic writings have yet come to light. But at least the Pharisaic reverence for the traditions of the fathers shows a very different attitude from the claim of new, ongoing, revelation that we find in the sectarian scrolls.[67]

Scripture and interpretation

Another innovation that we find in the Scrolls may be related to this. This is the clear separation between text and interpretation that we find especially in the *Pesharim*, but also in occasional instances of scriptural interpretation in other texts, notably the *Damascus Document*.[68] The distinction of text and commentary was in the spirit of the age. The earliest such commentaries are probably those of Aristobulus, writing in Greek in Alexandria in the second century BCE. But the Scrolls provide the earliest sustained examples in a Semitic language, although an instance of the clear separation of scripture and interpretation can be found already in Daniel 9, in the case of Jeremiah's prophecy of the seventy weeks.[69] The fact that such explicitly exegetical literature begins to appear after the Maccabean revolt testifies to the changed status of scripture in this period.[70]

How far these commentaries are controlled by exegetical concerns is a matter of dispute. No doubt the authors believed that they were unveiling what the texts "really meant." George Brooke has argued that in the continuous *Pesharim*

> the scriptural text takes priority. It can be played with, adjusted, punned, reordered, but it is the control. Secondly, the commentary ... is carefully constructed with all manner of allusions primarily to other scriptural texts which have not only suitable vocabulary but also suitable literary contexts of their own.[71]

But he also notes that when the *Pesharim* are read with due attention to their literary allusions, "an ideological and theological *Tendenz* emerges."[72] The *Pesharim* are not a disinterested exercise in literary interpretation. Their *Tendenz* has to do with establishing and reinforcing the identity of the community. Jutta Jokiranta argues that "the power of the *pesher* is to place the wicked enemies of its own nation on the

---

[67] James VanderKam, "Those Who Look for Smooth Things, Pharisees, and Oral Law," in Paul et al., eds., *Emanuel*, 464–77, points out that "their Essene opponents from Qumran and those who produced the Damascus Document consistently insulted them by using epithets that highlight abuse of speech – something that is not the case for their treatment of other enemies" (477).

[68] See Jonathan G. Campbell, *The Use of Scripture in the Damascus Document 1–8, 19–20* (Berlin: de Gruyter, 1995).

[69] Daniel is said to have perceived "in the books" the number of years prophesied by Jeremiah. Contrast Ezra 1, which refers to the fulfillment of the word of the Lord by the mouth of Jeremiah.

[70] Lange, "From Literature to Scripture," 101.

[71] George J. Brooke, "The Pesharim and the Origins of the Dead Sea Scrolls," in Wise et al., *Methods of Investigation*, 339–52 (350).

[72] *Ibid.*

same line as the Gentile enemies and oppressors."[73] The labels and identifications used in the interpretations "justify the group's existence and claims by juxtaposing the most relevant out-groups as the opposites of the in-group."[74] The fact that they are linked to scriptures gives them the aura of divine sanction. Moreover, the *Pesharim* help witness to, and help construct, a distinctive tradition of interpretation, which is essential to sectarian identity. In the words of Maxine Grossman:

> From a sectarian perspective, the ability to understand a text – to really know what it is saying – would separate a sectarian from an outsider, and a higher-ranking sectarian from a new volunteer. Understood in this way, textual interpretation becomes not only a marker of insider status but also a process for its formation, confirmation and internalization.[75]

The *Pesharim* witness to sectarian tradition in another respect. They interpret prophecy by correlating it with events and figures from the history of their own time. They presuppose an historical narrative that is never spelled out in narrative form. References to the Wicked Priest and Lion of Wrath, and even to the Teacher, are allusive in character and presuppose that readers are familiar with an account of events that is not provided in the *Pesharim*, or anywhere else in the Scrolls, for that matter. Presumably there was an oral tradition that preserved the memory of key events in the formation of the sect. Such a tradition would undoubtedly have been tendentious and not objective history, if such a thing exists. It is not the purpose of the *Pesharim* to narrate that history, but rather to inscribe the sectarian view of history in the prophetic texts, and give that account an aura of divine authority. But they presuppose an account of the sectarian view of history that has not been preserved in written form and must have been passed along in oral tradition.

The distinction between text and interpretation that we find in the *Pesharim*, and elsewhere in the Scrolls might seem to have the advantage of preserving the integrity of the biblical text, and to a degree, it has. Armin Lange has argued that

> for the time from Jason to Pompey, no evidence exists that argues for group specific canons. On the contrary, the evidence suggests a gradual growth of heterogeneous collections of authoritative writings common to all groups of ancient Judaism. The boundaries of the collection that was later called writings and the boundaries of the collections designated as Moses and prophets were still fluid.[76]

---

[73] Jutta Jokiranta, "Pesharim: A Mirror of Self-Understanding," in Kristin de Troyer and Armin Lange, eds., *Reading the Present in the Qumran Library. The Perception of the Contemporary by Means of Scriptural Interpretations* (SBL Symposium Series 30; Atlanta: Society of Biblical Literature, 2005) 23–34, here 31.

[74] Jutta Jokiranta, "Social Identity Approach: Identity-Constructing Elements in the Psalms Pesher," in Florentino García Martínez and Mladen Popović, eds., *Defining Identities: We, You, and the Other in the Dead Sea Scrolls* (STDJ 70; Leiden: Brill, 2008) 85–109 (here 97). Compare George W. E. Nickelsburg, "Polarized Self-Identification in the Qumran Texts," *ibid.*, 23–31.

[75] Maxine Grossman, "Cultivating Identity: Textual Virtuosity and 'Insider' Status," in García Martínez and Popović, eds., *Defining Identities*, 1–11 (4).

[76] Lange, "From Literature to Scripture," 98.

One could argue, of course, that to speak of canons at all in this period is anachronistic, but the issue is whether different groups regarded different corpora of writings as authoritative. Here it seems to me that Lange's claim needs to be qualified. It is true that different groups, Hasmoneans, Pharisees, Essenes, agreed that certain scriptures were authoritative, chiefly the Torah of Moses, but also the prophets and probably the psalms. This is the presupposition of 4QMMT, which appeals to a leader of Israel, probably a High Priest, on disputed matters of interpretation. There is some reason to believe that the sectarians of the Scrolls regarded additional texts, such as *Jubilees*, as authoritative.[77] I am not aware that we have any reason to think that the Pharisees, or the Hasmoneans, for that matter, would have accepted an argument based on *Jubilees* as authoritative. But at least there was a common corpus of authoritative scriptures, even if the boundaries and the text of these scriptures was still fluid.

But the fact that one could appeal to common scriptures is no guarantee that agreement, or even meaningful dialogue was possible. We do not have a response to the overture of 4QMMT, but according to 4QpPs[a] fragments 1–10, col. 4:8–9, the Wicked Priest sought to murder the Teacher "and the Torah which he sent to him." Elisha Qimron and John Strugnell made the attractive proposal that the document in question is none other than the text we know as 4QMMT,[78] and the proposal has been taken up by such diverse scholars as Michael Wise and Hanan Eshel.[79] If this is correct, then it would seem that the High Priest was not impressed by the fact that the author of MMT revered the same scriptures as his opponents. Tom Stoppard remarked forty years ago, in his play *Jumpers*, that in an election it is not the voting that matters, but the counting. Similarly in a halakhic dispute, the decisive factor was not the Scripture that was cited, but the way it was interpreted.

Conclusion

The Dead Sea Scrolls provide some of our earliest examples of explicit interpretation of authoritative scriptures. In the process, they shed some interesting light on

---

[77] See James C. VanderKam, "Questions of Canon Viewed through the Dead Sea Scrolls," in Lee Martin McDonald and James A. Sanders, eds., *The Canon Debate* (Peabody, MA: Hendrickson, 2002) 91–109, especially 107. VanderKam notes that 14 copies of *Jubilees* have been identified among the Scrolls and that it is quoted once as an authority, but also that its views are opposed in some instances.

[78] E. Qimron and J. Strugnell, *Qumran Cave 4. V. Miqsat Ma'ase Ha-Torah* (DJD 10; Oxford: Clarendon, 1994) 175.

[79] M. O. Wise, *The First Messiah* (San Francisco: HarperSanFrancisco, 1999) 65–8; Hanan Eshel, "4QMMT and the History of the Hasmonean Period," in J. Kampen and M. J. Bernstein, eds., *Reading 4QMMT. New Perspectives on Qumran Law and History* (SBL Symposium Series 2; Atlanta: Society of Biblical Literature, 1996) 53–65; idem, *The Dead Sea Scrolls and the Hasmonean State* (Grand Rapids: Eerdmans, 2008) 46–7.

the workings of tradition. On the one hand, the scriptures seem to provide a recognized anchor in the past, and to provide a measuring stick (canon?) of fidelity. On the other hand, the claim of revealed interpretation quite openly breaks with the traditions of the recent past, and provides a licence for the invention of new tradition in the name of revelation and interpretation. In fact, tradition is never a matter of simply passing on a *traditum*. While it provides continuity with the past in various ways, not least in language, it also gives us something upon which we can operate, which we can adapt, criticize, and change,[80] even while maintaining the illusion of stability.

---

[80] Cf. Karl Popper, above, note 3.

CHAPTER FIVE

The Interpretation of Genesis in the Dead Sea Scrolls

Few biblical stories have had more far-reaching impact on the history of culture than the story of Adam and Eve. In Jewish and especially in Christian tradition this story is associated with the Fall, whereby humanity, which had been created for immortality, lost its primeval innocence and became subject to death. "Who nowadays," asks James Kugel, "does not automatically think of the story of Adam and Eve in the Garden of Eden as telling about some fundamental change that took place in the human condition, or what is commonly called the Fall of Man? Who does not think of the 'serpent' in the story as the devil, or paradise as the reward of the righteous after death?"[1] Yet, these assumptions go far beyond what is stated explicitly in the biblical text.[2] From a modern perspective, the story is an etiology of the human condition as we know it, marked by pain and toil, and ultimately by mortality, the return to the dust from which we are taken. The story construes that condition as punishment for disobedience to a divine command not to eat the fruit of the tree of the knowledge of good and evil.[3] The punishment of death is not immediate; it is rather a matter of becoming mortal. It is not clear that humanity was created immortal, but it appears that Adam and Eve were not originally forbidden to eat from the tree of life, in which case they might have lived forever (cf. Gen 3:22). Insofar as Adam and Eve are driven from the Garden there is a change in the human condition, which has lasting consequences. While their act of disobedience is not called a sin in the text, it may be reasonably so characterized.[4] The story does not, however, suggest that sinfulness is transmitted to their descendants, as supposed by the traditional Christian doctrine of original sin. While the serpent in some way symbolizes temptation, he is not a Satanic figure in the context of Genesis, although he was so understood from around the beginning of the common era.[5] The role of

---

[1] James L. Kugel, *The Traditions of the Bible* (Cambridge, MA: Harvard, 1998) 94.

[2] See the incisive study of James Barr, *The Garden of Eden and the Hope of Immortality* (Minneapolis: Fortress, 1992).

[3] See further J. J. Collins, *Introduction to the Hebrew Bible* (Minneapolis: Fortress, 2004) 67–75.

[4] *Pace* Carol Meyers, *Discovering Eve. Ancient Israelite Women in Context* (New York: Oxford, 1988) 87.

[5] The earliest text that takes the snake as the devil is the Wisdom of Solomon 2:24: "through the Devil's envy, death entered the world." It is explicitly so identified in Rev 12:9.

the woman in the story continues to be controversial.[6] She does not bear either sole or primary responsibility for the "Fall," but she plays a role in leading Adam astray, and suffers some degree of subordination as a result, although the subordination has been exaggerated in later tradition. The story has enormous paradigmatic significance, in virtue of its place at the beginning of the Bible, but it must be read as an explanation of the way things are, not a prescription of how they should or must be. It is understood that the story in Genesis 2–3 is a different composition from that in Genesis 1, and that the two accounts have their distinct emphases and theological perspectives.

One of the benefits of the increased interest in the history of interpretation in recent years is that it makes us aware that what seems self-evident to one generation may not be evident at all to another.[7] In the case of the biblical stories of creation, the earliest surviving interpretations are often strikingly different, not only from modern critical readings but also from the interpretation that dominated most of Jewish and Christian tradition. This is the case with some of the discussions of the creation of humanity in the Dead Sea Scrolls.

The earliest interpretations

The scrolls provide some of our earliest witnesses to the understanding of the Genesis text.[8] The story of Adam and Eve is usually, and rightly, assigned to the Yahwist source in the Pentateuch, which until recently was regarded as one of the oldest strata of the Bible. The date, if not the existence, of this source has become controversial in recent years.[9] The echoes of Babylonian mythology in Genesis 1–11 lend some plausibility to arguments for an exilic or postexilic date, although an earlier date remains possible. In any case, there is strikingly little reference to the Eden story in the rest of the Hebrew Bible. The prophet Ezekiel taunts the king of Tyre by saying that he was in "Eden the garden of God" after he was created, and was sub-

---

[6] For a review of the debate see J. J. Collins, *The Bible after Babel. Historical Criticism in a Postmodern Age* (Grand Rapids: Eerdmans, 2005) 75–98.

[7] For a striking illustration, see the study of the interpretation of Jonah by Yvonne Sherwood, *A Biblical Text and Its Afterlives: The Survival of Jonah in Western Culture* (Cambridge: Cambridge University Press, 2000).

[8] The wide-ranging study of Gary Anderson, *The Genesis of Perfection. Adam and Eve in Jewish and Christian Imagination* (Louisville: Westminster John Knox, 2001), does not deal at all with Ben Sira, *1 Enoch*, or the Dead Sea Scrolls. Neither does the study of J. T. A. G. M. van Ruiten, "The Creation of Man and Woman in Early Jewish Literature," in Gerard P. Luttikhuizen, *The Creation of Man and Woman. Interpretations of the Biblical Narratives in Jewish and Christian Traditions* (Leiden: Brill, 2000) 34–62, which is focused on the issue of sexual differentiation in creation.

[9] See e.g. T. B. Dozeman and K. Schmid, *A Farewell to the Yahwist? The Composition of the Pentateuch in Recent European Interpretation* (SBL Symposium Series 34; Atlanta: Society of Biblical Literature, 2006).

sequently driven out by a cherub (Ezekiel 28:13–16).[10] Ezekiel presumably knew a story about the primal man. This story is somewhat different from what we find in Genesis, however. His Eden is "on the mountain of God" and the primal man is covered with precious stones. There is no mention of Eve. Neither is there any tree of life, nor any mention of good and evil, nor of a tempting serpent. Ezekiel may have known a different story about the primal man and Eden, even if it overlapped with the Genesis narrative in some details.[11] There is in fact no clear reference to the story of Adam and Eve in the Hebrew Bible. In view of the importance of the story in later tradition, this fact is quite amazing. Apparently, the questions of the origin of sin, and of what we know as the fallen human condition, were not felt to be as pressing by the biblical writers as by later theologians.

That situation changed, however, in the early second century BCE, when there seems to have been a lively debate about the origin of sin.[12] One colorful explanation, the myth of the fallen angels, which is propounded at length in the *Book of the Watchers* in *1 Enoch* 1–36, took as its point of departure the story in Genesis 6 of the "sons of God" who were attracted to the daughters of men. The *Book of the Watchers* also shows awareness of the Eden story. In *1 Enoch* 32, Enoch sees the tree of wisdom, and is told that this is the tree from which the primeval parents ate and learned wisdom, "and their eyes were opened, and they knew that they were naked, and they were driven from the garden." Moreover, we are told that the tree of life will be given to the righteous in the eschatological time, when it will be transplanted "to the holy place, by the house of God," presumably on Mt. Zion (*1 Enoch* 25:3–6). We may infer from this that humanity is denied access to the tree of life since the expulsion of Adam from the garden, although the punishment of death is not stated explicitly in *1 Enoch* 32. Yet the story of Adam and Eve does not seem to function as the primary account of the origin of sin in the *Book of the Watchers*. At least the spread of wickedness on earth is greatly intensified by the descent of the Watchers or fallen angels.[13]

The relation of the *Book of the Watchers* to the Mosaic Torah is a matter of debate. While the authors evidently knew the Torah, it is not clear whether they attributed to it normative status, or regarded it as uniquely authoritative.[14] They certainly drew on other mythological traditions besides. In contrast, the book of *Jubilees* follows

---

[10] M. Greenberg, *Ezekiel 21–37* (AB 22A; New York: Doubleday, 1997) 579–93, argues that the figure who is driven out is the cherub, and so that the allusion is the fall of a demi-god (cf. Helal ben-Shachar in Isaiah 14).

[11] The myth to which Ezekiel alludes remains elusive. See Greenberg, *Ezekiel 21–37*, 592–3.

[12] See J. J. Collins, *Apocalypticism in the Dead Sea Scrolls* (London: Routledge, 1997) 30–35.

[13] See further J. J. Collins, "Before the Fall: The Earliest Interpretations of Adam and Eve," in H. Najman and J. H. Newman, eds., *The Idea of Biblical Interpretation. Essays in Honor of James L. Kugel* (JSJSup 83; Leiden: Brill, 2004) 293–308.

[14] See A. Bedenbender, "The Place of the Torah in the Early Enoch Literature," in G. Boccaccini and J. J. Collins, eds., *The Early Enoch Literature* (Leiden: Brill, 2007) 65–80, and especially G. W. Nickelsburg, "Enochic Wisdom and Its Relationship to the Mosaic Torah," *ibid.*, 81–94.

the text of Genesis closely in the Eden story.¹⁵ The difference may be partly a matter of genre. However problematic the category "rewritten bible" may be as a genre designation, it expresses well the relation of *Jubilees* to Genesis. *Jubilees* has its own concerns, and these are primarily halakhic, but it addresses these concerns in the context of a retelling of the Genesis narrative.¹⁶ But *Jubilees* does not assign sole responsibility for the sinful state of humanity to the sin of Adam. It also adapts the story of the fallen angels from *1 Enoch* to explain the existence of demons as agents of temptation and affliction on earth.¹⁷ Moreover, Michael Segal has argued that some passages in *Jubilees* hint at a dualistic view of creation, according to which sin and evil had a place in God's plan from the beginning. Already in the account of creation in *Jub* 2:17–21 a distinction is drawn between "those who are partners in God's covenant (angels of the presence, angels of holiness, and Israel)" and "those destined for destruction (the spirits and the other nations)."¹⁸

Unlike *1 Enoch* and *Jubilees*, Ben Sira has no interest in fallen angels or demons. He famously identified wisdom with the book of the Torah, and his theology is basically covenantal. He reflects explicitly on the opening chapters of Genesis. In this case, the genre is wisdom *Instruction*, not narrative, and the author is free to pick out the motifs from Genesis that serve his purpose. His reflections raise some of the issues that are further developed in the Dead Sea Scrolls.¹⁹

Ben Sira

Ben Sira's best known allusion to Genesis 2–3 is a rather unfortunate one: "From a woman sin had its beginning, and because of her we all die" (Sir 25:24). This reading of Genesis, placing the primary blame and responsibility on Eve, became very common in later centuries. It was enshrined in the canonical New Testament in 1 Timothy 2:13–14, which forbade women to teach or have authority over men, since "Adam was not deceived, but the woman was deceived and became a transgressor." This line of interpretation, however, only becomes common in the first century of

---

¹⁵ J. T. A. G. M. van Ruiten, *Primaeval History Interpreted. The Rewriting of Genesis 1–11 in the Book of Jubilees* (JSJSup 66; Leiden: Brill, 2000) 71–111. The rewriting is characterized by harmonization of the two biblical accounts of creation.

¹⁶ Many of the differences between *Jubilees* and Genesis are due to the fact that *Jubilees* conceives Eden as a sanctuary, van Ruiten, *Primaeval History*, 111; idem, "Eden and the Temple: The Rewriting of Genesis 2:4–3:24 in the Book of *Jubilees*," in G. P. Luttikhuizen, ed., *Paradise Interpreted. Representations of Biblical Paradise in Judaism and Christianity* (Leiden: Brill, 1999) 63–94; M. Segal, *The Book of Jubilees. Rewritten Bible, Redaction, Ideology and Theology* (JSJSup 117; Leiden: Brill, 2007) 49. Segal distinguishes a "halakhic redaction" as a distinct layer in *Jubilees*.

¹⁷ *Jub* 10:7–11.

¹⁸ Segal, *The Book of Jubilees*, 241.

¹⁹ For a fuller treatment of Ben Sira's interpretation of Genesis see J. J. Collins, *Jewish Wisdom in the Hellenistic Age* (Louisville: Westminster John Knox, 1997) 80–84.

the common era. It is anomalous in Ben Sira, as it does not occur in the passages where he discusses the Genesis account of creation, but at the end of an outburst on the wickedness of women. Perhaps Ben Sira was carried away by his own rhetoric. In fact, it has been suggested that he was not referring to Eve at all when he said that sin had its beginning from a woman, but the suggestion is not persuasive.[20] There is only one comparable text in the Dead Sea Scrolls. This is a rather notorious fragment that was published by John Allegro under the title "The Wiles of the Wicked Woman" (4Q184).[21] This text describes a seductress, of whom it says: "She is the beginning of all the ways of iniquity ... for her ways are ways of death." The Qumran text is not alluding to Genesis, but rather to the description of the "strange woman" (אשה זרה) in Proverbs 7. In Proverbs, this evil woman is the anti-type of Wisdom, who is also portrayed as a female figure, and who is created as the beginning of the ways of God. The same Hebrew word (ראשית) is used for "beginning" in Proverbs and in 4Q184, whereas Sirach uses a different word (תהלה). In the Qumran text (as in Proverbs) the ways of death refer to spiritual death, which can be avoided. In contrast, Sirach says that "because of her we all die," and this is surely an allusion to Genesis. The point that I would like to emphasize, however, is that this reading of Genesis was exceptional in the pre-Christian period, although later it was espoused by Jews and Christians alike.[22]

Ben Sira draws directly on Genesis in an account of creation in chapter 17, in a passage where the Hebrew text is not preserved:

The Lord created human beings out of earth
and makes them return to it again.
He gave them a fixed number of days,
but granted them authority over everything on the earth.
He endowed them with strength like his own
and made them in his own image.
He put the fear of them in all living beings,
and gave them dominion over beasts and birds ...
He filled them with knowledge and understanding
and showed them good and evil ...
He bestowed knowledge upon them,
and allotted to them the law of life.

---

[20] J. R. Levison, "Is Eve to Blame? A Contextual Analysis of Sirach 25:24," *CBQ* 47 (1985) 617–23.

[21] J. M. Allegro, "The Wiles of the Wicked Woman. A Sapiential Work from Qumran's Fourth Cave," *PEQ* 96 (1964) 53–55; idem, *Qumran Cave 4. I (4Q158–4Q186)* (DJD 5; Oxford: Clarendon, 1968) 82–5. Note the corrections of Allegro's edition by John Strugnell, "Notes en marge du volume V des 'Discoveries in the Judaean Desert of Jordan,'" *RevQ* 7 (1970) 263–8. See also D. J. Harrington, *Wisdom Texts from Qumran* (London: Routledge, 1996) 31–35; M. J. Goff, *Discerning Wisdom. The Sapiential Literature of the Dead Sea Scrolls* (VTSup 116; Leiden: Brill, 2007) 104–21.

[22] For further examples of this line of interpretation see Kugel, *Traditions of the Bible*, 100–2 and 128–9; Anderson, *The Genesis of Perfection*, 99–116.

He established with them an eternal covenant,
and revealed to them his decrees (Sir 17:1–12).

Several points should be noted about this passage. First, Ben Sira makes no distinction between the account of creation in Genesis 1 and that in Genesis 2–3. The idea that human beings are taken from the earth is derived from Genesis 2, while the statements that God made them in his own image and gave them dominion over the beasts come from Genesis 1. Ancient exegetes were not unaware of the differences between the two accounts in Genesis, and could exploit them when it suited their purposes, as we shall see, but very often the two accounts are harmonized.

A second observation is more significant, as it concerns an apparent discrepancy between Ben Sira and the biblical text. According to Genesis, God explicitly forbade Adam and Eve to eat from the tree of the knowledge of good and evil. Ben Sira records no such prohibition. On the contrary, we are told, God filled them with knowledge and showed them good and evil. This is a bold reinterpretation of what seems to be the perfectly clear meaning of the biblical text. Wisdom and knowledge were unequivocally good things from the point of view of a wisdom teacher like Ben Sira. It was inconceivable that God would have restricted human access to them, especially since humanity, according to Genesis 1, was made in the image of God. So Ben Sira here simply skips the whole unpleasant incident of the Fall. There is no original sin here, and mortality is not imposed as a punishment. From the beginning, God intended that people would live a limited number of days. (This point is reiterated later in Sir 41:4, where we are told that death is simply "the decree of the Lord for all flesh"). The situation of Adam is no different from that of his descendants. Admittedly, Ben Sira is not entirely consistent on this point. At the end of the Praise of the Fathers he says that the glory of Adam surpassed that of every living thing (49:14). But in the passages that reflect most directly on Genesis, he takes Adam as generic humanity rather than as the exceptional primeval man. Genesis is read in light of Deuteronomy. Everyone has knowledge of the law, and is responsible for his or her own actions. In all of this, Sirach seems to read Genesis in light of everything else that he believes to be true. Genesis, as part of the revealed Torah, cannot contradict the truth, even if this means that some parts of the text must be disregarded.

But if God had endowed humanity with wisdom and given them knowledge of good and evil, how is the reality of human sin to be explained? Ben Sira addresses this problem in another passage:

Do not say, 'It was the Lord's doing that I fell away,'
for he does not do what he hates.
Do not say, 'It was he who led me astray,'
For he has no need of the sinful ...
God created humankind in the beginning
and placed him in the power of his inclination.
If you choose, you can keep the commandments,
and to act faithfully is a matter of your own choice (15:11–20).

The idea that it might be the Lord's doing was not altogether far-fetched. The Hebrew Bible had spoken of "an evil spirit from the Lord" that afflicted King Saul (1 Sam 19:9). We shall find a clear basis for such a view in the treatise on the Two Spirits in the Dead Sea Scrolls. Ben Sira himself seems to entertain such a possibility in another passage that refers to Genesis (Sir 33:10–13):

Every man is a vessel of clay, and Adam was created out of the dust. In the fullness of his knowledge the Lord distinguished them and appointed their different ways. Some he blessed and exalted, and some he made holy and brought near to himself; but some he cursed and brought low, and turned them out of their place. Like clay in the hand of the potter, to be molded as he pleases, so all are in the hand of their Maker, to be given whatever he decides.

In chapter 15, however, Ben Sira places the emphasis on human free will rather than on divine determinism. His way of doing this, however, is noteworthy. Human beings are in the power of their inclination. The Hebrew word here, יצר, comes from the verb meaning "to form" which is used in Gen 2:7 ("The Lord God formed man out of the dust of the ground"). There is no mention of an inclination in Genesis 2–3, but the word occurs twice in the Flood story: "every inclination of their thoughts is evil continually" (Gen 6:5) and "the inclination of the human heart is evil from youth" (Gen 8:21). The association of the "inclination" with evil is typical of biblical usage. Only two passages in the Hebrew Bible use the word in a positive sense (Isa 26:3 and 1 Chron 29:18). The negative sense of the inclination is attested in the book of *4 Ezra*, which was composed about 100 CE, and which attributes the sin of Adam to the fact that he was burdened with "an evil heart." Later, in rabbinic literature there was a developed doctrine of two inclinations.[23] The righteous are ruled by the good inclination, the wicked by the evil inclination and average people by both. The idea of two inclinations was derived from Genesis by a typical piece of rabbinic exegesis. The Hebrew word for "formed" in the phrase "the Lord God formed man" (וייצר) has the letter yod twice, and this was taken to indicate that there were two inclinations.[24] This distinction between good and bad inclinations is not yet found in Ben Sira, at least not clearly, but we can see that he is using the Genesis text to wrestle with the problem of the origin of evil. It should be noted that Ben Sira has no place for a devil, and that he ignores the snake of Genesis.[25]

---

[23] See G. F. Moore, *Judaism in the First Centuries of the Christian Era* (New York: Schocken, 1975) 1.474–96; E. E. Urbach, *The Sages: Their Concepts and Beliefs* (Jerusalem: Magnes, 1975) 1.471–83; G. H. Cohen Stuart, *The Struggle in Man between Good and Evil: An Inquiry into the Origin of the Rabbinic Concept of Yeser HaRa*ᶜ (Kampen: Kok, 1984).

[24] *Genesis Rabbah* 14:4.

[25] The Hebrew text of Sir 15:14 adds "and placed him in the power of his spoiler," but this statement is not found in the ancient translations and is evidently a late addition to the text.

Wisdom texts in the Scrolls

The idea that God endowed humanity with knowledge and wisdom from the beginning, which we have seen in Sir 17, is also found in several texts from Qumran. *4QWords of the Heavenly Luminaries* (4Q504), a liturgical text, weaves together motifs from Genesis 1 and Genesis 2. Adam is created in the image of God, and given dominion over the rest of creation. (As in several of the Qumran texts, the word for "dominion" is a form of משל rather than the biblical רדה. The setting is in the garden of Eden, and there is a prohibition imposed by God. When God fashioned Adam in the image of his glory: "the breath of life you blew into his nostril, and intelligence and knowledge."[26] The prohibition, then, can hardly be designed to prevent humanity from attaining knowledge of good and evil. This understanding of Genesis is also reflected in the fragmentary *4QMeditation on Creation* (4Q303), which mentions "the knowledge of good and evil" before the creation of Eve.[27] Like Ben Sira, these texts telescope Genesis 1 and Genesis 2–3 into a single account.

The *Words of the Heavenly Luminaries* explicitly refers to the prohibition, which led to the Fall:[28] "you imposed on him not to tu[rn away …]." The mention of disobedience is not preserved but the next line reads "he is flesh, and to dust …." The *Paraphrase of Genesis and Exodus* (4Q422), another fragmentary text that conflates the two creation accounts, is more explicit about the nature of the prohibition: "that he shoul[d n]ot eat from the tree that gives know[ledge of good and evil]."[29] It continues "he rose against Him and they forgot [His laws …] in evil inclination and for deed[s of injustice." In the *Words of the Heavenly Luminaries,* disobedience seems to be punished by mortality. The punishment is not preserved at all in the *Paraphrase*. The reference to the evil inclination, however, connects the sin of Adam to the sinful state of humanity before the Flood (Gen 6:5; 8:21). Esther Chazon detects an allusion to the setting of the Flood story also in the *Words of the Heavenly Luminaries* ("he is flesh," cf. Gen 6:3), although "very little of the Flood story has been preserved in this prayer."[30] In these texts, there is a pattern of sin and punishment, and it may be appropriate to speak of a "Fall," although the extent and significance of the punishment are obscured by the fragmentary nature of the texts.

---

[26] E. G. Chazon, "The Creation and Fall of Adam in the Dead Sea Scrolls," in J. Frishman and L. van Rampay, eds., *The Book of Genesis in Jewish and Oriental Christian Interpretation* (Leuven: Peeters, 1997) 15.

[27] T. H. Lim, "303. Meditation on Creation A," in T. Elgvin et al., *Qumran Cave 4. XV. Sapiential Texts, Part 1* (DJD 20; Oxford: Clarendon, 1997) 152–3; Goff, *Discerning Wisdom*, 268–70.

[28] Chazon, "The Creation and Fall," 16–17.

[29] T. Elgvin and E. Tov, "Paraphrase of Genesis and Exodus," in H. Attridge et al., *Qumran Cave 4 VIII: Parabiblical Texts, Part I* (DJD 13; Oxford: Clarendon, 1994) 421–2; T. Elgvin, "The Genesis Section of 4Q422 (4QparaGenExod)," *DSD* 1 (1994) 185. It also uses the hiphil of משל instead of the biblical רדה to indicate Adam's dominion over the rest of creation.

[30] Chazon, "The Creation and Fall," 15.

Not all texts from Qumran that discuss the story of creation, however, allow for a "Fall" at all.

4QInstruction

The most important of the wisdom texts found at Qumran is a long composition now known as *4QInstruction (Musar leMevin)*.[31] This text touches on the interpretation of Genesis at a number of points. One of the relevant passages is found in the fragmentary 4Q423:

> and every fruit that is produced and every tree which is good, pleasing to give knowledge. Is [it] not a ga[rden of pastu]re [and pleasant] to [gi]ve great knowledge? He set you in charge of it to till it and guard it .... thorns and thistles it will sprout forth for you, and its strength it will not yield to you ...in your being unfaithful.[32]

While much is unclear in this passage, it appears that the Genesis story is taken as a metaphor for the situation of the person addressed in the text. Most noteworthy is the interpretation of the trees. According to Gen 2:9: "Out of the ground the Lord God made to grow every tree that is pleasant to the sight and good for food, the tree of life also in the midst of the garden, and the tree of the knowledge of good and evil." Again in 3:6: "the woman saw that the tree was good for food, and that it was a delight to the eyes, and that the tree was to be desired to make one wise." The Qumran text picks up the idea that the trees are symbolic sources of wisdom and knowledge. It does not, however, seem to pick up the prohibition against eating from the tree of the knowledge of good and evil. Rather, it would seem, the garden is ambiguous. It gives knowledge and wisdom to the good, but thorns and thistles to those who are unfaithful. If this is correct (the text is too fragmentary to permit certainty), then the Qumran text is taking a position similar to what we found in Ben Sira: there is no prohibition of the knowledge of good and evil, and consequently no "Fall," but people may still choose to do wrong. If the earth produces thistles and brambles, this is not the fault of a primeval Adam but of each generation of human beings. The idea that nature responds differently to the righteous and to the wicked is found explicitly in Ben Sira 39:27: "All these are good for the godly, but for sinners they turn into evils."

Also like Ben Sira, the Qumran text posits a role for the human "inclination."[33] "Let not the thought of the evil inclination seduce you," the reader is told (4Q417 2

---

[31] J. Strugnell and D. J. Harrington, *Qumran Cave 4. XXIV. Sapiential Texts Part 2. 4QInstruction (Musar leMevin)* (DJD 34; Oxford: Clarendon, 1999). See also E. J. Tigchelaar, *To Increase Learning for the Understanding Ones. Reading and Reconstructing the Fragmentary Early Jewish Sapiential Text 4QInstruction* (STDJ 44; Leiden: Brill, 2001).

[32] The edition of 4Q423 in DJD 34 is by Torleif Elgvin.

[33] See J. J. Collins, "Wisdom, Apocalypticism and the Dead Sea Scrolls," in idem, *Seers, Sibyls and Sages* (JSJSup 54; Leiden: Brill, 1997) 369–83.

ii 12–13). Another passage speaks of "the inclination of the flesh" in the context of the need to distinguish between good and evil (4Q416 1 i 15–16). Yet another passage uses "inclination" in a positive sense, "to walk in the inclination of his understanding" (4Q417 1 i 11). It appears then that the human inclination may be either good or bad in this text.

The most important discussion of Genesis in the Qumran wisdom texts is found in *4QInstruction* in 4Q417 1 i 16–18.[34] The passage speaks of an engraved law that is decreed by God for all the wickedness of the sons of Seth (or Sheth), and a book of remembrance that is written before him for those who keep his word. This is also called "the Vision of Hagu" or Meditation. The book of Meditation is mentioned elsewhere in the Scrolls. Youths are supposed to be educated in it (1QSa 1:6–8) and judges are supposed to study it (CD 10:6; 13:2). It was obviously an important revelation of wisdom, but we cannot identify it with confidence with any extant writing. While the Vision of Hagu in this passage is surely related to the book mentioned elsewhere, the two are not necessarily identical. Then the passage continues:

and he gave it as an inheritance to Enosh with a spiritual people (עם רוח), for according to the likeness of the Holy Ones is his inclination (or: he formed him). Moreover, the Hagu (Meditation) was not given to the spirit of flesh (רוח בשר), for it did not know the difference between good and evil according to the judgment of its spirit.

The reference to "Enosh" has confused modern interpreters, because the word can be used in different ways.

The Hebrew word אנוש occurs numerous times in the Thanksgiving Hymns or *Hodayot* as a generic term for humanity.[35] "How will a man (אנוש) recount his sins?" asks the psalmist in 1QH 9:25. This usage would be problematic in the wisdom text, which distinguishes two kinds of human beings, a spiritual people and a spirit of flesh, and Enosh is only associated with the spiritual people. The word, then, cannot refer here to humanity at large.

אנוש can be read as a proper name, referring to the son of Seth, grandson of Adam, who is mentioned in Gen 4:26; 5:6–7, 9–11. This interpretation has been argued by Armin Lange, followed by Jörg Frey.[36] In the time of Enosh, people began

---

[34] Strugnell and Harrington, *Qumran Cave 4. XXIV*, 151–66. For more detailed analysis see J. J. Collins, "In the Likeness of the Holy Ones: The Creation of Humankind in a Wisdom Text from Qumran," in D. W. Parry and E. Ulrich, eds., *The Provo International Conference on the Dead Sea Scrolls* (Leiden: Brill, 1999) 609–18. See now also C. H. T. Fletcher-Louis, *All the Glory of Adam. Liturgical Anthropology in the Dead Sea Scrolls* (Leiden: Brill, 2002) 113–8; M. J. Goff, *The Worldly and Heavenly Wisdom of 4QInstruction* (STDJ 50; Leiden: Brill, 2003) 83–126.

[35] Strugnell and Harrington entertain the possibility both of a general reference and of a reference to Enosh (DJD 34, 164).

[36] So A. Lange, *Weisheit und Prädestination. Weisheitliche Urordnung und Prädestination in den Textfunden von Qumran* (STDJ 18; Leiden: Brill, 1995) 87; J. Frey, "Flesh and Spirit in the Palestinian Jewish Sapiential Tradition and in the Qumran Texts," in C. Hempel, A. Lange and H. Lichtenberger, eds., *The Wisdom Texts from Qumran and the Development of Sapiential Thought* (BETL CLIX; Leuven: Peeters, 2002) 393.

to call on the name of the Lord, and the book of *Jubilees* says that he was the first to do so. According to Sir 49:16, "Shem and Seth and Enosh were honored, but above every living being was the glory of Adam." But the evidence pertaining to Enosh in this period is quite limited. In the words of Steven Fraade:

> It is clear that Enosh was viewed as an important antediluvian figure in Jewish circles, at least as far back as the second century B.C.E. In most of these sources, however, his name is only cited as part of a 'chain' of such righteous antediluvians.[37]

In later, rabbinic tradition, the generation of Enosh was associated with the beginning of idolatry. Gen 4:26 is consistently read as referring to the worship of false gods.[38] Lange and Frey suppose that

> the passage seems to refer to a mythological tradition of the fall of the angels during the time of the sons of Seth, which presented Enosh and the עם רוח as the only pious of their time. So this primeval father and the עם רוח i.e. the obedient angels, gained the heavenly memorial as inheritance. In contrast, the book was not given to the רוח בשר because it was not able to discern between good and evil.[39]

Lange's argument assumes that the reference at the beginning of the passage to the wickedness of the sons of Seth refers to the father of Enosh. This reference, however, is not secure. The editors in the DJD edition read בני שות and suggest that the reference is to the Shuttu or sons of Sheth mentioned in Balaam's oracle in Num 24:17, a passage often cited in the Dead Sea Scrolls (1QM 11:6; CD 7:21; 4Q175 13).[40] The patriarch's name is not usually found with the plene spelling. The tradition of a fall of the angels in the time of Seth, which presented Enosh as a righteous remnant, remains hypothetical. The passage surely implies that the addressee belongs, at least potentially, to the "spiritual people,"[41] and if so that people cannot be entirely angelic. Moreover, some details of the passage are better explained on a different understanding of אנוש.

The word אנוש occurs in a different sense in the *Instruction on the Two Spirits* in the Community Rule. God created אנוש to rule the world. In this case the reference is to Adam in Gen 1:27–28.

The relevance of Adam to the passage from *4QInstruction* is shown by the qualifying phrase: "for according to the likeness of the Holy Ones is his inclination" (or, he formed him). The Holy Ones in the Dead Sea Scrolls and contemporary texts are heavenly beings, or angels. The Scrolls sometimes call these beings *elohim,* which

---

[37] Steven D. Fraade, *Enosh and His Generation: Pre-Israelite Hero and History in Postbiblical Interpretation* (SBLMS 30; Chico, CA: Scholars Press, 1984) 27.

[38] Fraade, *Enosh and His Generation*, 174, 226–7. P. Schäfer, "Der Götzendienst des Enosch: Zur Bildung und Entwicklung aggadischer Traditionen im nachbiblischen Judentum," in *Studien zur Geschichte und Theologie des Rabbinischen Judentums* (Leiden: Brill, 1978) 134–52.

[39] Frey, "Flesh and Spirit," 393. Frey understands the spirit of flesh as "sinful humanity."

[40] DJD 34: 163.

[41] Compare also 4Q418 43–45 6: "then you will distinguish between good and bad," and 4Q418 81 1–2: "he has separated you from every spirit of flesh."

can mean either gods, in the plural, or God in the singular. The Hebrew phrase "according to the likeness of the Holy Ones," is a paraphrase of Gen 1:27, which says that God created Adam (or humankind) "in the image of God." The Qumran text understands this as in the image of the Holy Ones or angels, rather than in the image of the Most High. אנוש is Adam, formed in the likeness of the heavenly beings. (Admittedly, this understanding of "the likeness of the Holy Ones" does not necessarily exclude a reference to the patriarch Enoch. According to *Genesis Rabbah* 23:6, Adam, Seth and Enosh were created in the image and likeness of God, "but from then on Centaurs were created.")[42]

A second allusion to the creation story is provided by the statement that the spirit of flesh did not distinguish between good and evil. Here we have a clear allusion to Genesis 2–3. God did not forbid humanity to eat of the tree of the knowledge of good and evil, according to this text, but some human beings, those who had a "spirit of flesh" failed to grasp the distinction. The spirit of flesh, however, stands in contrast to a "spiritual people" or "people of spirit," associated with "Enosh," who were deemed worthy to receive the revelation, and who presumably recognized the difference between good and evil.

The phrase רוח בשר, spirit of flesh, occurs in the *Hodayot* as a form of self-reference by the Hymnist: "for your servant is a spirit of flesh" (1QH^a 4:25) or as a designation of the human condition : "what is the spirit of flesh to understand all these matters ... What is someone born of a woman among all your awesome works?" (1QH^a 5:19–20). *4QInstruction*, however, tells the addressee: "He has separated you from every spirit of flesh, and you, separate yourself from everything he hates" (4Q418 81 1–2). In 4Q416 1.10–13 we are told that "every spirit of flesh" will be aroused in the context of a divine judgment, and there seems to be a contrast with "the sons of heaven" and "all the sons of his truth."[43] In this text, then, "spirit of flesh" does not simply connote the human condition, but rather a segment of humanity from which the elect must be separated.

We have seen that Ben Sira harmonized the two accounts in Genesis, and read them as one. *4QInstruction* also conflates the two accounts, since it uses the word יצר to fashion, from Gen 2:7 to describe the creation in the image of God.[44] But it still distinguishes between two kinds of human being who are created, the spiritual kind, whose creation is reported in Genesis 1 and the fleshly kind described in Genesis 2–3.[45] Only the fleshly kind fails to recognize the difference between good and evil, in accordance with the story in Genesis 2–3. This kind of interpretation of

---

[42] Fraade, *Enosh*, 132.
[43] See Frey, "Flesh and Spirit," 391.
[44] T. Elgvin, "An Analysis of 4QInstruction" (Diss. Jerusalem, 1997) 90.
[45] An alternative interpretation is proposed by Elgvin, *ibid.*, 91: "4QInstruction sees only one Adam in the biblical text. Before he sinned, he shared angelic glory and wisdom; after his fall he shared the conditions of רוח בשר." In that case, however, we should wonder why Adam failed to distinguish between good and evil, since he had been endowed with the vision of Hagu when he was created in the likeness of the holy ones.

Genesis, which explains the two creation stories as a double creation, is rare in antiquity, but not unique. Philo of Alexandria wrote in his *Allegorical Interpretation*:

> There are two types of men; the one a heavenly man, the other an earthly. The heavenly man, being made after the image of God, is altogether without part or lot in corruptible and terrestrial substance; but the earthly one was compacted out of the matter scattered here and there, which Moses calls clay.[46]

Philo interprets the two Adams in a framework derived from Greek philosophy, and this is very different from anything we find in the Dead Sea Scrolls. What he has in common with the Qumran wisdom text is the idea that the two accounts of creation in Genesis describe the creation of two different kinds of human being. Philo was apparently aware of other interpretations along the same lines.[47] The Qumran text suggests that there may have been a wider tradition of interpretation, found also in Hebrew in the land of Israel, that distinguished between the two creation accounts in Genesis.

The later rabbis were also aware of the duplication of creation. According to *Genesis Rabbah* 14:

> There were two formations [one partaking of the nature] of the celestial beings, [the other] of earthly creatures ... He created him with four attributes of the higher beings [i.e. the angels] and four of the lower creatures [i.e. the beasts] ... R. Tifdai said in R. Aha's name: The celestial beings were created in the image and likeness [of God] and do not procreate, while the terrestrial creatures procreate but were not created in [His] image and likeness. Said the Holy One, blessed be He: 'Behold, I will create him [man] in [My] image and likeness; [thus he will partake] of the [character of the] celestial beings, while he will procreate [as is the nature] of the terrestrial beings.' R. Tifdai [also] said in R. Aha's name: The Lord reasoned: 'If I create him of the celestial elements he will live [for ever] and not die; while if I create him of the terrestrial elements, he will die and not live. Therefore I will create him of the upper and lower elements; if he sins he will die, and if he dies he will live [in the future life].[48]

The midrash, however, differs from the Qumran text insofar as it combines the celestial and terrestrial elements in all human beings, whereas the Qumran text distinguishes two distinct types.

---

[46] Philo, *Allegorical Interpretation* 31; cf. *De Opificio Mundi* 134–5. See T. H. Tobin, *The Creation of Man: Philo and the History of Interpretation* (Washington, D.C.: Catholic Biblical Association, 1983) 108.

[47] Philo, *Questions on Genesis* 1:8 reports various answers that were given to the question "why does He place the moulded man in Paradise, but not the man who was made in his image?"

[48] *Midrash Rabbah* 14:3; trans. and ed. H. Freedman and M. Simon (New York: Soncino, 1983) 112.

The *Instruction on the Two Spirits*

The distinction between two types, each indicated by the word "spirit" ("people of spirit," "spirit of flesh") points us to another account of creation in the Dead Sea Scrolls, where the human being is also called אנוש. This is the *Instruction on the Two Spirits* in the *Community Rule*. According to that passage:

> From the God of Knowledge comes all that is and shall be. Before ever they existed He established their whole design .... He has created man (אנוש) to govern the world, and has appointed for him two spirits in which to walk until the time of His visitation: the spirits of truth and injustice. Those born of truth spring from a fountain of light, but those born of injustice spring from a source of darkness. All the children of righteousness are ruled by the Prince of Light, and walk in the ways of light, but all the children of injustice are ruled by the Angel of Darkness and walk in the ways of darkness ... (1QS 3:15–21).

This remarkable passage has often been taken as the quintessence of the distinctive theology of the sectarian scrolls. There is no precedent for warring spirits of light and darkness in the Jewish tradition. On the contrary, this concept has its closest parallel in Persian dualism, as has often been noted.[49] While the Jewish author certainly adapts the Persian myth for his purpose, the influence of that myth in shaping the idea of conflicting spirits of light and darkness cannot be doubted. And yet the passage is also an interpretation of Genesis, as we might expect in an account of the creation of humanity. Dependence on Genesis is signaled most clearly in the statement that God created man to rule the world – compare Gen 1:26. (The Hebrew word ממשלת recalls the use of המשיל in this context in other texts from Qumran.) I would argue, however, that even the doctrine of the two spirits should be understood in the context of the ongoing debate about the meaning of Genesis 1–3 and the origin of evil that we have seen in Ben Sira and in the wisdom texts from Qumran.

The insistence that "from the God of knowledge comes all that is" is at odds with at least one strand of Ben Sira's thought, which denied that sin comes from God (although we have seen that Ben Sira was not fully consistent on the subject). If everything comes from God, then sin must come from God too, even if indirectly. The text gives no exegetical justification for the statement that God created two spirits. A possible source may be suggested in Gen 2:7, which says that God breathed into his nostrils the breath of life, and he became a living being (נפש חיה); both the breath and the *nephesh* could be understood as spirits. The distinction could also be a development of the distinction between good and bad inclinations.[50] One of the earlier commentators on the passage, P. Wernberg-Moeller, argued that

---

[49] See Collins, *Apocalypticism in the Dead Sea Scrolls*, 41–43; idem, *Seers, Sibyls and Sages*, 287–99; M. Philonenko, "La Doctrine Qoumrânienne de Deux Esprits," in G. Widengren, A. Hultgård, M. Philonenko, *Apocalyptique Iranienne et Dualisme Qoumrânien* (Paris: Maisonneuve, 1995) 163–211.

[50] The term יצר is used in a positive sense in 1QS 4:5 and 8:3, and in a negative sense in 1QS 5:5, but it does not appear in the account of creation.

it is significant that our author regards the two 'spirits' as created by God, and that according to IV,23 and our passage both 'spirits' dwell in man as created by God. We are therefore not dealing here with a kind of metaphysical, cosmic dualism represented by the two 'spirits,' but with the idea that man was created by God with two 'spirits' – the Old Testament term for 'mood' or 'disposition' ... We have thus arrived at the rabbinic distinction between the evil and the good inclination.[51]

The attempt to deny any reference to metaphysical, cosmic dualism in the text is not convincing; the text clearly refers to Angels of Light and Darkness, and these are Spirits in one sense of the word. But the spirits also have a psychological dimension, and here Wernberg-Moeller was right to note the affinity of this distinction with that between the good and evil inclinations. The Persian myth provided the author of this Qumran passage with new language and a new concept to address an old problem – how could the creation of one omnipotent God have yielded evil as well as good? Here again nothing is said about a Fall; the assumption is that creation has continued in accordance with God's design. The *Instruction* concludes with a statement that God has allotted the two spirits to the children of men "that they may know good and evil," another clear allusion to Genesis. Like Ben Sira and *4QInstruction*, this text denies that God had ever forbidden humanity to know good and evil. Quite the contrary. Recognition of the distinction might be said to be one of the goals of creation.

Conclusion

We find then a spectrum of interpretations of the opening chapters of Genesis in the Dead Sea Scrolls, ranging from those that emphasize the sin of Adam to those that hold that humanity was created with different "spirits" from the beginning. Some aspects of what later became traditional interpretation do not appear in the Scrolls at all. The serpent is never identified as the devil, and indeed he receives no attention at all. Again, no scroll found at Qumran attaches any special blame to Eve. The people who preserved the Scrolls may not have done much to advance the cause of feminism in antiquity, but at least they did not use the text of Genesis to legitimate the subordination of women.[52]

The people who wrote these Scrolls were not isolated from the intellectual debates that were going in Judaism at the time. The issues raised in the Scrolls we have considered are fundamentally the same as those raised by Ben Sira and *1 Enoch*. Of course, it is not certain that the wisdom texts were sectarian in origin. They may

---

[51] P. Wernberg-Moeller, "A Reconsideration of the Two Spirits in the Rule of the Community (1Q Serek III,13 – IV,26)," *RevQ* 3 (1961) 422.

[52] The Scrolls do refer to the Eden story in connection with halakhic issues relating to marriage and divorce. See F. García Martínez, "Man and Woman: Halakhah based upon Eden in the Dead Sea Scrolls," in Luttikhuizen, ed., *Paradise Interpreted*, 95–115.

have been part of the wider literature preserved at Qumran (like the biblical books, or the books of Enoch). Some scholars even argue that the *Instruction on the Two Spirits* was composed before the Dead Sea sect separated from the rest of Judaism.[53] Nonetheless, both *4QInstruction* and the *Instruction on the Two Spirits* distinguish two types within humanity and this kind of distinction was foundational for the self-understanding of the sect. Yet we can see the beginnings of this kind of distinction in Ben Sira, who taught that all the works of the Lord come in pairs, one opposite the other (Sir 33:15), and that God blessed some people and cursed others (33:12). To be sure, the Dead Sea sect did not secede from the rest of Judaism because of their understanding of creation or their interpretation of Genesis, but these issues were part of the complex web of factors that shaped the distinctive self-understanding of the sect.

When we speak of biblical interpretation at Qumran, we most often think of the *pesharim*, which interpreted the prophetic texts as predictions of events in the Hellenistic and Roman periods. But this was not the only kind of biblical interpretation practiced at Qumran.[54] The readings of Genesis 1–3 implied in the texts we have considered resemble the *pesharim* insofar as they typically argue that the biblical texts describe the situation in which the sectarians found themselves. Adam was not a figure of ancient history, but a paradigmatic case with which the reader can identify. In the words of a later apocalypse, each of us is his own Adam (2 Bar 48:42). But we have found no readings of Genesis 2–3 that engage in one-to-one interpretations of elements in the text, such as "the snake is the devil." The interpretations are more subtle than that, and less atomistic. They involve interpretations of creation, not just of the words of Genesis, although verbal interpretation also plays a part.

A final conclusion concerns the freedom of interpretation that we find in these texts. For the modern interpreter, it is difficult to understand how a reader of Genesis could ignore the divine commandment to Adam and Eve that they not eat from the tree of good and evil. But all interpretation involves a correlation of what we find in the text with what we hold as true from other sources. This is what Gerald Bruns has called "the doctrine of charity" – "a way to interpret the utterances and behavior of a creature as revealing a set of beliefs largely consistent and true by our own standards."[55] Allegory, as practiced by Philo, provides an obvious example of the principle. For Ben Sira and the wisdom teachers whose work is preserved in the Scrolls, it was inconceivable that God would have forbidden people to acquire the knowledge of good and evil. Rather, we are told, people who had a "spirit of

---

[53] So Lange, *Weisheit und Prädestination*, 126–8; H. Stegemann, *The Library of Qumran* (Grand Rapids: Eerdmans, 1998) 110.

[54] For an overview see M. J. Bernstein, "Interpretation of Scriptures," in L. H. Schiffman and J. C. VanderKam, eds., *The Encyclopedia of the Dead Sea Scrolls* (New York: Oxford, 2000) 1.376–83.

[55] Gerald L. Bruns, *Hermeneutics Ancient and Modern* (New Haven: Yale, 1992) 203. The quotation is adapted from the philosopher Donald Davidson, *Inquiries into Truth and Interpretation* (Oxford: Clarendon, 1984) 137.

flesh" could not grasp the distinction, or the entire creation story unfolded in accordance with a divine plan, so that people would come to understand good and evil and their own mortality. The principle of correlation is also in evidence in the *Instruction of the Two Spirits*, which seems at first glance to be wildly at variance with the biblical account of creation. The author found in the Persian myth of Light and Darkness apt language to describe his experience of the universe. He then assumed that this must be a fair reflection of the process of creation described in Genesis. We would have appreciated a closer exegetical argument, such as we find later in the midrash, but the author provides sufficient allusions to Genesis to indicate that the two accounts were thought to correspond.

James Kugel has written of traditional Jewish and Christian intepretation as "the Bible as it was."[56] Our perusal of the interpretation of the early chapters of Genesis in the Dead Sea Scrolls, however, suggests that the earliest interpretations of the Bible were already diverse. Modern theorists have repeatedly emphasized that interpretation is never neutral and objective, but always depends on the presuppositions we bring to the text. Of course the presuppositions of the authors of the Scrolls are generally untenable in the modern world, because of the vast changes in science and philosophy over the last two thousand years. But the transparency of presuppositions in ancient interpretation can carry a salutary lesson for modern critics. The meaning of the Bible, as of any text, is never univocal, but is always viewed through the interpretive lens of the interpreter's culture and time.

---

[56] J. L. Kugel, *The Bible as It Was* (Cambridge, MA: Harvard, 1997).

CHAPTER SIX

The Interpretation of Psalm 2

At the beginning of the Epistle to the Hebrews, the author is concerned to establish the superiority of Christ over the angels. He does this by stringing together a series of quotations, beginning with verses from Psalm 2 and 2 Samuel 7:

For to which of the angels did God ever say,
'You are my son; today I have begotten you'? (Ps 2:7)

Or again,

'I will be his father, and he will be my son'? (2 Sam 7:14)[1]

In his commentary on Hebrews, Harold Attridge notes that "the form of this material resembles the *catenae* or *florilegia* found at Qumran, which share some of the texts found here."[2] He suggests that "such collections of messianic proof texts probably circulated in early Christian circles and it is likely that the author used such a traditional collection at this point."[3]

One of the texts that Attridge had in mind as a model for Hebrews is the so-called *Florilegium*, 4Q174.[4] This is not simply a catena, but a thematic interpretation of various passages from Deuteronomy 33, 2 Samuel 7, and Psalms 1, 2, and 5.[5] The extant fragment of the passage dealing with 2 Samuel 7 begins with 2 Sam 7:10–11a, which is interpreted using phrases from Exod 15:17 and Deut 23:3–4.[6] This is followed by the citation and interpretation of 2 Sam 7:11b. Then there is an abbreviated citation of 2 Sam 7:11c–14a, concluding with the passage cited in Hebrews: "I will be a father to him, and he will be a son to me." This, we are told, refers to the Branch of David, who will arise with the Interpreter of the Law at the end of days, and this interpretation is supported from Amos 9:11 ("I will raise up the booth of David

---

[1] The passage goes on to cite Deut 32:43 (LXX), Ps. 104:4; Ps. 45:6–7; Ps 102:25–7; and Ps 110:1.
[2] Harold W. Attridge, *Hebrews. A Commentary on the Epistle to the Hebrews* (Hermeneia; Philadelphia: Fortress, 1989) 50. He refers here to 4Q*Florilegium* and 4Q*Testimonia*.
[3] *Ibid.*
[4] Annette Steudel, *Der Midrasch zur Eschatologie aus der Qumrangemeinde (4QMidr-Eschat*[a.b]*)* (STDJ 13; Leiden: Brill, 1994) argues that 4Q174 is part of a longer work, of which another part is found in 4Q177. George Brooke, "*Florilegium*," *EDSS* 1.197 points out that there is no textual overlap between the two manuscripts and prefers to regard them as separate compositions.
[5] See the reconstruction by Steudel, *Der Midrasch zur Eschatologie*, 23–33.
[6] Fragments 1, 21, 2. Steudel, *Der Midrasch zur Eschatologie*, 25, assigns this material to column 3 of her reconstructed text.

which is fallen"). At this point there is a *vacat*, and a new section is introduced: "Midrash of 'Happy is the man who has not walked in the council of the wicked'" (Psalm 1:1). In this case the interpretation is introduced by the technical term *pesher*, which was not used in the interpretation of 2 Samuel 7. Only the opening half verse of Psalm 1 is cited, and it is interpreted with phrases drawn from Isa 8:11 and Ezek 37:23. Then the first two verses of Psalm 2 are cited. Only fragments of the interpretation are preserved.

The question arises whether there is any intrinsic relationship between the two passages that are cited, other than the fact that both are given an eschatological interpretation. George Brooke has argued that "consideration of the content of the interpretations themselves" suggests there was a closer relationship.[7] The opening verses of the two psalms, according to Brooke, function as *incipits*, which imply the rest of the psalm. The final section of the interpretation of 2 Sam 7:14 refers to the Branch of David, the kingly messiah. "The subsequent implied citation of the whole of Psalm 2 makes the interpretative purpose clear, since from Psalm 2.2 it is obvious that the son of Psalm 2.7 also refers to the Messiah, the kingly one, as Psalm 2.6 makes clear."[8] He concludes that 4Q174 "seems to offer citations and interpretations of 2 Samuel 7 and Psalm 2 which show that the two scriptural passages are mutually interdependent."[9] The intertextual relationship is confirmed by the citations in Hebrews 1. It may also be noted that in Acts 13:33–34 the citation of Psalm 2:7 is followed by a partial quotation of Isa 55:3: "I will give you the holy promises made to David," which entails an indirect allusion to 2 Samuel 7. While the two citations in the *Florilegium* are separated by a citation from Psalm 1, it must be borne in mind that Psalms 1–2 were often regarded as one in antiquity, as attested by rabbinic tradition and the western text of Acts.[10] That would appear to be the case here too. There is no introductory formula before the citation from Psalm 2.

Brooke's argument has been challenged vigorously by Annette Steudel, who argues that the fact that these two passages are both cited in 4Q*Florilegium* is coincidental.[11] In part, the disagreement concerns the structure and purpose of 4Q174, but

---

[7] George J. Brooke, "Shared Intertextual Interpretations in the Dead Sea Scrolls and the New Testament," in idem, *The Dead Sea Scrolls and the New Testament* (Minneapolis: Fortress, 2005) 70–94 (75). This article originally appeared in M. E. Stone and E. G. Chazon, eds., *Biblical Perspectives. Early Use and Interpretation of the Bible in Light of the Dead Sea Scrolls* (STDJ 28; Leiden: Brill, 1998) 35–57.

[8] *Ibid.*, 76.

[9] *Ibid.*

[10] Paul Maiberger, "Das Verständnis von Psalm 2 in der Septuaginta, im Targum, in Qumran, im frühen Judentum und im Neuen Testament," in Josef Schreiner, ed., *Beiträge zur Psalmenforschung. Psalm 2 und 22* (Forschung zur Bibel; Würzburg: Echter, 1988) 85–151 (85–9); H. L. Strack and P. Billerbeck, *Kommentar zum Neuen Testament aus Talmud und Midrasch* (München: Beck, 1924, 1989) 2.725; Berakot 9b; J. A. Fitzmyer, *The Acts of the Apostles* (AB 31; New York: Doubleday, 1998) 516.

[11] Annette Steudel, "Psalm 2 im antiken Judentum," in Dieter Sänger, ed., *Gottessohn und Menschensohn. Exegetische Paradigmen biblischer Intertextualität* (Neukirchen-Vluyn: Neu-

it also has broader implications for the understanding of Psalm 2, and of messianic expectation in late Second Temple Judaism. The messianic interpretation of Psalm 2 is well established in the New Testament, notably in connection with the baptism of Jesus,[12] and in connection with his exaltation,[13] and his role as messianic judge.[14] Steudel argues, however, that it is poorly attested in Second Temple Judaism, apart from *Psalms of Solomon* 17, and she suggests that while a messianic interpretation of the psalm as a whole is not impossible, a collective interpretation of Psalm 2 is implied in 4Q174.[15]

The relation between 2 Samuel 7 and Psalm 2 in 4Q174

A number of considerations weigh against the view that the passages from 2 Samuel 7 and Psalm 2 are juxtaposed in 4Q174 as messianic prooftexts. Steudel notes significant differences from the citations in Hebrews.[16] The Qumran text cites 2 Sam 7:10–14, not just 2 Sam 7:14, and cites Ps 2:1–2 rather than Ps 2:7.[17] There are formal differences between the two passages.[18] The interpretation of Psalm 1 is introduced as a "midrash." The phrase פשר הדבר is used in the interpretation of the psalms, but not of 2 Samuel 7. Messianic expectation is only one theme among many in 4Q174. In his article in the *Encyclopedia of the Dead Sea Scrolls*, Brooke sums up the concerns of the text as follows:

> Overall, this sectarian composition is concerned with the way various unfulfilled blessings and prophecies are being and will be fulfilled in the experiences of the community ... The principal fragments are primarily concerned with the sovereignty of God himself and with the character of the community as the eschatological Temple in anticipation and as the elect of Israel who are enduring a time of trials. There is also some interest in the Davidic messiah.[19]

Steudel sees the composition as a midrash on the "end of days."[20] Moreover, the section dealing with the psalms is marked off as a separate section by the heading

---

kirchener Verlag, 2004) 189–97: "Das gemeinsame Auftreten von Teilen von 2 Sam 7 und Ps 2 innerhalb von 4Q174 ist im Grunde zufälliger Natur."

[12] Matt 3:16–17; Mark 1:10–11; Luke 3:21–2.
[13] Acts 13:33–34.
[14] Rev 12:5; 19:15 rod of iron, cf. Ps 2:9. On the use of Psalm 2 in the New Testament see further Maiberger, "Das Verständnis," 113–18.
[15] Steudel, "Psalm 2," 197.
[16] Steudel, "Psalm 2," 195.
[17] The latter difference could be discounted if Brooke is right that the whole psalm is implied by the incipit.
[18] Maiberger, "Das Verständnis," 100–1. W. R. Lane, "A New Commentary Structure in 4Q*Florilegium*," *JBL* 78(1959) 343–6 suggested that two different works had been juxtaposed in 4Q174.
[19] Brooke, "*Florilegium*," 298.
[20] Steudel, *Der Midrasch der Eschatologie*, 214.

"Midrash," and preceded by a *vacat*. Steudel may be right that this section of the composition is "eine Art Psalmen-Kommentar."[21]

Moreover, as Brooke has also noted in his earlier work, the word משיחו in Ps. 2:2 is apparently taken as a plural and referred to "the elect ones of Israel." He concludes the passage quoted above by qualifying the interest of the composition in the Davidic messiah: "though 'his messiah' of Psalm 2:2 is interpreted to refer to 'the elect ones of Israel,' the community itself, rather than the Davidic messiah."[22] Admittedly, the word משיחו is not actually preserved, but it would seem to be the only possible antecedent for the "elect ones."

Steudel recognizes that the correlation of the word משיחו with "elect ones" does not rule out an interpretation of Psalm 2 in terms of an individual messiah. It is clear from the interpretation of 2 Samuel 7 that the author had a place for the Davidic messiah at the end of days. Several lines are missing from the end of column 4 as reconstructed by Steudel,[23] so it is quite possible that the "midrash" included a reference to the messianic king.[24] In the words of George Brooke: "It is just possible that 'his anointed' (Ps 2:2) is taken up in reference to a messianic figure who will reign on the Lord's holy hill and that this is done in terms of Exod 34:29, but nothing conclusive can be said on this score."[25] The extant interpretation of Psalm 2, however, does not address verses 6–7. The focus of the interpretation is on the time of upheaval and its implications for the community. But this does not imply a collective interpretation of the entire psalm.[26] We simply do not have an interpretation of the entire psalm in the extant fragments.

The messianic interpretation of Psalm 2

It is generally recognized that Psalm 2, or at least Psalm 2:1–9, is of pre-exilic origin,[27] and that in its original context it was not messianic in the eschatological sense,

---

[21] Steudel, "Psalm 2," 196. In *Der Midrasch der Eschatologie*, 129–34, she suggests that 4Q174+4Q177 comments on selected psalms from the "Davidic psalter" (Psalms 1–41). Cf. also Émile Puech, *La Croyance des Esséniens en la Vie Future: Immortalité, Résurrection, Vie Éternelle* (Paris: Gabalda, 1993) 573, n.20.

[22] Brooke, "*Florilegium*," 298. So also G. J. Brooke, *Exegesis at Qumran. 4QFlorilegium in its Jewish Context* (JSOTSup 29; Sheffield: JSOT, 1985) 148–9; Johannes Zimmermann, *Messianische Texte aus Qumran* (WUNT 2/104; Tübingen: Mohr Siebeck, 1998) 110; Steudel, "Psalm 2," 197.

[23] Steudel, *Der Midrasch zur Eschatologie*, 32.

[24] Brooke, *Exegesis at Qumran*, 158. Maiberger, "Das Verständnis," 100–1, argues against this possibility.

[25] Brooke, *Exegesis at Qumran*, 158–9.

[26] *Pace* Steudel, "Psalm 2," 197: "Die Interpretation des Zitats von Ps 2,1f deutet jedenfalls eher auf ein kollektives Verständnis des Gesamt-Psalms durch den Verfasser hin."

[27] See Hans-Joachim Kraus, *Psalms 1–59. A Continental Commentary* (Minneapolis: Fortress, 1993; translated from the 5th edition of *Psalmen 1. Teilband, Psalmen 1–59* [BK; Neukirchen-Vluyn: Neukirchener Verlag, 1978]) 126; Eckart Otto, "Psalm 2 in neuassyrischer Zeit. Assyrische Motive in der judäischen Königsideologie," in Klaus Kiesow and Thomas Meurer, eds.,

but reflects the ideology of the Judahite kingship in Jerusalem.[28] The oracle addressed to the king, "you are my son; today I have begotten you," is taken from an enthronement ceremony, and finds its closest parallels in Egyptian texts of the New Kingdom period.[29] Presumably, the Davidic kingship had taken over some of the rhetoric of kingship current in pre-Israelite Jerusalem, which had been under Egyptian control in the second millennium.[30] Some scholars, mainly German, date the psalm to the postexilic period, and argue that it was composed as a messianic, eschatological psalm.[31] This is unlikely. It makes far better sense in a context where the monarchy was still intact.[32] It is quite likely, however, that the psalm would have been read as messianic in the post-exilic period.

Arguments about how the psalms would have been read, however, are tenuous unless they are supported by changes in the text or by explicit interpretations. Brevard Childs argued that Psalm 2

has been given an eschatological ring, both by its position in the Psalter and by the attachment of new meaning to the older vocabulary through the influence of the prophetic message ... Indeed, at the time of the final redaction, when the institution of kingship had long since been destroyed, what earthly king would have come to mind other than God's Messiah?[33]

Christoph Rösel argues that Psalm 2 was the introduction to a "messianic psalter," which ended with Psalm 89, which picks up the theme of the king/messiah as "son of God" (Ps 89: 26–7).[34] Sue Gillingham, in contrast, argues that during the editori-

---

Textarbeit. Studien zu Texten und ihrer Rezeption aus dem Alten Testament und der Umwelt Israels. Festschrift für Peter Weimar (AOAT 294; Münster: Ugarit-Verlag, 2003) 335–49; idem, "Politische Theologie in den Königspsalmen zwischen Ägypten und Assyrien. Die Herrscherlegitimation in den Psalmen 2 und 18 in ihrem altorientalischen Kontexten," in E. Otto and E. Zenger, eds., *'Mein Sohn bist du,' (Ps 2,7). Studien zu den Königspsalmen* (Stuttgarter Bibelstudien 192; Stuttgart: Verlag Katholisches Bibelwerk, 2002) 33–65; Mark W. Hamilton, *The Body Royal. The Social Implications of Kingship in Ancient Israel* (Leiden: Brill, 2005) 60–1.

[28] J. A. Fitzmyer, *The One Who Is to Come* (Grand Rapids: Eerdmans, 2007) 20; S. E. Gillingham, "The Messiah in the Psalms," in John Day, ed., *King and Messiah in Israel and the Ancient Near East* (JSOTSup 270; Sheffield: Sheffield Academic Press, 1998) 212.

[29] See especially Otto, "Politische Theologie" (above n. 27); Klaus Koch, "Der König als Sohn Gottes," in Otto and Zenger, eds., *'Mein Sohn bist du,'* 11–15.

[30] The Canaanite background of Judahite kingship is reflected in Psalm 110, where the king is said to be a priest forever after the order of Melchizedek. See John Day, "The Canaanite Inheritance of the Israelite Monarchy," in Day, ed., *King and Messiah*, 72–90.

[31] E.g. Erhard S. Gerstenberger, *Psalms. Part One, with an Introduction to Cultic Poetry* (FOTL XIV; Grand Rapids: Eerdmans, 1988) 48. For an overview of the debate about the date of the Psalm see Friedhelm Hartenstein, "'Der im Himmel thront, lacht' (Ps 2,4)," in Dieter Sänger, ed., *Gottessohn und Menschensohn*, 158–88 (160). Hartenstein allows that vs. 7 is taken from a pre-exilic enthronement ritual (161).

[32] I discuss this further in Adela Yarbro Collins and John J. Collins, *Messiah, Son of God* (Grand Rapids: Eerdmans, 2008) chapter 1 (pp. 1–24).

[33] B. S. Childs, *Introduction to the Old Testament as Scripture* (Philadelphia: Fortress, 1979) 515–7 (516).

[34] Christoph Rösel, *Die messianische Redaktion des Psalters. Studien zu Entstehung und Theologie der Sammlung Psalm 2–89** (Stuttgart: Calwer, 1999).

al process in the postexilic period "psalmody was still understood at this time more in terms of its orientation backwards, into the time of the Davidic dynasty, rather than forwards, in terms of some great and glorious Messianic kingdom."[35] Following the argument of J. Clinton McCann, she argues that "the placing of strategic royal psalms ... gives the Psalter a sequence of critical events in the life of the monarchy – first, the inauguration of the covenant with David (Psalm 2), then the statement about the responsibilities of the Davidic king (Psalm 72), and finally the account of the downfall of the dynasty (Psalm 89)."[36] This explanation of the role of Psalm 2 is not entirely persuasive. (Unlike Psalm 89, Psalm 2 does not speak of a covenant with David.) But in fact any explanation of the placement of psalms is speculative, and cannot bear much weight in an argument.

Arguments based on the Greek translation of the Psalter have more evidence to support them, in cases where the translation departs from the Hebrew original. Joachim Schaper has shown that at least in some cases the figure of the king is enhanced.[37] For example, Psalm 110 (LXX 109) imputes pre-existence to the (messianic) king by saying that God has begotten him before the Day-Star.[38] But there is no such embellishment in Psalm 2.[39] The decree of the Lord, "you are my son, today I have begotten you," is rendered straightforwardly. There is no attempt to evade the declaration that the king is son of God, and certainly no hint of a collective interpretation, either here or in Ps 2:2, but the literal translation does not necessarily tell us how the psalm was understood. The fact that there are some signs of messianic interpretation elsewhere in the Septuagint lends support to the assumption that Psalm 2 was also understood messianically, but this remains a matter of inference.

Psalm 2 in the Pseudepigrapha

The strongest evidence for the interpretation of Psalm 2 as messianic in Second Temple Judaism is found in the Pseudepigrapha. In her discussion of the reception of Psalm 2, Steudel acknowledged only three texts among the Pseudepigrapha that

---

[35] Gillingham, "The Messiah in the Psalms," 225–6.

[36] *Ibid.*, 227. Cf. J. Clinton McCann, "Books I–III and the Editorial Purpose of the Hebrew Psalter," in idem, ed., *The Shape and Shaping of the Psalter* (JSOTSup 159; Sheffield: JSOT, 1993) 93–107.

[37] Joachim Schaper, *Eschatology in the Greek Psalter* (WUNT 2/76; Tübingen: Mohr Siebeck, 1995); idem, "Der Septuaginta-Psalter als Dokument jüdischer Eschatologie," in Martin Hengel and Anna Maria Schwemer, eds., *Die Septuaginta zwischen Judentum und Christentum* (Tübingen: Mohr Siebeck, 1994) 38–61.

[38] Schaper, *The Eschatology*, 102.

[39] On the LXX of Psalm 2 see Maiberger, "Das Verständnis," 89–91. Holger Gzella, *Lebenszeit und Ewigkeit. Studien zur Eschatologie und Anthropologie des Septuaginta-Psalters* (BBB 134; Berlin: Philo, 2002) 337, argues that the translation strengthens the messianic character of vs. 6, because the king rather than God is cast as the speaker, but it is not apparent why this change should bespeak messianic consciousness.

make use of this psalm: the *Psalms of Solomon*, especially *Psalm of Solomon* 17, *Sib Or* 3:664–8 and *T. Levi* 4:2. In *T. Levi*, the patriarch tells his sons that the Lord has heeded "your prayer ... that you should become a son to him, as minister and priest in his presence." This is an allusion to 2 Sam 7 rather than to Psalm 2, and it involves a reinterpretation of the promise to apply it to the priesthood. The passage in *Sibylline Oracles* 3 speaks of an attack of the nations on Jerusalem and the temple, but does not speak of a messianic figure. It is of interest here insofar as it shows that an allusion to Psalm 2 in an eschatological context does not necessarily entail a messiah. *Psalms of Solomon* 17 is an important text for the interpretation of Psalm 2, but Steudel overlooks two other major pseudepigraphic texts: the *Similitudes of Enoch* (*1 Enoch* 48:10) and *4 Ezra* 13.

The *Psalms of Solomon*

The 17th *Psalm of Solomon* is a plea for deliverance in the wake of the conquest of Jerusalem by Pompey in 63 BCE. The Roman general is identified as "a man alien to our race" and a "lawless one" who laid waste the land and expelled rulers to the west (17:11).[40] But Pompey is not the only villain of the story. The psalmist begins by affirming the kingship of God, but recalls that "Lord, you chose David to be king over Israel, and swore to him about his descendants forever that his kingdom should not fail before you" (17:4). Right kingship, then, is based on the covenant with David, as reported in 2 Samuel 7. But this had already been violated before Pompey arrived on the scene:

sinners rose up against us, they set upon us and drove us out.
Those to whom you did not (make) the promise ...
With pomp they set up a monarchy because of their arrogance;
They despoiled the throne of David with arrogant shouting (7:5–7).

The reference is to the Hasmoneans, who had usurped the throne although they were not of the line of David, and had brought upon Judea punishment in the form of the Romans.

The psalmist calls on the Lord to remedy this situation by raising up a Davidic messiah:

See Lord, and raise up for them their king,
the son of David, to rule over your servant Israel (17:21).

His task would be "to purge Jerusalem from gentiles." The description that follows draws heavily on Psalm 2:

in wisdom and righteousness to drive out sinners from the inheritance;

---

[40] Kenneth Atkinson, *I Cried to the Lord. A Study of the Psalms of Solomon's Historical Background and Social Setting* (JSJSup 84; Leiden: Brill, 2004) 135–6.

to smash the arrogance of sinners like a potter's jar;
to shatter all their substance with an iron rod;
to destroy the unlawful nations with the word of his mouth;
At his warning the nations will flee from his presence.

Compare Psalm 2:8–9:

Ask of me, and I will make the nations your heritage ...
You shall break them with a rod of iron,
And dash them in pieces like a potter's vessel.

In the background of the whole passage is the motif of the assault of the nations on Jerusalem, as envisioned in Psalm 2. The use of the plural "nations" echoes the psalm, and their discomfiture and flight alludes to a related formulation of the mythology of Zion in Psalm 48. Finally, the statement in *Pss Sol* 7:32: "and their king shall be the Lord messiah," which should probably be emended to "the Lord's messiah,"[41] also echoes the reference to "the Lord and his anointed" in Ps 2:2.

Psalms of Solomon 17 is not an exercise in exegesis. It weaves together motifs from various passages in its description of the messiah.[42] The motifs of wisdom and righteousness, and the word of his mouth, echo Isa 11:1–5.[43] The statement in *Pss Sol* 17:33 that "he will not rely on horse and rider and bow, nor will he collect gold and silver for war," echoes the law of the king in Deuteronomy 17.

The psalm is very clear that the messianic king is dependent on God: "The Lord himself is his king, the hope of the one who has a strong hope in God" (17:34). At the same time, he is endowed with semi-divine qualities of wisdom, strength and righteousness.[44] While his weapon is the word of his mouth, he is a violent warrior, as is typical of descriptions of the messiah in this period.[45]

Pss Sol 17:27 says that when the messianic king gathers the holy people "he shall know them that they are all children of their God." Steudel suggests that a collective interpretation of "sonship" is implied, or at least not excluded, here.[46] It is true that the messianic king is not explicitly called "son of God" here, as we might expect in view of the allusions to the Davidic covenant and to Psalm 2. But even if the sonship is "democratized," so to speak, and extended to the holy people, the status of the

---

[41] See H. E. Ryle and M. R. James, *Psalms of the Pharisees: Commonly Called the Psalms of Solomon* (Cambridge: Cambridge University Press, 1891) 141–3. The phrase occurs again in *Ps Sol* 18:7.

[42] See Kenneth Atkinson, *An Intertextual Study of the Psalms of Solomon Pseudepigrapha* (Lewiston, NY: Mellen, 2001) 336–41.

[43] On the description of the messiah see further Gene Davenport, "The 'Anointed of the Lord' in *Psalms of Solomon* 17," in G. W. E. Nickelsburg and J. J. Collins, eds., *Ideal Figures in Ancient Judaism* (SBLSCS 12; Chico: Scholars Press, 1980) 67–92 (72).

[44] See further G. W. E. Nickelsburg, *Jewish Literature between the Bible and the Mishnah* (revised ed.; Minneapolis: Fortress, 2005) 242.

[45] See further John J. Collins, *The Scepter and the Star. Messianism in Light of the Dead Sea Scrolls* (2nd ed.; Grand Rapids: Eerdmans, 2010) 52–78.

[46] Steudel, "Psalm 2," 197, n.29.

king is not thereby diminished. Paul speaks of the plural children of God, who are "conformed to the image of his son, in order that he might be the firstborn within a large family" (Rom 8:29), but the special status of Christ is not diminished thereby. There is no question of collective messianism in the *Psalms of Solomon*. The restoration of the people is accomplished through the agency of the messiah.

The *Similitudes of Enoch*

Psalm 2 is cited with reference to a very different kind of messiah in the *Similitudes of Enoch*. The *Similitudes* consist of three "parables" (chapters 38–44; 45–57; and 58–69), which are actually visions.[47] There are an introductory chapter (37) and two epilogues in chapters 70–72. The second and third parables are dominated by a figure variously called "the Chosen One," "the Righteous One," or "that Son of Man," who is also mentioned but not seen in the first parable.[48] The scene in which he is introduced, in *1 Enoch* 46, is clearly modeled on Daniel chapter 7, although the older scene is adapted freely. Enoch sees "one who had a head of days, and his head was like white wool. And with him was another, whose face was like the appearance of a man; and his face was full of graciousness like one of the holy angels" (46:1). In the third parable, this figure sits on the throne of glory, and presides over the judgment. Despite his human appearance, he is not a man, at least in the usual sense of the word. He is "like one of the holy angels" (46:1). While he is distinguished from other angels (Michael in 60:4–5; 69:14; 71:3; the four archangels in 71:8, 9, 13), his rank is higher than theirs.[49]

Much of the recent discussion of the Son of Man in the *Similitudes* has been concerned with his apparent identification with Enoch in *1 Enoch* 71:14, where Enoch is greeted on his ascent to heaven with the words: "You are that (or: a) son of man who was born for righteousness ..." We need not rehearse that debate here.[50] It must suffice to say that this passage occurs in a second epilogue, and is almost certainly a secondary addition. In the body of the *Similitudes* there is no hint that the figure Enoch sees in his visions is actually himself. Rather, he is a supernatural, heavenly

---

[47] G. W. E. Nickelsburg, "Discerning the Structure(s) of the Enochic Book of Parables," in Gabriele Boccaccini, ed., *Enoch and the Messiah Son of Man* (Grand Rapids: Eerdmans, 2007) 23–47 and M. A. Knibb, "The Structure and Composition of the Book of Parables," *ibid.*, 48–64. Citations from the *Similitudes* follow G. W. E. Nickelsburg and J. C. VanderKam, *1 Enoch. A New Translation* (Minneapolis: Fortress, 2004).

[48] J. C. VanderKam, "Righteous One, Messiah, Chosen One, and Son of Man in *1 Enoch* 37–71," in J. H. Charlesworth, ed., *The Messiah* (Minneapolis: Fortress, 1992) 169–91.

[49] On the transcendent character of the Son of Man see Christoph Böttrich, "Konturen des 'Menschensohnes in äthHen 37–71,'" in Sänger, ed., *Gottessohn und Menschensohn*, 76–9; H. S. Kvanvig, "The Son of Man in the Parables," in Boccaccini, ed., *Enoch and the Messiah Son of Man*, 179–215 (189).

[50] See my discussion in *The Apocalyptic Imagination* (revised ed.; Grand Rapids: Eerdmans, 1998) 187–91, and in Yarbro Collins and Collins, *Messiah, Son of God*, 90–94.

figure, although Enoch and other earthly righteous people are conformed to him to some degree.

The exalted nature of the Son of Man is especially in evidence in 48:2–3:

And in that hour that son of man was named in the presence of the Lord of Spirits, and his name before the Head of Days. Even before the sun and the constellations were created, before the stars of heaven were made, his name was named before the Lord of Spirits.

The passage continues in 48:6: "For this (reason) he was chosen and hidden in his presence before the world was created and forever." While the context of *1 Enoch* 48: 2 is either eschatological or the time of Enoch's ascent, 48:6 seems to state unequivocally that the Son of Man existed before the world was created.[51] Similarly, in *1 Enoch* 62:7 we read:

For from the beginning the son of man was hidden,
and the Most High preserved him in the presence of his might,
and he revealed him to the chosen.

It would seem that the *Similitudes* here have developed the identity of the Son of Man well beyond anything that we found in Daniel, by applying to him language that is elsewhere used of wisdom. Another significant parallel is found in the LXX translation of Psalm 110 where the king/messiah is begotten "before the Day Star."

The *Similitudes* also develop the role of the Son of Man beyond what was found in Daniel in other significant ways. Besides the association with wisdom, he is said to be "the light of the nations" like the servant in Second Isaiah.[52] Of special interest for our present inquiry are passages that associate the Son of Man with the Davidic messiah, although there is no hint of Davidic lineage.[53] The spirit of wisdom and insight that dwells in him (49:1–4) recalls the messianic oracle in Isaiah 11.[54] He is also installed on a glorious throne, and takes over the function of eschatological judge (51:3; 55:4; 61:8; 62:2; 69:29). The motif of enthronement is reminiscent of Psalm 110. Here again he functions in a manner reminiscent of the traditional messiah: "and the spirit of righteousness was poured out upon him, and the word of his mouth will slay all the sinners" (62:2).

Moreover, the kings of the earth are condemned in 48:10 for having denied "the Lord of Spirits and his Anointed One." As Johannes Theisohn recognized, this is a

---

[51] Gottfried Schimanowski, *Weisheit und Messias. Die jüdischen Voraussetzungen der urchristlichen Präexistenzchristologie* (Tübingen: Mohr/Siebeck, 1985) 153–94.

[52] For other allusions to the servant passages in 2 Isaiah, see Johannes Theisohn, *Der auserwählte Richter* (SUNT 12; Göttingen: Vandenhoeck & Ruprecht, 1975) 114–126; VanderKam, "Righteous One," 189.

[53] Stefan Schreiber, *Gesalbter und König. Titel und Konzeptionen der königlichen Gesalbtenerwartung in frühjudischen und urchristlichen Schriften* (BZNW 105; Berlin: de Gruyter, 2000) 338.

[54] Theisohn, *Der auserwählte Richter*, 138.

clear allusion to Psalm 2:2.[55] Again in 52:4, Enoch is told that all that he has seen "will serve the authority of his Anointed One." Again, the subjugation of the nations to the Lord and his Anointed in Psalm 2 forms the conceptual background. It is not suggested in the *Similitudes* that the Son of Man is a human descendent of David, but he is the Anointed, or Messiah, of the Lord, who takes over the functions of the Davidic king vis-à-vis the nations.

The *Similitudes* is one of a number of texts from around the turn of the era that attest to an exalted notion of the messiah, as a pre-existent, supernatural figure. These texts include the LXX translations of Psalm 110 and Isaiah 9, where the royal "child" is called an *angelos*, which should be understood as "angel."[56] Another important witness to this trend, from a slightly later time, can be found in *4 Ezra* 13.

4 Ezra 13

4 Ezra is a complex apocalypse, containing three dialogues and four visions.[57] The messiah figures prominently in the third dialogue and in the second and third visions.[58] Our present concern is with the third vision, in chapter 13. There Ezra reports that

> after seven days I had a dream in the night. I saw a wind rising from the sea that stirred up all its waves. As I kept looking, that wind brought up out of the depths of the sea something resembling a man and that man was flying with the clouds of heaven ...

The image of the man flying with the clouds of heaven is a clear allusion to Daniel 7. There is also an explicit reference to Daniel 7 in the preceding chapter, *4 Ezra* 12, where the interpreting angel tells Ezra explicitly: "The eagle you observed coming up out of the sea is the fourth kingdom that appeared in a vision to Daniel your brother. But it was not interpreted to him in the same way that I now interpret it to you" (*4 Ezra* 12:11). Moreover, the interpretation in chapter 13 provides a clear allusion to Daniel 2, when it says that the mountain on which the man takes his stand was "carved out without hands." This detail was not mentioned in the vision.

The allusions to Daniel in *4 Ezra* 13 are woven together with echoes of other sources. Anyone who hears the voice of the man from the sea melts like wax before a fire. (Compare the effect of the theophany in Micah 1:4, for the motif of melting

---

[55] *Ibid.*, 56: "Die Zeile klingt deutlich an Ps 2,2 an." Cf. also Schreiber, *Gesalbter und König*, 331.

[56] See further Yarbro Collins and Collins, *Messiah, Son of God*, chapter 3.

[57] For introductory matters see M. E. Stone, *Fourth Ezra: A Commentary on the Book of Fourth Ezra* (Hermeneia; Minneapolis: Fortress, 1990) 1–35; Collins, *The Apocalyptic Imagination*, 195–210.

[58] M. E. Stone, "The Question of the Messiah in *4 Ezra*," in J. Neusner, W. S. Green and E. Frerichs, eds., *Judaisms and Their Messiahs* (Cambridge: Cambridge University Press, 1987) 209–24.

like wax.) Most importantly, a great host comes to make war on the man. He carves out a mountain for himself and takes his stand upon it. Then he destroys the onrushing multitude with the breath of his lips. The onslaught of the multitude recalls Psalm 2. The mountain is Zion, the holy mountain (Ps 2:6). The breath of his lips is the weapon of the messianic king in Isa 11:4. Taken together, these allusions suggest that the man from the sea has taken on the role traditionally ascribed to the messianic king.

This impression is strengthened in the interpretation that follows, where the man is identified, in the Latin and Syriac versions, as "my son" (13:32, 37).[59] The messiah is also called "my son" in *4 Ezra* 7:28.[60] Michael Stone has argued that the Greek original in these passages read παῖς rather than υἱός because of variations in some of the versions, and suggested that the Hebrew original was 'servant' rather than 'son.'[61] But even if the Greek did read παῖς, the word can also mean child or son – compare Wis 2: 13, 16, where the righteous man claims to be παῖς of God and boasts that God is his father. In *4 Ezra* 13, in any case, the context, the assault of the nations against Mt. Zion, strongly suggests an allusion to Psalm 2, so the meaning is "son" rather than "servant."[62] The reference to "my son the messiah" in *4 Ezra* 7:28 is also most easily understood against the background of Psalm 2, although such a reference could also be derived from 2 Samuel 7.

Even though the messiah in *4 Ezra* appears to be pre-existent, he is nonetheless identified as a descendent of David, in *4 Ezra* 12:32: "this is the messiah whom the Most High has kept until the end of days, who will arise from the posterity of David." He is human, although he is endowed with supernatural powers. In chapter 7:29, he is said to die after a reign of 400 years. The apocalypse does not explain why a descendent of David should arise from the sea on clouds. In the judgment of Michael Stone, his Davidic ancestry is "a traditional element and not at all central to the concepts of the book."[63] What is important is that he takes over the functions traditionally associated with the Davidic messiah.

Together with *Pss Sol* 17 and the *Similitudes of Enoch*, *4 Ezra* constitutes a significant body of evidence for the messianic interpretation of Psalm 2 in Jewish texts around the turn of the era. There is some variation in the ways that the psalm is used. *Pss Sol* 17 and *4 Ezra* explicitly associate the messiah with the line of David. The *Similitudes* does not. In *Pss Solomon* and *4 Ezra* he is human, however exalted. In the *Similitudes* he has a human form, but is higher than the angels. Only *4 Ezra* emphasizes his divine sonship. Both *4 Ezra* and the *Similitudes*, however, see him

---

[59] See further Collins, *The Scepter and the Star*, 184–5.

[60] Schreiber, *Gesalbter und König*, 349, raises the possibility of Christian tampering with the text, but there is little other evidence for this in *4 Ezra*.

[61] Stone, *Fourth Ezra*, 207–13 ("Excursus on the Redeemer Figure").

[62] Cf. M. Knibb and R. J. Coggins, *The First and Second Books of Esdras* (Cambridge Bible Commentary; Cambridge: Cambridge University, 1979) on 7:28.

[63] M. E. Stone, *Features of the Eschatology of Fourth Ezra* (Atlanta: Scholars Press, 1989) 131–32; compare Schreiber, *Gesalbter und König*, 351.

as a pre-existent figure, who will be revealed in the eschatological age. They testify to a tendency in the late Second Temple period to regard the messiah as a supernatural, heavenly figure, although this understanding of the messiah was by no means uniform or standard.

The Scrolls

It remains true, as Steudel has noted, that Psalm 2 is not among the texts commonly cited in the messianic passages in the Dead Sea Scrolls.[64] The most common, by far, are Balaam's Oracle and Isaiah 11, while the common messianic title צמח דויד, may allude either to Jeremiah or to Zechariah.[65] Other passages (Genesis 49 in 4Q252, Isaiah 9 in 1QH[a] 11) are cited rarely. Even 2 Samuel 7 is only adduced as a messianic reference in the *Florilegium*. We should not conclude that because a passage is not commonly cited it was not understood messianically at all. It is remarkable, however, that the Scrolls seldom if ever appeal to the royal psalms in this regard.

There are, however, some notable if controversial exceptions.[66] The "Rule of the Congregation" specifies the order of assembly for the occasion "when God begets the messiah with them" (1QSa 2:11–12). The reading יוליד (begets) is unclear in the manuscript, and has been endlessly disputed.[67] The scholars who examined the manuscript in the 1950's agreed that the manuscript reads יוליד although Milik and Cross favored emending it to יוליך (causes to come).[68] Geza Vermes, who has vacillated on the reading, claims that "it seems to be confirmed by computer enhancement."[69] The statement that God begets the messiah "with them" is odd, however, and gives some pause. If the reading is correct, it is simply picking up and endorsing the language of the Psalms. Indeed, Jan Willem van Henten states unequivocally: "This passage alludes to Psalm 2."[70]

[64] Steudel, "Psalm 2," 192.
[65] Collins, *The Scepter and the Star*, 62–71.
[66] These are noted by Steudel, "Psalm 2," 191, but she does not take them seriously.
[67] Maiberger, "Das Verständnis," 101–5.
[68] P. W. Skehan, "Two Books on Qumran Studies," *CBQ* 21 (1959) 74, cites "the testimony of half a dozen witnesses, including Allegro, Cross, Strugnell, and the writer [Skehan], as of the summer of 1955," that the text reads יוליד. F. M. Cross, *The Ancient Library of Qumran* (3rd ed.; Sheffield: Sheffield Academic Press, 1995) 76, n. 3. The reading יועד "will be assembled," originally proposed by Theodore Gaster and Jacob Licht, and accepted by L. H. Schiffman, *The Eschatological Community of the Dead Sea Scrolls* (SBLMS 38; Atlanta: Scholars Press, 1989) 54, is emphatically rejected by Cross on palaeographic grounds. Emile Puech, "Préséance sacerdotale et messie-roi dans la Règle de la Congrégation (1QSa ii 11–22)," *RevQ* 16 (1993–1995) 361, proposes to read יתגלה "will be revealed."
[69] G. Vermes, *The Complete Dead Sea Scrolls in English* (revised ed.; London: Penguin, 2004) 161.
[70] J. W. van Henten, "The Hasmonean Period," in M. Bockmuehl and J. C. Paget, eds., *Redemption and Resistance.The Messianic Hopes of Jews and Christians in Antiquity* (New York/London: T. & T. Clark, 2007) 22.

An even more controversial case is provided by 4Q246, the so-called "Aramaic Apocalypse" or "Son of God" text, which refers to a figure who will be called "Son of God" and "Son of the Most High." I have argued at length elsewhere for the messianic interpretation of this text, and will not repeat the arguments here.[71] Steudel subscribes to the view originally proposed by Milik, that the figure who is called "Son of God" is a negative figure, and argues that the future hope in this text rests collectively with the people of God.[72] I find this interpretation highly unlikely. By far the closest parallel to the titles in question is explicitly messianic. In Luke 1:32–33 the angel Gabriel tells Mary that her child "will be great, and will be called the Son of the Most High, and the Lord God will give to him the throne of his ancestor David. He will reign over the house of Jacob forever, and of his kingdom there will be no end." In 1:35 he adds: "he will be called the Son of God." The Greek titles "Son of the Most High" and "Son of God" correspond exactly to the Aramaic fragment from Qumran. Both texts refer to an everlasting kingdom. The fact that these parallels are found in the New Testament does not lessen their relevance to the cultural context of the Qumran text. No significance can be attached to the fact that he is said to be *called* rather than to *be* the son of God. In the Hellenistic ruler cults, divine titles were honors, conferred in appreciation for acts of beneficence.[73] If the author wished to imply that the titles were not appropriate, we should expect that the one so called would be subject to judgment, just as Daniel leaves no doubt that the *hybris* of Antiochus Epiphanes leads to his downfall. The fact that the people of God arises, or is raised up, in the latter part of the text in no way excludes a role for the messianic king, any more than the collective interpretation of משיחו excludes a role for the Branch of David in 4Q174, or the exaltation of Israel excludes a role for Michael in 1QM 17:7, which reads: "to exalt the sway of Michael above all the gods, and the dominion of Israel over all flesh." In part Steudel is misled by a mistaken collective interpretation of Daniel 7, where the "one like a son of man" is not a collective symbol for Israel, but its heavenly leader, as is clear from the parallel with chapter 12.[74] The restoration typically involves a role for a leader who is God's agent in the end-time.

If then it is the messianic king who is called "son of God" in 4Q246, the most obvious basis for that title is found in Psalm 2. The Aramaic text does not cite the psalm directly, but the psalm may well inform not only the titles but the entire depiction of the turmoil of the nations.

---

[71] Collins, *The Scepter and the Star*, 154–72; Yarbro Collins and Collins, *Messiah, Son of God*, 65–74. See also Johannes Zimmermann, *Messianische Texte aus Qumran*, 128–69.

[72] Annette Steudel, "The Eternal Reign of the People of God – Collective Expectations in Qumranic Texts," *RevQ* 17 (1996) 507–25.

[73] See Yarbro Collins and Collins, *Messiah, Son of God*, 48–54.

[74] John J. Collins, *Daniel. A Commentary on the Book of Daniel* (Hermeneia; Minneapolis: Fortress, 1993) 304–10.

Florentino García Martínez has argued that the "son of God" in 4Q246 is "a heavenly being similar to Melchizedek of 11QMelch or the Son of Man of Dan 7... He is thus a messiah, an almost divinized messiah, similar to Melchizedek and the heavenly Son of Man."[75] I do not think the title "son of God" necessarily implies a heavenly being. He could be imagined along the lines of the messiah in the *Psalms of Solomon* 17. But García Martínez is certainly right that the messiah was sometimes viewed as a heavenly figure. We have seen that Psalm 2 was applied to a heavenly messiah in the *Similitudes of Enoch* and *4 Ezra*. The widely recognized echoes of Daniel in 4Q246 lend some support to the possibility that the messiah in this text is also a heavenly figure. But in any case I would argue that this text too is a witness to the widespread messianic interpretation of Psalm 2.

The *Florilegium* again

None of this necessarily determines the way Psalm 2 is interpreted in 4Q174. If the word משיחו is interpreted as a collective reference to the elect of Israel, then the interpretation offered in the psalm is unusual in any case. But despite the best efforts of Joseph Fitzmyer, messianic expectation cannot be reduced to the use and interpretation of the word משיח.[76] Despite the collective interpretation of משיחו, the *Florilegium* still has an explicit role for the Branch of David in the end of days, as Steudel also recognizes. The author did not find it necessary to exploit every possible exegetical opportunity to make this point. In view of the common messianic interpretation of Psalm 2, and the fact that it explicitly addresses the king as son of God, I, like George Brooke, find it difficult to believe that the juxtaposition of 2 Samuel 7 and Psalms 1–2 is coincidental. To be sure, messianic expectation is not the primary focus of the *Florilegium*, and it is not a catena of messianic texts, but the fact that both were associated with the kingship of God and his messiah may still explain why these two texts are juxtaposed in this midrash on the end of days.[77]

---

[75] Florentino García Martínez, "Two Messianic Figures in the Qumran Texts," in idem, *Qumranica Minora II. Thematic Studies on the Dead Sea Scrolls* (STDJ 64; Leiden: Brill, 2007) 13–32 (24).

[76] Joseph A. Fitzmyer, *The One Who Is to Come* (Grand Rapids: Eerdmans, 2007).

[77] Brooke, *Exegesis at Qumran*, 169–74, has made the interesting suggestion that the texts cited in the *Florilegium* were associated liturgically, perhaps at the Feast of Tabernacles.

CHAPTER SEVEN

The Book of Daniel and the Dead Sea Scrolls

Fragments of the Book of Daniel are found in eight manuscripts at Qumran.[1] These fragments contain verses from the first eleven chapters of Daniel. (Daniel 12 is attested in 4Q174 *Florilegium*.)[2] The Qumran fragments attest the same combination of Hebrew and Aramaic as the MT. The shift from Hebrew to Aramaic is attested in 4QDan^a. The shift from Aramaic to Hebrew is attested in 4QDan^a and 4QDan^b. The Hebrew prayer in Daniel 9 is attested in 4QDan^e, but no equivalents of the prayers found in the Greek additions to Daniel are attested.[3] Two of the manuscripts, 4QDan^c (4Q114) and 4QDan^e (4Q116) are dated to the late second or early first century BCE, less than a century after the composition of the book.[4]

The relatively high number of manuscripts,[5] distributed in three caves, suggests that Daniel had some importance for the sect known to us from the scrolls. This impression is confirmed by a small but significant number of allusions and explicit citations in sectarian texts. There are also several other compositions found in the Scrolls that are related to Daniel in various ways, but are not clearly sectarian.[6]

Explicit citations

Explicit citations of Daniel are found in 4Q174 (*Florilegium*) and *11QMelchizedek*.

The citation in the *Florilegium* has a slight variant of Dan 12:10: " ... a]s it is written in the book of Daniel the prophet: '[For the wicked] to act wicked[ly ...]' and the righteous 'shall pu[rify themselves, and make themselves w]hite, and be refined.'" It is introduced to illustrate the "time of trial," which the author evidently

---

[1] E. C. Ulrich, "The Text of Daniel in the Dead Sea Scrolls," in J. J. Collins and P. W. Flint, eds., *The Book of Daniel. Composition and Reception* (VTSup 83.2; Leiden: Brill, 2001) 573–85.
[2] *Ibid.*, 575.
[3] See also J. J. Collins, *Daniel* (Hermeneia; Minneapolis: Fortress, 1993) 2–3.
[4] Ulrich, "The Text of Daniel," 574.
[5] Daniel is outnumbered by only eight other compositions: Psalms, Deuteronomy, Isaiah, Genesis, Exodus, *Jubilees, 1 Enoch* and Leviticus. See P. W. Flint, "The Daniel Tradition at Qumran," in Collins and Flint, eds., *The Book of Daniel*, 328.
[6] Flint, "The Daniel Tradition," 332; L. T. Stuckenbruck, "The Formation and Re-Formation of Daniel in the Dead Sea Scrolls," in J. H. Charlesworth, ed., *The Bible and the Dead Sea Scrolls. The Princeton Symposium on the Dead Sea Scrolls* (Waco, TX: Baylor University Press, 2006) 101–30.

believed was at hand, but the context is fragmentary. Perhaps the most significant point about this citation is the reference to "Daniel the prophet." Presumably the author would have classified the book of Daniel among "the prophets" which are often juxtaposed with the Torah of Moses as authoritative sources.[7] At the very least, the citation serves to question the idea that the collection of "the prophets" had been closed before the book of Daniel was composed, and lends credence to the view that Daniel was originally among the prophets (as it is in the Greek Bible) and only assigned to the Writings by the rabbis.[8]

The citation in *11QMelchizedek* is more intriguing. It is introduced as a secondary quotation to clarify the "messenger" (מבשר) who is mentioned in Isa 52:7: "And the messenger i[s] the anointed of the spir[it] as Dan[iel] said [...]" (*11QMelch* col. 2:18). The (partial) restoration of the name of Daniel is not in doubt, but it is unfortunate that the actual citation is not preserved. There are two verses in Daniel that mention a משיח: Dan 9:25 refers to the coming of "an anointed prince" (משיח נגיד), who is usually identified with Joshua, the post-exilic High Priest, in the context of Daniel.[9] The following verse refers to another "anointed one," sixty-two "weeks" (of years) later, who would be "cut off." This is usually taken as a reference to the High Priest Onias III who was murdered during the so-called "Hellenistic Reform" in Jerusalem in the second century BCE.[10] Most commentators restore Dan 9:25 in *11QMelchizedek*.[11] An exception is Michael Wise, who opts for Dan 9:26.[12] In this, he accepts the arguments put forward by Michael Douglas in an unpublished paper.[13] While either Danielic verse would fit the lacuna reasonably well, the context in *11QMelchizedek* requires that the messiah in question appears in the tenth jubilee, and so the later "messiah" mentioned in Daniel provides the more plausible reference.[14]

Wise takes the "messenger" to be the Teacher, and infers that his followers had turned to Daniel to explain the death of their leader: "For they found predicted in Daniel 9:24–27 the death of an Anointed One, a messiah... According to Daniel, the

---

[7] See J. Barton, "The Law and the Prophets" = chapter 2 in idem, *Oracles of God* (rev. ed.; Oxford: Oxford University Press, 1997).

[8] K. Koch, "Is Daniel Also among the Prophets?" *Interpretation* 39 (1985) 117–30.

[9] Collins, *Daniel*, 355. The title could refer either to a priest or to a king. J. A. Fitzmyer, *The One Who Is to Come* (Grand Rapids: Eerdmans, 2007) 62–4, regards this passage as referring to "some sort of Messiah in a narrow sense," although he recognizes the historical reference.

[10] Collins, *Daniel*, 356. Compare 2 Macc 4:33–38.

[11] P. J. Kobelski, *Melchizedek and Melchiresha*ʿ (CBQMS 10; Washington, D.C.: Catholic Biblical Association, 1981) 6, 9; É. Puech, *La Croyance des Esséniens en la Vie Future: Immortalité, Resurrection, Vie Éternelle* (Paris: Gabalda, 1993) 523.

[12] M. Wise, M. Abegg, Jr., and E. Cook, *The Dead Sea Scrolls. A New Translation* (San Francisco: HarperSanFrancisco, 1996) 457.

[13] M. Douglas, "*11QMelchizedek* and a Dying Eschatological Figure," paper presented at the Society of Biblical Literature Meeting in Washington, DC, 1993). See M. Wise, *The First Messiah. Investigating the Savior before Christ* (San Francisco: HarperSanFrancisco. 1999) 325–7 (note 19).

[14] É. Puech, "Notes sur le manuscript de XIQ Melkîsédeq," *RevQ* 12 (1985–87) 509, acknowledges that the restoration of Dan 9:25 is not certain in view of the availability of Dan 9:26.

messiah was to be 'cut off.'"[15] The death of the Teacher, then, could be taken as confirmation that the "seventy weeks of years" of which Daniel had prophesied had nearly run their course. The idea that the end should be expected forty years after the death of the Teacher is explicit in CD 20:14–15. Long ago, F. F. Bruce suggested that the "seventy weeks of years" were an important factor in Essene eschatological calculations. The 390 years of CD 1:5–6 (admittedly based on the 390 days of Ezek 4:5) can be reconciled with the 490 years of the "seventy weeks," by taking the 20 years of groping before the arrival of the Teacher (CD 1:10), allowing 40 years for his career, and then a period of 40 years from his death to the eschaton.[16]

It must be noted, however, that the extant fragments of *11QMelchizedek* say nothing of the death of the messianic messenger, and certainly do not use that event as a marker in the chronology of the eschaton. Even if the passage cited from Daniel was 9:26, we do not know how it was interpreted. Wise's theory is intriguing, but it depends entirely on how one fills in the lacuna, and this does not provide a sound basis for further speculation.

It is clear, however, that the book of Daniel, or at least Daniel 7–12, was read as prophecy in *11QMelchizedek*, as it was in *4QFlorilegium*. In both cases, Daniel was believed to predict the events of the eschatological upheaval.

Allusions to Daniel in sectarian literature

Perhaps the clearest indication of the importance of Daniel for the *yahad* is the way key sectarian terminology is drawn from the book. According to Dan 11:33, the wise among the people (משכילי עם) would instruct the common people (רבים). After the resurrection the (משכילים) would shine like the stars. In the *Community Rule* from Qumran, the official who is to "instruct all the sons of light and teach them the nature of all the children of men" is called a *maskil*.[17] In the Scroll of Blessings (1QSb), this individual is charged with blessing those who fear God, the sons of Zadok, the priests, and the "prince of the congregation." The rank and file of the community are called the *rabbim*.[18] While the word *maskil* for the Instructor could easily be derived

---

[15] Wise, *The First Messiah*, 232.

[16] F. F. Bruce, "The Book of Daniel and the Qumran Community," in E. Earle Ellis and M. Wilcox, eds., *Neotestamentica et Semitica: Studies in Honour of Matthew Black* (Edinburgh: Clark, 1969) 232; A. Mertens, *Das Buch Daniel im Lichte der Texte vom Toten Meer* (Würzburg: Echter, 1971) 86. See further J. J. Collins, *Apocalypticism in the Dead Sea Scrolls* (London: Routledge, 1997) 52–70.

[17] C. A. Newsom, "The Sage in the Literature of Qumran: The Function of the Maskil," in J. G. Gammie and L. G. Perdue, eds., *The Sage in Israel and the Ancient Near East* (Winona Lake: Eisenbrauns, 1990) 373–82; A. Lange, "Sages and Scribes in Qumran Literature," in L. G. Perdue, ed., *Scribes, Sages and Seers: The Sage in the Eastern Mediterranean World* (FRLANT 219; Göttingen; Vandenhoeck & Ruprecht, 2008) 271–93.

[18] See Mertens, *Das Buch Daniel*, 63–4; Collins, *Daniel*, 73.

from other sources, including the Psalms, the linkage with the *rabbim* makes it likely that the terms are drawn from Daniel. The same passage in Daniel complains that many will join the *maskilim* in deceit (בחלקלקות). The sectarian scrolls polemicize against people whom they call דורשי החלקות "seekers after smooth things."[19] The seekers after smooth things are usually identified with the Pharisees, and חלקות is taken as a play on *halakot*, the legal rulings of the Pharisees, but an allusion to Daniel also seems probable.

Further significant allusions to Daniel are found in the *War Scroll*.[20] The opening column of the *Scroll* has various terminological echoes of Daniel 11–12. These include "violators of the covenant" in 1QM 1:2, Kittim *passim*, one who will "go forth in great wrath ... to destroy" (1QM 1:4), no helper for Assyria (1QM 1:6, cf. Dan 11:42, 45). The time of the battle is a time of distress (1QM 1:11–12; Dan 12:1). The archangel Michael, prince of Israel, who arises in victory in Dan 12:1, is also exalted in 1QM 17:7. The *War Scroll* takes these terms and applies them in a new context. For example, the Kittim in Daniel are clearly the Romans, and they have only an incidental role in the drama of the end-time. In the *War Scroll*, they are the primary enemy, and it is arguable that "the Kittim of Assyria" are the Seleucids.[21] David Flusser, followed now by Brian Schultz, has argued that the dependence on Daniel is not only terminological: "the eschatological vision of the *War Scroll* is predicated on an actualizing interpretation of Daniel's unfulfilled prophecy."[22] The wicked king must yet be destroyed. Schultz argues that while the new scenario offered by the *War Scroll* is less dependent than Daniel on precise historical events, yet it reflects the same socio-political dynamics: "there is still conflict between Egypt in the south and Syria in the north; within Judea, those who violate the covenant do so by their alliance with Syria."[23] He argues that this supports an early (Seleucid period) date at least for this section of the *War Scroll*:

From the perspective of realism, the sooner it is composed after the people have realized that that portion of Daniel's prophecy did not come to fruition, the easier it is to reflect the same socio-political environment and the more plausible the scenario will seem to its readers.[24]

---

[19] See especially 4Qpesher Nahum. A. I. Baumgarten, "Seekers after Smooth Things," *EDSS* 857–9.

[20] Mertens, *Das Buch Daniel*, 79–83; Collins, *Daniel*, 73–74; D. Flusser, "Apocalyptic Elements in the *War Scroll*," in idem, *Judaism of the Second Temple Period. Vol. 1. Qumran and Apocalypticism* (Grand Rapids: Eerdmans, 2007) 140–58; B. Schultz, *Conquering the World. The War Scroll (1QM) Reconsidered* (STDJ 76; Leiden: Brill, 2009) 91–102.

[21] Flusser, "Apocalyptic Elements," 149; Schultz, *Conquering the World*, 393; D. J. Harrington, "Holy War Texts among the Qumran Scrolls," in P. W. Flint, E. Tov and J. C. VanderKam, eds., *Studies in the Hebrew Bible, Qumran, and the Septuagint presented to Eugene Ulrich* (VTSup 101; Leiden: Brill, 2006) 178. The "Kittim in Egypt" would then refer to a Seleucid invasion of Egypt.

[22] Flusser, "Apocalyptic Elements," 156. Compare Schultz, *Conquering the World*, 93–99.

[23] Schultz, *Conquering the World*, 101.

[24] *Ibid.*, 102.

The Seleucid context in itself does not require a date before the first century BCE.[25] Schultz argues that the apparent independence of Edom, Moab, Ammon, and Philistia, argues for a date before the time of Alexander Jannaeus.[26] In any case, the dependence of the opening column of the *War Scroll* on Daniel is clear.

The influence of the Book of Daniel on the Dead Sea Scrolls is considerably more extensive than what we have considered here. Daniel's interpretation of dreams may be a fore-runner of *pesher*-style exegesis. The concept of mystery (*raz*) is important in both corpora, as is the periodization of history. The eventual exaltation of the *maskilim* to shine like the stars may be a model for the sectarian idea of fellowship with the angels, which is realized, however, in this life.[27] Some of these features, however, may be attributed more broadly to the apocalyptic worldview, which was shared with the early *Enoch* writings and some other compositions, rather than specifically to influence of the Book of Daniel.

Texts related to Daniel

Apart from the question of influence of Daniel on the sectarian scrolls, there are five texts among the Scrolls that are not distinctively sectarian but that arguably have a genetic relationship to Daniel in some way. The *Prayer of Nabonidus* (4Q242) is arguably a source on which the biblical author drew; *Pseudo-Daniel*$^{a-b}$ (4Q243–4), *Pseudo-Daniel*^{c} (4Q245), the so-called *"Aramaic Apocalypse"* or *"Son of God"* text (4Q246) and the *"four Kingdoms text"* (4Q552–553) are arguably influenced by Daniel.[28] Whether in fact there is direct influence in any of these cases, however, is still debatable. We shall discuss the texts in the order in which they were made known to the public.

---

[25] Collins, *Apocalypticism in the Dead Sea Scrolls*, 106–7.

[26] Schultz, *Conquering the World*, 101–2.

[27] Collins, *Apocalypticism in the Dead Sea Scrolls*, 110–29; Stuckenbruck, "The Formation and Re-Formation of Daniel," 123–9.

[28] See my article "New Light on the Book of Daniel from the Dead Sea Scrolls," in F. García Martínez and E. Noort, eds., *Perspectives in the Study of the Old Testament and Early Judaism* (VTSup 73; Leiden: Brill, 1998) 180–96. The earlier article also discussed *4Q Historical Text* (4Q248) which has been claimed to have influenced Dan 12:7 by M. Broshi and E. Eshel, "The Greek King Is Antiochus IV (4QHistorical Text – 4Q248)," *JJS* 48 (1997) 120–9. See now their edition in P. Alexander et al., *Qumran Cave 4. XXVI. Miscellanea, Part 1* (DJD 36; Oxford: Clarendon, 2000) 192–200. The point of contact with Daniel rests on a doubtful reading. But even if the Broshi-Eshel reading were correct, the relation between this text and Daniel would still be incidental. 4Q248 is not in any sense a "Danielic" text. See also P. W. Flint, "The Daniel Tradition at Qumran," in Collins and Flint, eds., *The Book of Daniel*, 329–67; Stuckenbruck, "The Formation and Re-Formation of Daniel," 104–20.

The *Prayer of Nabonidus* (4QPrNab)

The *Prayer of Nabonidus* was published by J. T. Milik in 1956.[29] An additional fragment was published by Rudolf Meyer in his 1962 monograph,[30] but no new fragments have come to light in recent years. The reconstruction of the text, however, remains in dispute, in part because there is disagreement as to how large a lacuna should be allowed between fragments that contain portions of the same lines.[31] The reconstruction is also influenced by the relationship that one posits between this text and the Book of Daniel. My own edition was published in DJD XXII in 1996.[32] Émile Puech also published a study of the text in 1996.[33]

The major cruces of interpretation are presented by lines 3 and 4 of column 1. The lacuna in line 3 is preceded by the word מן and followed by the word שוי. Milik took the verb שוי in the sense of "put, placed," and rendered "loin des hommes je fus relégué."[34] Meyer read "I was far from my throne."[35] These translations are influenced by Dan 4:32, "and driven out from among men." The semantic range of שוי however, can scarcely extend to "banish" or "drive out."

Several scholars have taken שוי as "to be equal or like." Frank Cross's placement assumes a very short lacuna and so he restores מן [די] שוי א[נ]ה לחיוא which he translates as "and from that (time) I was like unto a beast."[36] Cross's restoration is inspired by Dan 5:21: ולבבה עם חיותא שוי.

If Cross's reconstruction were correct, we would have a simple metaphorical comparison with a beast (cf. Ps. 73:21: "I was stupid and ignorant; I was like a brute beast toward you") and this might then have provided the jumping off point for the elaborate legend of transformation that we find in Daniel 4. It must be emphasized, however, that there is no mention of a beast in the extant fragments and the restoration is highly questionable.

There is, moreover, an orthographic problem with the word שוי which was pointed out to me by Douglas Gropp. Most scholars have read the word as a passive participle, followed by the first person pronoun: I was placed, or I was made like. The

---

[29] J. T. Milik, "'Prière de Nabonide' et autres écrits d'un cycle de Daniel," *RB* 63 (1956) 407–15.

[30] R. Meyer, *Das Gebet des Nabonid. Eine in den Qumran-Handschriften wiederentdeckte Weisheitserzählung* (Berlin: Akademie Verlag, 1962) 16.

[31] F. M. Cross, "Fragments of the *Prayer of Nabonidus*," *IEJ* 34 (1984) 260–4, reconstructs the text with smaller lacunae than Milik had proposed.

[32] J. J. Collins, "242. 4Q*Prayer of Nabonidus* ar," in G. Brooke et al., *Qumran Cave IV. XVII* (DJD 22; Oxford: Clarendon, 1996) 83–93.

[33] É. Puech, "La prière de Nabonide (4Q242)," in K. J. Cathcart and M. Maher, eds., *Targumic and Cognate Studies: Essays in Honour of Martin McNamara* (JSOTSup 230; Sheffield: Sheffield Academic Press, 1996) 208–28.

[34] Cf. F. García Martínez, "The *Prayer of Nabonidus*: A New Synthesis," in idem, *Qumran and Apocalyptic* (Leiden: Brill, 1992) 116–36: "banished far from men" (p. 120). Similarly, Meyer, *Das Gebet*, 23.

[35] Meyer, *Das Gebet*, 23.

[36] So also É. Puech, "La prière de Nabonide (4Q242)."

passive participle, however, is spelled with an *aleph* or *he* rather than with a *yod*. I do not think an anomalous spelling with a *yod* can be completely ruled out, but we should assume normal spelling unless we have compelling evidence to the contrary. The word שוי then should be read as a third person singular, most probably a pael, active verb. Pierre Grelot read the word in this way: "and after this God set his face on me" (i.e. paid attention to me; the idiom is attested in the Targumim).[37] Grelot assumed the longer lacuna proposed by Milik. If Cross's placement is correct we must read simply "but from the time that God set his face on me," or "since God set his face on me" (taking מן די in a causal sense, as in line 8). Grelot goes on to restore "and he healed me." This reading is at least free of grammatical problems and also provides a plausible transition to the remission of sin in the following line.

The second major crux in this passage concerns the manner in which sin is remitted in line 4. Milik took גזר as the object of שבק and supplied a verb in the lacuna to govern "my sins" ("After I had confessed my sins and my faults, God granted me a diviner"). This interpretation has been widely rejected. The verb שבק is too often associated with sin, in the sense of "remit," for the juxtaposition here to be coincidental. Dupont-Sommer argued that the word order most naturally leads to the assumption that גזר is the subject of the verb שבק, taking לה as a *dativus ethicus* ("he remitted for himself my sin," treating the pronoun, in effect, as redundant).[38] Both Cross and Grelot render "and, as for my sin, he forgave it," taking God as subject. If we follow Grelot in line 3, and restore "God set his face on me," then God must also be the subject of שבק. God is the most usual remitter of sin. As the scribes ask in the Gospels (Mark 2:7, Luke 5:21), "Who can forgive sins but God alone?" There is no reason in principle why the power to remit sin should not be exercised by a human agent.[39] But if God is restored as the subject of שוי in line 3, he must also be the subject in line 4.

On the reconstruction proposed here, the king is healed by a gratuitous act of divine favor, even though acknowledgement is subsequently demanded. We are told in line 7 that the king had been praying to false gods for seven years, without result. Most other reconstructions presuppose that the king underwent an unexplained conversion before the introduction of the Jewish גזר in 1.4. But if these restorations were correct the king would already know the nature of his sin and the identity of the true God. The Jewish גזר would then have little purpose. Line 7 makes clear that the king prayed at first to the gods represented by idols, but this prayer was of no avail. Then, when he was suddenly healed, the Jewish diviner came forward and

---

[37] P. Grelot, "La Prière de Nabonide (4Q Or Nab). Nouvelle Essai de Restauration," *RevQ* 9 (1978) 483–95.

[38] A. Dupont-Sommer, "Exorcismes et guérisons dans les écrits de Qoumrân," in J. A. Emerton, ed., *Oxford Congress Volume* (VTSup 7; Leiden: Brill, 1960) 258–9.

[39] Dupont-Sommer, *ibid.*, 260, adduces the parallel of CD 13:10 which says that the Guardian "shall loosen all the fetters."

identified the Most High God as the one that had acted, and told the king to give praise to Him.

Long before the discovery of the *Prayer of Nabonidus* at Qumran, scholars had surmised that the exile of Nabonidus at Teima underlay the legend of Nebuchadnezzar's madness in Daniel 4.[40] To a great degree, the *Prayer* supplies the missing link between the Babylonian traditions and the biblical book. It makes explicit mention of Nabonidus and Teima. The *Prayer* agrees with Daniel 4, against the Babylonian accounts of the sojourn, in putting the length of the sojourn at seven years rather than ten. It also agrees with the biblical book in giving a Jewish exile a pivotal role in the king's recovery. There can be little doubt that the *Prayer* occupies an intermediate place in the tradition between the Babylonian accounts of an historical incident and the formation of the biblical legend. This is not to say that the author of Daniel 4 necessarily had a copy of the Prayer before him or even that the *Prayer* as we have it is older than Daniel 4. The point is that the *Prayer* preserves some features of an older stage of the tradition that are not preserved in the biblical story.

Some other possible points of analogy remain controversial. Some scholars, most notably Cross, reconstruct a reference to a beast in line 3. Another disputed analogy with Daniel lies in the putative reference to a dream in frg. 4. The word in question (אחלמת) should be understood as a reference to the king's recovery rather than to a dream. Meyer's attempt to reconstruct a dream about a cosmic tree is without foundation in the Qumran fragments.[41] Milik's restoration of the name Daniel in fragment 4, line 4 ("how you are like Daniel"), is also gratuitous.[42]

The Pseudo-Daniel texts

In his 1956 article in *Revue Biblique*, Milik also published fragments of three manuscripts that mention the name of Daniel: Ps. Daniel a, b, and c. The first two of these overlap and are clearly manuscripts of the same text. Milik admitted that *Ps. Daniel*[c] was not necessarily part of the same text, but proposed that it was. In this case an important new fragment has come to light in the meantime. This is a list of priests, from Qahat down to the Hellenistic period, followed by a list of kings beginning with David and Solomon.[43] It is difficult to see how this list could be fitted into

---

[40] See Collins, *Daniel*, 217. On the Babylonian sources relevant to Daniel 4 see K. Koch, "Gottes Herrschaft über das Reich des Menschen. Daniel 4 im Licht neuer Funde," in A. S. van der Woude, *The Book of Daniel in the Light of New Findings* (BETL 106; Leuven: Leuven University Press, 1993) 77–119.

[41] Meyer, *Das Gebet*, 42–51.

[42] Milik, "Prière," 410.

[43] See J. J. Collins and P. W. Flint, "243–245. 4Qpseudo-Daniel[a-c]," in Brooke et al., DJD 22, 95–164. See also J. J. Collins, "Pseudo-Daniel Revisited," *RevQ* 17 (1996) 111–35 and P. W. Flint, "4Qpseudo-Daniel ar[c] (4Q245) and the Restoration of the Priesthood," *ibid.*, 137–50.

the chronological framework of *Ps. Daniel*ᵃ⁻ᵇ. It now seems likely that *Ps. Daniel*ᶜ is part of a distinct text.

In addition to the name of Daniel, Milik found significant points of contact between *Ps. Daniel*ᵃ⁻ᵇ and the biblical book in an allusion to "seventy years" and a schema of four kingdoms.⁴⁴ The fragment in question (4Q243.16) reads:

] oppressed (?) for [seven]ty years [
with] his great [ha]nd and he will save th[em
]powerful [ ] and the kingdoms of [the] peoples
]It is the fi[rst]?/h[oly]? Kingdom [

The word seventy is not actually preserved; only the ending ין is clearly legible. The preceding letter is probably *ayin*. "Seventy" (שבעין) is the most likely restoration. The seventy years, however, does not necessarily refer to the Babylonian exile as it did in Daniel 9. In 4Q390, the Pseudo-Moses text, somebody is delivered into the hands of the sons of Aaron for seventy years, and again people quarrel among themselves for seventy years, before God intervenes to punish them. A reference to seventy years, then, can have more than one possible reference, and is not necessarily an allusion to Daniel 9.

The presence of a four kingdom schema in Ps. Daniel depends on the disputed reading of the last line of the fragment cited above, which reads היא מלכותא קד[. Milik restored קדמיתא, first. But this suggestion is problematic. The fragment has already said that God "will save them." It is unlikely that an act of salvation would be followed immediately by a sequence of Gentile kingdoms. If the salvation refers to deliverance from the Babylonian exile, then it would be extraordinary to have the sequence of four kingdoms inaugurated after the Exile. In the *DJD* edition, the word is restored as קדישתא, the holy kingdom, and the passage is related to the eschatological age.

Milik also found a parallel to the Book of Daniel in *Ps. Dan*ᶜ in a passage that he read as a reference to resurrection. The fragment reads:

...] these in blindness, and error
... th]ese then will arise

Milik related the contrast between those who are in blindness and those who will arise to the two groups who will rise to different fates in Daniel 12.⁴⁵ But it is surely unlikely that those who are in blindness and error are risen from the dead. The verb קום does not necessarily refer to resurrection. (Daniel 12 uses the verb "awake.") It may equally well refer to the rise of a group, such as we find in such texts as the *Apocalypse of Weeks*, the *Animal Apocalypse* or the *Damascus Document*, and this meaning seems more appropriate to the context here.

---

⁴⁴ Milik has been followed by several scholars, e.g. García Martínez, *Qumran and Apocalyptic*, 137–49; Mertens, *Das Buch Daniel*, 42–50; Collins, *Daniel*, 76, but see the DJD edition where this position is reversed.

⁴⁵ So also Puech, *La croyance des Esséniens*, 568–70.

Both *Ps. Dan*ᵃ⁻ᵇ and *Ps. Dan*ᶜ mention the name of Daniel. *Ps. Dan*ᵃ⁻ᵇ assumes that Daniel is at the Babylonian court. (Belshazzar is mentioned in 4Q243.2.) Apart from the setting, however, there is little to suggest that these texts depend on the biblical book of Daniel. Both texts refer to writings that appear to be the sources of the revelations that follow. These revelations resemble what we find in Daniel insofar as they give an overview of history and look to an eschatological future. But the specific motifs that these texts were thought to share with the Book of Daniel disappear on closer examination. Moreover, as Lorenzo DiTommaso has argued, the theological perspective is different from that of the canonical book.[46] It is likely then that there were several writings in the name of Daniel circulating in the second century BCE, and that only a selection found their way into the biblical book.

The *Aramaic Apocalypse*

DJD XXII contains another text called "4QApocryphe de Daniel ar."[47] This is 4Q246, better known as the *Aramaic Apocalypse* or the *Son of God Text*, first presented by Milik in a lecture in 1972, and published by Émile Puech twenty years later.[48] In this case, the association with Daniel is controversial, since the name does not occur in the extant fragments. Like *Ps. Daniel*ᵃ⁻ᵇ, this text is set in a royal court. Someone falls before a throne, and interprets a vision. The vision concerns warfare and a succession of kings, culminating with the advent of one who is called Son of God and Son of the Most High. The text concludes with the rise of the people of God and an eternal kingdom.

Much of the discussion of this text has focused on the identity of the figure who is called the Son of God. Some scholars, beginning with Milik, have argued that he is a Seleucid king.[49] Others, including F. M. Cross and myself, have argued that he is a Jewish messiah.[50] One factor in this debate concerns the relation of the text to the Book of Daniel. In addition to the court setting, the text uses some phrases that correspond directly to phrases in Daniel: "his (or its) kingdom is an everlasting

---

[46] L. DiTommaso, "4Qpseudo-Danielᵃ⁻ᵇ (4Q243–4Q244) and the Book of Daniel," *DSD* 12 (2005) 101–33. The theology of history in the fragments is Deuteronomistic rather than apocalyptic.

[47] É. Puech, "246. 4QApocryphe de Daniel ar," in Brooke et al., DJD 22, 165–84.

[48] É. Puech, "Fragment d'une apocalypse en araméen (4Q246=pseudo-Danᵈ) et le "royaume de Dieu," *RB* 99 (1992) 98–131.

[49] The most elaborate argument for this position is presented by E. Cook, "4Q246," *Bulletin for Biblical Research* 5 (1995) 43–66.

[50] F. M. Cross, *The Ancient Library of Qumran* (3rd ed.; Sheffield: Sheffield Academic Press, 1995) 189–91; J. J. Collins, "The *Son of God* Text from Qumran," in M. de Boer, ed., *From Jesus to John. Essays on Jesus and New Testament Christology in Honour of Marinus de Jonge* (JSNT 84; Sheffield: JSOT Press, 1993) 65–82; idem, "The Background of the 'Son of God' Text," *Bulletin for Biblical Research* 7 (1997) 1–12. For the most recent analysis see my treatment in Adela Y. Collins and John J. Collins, *King and Messiah as Son of God* (Grand Rapids: Eerdmans, 2008) 65–74.

kingdom" (2:5; cf. Dan 4:3; 7:27) and "his sovereignty is an everlasting sovereignty" (2:9; cf. Dan 4:34; 7:14). Moreover, the conflict between the nations in col. 1 is reminiscent in a general way of Daniel, and there is a possible allusion to Daniel 7 in the use of the word "trample" (דוש) in 2:3.[51]

These correspondences can be interpreted in various ways. Puech takes them as indications that the text comes from the same general milieu as Daniel.[52] In this case, phrases such as "his kingdom is an everlasting kingdom" are presumably eschatological commonplaces. But these phrases are not in fact common in the literature of this period, and the specificity of the parallels suggests a more direct relationship between the texts. If 4Q246 is messianic, as I believe it is, this would favor a later date for the Qumran text than for Daniel, since there is no evidence of messianic expectation in the Maccabean period. In this case, 4Q246 is more likely to derive the common phrases from Daniel than *vice versa*.

If the Qumran text indeed takes these phrases from Daniel, then a further intriguing question arises. Should the figure who is called the Son of God be understood as an interpretation of the famous "one like a son of man" in Daniel 7? Both texts go on to speak of the rise of the people of God or of the holy ones, and the eternal kingdom. I have argued at length elsewhere that the "one like a son of man" is not simply identical with the people of holy ones, but is their representative and leader, who in Daniel is the archangel Michael.[53] If the "Son of God" is understood as the messiah, he too must be understood as the representative and leader of the people of God. In this case, the understanding of the figure in question is different from that which was implied in Daniel 7 itself. We know, however, that Daniel 7 was understood to refer to a messianic figure in the first century CE, in the *Similitudes of Enoch* and again in *4 Ezra 13*.[54] It is possible that 4Q246 provides the earliest instance of the messianic interpretation of Daniel 7.

The *Four Kingdoms Text*

Like 4Q246, the *Four Kingdoms Text* does not mention Daniel explicitly. This text is found in two very fragmentary Aramaic manuscripts, 4Q552–553. While this text was published in a very preliminary way by Eisenman and Wise in 1992,[55] and Bey-

---

[51] Note however the cautions of Stuckenbruck, "The Formation and Re-Formation of Daniel," 118–9, who concludes that the correspondences neither exclude nor fully corroborate dependence on Daniel.

[52] Puech, "4QApocryphe de Daniel ar," 183.

[53] Collins, *Daniel*, 304–10.

[54] J. J. Collins, "The Son of Man in First Century Judaism," *New Testament Studies* 38 (1992) 448–66; *The Scepter and the Star. The Messiahs of the Dead Sea Scrolls and Other Ancient Literature* (New York: Doubleday, 1995) 173–94.

[55] R. Eisenman and M. Wise, *The Dead Sea Scrolls Uncovered* (Rockport, MA: Element, 1992) 71–74. They list the text as 4Q547.

er in 1994,[56] the official *DJD* edition by Émile Puech only appeared in 2009.[57] It is a vision of four trees, which represent four kingdoms. The first is identified as Babylon, and it is said to rule over Persia.[58] The setting is apparently a royal court, as there is mention of a conversation involving a king. Puech restores "Daniel" as the name of the visionary, but this is gratuitous.[59] Nonetheless, it has been considered "a parabiblical work that provides an interpretive elaboration on Danielic themes."[60]

Apart from the visionary language and the court setting, the main reason for associating this text with Daniel is its use of the four-kingdom schema with Babylon as the first kingdom. This schema was known more widely than Daniel in the Hellenistic age, but traditionally, the first kingdom was that of Assyria, so the choice of Babylon here is significant.[61] The tree symbolism may be suggested by Daniel 4, where Nebuchadnezzar is represented as a tree,[62] but other, arguably better, parallels are available in Ezek 31:1–14 and 17:1–24.[63] Of course, the four kingdom schema is altered here, as can be seen from the subordination of Persia to Babylon, which makes it unlikely that Media had any place in the sequence. Despite the fragmentary nature of the text, it is plausible that it "includes a contemporizing exegesis of the four kingdoms,"[64] which necessarily entails revision and updating.

Albert Hogeterp has argued that this text also "exhibits underlying textual variety in the Daniel tradition."[65] The evidence for this is subtle; it consists of a couple of parallels (mention of angels, El Elyon or the Most High God) between this Aramaic text and the LXX but not the Aramaic of Daniel 4. These parallels are neither extensive nor distinctive enough to prove the point, although they raise an intriguing possibility. It is generally assumed that there existed an Aramaic Vorlage for the LXX text of Daniel 4, which differs considerably from the MT, but as yet no such Aramaic text has come to light.

A few other texts, of lesser importance for the study of Daniel, may be mentioned. J. T. Milik proposed that a very fragmentary Aramaic text, 4Q551 was a fragment of

---

[56] K. Beyer, *Die aramäischen Texte vom Toten Meer: Ergänzungsband* (Göttingen: Vandenhoeck & Ruprecht, 1994) 108–9.

[57] É. Puech, *Qumrân Grotte 4.XXVII: Textes araméens, deuxième partie (4Q550–4Q575a, 4Q580–4Q587)* (DJD 37; Oxford: Clarendon, 2009) 57–90.

[58] Puech, DJD 37, 64, 78, restores Media and Greece as the second and third kingdoms, but the names are not preserved.

[59] Puech, DJD 37, 61 (4Q552 1 6).

[60] So A. L. A. Hogeterp, "Daniel and the Qumran Daniel Cycle: Observations on 4QFour Kingdoms[a-b] (4Q552–553)," in M. Popović, ed., *Authoritative Scriptures in Ancient Judaism* (JSJSup 141; Leiden: Brill, 2010) 173–91 (here, 190). See also Flint, "The Daniel Tradition at Qumran," 362–3; Stuckenbruck, "The Formation and Re-Formation of Daniel," 120.

[61] See Collins, *Daniel*, 166–70.

[62] Flint, "The Daniel Tradition at Qumran," 362; Stuckenbruck, "Formation and Re-Formation of Daniel," 120; Hogeterp, "Daniel and the Qumran Daniel Cycle," 189.

[63] Stuckenbruck, "Formation and Re-Formation of Daniel," 120.

[64] Hogeterp, "Daniel and the Qumran Daniel Cycle," 190.

[65] *Ibid.*, 190.

an Aramaic counterpart of the story of Susanna.[66] This suggestion has been decisively rejected, however. The fragment in question has closer parallels with Judges 19:15–23 and Gen 19:4–7.[67] Another fragmentary Aramaic text, 4Q489 (*pap4Qapocalypse ar*), published by M. Baillet,[68] contains the Aramaic words for "its appearance" and "you saw." It is obviously a visionary text, but the words in question are too few and common to provide a basis for any literary connection, to Daniel or any other text.[69]

Finally, Milik also noted interesting parallels between throne theophany in the *Book of Giants* (4QGiants[b], 4Q530, frag. 2) and Daniel 7, and suggested that the *Giants* text was "inspired by Dan 7:9–10."[70] Loren Stuckenbruck, in several studies, has argued persuasively that the *Book of Giants* preserves an earlier form of the tradition.[71] He concludes, however: "It is important to stress that these comparisons do not lead to a conclusion that either the *Book of Giants* or Daniel has taken the vision directly from the other ... Rather, it seems best to conclude that Daniel has taken up a tradition that, at least in some details, has been more faithfully preserved in the *Book of Giants*."[72]

Conclusion

It is apparent that the book of Daniel is closely related to several Aramaic compositions that were current in Judea in the last centuries before the common era. In the case of the *Prayer of Nabonidus*, the relationship is not necessarily direct. The importance of that Aramaic text for Daniel is that it throws light on the traditional story that underlies Daniel 4, whether the author of Daniel knew this specific text or not. The same might be said for the parallels between Daniel 7 and 4QGiants[b]. The relationship between Daniel and the *Pseudo-Daniel* texts is more elusive. It now seems that 4Q243–244 and 4Q245 are largely independent of the biblical book.

---

[66] J. T. Milik, "Daniel et Susanne à Qumrân?" in J. Doré et al., eds., *De la Tôrah au Messie* (Paris: Desclée, 1981) 337–59.

[67] Puech, DJD 37, 48.

[68] M. Baillet, *Qumrân Grotte 4.III (4Q482–4Q520)* (DJD 7; Oxford: Clarendon, 1982) 10–11 + pl. II.

[69] Flint, "The Daniel Tradition at Qumran," 361.

[70] J. T. Milik, *The Books of Enoch: Aramaic Fragments from Qumran Cave 4* (Oxford: Clarendon, 1976) 305.

[71] L. T. Stuckenbruck, *The Book of Giants from Qumran: Text, Translation, and Commentary* (Tübingen: Mohr Siebeck, 1997) 119–23; idem, "The Throne-Theophany of the Book of Giants: Some New Light on the Background of Daniel 7," in S. E. Porter and C. A. Evans, eds., *The Scrolls and the Scriptures. Qumran Fifty Years After* (JSPSup 26; Sheffield: Sheffield Academic Press, 1997) 211–20; idem, "The Formation and Re-Formation of Daniel," 106–112. The fragments of the 4QGiants[b] are published by É. Puech, *Qumrân Grotte 4. XXII. Textes Araméens, Première Partie, 4Q529–549* (DJD 31; Oxford: Clarendon, 2001) 19–47.

[72] Stuckenbruck, "The Formation and Re-Formation of Daniel," 112.

Conclusion

Daniel evidently gave his name to more compositions than were accepted into the canon of scripture. A stronger case for dependence can be made in the case of 4Q246, the *"Son of God"* text, since here we have phrases that correspond exactly to the language of Daniel. I believe that this text does in fact depend on Daniel. Whether that dependence is only a matter of a few phrases, or whether the whole text should be seen as an interpretation or updating of Daniel, remains uncertain. Similarly, the *Four Kingdoms Text* (4Q552–553) appears to be a contemporizing exegesis of Daniel 2 or 7, although the exact relationship of this text to Daniel is obscured by its fragmentary nature.

It is noteworthy that all this "Danielic" or "para-Danielic" literature is in Aramaic, and not distinctively sectarian. The Torah of Moses does not appear in it at all. Daniel was, however, influential within the sect, as can be seen from the number of copies preserved and the citations and allusions in the sectarian scrolls.

Part Two
History and Sectarianism

CHAPTER EIGHT

Historiography in the Dead Sea Scrolls

To speak of historiography in the Dead Sea Scrolls is largely to speak of an absence. The Scrolls contain no historical narratives that could be compared to the books of Maccabees or the writings of Josephus. In the words of Armin Lange,

> The classical Greek and modern concepts of historiography do not apply to this type of literature. At Qumran, only a few fragments were found that appear to recall history by mentioning historical personae and their deeds by name (e.g. 4Q332–33, 4Q468e) and are in some way comparable to Greek historiography.[1]

It is not the case that the people who wrote and gathered the Scrolls had no interest in the past, but they were interested in it for the light it might shed on their own situation in the present. In part, their interest in history resembles what we find in the apocalyptic writings: a concern for the broad sweep of history and their own place within it, and for the patterns they perceived on the macro-historical level.[2] In other part, their treatment of history is more distinctive, especially in their intense interest in the fulfillment of prophecy in the history of their time. The lack of historical narrative, however, is striking, as is the absence of details such as the name of their Teacher. It has been noted that even the historical books that we know as biblical, the books of Kings and Chronicles, are poorly represented in the Scrolls. There are only three manuscripts of Kings, one each from caves 4, 5, and 6. One manuscript, 4Q118, has been identified as a copy of Chronicles. Part of one column corresponds to 2 Chron 28:27–29:3. But the other column has no parallel in Chronicles, and so it is questionable whether this actually is a copy of the book as such.[3] It has been suggested that the sectarians avoided Chronicles because of its strong focus on Jerusalem and the temple,[4] but this seems unlikely. There are plenty of texts that focus on

---

[1] Armin Lange with U. Mittmann-Richert, "Annotated List of the Texts from the Judaean Desert Classified by Content and Genre," in Emanuel Tov et al., *The Texts from the Judaean Desert. Indices and an Introduction to the Discoveries in the Judaean Desert Series* (DJD 39; Oxford: Clarendon, 2002) 120.

[2] On apocalyptic historiography see now Michael E. Stone, *Ancient Judaism. New Visions and Views* (Grand Rapids: Eerdmans, 2011) 59–89.

[3] George J. Brooke, "Types of Historiography in the Dead Sea Scrolls," in George J. Brooke and Thomas Römer, eds., *Ancient and Modern Scriptural Historiography. L'Historiographie Biblique, Ancienne et Moderne* (BETL 207; Leuven: Leuven University, 2007) 214.

[4] J. C. VanderKam and P. W. Flint, *The Meaning of the Dead Sea Scrolls: Their Significance for Understanding the Bible, Judaism, Jesus, and Christianity* (San Francisco, CA: HarperSanFrancisco, 2002) 118.

Jerusalem and the temple among the Scrolls. There is nothing to indicate that Chronicles was regarded as authoritative scripture by the sectarians, or that they attached any special importance to it. Ideological considerations probably do account, however, for the absence of 1 Maccabees from the caves. While the relations of the sectarians to the Hasmonean dynasty may have been more complex than is often supposed, they surely did not share the enthusiasm for the Maccabees that is reflected in the Hasmonean court history.

Apocalyptic historiography

Probably the best-known historiographical, or quasi-historiographical passage in the sectarian Scrolls is found in the opening column of the *Damascus Document*:

For when they were unfaithful in forsaking him, he hid his face from Israel and from his sanctuary and delivered them up to the sword. But when he remembered the covenant with the forefathers, he saved a remnant for Israel and did not deliver them up to destruction. And in the period of wrath, 390 years after delivering them into the hand of Nebuchadnezzar, king of Babylon, he visited them and caused to sprout from Israel and from Aaron a root of planting, in order to possess his land and to become fat with the good things of its soil. And they realized their iniquity and knew that they were guilty, but they were like blind people and those who grope for a path over twenty years. And God appraised their deeds, because they sought him with an undivided heart, and raised up for them a Teacher of Righteousness, in order to direct them in the path of his heart. (CD 1:3–11)

This passage is highly schematic. It presupposes the pattern of sin-punishment-restoration familiar from the Deuteronomistic History. The rise of the sect is located a significant time after the Babylonian Exile, but the figure of 390 is symbolic – it is the number of years assigned for the punishment of Israel in Ezekiel 4:5. Although this has often been taken to indicate an approximate date for the origin of the sect, it has no reliable chronological value – any more than the seventy weeks of years, or 490 years, which is given in Daniel 9 as the period from the destruction of Jerusalem to the time of Antiochus Epiphanes. (The actual period was approximately 420 years.) The *Damascus Document* is not concerned with chronology (although the 20 years of groping has some value for understanding the way in which the movement developed). Rather, it is concerned to illustrate the ways in which God works in history, and to suggest that the author's group represented the elect of the last days.[5]

In the *Damascus Document*, this passage is found in a hortatory section of the text, known as the Admonition. The use of history, however, is reminiscent of the

---

[5] This is not the only passage in the *Damascus Document* that uses history for parenetic purposes. For a fuller treatment see Albert I. Baumgarten, "The Perception of the Past in the *Damascus Document*," in J. M. Baumgarten, E. G. Chazon and A. Pinnick, eds., *The Damascus Document: A Centennial of Discovery. Proceedings of the Third International Symposium of the Orion Center for the Study of the Dead Sea Scrolls and Associated Literature, 4–8 February, 1998* (STDJ 34; Leiden: Brill, 2000) 1–15.

apocalypses of the early second century. The *Apocalypse of Weeks* in *1 Enoch* is at least as schematic in its overview of history. There too plant imagery is used to identify the elect group that arises at the end of history. In Daniel, this role is taken by the *maskilim*, or wise teachers, who arise in the time of persecution in Daniel 11, although that passage is somewhat atypical in its historical detail. The schematic overview of history, culminating in the rise of an elect group, is so typical of the apocalyptic writings of the Maccabean era that scholars like Martin Hengel assumed that they must all refer to the same movement, the Hasidim. That view is no longer compelling. There was more than one elect group in this era. But these texts do testify to a common way of viewing history in highly schematic terms, to highlight the rise of an elect group in the final period.

The book of Daniel and most of the books of Enoch (except for the *Similitudes*) are found at Qumran in multiple copies. There are also some previously unknown texts that present history in the form of *ex eventu* prophecy. Examples are found in 4Q390, which has been variously identified as *pseudo-Jeremiah* or *pseudo-Moses*, and in the *pseudo-Daniel* texts (4Q243–4, 245).

4Q390 is notable for exempting the first generation after the Exile from the general corruption of the post-Exilic period, which was subject to the "angels of destruction." The text is fragmentary, and does not extend to the final restoration, but it evidently deals with the broad sweep of history in schematic terms. It is unlikely that the positive judgment on the first generation after the Exile has any basis beyond the traditional scriptures.

The Aramaic *pseudo-Daniel* texts (4Q243–4) are also largely paraphrases of biblical history in the guise of prophecy. They offer a few interesting variations. The destruction at the hand of Nebuchadnezzar is attributed to the sacrifice of children to the demons of error, but again it is unlikely that this statement was based on any independent tradition. It is apparent, however, that *Pseudo-Daniel* included some historical information beyond what is found in the traditional scriptures, in the prophecy of the Hellenistic period. There is a fragmentary name ending in "–rhos, son of . . ." (the Aramaic "rh" reflects a double *rho* in Greek) and mention of a figure called Balacros (a relatively common Hellenistic name). Unfortunately, the text is too fragmentary to allow us to reconstruct the historical events to which it refers. The text ends with the ingathering of the elect.

The second *Pseudo-Daniel* text, 4Q245, also contains historical information that is not derived from the traditional scriptures.[6] Fragments of two columns survive. The first column mentions Daniel's name, and "a book that was given." Then it gives a list of names. The first part of the list gives the names of High Priests, beginning with Levi and Qahath. This is followed by a list of kings beginning with David and

---

[6] For the text, see John J. Collins and Peter W. Flint, "245. 4Qpseudo-Daniel^c ar," in George Brooke et al., *Qumran Cave 4. XVII. Parabiblical Texts, Part 3* (DJD 22; Oxford: Clarendon, 1996) 153–64.

Solomon. The second fragment refers to the end of wickedness and eschatological restoration.

The list of priests preserves the names of Bukki, Uzzi, Zadok, Abiathar and Hilkiah. All of these except for Abiathar are found in 1 Chron 5:27–41. Since no other list begins as far back as Levi and Qahath, this may suggest that *Pseudo-Daniel* drew on Chronicles here (despite the near absence of manuscripts of Chronicles from the Scrolls). It is also possible, however, that *Pseudo-Daniel* and the Chronicler had a common source, which they adapted in slightly different ways. The inclusion of Abiathar shows that, unlike Chronicles, *Pseudo-Daniel*'s list was not confined to the Zadokite line. Michael Wise argues that the list would also have included the five High Priests descended from Ithamar, beginning with Eli, who held office immediately before Zadok according to Josephus.[7] (The argument is based on the space available.) If this were so, then *Pseudo-Daniel* must have had available a list of High Priests similar to that presupposed by Josephus, but that argument depends on the filling of a lacuna.

The most interesting part of *Pseudo-Daniel*'s list of High Priests, however, lies in the extension of the list beyond the period covered by Chronicles. The names חוניה (Onias) and שמעון (Simon) are clearly preserved, and the name before the latter ends with -תן and can only be Jonathan. So the list included at least two Hasmonean High Priests. Wise reasons that the list skipped at least eleven High Priests in the Persian and early Hellenistic period and resumed about the year 200 BCE. Wise also supposes that the list continued to John Hyrcanus and perhaps Judah Aristobulus, but Simon is the last name actually preserved. The last king whose name is preserved is Joash, but that list probably extended down to the Babylonian exile.

4Q245 raises various interesting questions about the attitude of its author to the Hasmonean priest kings. The list contains no comment. Jonathan and Simon appear as legitimate as their Zadokite predecessors. My concern in this paper, however, is not with the substance of the history preserved, but with *Pseudo-Daniel* as historiography, or at least as witness to a kind of historiography that is poorly attested in the Scrolls. This consists of preserving historical memory in the form of lists. The lists, no doubt, were made for a purpose. In this case, the separate lists of High Priests and Kings may have been meant to show that the two offices should not be combined, as they eventually were, at least by Alexander Jannaeus. But in the process, they preserve a record of historical succession. In large part the lists are compiled from traditional scriptures, but it is apparent that the author was prepared to modify the traditional lists (by including at least Abiathar in the list of High Priests) and to extend it, whether the extension was based on written sources or on oral tradition.

---

[7] Michael O. Wise, "4Q245 and the High Priesthood of Judas Maccabaeus," *DSD* 12 (2005) 329–31; cf. Josephus *Ant* 5. 361–2.

In 4Q245, the mention of Daniel suggests that the lists were presented as part of a revelation, although the text is too fragmentary to be sure. There are other lists among the Scrolls, mostly culled from the Scriptures. 4Q339 gives a list of "the false prophets who arose in [Israel]". The last line of the fragment only preserves the letters עון. Alexander Rofé and Elisha Qimron proposed that the line should be restored to read "Yohanan ben Shim'on," or John Hyrcanus, who was said to have the gift of prophecy.[8] The editors, Magen Broshi and Ada Yardeni decided that it was simpler to restore "the prophet from Gibeon," since Hananiah son of Azur was from Gibeon.[9] If the restoration of Hyrcanus were correct, the list would be compiled for the purpose of stigmatizing a recent or contemporary figure. If the reference is to Hananiah, then it is simply a matter of classifying information from the biblical text. 4Q340 provides a list of *netinim*, or temple servants. Such lists can be found in Ezra 2:43–54 and Nehemiah 7:46–56, but the very fragmentary list from Qumran does not correspond to these. Later, in the Talmud, they are prohibited from marrying unblemished Israelites, and they were equated with bastards (m. Qidd. 4:1). The editors suggest that this is a list of blemished people unfit for marriage.[10] They restore the name Tobiah in the last line, but only טו is preserved. This interpretation of the text was challenged by Shaye Cohen, who saw no polemical purpose at work.[11] Cohen saw the making of lists as a scholarly activity, and evidence for the Hellenization of Judaism. Whether list-making requires Hellenistic influence seems to me doubtful, but I agree with Cohen that this is scholarly activity. Insofar as the data listed are historical, it is also a kind of rudimentary historiography. At least it displays an interest in preserving and organizing information about the past. This remains true even if the compositions had a polemical purpose.

The *Pesharim*

Another aspect of historiography in the Scrolls is highlighted by the *pesharim*. George Brooke has properly insisted that "the *pesharim* are not an overt form of history writing, are not outlines of past events, recent or otherwise."[12] Nonetheless he suggests that "the *pesharim* may indeed be considered as a type of historiography."[13] As stated explicitly in *Pesher Habakkuk* (6:12–7:8), the prophets did not

---

[8] As reported by M. Broshi and A. Yardeni, "4Q List of False Prophets ar," in Magen Broshi et al., *Qumran Cave 4. XIV. Parabiblical Texts Part 2* (DJD 19; Oxford: Clarendon, 1995) 79.

[9] Broshi and Yardeni, *ibid.*

[10] Broshi and Yardeni, "4QList of Netinim," *ibid.*, 82.

[11] Shaye J. D. Cohen, "Hellenism in Unexpected Places," in John J. Collins and Gregory E. Sterling, eds., *Hellenism in the Land of Israel* (Notre Dame, IN: Notre Dame University, 2001) 220.

[12] Brooke, "Types of Historiography," 218. Whether this means that they cannot be used for modern historical reconstruction, as Brooke argues, is a different issue. Historical information can be inferred from texts that were not composed for the purpose of conveying it.

[13] *Ibid.*, 219.

properly understand their own oracles. These refer not to the time of the prophets, but to the time of the interpreter. Consequently, the prophecies were still unfulfilled, and could be used to shed light on the time of the interpreter. The validity of the interpretations, according to Brooke, is discernible in the use of "a variety of hermeneutical methods as keys to unlocking the present meaning of past utterances."[14]

My own view of the relevance of the *pesharim* to the question of historiography in the Scrolls is somewhat different. They do convey historical information, but this is not their primary purpose, and so I would hesitate to describe them as "historiographical." Moreover, while the *pesharim* certainly make use of "a variety of hermeneutical methods," this is not what establishes the validity of their interpretations. That validity derives from the authority of the Teacher of Righteousness, even though he personally cannot have been the author of all the *pesharim*. This is stated explicitly in *Pesher Habakkuk* 7:3–5: "And when it says, so that he can run who reads it, its interpretation concerns the Righteous Teacher, to whom God made known all the mysteries of the words of his servants the prophets." In the early days of the interpretation of the Scrolls there was a debate as to whether the *pesharim* were guided by hermeneutical principles such as we find in the later Midrash (so Brooke's teacher, William Brownlee)[15] or rather claimed to be inspired interpretation, in the tradition of Daniel 9 (so Karl Elliger).[16] The dichotomy was shown to be unnecessary by Lou Silberman: even the "revealed" interpretation of Jeremiah in Daniel 9 makes use of hermeneutical principles.[17] But it is important to note that the *pesharim* do not base their claim to validity on hermeneutical techniques, but rather on the authority of the Teacher.

The *pesharim* are written to assure the faithful that their vindication is guaranteed by prophecy, and that prophecy is being fulfilled in their time. In order to show that prophecy is being fulfilled they identify certain historical events that have already taken place as fulfillment of prophecy, and this provides assurance that the prophecies are also reliable with regard to things that have not yet come to pass. In this regard, the logic of the *pesharim* resembles that of *ex eventu* prophecies in apocalypses. It requires that they refer to some actual events that were known to the intended readers. Fictional characters and events would provide no evidence of the reliability of prophecy.[18] Moreover, the *pesharim* do not construct a full narrative of the events to which they allude. Rather, they allude to isolated events as the biblical

---

[14] *Ibid.*

[15] W. H. Brownlee, "Biblical Interpretation among the Sectaries of the Dead Sea Scrolls," *BA* 14 (1951) 54–76.

[16] Karl Elliger, *Studien zum Habakkuk Kommentar vom Toten Meer* (Tübingen: Mohr, 1953) 157–64.

[17] Lou H. Silberman, "Unriddling the Riddle," *RevQ* 3 (1961) 326–7.

[18] See my articles, "Prophecy and Fulfillment in the Qumran Scrolls," in my book, *Seers, Sibyls and Sages in Hellenistic-Roman Judaism* (JSJSup 54; Leiden: Brill, 1997) 301–14; "Prophecy and History in the *Pesharim*," in M. Popović, ed., *Authoritative Scriptures in Ancient Judaism* (JSJSup 141; Leiden: Brill, 2010) 209–26.

text offers occasion. These events are primarily events in the first half of the first century BCE, not events from the biblical period.[19] In order to refer to these events, the *pesharim* have to rely on tradition, whether oral or written, and in many cases that tradition is no longer available to us. They show, however, that an account of historical events from the early first century BCE was known to the authors and presumed readers of the *pesharim*, even though that account has not been preserved apart from its secondary usage in the commentaries. Herein, I suggest, lies the main importance of the *pesharim* for the question of historiography in the Dead Sea Scrolls.

The use of history in the *pesharim* is most clearly evident in *Pesher Nahum*, which explicitly mentions "Deme]trius King of Greece," who sought to enter Jerusalem on the advice of the "Seekers after Smooth Things."[20] There follows a statement that "[Jerusalem was not given] into the hand of the kings of Greece from Antiochus to the rise of the rulers of the Kittim, but afterwards it will be trampled" (4Q169 3–4 i 3). The reference here is to Demetrius III Akairos (94–88 BCE) who was invited by the Jewish opponents of King Alexander Jannaeus. He defeated Jannaeus in battle but suffered heavy losses and withdrew from Judea.[21] The Kittim in the *pesharim* are universally recognized as the Romans, and the reference to the trampling of Jerusalem may well be *ex eventu*, written after the conquest of Jerusalem by Pompey. This passage is exceptional in mentioning actual names, but, as Timothy Lim has put it, it gives the reader

the clearest indication that the pesherist was indeed interested in history. His commentary was not just an exegetical and literary play on the words and oracles of the prophet Nahum, but in it was also a concern for contemporary life and events.[22]

The following passage in *Pesher Nahum* is an interpretation of Nah 2:13: "the lion tears enough for his cubs, and strangles prey for his lionesses." This is interpreted as "concerning the Lion of Wrath, who would strike with his great ones and the men of his counsel" (4Q169 3–4 i 5). Nahum 2:13b, "and it fills up] its cave [with prey], and its den with torn flesh," is interpreted with reference to "the Lion of Wrath" and "the Seekers after Smooth Things," and says that "he would hang men up alive." The "Lion of Wrath" is almost universally identified as Alexander Jannaeus, who had eight hundred of his opponents crucified.[23] It is generally accepted that the opponents, the "Seekers after Smooth Things," are the Pharisees. While this interpre-

---

[19] Michael O. Wise, "Dating the Teacher of Righteousness and the *Floruit* of His Movement," *JBL* 122 (2003) 53–87.

[20] 4Q169 3–4 i 1–2. The commentary is on Nah 2:12–14. See Shani Berrin, *The Pesher Nahum Scroll from Qumran: An Exegetical Study of 4Q169* (STDJ 53; Leiden: Brill, 2004) 87.

[21] Josephus, *Ant.* 13.372–416.

[22] Timothy H. Lim, *Pesharim* (London: Continuum, 2002) 68–69.

[23] Berrin, *Pesher Nahum*, 104–9. Gregory L. Doudna, *4Q Pesher Nahum: A Critical Edition* (London: Sheffield Academic Press, 2001) 557–73, regards him as a gentile king. The "Lion of Wrath" is also mentioned in 4QpHos[b] 2 2–4.

tation is prompted by the violent actions of the lion in the biblical text, it is apparent that the details of the interpretation are not derived exegetically, but allude to historical events known to the reader. In this case, we are fortunate to know what the events were, because they are described in some detail by Josephus (*Ant.* 13.379–383). The authors of the *pesher* did not have Josephus, or any other written historical narrative of these events known to us. But they evidently had a tradition about these events, whether written or oral, that corresponds in some details to the account found more than a century later in Josephus. The sectarian community evidently had historical traditions that are not preserved in narrative form in the Dead Sea Scrolls. Just as the authors of *Pseudo-Daniel* had information about someone called "Balacros," so the authors of the *pesharim* had traditions about the conflicts in the reign of Alexander Jannaeus.

Historiographical texts among the Scrolls

While we do not have the sources from which the authors of the *pesharim* drew their information, we do have some fragmentary texts that modern scholars have regarded as historiographical.

4Q248, formerly identified as "Acts of a Greek King," was published in DJD 36 as Historical Text A, by Magen Broshi and Esther Eshel.[24] It consists of a single fragment, translated by its editors as follows:

]Egypt and in Greece and [
] he shall magni[fy (himself)] thus they shall eat
[of] their [son]s and daughters in the siege in [
[and] the Lord shall cau[se] a spirit to go [ ]their lands and [
[And] he shall come to Egypt and sell its land. And he shall come
to the Temple city and seize it and al[l
and he shall overthrow lands of (foreign nations and (then) return to Egyp[t]
And when the shattering of the power of the ho[ly] people [comes to an end]
[then shall] all these things [be fulfilled] the children of [Israel] shall return [

This text was originally dubbed "Acts of a Greek King." In the DJD edition the editors suggest that it is "a genuine historical composition which is part of an apocalyptic work. Historical events are represented in apocalyptic works in an accurate way in order to persuade the reader that the apocalyptic vision will soon also be fulfilled."[25] They understand it on the analogy of Daniel 11, and take it to refer to the career of Antiochus IV Epiphanes, who invaded Egypt twice. Crucial to their interpretation is their construal of the second to last line, which they read as
וככלות] נפץ יד עם הק[דש

---

[24] DJD 36, 192–200.
[25] *Ibid.*, 192.

Precisely this sequence of words is found in Dan 12:7: "when the shattering of the power of the holy people is complete." Many scholars have emended the Danielic text by transposing the words יד and נפץ and translating "when the power of the shatterer of the holy people comes to an end." Broshi and Eshel take the Qumran text as confirmation of the order of the words in Daniel, and suggest that it was a source for Daniel, written before the outbreak of persecution in Jerusalem. This ingenious interpretation, however, is highly questionable. Epiphanes besieged Alexandria twice, but neither siege was severe, and the editors have to regard the reports of cannibalism as gross exaggeration. There is no record of Epiphanes selling land in Egypt, although he did this in Jerusalem, according to Dan 11:39. The reference to the return of the children of Israel at the end is reconstructed. The text may have referred to a mundane, not eschatological, return of some group. Most crucially, however, the reading נפץ יד is problematic. Only the ligature of the *nun* of נפץ is preserved, and the *pe* looks more like a bet. J. T. Milik read this line as וב[בציד עם הק]יץ.[26] Michael Wise translates "[The destroyer shall fall] upon the vintage and the sum[mer fruits]."[27] This reading has its own problems. The fourth letter seems to be a *daleth* rather than a *resh*, and should perhaps be read as בציד, "with provisions." In this case, line 9 is not an eschatological turning point in the text, but simply a continuation of the prediction, whether *ex eventu* or not, and the text is related to Daniel 11–12 only in a general way.[28]

Since the events in this passage are narrated in the future tense, Broshi and Eshel are probably right that this text is a fragment of a pseudo-prophetic work. It may be an *ex eventu* account, such as we find in Daniel 11. It may possibly refer to Antiochus Epiphanes. In that case, it preserves some historical tradition, notably the information that he came to Jerusalem after his first invasion of Egypt, as claimed by 1 Macc 1:20–28. It may even constitute evidence that Epiphanes sold land in Egypt. But none of this is certain. Wise suggests that the narrative relates to Ptolemy I Soter, who first captured Jerusalem and then returned there to rule. Moreover, the entire sequence could conceivably be a fantasy of future events. The designation of this composition as an "Historical Text" then seems dubious. It is more likely to be a pseudo-prophetic text, which may incorporate historical traditions, in the manner of Daniel 11 or the *Pseudo-Daniel* texts. It is not a primary historiographical document.

---

[26] B. Z. Wacholder and M. G. Abegg, *A Preliminary Edition of the Unpublished Dead Sea Scrolls* (Washington: Biblical Archeology Society, 1995) 3.33.

[27] M. Wise, M. Abegg, E. Cook, *The Dead Sea Scrolls, A New Translation* (San Francisco: Harper, 1996) 271.

[28] See further my article, "New Light on the Book of Daniel from the Dead Sea Scrolls," in Florentino García Martínez and Ed Noort, eds., *Perspectives in the Study of the Old Testament and Early Judaism. A Symposium in Honour of Adam S. van der Woude on the Occasion of His 70th Birthday* (VTSup 73; Leiden: Brill, 1998) 191–5.

The same can be said for 4Q386, a pseudo-Ezekiel prophetic text, which contains an *ex eventu* prophecy.²⁹ The relevant passage is in col. 2:

> And the Lord said, 'A Son of Belial will scheme to oppress my people, but I will not allow him; and his kin will not survive, nor will there be left from the impure one any seed; and from the caperbush there shall be no wine, nor will a hornet make any honey. [*vacat*]. And the wicked one I will slay at Memphis but my children I will bring forth from Memphis, and their rem[na]nt I shall return.

Devorah Dimant, in the DJD edition, argued that the "son of Belial" and the "wicked one" were two different people. She identified the former with Antiochus Epiphanes and the latter with some historical figure active in Memphis during the reign of Epiphanes or shortly thereafter.³⁰ A more plausible interpretation was offered by Hanan Eshel, who argued that both references are to the same figure, and that he should be identified as Pompey, who was murdered on a boat outside the port of Pelusium in 48 BCE.³¹ A more accurate reference to Pompey's death can be found in the Psalms of Solomon 2, and this shows that the details of his death were known in Judea. Eshel argues that 4Q386 mentions Memphis as the place of death to make it accord with prophecy (Hos 9:6: "but Egypt shall gather them, Memphis shall bury them"). For our present purposes, the point to note is that the author was aware of, and drew on, historical traditions, even though his work was not directly historiographical.

The so-called "annalistic lists"

More promising for our quest for historiographical works among the Scrolls are a few fragmentary scrolls, 4Q331–333, that mention the names of historical individuals and also mention priestly courses.³² Three different manuscripts are distinguished, and they do not overlap, but it remains uncertain whether they are copies of a single text or of three similar compositions. Milik associated these fragments with the *Mishmarot* (texts relating to the priestly courses).³³ The priesthood was divided into 24 courses, which took turns serving in the Temple for a week at a time.

---

²⁹ Devorah Dimant, *Qumran Cave 4, XXI, Parabiblical Texts, IV* (DJD 30; Oxford: Clarendon, 2001) 53–69.
³⁰ Dimant, DJD 30, 56.
³¹ Eshel, *The Dead Sea Scrolls and the Hasmonean State*, 157–9.
³² Kenneth Atkinson, "Representations of History in 4Q331 (4QPaphistorical Text C), 4Q332 (4QHistorical Text D), 4Q333 (4QHistorical Text E), and 4Q468E (4QHistorical Text F): An Annalistic Calendar Documenting Portentous Events?" *DSD* 12 (2007) 125–51; Eshel, *The Dead Sea Scrolls and the Hasmonean State*, 133–50.
³³ See J. A. Fitzmyer, "331. 4QpapHistorical Text C," in J. C. VanderKam and Monica Brady, eds., *Qumran Cave 4. XXVI: Cryptic Texts and Miscellanea, Part I* (DJD 36; Oxford: Clarendon, 2000) 275. For the texts classified as Mishmarot see Donald W. Parry and Emanuel Tov, *Calendrical and Sapiential Texts* (The Dead Sea Scrolls Reader 4; Leiden: Brill, 2004) 2–53.

Consequently the name of a priestly course could be used to identify a particular week. The Mishmarot texts typically co-ordinate the service of the priestly courses with other details of the calendar, including the festivals:

The (first day of the) seventh (month falls) in (the week of Immer; this is the Day of Remembrance. In (the week of) Hezir, in it (falls) the Day of Atonement; in (the week of) Happi]sses, in it (falls) the Festival of Booths ... (4Q329 col. 8, verse 9)

4Q331–333 are distinctive in mentioning names of historical figures. Consequently, they were eventually labeled "Historical Texts." The genre and purpose of these texts, however, is still disputed, and the dispute is aggravated by the fragmentary nature of the texts.

4Q331 has ten fragments, but some of these only contain a few letters. Most notable are the names that are preserved. Frag 1 i mentions "priest who all" and, on the next line "Yohanan to bring to." This Yohanan is usually taken to be John Hyrcanus, but Hanan Eshel notes that all the other names in these fragments date from the first century BCE.[34] Frag 1 ii mentions Shelamzion (Queen Salome Alexandra, widow of Alexander Jannaeus), without any indication of context. Another fragment mentions Eliashib, the ancestral name of one of the priestly courses.

4Q332 has only three fragments. They are slightly better preserved than those of 4Q331, but still have no complete sentences. The first refers to the priestly course of Jedaiah, but goes on to mention that some people were "embittered in soul," and refers to "prisoners." The second fragment reads:

to give him honor among the Arabs
on the ninth of Shebat, this (is)
which is the [tw]entieth in the month
with secret counsel Salome came
to confront the
Hyrcanus rebelled
to confront

Michael Wise[35] and Joseph Fitzmyer[36] reconstructed the second last line as "Hyrcanus rebelled against Aristobulus. If this is correct, the reference is to the conflict between the brothers that preceded the coming of Pompey, written from a perspec-

---

[34] Eshel, *The Dead Sea Scrolls and the Hasmonean State*, 137.
[35] M. O. Wise, "An Annalistic Calendar from Qumran," in M. O. Wise et al., eds., *Methods of Investigation of the Dead Sea Scrolls and the Khirbet Qumran Site. Present Realities and Future Prospects* (Annals of the New York Academy of Sciences 722; New York; The New York Academy of Sciences, 1994) 397–8. See also Wise, "*Primo Annales Fuere*: An Annalistic Calendar from Qumran," in idem, *Thunder in Gemini and Other Essays on the History, Language and Literature of Second Temple Palestine* (JSPSup 15; Sheffield: Sheffield Academic Press, 1994) 208–10. Note that the numbers assigned to the text were changed after Wise wrote. He refers to these texts as 4Q322–324c.
[36] DJD 36, 283–4.

tive favorable to Aristobulus. The third fragment says that [the leader of the Kit]tim killed someone. The following line refers to "the fifth in (the course) of Jedaiah."

4Q333 has only two fragments. The first of these refers to the priestly course of Jehezkel, followed by "Aemilius killed" and to "the entrance to the priestly course of Gamul," followed by "Aemilius killed." The Aemilius in question is Marcus Aemilius Scaurus, whom Pompey appointed governor of Syria in 66 BCE. Only two words are preserved in the second fragment: איש יהודי, "a Judean man."

Opinion has vacillated as to whether these fragments are primarily calendrical or primarily historical. Some scholars (Michael Wise and Kenneth Atkinson) finesse the issue by referring to "an annalistic calendar." Brooke argues that

in the light of the Mishmarot texts and the hints of the names of priestly courses in some fragments, it is likely that the mention of historical personages is entirely secondary to the overall concern in the fragments for the rotation of the priestly courses. To label this text historical is probably inappropriate.[37]

In contrast, Shemaryahu Talmon and Jonathan Ben-Dov argued that the fragments represented historical events and referred to the priestly courses as a way of dating them.[38] The latter view is also affirmed by Fitzmyer, and in my view is clearly right. The references to historical events shed no light on the succession of priestly courses; conversely, the references to the courses provide a way of dating the historical events.

Milik referred to these fragments as "an Essene calendar giving the dates of certain historical events which were celebrated annually."[39] There is a well-known example of such a text in *Megillat Ta'anit*, a list of memorable days associated with important historical events, on which it is prohibited to fast and, in some cases, to deliver eulogies.[40] It was written in Aramaic, and later elaborated in Hebrew. It is generally regarded as pre-Mishnaic. Vered Noam has recently argued for a date before 70 CE, but the evidence is open to question.[41] The identifiable events mostly belong to the Maccabean period, although a few appear to be later. The events in question are all causes of rejoicing: the dedication of the wall of Jerusalem, the departure of the (Syrian) garrison, cessation of tribute (to the Seleucids), the suspension of the decrees (of Antiochus IV), the festival of Hanukkah. In contrast, the Qumran fragments refer to some events that would have been perceived negatively (killing perpetrated by Scaurus, the "rebellion" of Hyrcanus II) or as neutral. *Pace* Milik, there is no evidence that these events were commemorated. The list does not

---

[37] Brooke, "Types of Historiography," 227.
[38] Talmon and Ben-Dov, *Qumran Cave 4. XVI: Calendrical Texts* (DJD 21; Oxford: Clarendon, 2001) 12–13.
[39] J. T. Milik, *Ten Years of Discovery in the Wilderness of Judaea* (London: SCM, 1959) 73.
[40] Noted by Wise, "An Annalistic Calendar," 396; Eshel, *The Dead Sea Scrolls and the Hasmonean State*, 136.
[41] Vered Noam, *Megillat Ta'anit. Versions, Interpretation, History* (Jerusalem: Yad Ben-Zvi, 2003) (Heb.). See the review by Sacha Stern in *JJS* 57 (2006) 184–6.

appear to have a liturgical or halakhic purpose. It is simply a record of events that are dated by reference to the priestly courses. This is a peculiarly priestly kind of historiography, but historiography it surely is.

There is also dispute as to whether these fragments are sectarian (i.e. a product of the community of the new covenant or of the *yahad*). Eshel argues that they are not, since they use personal names, and in one case use the Babylonian name for a month.[42] If the use of personal names were a criterion, we should have to deem *Pesher Nahum* non-sectarian, which is plainly wrong. Brooke argues that they are sectarian, because of their presumed similarity to the *Mishmarot*, and the fact that they date from the first century BCE.[43] The latter argument reflects an outdated assumption that "the Qumran community" was hermetically sealed once it took up residence in the wilderness. Similarity to the *Mishmarot* would be significant if we may assume that these fragments presuppose the same, solar, calendar. The historical fragments are not polemical and do not refer to events in distinctively sectarian terms. They do not, for example, refer to the Teacher or the Wicked Priest. Ken Atkinson infers that "these texts were written for insiders, who already shared the values of their authors and also accepted their calendar."[44] This may be, but the fragments are not explicit about the calendar they presuppose, and the events they record were of interest to all Judeans. All we may infer from the presence of these fragments in Qumran Cave 4 is that they were known to the people who collected the Scrolls.

A couple of other very fragmentary works from Qumran may also have been historical records. 4Q468e is a tiny fragment that preserves the lines:

ki]lling the multitude of me[n
] Potlais and the people [

The Potlais in question is most probably Peitholaus, a Jewish officer who joined Gabinius in his war against Alexander, the son of Aristobulus in 57 BCE.[45] Eshel suggested that this fragment was related to 4Q331–33, but the fragment is too small to allow much by way of inference. It is, however, further evidence of the presence of historical traditions in the Scrolls. Another possibly historical text, 4Q322a, is even more fragmentary. The editor, Eibert Tigchelaar, suggests that it may refer to Aristobulus, but only the letters אר are preserved.[46]

Also uncertain is the importance of this material for the sectarians of the *yahad*. Arguably, four or five such texts were hidden in Cave 4, or alternatively, four or five copies of one text. The fact that the manuscripts are so poorly preserved is a matter

---

[42] Eshel, *The Dead Sea Scrolls and the Hasmonean State*, 136, n.9.
[43] Brooke, "Types of Historiography," 227.
[44] Atkinson, "Representations of History," 130.
[45] Eshel, *The Dead Sea Scrolls and the Hasmonean State*, 143, following Daniel Schwartz, John Strugnell and William Horbury.
[46] Eibert Tigchelaar, "322a. 4QHistorical Text H?," in M. Bernstein et al., *Qumran Cave 4. XXVIII. Miscellanea, Part 2* (DJD 28; Oxford: Clarendon, 2001) 125–8.

of coincidence. Even if single copies of each text were deposited, this would not necessarily mean that they were of little significance. The *pesharim* only survived in single copies. To be sure, there is nothing to indicate that these texts were of central importance to the *yahad*, in the way that Isaiah or the Community Rule were. But they were not necessarily unimportant. It is apparent from the *pesharim* that the *yahad* had access to historical traditions in some form. These annalistic fragments are, in the words of Michael Wise, "the nearest thing to historiography yet to emerge from the DSS."[47]

Conclusion

The Dead Sea Scrolls have vastly increased our knowledge of Jewish literature between the Bible and the Mishnah. We should remember, however, that these Scrolls were discovered by chance, and that they are unlikely to exhaust the Jewish literature that existed in this period, or even the literature of the community of the new covenant or the *yahad*. Historiographical writing is woefully under-represented in the Scrolls. This fact may be due in part to ideological reasons. The sectarians were not disposed to preserve the praises of the Maccabees, and they seem to have been far more interested in the niceties of halakah than in historical records. But in part it is also due to chance. The *pesharim* presuppose familiarity with historical traditions, whether oral or written, that have not survived. The so-called annalistic texts provide a glimpse of the form those traditions may have taken. These texts are not historiography on the grand scale of the books of Maccabees or Josephus, but they are historical records, however minimal, and they show that Judeans between the Maccabees and Josephus, including the sectarians known from the Scrolls, were not entirely indifferent to historical memory.

---

[47] Wise, *Thunder in Gemini*, 221.

CHAPTER NINE

Reading for History in the Dead Sea Scrolls

No scholar of the Dead Sea Scrolls in this generation was more committed to the quest for historical reality than Hanan Eshel. While his contributions to the field have been tragically cut short,[1] we are fortunate that he left us a concise summary of the historical data he distilled from the Scrolls, published less than two years before his death.[2] He was well aware of the difficulty of historical reconstruction. Only ten of approximately nine hundred scrolls mention known historical figures of the Hellenistic and early Roman periods by name.[3] As a result, most of his book is concerned with analyzing elliptic references in fragmentary texts, and the results are inevitably controversial. While Hanan made many important contributions in identifying historical allusions, his most enduring legacy may lie in the questions he raised and his insistence on the importance of historical study for understanding the Scrolls.

The Scrolls contain no historical narratives that could be compared to the books of Maccabees or the writings of Josephus. As George Brooke has noted:

It is not that the Qumran library is bereft of historical works and certainly it is not lacking in various historical perspectives, but that the kind of sequential narration of events such as is found in the books of Kings and Chronicles and also in 1 and 2 Maccabees does not seem to be the way that historiography is represented in the collection.[4]

---

[1] Hanan had undertaken to write the survey of Judean history in the Hellenistic and early Roman periods for J. J. Collins and D. Harlow, eds., *The Eerdmans Dictionary of Early Judaism* (Grand Rapids: Eerdmans, 2010) and an article on the history of the sectarian movement for T. H. Lim and J. J. Collins, eds., *The Oxford Handbook of the Dead Sea Scrolls* (Oxford: Oxford University Press, 2010) but had to withdraw from both assignments. He did, however, contribute four articles to the *Dictionary*, and was a generous adviser to both projects.

[2] Hanan Eshel, *The Dead Sea Scrolls and the Hasmonean State* (Grand Rapids: Eerdmans, 2008).

[3] *Ibid.*, 3. For lists of historical references in the Scrolls see Michael O. Wise, "Dating the Teacher of Righteousness and the *Floruit* of His Movement," *JBL* 122 (2003) 53–87 (67–81); Geza Vermes, "Historiographical Elements in the Qumran Writings: A Synopsis of the Textual Evidence," *JJS* 58 (2007) 121–39 (134–8). Vermes's article is mainly concerned with the designations "Kittim" and "Yawan."

[4] George J. Brooke, "Types of Historiography in the Qumran Scrolls," in George J. Brooke and Thomas Römer, eds., *Ancient and Modern Scriptural Historiography* (BETL 207; Leuven: Peeters, 2007) 211–30 (211).

The *Damascus Document* uses history for didactic purposes, to construct the identity of the movement, but its use of history is allusive.[5] Some texts such as *11QMelchizedek* entail sweeping periodization of all of history.[6] There are a few annalistic texts (4Q322a, 4Q331–333, 4Q468e-f, 4Q578),[7] but they are extremely fragmentary. History is sometimes presented in the guise of *ex eventu* prophecy (e.g. 4Q243–4, 4Q245, 4Q248, 4Q390), but it is elliptic and schematic. None of these texts provides a clear narrative of historical events pertaining to the history of the sectarian movement. Consequently, scholars who want to reconstruct that history have to rely on oblique references in works that are not constructed as historical narratives. This task is neither impossible nor invalid, but it presents considerable difficulties, and these have often been underrated. Ever since the discovery of the Scrolls, scholars have been intrigued by the veiled allusions to historical figures. These allusions are found primarily in the *Damascus Document* and in the *pesharim*, but there has also been a noteworthy attempt to distill history from the "Teacher Hymns" in the *Hodayot*. In general, however, the trend in recent scholarship has been to refrain from historical identification, and to concentrate on the literary character of the works in question. In this respect, the work of Hanan Eshel is atypical of the current field, as also is the work of Michael Wise, who has presented an important alternative to Eshel's approach but is no less concerned with historical realism.[8]

The turning away from positivistic historical search is mainly due to literary considerations. As Joseph Angel puts it in a recent monograph:

Historical conclusions based on literary works so forcefully controlled by the stereotypical motifs and stock phrases of scriptural sources are, in the words of George Brooke, 'at best somewhat forced, at worst merely arbitrary.'[9]

[5] Albert I. Baumgarten, "The Perception of the Past in the *Damascus Document*," in J. M. Baumgarten, E. G. Chazon, and A. Pinnick, eds., *The Damascus Document: A Centennial of Discovery. Proceedings of the Third International Symposium of the Orion Center for the Study of the Dead Sea Scrolls and Associated Literature, 4–8 February, 1998* (STDJ 34; Leiden: Brill, 2000) 1–15.

[6] Brooke, "Types of Historiography," 220–1. Brooke identifies several other types of historiography, including "liturgical history," and "listed history."

[7] Armin Lange with Ursula Mittmann-Richert, "Annotated List of the Texts from the Judaean Desert Classified," in Emanuel Tov, ed., *The Texts from the Judaean Desert: Indices and an Introduction to the Discoveries in the Judaean Desert Series* (DJD 39; Oxford: Clarendon, 2002) 115–64 (120): "Only a few fragments were found that appear to recall history by mentioning historical personae and their deeds by name (e.g. 4Q332–333, 4Q468e)."

[8] Michael O. Wise, *The First Messiah* (San Francisco: Harper, 1999); idem, "Dating the Teacher of Righteousness," 53–87; idem, "The Origins and History of the Teacher's Movement," in Lim and Collins, eds., *The Oxford Handbook of the Dead Sea Scrolls*, 92–122. Also exceptional, but relying on older scholarship, is James H. Charlesworth, *The Pesharim and Qumran History: Chaos or Consensus?* (Grand Rapids: Eerdmans, 2002).

[9] Joseph L. Angel, *Otherworldly and Eschatological Priesthood in the Dead Sea Scrolls* (STDJ 86; Leiden: Brill, 2010) 4, citing George J. Brooke, "The *Pesharim* and the Origin of the Dead Sea Scrolls," in M. O. Wise et al., eds., *Methods of Investigation of the Dead Sea Scrolls and the Khirbet Qumran Site: Present Realities and Future Prospects* (Annals of the New York Academy of Sciences 722; New York: The New York Academy of Sciences, 1994) 339–52 (348). Compare the

Philip Davies suggested that the authors of the *pesharim* may have inferred historical events not only from the biblical text but also from the *Hodayot*.[10] Maxine Grossman further complicated the topic by arguing for a "new historiography," that is not concerned with the original meaning. The meaning of texts depends on how they are interpreted, and interpretations can change over time.[11] While her focus is different, Grossman shares with scholars like Brooke and Davies, the insistence that the scrolls "are, themselves, literary texts presenting ideological constructions of history and not simple statements of fact."[12] Most recently, Davies has proposed that the scrolls be viewed through the lens of "collective memory," a category formulated by Maurice Halbwachs some thirty years ago,[13] and popularized in biblical and ancient Near Eastern studies by Jan Assmann's *Moses the Egyptian: The Memory of Egypt in Western Monotheism*.[14] Such history "is not to be understood in the sense of a reliable recollection, but as a shared understanding of the past that serves to create or sustain a group identity."[15] Davies then attempts to trace the way this cultural memory developed, or the "mnemohistory" of the sect.

The appreciation of the literary and ideological character of the texts is salutary and necessary. Grossman has certainly expanded the scope of historical interest in the Scrolls in interesting ways. But like Hanan Eshel, I contend that the search for historical allusions in the Scrolls is still legitimate and even necessary, if we are to understand the texts in their historical context. To say that this search has often been carried out in a naïve manner is not to say that it cannot be carried out responsibly at all. Even Davies allows that "a reconstruction of cultural memory permits some deductions about 'real' history," although his deductions are minimalist.[16]

In fact, the problems presented by our different sources vary with their genre. In no case do the texts yield a clear historical narrative, but they do yield clues of various sorts as to their historical context. I will begin with the *Damascus Document*,

---

remarks of Matthew A. Collins, *The Use of Sobriquets in the Qumran Dead Sea Scrolls* (Library of Second Temple Studies 67; London: T&T Clark, 2009) 16–18, on the problems of "naïve historicism."

[10] Philip R. Davies, "History and Hagiography," in *Behind the Essenes: History and Ideology in the Dead Sea Scrolls* (Atlanta: Scholars Press, 1987) 87–106 (91). See now also idem, "What History Can We Get from the Scrolls, and How," in C. Hempel, ed., *The Dead Sea Scrolls: Texts and Context* (STDJ 90; Leiden: Brill, 2010), 31–46 (41–42). Davies also suggests that the figure of the Wicked Priest was inferred from 4QMMT.

[11] Maxine L. Grossman, *Reading for History in the Damascus Document: A Methodological Study* (STDJ 45; Leiden: Brill, 2002) ix.

[12] *Ibid.*, x.

[13] Maurice Halbwachs, *The Collective Memory* (New York: Harper Colophon, 1980); idem, *On Collective Memory* (ed. and trans. L. A. Coser; Chicago: University of Chicago, 1992).

[14] Jan Assmann, *Moses the Egyptian: The Memory of Egypt in Western Monotheism* (Cambridge, MA: Harvard, 1997). See further Davies, "What History?" 32–34.

[15] Davies, "What History?" 32–33.

[16] *Ibid.*, 45.

which has often served as the starting point for reconstructions of sectarian history, and then proceed to the *Hodayot* and the *pesharim*.[17]

The *Damascus Document*

The first column of the *Damascus Document* is arguably as close to an historical narrative as any passage in the Dead Sea Scrolls. It, or rather the longer section CD 1:1–6:7, has been compared to the "antecedent history" of the covenant formulary, or of ancient Near Eastern treaties.[18] On a surface reading it appears to give a chronology for the beginning of the sectarian movement, three hundred and ninety years after the fall of Jerusalem to Nebuchadnezzar, followed twenty years later by the advent of the Teacher of Righteousness. But this is not historiography in the modern, critical sense. The problem is not just that it is "mnemohistory," or a tendentious reconstruction of history, but rather that it is highly schematized and formulated with a tissue of biblical allusions.

All scholars recognize that the figure of three hundred and ninety years is symbolic – it is the time allotted for the punishment of Israel in Ezek 4:5. It may well be related to the "seventy weeks of years" (= four hundred and ninety years) of Dan 9.[19] In any case, it cannot be taken as a realistic calculation of the duration from the fall of Jerusalem to the rise of the sect, any more than Daniel's four hundred and ninety years, which we know to be inaccurate. Nonetheless, even scholars who recognize that the number is symbolic, have continued to use it as a rough chronological indicator. Hanan Eshel is typical in this regard. Even though he declares, rightly, that "the number should not be understood as an exact historical reckoning," and moreover that "since the Judaeans of the Second Temple period were not aware that the Persian period had lasted more than two hundred years ... the Qumranites could not have accurately calculated the time that had elapsed from the destruction of the First Temple ...", he concludes blithely that "in any case, the group probably came into being before the Hasmonean revolt, most likely about the year 170 BCE."[20] He further claims that the reference to three hundred and ninety years is "one of the three major arguments for the identification of the Wicked Priest with Jonathan Macca-

---

[17] My concern here is with the derivation of historical information from literary texts. For a discussion of the archeological evidence, see my book, *Beyond the Qumran Community: The Sectarian Movement of the Dead Sea Scrolls* (Grand Rapids: Eerdmans, 2010) 166–208.

[18] Philip R. Davies, *The Damascus Covenant: An Interpretation of the "Damascus Document"* (JSOTSup 25; Sheffield: JSOT, 1983) 51.

[19] So Frederick F. Bruce, *Biblical Exegesis in the Qumran Texts* (Grand Rapids: Eerdmans, 1959) 59–62. If one adds the twenty years of wandering, allows forty years for the career of the Teacher, the time predicted for the eschaton (forty years after the Teacher's death, CD 20:14) would bring the total to four hundred and ninety years. See further Eshel, *The Dead Sea Scrolls and the Hasmonean State*, 57 n. 76; Collins, *Beyond the Qumran Community*, 92.

[20] Eshel, *The Dead Sea Scrolls and the Hasmonean State*, 31.

bee."[21] But as he himself had shown cogently, the figure cannot be taken literally, and it is very unlikely that the sectarians knew (or cared) how many years had passed since the exile.[22] The number cannot be salvaged by appeal to the Hellenistic Jewish historian, Demetrius the Chronographer, who calculated that the time from the fall of Jerusalem to the reign of Ptolemy IV (221–204 BCE) was three hundred and thirty-eight years and three months.[23] On this reckoning, three hundred and ninety years after the fall of Jerusalem would be 169 BCE. But there is absolutely no reason to believe that the author of CD 1 was acquainted with Demetrius, or that the latter's calculations were known in Judea. The appeal to Demetrius only becomes credible if we have prior reason to believe that the origin of the sect should be sought in the Maccabean era, and in fact we do not. We can probably infer from CD 1 that a considerable time had elapsed since the exile, and that the movement was in existence for some years before the advent of the Teacher, but cannot infer even approximate dates for the rise of the movement.

CD 1 provides one other piece of possible historical information. We are told that around the time of the advent of the Teacher, "a man of mockery arose who sprinkled upon Israel waters of falsehood and led them astray."[24] These people "sought smooth things" (דרשי בחלקות; CD 1:18). The rival figure appears again in CD 20:14–15, which refers to people who turned back with "the Man of the Lie." Hartmut Stegemann argued that the latter figure was a leader within the sectarian movement, who refused to accept the authority of the Teacher, and led a splinter group that became the Pharisees.[25] (The reference to "smooth things," חלקות, is often taken as a pun on the Pharisaic halakah.[26]) Jerome Murphy-O'Connor suggested that he was the lead-

---

[21] *Ibid.*, 43 n. 35.

[22] The latter point has also been made by Geza Vermes, "Eschatological World View in the Scrolls and in the New Testament," in S. M. Paul et al., eds., *Emanuel: Studies in the Hebrew Bible, Septuagint, and Dead Sea Scrolls in Honor of Emanuel Tov* (VTSup 94; Leiden: Brill, 2003) 479–94 (482 n. 4).

[23] Demetrius, fragment 6, from Clement of Alexandria, *Strom.* 1.21.141.1–2. See Carl R. Holladay, *Fragments from Hellenistic Jewish Authors, Volume 1: Historians* (Chico, Calif.: Scholars Press, 1983) 78–79. The appeal to Demetrius was made by Hartmut Stegemann, "The Qumran Essenes – Local Members of the Main Jewish Union in Late Second Temple Times," in J. Trebolle Barrera and L. Vegas Montaner, eds., *The Madrid Qumran Congress: Proceedings of the International Congress on the Dead Sea Scrolls, Madrid, 18–21 March 1991* (2 vols.; STDJ 11; Leiden: Brill, 1992) 1:83–166 (141–42); idem, *The Library of Qumran: On the Essenes, Qumran, John the Baptist, and Jesus* (Grand Rapids: Eerdmans, 1998) 123, and has been endorsed by several scholars.

[24] CD 1:14–15. Translation from Joseph M. Baumgarten and Daniel R. Schwartz, "*Damascus Document*," in *The Dead Sea Scrolls: Hebrew, Aramaic, and Greek Texts with English Translations, Vol. 2* (Louisville: Westminster/Tübingen: Mohr Siebeck, 1995) 13.

[25] Hartmut Stegemann, *Die Entstehung der Qumran Gemeinde* (Bonn: published privately, 1971) 227–28; Stephen Hultgren, *From the Damascus Covenant to the Covenant of the Community* (STDJ 66; Leiden: Brill, 2007) 307, regards him as a proto-Pharisee, but not as the founder of Pharisaism.

[26] See e.g. Albert I. Baumgarten, "Seekers after Smooth Things," *EDSS* 2:857–59; James C.

er of "non-Qumran Essenism," which refused to follow the Teacher into the desert.[27] But in fact all we can reasonably infer from CD is that he was a rival teacher, and that some erstwhile followers of the Teacher of Righteousness defected to him. His association with the Pharisees is plausible, even if not provable. He was evidently contemporary with the Teacher, at the formative stage of the latter's movement.

Davies makes much of the fact that CD 20:11 speaks of people who "turned away with the Men of Mockery" (plural) while CD 20:15 and CD 1:14 speak of a singular "Man of the Lie," or "Man of Mockery."[28] He suggests that there is a development from "the ideological, essentially halakhic conflict of 'Israels'" remembered at an earlier stage to a conflict of personalities. But there is no good literary reason to say that CD 20:11 and CD 20:15 reflect different stages of communal memory. The Man of the Lie was the leader of the Men of Mockery. The author is simply varying his way of referring to them. The Man of the Lie is as likely to be historical as the Teacher.[29]

One other passage from CD has been controversial in regard to the history of the movement. CD 6:7 refers to a figure called "the Interpreter of the Torah" who is clearly in the past, but the passage goes on to refer to one who will teach righteousness in the end of days. Davies has argued repeatedly that this passage comes from a time before the advent of the historical Teacher of Righteousness, and that the Interpreter was the founder of the "parent community."[30] Then the historical Teacher was identified as the one who would teach righteousness at the end of days, and he eclipsed the Interpreter in the memory of the community. I have never found this interpretation persuasive. As CD now stands, it refers both to a Teacher who was already dead when the document was finally redacted and to "one who will teach righteousness at the end of days." (In the early days of Scrolls scholarship, there was some rather wild speculation about the resurrection of the Teacher.[31]) It also refers to the Interpreter of the Law as an eschatological figure, the "star" of Balaam's oracle, in CD 7:18. The Interpreter is also a figure who will appear in the end of days in the *Florilegium* (4Q174 1–2 i 11–12).[32] In light of this, it seems easier to suppose that "Teacher of Righteousness" and "Interpreter of the Law" are interchangeable titles,

---

VanderKam, "Those Who Look for Smooth Things, Pharisees and the Oral Law," in Paul et al., eds., *Emanuel*, 465–77.

[27] Jerome Murphy-O'Connor, "The Essenes and Their History," *RB* 81 (1974) 215–44 (235); idem, "Judah the Essene and the Teacher of Righteousness," *RevQ* 10 (1981) 579–86.

[28] Davies, "What History?" 37–38. Davies also suggests that the "Israel" the mocker led astray was the original sectarian movement, but this seems gratuitous.

[29] Davies allows that the historicity of the Teacher is overwhelmingly probable ("What History?" 45), but is not sure whether the Scoffer represents an historical individual.

[30] Davies, *The Damascus Covenant*, 124; idem, "The Teacher of Righteousness at the End of Days," *RevQ* 13 (1988) 313–17; idem, "What History?" 36.

[31] André Dupont-Sommer, *The Essene Writings from Qumran* (trans. G. Vermes; Gloucester, Mass.: Peter Smith, 1973) 121. See the rebuttal by Jean Carmignac, "Le retour du docteur de Justice à la fin des jours?" *RevQ* 1 (1958–59) 235–48.

[32] The fact that the Interpreter appears both as a past and as a future figure undercuts the objec-

and that they can refer both to historical and to eschatological figures. The Interpreter in CD 6:7, then, is most probably the figure elsewhere known as the Teacher. At the least, this is surely how the text would have been read in the Teacher's community, and it is not apparent that it need ever have been read otherwise.[33] The attempt to reconstruct a "pre-Teacher" stratum in the *Damascus Document* is dubious at best.[34]

Our historical gleanings from this admittedly partial review of the *Damascus Document* are modest, but they are not without significance. It is apparent that the movement of the New Covenant had its origin in disputes over the correct interpretation of the Torah. The figures called Teacher of Righteousness/Interpreter of the Law and Man of the Lie had prominent roles in these disputes. The Document, however, gives us no clue as to their specific identity, or to the specific time at which they lived. In light of the fragments of the *Damascus Document* found at Qumran, they cannot have lived later than the middle of the first century BCE, but the *terminus a quo* is an open question.[35]

But we should also notice what the *Damascus Document* does not say. There is nothing to suggest that dispute over the High Priesthood played any part in the origin of the sect. There is no mention of a Wicked Priest. However we explain the latter fact, the silence of the *Damascus Document* on the question of High Priestly succession should cast some doubt on the popular theory that this issue was at the root of the genesis of the sect.[36] If we are to look for a plausible setting for the Teacher, the main clue provided by the *Damascus Document* is that it was a time when there were vehement disputes over halakhic interpretation.

---

tion that nowhere else is an eschatological counterpart to the Teacher implied (Davies, "The Teacher of Righteousness at the End of Days," 313; Collins, *The Use of Sobriquets*, 45).

[33] Davies's interpretation of CD 6 was refuted already by Michael Knibb, "The Teacher of Righteousness – A Messianic Title?" in P. R. Davies and R. T. White, eds., *A Tribute to Geza Vermes: Essays on Jewish and Christian Literature and History* (JSOTSup 100; Sheffield: JSOT, 1990) 51–65. Cf. John J. Collins, "Teacher and Messiah? The One Who Will Teach Righteousness at the End of Days," in E. Ulrich and J. C. VanderKam, eds., *The Community of the Renewed Covenant: The Notre Dame Symposium on the Dead Sea Scrolls* (Notre Dame: University of Notre Dame, 1994) 193–210 (194); Angel, *Otherworldly and Eschatological Priesthood*, 191–93.

[34] Collins, *The Use of Sobriquets*, 38–51, relies on Davies for his characterization of the "Formative Sectarian Period," and more generally for his developmental understanding of the terminology of the Scrolls.

[35] The earliest of these fragments dates to "the first half or middle of the first century BCE." See Joseph M. Baumgarten, "*Damascus Document*," in J. H. Charlesworth and H. W. M. Rietz, eds., *The Dead Sea Scrolls: Hebrew, Aramaic, and Greek Texts with English Translations, Vol. 3* (Louisville: Westminster/Tübingen: Mohr Siebeck, 2006) 1.

[36] See the overview of scholarship in James C. VanderKam, "Identity and History of the Community," in P. W. Flint and J. C. VanderKam, eds., *The Dead Sea Scrolls after Fifty Years: A Comprehensive Assessment* (Leiden: Brill, 1999) 487–533.

The *Hodayot*

In his article on the origins and history of the Teacher's movement for the *Oxford Handbook of the Dead Sea Scrolls*, Michael Wise takes as his basis not the *Damascus Document* or the *pesharim* but the so-called "Teacher Hymns" in the *Hodayot* (1QH^a 9:1–18:14).[37] His argument is that "the genesis of the movement would most reasonably be sought in the genuine writings of the founder, the Teacher of Righteousness, if such are available."[38] Wise argues that the "Teacher Hymns" are such writings.[39] The speaker in these hymns is a figure of great verbal power, who makes claims to divine inspiration and unique authority. Wise argues that it is inconceivable that there were two such figures within a short time in the same community.[40] I find this claim compelling, but it is far from universally accepted, and it is ultimately unprovable.[41] Accordingly, I do not think the *Hodayot* can provide as sound a foundation for historical research as Wise thinks.[42]

Nonetheless, his reading of the "Teacher Hymns" is illuminating. He rightly observes that "the question of when the movement arose is closely intertwined with the reason why it did. The heart of the matter was apparently a new interpretation of biblical and ritual law that the Teacher promulgated."[43] This observation remains significant even if the speaker in these hymns should prove to be an ideal sectarian persona, in the manner suggested by Carol Newsom,[44] rather than the historical Teacher.

Wise has no difficulty in assembling a range of citations from the *Hodayot* that show that the interpretation of the Law was the point at issue between the speaker of the "Teacher Hymns" and his opponents, for example, "They plot destruction against me, wishing to coerce me into exchanging your law which you spoke so audibly within my mind for accommodation (lit. "smooth things") for your people," 1QH^a 12:11–12. He notes the use of the expression דורשי חלקות for the opponents,

---

[37] Michael O. Wise, "The Origins and History of the Teacher's Movement," in Lim and Collins, eds., *The Oxford Handbook*, 92–122.

[38] *Ibid.*, 103.

[39] Wise accepts and builds on the work of Michael Douglas, "Power and Praise in the Hodayot: A Literary Critical Study of 1QH 9:1–18:14" (Ph.D. diss., University of Chicago, 1998) and idem, "The Teacher Hymn Hypothesis Revisited: New Data for an Old Crux," *DSD* 6 (1999) 239–66.

[40] So already Gert Jeremias, *Der Lehrer der Gerechtigkeit* (Göttingen: Vandenhoeck & Ruprecht, 1963) 176.

[41] See the sophisticated discussion of the authorship of the "Teacher hymns" by Carol Newsom, *The Self as Symbolic Space. Constructing Identity and Community at Qumran* (STDJ 52; Leiden: Brill, 2004) 287–300. Newsom grants that the Teacher hypothesis is one plausible explanation of the evidence, but favors the alternative view that these hymns should be associated with an institutional role held by successive leaders.

[42] Wise is on firmer methodological ground, in my view, in his earlier article, when he takes as his starting point the recognizable historical allusions in the Scrolls. See Wise, "Dating the Teacher of Righteousness," 65–81.

[43] Wise, "The Origins and History," 105.

[44] Above, n. 41.

and the apparent association of this phrase with the Pharisees in the *pesharim*. Wise takes seriously the references to exile in the *Hodayot*, and construes this as a political punishment imposed on the Teacher. I am not sure that the poetic language of the *Hodayot* can be pressed in this way. But essentially Wise's reading of the "Teacher Hymns" confirms the findings from the *Damascus Document* that the main point at issue was halakhic interpretation of the Torah. The *Hodayot* in themselves do not give any clear indication of the time at which these disputes took place.

The *Pesharim*

The Teacher, Man of the Lie, and Seekers after Smooth Things all reappear in the *pesharim*.

While it is universally agreed that "the *pesharim* are not history in the normal sense of the word,"[45] and that it is not their primary purpose to convey historical information, they do nonetheless contain historical references.[46] The *pesharim* are written to assure the faithful that their vindication is guaranteed by prophecy, and that prophecy is being fulfilled in their time. In order to show that prophecy is being fulfilled they refer to certain historical events that have already taken place, and this provides assurance that the prophecies are also reliable with regard to things that have not yet come to pass. In this regard, the logic of the *pesharim* resembles that of *ex eventu* prophecies in apocalypses. It requires that they refer to some actual events that were known to the intended readers. Fictional characters and events would provide no evidence of the reliability of prophecy.[47] Moreover, the *pesharim* do not construct a full narrative of the events to which they allude. Rather, they allude to isolated events as the biblical text offers occasion. In order to do this they have to rely on tradition, whether oral or written, and in many cases that tradition is no longer available to us.

The use of history in the *pesharim* is most clearly evident in *Pesher Nahum*, which explicitly mentions "[Deme]trius King of Greece," who sought to enter Jerusalem on the advice of the "Seekers after Smooth Things."[48] There follows a statement that "[Jerusalem was not given] into the hand of the kings of Greece from

---

[45] Jutta Jokiranta, "*Pesharim*: A Mirror of Self-Understanding," in *Reading the Present in the Qumran Library: The Perception of the Contemporary by Means of Scriptural Interpretations* (ed. K. De Troyer and A. Lange; Atlanta: SBL, 2005) 23–34 (27).

[46] Brooke, "Types of Historiography," 219, declares, somewhat surprisingly, that "the *pesharim* may indeed be considered as a type of historiography," because they identify references to historical events in the prophetic texts.

[47] See my articles, "Prophecy and Fulfillment in the Qumran Scrolls," in *Seers, Sibyls and Sages in Hellenistic-Roman Judaism* (JSJSup 54; Leiden: Brill, 1997) 301–14; "Prophecy and History in the *Pesharim*," in Popović, ed., *Authoritative Scriptures in Ancient Judaism*, 209–26.

[48] 4Q169 3–4 i 1–2. The commentary is on Nah 2:12–14. See Shani Berrin, *The Pesher Nahum Scroll from Qumran: An Exegetical Study of 4Q169* (STDJ 53; Leiden: Brill, 2004) 87.

Antiochus to the rise of the rulers of the Kittim, but afterwards it will be trampled" (4Q169 3–4 i 3). The reference here is to Demetrius III Akairos (94–88 BCE) who was invited by the Jewish opponents of King Alexander Jannaeus. He defeated Jannaeus in battle but suffered heavy losses and withdrew from Judea.[49] The Kittim in the *pesharim* are universally recognized as the Romans, and the reference to the trampling of Jerusalem may well be *ex eventu*, written after the conquest of Jerusalem by Pompey. This passage is exceptional in mentioning actual names, but, as Timothy Lim has put it, it gives the reader "the clearest indication that the *pesher*ist was indeed interested in history. His commentary was not just an exegetical and literary play on the words and oracles of the prophet Nahum, but in it was also a concern for contemporary life and events."[50]

The following passage in *Pesher Nahum* is an interpretation of Nah 2:13: "the lion tears enough for his cubs, and strangles prey for his lionesses." This is interpreted as "concerning the Lion of Wrath, who would strike with his great ones and the men of his counsel" (4Q169 3–4 i 5). Nahum 2:13b, "and it fills up] its cave [with prey], and its den with torn flesh," is interpreted with reference to "the Lion of Wrath" and "the Seekers after Smooth Things," and says that "he would hang men up alive."[51] The "Lion of Wrath" is almost universally identified as Alexander Jannaeus, who had eight hundred of his opponents crucified.[52] It is generally accepted that the opponents, the "Seekers after Smooth Things," are the Pharisees.[53] While this interpretation is prompted by the violent actions of the lion in the biblical text, it is apparent that the details of the interpretation are not derived exegetically, but allude to historical events known to the reader. In this case, we are fortunate to know what the events were, because they are described in some detail by Josephus.[54] The authors of the *pesher* did not have Josephus, or any other written historical narrative of these events known to us. But they evidently had a tradition about these events, whether written or oral, that corresponds in some details to the account found more than a

---

[49] Josephus, *Ant.* 13.372–416.

[50] Timothy H. Lim, *Pesharim* (London: Continuum, 2002) 68–69.

[51] Translation from Maurya P. Horgan, "Nahum *Pesher*," in J. H. Charlesworth et al., eds., *The Dead Sea Scrolls: Hebrew, Aramaic, and Greek Texts with English Translations, 6B: Pesharim, Other Commentaries and Related Documents* (Louisville: Westminster/Tübingen: Mohr Siebeck, 2002) 149.

[52] Berrin, *Pesher Nahum*, 104–9. Gregory L. Doudna, *4Q Pesher Nahum: A Critical Edition* (London: Sheffield Academic Press, 2001) 557–73, regards him as a gentile king. The "Lion of Wrath" is also mentioned in 4QpHos^b 2 2–4.

[53] Admittedly, this is not universally accepted. See Philip R. Callaway, *The History of the Qumran Community: An Investigation* (Sheffield: JSOT, 1988) 164–8; Håkan Bengtsson, *What's in a Name? A Study of Sobriquets in the Pesharim* (Uppsala: Uppsala University, 2000) 110–14. Matthew Collins, *The Use of Sobriquets*, 186–91, following Davies, argues that it was originally "an indefinite scripturally-grounded description" which only later became "a definite titular form" (191). He does not discuss the identity of the "specific group" to which the title refers in the *pesharim*.

[54] *Ant.* 13.379–383.

century later in Josephus. The sectarian community evidently had historical traditions that are not preserved in narrative form in the Dead Sea Scrolls.

In contrast to my reasoning here, Davies seems to assume that the authors of the *pesharim* had no information available to them except what could be inferred, rightly or wrongly, from texts now available to us. So he claims that "there is no evidence of the creation and preservation of a body of tradition, oral or written, about the 'teacher' such as gathered about many religious leaders."[55] It is true that we have no narratives about the Teacher, but it would be surprising indeed if not even oral narratives had existed. Indeed, many scholars would claim that the *pesharim* provide evidence of such traditions. Davies, however, claims that the ostensibly historical references to the Teacher in the *pesharim* are inferred from "textual clues and nothing else."[56] Specifically he claims that many of the references in *Pesher Habakkuk* are inferred from the *Hodayot*, which, he suggests, were read as works of the Teacher just as the biblical psalms were read as works of David.[57]

It is likely that the language of the *pesharim* is influenced by the *Hodayot* at some points, though not to the extent that Davies supposes. (For example, he claims that the "swallowing" of the Teacher by the Wicked Priest in 1QpHab 11:5 "is nothing else than an allusion to the 'devilish scheming' (*zmmu bly^{c}l*)" of 1QH^a 12:10.[58] But the obvious source of this language is Hab 1:13: "when the wicked swallows one more righteous than he.") Whether the *pesharim* infer historical events or persons from the *Hodayot* is another matter. The idea that historical events might be inferred from poetic material is not unreasonable in itself. It is arguable that the prose account of Exod 14 is inferred from the Song of the Sea in Exod 15,[59] and that the prose account of the death of Sisera in Judg 4 was inferred from the Song of Deborah in Judg 5.[60] But in each of these cases the prose account produces a clear narrative, however fictional, out of the allusive poetry. The *pesharim*, in contrast, are almost as allusive as the *Hodayot*. They are not fully intelligible to us as they stand, since they seem to allude to a fuller narrative, which they do not recount. If the authors and original readers of the *pesharim* had no further stories about the Teacher, but only the allusive language of the *Hodayot*, the disjointed references in the commentaries would have been as enigmatic to them as they are to us.

The *Hodayot* refer to "scornful liars" (מליצי כזב) at 1QH^a 10:31 and 12:9–10. These are paralleled with דרשי חלקות, seekers after smooth things, in 10:31–2, and these are further paralleled with "men of deceit" (אנשי רמיה) in 10:15–16. Davies makes

---

[55] Davies, "What History?" 41.

[56] *Ibid.*

[57] Davies, "History and Hagiography," in idem, *Behind the Essenes: History and Ideology in the Dead Sea Scrolls* (Atlanta: Scholars Press, 1987) 87–105.

[58] Davies, "History and Hagiography," 95. See Collins, "Prophecy and History," 222.

[59] Frank Moore Cross, *Canaanite Myth and Hebrew Epic: Essays in the History of the Religion of Israel* (Cambridge, Mass.: Harvard University Press, 1973) 123–44.

[60] Baruch Halpern, *The First Historians: The Hebrew Bible and History* (San Francisco: Harper & Row, 1988) 76–104.

three inferences from this usage. First, "the terms do not designate specific groups, but appear as stereotyped terms for undifferentiated, generalized opposition"; second, "there are no individual opponents at all in the *Hodayoth*"; and third, "the opposition seems to be expressed within a group to which the author once belonged."[61] In the *pesharim*, some of these terms become sobriquets for specific groups, and the man of the lie is individualized. A similar process must be posited for the *Damascus Document*.[62] "The inevitable conclusion," writes Davies,

is that H constitutes the original source of the vocabulary. We cannot conclude that H, D and the *pesharim* are all independent witnesses to real events because H makes no reference to groups or to any individuals ... Nor can we easily explain why groups in the *pesharim* should become generalized phrases in 1QH, including the pluralizing of individual terms, while key individuals should disappear in H.[63]

None of these conclusions is inevitable. As Davies himself recognizes, the generalized plurals of the *Hodayot* are "absolutely typical of the biblical Psalms."[64] Their use is a matter of genre, whether they refer to specific groups or not. The generic usage also explains the absence of individual enemies. It cannot be used as evidence that the author of the *Hodayot* did not have specific individuals or groups in mind, or that these had to be created later by exegetical inference. Neither is it apparent that all the opposition came from within a group to which the author once belonged. *Pesher Habakkuk*, at least, distinguishes three kinds of traitors (בגדים): those associated with the Man of the Lie, who did not accept the authority of the Teacher; traitors to the New Covenant, and traitors at the end of days.[65] Of these, only the second category clearly belonged to the same movement as the Teacher. There was some internal dissension, but there was also conflict with people outside the movement. This is also the situation reflected in the *Damascus Document*.

Davies's boldest suggestion, however, concerns the Wicked Priest. It is indeed noteworthy that this individual is not mentioned at all in either the *Hodayot* or the *Damascus Document*. His absence from these texts should already cast doubt on the popular theory that the sect seceded because of the succession of the High Priesthood. But this does not mean that he was invented out of whole cloth. As argued already, the ostensibly historical references in the *pesharim* would not serve any purpose if they did not correspond to a narrative that was already known to the readers.

The expression "the wicked priest," הכוהן הרשי, occurs several times in *Pesher Habakkuk* and once in *Pesher Psalms*ᵃ (4Q171). There is also a reference in 1QpHab

---

[61] Davies, "What History?" 40.
[62] Davies' understanding of the development of the terminology underlies M. A. Collins' developmental view of the use of sobriquets. Collins, *The Use of Sobriquets*, 182–207.
[63] Davies, "What History?" 40.
[64] *Ibid.*
[65] 1QpHab 2:1–6.

8:16 to "the priest who rebelled."⁶⁶ In none of these cases does the underlying biblical text mention a priest, so the inference that the wicked person in question was a priest is not derived exegetically. Neither is there any mention of a priestly adversary in the *Hodayot*. Davies suggests that the existence of the Wicked Priest was inferred from 4QMMT, which has often been read by modern scholars as a letter from the Teacher to the High Priest of the day.⁶⁷ But 4QMMT does not refer to the addressee as a priest – the idea that he was in fact a High Priest is inferred from the phrase "the welfare of your people" (Composite Text, C 27).⁶⁸ Neither is there any indication that the addressee of 4QMMT was wicked. On the contrary, he is told "we have seen (that) you have wisdom and knowledge of the Torah" (Composite Text C 27–28). It is hard to see how anyone could infer from this text that the recipient was a "Wicked Priest," unless there was also a tradition that the High Priest had rejected the overture. Some scholars have indeed suggested that such a tradition is reflected in 4QpPsᵃ 3–10 iv 8–9, which says that the Wicked Priest tried to kill the Teacher "and the Torah that he sent to him,"⁶⁹ and this may well be correct. But the rejection of the "Torah" cannot be inferred from the text of 4QMMT; it requires some independent memory or tradition.

But if the Wicked Priest was an historical figure whose conflict with the Teacher was a subject of tradition, why is he not mentioned in the *Damascus Document* or the *Hodayot*? Nothing in the *pesharim* suggests that the conflict between the Teacher and the Wicked Priest was responsible for the formation of the Teacher's movement or its withdrawal from Judean society. It did not pertain to the origin of the movement. It most probably happened late in the Teacher's career, when he had already formulated his "Torah." The simplest explanation of the absence of the Wicked Priest from the *Hodayot* is that this conflict had not yet taken place when the hymns were composed. The *Damascus Document* contains references to the death of the Teacher, but these are generally recognized as secondary up-dates. The core of that work too, including columns 1–6, may well have pre-dated the conflict with the Wicked Priest.

The identification of the Wicked Priest is beset with difficulties, not only because of the use of sobriquets but also because the *pesharim* are full of biblical allusions, and it is often difficult to discern what should be taken literally. So for example 1QpHab 11:12–15 says that the Wicked Priest "walked in the ways of inebriety, in order that the thirst might be consumed." This brings to mind Alexander Jannaeus,

---

⁶⁶ Timothy H. Lim, "Wicked Priest," *EDSS* 2:973–76 (973).

⁶⁷ Davies, "What History?" 43.

⁶⁸ Elisha Qimron and John Strugnell, *Qumran Cave 4. V. Miqsat Maʿase Ha-Torah* (DJD 10; Oxford: Clarendon, 1994) 63.

⁶⁹ DJD 10:175; Hanan Eshel, "4QMMT and the History of the Hasmonean Period," in *Reading 4QMMT: New Perspectives on Qumran Law and History* (ed. J. Kampen and M. Bernstein; SBLSymS 2; Atlanta: SBL, 1996) 53–65; idem, *The Dead Sea Scrolls and the Hasmonean State*, 46–47; Wise, *The First Messiah*, 65–68.

whose death from quatrain fever was attributed to heavy drinking,[70] or Simon Maccabee, who was drunk at a banquet when he was killed.[71] But Józef Milik pointed out that the language of the passage draws on Deut 29:18, "to devastate the dry and the irrigated land together," and concluded that the drunkenness was metaphorical.[72] The reference would be all the more appropriate if the priest in question had a reputation for drinking, but it is difficult to be sure. Moreover, the possibility that the expression "the Wicked Priest" was used to refer to more than one figure cannot be ruled out.[73] The crucial passages for our present purpose are those that refer to a conflict with the Teacher.[74]

The Wicked Priest has most often been identified with Jonathan Maccabee, with a minority vote for his brother Simon. Hanan Eshel argued that the identification with Jonathan was supported by three main considerations: the reference to three hundred and ninety years in CD 1, the death of the Wicked Priest at the hands of enemies who abused his body, and "the fact that he was first associated with the true faith and betrayed the laws only after becoming ruler of Israel."[75] We have already seen that the reference to three hundred and ninety years can bear no chronological weight. It is not explicitly stated that the Wicked Priest met his death at the hands of his enemies, although he was given into their hands (4QpPs[a] 3–10 iv 10; 1QpHab 9:10) and suffered some form of affliction. The language describing the affliction is vague: "and horrors of evil diseases were at work in him, and acts of vengeance on his carcass of flesh,"[76] or "God gave into the hands of his enemies to humble him with disease for annihilation in bitterness of soul."[77] Jonathan Maccabee was certainly "given into the hands of his enemies." He was captured by the Syrian general Trypho, held for a time, and then killed.[78] We are not told that he was tortured or mutilated, although Milik pleaded that this was "a most probable deduction."[79] The passage could be applied at least as well to Hyrcanus II, whose ears were mutilated while he was in Parthian custody.[80] Jonathan Maccabee presumably had a good

---

[70] *Ant.* 13.398.

[71] 1 Macc 16:16.

[72] Józef T. Milik, *Ten Years of Discovery in the Wilderness of Judaea* (London: SCM, 1959) 69–70.

[73] The suggestion of Adam S. van der Woude, "Wicked Priest or Wicked Priests? Reflections on the Identification of the Wicked Priest in the Habakkuk Commentary," *JJS* 33 (1982) 349–59, that *Pesher Habakkuk* refers to several Hasmonean priests in sequence, is untenable, but the possibility that there is reference to more than one individual remains. See Timothy H. Lim, "The Wicked Priests of the Groningen Hypothesis," *JBL* 112 (1993) 415–25.

[74] See Collins, *Beyond the Qumran Community,* 111–13.

[75] Eshel, *The Dead Sea Scrolls and the Hasmonean State,* 43 n. 35.

[76] 1QpHab 9:2. Translation from Maurya P. Horgan, "Pesharim," in Charlesworth, ed., *The Dead Sea Scrolls. Hebrew, Aramaic, and Greek Texts with English Translations. Vol. 6B. Pesharim,* 1–247 (177).

[77] 1QpHab 9:10–11. Translation from Horgan, ibid.

[78] 1 Macc 16:16; Josephus, *Ant.* 13.228.

[79] Milik, *Ten Years,* 69.

[80] Josephus, *J.W.* 1.107–119; *Ant.* 13.405–432.

reputation when he came to power. Whether he subsequently changed his attitude to the laws (cf. 1QpHab 8:10) is not clear. Again, this passage is a better fit for Hyrcanus II. He first came to power as High Priest when his mother Salome Alexandra became queen. His father, Alexander Jannaeus, had been at odds with the Pharisees, but Salome made peace with them, and followed their legal rulings. According to Josephus, "she permitted the Pharisees to do as they liked in all matters, and also commanded the people to obey them."[81] The Pharisees, the Seekers after Smooth Things, were the archenemies of the Teacher and his followers. The latter would reasonably have expected Hyrcanus II, as High Priest, to continue the policies of his father, but when he came to power he adopted the rival interpretation of the laws.

The one point on which all our sources agree is that the interpretation of the laws (and not the High Priestly succession) was the *raison d'être* of the Teacher's movement. The transition from Alexander Jannaeus to Salome Alexandra and Hyrcanus II provides a very plausible occasion for conflict between the Teacher and a High Priest.[82] The "Torah" that the Teacher is said to have sent to the Wicked Priest can be understood plausibly as an attempt to win him back from accepting the Pharisaic halakah, and the identification with 4QMMT is attractive, even if it is not ultimately provable.[83] We do not know of any such conflict over the interpretation of the Torah in the time of Jonathan Maccabee.

Many scholars have dismissed Hyrcanus II as simply too late to be identified with the Wicked Priest, but these scholars have generally accepted the three hundred and ninety years of CD 1 as approximately correct, and have also assumed that the conflict between the Teacher and the Priest pertained to the origin of the sect. Neither of these assumptions is reliable. The Teacher's movement may have been in existence for a considerable time before the conflict with the High Priest. If that conflict took place about 75 BCE near the end of the Teacher's career and the beginning of that of Hyrcanus, the chronology poses no great difficulties. The conflict with the Man of the Lie, in contrast, would have to be placed earlier in the Teacher's career.

There are indications in the Scrolls that the "end" was expected about forty years after the death of the Teacher (CD 20:14; 4QpPs^a 3–10 ii), and also that the end was felt to be overdue when *Pesher Habakkuk* was composed (1QpHab 7:7). "Forty

---

[81] *Ant.* 13.408–409.

[82] See especially Wise, "The Origins and History of the Teacher's Movement," 107–9.

[83] The editors of 4QMMT argued that "the 'they' group is the Pharisees. This is evident from the similarity between the halakah of the opponents of the sect and rabbinic halakah: the 'they' group must have been the predecessors of the rabbis, namely the Pharisees" (DJD 10:175). This is disputed by Charlotte Hempel, "The Context of 4QMMT and Comfortable Theories," in Hempel, ed., *The Dead Sea Scrolls: Texts and Context*, 275–92 (287–8), who suggests that the "they" group is "a misguided priestly group." She does not address, however, the alleged similarity between the halakha of this group and that attributed to the Pharisees in the rabbinic writings. The point at issue is what halakhic teaching was being opposed. Hempel is probably correct, however, that MMT does not speak of sectarian origins, in the sense of the initial formation of the group it represents, although it may relate to a widening breach between that group and the ruling powers of the day.

years," to be sure, was a round number, indicating the approximate length of a generation. There is no indication in *Pesher Habakkuk* or elsewhere that the "end" was expected on a specific date. We do not know exactly when the *pesharim* were written. They are clearly later than the Roman conquest of Jerusalem in 63 BCE. If Hyrcanus II is identified as the Wicked Priest, then *Pesher Habakkuk* must be later than his mutilation in 40 BCE. Michael Wise argues that 1QpHab 9:4–7 refers to the plundering of Jerusalem by the Roman general Sosius in 37 BCE.[84] This is not certain, but a date in the 30's seems likely. There is no reference to the reign of Herod (37–4 BCE). If *Pesher Habakkuk* was composed in the 30's, then a date in the 70's is likely for the death of the Teacher. It is not implausible that he lived through the death of Jannaeus and the inauguration of Hyrcanus II as High Priest.

Conclusion

I would argue then that some historical information can be inferred from the Dead Sea Scrolls, especially the *pesharim*, although this information is neither as ample nor as certain as has often been supposed. The authors of the *pesharim* clearly had traditions available to them, whether oral or written, that we do not now have in textual form. Figures like the "Man of the Lie" and "Wicked Priest" cannot be dismissed as fictional, even if their identities are obscure. While the ostensibly historical allusions in the Scrolls are always tendentious, they do at least permit us to infer the general context in which the sect developed.

As Wise has observed, "the question of when the movement arose is closely intertwined with the reason why it did."[85] All indications are that this reason was a conflict over the interpretation of the Torah. It was not a dispute over the High Priesthood. The conflict between the Teacher and the Wicked Priest was not the *raison d'être* of the movement, but probably happened late in the Teacher's career. A very plausible occasion for that conflict is provided by the transition of power after the death of Alexander Jannaeus, when Alexandra Salome and Hyrcanus II decided to adopt the halakah of the Pharisees. It may be noted in passing that this dating of the Teacher's activity is compatible with the revised dating of the Qumran settlement by Jodi Magness,[86] but the relation between the archaeology and the texts is a matter that goes beyond the agenda of this essay.

I should be reluctant to speculate further on the career of the Teacher on the basis of allusions in the *Hodayot*, and also reluctant to postulate a mnemohistory of sectarian traditions, based on hypothetical ordering of passages within the *Damascus Document* (other than the passages that refer to the death of the Teacher) or on as-

---

[84] Wise, "Dating the Teacher," 81.
[85] Wise, "The Origins and History," 105.
[86] Jodi Magness, *The Archaeology of Qumran and the Dead Sea Scrolls* (Grand Rapids: Eerdmans, 2002) 65.

sumptions that all the allusions in the *Hodayot* must be derived from extant textual allusions.

The historical information that can be gleaned from the Scrolls is quite limited, and there was no doubt an element of 'naïve historicism' in earlier scholarship in this regard. But the little information that can be gleaned is very important for understanding the context of the Scrolls, as Hanan Eshel, more than most scholars of his generation, appreciated.

CHAPTER TEN

"Enochic Judaism" and the Sect of the Dead Sea Scrolls

The oldest extant copies of books of Enoch are found among the Dead Sea Scrolls. Since they are found in multiple copies, it is reasonable to assume that they were of more than passing interest to the people who hid the scrolls in the caves. Moreover, there are clear and well-known affinities between the early Enochic books and some of the core sectarian writings from the Scrolls. The *Apocalypse of Weeks* and the *Animal Apocalypse* each describes the rise of an elect group, in veiled language that is commonly understood to point to events in the Hellenistic age. A similar development is described in the opening column of the *Damascus Document*, which refers to a "plant root" that rises from Aaron and Israel, 390 years after the Exile. The Enochic apocalypses share with the *Damascus Document* a theology of history which regards the emergence of this group as climactic, and also an interest in the agency of supernatural powers, which is typical of apocalyptic literature and of other sectarian texts found at Qumran, such as the *Community Rule* and the *War Scroll*. In light of these affinities it is widely accepted that the Enochic texts are representative of the milieu in which the movement described in the *Damascus Document* developed. The authors of the sectarian scrolls were evidently familiar with the Enochic writings and were influenced by them in various ways. All of this has been widely accepted from a relatively early point in the history of research on the scrolls.[1]

Much less clear, however, is the exact relationship between the authors and tradents of the early Enoch literature ("Enochic Judaism") and the members of the "new covenant" of the *Damascus Document*, or the followers of the Teacher of

---

[1] The relation between the Scrolls and the Enochic literature, or more broadly "the Palestinian apocalyptic tradition," is discussed with various nuances by P. Grelot, "L'eschatologie des Esséniens et le livre d'Hénoch," *RevQ* 1(1958) 113–31; M. Hengel, *Judaism and Hellenism* (Philadelphia: Fortress, 1974) 1.175–210; D. Dimant, "Qumran Sectarian Literature," in M. E. Stone, ed., *Jewish Writings from the Second Temple Period* (CRINT 2/2; Philadelphia: Fortress, 1984) 483–550, esp. 544–5; F. García Martínez, "Qumran Origins and Early History: A Groningen Hypothesis," *Folia Orientalia* 25 (1988) 113–36, esp. 119; P. R. Davies, "Three Essene Texts," in P. R. Davies, *Behind the Essenes. History and Ideology in the Dead Sea Scrolls* (BJS 94; Atlanta: Scholars Press, 1987) 107–34; "The Prehistory of the Qumran Community," in D. Dimant and U. Rappaport, eds., *The Dead Sea Scrolls. Forty Years of Research* (Leiden: Brill, 1992) 116–25, esp. 123; J. J. Collins, "Was the Dead Sea Sect an Apocalyptic Movement?" in L. H. Schiffman, ed., *Archaeology and History in the Dead Sea Scrolls* (JSPSup 8; Sheffield: Sheffield Academic Press, 1990) 25–51; idem, *Apocalypticism in the Dead Sea Scrolls* (London: Routledge, 1997) 18–24; G. Boccaccini, *Beyond the Essene Hypothesis. The Parting of the Ways between Qumran and Enochic Judaism* (Grand Rapids: Eerdmans, 1998).

Righteousness. This relationship has been formulated in various ways. In recent years, Gabriele Boccaccini has staked out a distinctive position on this issue, arguing that "Enochic Judaism is the modern name for the mainstream body of the Essene party, from which the Qumran community parted as a radical, dissident, and marginal offspring."[2]

This radical proposal is based on several assumptions about the Essenes and "the Qumran community" that have taken hold in the course of the history of research. In my judgment, several of these underlying assumptions are seriously flawed and confuse rather than clarify the relationship between the Enochic writings and the sect known to us from the Scrolls.

The Essenes

The idea that the Dead Sea Scrolls were of Essene provenance was proposed almost immediately after the discovery of the first scrolls in 1947 by E. L. Sukenik and Millar Burrows, and argued in some detail by A. Dupont-Sommer as early as 1950.[3] Two considerations were fundamental to this identification. One was the testimony of Pliny the Elder that there was an Essene settlement near the shore of the Dead Sea.[4] The excavation of the site by Roland de Vaux was widely accepted as confirming the view that the ruins at Khirbet Qumran were the remains of this Essene settlement.[5] The other was the similarity between the kind of community described in the *Community Rule* and the Essenes as described by Josephus and Philo. The similarity lay in the segregated life of a community with common possessions, and the multi-year process of admission.[6] As many scholars have pointed out in later years, the correspondences are by no means perfect. Pliny and Philo emphasize that the Essenes lived without women, although Josephus reports that a second order of the sect allowed marriage.[7] Celibacy is not explicitly required in the Scrolls, although the *Community Rule* makes no mention of women or children. Whether women were present at the site of Qumran remains a contentious issue, especially with regard to the number of female skeletons in the cemetery.[8] Moreover, many concerns

---

[2] Boccaccini, *Beyond the Essene Hypothesis*, 16.

[3] A. Dupont-Sommer, *Aperçus préliminaires sur les manuscrits de la mer Morte* (Paris: Maisonneuve, 1950); *The Essene Writings from Qumran* (trans. G. Vermes; Gloucester, MA: Smith, 1973) 11.

[4] For the text see G. Vermes and M. Goodman, *The Essenes according to the Classical Sources* (Sheffield: Sheffield Academic Press, 1989) 32–3.

[5] R. de Vaux, *Archaeology and the Dead Sea Scrolls* (rev. ed.; Oxford: Oxford University Press, 1973).

[6] T. S. Beall, *Josephus' Description of the Essenes Illustrated by the Dead Sea Scrolls* (SNTSMS 58; Cambridge: Cambridge University Press, 1988); J. J. Collins, "Essenes," *ABD* 2.619–26.

[7] *JW* 2.160.

[8] See J. Magness, *The Archaeology of Qumran and the Dead Sea Scrolls* (Grand Rapids: Eerdmans, 2002) 163–87.

that are prominent in the Scrolls (messianic expectations, apocalyptic beliefs) do not figure at all in the accounts of the Essenes. Whether or not one accepts the identification of the community as Essene depends on whether one is more impressed by the quite distinctive similarities or by the absence of prominent features of the Scrolls from the Greek and Latin accounts. Two points should be stressed, however.

First, the Qumran text that provides the strongest basis for the Essene identification is the description of the *yahad* in the *Community Rule*. There are also significant points of contact with the *Damascus Rule*. The latter provides explicitly for women and children, but Josephus informs us that there was a second order of Essenes who married and had children. Hence the view arose that the differences between the two Rules could be explained on the assumption that the *Community Rule* related to the "monastic" Essenes who lived at Qumran, while the Damascus Rule related to the "marrying" Essenes who lived at other locations.[9] This view is problematic, as we shall see, but in any case the attribution of any of these texts to the Essenes depends primarily on their description of community structures. The case for identifying texts (such as the *Enoch* books or *Jubilees*), that do not describe community structures, as Essene, is much more tenuous than the case for the rule books.

The second point to be stressed is that the accounts of the Essenes in Pliny, Philo and Josephus do not on any reckoning give a complete or accurate description of the communities known from the Hebrew rule books. This in itself is not surprising. Philo and Josephus most probably relied on a source that stood in the tradition of Greek ethnography, whether its author was Jewish or Gentile.[10] They are not eyewitness accounts, despite the claim of Josephus that he had experimented with life as an Essene.[11] Given the unreliability of the Greek and Latin accounts, one may question whether anything is gained by referring to the communities known from the Scrolls as Essene. To do so is to privilege outsider accounts over the primary evidence. It is even more problematic when texts that do not correspond to these accounts at all are labelled "Essene" because they correspond at some point with the Dead Sea Scrolls.

The Hasidim

At an early point in research on the scrolls, a consensus developed that the sect described in the Dead Sea Scrolls had its origin in the Hasidim who are mentioned in the books of Maccabees.[12] The reasons for this consensus were circumstantial, and

---

[9] E.g. G. Vermes, *The Complete Dead Sea Scrolls in English* (London: Penguin, 1997) 34–45.

[10] See R. Bergmeier, *Die Essener-Berichte des Flavius Josephus* (Kampen: Kok Pharos, 1993) 60–72; M. Smith, "The Descriptions of the Essenes in Josephus and the Philosophoumena," *HUCA* 29 (1958) 273–313.

[11] Josephus, *Life*, 9–11.

[12] J. T. Milik, *Ten Years of Discovery in the Wilderness of Judaea* (SBT 26; London: SCM,

were related to the intuition that the emergence of the sect was related to the usurpation of the high priesthood by the Hasmoneans. Since the phrase "sons of Zadok" is used as an honorific title in the *Damascus Document*, the sectarians were assumed to be supporters of the Zadokite line. The Hasidim, we are told, abandoned their resistance to the Seleucids when a Zadokite, Alcimus, was appointed high priest.[13] Moreover, the movement described in CD 1 had wandered like blind men for twenty years, a period that could be equated with the years from the rise of the Hasidim to the usurpation of the high priesthood by Jonathan Maccabee in 152 BCE.

Unfortunately, we have very little information about the Hasidim.[14] Nonetheless, some scholars painted an elaborate picture of them, and saw them as the authors of the apocalyptic books of Enoch and Daniel, which refer to the rise of some distinctive group around the time of the Maccabean revolt.[15] It was in this context that the idea that the tradents of the Enoch literature were the forerunners of "the Qumran community" was first introduced into scholarship.

The scholarly reconstruction of the Hasidim, however, was highly hypothetical and was widely criticized.[16] It does not seem possible to attribute every book that refers to the rise of a group in the Maccabean era to a single party. The references to the Hasidim in the books of Maccabees do not hint at the kind of apocalyptic ideas found in the books of Enoch. Accordingly, the "Hasidim hypothesis" fell into disrepute. Philip Davies questioned whether the Hasidim existed as an organized party at all.[17] It is apparent that some group of people, whether organized or not, were identified as Hasidim at the time of the Maccabean revolt, but unfortunately very little can be said about them except that for a time they supported the Maccabees.

1958) 80. F. M. Cross, *The Ancient Library of Qumran* (3rd ed.; Sheffield: Sheffield Academic Press, 1995, originally published in 1961) 104; Hengel, *Judaism and Hellenism*, 1.175–80; H. Stegemann, *Die Entstehung der Qumrangemeinde* (Bonn: published privately, 1971) 250.

[13] 1 Macc 7:12–13.

[14] In addition to the reference in 1 Macc 7, they are mentioned in 1 Macc 2:42, where they are described as "mighty warriors of Israel, everyone who offered himself willingly for the law," and in 2 Macc 14:6, where they are said to be followers of Judas Maccabee. See J. Kampen, *The Hasideans and the Origin of Pharisaism* (SCS 24; Atlanta: Scholars Press, 1988); "Hasidim," *ABD* 3.66–67.

[15] Hengel, *Judaism and Hellenism*, 1.175–80; O. Plöger, *Theocracy and Eschatology* (Richmond: Knox, 1968) 23; M. Delcor, "Le milieu d'origine et le développement de l'apocalyptique juive," in W. C. van Unnik, ed., *La Littérature Juive entre Tenach et Mischna* (Leiden: Brill, 1974) 101–17.

[16] J. J. Collins, *The Apocalyptic Vision of the Book of Daniel* (HSM 16; Missoula: Scholars Press, 1977) 201–5; P. R. Davies, "Hasidim in the Maccabean Period," *JJS* 28 (1977) 127–40; G. W. E. Nickelsburg, "Social Aspects of Palestinian Jewish Apocalypticism," in D. Hellholm, ed., *Apocalypticism in the Mediterranean World and the Near East* (Tübingen: Mohr Siebeck, 1983) 641–54, esp. 647–8.

[17] Davies, "Hasidim," 140; idem, "The Prehistory of Qumran," 118.

A split in the emerging movement

The discussion of the origins of the sectarian movement was given a new impetus by the dissertation of Hartmut Stegemann, *Die Entstehung der Qumrangemeinde* which was completed in 1965 and published privately in 1971. Building on the earlier work of G. Jeremias,[18] Stegemann distinguished clearly between the figures known in the scrolls as "the wicked priest" and "the man of the lie." The latter was a figure within the Hasidim, who rejected the claims to authority of the Teacher of Righteousness. The followers of "the man of the lie" became the Pharisees. Those who accepted the authority of the Teacher became the Essenes or "the Qumran community." Stegemann argued that the Teacher was actually the legitimate High Priest in Jerusalem, and that he was displaced by Jonathan Maccabee.[19] This view is highly hypothetical, and rests on an unwarranted inference from the fact that the Teacher is called "the priest" without qualification (4Q171 3:15 =4QpPs^a).[20] In his later work, Stegemann realized that the movement founded by the Teacher could not be equated with "the Qumran community." Rather, he argued that "the Essene union" founded by the Teacher was "the largest religious organization in the Palestinian Judaism of that time."[21] The Qumran settlement was only established around 100 BCE, some 50 years after the foundation of the "union."[22] Stegemann was not concerned with the place of the Enoch literature in this process. He was essentially in continuity with the work of earlier scholars such as Cross and Milik insofar as he regarded the Essenes, or "the Qumran community" as an offshoot of the Hasidim.

Stegemann's work was taken up by Jerome Murphy-O'Connor, who added to it some hypotheses of his own.[23] Most important of these was the suggestion that "Damascus" in the *Damascus Document* was a code name for Babylon, and that the movement had actually originated in the eastern Diaspora. Murphy-O'Connor claimed that the laws preserved in the *Damascus Document* reflect this early stage in the history of the movement. The movement did not originate in Palestine as a reaction to Hellenism, but arose from reflection on the causes of the Exile.[24] Consequently, Murphy-O'Connor did not associate the early stage of this movement with the Hasidim, but referred to it as "Essene" from the beginning. He accepted Stege-

---

[18] G. Jeremias, *Der Lehrer der Gerechtigkeit* (Göttingen: Vandenhoeck & Ruprecht, 1963).

[19] Stegemann, *Die Entstehung*, 102.

[20] See my criticism of this position in J. J. Collins, "The Origin of the Qumran Community," in J. J. Collins, *Seers, Sibyls, and Sages in Hellenistic-Roman Judaism* (JSJSup 54; Leiden: Brill, 1997) 246–7; also M. O. Wise, "The Teacher of Righteousness and the High Priest of the Intersacerdotium: Two Approaches," *RevQ* 14 (1989–90) 587–613.

[21] Stegemann, *The Library of Qumran. On the Essenes, Qumran, John the Baptist and Jesus* (Grand Rapids: Eerdmans, 1998) 150.

[22] Magness, *The Archaeology of Qumran*, 65, dates the ocupation of the site to "some time between 100–50 B. C. E."

[23] J. Murphy-O'Connor, "The Essenes and Their History," *RB* 81 (1974) 215–44.

[24] *Ibid.*, 222.

mann's view that the Teacher was High Priest, deposed by Jonathan. Then "the ejected Sadokite took refuge with the Essenes."[25] An effect of his arrival was "a split within the Essene movement in which he found himself confronted by the Man of Lies."[26] In Murphy-O'Connor's reconstruction, both the followers of the Teacher and those of "the man of the lie" were Essenes. The followers of the Teacher withdrew to the desert and established the community at Qumran, while the others became "non-Qumran Essenism," which, claims Murphy-O'Connor, "preserved its identity long after the split."[27]

At no point does Murphy-O'Connor attempt to justify his use of the name "Essene" with reference to the movement before the arrival of the Teacher. Even if one accepts his theory that the laws of the *Damascus Document* belong to that phase,[28] they provide little if any basis for such an identification. As we have noted already, the key points of similarity with the Greek accounts of the Essenes are found in the *Community Rule*, which Murphy-O'Connor regards as the rule for the Teacher's community at Qumran. Moreover, while Josephus says that there was a second order of Essenes, and both he and Philo claim that the Essenes were numerous and not confined to one location, neither gives any hint that there was a schism between the two orders, or that the "monastic" Essenes were confined to one location. On the contrary, he says that the marrying Essenes were in agreement with the others on "the way of life, usages and customs," except for the issue of marriage.[29] Underlying Murphy-O'Connor's theory is the unexamined assumption that the *Community Rule* was written specifically for Qumran, and that that community was *sui generis*. As we shall see below, this assumption cannot withstand a careful reading of the *Community Rule*.

Murphy-O'Connor's theses were taken up enthusiastically by Philip Davies. Davies also added his own distinctive suggestions, most notably that CD 6:10–11 reflected the expectation of the Teacher of Righteousness as a future messianic figure and so belonged to a "pre-Qumran" stage of the history of the sect.[30] In Davies' view "CD has been now seen to reflect the organization of the *parent* community

---

[25] *Ibid.*, 233.

[26] *Ibid.*

[27] *Ibid.*, 235.

[28] For subsequent literature on this issue, see C. Hempel, *The Damascus Texts* (Sheffield: Sheffield Academic Press, 2000) 49–53.

[29] *JW* 2.160.

[30] P. R. Davies, *The Damascus Covenant* (JSOTS 25; Sheffield: JSOT, 1983) 124; idem, "The Teacher of Righteousness at the End of Days," *RevQ* 13 (1988) 313–7. See the criticism of this position by M. Knibb, "The Teacher of Righteousness – A Messianic Title?" in P. R. Davies and R. T. White eds., *A Tribute to Geza Vermes: Essays on Jewish and Christian Literature and History* (JSOTSup 100; Sheffield: Sheffield Academic Press, 1990) 51–65, and J. J. Collins, "Teacher and Messiah? The One Who Will Teach Righteousness at the End of Days," in E. Ulrich and J. VanderKam, eds., *The Community of the Renewed Covenant* (Notre Dame, IN: University of Notre Dame, 1994) 193–210.

from which the Qumran group emerged."³¹ The "Qumran community" was formed by breaking away from this parent group, not by breaking away from the rest of Judaism. References to the Teacher as a past figure at the beginning and end of CD were attributed to a "Qumran recension." Davies equated "Essene" with "pre-Qumran,"³² and regarded the "Qumran Essenes" as an offshoot of the main body of Essenes. Finally, he declared that "it seems unnecessarily pedantic" not to call the *Apocalypse of Weeks* or *Jubilees* "Essene,"³³ thereby in effect reconstituting the all-inclusive Hasidim of earlier scholarship under a new name.³⁴

Unlike Davies, Florentino García Martínez and Adam van der Woude wrote in part to correct the proposal of Murphy-O'Connor, by reasserting the Palestinian roots of the movement. Nonetheless, they accepted some key features of his proposal. So they proposed, *inter alia*, "to make a clear distinction between the origins of the Essene movement and those of the Qumran group" and "to seek the origins of the Qumran group in a split which occurred within the Essene movement in consequence of which the group loyal to the Teacher of Righteousness was finally to establish itself in Qumran."³⁵ García Martínez and van der Woude differed clearly from Murphy-O'Connor and Davies insofar as they rejected the proposed Babylonian origin of the movement. They also postulated "ideological roots in the apocalyptic tradition in which we find determinism, the type of biblical interpretation, the angelology, the idea of the eschatological temple, etc., that emerge as characteristic of the Essene ideology."³⁶ Murphy-O'Connor had not concerned himself with the ideological roots of the movement, but Davies, as we have seen, was eager to extend the name "Essene" to the *Epistle of Enoch* and *Jubilees*.

Gabriele Boccaccini builds explicitly on the work of Davies and García Martínez. "Their approach," he writes, "has the great merit of having introduced a fundamental distinction between Essene origins and Qumran origins ... The history of the Qumran community may not coincide with the history of the Essene movement."³⁷ Boccaccini, however, is more specific in his identification of Essenism: "what the ancient historians called Essenism encompasses not only the Qumran community but also what modern scholars have identified, on the basis of its extant documents, as Enochic Judaism."³⁸ His understanding of "Enochic Judaism" is a reformulation

---

[31] Davies, *Behind the Essenes*, 18.
[32] *Ibid.*, 30.
[33] Davies, *ibid.*, 109, 129.
[34] Davies ("The Prehistory of Qumran," 118) protests that "Murphy-O'Connor's designation 'Essenes' at least corresponds to a real movement attested and described in several ancient sources." He does not bother to ask whether these descriptions in any way correspond to the entities associated with "the prehistory of Qumran."
[35] F. García Martínez and A. S. van der Woude, "A Groningen Hypothesis of Qumran Origins," *RevQ* 14 (1990) 521–41, esp. 537.
[36] García Martínez and van der Woude, "A Groningen Hypothesis," 537.
[37] Boccaccini, *Beyond the Essene Hypothesis*, 7.
[38] *Ibid.*, 11.

of the view of "apocalyptic" proposed by his teacher, Paolo Sacchi.[39] It was a stream of thought, or intellectual movement, characterized by a "generative idea": the understanding of evil as "an autonomous reality antecedent to humanity's ability to choose."[40] Boccaccini does not confine "Enochic Judaism" to the Enoch literature, but extends it to writings in which the figure of Enoch is not central, such as *Jubilees*, the *Testaments of the Twelve Patriarchs*, or *4 Ezra*. In his view, however, it does not include all apocalyptic literature, but is ideologically opposed to such works as Daniel and Revelation. "Enochic Judaism" originated in an ancient schism within the Jewish priesthood, and emerged as a distinct, anti-Zadokite, movement somewhere in the fourth or third centuries BCE.[41] *Jubilees*, dated to the Maccabean era after the overthrow of the Zadokite line, marks an important transition in the development of this tradition, as it "makes Moses a revealer like Enoch and Jacob."[42] It thus paves the way for the emphasis on Mosaic revelation in the Dead Sea Scrolls. The *Damascus Document* is regarded as "pre-Qumran." The split between the group that became the Qumran community and the main body of the Essenes came about because the Teacher called for a greater degree of separation from Israel and the temple than many were willing to accept.[43] In Boccaccini's view, "the Qumran sectarians did not seek an organized relationship with the Essenes."[44] Rather, "the community of the Dead Sea Scrolls virtually ignored other groups, including its parent movement, and received from them an equally open disdain."[45]

Boccaccini relates the "split" between Qumran and the Essenes to the different accounts of the latter in the Greek and Latin sources. Pliny knew only one Essene settlement, by the Dead Sea. Philo and Josephus speak of an association spread throughout the land. Boccaccini suggests that the Jewish authors were referring to the main body of the Essenes, while Pliny knew only the marginal group at Qumran. Neither the Jewish nor the Gentile authors, however, show any awareness of a schism in the Essene movement.

Boccaccini is certainly right that the Essenes cannot be equated without remainder with the Qumran community. He is also right that there is significant ideological continuity between "Enochic Judaism" and the *yahad*. At several points, however, the discussion is confused by the uncritical acceptance of hypotheses advanced in earlier discussion that have gradually, and mistakenly, been treated as established facts.

---

[39] P. Sacchi, *Jewish Apocalyptic and Its History* (JSPSup 20; Sheffield: Sheffield Academic Press, 1997).
[40] Boccaccini, *Beyond the Essene Hypothesis*, 12.
[41] *Ibid.*, 77.
[42] *Ibid.*, 89.
[43] *Ibid.*, 152.
[44] *Ibid.*, 188.
[45] *Ibid.*

"The Qumran community"

Perhaps the most basic and widespread confusion concerns what is called "the Qumran community." It is widely assumed that the *Community Rule, Serek haYahad*, was the rule for the Qumran settlement, which could therefore be regarded as a distinct entity. This view is untenable. The Rule explicitly refers to "all their places of residence" (1QS 6:2) and to "every place where there are ten men of the Community council" (6:3).[46] It is, then, in Stegemann's words, "composed not for the Qumran settlers especially but for all of the Essenes everywhere in the country,"[47] or at least for all members of the *yahad*. The *yahad* is not a single community, but an association of people who live in many communities.

Whether the Qumran settlement (assuming that it was a sectarian settlement) was at all distinctive is unclear. Stegemann regards Qumran as a "settlement for the large-scale production of writing scrolls," established after the death of the Teacher.[48] Many scholars have seen a reference to the founding of the Qumran settlement in a passage in 1QS 8:

And when these have become a community in Israel in compliance with these arrangements, they are to be segregated from within the dwelling of the men of sin to go to the desert, to prepare there the way of Him, as it is written, "in the desert prepare the way of ..." (8:13–14).[49]

While the passage goes on to equate the preparation of the way with the study of the Law, it is quite possible that it refers to an actual withdrawal to the desert.[50] The group that withdraws, however, is not schismatic, but is specially set aside and trained within the *yahad* for a period of two years, and instructed in everything that is hidden from Israel but discovered by the Interpreter (8:11–12). These, in short, are "the men of perfect holiness" who constitute an elite within the *yahad* but do not "break away" from it. If this passage refers to the establishment of the Qumran settlement, which is an attractive possibility but not provable, then we should think of Qumran as a place where the same law and rules were observed as in other settlements, but in a higher degree of perfection.[51]

Much remains unclear about the relation between the Damascus Rule and the *yahad* described in the *Serek*. It will not do, however, to assign the *Serek* to Qumran

---

[46] See J. J. Collins, "Forms of Community in the Dead Sea Scrolls," in S. M. Paul, R. A. Kraft, L. H. Schiffman, and W. W. Fields, eds., *Emanuel. Studies in Hebrew Bible, Septuagint and Dead Sea Scrolls in honor of Emanuel Tov* (Leiden: Brill, 2003) 97–111; idem, "The *Yahad* and the Qumran Community," in C. Hempel and J. M. Lieu, eds., *Biblical Traditions in Transmission. Essays in Honour of Michael A. Knibb* (Leiden: Brill, 2006) 81–96.

[47] Stegemann, *The Library of Qumran*, 142.

[48] *Ibid.*, 156.

[49] E. F. Sutcliffe, "The First Fifteen Members of the Qumran Community," *JSS* 4 (1959) 134–8; J. Murphy-O'Connor, "La genèse littéraire de la Règle de la Communauté," *RB* 76 (1969) 528–49.

[50] G. J. Brooke, "Isaiah 40:3 and the Wilderness Community," in G. J. Brooke and F. García Martínez, eds., *New Qumran Texts and Studies* (Leiden: Brill, 1994) 117–32.

[51] Collins, "Forms of Community," 105–7.

and the Damascus Rule to the "non-Qumran Essenes." Both rules envision a network of communities. Both also make some distinction between those who pursue perfect holiness and other members of the association – compare CD 7:5–8. In the case of the Damascus Rule, some members marry and have children. It is possible that one rule reflects an earlier phase of the same movement than the other, but then it is difficult to explain why copies of both rules continued to be copied contemporaneously. And while the Damascus Rule *may* preserve rules that were formulated before the arrival of the Teacher, the extant text clearly looks back to the Teacher as an authoritative figure. Despite the widespread assumption that the *yahad* was the movement of the Teacher's followers, which may well be correct, the fact remains that the Teacher is acknowledged in the Damascus Rule but not in *Serek ha-Yahad*.

In light of this situation, it makes little sense to distinguish between "Qumranic" and "pre-Qumranic" or "non-Qumranic." With the possible exception of the passage in 1QS 8, we have no literature that can be said with confidence to have been composed specifically for the Qumran settlement. There is no evidence at all that the Qumran settlement resulted from a schism within the *yahad*, or that *Serek ha-Yahad* and the *Damascus Rule* reflect the two sides of a "split."

The Essenes revisited

As noted already, the main correspondences between the accounts of the Essenes in Philo and Josephus and the Dead Sea Scrolls are found in *Serek ha-Yahad*. It is here that we find the multi-year process of admission, and the detailed stipulations for living in community. It is also here that we find striking similarities in eschatological expectations, formulated in terms of reward and punishment after death but not of resurrection. There are, to be sure, discrepancies. The *Serek* does not explicitly forbid marriage, and the Greek authors do not mention spirits of light and darkness or messiahs. But neither do they mention a covenant, the central category of the Damascus Rule. Whatever problems there may be in identifying the *yahad* described in the *Serek* as Essene, these problems are infinitely greater if we extend the term to any other literature found at Qumran. It seems to me quite unjustifiable to apply the label "Essene" to the Enochic books or even *Jubilees*, which contain no description of community life and have only incidental features in common with the accounts in Philo and Josephus.[52] We simply do not know how "the chosen righteous" of the *Apocalypse of Weeks* were organized, but we have no warrant for assuming that they lived a common life in the manner attributed to the Essenes.

There are, however, still substantial grounds for relating the Hebrew rule books to the Essenes. Like the *yahad*, and the camps of the Damascus Rule, the Essenes were not confined to one location. The two orders of the Essenes, one of which mar-

---

[52] For these features, see Boccaccini, *Beyond the Essene Hypothesis*, 166–70.

ried, can be correlated with the distinction in the Damascus Rule between those who walk in perfect holiness and those who live in camps according to the order of the land and marry and have children (CD 7:4–8). Neither Josephus nor the *Damascus Rule* suggests that there was any schism; rather they suggest that the movement tolerated more than one life-style. In short, there is still a good case to be made that the movement initiated by the Teacher of Righteousness should be identified with the Essenes. There is no justification, in my view, for extending that label to the so-called "parent community" that existed before his arrival.

Enochic Judaism and the Scrolls

If we leave aside the question of identification with the Essenes, however, how should we describe the relation between the early Enoch literature and the movement described in the Scrolls? Or more specifically, what is the relationship between the "chosen righteous" of the *Apocalypse of Weeks*, or the "lambs" of the *Animal Apocalypse* and the "plant root" described in the opening column of the *Damascus Document*?

Many scholars have been impressed by the fact that the Enochic apocalypses describe the rise of a distinct group on the eve of the Maccabean revolt and have noted that the chronology can be reconciled with that of the "plant root" described in CD 1. Unfortunately, we know nothing of the organization of these groups. We can, however, infer a certain amount about their beliefs and ideology from the texts in which they are mentioned. The Enochic texts may be said to have an apocalyptic view of history. Its course is predetermined; it is the arena of conflict between angels and demons; it will culminate in a judgment. The destiny of the righteous dead is to live with the angels in heaven. The angelic life has no place for sex and marriage (*1 Enoch* 15–16), and the idealization of this life-style could easily lead to a rejection of marriage, although there is no such rejection in the early Enoch literature. This view of history and of human destiny is broadly similar to what we find in the Dead Sea Scrolls. But it is also similar to what we find in Daniel, a book which, as Boccaccini recognizes, cannot be attributed to the same circles as the Enoch apocalypses. The ways in which this worldview is articulated varies. Boccaccini acknowledges that

The sectarian literature of Qumran gave a distinctive emphasis to the generative idea of Enochic Judaism, that is, the superhuman origin of evil. The concepts of cosmic dualism and individual predestination ultimately made God the origin of evil on both the cosmic and the individual level.[53]

The story of the Watchers, which is foundational in the Enoch literature, was known to the sectarian authors, but it did not provide the basic paradigm for the origin of

---

[53] *Ibid.*, 170.

evil in the sectarian scrolls. Boccaccini claims that "the denial of angelic and human freedom became the main cause of disagreement between Qumran and the larger Essene movement."[54] But the Scrolls give no indication that such issues were the main cause of disagreement with anyone. The grounds for separation from the rest of Judaism were disagreement over the calendar and halakhic issues, while the dispute with the Man of the Lie concerned the authority of the Teacher and the interpretation of the Law. The ideological continuity between "Enochic Judaism" and the Scrolls is a matter of a common apocalyptic worldview, which was also shared by others, such as the authors of Daniel. This common apocalyptic worldview might be described as an intellectual movement, in Boccaccini's terms, but it is not so specific as to require that the authors of the Enoch apocalypses and the sectarian rule books once belonged to the same group or organization. Accordingly, when we find variations in the worldview, such as the different myths about the origin of evil in the *Book of the Watchers* and the *Community Rule*, there is no need to suppose that a schism has occurred in an organization that was previously unified.

By far the most important feature shared by the Enochic books and the sectarian scrolls is adherence to the 364-day calendar. Related to this is a critical attitude towards the temple. On both of these counts, the Enochic books differ from Daniel. The calendar was a fundamental issue for the sectarians of the Scrolls, and so the common calendar is an important link between them and the Essenes. Nonetheless, the significance of the common calendar is disputed. James VanderKam has noted that the cultic calendar was disrupted during the persecution by Antiochus Epiphanes, and suggested that the luni-solar cultic calendar was introduced by the Seleucids or by the Hasmoneans.[55] If this were correct, then adherence to a traditional solar calendar need not be taken as a marker of sectarian identity. Nonetheless, the emphasis on the solar calendar is a distinctive feature in the literature that survives from this period.

But while the calendar, and the critical attitude towards the temple, suggest some link between the sect of the Dead Sea Scrolls and Enochic Judaism, some other considerations weigh against it. Both the *Damascus Document*, in all its stages, and the *Community Rule* ascribe central importance to the Torah of Moses. In contrast, in the early Enoch literature, Enoch, not Moses, is the mediator of revelation. In the words of George Nickelsburg, "to judge from what the authors of *1 Enoch* have written, the Sinaitic covenant and Torah were not of central importance to them."[56] This is not to say that the Torah was unknown or unheeded in Enochic circles; the

---

[54] *Ibid.*, 170.

[55] J. VanderKam, "The Origin, Character, and Early History of the 364-Day Calendar: A Reassessment of Jaubert's Hypotheses," *CBQ* 41 (1979) 390–411; "2 Maccabees 6,7a and Calendrical Change in Jerusalem," *JSJ* 12 (1981) 1–23; idem, *Calendars in the Dead Sea Scrolls: Measuring Time* (London: Routledge, 1998) 114–6. Evidence for calendrical change is found in Dan 7:25 and 2 Macc 6:7.

[56] G. W. E. Nickelsburg, *1 Enoch 1: A Commentary on the Book of 1 Enoch, Chapters 1–36; 81–108* (Hermeneia; Minneapolis: Fortress, 2001) 50.

entire *Animal Apocalypse* is a paraphrase of biblical history.[57] But nowhere in the Enochic corpus does the Torah occupy a central place as it does in the Scrolls. The sectarian rule books do not invoke Enoch as an authoritative figure, nor do they resort to pseudepigraphy at all. The reason for this seems to be the authority accorded to the Torah and to the Teacher as its interpreter.[58]

Boccaccini asserts that "the honor given to Moses does not contradict the association of the Essenes with Enochic Judaism."[59] He grants that the Torah is conspicuously absent from the earlier Enochic literature, but claims that "thanks to *Jubilees*, Moses became an important figure in the Enochic movement."[60] But whether *Jubilees* can be assigned to "the Enochic movement" is questionable. It was certainly influenced by the early Enoch literature, but does that necessarily require that it was written within the same group? Whether it even belongs to the same intellectual movement depends on how that movement is defined. Boccaccini defines Enochic Judaism on the basis of a supposedly generative idea – the autonomous existence of evil. But, as he himself notes in another context, a shared worldview does not require that two texts have originated in the same group or party.[61] *Jubilees* draws some material from the Enoch tradition, but it also has far-reaching halakhic interests that are not attested at all in the Enochic corpus. In the matter of Mosaic authority and interest in halakah, the contrast between "Enochic Judaism," on the one hand, and *Jubilees* and the Scrolls on the other, is far more impressive than the continuity.

We should also bear in mind that the Enochic literature is not the only corpus that has affinities with the Scrolls. We have already noted the case of Daniel, which figures very prominently at Qumran. The publication of *4QInstruction* has demonstrated that there were also significant links between the sectarian scrolls, even in apocalyptic passages such as the *Instruction on the Two Spirits*, and the Jewish wisdom tradition.[62]

---

[57] Compare A. Bedenbender, *Der Gott der Welt tritt auf den Sinai. Entstehung, Entwicklung und Funktionsweise der frühjüdischen Apokalyptik* (Berlin: Institut Kirche und Judentum, 2000) 215–30, who speaks of *1 Enoch* 1–5 as "Mosaisierung des Wächterbuches."

[58] See further J. J. Collins, "Pseudepigraphy and Group Formation in Second Temple Judaism," in E. G. Chazon and M. Stone, eds., *Pseudepigraphic Perspectives: The Apocrypha and Pseudepigrapha in Light of the Dead Sea Scrolls* (Leiden: Brill, 1999) 43–58.

[59] Boccaccini, *Beyond the Essene Hypothesis*, 167.

[60] Ibid.

[61] Ibid., 14–15.

[62] See J. J. Collins, G. E. Sterling, and R. A. Clements, *Sapiential Perspectives: Wisdom Literature in Light of the Dead Sea Scrolls* (STDJ 51; Leiden: Brill, 2004).

Conclusion

That there were close links between "Enochic Judaism" and the sectarian movement described in the Scrolls is not in doubt. The foregoing analysis suggests, however, that it is far too simple to equate Enochic Judaism with the "parent-community" of the *Damascus Document*, and that there is no basis for identifying it with the Essenes. Both the accounts of the Essenes and the sectarian rule books describe a form of Judaism that was, whatever else, "Mosaic." If the movement that produced the early Enoch literature was absorbed into the "new covenant" of the *Damascus Document*, it must have radically changed its character. And while the movement described in the Scrolls may well have drawn both ideas and personnel from the Enoch movement, there is ample evidence that it also drew from other sources.

There is always a strong tendency in scholarship to reduce chaos to order and to schematize historical evidence. James VanderKam has highlighted the recurring tendency to explain Second Temple Judaism in terms of binary oppositions, whether hierocrats vs. visionaries or Zadokites vs. Enochians.[63] Despite its attractions, such tendencies should be resisted. Historical reality is always less tidy than we would wish it to be.

---

[63] James C. VanderKam, "Mapping Second Temple Judaism," in Gabriele Boccaccini and John J. Collins, ed., *The Early Enoch Literature* (JSJSup 121; Leiden: Brill, 2007) 1–20.

CHAPTER ELEVEN

Sectarian Consciousness in the Dead Sea Scrolls

The terms "sect" and "sectarian" admit of various nuances and are used in various ways not only by biblical scholars and historians of religion but also by sociologists.[1] There is broad agreement, however, that a sect is a group that has separated to some degree from a parent body, and has boundary markers to indicate its separate identity.[2] Recent studies of sectarianism often posit a continuum in the degree of separation, or alienation.[3] The break may be more or less decisive, and the separation more or less extreme. Consequently, whether a particular group is sectarian or not is a matter of where one draws the line. In the context of ancient Judaism, the Dead Sea Scrolls are often thought to provide a paradigm example of sectarianism in an extreme form. The *Community Rule* and *Damascus Document*, both of which are found in multiple copies in the Scrolls, describe a community (or communities) in tension with the larger entity of Israel, from which it has separated. There are clear boundary markers, indicated especially in the elaborate admission process in the *Community Rule*, and claims of unique legitimacy for the group in question. The use of the term "sect" with reference to this group has not been very controversial, because of its clear separation "from the majority of the people," in the phrase of 4QMMT.

When we attempt to categorize the literature of the Dead Sea Scrolls, however, the use of the adjective "sectarian" becomes more problematic. In an influential, pioneering, article, Carol Newsom proposed "at least three different things that one

---

[1] For a helpful overview, see J. M. Jokiranta, "'Sectarianism' of the Qumran 'Sect': Sociological Notes," *RevQ* 20 (2001) 223–40. Among many recent treatments, see B. R. Wilson, *Magic and the Millennium. A Sociological Study of Religious Movements of Protest among Tribal and Third-World Peoples* (London: Heinemann, 1973); idem, *The Social Dimensions of Sectarianism* (Oxford: Clarendon, 1990); R. Stark and W. S. Bainbridge, *The Future of Religion. Secularization, Revival and Cult Formation* (Berkeley: University of California Press, 1985); R. Wallis, ed., *Sectarianism. Analyses of Religious and Non-Religious Sects* (London: Owen, 1975); L. L. Dawson, "Creating 'Cult' Typologies: Some Strategic Considerations," *Journal of Contemporary Religion* 12 (1997) 363–81.

[2] Compare the definition offered by Al Baumgarten: "a voluntary association of protest, which utilizes boundary marking mechanisms – the social means of differentiating between insiders and outsiders – to distinguish between its own members and those otherwise normally regarded as belonging to the same national or religious entity" (*The Flowering of Jewish Sects in the Maccabean Era: An Interpretation* [JSJSup 55; Leiden: Brill, 1997]) 7.

[3] Jokiranta, "Sectarianism," 226–31.

might mean by referring to a scroll as sectarian."[4] The first, and most common, was that "it had been written by a member of the Qumran community." A second possibility was that it was used by the Qumran community, regardless of its origin; that it was adopted, so to speak. Finally, the term sectarian might refer to "a rhetorical stance." The latter category would apply to texts "that speak specifically of the unique structures of the community and the history of its separation from a larger community, and/or that develop its distinctive tenets in a self-consciously polemical fashion." This last category might not include everything written by members of a sectarian community, only that which is "sectually explicit."

Throughout this discussion, Newsom was tacitly assuming that "sectarian," in the context of the Dead Sea Scrolls, implies a relation to "the Qumran community." This assumption is problematic in several respects. First, the community described in the Scrolls was surely not the only sectarian group in ancient Judaism. Even within the corpus of the Scrolls, it is quite conceivable that some literature derived from a different sect. Moreover, in the time since Newsom wrote her article, the notion of "the Qumran community" has become more problematic. The term *yahad*, which has often been taken as a technical name for that community in the *Community Rule*, does not refer to a single settlement such as the one at Qumran but is an umbrella term for a network of smaller groups of ten or more members.[5] Further, the relation between the *yahad* and "the new covenant in the land of Damascus," described in the *Damascus Document*, remains controversial.[6] There was evidently some relationship between them, as can be seen from the presence of the 4QD manuscripts at Qumran and from the overlaps between these manuscripts and the copies of the *Community Rule* from Cave 4.[7] But if the *Damascus Rule* and the *Community Rule* are taken to represent variant forms of the same movement or sect, then this movement must have been somewhat diverse, embracing some people who married and had children, as well as "the men of perfect holiness" who withdrew to the wilderness to walk in perfection of the way. The latter were evidently separated more sharply from the parent society than were their married brethren.

Newsom's study was seminal insofar as she called for a distinction between texts that can be clearly attributed to the *yahad* and those that can not. Some texts, such

---

[4] C. A. Newsom, "'Sectually Explicit' Literature from Qumran," in W. H. Propp, B. Halpern and D. N. Freedman, eds., *The Hebrew Bible and Its Interpreters* (Winona Lake, IN: Eisenbrauns, 1990) 167–87. The quotation is from pp. 172–73.

[5] J. J. Collins, "Forms of Community in the Dead Sea Scrolls," in S. M. Paul, R. A. Kraft, L. H. Schiffman and W. W. Fields, eds., *Emanuel. Studies in Hebrew Bible, Septuagint and Dead Sea Scrolls in Honor of Emanuel Tov* (Leiden: Brill, 2003) 97–111.

[6] C. Hempel, "Community Structures in the Dead Sea Scrolls: Admission, Organization, Disciplinary Procedures," in P. W. Flint and J. C. VanderKam, eds., *The Dead Sea Scrolls after Fifty Years. A Comprehensive Assessment* (Leiden: Brill, 1999) 67–92.

[7] See S. Metso, "The Relationship between the *Damascus Document* and the *Community Rule*," in J. M. Baumgarten, E. G. Chazon and A. Pinnick, eds., *The Damascus Document. A Centennial of Discovery* (Leiden: Brill, 2000) 85–93.

as those that refer to the Teacher, can be attributed to the *yahad* with confidence. There remains, however, a huge grey area of texts that seem compatible with the sectarian movement, in some of its forms, but lack unambiguous indicators. Perhaps Newsom's most interesting contribution was to direct the discussion away from the question of authorship, which is often elusive, to "the rhetorical function of the texts." Regardless of their provenance, several texts found among the Scrolls contain "some self-conscious reference to separation from the larger religious community."[8] It is this phenomenon of separatist self-consciousness that I want to consider here. I will proceed by reviewing the sectarian self-understanding found in the undisputedly sectarian works, the rule books and 4QMMT, and then turn to the more problematic case of a wisdom text, *4QInstruction*.

The *yahad*

For much of the history of scholarship on the scrolls, the understanding of the sectarian character of the underlying community was based on a passage in col. 8 of the *Community Rule*:

And when these become members of the community in Israel according to all these rules, they shall separate from the habitation of unjust men and shall go into the wilderness to prepare there the way of Him; as it is written: "Prepare in the wilderness the way of ..., make straight in the desert a path for our God."

This passage, together with the apparent isolation of the Qumran site, gave rise to the view of a community that was physically isolated from the rest of Judaism and had minimal contact with outsiders. Leaving aside the interpretation of the Qumran site, which is increasingly contested,[9] this view is problematic even within the context of the *Community Rule*. The antecedent of "these" who are to go out into the wilderness are the mysterious "twelve men and three priests." They are said to be set apart as holy in the midst of the council of the community, after they have been confirmed for two years among the perfect of the way. Only then are they to separate themselves and go out into the wilderness. It may be that these were "the first fifteen members of the Qumran community" as E. F. Sutcliffe argued,[10] but they are not the first mem-

---

[8] Newsom, "'Sectually Explicit' Language," 179.

[9] For a concise bibliography, see J. Magness, *The Archaeology of Qumran and the Dead Sea Scrolls* (Grand Rapids: Eerdmans, 2002) 18, and her refutation of attempts to see Qumran as a country villa, *ibid.*, 90–104. Prominent dissidents include N. Golb, *Who Wrote the Dead Sea Scrolls?* (New York: Scribner, 1995) and Y. Hirschfeld, "Early Roman Manor Houses in Judea and the Site of Khirbet Qumran," *JNES* 57 (1998) 161–89; idem, "The Architectural Context of Qumran," in L. H. Schiffman, E. Tov, and J. C. VanderKam, eds., *The Dead Sea Scrolls Fifty Years after Their Discovery* (Jerusalem: Israel Exploration Society in cooperation with The Shrine of the Book, Israel Museum, 2000) 673–83.

[10] E. F. Sutcliffe, S.J., "The First Fifteen Members of the Qumran Community," *JSS* 4 (1959) 134–8.

bers of "the council of the community." They are initially members of a larger group. Their separation from that group is not schismatic. They are trained and tested in "the council of the community," but are set aside to live a more holy life, and atone for the land. Their atoning role may be taken to imply a criticism of the efficacy of the atonement rituals practiced in the Jerusalem temple. While they may be sectarian in relation to Jewish society as a whole, however, they are not sectarian vis-à-vis their parent community. The group that goes to the wilderness is not all of the *yahad*, but it is part of it. It does not have a separate identity or purpose.[11]

The larger community, or *yahad*, within which these people are set aside, is also separatist, although to a less extreme degree. They are supposed to "separate themselves from the congregation of the men of injustice, and unite, with respect to the Law and possessions," under the authority of the sons of Zadok, and/or the multitude of the men of the community.[12] This *yahad* is embodied in clusters of ten or more members, and has a set of regulations governing common life, such as we also find in Hellenistic voluntary associations.[13] It appears, however, to be a more greedy institution than its Hellenistic counterparts, insofar as it lays greater claims on the lives of its members. It also has an adversarial stance towards the larger society, and this is atypical of voluntary associations in the Hellenistic world.

The *raison d'être* of the *yahad* in the *Community Rule* is primarily its distinctive interpretation of the Torah of Moses, which was allegedly revealed to the sons of Zadok and to the multitude of the men of the community. While this interpretation was contested, it did not question the foundational importance of the Torah of Moses. In this sense, both the *yahad* and its elite offshoot in the wilderness are reformist movements. According to 1QS 5,

whoever approaches the Council of the Community shall enter the Covenant of God in the presence of all who have freely pledged themselves. He shall undertake by a binding oath to return with all his heart and soul to every commandment of the Law of Moses

in accordance with the community's interpretation. An elaborate covenant renewal ceremony is prefixed to the rules of the community in 1QS. The community, then, sees itself as fulfilling God's covenant with Israel.[14] The members are "the multitude

---

[11] See further Collins, "Forms of Community," 105–6.

[12] 1QS 5:1–3. The reference to the sons of Zadok is not found in some manuscripts of the rule. See S. Metso, "In Search of the *Sitz im Leben* of the *Community Rule*," in D. W. Parry and E. Ulrich, eds., *The Provo International Conference on the Dead Sea Scrolls* (Leiden: Brill, 1999) 306–15, who regards the shorter text as older, and P. S. Alexander, "The Redaction History of *Serekh ha-Yahad*: A Proposal," *RevQ* 17 (1996) 437–53, who defends the priority of the longer text.

[13] M. Weinfeld, *The Organizational Pattern and the Penal Code of the Qumran Sect. A Comparison with Guilds and Religious Associations of the Hellenistic-Roman Period* (Göttingen: Vandenhoeck & Ruprecht, 1986); M. Klinghardt, "The Manual of Discipline in the Light of Statutes of Hellenistic Associations," in M. O. Wise et al., eds., *Methods of Investigation of the Dead Sea Scrolls and the Khirbet Qumran Site. Present Realities and Future Prospects* (Annals of the New York Academy of Sciences 722; New York: The New York Academy of Sciences, 1994) 251–70.

[14] See further J. J. Collins, "The Construction of Israel in the Sectarian Rule Books," in A. J.

of Israel who have freely pledged themselves in the Community to return to His covenant" (1QS 5:22). Its priests are "the sons of Aaron." The *Community Rule* clearly envisions an ongoing process whereby people from "old Israel" can still enter the new covenant. The goal, however, does not seem to be to reform existing Jewish society from within, but to replace it with an intentional community in which the Torah is observed according to ideal norms. Despite its reformist self-understanding, the *yahad* can reasonably be called a sect, since it is clearly separated from the parent society of Judaism by its distinctive rituals of admission and its avowed intention to separate from the rest of Jewish society.

The *Damascus Document* differs from the *Community Rule* insofar as it offers an historical narrative of the origin of its community.[15] The best-known passage, in CD col. 1, describes how God visited Israel 390 years after the destruction by Nebuchadnezzar, and caused a plant root to spring from Aaron and Israel "to inherit his land and prosper on the good things of his earth." The new community, then, is an offshoot, or a remnant, of historic Israel. The association of this community with "Aaron and Israel" is an obvious point of affinity with the *Community Rule*. The CD passage specifies that the movement was initially penitential in character, and that it only achieved clarity with the advent of the Teacher of Righteousness.

The *Damascus Document* also speaks of a new covenant. The members of the first covenant sinned and were delivered up to the sword, "but with the remnant which held fast to the commandments of God He made His covenant with Israel for ever, revealing to them the hidden things in which all Israel had gone astray" (CD 3:12–13). Here again, the *raison d'être* of the new community is the correct interpretation of the Torah. CD 6 interprets a reference to "the well which the princes dug" in Numbers 21 as follows: "The Well is the Law, and those who dug it were the converts of Israel who went out of the land of Judah to sojourn in the land of Damascus." The word translated "converts" here, שבי, from שוב, is another point of affinity with the *Community Rule*, where the members swore to return to the Torah of Moses.[16] The theme of separation is reflected in the statement that they "went out from the land of Judah to sojourn in the land of Damascus." There has been endless debate as to whether Damascus is a cipher for Qumran, or whether there actually was a migration to Damascus.[17] We should also reckon with the possibility that the reference is not geographical at all, but that Damascus is a symbol for a state of sep-

---

Avery-Peck, J. Neusner and B. D. Chilton, eds., *Judaism in Late Antiquity. Part 5: The Judaism of Qumran: A Systemic Reading of the Dead Sea Scrolls. 1. Theory of Israel* (Leiden: Brill, 2001) 25–42.

[15] For a recent review of the accounts of the origin of the sect in the *Damascus Document* see C. Hempel, "Community Origins in the *Damascus Document* in the Light of Recent Scholarship," in Parry and Ulrich, eds., *The Provo International Conference*, 316–29.

[16] For a summary of the debate about this phrase in the *Damascus Document*, see C. Hempel, *The Damascus Texts* (Sheffield: Sheffield Academic Press, 2000) 57–8.

[17] Hempel, *ibid.*, 58–59. A migration to Damascus is assumed by M. O. Wise, *The First Messiah. Investigating the Savior before Christ* (San Francisco: HarperSanFrancisco, 1999) 135–38.

aration from the religious establishment of Judah. CD 8:16 refers to "the converts of Israel who depart from the way of the people." Conversely, "the princes of Judah" are criticized because "they have not kept apart from the people."

There has been a tendency in recent scholarship to emphasize the differences between the *Community Rule* and the *Damascus Document*.[18] Most famously, the latter document legislates for people who live in camps according to the order of the land, and who marry and have children. Women and children are conspicuous by their absence in the *Community Rule*, but that rule book too provides for smaller congregations, which may be analogous to the camps. Other significant differences include the absence of discussion of admission procedures in CD and the failure of the *Community Rule* to situate its community in the history of Israel. Most significant, perhaps, is the fact that several laws in CD envision life in a Gentile context. These differences, however, must be weighed against the affinities between the two documents. The sectarian consciousness of the two documents seems remarkably similar. The covenant that God made with Israel is not repudiated, but now individuals must decide whether to "enter" this covenant anew. CD refers several times to "the new covenant in the land of Damascus" (CD 6:19; 8:21; 19:33–34). The "new covenant" is an allusion to Jer 31:31. Its continuity with the "old" covenant is not in doubt, but not all Israelites qualify as members. They must join voluntarily, and their children too must be enrolled when they reach the appropriate age (CD 15:5–6). The *Damascus Document* envisions a period in which any Israelite or proselyte may join the new covenant, but when this period is completed "there shall be no more joining to the house of Judah" (CD 4:10–11).

The community of the new covenant, in CD as in the *Community Rule*, is reformist in the sense that its goal is a return to the Law of Moses, but it is also a separatist, exclusivist, movement that claims to have new revelation about the proper interpretation of that law. As such, it may reasonably be called a sect. Attempts to reconstruct from the laws of CD a movement that was less separatist, and therefore less sectarian than the document in its final form, are very hypothetical.[19]

4QMMT, the so-called "Halakhic Letter," also addresses explicitly the separation of a community from the majority of the people. In this case there is no historical perspective, and no indication of the form of the author's community. The author sets out a series of halakhic issues, which are the reason for the separation. These issues are matters of scriptural interpretation and allow an appeal to the common ground on which both parties base their beliefs. "We have [written] to you so that you may study the book of Moses and the books of the Prophets and (the writings

---

[18] See Hempel, "Community Structures"; P. R. Davies, "The Judaism(s) of the *Damascus Document*," in J. M. Baumgarten, E. G. Chazon and A. Pinnick, eds., *The Damascus Document. A Centennial of Discovery* (Leiden: Brill, 2000) 27–43.

[19] For such an attempt, see C. Hempel, *The Laws of the Damascus Document. Sources, Traditions and Redaction* (Leiden: Brill, 1998).

of) David," in the hope that such study would confirm the author's interpretation.[20] These scriptures constituted a common basis for the author and the addressee.[21] The separation of the author's community was not based on ontological considerations, but on different interpretation, and the authority of different interpreters.

Creation and election

There is, however, another way in which sectarian consciousness is conceived, whereby the division is located not in the recent history of Israel but at creation.

The idea that some people were chosen at creation and some were rejected is found already in Ben Sira, where the contrast seems to be between Israel and the Canaanites.[22] The *Damascus Document* only hints at such a predestinarian theology in col. 2. Here we are told that destruction is in store for "those who turn from the way," for "from the beginning God chose them not. He knew their deeds before ever they were created and He hated their generations."[23] Those who turn from the way are presumably Jews rather than Gentiles. More specifically, they are those who followed "the Scoffer" rather than the Teacher in CD 1. If these people were predestined for destruction, it seems reasonable to suppose that those who held fast to the commandments were also chosen from the beginning. This theme, however, is not developed in the *Damascus Document*, which is primarily covenantal in its theology.

The *Discourse on the Two Spirits*, in 1QS 3–4, also appeals to creation: "From the God of knowledge stems all there is and is to be . . . He created man to rule the world and placed within him two spirits so that he would walk with them until the moment of his visitation." For (אנוש) Our present purposes, the point to note here is that the division between the elect and their adversaries is not attributed to choices made by human beings in the period after the Babylonian exile but is rooted in creation.

There is no doubt that the dualistic theology of the two spirits is sectarian in Newsom's second sense, that it was used by sectarian authors to legitimate and lend significance to a social division. The more difficult question is whether a dualistic

---

[20] 4QMMT C 10. E. Qimron and J. Strugnell, *Qumran Cave 4. V. Miqsat Maʿase Ha-Torah* (DJD 10; Oxford: Clarendon, 1994) 58–59. See however the article of Eugene Ulrich, "The Non-Attestation of a Tri-Partite Canon in 4QMMT," *CBQ* 65 (2003) 202–14, which questions the editors' reading of this passage.

[21] Steven Fraade has made an interesting argument that 4QMMT is intended not for external polemic but for internal parenesis. Even if this is correct, however, the rhetoric of the document attempts to ground the distinctive views of the group in scriptures that are also accepted by outsiders.

[22] Sir 33:10–13: "In the fullness of his knowledge he distinguished them and appointed their different ways. Some he blessed and exalted. Some he made holy and brought near to himself; but some he cursed and brought low and turned them out of their place."

[23] CD 2:7–8. On the predestinarian theology of this passage see A. Lange, *Weisheit und Prädestination* (STDJ 18; Leiden: Brill, 1995) 233–70.

creation theology is inherently sectarian. Since the dualism of the two spirits was scarcely known in a Jewish context before the discovery of the Dead Sea Scrolls, most scholars have assumed that it is "a paradigmatic expression of the sectarian theology."[24] In contrast, Hartmut Stegemann[25] and Armin Lange[26] have argued that the *Discourse on the Two Spirits* is an older, pre-sectarian text, that was incorporated into the sectarian rule book. The *Damascus Document* was influenced by the *Discourse*, but not profoundly. On this view, the *Discourse* itself was a sapiential text that sought to explain the division of the world between good and evil, but was not necessarily the product of a sectarian group. Nonetheless, it appears remarkably congenial to sectarian ideology, and the argument that it is pre-sectarian appears rather counter-intuitive.[27]

4QInstruction

The sectarian implications of dualism in the *Community Rule* and *Damascus Document* are clear enough, because these documents explicitly describe separatist communities. A more difficult case is provided by the recently published wisdom text, *4QInstruction*.[28] This text says nothing about a *yahad* or community life, and makes no mention of a new covenant.[29] It assumes marriage and family life, and discusses financial matters without any suggestion of communal possessions. Nothing in the text suggests the kind of communal structures we find in the *Community Rule* or the *Damascus Document*. Moreover, while it alludes to the Torah of Moses at several points,[30] it does not speak of it explicitly as a source of authority, in marked contrast to the wisdom book of Ben Sira. In the few cases where it reflects halakhic interpre-

---

[24] So e.g. D. Dimant, "Qumran Sectarian Literature," in M. E. Stone, ed., *Jewish Writings of the Second Temple Period* (Philadelphia: Fortress, 1984) 483–550, especially 533–38.

[25] H. Stegemann, *Die Essener, Qumran, Johannes der Täufer und Jesus* (Freiburg: Herder, 1993) 154. The English translation of this book, however, *The Library of Qumran. On the Essenes, Qumran, John the Baptist and Jesus* (Grand Rapids: Eerdmans, 1998) 108, says that the passage "is surely of Essene origin."

[26] Lange, *Weisheit und Prädestination*, 126–8.

[27] See further J. J. Collins, *Apocalypticism in the Dead Sea Scrolls* (London: Routledge, 1997) 43–45.

[28] J. Strugnell, D. Harrington and T. Elgvin, *Qumran Cave 4. XXIV. Sapiential Texts, Part 2* (DJD 34; Oxford: Clarendon, 1999).

[29] The word *yahad* occurs several times in *4QInstruction* in an adverbial sense. There is one possible exception in 4Q417 2 i 17 where the editors restore the word *yahad* and translate "then thy surpluses [bring in together/into the community/into thy associate's possession]". Even if the restoration on the basis of a tiny fragment, 4Q199 1, is accepted, it is by no means clear that the reference is to a community. The passage is discussed by C. M. Murphy, *Wealth in the Dead Sea Scrolls and in the Qumran Community* (STDJ 40; Leiden: Brill, 2002) 179.

[30] G. J. Brooke, "Biblical Interpretation in the Wisdom Texts from Qumran," in C. Hempel et al., eds., *The Wisdom Texts from Qumran and the Development of Sapiential Thought* (Leuven: Peeters, 2002) 201–20.

tation of the Torah, its interpretation does not accord with that of the sectarian texts from Qumran, as Larry Schiffman has shown.[31] Consequently the editors regard it as an example of "common Israelite wisdom" addressed "not to any closed community like that at Qumran, nor to any earlier and theologically cognate population, but to a typical junior sage."[32] Eibert Tigchelaar has argued that the addressee could be "anyone in society."[33] Yet Geza Vermes argues that it is "unquestionably sectarian and displays a terminology akin to the *Community Rule*, the *Damascus Document* and the Thanksgiving Hymns"[34] and other scholars have also been impressed with its affinities with texts that are accepted as sectarian.

There are indeed numerous points of correspondence between *4QInstruction* and the *Hodayot*, especially 1QH[a] 5, and between the wisdom text and the *Discourse on the Two Spirits*. The correspondences with the *Hodayot* include such phrases as "wondrous mysteries," "eternal visitation," "eternal glory," "eternal foundations," "spirit of flesh" and other phrases.[35] These correspondences may be explained by supposing that the hymnist was influenced by the wisdom text, and thus do not necessarily require sectarian provenance for the latter. The correspondences with the *Discourse on the Two Spirits* are more intriguing. Here again there is a long list of common phrases: "period of peace," "all periods of eternity," "God of knowledge," "children of iniquity," "sons of heaven," etc.[36] Tigchelaar has observed that these phrases are found primarily in the opening and closing paragraphs of the Discourse (1QS 3:13–18; 4:15–26). The *Instruction* does not use the terminology of light and darkness, does not speak of Spirits as angels, and does not say that two spirits feud in the human heart. In short, *4QInstruction* lacks the most distinctive elements of the *Discourse*. If the wisdom text were dependent on the *Discourse on the Two Spirits*, we should have to explain why it only alludes to part of it. It seems more plausible then that the authors or editors of the *Discourse* drew terminology from *4QInstruction*. Moreover, as Lange has noted, the *Discourse* has a more developed presentation of dualism and eschatology than the wisdom text, and this too suggests that it is the later of the two.[37]

---

[31] L. H. Schiffman, "Halakhic Elements in the Sapiential Texts from Qumran," in J. J. Collins, G. E. Sterling and Ruth A. Clements, eds., *Sapiential Perspectives: Wisdom Literature in Light of the Dead Sea Scrolls. Proceedings of the Sixth International Symposium of the Orion Center, 20–22 May, 2001* (STDJ 51; Leiden: Brill, 2004) 89–100.

[32] *Ibid.*, 36.

[33] E. J. C. Tigchelaar, "The Addressees of *4QInstruction*," in D. K. Falk et al., eds., *Sapiential, Liturgical and Poetical Texts from Qumran. Proceedings of the Third Meeting of the International Organization for Qumran Studies, Oslo 1998* (Leiden: Brill, 2000) 62–75 (quotation from p. 75).

[34] G. Vermes, *The Complete Dead Sea Scrolls in English* (London: Penguin, 1997) 402.

[35] These parallels have been discussed by T. Elgvin, "An Analysis of *4QInstruction*" (Diss. Hebrew University, Jerusalem, 1997) 160–61; E. J. C. Tigchelaar, *To Increase Learning for the Understanding Ones* (Leiden: Brill, 2001) 203–6. The parallels to 1QH[a] 5 are concentrated in 4Q417 1.

[36] Tigchelaar, *To Increase Learning*, 194–203; Lange, *Weisheit und Prädestination*, 127–28.

[37] Lange, *Weisheit und Prädestination*, 130.

The relationship between *4QInstruction* and the *Discourse* is especially interesting, as both texts envisage a division of humanity into two kinds of people. In 4Q417 fragment 1, we are told that God disclosed the vision of Hagu, or book of memorial, which contains the destiny of righteous and wicked, to אנוש, with a spiritual people, but did not give it to "the spirit of flesh," because it failed to distinguish between good and evil. אנוש, we are told, is fashioned after the pattern of the holy ones, or angels. The language of the passage alludes to the opening chapters of Genesis.[38] אנוש is most probably not the name of the patriarch Enoch,[39] but refers to humanity as originally created. The *Instruction on the Two Spirits* similarly says that God "created אנוש to rule the world," where the reference is clearly to Adam or humanity. The statement that אנוש and the spiritual people are formed after the pattern of the holy ones is a paraphrase of Gen 1:27, where humanity is created in the image of God. The failure of the spirit of flesh to discern good and evil alludes to the story in Gen 2–3, where Adam and Eve eat from the tree of the knowledge of good and evil with disastrous results.

There is some debate as to whether the spirit of flesh initially had access to the revelation of Hagu, and lost it by a "fall," or whether it was inherently incapable of receiving the revelation. The Hebrew reads: "and Hagu was no longer given to the spirit of flesh."[40] It is not apparent, however, that the revelation was withdrawn from the spiritual people. Rather, there seem to be two kinds of people from the beginning, and if one kind loses its access to revelation, this is because it had a spirit of flesh.[41]

It seems reasonable to suppose that *4QInstruction* is addressed to "spiritual people" who are capable of grasping revelation. To be sure, the addressees of this text are a matter of some controversy. Tigchelaar has noted that it often addresses hypothetical situations, how to behave if one is poor, or subjected to a beating, or if one enjoys good fortune, etc. But he also notes that "the composition is not merely a collection of instructions for different kinds of addressees."[42] The addressee is consistently called a מבין, or "understanding one," although the understanding may be a matter of aspiration rather than accomplished fact. The understanding in question is not confined to practical wisdom, of the kind familiar from Proverbs and Ben Sira.

---

[38] See J. J. Collins, "In the Likeness of the Holy Ones: The Creation of Humankind in a Wisdom Text from Qumran," in Perry and Ulrich, eds., *The Provo International Conference*, 595–618.

[39] Contra Lange, *Weisheit und Prädestination*, 87–88; Brooke, "Biblical Interpretation in the Wisdom Texts from Qumran," 213.

[40] So Strugnell and Harrington, in DJD 34, 155. They suggest that "since the days of Enosh the fleshly in spirit have not possessed the power of meditation" (p. 166). If the passage is read in the context of creation, one might suggest that the power of meditation was lost in the "Fall" of Adam.

[41] On the spirit of flesh see J. Frey, "The Notion of Flesh in *4QInstruction* and the Background of Pauline Usage," in Falk et al., *Sapiential, Liturgical and Poetical Texts*, 197–226; idem, "Flesh and Spirit in the Palestinian Jewish Sapiential Tradition and in the Qumran Texts: An Inquiry into the Background of Pauline Usage," in Hempel et al., eds., *The Wisdom Texts from Qumran*, 367–404.

[42] Tigchelaar, "The Addressees of *4QInstruction*," 73.

Throughout the document, the addressee is urged to contemplate "the mystery that is to be" (רז נהיה).⁴³ This mystery embraces past, present and future, but it includes the eschatological destiny of righteous and wicked, which is also the subject of the "vision of Hagu." Presumably the mystery is available to the addressee, and it is either identical with or overlaps with the vision of Hagu, which was given to Enosh and the spiritual people, according to 4Q417 1. The spiritual people, then, were not confined to pre-lapsarian utopia, but were a group to be fostered in the author's own time. They do not appear to live in community, and they may pursue various professions. They do not appear to be a social elite, since there is extensive discussion of poverty.⁴⁴ They are not just "anyone in society," however, but are regarded as a spiritual elite.

A further key passage for the question of sectarian consciousness in *4QInstruction* is found in 4Q418. In 4Q418 69 ii the addressees are called the "chosen ones of truth," in contrast to the "foolish of heart" who are doomed to destruction. The passage is fragmentary, but the chosen ones are associated with the pursuit of knowledge. The key passage is found in 4Q418 fragment 81:

[for the utterance of] your lips He has opened up a spring so that you may bless the Holy Ones, and (so that) as (with) an everlasting fountain you may praise His n[ame. The]n has He separated you from every fleshly spirit, so that you may be separated from everything that He hates, and may hold yourself aloof from all that His soul abominates. For He has made everyone and has made them to inherit each his own inheritance; but he is your portion and your inheritance among the children of mankind ... just as He has appointed you as a Holy of Holies [over all the] earth, And (just as) among all the [Go]dly [ones] has He cast your lot. And He has magnified your glory greatly. He has appointed you for himself as a first-born among ...

This passage alludes to the promise to Aaron in Num 18:20: "I am your inheritance and your lot among all the sons of Israel." In Num 8:14 and 16:9 the same verb "to separate" that is used here occurs with reference to the Levites, who are set aside from the midst of the Israelites.⁴⁵ The significance of this passage in the context of *4QInstruction* is much disputed. Fletcher-Louis has argued that the addressee is a priest,⁴⁶ and his argument may seem to lend support to Lange's thesis that *4QInstruction* derives from a priestly milieu.⁴⁷ There is, however, remarkably little evidence of priestly concerns in the work as a whole.⁴⁸ Tigchelaar, in line with his ar-

---

⁴³ For a thorough recent discussion see M. J. Goff, *The Worldly and Heavenly Wisdom of 4QInstruction* (Leiden: Brill, 2003) chapter 2.

⁴⁴ *Ibid.*, chapter 4.

⁴⁵ Tigchelaar, *To Increase Learning*, 232.

⁴⁶ C. Fletcher-Louis, *All the Glory of Adam. Liturgical Anthropology in the Dead Sea Scrolls* (STDJ 42; Leiden: Brill, 2002) 176–87.

⁴⁷ A. Lange, "In Diskussion mit dem Tempel. Zur Auseinandersetzung zwischen Kohelet und Weisheitlichen Kreisen am Jerusalemer Tempel," in A. Schoors, ed., *Qohelet in the Context of Wisdom* (Leuven: Peeters, 1998) 113–59.

⁴⁸ See the thorough analysis of this issue by T. Elgvin, "Priestly Sages? The Milieus of Origin

gument that people of various professions are addressed, suggests that the addressees are priests in this passage, but not in others.[49] Elgvin, at the other end of the spectrum, notes that the passage includes royal motifs as well as priestly, especially in the reference to the first-born son.[50] He argues that both priestly and royal motifs are applied symbolically to the elect addressee.

The nature of the allusions to the priestly passages in Numbers tells in favor of Elgvin's position. Whereas the Lord is the inheritance of Aaron "among all the sons of Israel," He is the inheritance of the addressee "among the children of humankind." Again, the addressee is not separated from Israel, but from "the spirit of flesh." In light of what we have seen of the spirit of flesh in 4Q417, we should conclude that the addressee is being included in the spiritual people, and that this requires separation, in some sense, from the mass of humankind. This is not just the separation of priest from people, but the separation of the elect from "everything He hates."

Two other aspects of this passage are significant. First, while the end of line 4 is fragmentary, it most probably says that God has cast the lot of the addressee with the holy ones. This language is applicable to priests, to be sure, but it also recalls the familiar motif of fellowship with the angels in the sectarian scrolls. It is also in accordance, however, with the statement in 4Q417 that the spiritual people are created after the pattern of the holy ones. Second, the statement that "He has appointed you as a Holy of Holies [over all the] earth" is reminiscent of 1QS 8, where the community becomes a holy of holies to atone for the land.[51] In the rule book, it is generally assumed that a criticism of the temple cult is implied. The same may be true in *4QInstruction*, but the passage is too oblique to prove that the addressees are in schism with the temple.

Elgvin has argued strongly that this passage does not reflect a single wisdom teacher speaking to his disciple, but rather that "teacher and addressee belong to circles with a distinct identity, some kind of 'remnant' community."[52] In part, his argument rests on a reference in 4Q418 81, line 13, to an "everlasting plantation," language similar to that used to describe the elect community in the *Apocalypse of Weeks*. Unfortunately, the context in *4QInstruction* is fragmentary, and the reference of the "everlasting plantation" is not clear. The passage is indeed reminiscent of the community in 1QS 8, but it does not make any explicit reference to a community, or describe any communal structures. We have, in short, a text that exhibits sectarian consciousness, insofar as it envisions a class of people who are separated

---

of 4QMysteries and *4QInstruction*," in Collins, Sterling, and Clements, eds., *Sapiential Perspectives*, 67–87. Compare Tigchelaar, *To Increase Learning*, 235–6.

[49] Tigchelaar, *To Increase Learning*, 231–6.

[50] Elgvin, "Priestly Sages." See also his discussion of this passage in "An Analysis," 125–38.

[51] In 1QS 8, the community is called "chosen ones of favor." 4Q418 81 line 10 says "it is in your power to turn away anger from the men of favor."

[52] Elgvin, "An Analysis," 138.

from the "spirit of flesh," but lacks any reference to communal organization, and does not articulate its distinctive consciousness in terms of the covenant and the law, in the manner of the sectarian rule books from Qumran.

Charlotte Hempel has suggested that the peculiar character of *4QInstruction* might be explained by redaction criticism. She suggests that *4QInstruction* is a composite work, parts of which are traditional wisdom, while other parts originated in "a particular strand in Second Temple Judaism, though not the *yahad*, but perhaps its forerunners."[53] The quasi-sectarian character of *4QInstruction*, however, does not derive only from a few passages such as 4Q418 81, but depends largely on the appeal to a mystery, the *raz nihyeh*, to which some people have access while others do not. Appeals to this mystery are ubiquitous in the text, and cannot be removed by redaction-critical surgery.

Hempel may, however, be on the right track when she suggests that the authors of *4QInstruction* were in some sense forerunners of the *yahad*. Al Baumgarten has suggested that one can divide

the course of a successful idea or institution into vague antecedents, forerunners, maturity, and after-effects. What separates any one stage from the others is the extent to which the idea or institution served as a basis for social cohesion and action. This determination is only possible with the benefit of hindsight: a historian must first know when full maturity was reached, and only then can the story be organized in a meaningful way.[54]

The account of the development of a sectarian community in CD 1 is an example of this kind of retrospective assessment. Before the arrival of the Teacher, the penitents were like blind men groping for the way. They did not necessarily see themselves that way at the time. We do not know whether *4QInstruction* was a product of these "blind men" of the *Damascus Document*. There were several proto-sectarian groups in Judea in the third and second centuries BCE, as can be seen from the Enoch literature and other pseudepigrapha. It does appear, however, that *4QInstruction* reflects a stage of spiritual separatism that was not yet embodied in social action. The "spiritual people" were aware of their need to separate from "the spirit of flesh," but they had not yet found their Teacher. They had not yet developed the kind of systematic focus on Torah interpretation that we find in the "mature" sectarian scrolls from Qumran, and they had not yet set up the social structures that would enable them to separate themselves from the multitude of the people.

---

[53] C. Hempel, "The Qumran Sapiential Texts and the Rule Books," in Hempel et al., eds., *The Wisdom Texts from Qumran*, 282. The idea of editorial strata in *4QInstruction* has been argued especially by T. Elgvin, "Wisdom and Apocalypticism in the Early Second Century BCE: The Evidence of *4QInstruction*," in Schiffman et al., eds., *The Dead Sea Scrolls Fifty Years after Their Discovery*, 226–47. Goff, *The Worldly and Heavenly Wisdom*, argues strongly against separating the different kinds of material.

[54] Baumgarten, *The Flourishing of Jewish Sects*, 24.

Part Three
The Sectarian Worldview

CHAPTER TWELVE

Covenant and Dualism in the Dead Sea Scrolls

The sectarian movement known from the Scrolls was first of all a movement of covenant renewal.[1] This is especially clear in the *Damascus Document*, which like most but not all scholars I take to contain an earlier formulation of sectarian rules than the *Community Rule*,[2] but the latter, too, at least in the form preserved in 1QS, begins with a covenant renewal ceremony.

Covenantal nomism

The centrality of the Mosaic covenant for Second Temple Judaism is amply clear. E. P. Sanders argued that most Jewish literature of that period subscribed to a pattern of religion that he dubbed covenantal nomism. By a pattern of religion he meant "how a religion is perceived by its adherents to function," specifically "how getting in and staying in are understood."[3] The biblical basis of this pattern was set out especially in the book of Deuteronomy, although Sanders expounds it primarily on the basis of Tannaitic literature. At the heart of the covenant was the demand for obedience to the commandments, with curses for disobedience and blessings for observance.[4] But there was also an antecedent history, which explained how the covenant was initiated by the gracious acts of God. Sanders was at pains to counteract Christian caricatures of Jewish legalism. He insisted that "entrance into the covenant was prior to the fulfillment of commandments; in other words, that the covenant was not earned, but that obedience to the commandments is the consequence of the prior election of Israel by God."[5] Again, "the election was of all Israel... the individual's place in God's plan was accomplished by his being a member of the group ... The

---

[1] For a comprehensive treatment of the covenantal ideologies in the scrolls see Stephen Hultgren, *From the Damascus Covenant to the Covenant of the Community* (STDJ 66; Leiden: Brill, 2007).

[2] John J. Collins, *Beyond the Qumran Community. The Sectarian Movement of the Dead Sea Scrolls* (Grand Rapids: Eerdmans, 2010) 12–87.

[3] E. P. Sanders, *Paul and Palestinian Judaism. A Comparison of Patterns of Religion* (Philadelphia: Fortress, 1977) 17.

[4] For a lucid exposition, see Jon D. Levenson, *Sinai and Zion: An Entry into the Jewish Bible* (San Francisco: Harper, 1987) 15–86.

[5] Sanders, *Paul and Palestinian Judaism*, 85.

question is whether or not one is an Israelite in good standing."[6] While Deuteronomy envisioned the consequences of the covenant in this-worldly terms, many Jews in the later Second Temple period believed in resurrection and a differentiated afterlife. In the rabbinic literature, the pervasive view is that "all Israelites have a share in the world to come" (*Sanhedrin* 10.1) although there are exceptions.[7]

A sectarian covenant?

A sectarian movement, which distinguished itself from "the majority of the people" in the phrase of 4QMMT, obviously required some modification of this understanding of the covenant. In fact, as Sanders also noted, the sectarian view of the covenant is formulated in two distinct ways in the Scrolls. On the one hand, we read of a *new* covenant (1QpHab 2:3), sometimes specified as "the new covenant in the land of Damascus" (CD 6:19; 8:21; 20:12).[8] On the other, the covenant is the one God made with Moses, but it contained hidden things that are known only to this community. So we read in CD 3:12–15:

But with those who remained steadfast in God's precepts, with those who were left from among them, God established his covenant with Israel forever, revealing to them hidden matters in which all Israel had gone astray: his holy Sabbaths and his glorious feasts, his just stipulations and his truthful paths, and the wishes of his will which man must do in order to live by them.

The sectarians believed that they had the only correct interpretation of the Torah of Moses, even though it was meant for all Israel. Consequently, the members are said to enter the covenant for all Israel (CD 15:5) and take "the oath of the covenant which Moses established with Israel, the covenant to return to the Torah of Moses with all one's heart and with all one's soul" (CD 15:8–9). Also, the sectarians believed that all Israel would walk according to their regulations in the end of days (1QSa 1:1–2). Sanders notes

both in 1QSa and 1QM a terminological difference from 1QH and 1QS. In the latter two, the sect does not employ the title Israel for itself, and its enemies are non-sectarian Israelites. In the former, the saved become 'Israel,' and the enemies are Gentiles. The distinction is clearly

---

[6] *Ibid.*, 237, citing Ephraim Urbach, *The Sages. Their Concepts and Beliefs* (Jerusalem: Magnes, 1975) 538–40.

[7] Israel J. Yuval, "All Israel Have a Portion in the World to Come," in Fabian Udoh, with Susannah Heschel, Mark Chancey, and Gregory Tatum, eds., *Redefining First-Century Jewish and Christian Identities. Essays in Honor of Ed Parish Sanders* (Notre Dame: University of Notre Dame Press, 2008) 114–138, argues that the statement about all Israel sharing in the world to come is a late anti-Christian addition to the Mishnah. I will return to this issue at the end of the article.

[8] On the biblical and theological foundations, see Hultgren, *From the Damascus Covenant*, 77–140. See also my article, "The Construction of Israel in the Sectarian Rule Books," in Alan J. Avery-Peck, Jacob Neusner and Bruce Chilton, eds., *Judaism in Late Antiquity. Part 5, Volume 1; The Judaism of Qumran: A Systemic Reading of the Dead Sea Scrolls* (Leiden: Brill, 2001) 25–42.

that 1QSa and 1QM are addressed to the time of the eschatological war. *At that time* the sect will become identical with Israel.[9]

For the present, however, even if all Israel *should* follow the "correct" interpretation of the Torah, it was painfully obvious that it did not. Consequently, "'returning to the Law of Moses' is in fact equivalent to joining the 'new covenant'."[10] It required admission to a voluntary association, with its own rituals for admission and expulsion, and Instruction in the rulings peculiar to that association. Similarly in 1QS 5:8–9:

> Whoever enters the council of the *yahad* enters the covenant of God ... He shall swear with a binding oath to revert to the Law of Moses, according to all that he commanded, with whole heart and whole soul, in compliance with all that has been revealed of it to the sons of Zadok, the priests who keep the covenant ... and to the multitude of the men of their covenant.

The expression "their covenant" is telling. Even though it is identified as "the covenant of God," it is defined by the distinctive interpretation of the *yahad*.

Since the *Community Rule*, unlike the *Damascus Document*, does not locate the community in the history of Israel, its consciousness of belonging to a covenant people has been questioned,[11] but in fact it clearly affirms the need "to return to his covenant through the community" (1QS 5:22). There is some ambiguity as to how one comes to be in the covenant in the first place. God establishes his covenant with those who remained faithful (CD 3:12–15). Those who formed "the new covenant" have often been categorized as a penitential movement. They realized their iniquity and realized that they were guilty (CD 1:8–9). Yet this alone would have been of no avail had God not raised up for them a Teacher of Righteousness. There is, in short, a dialectic between human merit and divine grace.[12] It remains true, however, that the covenant provides the context in which people can please God by obeying his commandments, and this covenant is clearly continuous with the traditional Mosaic covenant.

Sanders insisted that all of this could comfortably be subsumed under the heading of "covenantal nomism," but some of the modifications of Deuteronomic theology are significant. The Scrolls never deny that the covenant is intended for all Israel, and the authors were well aware that their movement was not identical with all Israel in the present. They hoped it would be so in the eschatological future, but even then the *War Scroll* acknowledged that "the violators of the covenant" would share

---

[9] Sanders, *Paul and Palestinian Judaism*, 249–50.

[10] *Ibid.*, 241.

[11] Ellen Juhl Christiansen, "The Consciousness of Belonging to God's Covenant and What it entails, according to the *Damascus Document* and the *Community Rule*," in F. H. Cryer and T. L. Thompson, eds., *Qumran between the Old and New Testaments* (Sheffield: Sheffield Academic Press, 1998) 87.

[12] David Lambert, "Was the Dead Sea Sect a Penitential Movement?" in Timothy Lim and John J. Collins, eds., *The Oxford Handbook of the Dead Sea Scrolls* (Oxford: Oxford University Press, 2010) 501–13, questions the appropriateness of describing the sect as a penitential movement.

the lot of the Kittim. In short, from the perspective of the sect, it is not true that all Israel has a share in the world to come.

The Two Spirits

The manuscript 1QS, however, introduces another pattern of thought that is quite different from Deuteronomic theology, in the *Instruction on the Two Spirits*. Here we read that "from the God of knowledge comes all that is and shall be. Before ever they existed He established their whole design." Not only has God created man to rule the world, as described in Genesis 1, but he also

> appointed for him two spirits in which to walk until the time of his visitation: the spirits of truth and injustice. Those born of truth spring from a fountain of light, but those born of injustice spring from a source of darkness. All the children of righteousness are ruled by the Prince of Light and walk in the ways of light, but all the children of injustice are ruled by the Angel of Darkness and walk in the ways of darkness. The Angel of Darkness leads all the children of righteousness astray, and until his end, all their sin, iniquities, wickedness, and all their unlawful deeds are caused by his dominion in accordance with the mysteries of God. (1QS 3:15–23)

The *Instruction on the Two Spirits* is a complex and carefully constructed passage. As Philip Alexander has remarked, it is one of the most remarkable theological texts to survive from early Judaism, at least in Hebrew or Aramaic. "I know of no other theological work in either of these languages so systemic and so propositional in its presentation, until we come to the little cosmological instruction known as the *Sefer Yesirah*," many centuries later.[13] It begins with a veritable table of contents: "It is for the Maskil to instruct and teach all the Sons of Light concerning the nature of all the sons of man, with respect to all the kinds of spirits with their distinctions for their works in their generations, and with respect to the visitation of their afflictions together with their times of peace" (3:13–15a). This is followed by an account of creation (3:15–18), then an outline of the two spirits (3:18–4:1), then the effects of the two spirits in the world (4:2–14; 2–8 on the spirit of light and 9–14 on the spirit of darkness). Finally, the last section, 4:15–26, describes the struggle of the two spirits for control of humanity.[14]

---

[13] Philip Alexander, "Predestination and Free Will in the Theology of the Dead Sea Scrolls," in John M. G. Barclay and Simon Gathercole, eds., *Divine and Human Agency in Paul and His Cultural Environment* (Library of New Testament Studies 335; London/New York: T & T Clark, 2006) 27–46, here 26.

[14] See Jutta Leonhardt-Baltzer, "Evil, Dualism and Community: Who/What Did the Yahad Not Want to Be," in Geza G. Xeravits, ed., *Dualism in Qumran* (LSTS [JSPSup] 76; London and New York: T&T Clark, 2010) 131. Compare Jörg Frey, "Different Patterns of Dualistic Thought in the Qumran Library," in Moshe Bernstein, Florentino García Martínez and John Kampen, eds., *Legal Texts and Legal Issues* (Leiden: Brill, 1997) 290.

Several scholars have attempted to distinguish redactional layers in this text.[15] So, for example, Peter von der Osten-Sacken posited a first expansion in 1QS 4:15–23a, which introduces the idea of a division within every human being, and a second one in 4:23b-26, which elaborates the first addition.[16] Jean Duhaime added another layer of additions in 1QS 3:18b–25.[17] Against such proposals, Jörg Frey has argued that the extant text conforms to the introductory heading, and should be read as a literary unit.[18] Frey finds a "multi-dimensional pattern of dualism" in the text, combining *cosmic dualism*, in the opposition of two spiritual beings, the Prince of Light and the Angel of Darkness; *ethical dualism*, in the opposition of two classes of human beings with virtues and vices, and *psychological dualism*, which posits the presence of the two spirits within each individual. Cosmic dualism is found without the other layers in some other texts from Qumran (*Testament of Amram*, the *War Scroll*). Ethical dualism is rooted in the wisdom tradition. The psychological dualism is peculiar to the *Instruction on the Two Spirits*. Only one other text, 4Q186, a physiognomic text in Aramaic, posits partial shares in light and darkness within individuals, and its relevance to the *Instruction* in 1QS is disputed, since its frame of reference is astrological rather than a doctrine of creation.[19] This "psychological dualism" stands in some logical tension with the cosmological dualism, which more easily envisions a clean separation into two parties, but if a redactor of the *Instruction* could regard them as compatible, it is not apparent why the author of the *Instruction* could not have done so. The tension lies between the underlying traditions, which are brought together in a distinctive way in 1QS.

As Philip Alexander has remarked, "haggadah and midrash are conspicuous by their absence" from the *Instruction*, and there is no explicit appeal to normative scripture.[20] Nonetheless, it presupposes a distinctive reading of Genesis 1–3.[21] The statement that God created 'enosh to rule the world echoes Gen 1:28. God gave the

---

[15] For a convenient overview see Charlotte Hempel, "The *Instruction on the Two Spirits*," in Xeravits, ed., *Dualism in Qumran*, 110–13.

[16] Peter von der Osten-Sacken, *Gott und Belial. Traditionsgeschichtliche Untersuchungen zum Dualismus in den Texten aus Qumran* (SUNT 6; Göttingen: Vandenhoeck & Ruprecht, 1969) 17–27; 116–89.

[17] Jean Duhaime, "Dualistic Reworking in the Scrolls from Qumran," *CBQ* 49 (1987) 32–56, especially 40–43. For a different redactional analysis, based on varying levels of terminological and theological overlap with *4QInstruction*, see Eibert Tigchelaar, *To Increase Learning for the Understanding Ones: Reading and Reconstructing the Fragmentary Early Jewish Sapiential Text 4QInstruction* (STDJ 44; Leiden: Brill, 2001) 201–3.

[18] Jörg Frey, "Different Patterns of Dualistic Thought," 289–95. Alexander, "Predestination and Freewill," also favors literary unity.

[19] Mladen Popović, *Reading the Human Body. Physiognomics and Astrology in the Dead Sea Scrolls and Hellenistic–Early Roman Period Judaism* (STDJ 67; Leiden: Brill, 2007) 186–91.

[20] Alexander, "Predestination and Free Will," 27.

[21] See my essay "The Interpretation of Genesis in the Dead Sea Scrolls," in Akio Moriya and Gohei Hata, eds., *Pentateuchal Traditions in the Late Second Temple Period. Proceedings of the International Workshop in Tokyo, August 28–31, 2007* (JSJSup 158; Leiden: Brill, 2012) 157–75 (= chapter 5 in this volume).

two spirits to human beings "so that they might know good [and evil]."²² The ultimate goal is to inherit "the glory of Adam" (4:23). In Genesis, the primal couple are forbidden to eat the fruit of the tree of knowledge of good and evil. Here, however, God wants people to have that knowledge.

The *Instruction on the Two Spirits* was not the first or only text that claimed that God had given humanity the knowledge of good and evil. According to Ben Sira,

The Lord created human beings out of the earth
and makes them return to it again ...
He endowed them with strength like his own
And made them in his own image...
He filled them with knowledge and understanding
And showed them good and evil. (Sir 17:1–7)

It was inconceivable to the sage that God would have denied people knowledge and understanding, and he read the creation story accordingly. Ben Sira also hints at a dualistic structure in creation.

All human beings come from the ground
and humankind was created out of the dust.
In the fullness of his knowledge the Lord distinguished them
And appointed their different ways.
Some he blessed and exalted,
And some he made holy and brought near to himself;
But some he cursed and brought low,
And turned them out of their place.
Like clay in the hand of the potter to be molded as he pleases
So all are in the hand of their maker, to be given whatever he decides. (Sir 33:10–13)

Ben Sira goes on to say that all the works of the Most High come in pairs, one the opposite of the other. Ben Sira is notoriously inconsistent, and on other occasions he affirms a vigorous belief in the human freedom to choose. He is still far from the dualism of the Two Spirits, but his musings may well reflect an early stage of the debate in wisdom circles about the origin of evil.²³

Another important stage in that debate is illustrated by *4QInstruction*, a long wisdom text from Qumran that was only published in the 1990's. In a much disputed passage we read:

Engraved is the ordinance, and ordained is all the punishment. For engraved is that which is ordained by God against all the iniquities of the children of Seth. And written in His presence is a book of remembrance of those who keep His word, and it is the Vision of Meditation (Hagu/i) and a Book of Remembrance. He gave it as an inheritance to 'enosh, together with a spiritual people, for he fashioned him after the likeness of the Holy Ones. But the Meditation

---

²² 1QS 4:26. [and evil] has to be restored.
²³ See my essay, "Wisdom, Apocalypticism and the Dead Sea Scrolls," in my book, *Seers, Sibyls and Sages in Hellenistic-Roman Judaism* (JSJSup 54; Leiden: Brill, 1997) 369–83.

is no longer given to the spirit of flesh, for it did not distinguish between good and evil, according to the judgment of its spirit. (4Q417 1 i.14–18).[24]

While many details of this passage are disputed, it clearly envisions a binary division of humanity. In the words of Jörg Frey:

it is obvious that wisdom is not accessible to everyone, but limited to a certain group of people, and that the fact that only the knowledgeable have access to that hidden wisdom is explained from a primordial act in which insight was revealed to the 'spiritual people', not to the 'fleshly spirit'.[25]

The statement that the "spiritual people" was fashioned in the likeness of the Holy Ones, or angels, is a reading of Gen 1:26, in which *adam* is created in the image of *elohim*. The statement that the Hagu was denied to the spirit of flesh because it did not distinguish between good and evil, alludes to the second creation story in Genesis 2–3. In this text, however, God does not prevent people from attaining the knowledge of good and evil. Rather, because the spirit of flesh fails to distinguish, God denies it the revelation.[26]

Armin Lange and Jörg Frey have argued that these sapiential reflections on the creation stories provide the context for the emergence of dualism in the *Instruction on the Two Spirits*.[27] They certainly provide one relevant context, but as Frey admits, they provide no precedent for cosmic dualism, the idea of two conflicting Spirits or Light and Darkness, Truth and Falsehood. (Another wisdom text, 1Q27, or *1QMysteries*, says that evil will vanish as darkness before the light, but this metaphorical usage is quite different from the cosmic dualism of the Two Spirits.) The only precedent for cosmic dualism of this sort is found in another Qumran text, the *Testament of Amram* (4Q453–58, 459?), an Aramaic text that has been dated to the late third or early second century BCE on the basis of language and palaeography, and so appears to come from a time before the emergence of the sectarian movement known from the Scrolls.[28] In one of the fragments of this work, Amram recounts a vision of two angelic beings, who are fighting over him. One of them rules over darkness and

---

[24] John Strugnell and Daniel J. Harrington, *"Instruction,"* in John Strugnell, Daniel J. Harrington and Torleif Elgvin, *Qumran Cave 4. XXIV. Sapiential Texts, Part 2* (DJD 34; Oxford: Clarendon, 1999) 151–72.

[25] Jörg Frey, "Apocalyptic Dualism," in John J. Collins, ed., *The Oxford Handbook of Apocalyptic Literature* (New York: Oxford, 2014) chapter 16.

[26] See further my essay, "In the Likeness of the Holy Ones: The Creation of Humankind in a Wisdom Text from Qumran," in D. W. Parry and E. Ulrich, eds., *The Provo International Conference on the Dead Sea Scrolls* (Leiden: Brill, 1999) 609–18.

[27] Armin Lange, *Weisheit und Prädestination: Weisheitliche Urordnung und Prädestination in den Textfunden von Qumran* (STDJ 18. Leiden: Brill, 1995) 121–70; idem, "Die Weisheitstexte aus Qumran: Eine Einleitung" in C. Hempel, A. Lange, and H. Lichtenberger, eds., *The Wisdom Texts from Qumran and the Development of Sapiential Thought* (BETL 159; Leuven: Peeters, 2002) 3–30, especially 25–26; Frey, "Different Patterns of Dualistic Thought," 295–300.

[28] Émile Puech, *Qumrân Grotte 4. XXII. Textes Araméens. Première Partie. 4Q529–549* DJD 31; Oxford: Clarendon, 2001) 283–405. On the dating, see pp. 285–87.

all that pertain to it, while the other rules over the sons of light. They ask him by which of them he chooses to be ruled. The two angelic beings each have three names, but only one of the names of the Angel of Darkness is preserved: Melchiresha.[29] It is reasonable to infer that his adversary is Melchizedek, who is known as an angelic or divine figure from *11QMelchizedek*. It is apparent from this text that humanity was thought to be divided between sons of light and sons of darkness, or "sons of the lie" and "sons of truth." The surviving fragments do not list the ethical characteristics of either group, and Amram at least appears to have a choice between them.[30] There is no precedent for this kind of dualism in the Hebrew Bible. When Deutero-Isaiah says that YHWH forms light and creates darkness (Isa 45:7) he is not speaking of spirits in which humanity must walk.

Persian dualism

There was, of course, a well-known precedent for cosmic dualism in the Hellenistic Near East, in the teachings of the Persian prophet Zoroaster.[31] While most of the Zoroastrian writings are preserved in Pahlavi texts from the early Middle Ages, the Gathas are recognized as old, possibly deriving from Zoroaster himself,[32] and we also have accounts in Greek and Roman authors, most notably in Plutarch, who claims to derive his account from Theopompus (c. 300 BCE).[33] The Gathas already speak of two spirits:

In the beginning those two spirits who are the well-endowed twins were known as the one good and the other evil, in thought, word, and deed. Between them the wise chose rightly, not so the fools. And when these Spirits met they established in the beginning life and death that in the end the followers of the Lie should meet with the worst existence, but the followers of Truth with the Best Mind. Of these two spirits he who was of the Lie chose to do the worst

---

[29] 4Q544 2 13. See also Paul J. Kobelski, *Melchizedek and Melchiresha'* (CBQMS 10; Washington, DC: The Catholic Biblical Association of America, 1981) 24–36.

[30] Liora Goldman, "Dualism in the Visions of Amram," *RevQ* 95 (2010) 421–32, underlines the differences between the dualism of *4QAmram* and that of 1QS, insofar as the Aramaic text is not so clearly deterministic. She also questions whether 4Q548, which mentions "sons of light" and "sons of darkness," belongs to the same text as the other fragments.

[31] Geo Widengren, Anders Hultgård, Marc Philonenko, *Apocalyptique Iranienne et Dualisme Qoumrânien* (Paris: Maisonneuve, 1995); Anders Hultgård, "Persian Apocalypticism," in John J. Collins, ed., *The Encyclopedia of Apocalypticism. Vol. 1. The Origins of Apocalypticism in Judaism and Christianity* (New York: Continuum, 1998) 39–83; Prods Oktor Skjaervø, "Zoroastrian Dualism," in Armin Lange, Eric M. Meyers, Bennie H. Reynolds III, Randall Styers, eds., *Light against Darkness* (JAJSup 2; Göttingen: Vandenhoeck & Ruprecht, 2011) 55–91.

[32] Albert de Jong, "Iranian Connections in the Dead Sea Scrolls," in Timothy H. Lim and John J. Collins, eds., *The Oxford Handbook of the Dead Sea Scrolls* (Oxford: Oxford University Press, 2010) 480.

[33] Albert de Jong, *Traditions of the Magi. Zoroastrianism in Greek and Latin Literature* (Leiden: Brill, 1997) 157–204 on Plutarch.

things; but the Most Holy Spirit, clothed in rugged heaven, [chose] Truth as did [all] who sought with zeal to do the pleasure of the Wise Lord by [doing] good works.[34]

The Gathas do not associate the two spirits with light and darkness, but Plutarch, citing Theopompus, says that "Horomazes (Ahura Mazda) is born from the purest light and Areimanius (Ahriman) from darkness, and they are at war with one another."[35]

In classical, medieval, Zoroastrianism, the two spirits are coeval, uncreated beings, and this seems to be the case already in Plutarch's account. In the Gathas, however, at least on the usual interpretation, the two spirits (identified as Spenta Mainyu and Angra Mainyu) were thought to be the twin children of Ahura Mazda, who was therefore the sole supreme god above them.[36]

The affinity of the *Instruction on the Two Spirits* in 1QS to Persian, Zoroastrian, dualism was pointed out by the German scholar K. G. Kuhn shortly after the text was published, and remains compelling.[37] In the words of Albert de Jong,

> If we restrict ourselves, for the sake of the argument, to the description of the two spirits, the system of 1QS is almost wholly parallel to the Iranian one. That is to say, the two spirits are wholly opposed to each other and do not share a single common trait. They are associated with two distinct realms, described in (predictable) opposing terms. The one is described as 'truth,' has his origins in a source of light, and is located – occasionally – in the highest realms of reality, being with God. The other is described as 'deceit,' has his origins in a source of darkness, and belongs, more clearly, to a lower realm (the 'abyss') where darkness itself is located.[38]

But there are differences too. As de Jong also points out, "the Zoroastrian sources ... do not at any moment suggest that Ahura Mazda has pre-ordained everything."[39] In that respect, the Testament of Amram, where Amram is supposed to choose between the two spirits, provides a closer parallel to the Gathas than does the *Instruction on the Two Spirits*. But the structural similarity is striking, and can hardly be coincidental. Judah had been ruled by Persia for two hundred years, and the distinctive Persian beliefs aroused the interest of Greek writers in the Hellenistic and Roman periods, so while we do not know the doctrine of the two spirits came to the attention of an Essene, the possibility of an encounter with Persian ideas poses no great problem.

---

[34] Yasna 30; trans. R. C. Zaehner, *The Dawn and Twilight of Zoroastrianism* (London: Weidenfeld & Nicolson, 1961) 42.

[35] Plutarch, *Isis and Osiris* 47; J. Gwyn Griffiths, *Plutarch's De Iside et Osiride* (Cardiff: University of Wales, 1970) 46–7. Amazingly, Leonhardt-Balzer, "Evil, Dualism and Community," 129, claims that "the contrasting terms light-darkness do not play any part in the Iranian myth."

[36] de Jong, "Iranian Connections," 481. He notes that this interpretation has been questioned on philological grounds by Jean Kellens and Eric Pirart, "La strophe des jumeaux: stagnation, extravagance et autres methods d'approche," *JA* 285 (1997) 31–72.

[37] K. G. Kuhn, "Die Sektenschrift und die iranische Religion," *ZTK* 49 (1952) 296–316. See John J. Collins, *The Dead Sea Scrolls. A Biography* (Princeton: Princeton University Press, 2012) 154–7.

[38] de Jong, "Iranian Connections," 493–4.

[39] *Ibid.*, 492.

Many scholars have been reluctant to accept the idea of Persian influence in the Scrolls, for various reasons. For Paul Heger, it is decisive that "dualism conflicts with Israelite doctrines," as if these were always and ever the same, and he insists that the *Instruction on the Two Spirits* must be explained from Scripture.[40] Other scholars are deterred by their lack of familiarity with Persian religion, and the problems of dating the Persian sources. It is not uncommon for serious scholars to suggest that if we can find Jewish parallels for ideas in the Scrolls we can spare ourselves the exertion of looking farther. There is no doubt that the *Instruction* draws phraseology from the older scriptures, or that it relates to Jewish traditions in many ways. It is a Jewish text, not a Persian one, and it was not attempting to reproduce Persian ideas as they might have been understood in their original context. Cultural influence is always shaped to meet the needs of the borrower. Even if the author of the *Instruction* had encountered a form of Persian dualism in which the two spirits were primeval, he would surely have subordinated them to the creator God, in accordance with Isa 45:7. But nonetheless the *Instruction on the Two Spirits* was a novelty in Jewish tradition, and its novelty is due primarily to its balanced cosmic dualism, that is characteristic of Zoroastrianism and alien to the biblical tradition.

But it is also apparent that the *Instruction* adapted the dualism of the Two Spirits for its purposes. Most notably, human beings are not allowed to choose between them, but their allegiance is determined at creation. The idea that the conflict between the spirits takes place within the individual person, and that everyone has a share in both spirits is also most probably an innovation.

The provenance of the *Instruction*

It is now apparent that the *Instruction on the Two Spirits* was not an invariable part of the *Community Rule*. It is found in only one other manuscript besides 1QS, a papyrus manuscript 4QS^c.[41] It was clearly not part of 4QS^e and 4QS^d, which began at 1QS 5, and Sarianna Metso has argued persuasively that they contain a form of the Rule that is more original than 1QS.[42] Hartmut Stegemann suggested that "the Essenes adopted this didactic piece unchanged from older tradition"[43] and in this he

---

[40] Paul Heger, "Another Look at Dualism in Qumran Writings," in Xeravits, ed., *Dualism in Qumran*, 39–101 (quoted from p. 41). This essay is reprinted in idem, *Challenges to Conventional Opinions on Qumran and Enoch Issues* (STDJ 100; Leiden: Brill, 2012) 227–310.

[41] Alexander, "Predestination and Free Will," 38; Hempel, "The *Instruction on the Two Spirits* and the Literary History of the Rule of the Community," 102–20.

[42] Sarianna Metso, *The Textual Development of the Qumran Community Rule* (STDJ 21; Leiden Brill, 1997) 107. This is disputed by Philip Alexander, "The Redaction-History of *Serek ha-Yahad*: A Proposal," *RevQ* 17 (1996) 437–53.

[43] Hartmut Stegemann, *The Library of Qumran. On the Essenes, John the Baptist and Jesus* (Grand Rapids: Eerdmans, 1998) 110.

has been followed by Armin Lange[44] and Jörg Frey.[45] One way of testing this hypothesis is to see whether the doctrine is modified when it appears in a text that is clearly sectarian.

Covenant and dualism

In 1QS, the *Instruction on the Two Spirits* follows immediately on a covenant renewal ceremony, which has itself a distinctly dualistic coloring. The juxtaposition raises the question how such a dualistic and deterministic worldview can be reconciled with the covenantal nomism that is so widely attested in the Scrolls. Klaus Baltzer argued that the *Instruction* itself could be understood as an adaptation of what he called "the covenant formulary." To be sure, the historical prologue that characterized the covenantal texts in the Hebrew Bible is replaced here by a "dogmatic section," which gives a dualistic account of the human condition. But since the passage goes on to contrast two ways of living, and associate them with different outcomes, he reasoned that the covenantal structure is intact.[46] But this is to miss the significance of the account of cosmic dualism. The traditional covenant presupposed a vigorous doctrine of free will, by which the Israelites were to choose to obey the commandments or not, and were fully responsible for their actions. The suggestion that human beings are determined by angelic or demonic forces, and that their design is established in advance, departs radically from this view, and has very little precedent in the Hebrew Bible.

The covenant ceremony at the beginning of the *Community Rule* is designed for those who enter "the covenant of God" during the reign of Belial. The priests recount the wondrous works of God and his merciful acts of love towards Israel. Then the Levites enumerate the iniquities of the sons of Israel and all their guilty transgressions during the reign of Belial. And all those who cross over into the covenant shall confess after them, saying "We have perverted ourselves, we have rebel[led], we [have sin]ned, we have acted impiously, we [and] our [fath]ers before us ..." They acknowledge that God had been righteous in his judgment "against us and our fathers."

The confession of sin would seem to presuppose free will, and go against the deterministic theology of the *Instruction on the Two Spirits*. The passage continues, however, by blessing "the men of God's lot who walk perfectly in all his ways," and cursing the lot of Belial. At this point it is not apparent that those who "walk perfectly" have any sin to confess. The question arises whether the sins confessed by the Levites are those of the members of the *yahad*, or those of their ancestors. In short,

---

[44] Armin Lange, *Weisheit & Prädestination. Weisheitliche Urordnung & Prädestination in den Textfunden von Qumran* (STDJ 18; Leiden: Brill, 1995) 127–8.
[45] Frey, "Different Patterns of Dualistic Thought," 289.
[46] Klaus Baltzer, *The Covenant Formulary* (Oxford: Blackwell, 1971) 99–109.

those entering the covenant acknowledge the righteousness of God's judgment on past generations, in accordance with traditional covenantal theology, but they give thanks that they have been assigned a better lot, and correspondingly curse those who have not.

The question of free will arises again in connection with defection from the community: "Cursed be he who enters into this covenant and puts the stumbling-block of his iniquity before him so that he backslides (stumbling) over it.... May his spirit be destroyed, (suffering) thirst along with saturation, without forgiveness ... May all the curses of this covenant stick to him" (1QS 2:11–17). It is not clear here whether the backsliders are thought to have been genuinely members of the covenant, who changed over time, or impostors, who were never truly members of the covenant in the first place.

The covenant renewal ceremony in 1QS 1:16–3:13 says nothing about spirits battling within the individual heart. Consequently, Jörg Frey judges it to exhibit a different kind of dualism from the *Instruction on the Two Spirits*, and to confirm that the latter is not itself a product of the *yahad*.[47] There is no room for ambiguity, or for partial adherence, in the covenant. It seems to me, however, that the evidence could be read otherwise. If the spirits struggle within the individual, then presumably a person may be tugged this way or that. If a person sins, this is due to the Spirit of Darkness, but the person is culpable nonetheless. As Philip Alexander has argued,

> whether a man is counted righteous or wicked depends on the preponderance of Truth and Falsehood in his make-up: 'According to a man's share in Truth shall he be righteous and thus hate falsehood, and according to his inheritance in the lot of Falsehood shall he be wicked'.[48]

The very fact that the covenantal ceremony makes provision for expulsion, shows that a member's status may vary, even if his end-state is pre-determined.

Various scholars have pointed to aspects of life in the *yahad* that seem to imply free will. These include the use of petitionary prayer,[49] or voluntary actions such as entering the community, or the presence of a penal code.[50] Some might infer that the *Instruction on the Two Spirits* is atypical of the movement, but Alexander has recently argued for extensive influence.[51] In addition to the *War Rule*, which clearly exhibits cosmic dualism, he points to 4Q502, the so-called "Ritual of Marriage," which appears to quote 1QS 4:4–6; 4Q186, the physiognomic text, where he finds "strong intertextuality" with the *Instruction*, and the *Songs of the Sabbath Sacrifice*, which contain "a significant allusion" to it ("For from the God of knowledge comes

---

[47] Frey, "Apocalyptic Dualism."

[48] 1QS 4:24; cf. 4:15–16.

[49] Eileen Schuller, "Petitionary Prayer and the Religion of Qumran," in J. J. Collins and R. A. Kugler, eds., *Religion in the Dead Sea Scrolls* (Grand Rapids: Eerdmans, 2000) 29–45.

[50] See Mladen Popovic, "Apocalyptic Determinism," in Collins, ed., *The Oxford Handbook of Apocalyptic Literature*, chapter 15.

[51] Alexander, "Predestination and Free Will," 39–47.

all that exists forever ...").⁵² Most notable for our purposes is the presence of dualistic elements in the *Damascus Document*. One recension of the *Document* begins with an exhortation "for the So]ns of Light to keep apart from the wa[ys of Darkness."⁵³ CD 5:17–19 portrays the struggle between Moses and Aaron and the Egyptian magicians Jannes and Jambres in terms of the struggle between the Prince of Light and Belial. CD 2:2–13 is introduced as an address to those who enter the covenant. It does not mention spirits of Light and Darkness, but it has a strongly deterministic tone. It says of the wicked: "From the beginning God chose them not. He knew their deeds before ever they were created and he hated their generations." Conversely, in every generation he called for himself men called by name that a remnant might be left to the Land.⁵⁴ This kind of deterministic language seems to be at odds with the centrality of the covenant, which is usually thought to require free will. We should remember, however, that even Ben Sira, who is usually regarded as a staunch defender of free will, used deterministic language on occasion and said that human beings are left in the power of their *yeser*, or inclination.⁵⁵ The *yeser* is not an external force as the spirits are, but nonetheless it cannot be equated with free will, and it is not entirely subject to rational control.⁵⁶ Many Judeans in the late Second Temple period subscribed to some combination of fate and free will. According to Josephus, the Pharisees "attribute everything to fate and to God; they hold that to act rightly or otherwise rests, indeed, for the most part with men, but that in each action fate cooperates."⁵⁷ Or, in the famous dictum of Rabbi Akiba, "all is foreseen, yet freedom of choice is granted."⁵⁸ There are, to be sure, significant differences between the positions attributed to the Pharisees and the Essenes, but they are differences along a spectrum rather than absolute contrast.⁵⁹

Traces of dualism and determinism in the *Damascus Document* pose a problem for those, including myself, who think that the *Document* preserves an earlier sectarian rule than the *Serek*. Jean Duhaime suggested that the reference to the Prince of Light and Prince of Darkness in CD 5:17–19 was an instance of "dualistic rework-

---

⁵² 4Q402 4 12–15; 4Q406 1 1–2; Mas1k i 1–7. Carol A. Newsom, *Angelic Liturgy: Songs of the Sabbath Sacrifice* (Louisville: WestminsterJohnKnox/Tübingen: Mohr Siebeck, 1999) 152–3.

⁵³ 4Q266 (4QDᵃ).

⁵⁴ Alexander, "Predestination and Free Will," 42–44; Lange, *Weisheit & Prädestination*, 233–70.

⁵⁵ Sir 15:14. See John J. Collins, *Jewish Wisdom in the Hellenistic Age* (Louisville: Westminster, 1997) 80–84.

⁵⁶ On the *yeser* in rabbinic literature, see now Ishay Rosen-Zvi, "Two Rabbinic Inclinations? Rethinking a Scholarly Dogma," *JSJ* 39 (2008) 513–39, who argues that the idea of two inclinations is marginal in the rabbinic corpus, and that the evil *yeser* is predominant.

⁵⁷ Josephus *JW* 2.163. Compare *Ant* 18.13.

⁵⁸ m. Avot 3.16.

⁵⁹ See the discussion of various kinds of "compatibilism" in ancient Judaism by Jonathan Klawans, *Josephus and the Theologies of Ancient Judaism* (New York: Oxford University Press, 2012) chapter 2.

ing."⁶⁰ 4QDᵃ may reflect a recension of the older rule to bring it into line with the Serek. Perhaps. The interactions between the two rules are complex and should not all be attributed to one-way influence. But in any case, the forms of the Damascus rule that have survived include dualistic and deterministic language at several points.

Philip Alexander has argued, following the philosopher P. F. Strawson, that

however philosophically strong the arguments may be for determinism, we all, – even those of us who may theoretically subscribe to it – normally interact with each other in everyday life on the assumption that we are free agents.⁶¹

This was undoubtedly true for the Essenes as well as for anyone else. Seth Schwartz has argued that the doctrine of the Two Spirits is only the "most poignant and self-conscious form" of "the juxtaposition of incongruous systems" that characterized much of Judaism around the turn of the era.⁶² In his view, what he calls "the apocalyptic myth" in all its forms is in "stark contradiction of the covenantal ideology."⁶³ I would like to suggest, however, that what we find in the *Community Rule* is not merely the juxtaposition of incongruous systems. Rather, the dualistic and deterministic ideas are combined with the idea of covenant in an integral way, which entailed a serious revision of the traditional covenant. Those who entered the covenant affirmed their election, and their allegiance to the lot of Light, and this was regarded as meritorious, even though they were predetermined to do so. Conversely, those who rejected the covenant or defected from it displayed the abject nature that had been assigned to their lot, and were rightly cursed for it. The new covenant, in short, operated differently from Deuteronomy. Election was not only an offer made by God to select humans, but actually determined their fate. As Jeremiah might have said, it was a covenant written in the heart (Jer 31:33). The covenant left to human free choice had long ago been shown to be a failure.

Unlike the rabbis, the authors of these scrolls, the *Damascus Document* as well as the *Serek*, rejected the notion that all Israel has a share in the world to come, even if they still tended to equate the Sons of Light with Israel in texts like the *War Scroll* that referred to the eschatological time. The division between Sons of Light and Sons of Darkness was not universalistic – Gentiles were assumed to belong to the Sons of Darkness except for the poorly attested case of proselytes. But the covenantal community was no longer equated with ethnic Israel. The continued use of covenantal language then gives an impression of continuity but in fact masks a sharp rupture with biblical tradition.

---

⁶⁰ Duhaime, "Dualistic Reworking," 51–55
⁶¹ Alexander, "Predestination and Free Will," 49, citing P. F. Strawson, *Freedom and Resentment, and Other Essays* (London: Methuen, 1974).
⁶² Seth Schwartz, *Imperialism and Jewish Society, 200 B.C.E. to 640 C.E.* (Princeton: Princeton University Press, 2001) 79.
⁶³ *Ibid.*, 78.

This rupture was not necessarily peculiar to the communities that produced the Scrolls. Israel Yuval claims that the Pharisees "believed that only the righteous shall be worthy of a place in the world to come," although he does not document the claim.[64] (His claim seems to be an inference from the importance the Pharisees attached to the observance of the Torah.) Moreover, the following statement in the Mishnah, that one who denies the resurrection has no share in the world to come, would seem to exclude the Sadducees. Yuval also notes that the saying of Jesus that the meek will inherit the earth (Matt 5:5) assumes "an ethical and personal criterion."[65] Nonetheless, the idea that "all Israel will be saved" is affirmed by Paul in Romans 11:26, an affirmation that is all the more remarkable because Paul believed that salvation depended on faith in Christ, and that "a hardening" had come upon part of Israel (Rom 11:25). As Joseph Fitzmyer has shown, the phrase "all Israel," which occurs 148 times in the Old Testament, "always designates historic, ethnic Israel, usually in the synchronic sense of the generations of Israel contemporary with the author."[66] The Pauline statement shows that the idea that all Israel has a share in the world to come was current in the first century CE, but in fact it had been undercut to a great degree by the belief in a judgment after death that was not based on ethnicity but on individual merit.

The sectarian scrolls envision a new kind of community, one that is determined by divine election, even if the members can still be held responsible for their actions. This theology was shaped not only by Israelite and Judean traditions, but also by ideas derived from Persian dualism, although these ideas were also adapted and reformulated to produce a theology that was new and distinctive in the ancient world. The "profoundly dualistic and deterministic worldview"[67] expressed in *Instruction on the Two Spirits* fits a sectarian mentality remarkably well. I am not persuaded that it was an older composition taken over by the Essenes; I think it is more easily explained as a sectarian composition. Whether it was "all-pervasive in Qumran theology," as Alexander argues,[68] may still be debatable, but the fact that the *Instruction* was included in some editions of the *Community Rule* cannot be lightly dismissed. In any case, even compositions like the Damascus Rule, where dualism and determinism are present but not central, still entail a radical revision of the traditional covenant, and a redefinition of what it meant to belong to the Israel of God.

Seth Schwartz has argued that "the repeated juxtaposition of the covenant and the [apocalyptic] myth in ancient Jewish writing indicates that though the systems are logically incongruous, they did not for the most part generate social division."[69] The

---

[64] Yuval, "All Israel," 170.
[65] *Ibid.*, 120.
[66] Joseph A. Fitzmyer, S. J., *Romans* (AB 33; New York: Doubleday, 1992) 623. Yuval assumes that Paul is referring to Israel according to the spirit, or Christianity.
[67] Alexander, "Predestination and Free Will," 47.
[68] *Ibid.*
[69] Schwartz, *Imperialism and Jewish Society*, 81.

case of the new covenant and the *yahad*, however, is clearly an exception to this. (The case of the Enoch literature is less clear, but may well imply social division too.) The dualism of light and darkness went hand in hand with the separation of the sect from the rest of Judaism. It is probably fruitless to argue whether the division or the myth came first. If we may judge by 4QMMT, the separation of the sect was primarily due to legal disagreement, and so we might suppose that the doctrine of the two spirits was adopted secondarily to provide a theological explanation of the social division. It did not entail a rejection of the covenantal tradition, but it did entail a new way of understanding that tradition that had far-reaching implications for the Jewish identity of the sectarian movement.

CHAPTER THIRTEEN

The Angelic Life

The idea that human beings can be transported to the world of the gods is an ancient one, in the Near East as well as in Greece. One can think, for example, of Utnapishtim in Mesopotamia, or of Enoch and Elijah in the biblical tradition. In ancient Israel, however, such exaltation was exceptional. It is only at the end of the biblical period that the idea takes hold that righteous human beings, or at least righteous Israelites, would join the heavenly host after death. In Jewish tradition, this belief is first attested in the apocalyptic books of Daniel and Enoch, in the early second century BCE.[1]

Angelic afterlife

Most explicit is the *Epistle of Enoch*:

Be hopeful! For you were formerly put to shame through evils and afflictions, but now you will shine like the lights of heaven and will be seen, and the gate of heaven will be opened to you ... for you will have great joy like the angels of heaven ... for you will be companions of the host of heaven. (*1 Enoch* 104:2–6).

Essentially the same hope is attested in Daniel 12:

Many of those who sleep in the land of dust will awake, some to everlasting life and some to reproach and everlasting disgrace. The wise will shine like the splendor of the firmament, and those who lead the common people to righteousness will be like the stars forever and ever.[2]

It should be noted that these formulations cannot be categorized in terms of the familiar binary contrast of resurrection of the body and immortality of the soul. It is probably true that most conceptions of afterlife assume some kind of body. As Dale Martin has argued, "most philosophers speak of the soul as if it were composed of some substance that we would consider 'stuff,' even if they would not say that it is

---

[1] See my essay, "The Afterlife in Apocalyptic Literature," in Alan J. Avery-Peck and Jacob Neusner, eds., *Judaism in Late Antiquity. Part Four. Death, Life-After-Death, Resurrection and the World-to-Come in the Judaisms of Late Antiquity* (Handbuch der Orientalistik 1/49; Leiden: Brill, 2000) 119–39.

[2] John J. Collins, *Daniel. A Commentary on the Book of Daniel* (Hermeneia; Minneapolis: Fortress, 1993) 393–8.

composed of *hyle*."[3] But it is not apparent that either Daniel or *Enoch* implies a resurrected body of flesh and blood, or bones in the manner of Ezekiel. The "land of dust" from which the dead are raised in Daniel is probably Sheol rather than the grave. (Compare Job 17:16 where Sheol and 'the dust' are used in parallelism.) The resurrection seems to involve elevation from the Netherworld to the heavenly realm. The immortal body is often conceived as fiery or airy, and akin to the stars in Greek thought.[4] In *Enoch* and Daniel, too, the imagery is astral. The righteous dead will shine like the stars or like the host of heaven. In Hebrew tradition, the stars were the host of heaven, or what would be called the angelic host in Hellenistic times. In the book of *Jubilees*, similarly, it is said of the righteous that "their bones shall rest in the earth and their spirits will have much joy" (*Jub* 23:31). Here again we have a form of resurrected life that is neither resurrection of the physical body nor immortality of the soul in the Platonic sense. This literature is not philosophical, and we do not find the kind of discussion of the nature of the resurrected body that we find e.g. in Paul. But the idea of an incorruptible "body" that is not flesh and blood is by no means unusual in the Hellenistic world, and is in fact more typically Hellenistic than the Platonic idea of immortality.[5] The idea of a bodily resurrection in physical terms is attested in Judaism early on, for example in 2 Maccabees 7, but it is by no means normative or standard.

The early apocalypses do not provide much description of the transformed state. Both Daniel and *Enoch* refer to the elevated righteous as luminous or shining. Later apocalypses sometimes describe the transformation in terms of donning glory as a garment. In the later apocalypse of *2 Enoch*, when Enoch ascends to heaven the Lord instructs the archangel Michael to "take Enoch, and extract (him) from the earthly clothing. And anoint him with the delightful oil, and put (him) into the clothes of glory" (*2 Enoch* 22:8). The oil, we are told, is "greater than the greatest light." When Enoch is clad in his new garments, he tells us: "I gazed at all of myself, and I had become like one of the glorious ones, and there was no observable difference." In the words of Martha Himmelfarb, "donning such a garment can imply equality with the angels (or better!)."[6] In *Apoc Abraham* 13:14, Azazel is told that he cannot tempt Abraham, for "the garment which in heaven was formerly yours has been set aside for him, and the corruption which was on him has gone over to you."

---

[3] Dale B. Martin, *The Corinthian Body* (New Haven: Yale, 1995) 104–36, especially 115.

[4] *Ibid.*, 118, on heavenly bodies, which were usually thought to be fiery.

[5] See further Martin, *The Corinthian Body*, 1–37, and Troels Engberg-Pedersen, "Total Transformation in 1 Corinthians 15 – a Philosophical Reading of Paul on Body and Spirit," in Turid Karlsen Seim and Jorunn Økland, eds., *Metamorphoses. Resurrection, Body and Transformative Practices in Early Christianity* (Ekstasis 1; Berlin: de Gruyter, 2009) 123–46. See also the reflections on the nature of the resurrected body in early Christian and Gnostic texts in the essays of Jorunn Økland, Outi Lehtipou and Hugo Lundhaug in the same volume.

[6] Martha Himmelfarb, *Ascent to Heaven in Jewish and Christian Apocalypses* (New York: Oxford, 1993), 40, suggests that "the process by which Enoch becomes an angel is a heavenly version of priestly investiture."

These admittedly later parallels describe the transformed, angelic state as donning a garment of glory. Compare also the desire of Paul to put off the "earthly tent" of the body, "because we wish not to be unclothed but to be further clothed, so that what is mortal may be swallowed up by life" (2 Cor 5:4).[7]

Angelic afterlife in the Scrolls

The people who wrote the sectarian scrolls found at Qumran were certainly familiar with the books of Daniel and Enoch. Both are found there in multiple copies. They also assume that the righteous can expect a beatific afterlife, not just the dreary afterlife in Sheol as traditionally imagined. The destiny of the righteous is described as follows in the *Instruction on the Two Spirits*:

healing and great peace in length of days, fruitfulness of seed with all everlasting blessings, everlasting joys in eternal life, and a crown of glory with majestic raiment in everlasting light (1QS 4:6–8).

The "fruitfulness of seed" has been controversial, since it would seem to imply continued earthly existence.[8] Some of the other features, however, suggest a transcendent life that surpasses earthly experience.

"Everlasting joys in eternal life" (שמחת עולמים בחיי נצח) echoes Dan 12:2, where the phrase is חיי עלם.[9]

A crown of glory (usually עטרת rather than כליל) is a symbol of honor in the Hebrew Bible. In Psalm 8:5, humanity is crowned with glory and honor, as an indication of being only a little lower than אלהים. In 1QHª 27:25 the scoffing of an enemy is transformed into a crown (כליל) of glory. It can also have an eschatological connotation. According to Wis 5:15–16, "the righteous live forever, and their reward is with the Lord . . . Therefore they will receive a glorious crown and a beautiful diadem from the hand of the Lord." In Rev 2:10, a crown of life is a reward for fidelity unto death.[10]

Majestic raiment (מדת הדר) may be illustrated from the transformation of the righteous on the day of judgment in *1 Enoch* 62:15–16:

---

[7] Cf. also the promise of white robes in Rev 3:5. See further Émile Puech, *La Croyance des Esséniens en la Vie Future: Immortalité, Resurrection, Vie Éternelle?* (Paris: Lecoffre, 1993) 436.

[8] A. R. C. Leaney, *The Rule of Qumran and Its Meaning* (Philadelphia: Westminster, 1966) 152. J. Duhaime, "La Doctrine des Esséniens de Qumran sur l'après-mort," in Guy Couturier et al., eds., *Essais sur la Mort* (Montreal: Fides, 1985) 107, questions whether the passage refers to the afterlife at all.

[9] Puech, *La Croyance des Esséniens*, 435. Cf. also 1QHª 5:23, "everlasting peace and length of days,"

[10] Cf. Rev. 3:11. Similarly in 1 Peter 5:4 it is a reward given when "the chief shepherd" appears in judgment.

And the righteous and the chosen will have arisen from the earth, and have ceased to cast down their faces, and put on the garment of glory. And this will be your garment, the garment of life from the Lord of Spirits; and your garments will not wear out, and your glory will not fade in the presence of the Lord of Spirits.

We have already noted the tendency to conceive the immortal state in terms of a garment of glory in later apocalypses.[11]

"Eternal light" is associated especially with the divine presence. Compare for example 1QH^a 12:22–23: "you reveal yourself in me ... as perfect light." Likewise, 1QS 11:3: "from the source of his knowledge he has disclosed his light."

Wernberg-Møeller has astutely remarked that this whole passage in the *Instruction on the Two Spirits* is indebted to Psalm 21, where the blessings are those enjoyed by the king:

For you meet him with rich blessings; you set a crown of fine gold on his head. He asked you for life; you gave it to him – length of days forever and ever. His glory is great through your help; splendor and majesty you bestow on him. You bestow on him blessings forever; you make him glad with the joy of your presence.[12]

It is disputed whether this psalm promises eternal life to the king.[13] If so, the king was considered an exception to the common human lot, but that is quite conceivable. Some of the blessings, the crown, splendor and majesty were commonly associated with royalty. They are democratized in the Qumran text, but they also take on otherworldly associations in the apocalyptic worldview of the Scrolls.

The final reward of the righteous is also expressed as "the glory of Adam," in 1QS 4:22–3. The same motif is found in 1QH^a 4:14–15 and in CD 3:20, which also says that the elect will live for a thousand generations.[14] 4QpPs^a (4Q171) 3:1–2 says that those who return from the wilderness will live for a thousand generations and that they and their descendants forever will possess all the inheritance of Adam. Crispin Fletcher-Louis has pointed out that Adam was associated with the divine glory qua image of God.[15] A fragmentary passage in the Words of the Heavenly Luminaries, 4QDib Ham, 4Q504 8 4–6 is plausibly reconstructed to read: "Adam,] our [fat]her,

---

[11] Note also the splendor of the risen righteous in 2 Baruch 51:3: "their faces will shine even more brightly and their features will assume a luminous beauty, so that they may be able to attain and enter the world which does not die." See the discussion by Liv Ingeborg Lied, "Recognizing the Righteous Remnant? Resurrection, Recognition, and Eschatological Reversals in 2 Baruch 49–51," in Karlsen Seim and Økland, *Metamorphoses*, 311–35.

[12] P. Wernberg-Møeller, *The Manual of Discipline. Translated and Annotated with an Introduction* (STDJ 1; Leiden: Brill, 1957) 80.

[13] The argument for the immortality of the king has been made by John Healey, "The Immortality of the King: Ugarit and the Psalms," *Or* 53 (1984) 245–54. It is disputed by John Day, "The Canaanite Inheritance of the Israelite Monarchy, " in J. Day, ed., *King and Messiah in Israel and the Ancient Near East* (JSOTSup 270; Sheffield: Sheffield Academic Press, 1998) 85–6.

[14] The promise that those who walk in perfect holiness will live a thousand generations is also found in CD 7:5–6.

[15] C. Fletcher-Louis, *All the Glory of Adam. Liturgical Anthropology in the Dead Sea Scrolls* (STDJ 42; Leiden: Brill, 2002) 91–95.

you fashioned in the image of [your] glory ... [the breath of life] you [b]lew into his nostril, and intelligence and knowledge ... [in the gard]en of Eden, which you had planted."[16] *Genesis Rabbah* 20:12 reports that Rabbi Meir read Gen 3:21 to say that God dressed Adam and Eve in "garments of light" rather than garments of skin. But the glory was lost when Adam was expelled from the garden. The glory of Adam, then, may coincide with the majestic raiment of light promised in 1QS 4.

Fellowship with the angels in this life

The investment with majestic raiment of light, and the glory of Adam, is an eschatological blessing in 1QS 4. Many texts in the Dead Sea Scrolls, however, appear to speak of fellowship with the angels as a present experience for members of the sect. So in 1QS 11:7–8 we read:

To those whom God has selected he has given them as an everlasting possession; and he has given them an inheritance in the lot of the holy ones. He unites their assembly to the sons of the heavens in order (to form) the council of the community and a foundation of the building of holiness to be an everlasting plantation throughout all future ages.

Again, in 1QH^a 11:19–21, the psalmist thanks the Lord

because you saved my life from the pit, and from the Sheol of Abaddon have lifted me up to an everlasting height, so that I can walk on a boundless plain. And I know that there is hope for someone you fashioned out of dust for an everlasting community. The depraved spirit you have purified from great offence so that he can take a place with the host of the holy ones, and can enter in communion with the congregation of the sons of heaven.

In these and other such passages the fellowship with the angels promised to the righteous after death in the *Epistle of Enoch* and Daniel is claimed for the members of the sectarian community. The question is whether, or to what extent, they can be said to live an angelic life in the present. The constant use of the perfect tense in these hymns suggests that the deliverance has already taken place.[17] Émile Puech,

---

[16] Trans. F. García Martínez and E. J. Tigchelaar, *The Dead Sea Scrolls Study Edition* (Leiden: Brill, 1998) 1009. According to the *Greek Apocalypse of Baruch* (*3 Bar* 4:16), Adam was stripped of the glory of God after the Fall. According to *Deuteronomy Rabbah* 11:3, Adam claimed to be greater than Moses because he was created as the image of God. Moses replied "I am far superior to you, for your glorious light was taken away, but as for me, the radiant countenance that God gave me still abides." See further G. A. Anderson, "Garments of Skin," in idem, *The Genesis of Perfection. Adam and Eve in Jewish and Christian Imagination* (Louisville: Westminster John Knox, 2001) 117–34.

[17] See H.-W. Kuhn, *Enderwartung und gegenwärtiges Heil* (Göttingen: Vandenhoeck & Ruprecht, 1966); G. W. E. Nickelsburg, *Resurrection, Immortality and Eternal Life in Intertestamental Judaism* (HTS 26; Cambridge, MA: Harvard, 1972) 146–56; J. J. Collins, *Apocalypticism in the Dead Sea Scrolls*, 117–23; D. Dimant, "Men as Angels: The Self-Image of the Qumran Community," in A. Berlin, ed., *Religion and Politics in the Ancient Near East* (Bethesda, MD: University of Maryland, 1996) 93–103.

however, has argued that the verbs should be read as "prophetic perfects" which bespeak a state that is assured but essentially in the future.[18]

It is certainly true that hymns in the Scrolls do not envision a world fully redeemed. But it is also apparent that they claim some measure of transformation as a present reality. The hymn at the end of the *Community Rule* says that God has given the elect "an inheritance in the lot of the holy ones" (1QS 11:7–8). The inheritance, in principle, could still be in the future. But the passage goes on to say that "He unites their assembly to the sons of the heavens into a council of the community and a foundation of the building of holiness to be an everlasting plantation throughout all future ages." (11:8). The phrase "council of the community" is the technical name for the sectarian community in the *Community Rule*. The word for community is יחד, *yahad*, which means "union."[19] (Used adverbially, it means "together.") This passage suggests that togetherness with the angels is constitutive of the community on earth.

The *yahad*

The kind of community designated as *yahad* was a new phenomenon in the history of Judaism, when it came into being in the second or early first century BCE. On a few occasions in the Second Temple period there were attempts to implement "a return to the law of Moses" in a way that involved a new commitment and the formation of a new community. In Nehemiah 10:29 certain people "enter into a curse and an oath to walk in God's law, which was given by Moses the servant of God, and to observe and do all the commandments of the Lord our God and his ordinances and his statutes."[20] The movement described in the *Damascus Document*, of which fragments were found at Qumran, was analogous to this. The individual "must impose upon himself to return to the law of Moses with all his heart and soul" (15:12). The *Damascus Document* is primarily concerned with a family based movement, whose members "live in camps according to the order of the land and marry and have children," and who contribute two days' salary a month to the common fund (CD 14:13). The reason for the formation of that movement was the sense that the law was not being properly observed by other Jews of the time. Problems included

---

[18] Puech, *La Croyance des Esséniens*, 335–419. Note that Kuhn, *Enderwartung*, 176, also insists that "die futurische Eschatologie nicht aufgehoben ist" even if it is "ganz in der Hintergrund."

[19] Fletcher-Louis, *All the Glory of Adam*, 90, suggests that the designation יחד may refer to communion with the angels. Alternatively, it may be borrowed from Deut 33:5, which refers to "the union of the tribes of Israel."

[20] The analogy with the Dead Sea Scrolls was already noted by Morton Smith, "The Dead Sea Sect in Relation to Ancient Judaism," *NTS* 7 (1961) 347–60. See also Alexei Sivertsev, "Sects and Households: Social Structure of the Proto-Sectarian Movement of Nehemiah 10 and the Dead Sea Sect," *CBQ* 67 (2005) 59–78; idem, *Households, Sects, and the Origins of Rabbinic Judaism* (JSJSup 102; Leiden: Brill, 2005) 94–118.

"defilement of the temple," which was identified as one of the "three nets of Belial" in CD 4:18.

The *yahad* would seem to have developed out of the movement described in the *Damascus Document*. Like the latter, it involves a new covenant, with provision for admission and expulsion. But it makes greater demands on its members. All property is in common, and there is no mention of women or children. This association has much in common with the Essenes described by Philo, Josephus and Pliny, and most scholars believe that it should be identified as Essene. The silence on women and children in the *Community Rule* is compatible with reports that the Essenes, or at least one branch of them, were celibate, although celibacy is never required explicitly.

The *raison d'être* of the more demanding community of the *yahad* is spelled out most fully in column 8 of the *Community Rule*:

the council of the community shall be founded in truth to be an everlasting plantation, a holy house for Israel and the foundation of the holy of holies for Aaron ... to atone for the land and to render to the wicked their retribution" (1QS 8:5–6, cf. 9:3–6). Then, "when these have become a community in Israel in compliance with these arrangements, they are to be segregated from within the dwelling of the men of sin to go to the desert in order to prepare there the path of Him, as it is written, "In the desert prepare the way of *** ...

It is apparent that the *raison d'être* of the community is to substitute for the temple cult, which was rejected as defiled.[21] The members of the *yahad* would atone for sin "without the flesh of burnt offerings and without the fats of sacrifice – the offering of the lips in compliance with the decree will be like the pleasant aroma of justice and the perfectness of behavior will be acceptable as a freewill offering" (1QS 9: 3–5). In the phrase found in the *Florilegium*, 4Q174 1.6, they would constitute a מקדש אדם, a sanctuary consisting of men.[22] The passage in 1QH 11 adds to this profile the idea that fellowship with the angels would be a constitutive factor in establishing this purified worship.[23]

---

[21] See e.g. Georg Klinzing, *Die Umdeutung des Kultus in der Qumrangemeinde und im Neuen Testament* (SUNT 7; Göttingen:Vandenhoeck & Ruprecht, 1971) 50–106; L. H. Schiffman, "The Qumran Community's Withdrawal from the Jerusalem Temple," in Beate Ego, Armin Lange und Peter Pilhofer in Zusammenarbeit mit Kathrin Ehlers, eds., *Gemeinde ohne Tempel = Community without temple : zur Substituierung und Transformation des Jerusalemer Tempels und seines Kults im Alten Testament, antiken Judentum und frühen Christentum* (Tübingen: Mohr Siebeck, 1999) 267–84.

[22] The phrase may have more than one level of reference. See George Brooke, "Miqdash Adam, Eden, and the Qumran Community," in Ego et al., *Gemeinde ohne Tempel*, 285–301.

[23] The liturgical context of fellowship with the angels is explored at length by Bjorn Frennesson, *"In a Common Rejoicing." Liturgical Communion with Angels in Qumran* (Acta Universitatis Upsaliensis. Studia Semitica Upsaliensia 14; Uppsala: Uppsala University, 1999). Cf. Michael Mach, *Entwicklungsstudien des jüdischen Engelglaubens in vorrabbinischer Zeit* (TSAJ 34; Tübingen: Mohr Siebeck, 1992) 216–40.

The *Songs of the Sabbath Sacrifice*

The main evidence that the fellowship with the angels is focused on the heavenly temple is found in the *Songs of the Sabbath Sacrifice*.[24] These are compositions for each of thirteen Sabbaths, which call on the angels to give praise and provide descriptive statements about the angels and their praise-giving. They do not give the words of the angels or cite any angelic hymns of praise. We are told that God "has established for himself priests of the inner sanctum, the holiest of the holy ones" (4Q400 fragment 1). They are also called "ministers of the presence in his glorious *debir*." The angelic priests are depicted as divided into "seven priesthoods," "seven councils," and as occupying "seven precincts" in the heavenly temple. The ninth to thirteenth songs appear to contain a systematic description of the heavenly temple that is based in part on Ezekiel 40–48.

The heavenly temple is evidently imagined by analogy with the earthly temple, except that no attention is paid to any outer courts. The holy place is an *ulam*, while the holy of holies is the *debir*, which contains the *merkavah* throne. Everything is sevenfold, so there are apparently seven temples.[25] It is not clear how they relate to each other. The text gives no indication of their spatial relationship, and there is no reason to correlate them with seven heavens. The motif of seven heavens only becomes common after the turn of the era.[26]

The *Songs* are recited by the *Maskil*, in the presence of the community members, who are referred to as "we" in the second song, and whose priesthood is compared to that of the angels. In the words of Philip Alexander,

> we have here a public liturgy, in which a prayer-leader leads a congregation, who may join him in reciting in whole or in part the words of the hymns. That congregation exhorts the angels in heaven to perform their priestly duties in the celestial temple, and somehow through this liturgical act it feels drawn into union with the angels in worshipping God.[27]

This does not require that the community members have ascended to heaven in a spatial sense. As Alexander has argued, "sophisticated Jews in the Second Temple

---

[24] C. A. Newsom, *Songs of the Sabbath Sacrifice: A Critical Edition* (HSS 27; Atlanta: Scholars Press, 1985); eadem, "4QShirot 'Olat HaShabbatª," in E. Eshel et al., *Qumran Cave 4. VI. Poetical and Liturgical Texts, Part 1* (DJD 11; Oxford: Clarendon, 1998) 173–401; P. Alexander, *The Mystical Texts. Songs of the Sabbath Sacrifice and Related Manuscripts* (Library of Second Temple Studies 61; London and New York: T. & T. Clark, 2006) 13–61.

[25] R. Elior, *The Three Temples. On the Emergence of Jewish Mysticism* (Oxford/ Portland, Oregon: Littmann, 2004) 34–44.

[26] Adela Yarbro Collins, "The Seven Heavens in Jewish and Christian Apocalypses," in eadem, *Cosmology and Eschatology in Jewish and Christian Apocalypticism* (JSJSup 50; Leiden: Brill, 1996) 21–54.

[27] Alexander, *The Mystical Texts*, 44. Alexander is following the interpretation proposed by Carol Newsom. Fletcher-Louis has argued that the exhortations are addressed not to angels but to "angelomorphic" humans (*All the Glory of Adam*, 252–394). See the critique by Alexander, *The Mystical Texts*, 45–7.

period were perfectly capable of conceiving of heaven as 'another dimension' or a 'parallel universe,' and not literally as 'up there.'"[28]

The *Songs* suggest that the main activity of angels is giving praise to God. Beyond that, they offer a few characterizations of the angelic life:[29]

Angels are "spirits," which is to say that they are not "flesh," which is corruptible and mortal, and also subject to impurity.[30]

There is an angelic priesthood, including "ministers of the Face," which represents the higher forms of angelic life.[31] The offerings in the heavenly temple are bloodless, and can be described as a "spiritual portion" or "an offering of the tongue."[32]

The priestly angels are repeatedly referred to as "*Elim* of knowledge," just as God is the "God of knowledge" and heaven is a place of knowledge. These angels can pass on to human beings the knowledge they have received. The precise nature of this knowledge is never clarified in the *Songs*, but we shall encounter it again in other sectarian texts.

The ideas about heavenly worship in the *Songs of Sabbath Sacrifice* were not peculiarly sectarian. But they are representative of the assumptions that inform the life of the *yahad*. As Philip Alexander has noted, many of the key ideas of the *Sabbath Songs* are alluded to in works with impeccable sectarian credentials, such as the *Hodayot*, the *Community Rule, the Rule of the Congregation* (1QS[a]), the *Rule of Benedictions* and the *War Rule*.[33] Life in the *yahad* was structured to enable and facilitate participation in the heavenly cult. There is great emphasis on purity in the community regulations.[34] According to the *Rule of the Congregation*,

No man defiled by any of the impurities of a man shall enter the assembly of these [the council of the community]; and no one who is defiled by these should be established in his office in the midst of the congregation, everyone who is defiled in his flesh, paralyzed in his feet or in his hands, lame, blind, deaf, dumb or defiled in his flesh with a blemish visible to the eyes, or the tottering old man who cannot keep upright in the midst of the assembly; these shall not

---

[28] Alexander, *The Mystical Texts*, 54.

[29] Maxwell J. Davidson, *Angels at Qumran* (JSPSup 11; Sheffield: Sheffield Academic Press, 1992) 290–1.

[30] On the notion of "flesh" in the texts from Qumran see Jörg Frey, "Flesh and Spirit in the Palestinian Jewish Sapiential Tradition and in the Qumran Texts: An Inquiry into the Development of Pauline Usage," in C. Hempel, A. Lange and H. Lichtenberger, eds., *The Wisdom Texts from Qumran and the Development of Sapiential Thought* (BETL 159; Leuven: Peeters, 2002) 367–404; idem, "The Notion of 'Flesh' in 4QInstruction and the Background of Pauline Thought," in D. Falk et al., eds., *Sapiential, Liturgical and Poetical Texts from Qumran* (STDJ 35; Leiden: Brill, 2000) 197–226.

[31] Alexander, *The Mystical Texts*, 57: "Highest of all the angels is the celestial high priest (Melchizedek/Michael). Below him stand the Deputy High Priest and the rest of the Angels of the face. Then come the ordinary priestly angels, followed by the hosts of non-priestly angels."

[32] *Ibid.*, 58.

[33] *Ibid.*, 71. See also Frennesson, *"In a Common Rejoicing."*

[34] Cf. Frennesson, *"In a Common Rejoicing,"* 114: "Purity and Knowledge were qualities representing the *sine qua non* on the part of man."

enter to take their place among the congregation of the men of renown, for the angels of holiness are among their congregation. (1QS^a 2:3–9)[35]

The prominence of priests in the leadership of the sect is well-known, even if it is not clear whether the title "sons of Zadok" has any genealogical significance, and if their prominence fluctuates in different recensions of the *Community Rule*.

The company of angels is probably also the reason for the absence of women and children in *Serek ha-Yahad*. The logic of celibacy in an angelic context is most explicitly set forth in the *Book of the Watchers* in *1 Enoch* 15. Enoch is told to chide the Watchers for having lain with women, and defiled themselves with the daughters of men, and taken for themselves wives, and done as the sons of earth. God had given women to human beings so that they might beget children and not vanish from the earth. But God did not give women to those who existed as spirits, living forever, and not dying for all the generations of eternity. Sex has no place in the angelic or heavenly life. (Compare the saying of Jesus in Mark 12:25: "when they rise from the dead, they neither marry nor are given in marriage but are like angels in heaven.") While neither the *Damascus Rule* nor the *Serek* ever explicitly requires celibacy, this same logic most probably underlies the guarantee in CD 7:5–6 that those who walk in perfect holiness shall live a thousand generations. (This is followed immediately by the statement "And if they live in camps in accordance with the rule of the land, and take women and beget children ...") When the community is regarded as a metaphorical temple, as is the case in the *Serek*, requirements of purity create an additional obstacle to sexual relations.

Personal transformation

Like the *Songs of Sabbath Sacrifice*, the hymn at the end of the *Community Rule* is put on the lips of the *Maskil*.[36] In addition to what it says about the *yahad*, it makes some claims that have a more personal ring to them:

As for me, to God belongs my judgment; in his hand is the perfection of my behavior with the uprightness of my heart; and with his just acts he cancels my iniquities. For from the source of his knowledge he has disclosed his light, and my eyes have observed his wonders, and the light of my heart the mystery that is to be (רז נהיה) ... From the spring of his justice is my judgment and from the wonderful mystery is the light of my heart. My eyes have gazed on that which is eternal, wisdom hidden from humankind, knowledge and prudent understanding (hidden) from the sons of man, fount of justice and well of strength and spring of glory (hidden) from the assembly of flesh. (1QS 11:2–7)

---

[35] 1QSa 2:3–9; J. A. Fitzmyer, "A Feature of Qumran Angelology and the Angels of 1 Cor 11:10," in J. Murphy-O'Connor and J. H. Charlesworth, eds., *Paul and the Dead Sea Scrolls* (New York: Crossroad, 1990) 31–47.

[36] Newsom, *The Self as Symbolic Space*, 165–74.

Here is a claim of special revelation that is rather different from the specific revelations that we typically find in apocalypses.[37] The phrase *raz nihyeh* also occurs in *4QInstruction*, a wisdom text that is not explicitly sectarian, and in *1Q/4QMysteries*. It is variously translated as "the mystery that is to be" or "the mystery of Being/existence."[38] It entails comprehensive understanding, rather than specific information. It is probably to be understood as referring to the plan of God for the world, rather than to experiential knowledge of the divinity. (Compare 1QS 3:15: "from the God of knowledge comes all that is and shall be, כל הויה ונהייה.) The claim of enlightenment is offset by a self-deprecatory passage, in verses 9–10: "I belong to evil humankind, to the assembly of unfaithful flesh . . ." But this is the condition from which the speaker has been rescued, which serves only to underline the wonderful character of the transformation. It may be that the author of this hymn was an exceptional individual who had a mystical experience. But as Carol Newsom has argued, the placement of this hymn at the end of the *Community Rule* suggests that it represents the culmination of formation within the community. "The character constructed for the *Maskil* in the instructions and hymn is one that embodies the values of the sect in a particularly pronounced fashion."[39] The experience articulated in this hymn is paradigmatic for the community. Moreover, we are told that God has given such knowledge and understanding to the elect, whom he has united with the holy ones. Knowledge and understanding of heavenly realities is also entailed by fellowship with the angels.

There is also some dialectic between individual and communal experience in the *Hodayot*. One bloc of the hymns (cols. 10–17) is usually distinguished as "hymns of the Teacher," while the remainder is classified as "hymns of the community."[40] The attribution to the Teacher is impossible to verify, but at least these hymns reflect a distinctive, individual voice. Nonetheless, these hymns too were used in the community. Precisely *how* they were used is difficult to say. There is a long-standing debate as to whether they were primarily cultic or instructional in purpose.[41] They are distinctly different from other liturgical compositions found at Qumran.[42] They are not designated for specific occasions, and some are very long. As Daniel Falk has put it, "they are not functionally analogous to collections of prayers for specific

---

[37] Cf. Mach, *Entwicklungsstudien*, 210–11.

[38] Matthew J. Goff, *The Worldly and Heavenly Wisdom of 4QInstruction* (STDJ 50; Leiden: Brill, 2003) 51–79.

[39] Newsom, *The Self as Symbolic Space* (STDJ 52; Leiden: Brill, 2004) 173.

[40] Gert Jeremias, *Der Lehrer der Gerechtigkeit* (SUNT 2; Göttingen: Vandenhoeck & Ruprecht, 1963) 168–267; Michael C. Douglas, "The Teacher Hymn Hypothesis Revisited: New Data for an Old Crux," *DSD* 6 (1999) 239–66

[41] Svend Holm-Nielsen, *Hodayot. Psalms from Qumran* (Acta Theologica Danica 2; Aarhus: Universitetsvorlaget, 1960) 332–48. For bibliography on the debate see Daniel Falk, *Daily, Sabbath, and Festival Prayers in the Dead Sea Scrolls* (STDJ 27; Leiden: Brill, 1998) 103, n.18.

[42] Bilhah Nitzan, *Qumran Prayer and Religious Poetry* (STDJ 12; Leiden: Brill, 1994) 324.

occasions such as *Daily Prayers* and *Words of the Luminaries*."[43] Nonetheless, they contain some indications of cultic use, such as references to communal singing, first person plural speakers, calls for congregational response and references to the *Maskil*, who may have functioned as a liturgical leader.[44] Even in cases where *Hodayot* reflect the experiences of an individual, they may have been appropriated by the community through common recitation.[45]

Both the Hymns of the Teacher and the Community Hymns speak of fellowship with the angels.[46] From the Teacher Hymns, we have already cited 1QH^a 11:19–21: "I thank you Lord, because you saved my life from the pit, and from Sheol of Abaddon you have lifted me up to an everlasting height so that I can walk on a boundless plain." The language here reflects the same understanding of resurrection that we have seen in Daniel 12, except that the deliverance is already effected. In this case, the hymnist shows an acute consciousness of an ongoing human condition: "But I, a creature of clay, what am I? ... For I find myself at the boundary of wickedness and share the lot of the scoundrels" (1QH^a 11:23–25).[47] Nonetheless, he has been purified for admission into communion with the angels. Moreover, "you cast eternal destiny for man with the spirits of knowledge, so that he praises your name in the community of jubilation." The hymnist, then, has a two-sided existence. On the one side, he is still beset by enemies (and the Teacher Hymns spend a good deal of time complaining of persecution and adversity). On the other side, he is set apart from all that and can join with the angels in praising God. Elsewhere in the Teacher Hymns we read that "those who walk in the way of your heart have listened to me; they have arrayed themselves for you in the assembly of the holy ones" (1QH^a 12:24–25), and that "you have brought [your truth and] your [glo]ry to all the men of your council, and in a common lot with the angels of the presence."

The themes of purification and knowledge are also prominent in 1QH^a 19:3–14, a community hymn.[48] This hymn thanks God for having done wonders with dust. In part, this is a matter of instruction: "you have taught me the basis of your truth and have instructed me in your wonderful works."[49] In part it is a matter of purification:

For the sake of your glory you have purified man from offence so that he can make himself holy for you ... to become united with the sons of your truth and in the lot with your holy ones

---

[43] Falk, *Daily, Sabbath, and Festival Prayers*, 101.

[44] For references see Russell C. D. Arnold, *The Social Role of Liturgy in the Religion of the Qumran Community* (STDJ 60; Leiden: Brill, 2006) 211. For the hymns of the *Maskil*, see Falk, *Daily, Sabbath, and Festival Prayers*, 100–103, citing 1QH^a 20:4–11 and 1QH^a 5.

[45] Compare Arnold, *The Social Role of Liturgy*, 214–21.

[46] Puech, *La Croyance*, 417: "Que ce soit dans l'un ou l'autre type d'hymnes (du Maître ou de la Communauté) la conception de l'eschatologie n'est pas différente."

[47] Whether this is in fact a Teacher hymn is disputed. See Puech, *La Croyance*, 366. Kuhn, *Enderwartung*, 65–66, denies that it can be attributed to the Teacher.

[48] Kuhn, *Enderwartung*, 78–112.

[49] On the motif of knowledge in these hymns, see Kuhn, *Enderwartung*, 113–75.

... so that he can take his place in your presence with the perpetual host ... and with those who know in a community of jubilation.

In another Community Hymn, 1QH^a 7: 7 we read, "and we are gathered in the community (יחד) with those who know ... and we shall shout (for joy)."

There is also a dialectic between individual and community in the so-called *"Self-Exaltation Hymn,"* of which four very fragmentary copies have survived, at least one of which was part of a scroll of *Hodayot*.[50] Two recensions may be distinguished, the shorter form in 4Q491c and the longer in 4Q427 7 and 4Q471b.[51] The first part of this hymn refers to "a mighty throne in the congregation of the gods" on which the speaker apparently claims to have sat. He goes on to boast "I am reckoned with the gods, and my dwelling is in the holy congregation," and "there is no teaching comparable [to my teaching]." He also asks "who suffers evil like me?" and boasts that his glory is with the sons of the king (i.e. God). Other striking phrases are found in the other fragments. The speaker is "beloved of the king, companion of the holy ones," and even asks "who is like me among the gods?" (4Q471b). In 4Q491c this *Self-Exaltation Hymn* is marked off from the following "canticle of the righteous" by a large *lamed*, which has been taken to indicate a separate composition. The marker is not found in other copies of the text. The canticle is most fully preserved in 4Q427: "Sing a hymn, beloved ones, to the king ... Exalt together with the eternal host, ascribe greatness to our God and glory to our King."

There is no consensus as to the identity of the speaker in this hymn. The Teacher of Righteousness has inevitably been proposed, but the hymn conspicuously lacks the protestations of human unworthiness that we find in the *Hodayot*. On the contrary, the speaker boasts that his desire is not like that of flesh. Several other interpretations are possible: the hymn could have been ascribed to the Teacher after his death,[52] or it could be the work of a later teacher,[53] or it might be put on the lips of an

---

[50] E. Eshel, "The Identification of the 'Speaker' of the Self-Glorification Hymn," in D. W. Parry and E. Ulrich, eds., *The Provo International Conference on the Dead Sea Scrolls* (STDJ 30; Leiden: Brill, 1999) 619–35; M. O. Wise, "מי כמוני באלים: A Study of 4Q491c, 4Q471b, 4Q427 7 and 1QH^a 25:35–26:10," *DSD* 7 (2000) 173–219. The text is found in 4Q427 fragment 7, 4Q491c, 4Q471b, and in smaller fragments in 4Q431, which is part of the same manuscript as 4Q471b, and 1QH^a 25:35–26:10.

[51] Florentino García Martínez, "Old Texts and Modern Mirages: The 'I' of Two Qumran Hymns," in idem, *Qumranica Minora I. Qumran Origins and Apocalypticism* (STDJ 63; Leiden: Brill, 2007) 105–25 (114–8). See also his longer treatment, "Ángel, hombre, Mesías, Maestro de Justicia? El Problemático 'Yo' de un Poema Qumránico," in J. J. Fernández Sangrador and S. Guijarro Oporto, eds., *Plenitudo Temporis. Miscelánea Homenaje al Prof. Dr. Ramón Trevijano Etcheverría* (Bibliotheca Salmanticensis, Estudios 249; Salamanca: Universidad Pontificia, 2002) 103–31.

[52] Wise, "מי כמוני באלים," 418, argues that the redactor who inserted this hymn into the *Hodayot* meant for the reader to think of the Teacher.

[53] I. Knohl, *The Messiah before Jesus: The Suffering Servant of the Dead Sea Scrolls* (Berkeley, CA: University of California, 2000) 52–5, suggests Menahem the Essene, who is mentioned by Josephus.

eschatological teacher or High Priest, the messiah of Aaron.⁵⁴ The original editor, Baillet, suggested the archangel Michael. That suggestion has been widely rejected, but it has recently been revived by García Martínez, at least for 4Q491c, which appears to be part of the *War Scroll*.

In the *Hodayot* recension, at least, the composition is designated as a מזמור for the משכיל. Even the 4Q491 manuscript indicates a hymnic context ("let the holy ones rejoice," line 2). This hymnic context is strengthened in the *Hodayot* redaction, where the second composition is fused with the first one, so that the hymn both begins and ends with communal praise. Wise draws a direct inference about the speaker in the first person section from the context of communal praise: "each individual member of the user group spoke of himself or herself. At least by the stage of the *Hodayot* redaction, they declaimed in unison and chanted, singing of their singular significance at the behest of a worship leader, the *Maskil*." ⁵⁵ It is true that the community would have appropriated the "I" of the speaker to some degree, but the identification need not be complete. The community could also give praise and thanks for the exaltation of a leader, whether historical or eschatological. As Philip Alexander argues, the speaker is "someone special. His experience is not something that anyone can achieve, though he can still lead others into a state of closer communion with the heavenly host."⁵⁶ Alexander regards this hymn as evidence for the experience of ascent, on the assumption that the speaker has returned to earth. This assumption is not necessarily valid, however. It may be that the heavenly throne reflects a permanent or eschatological abode, and that the speaker is not the actual author of the hymn, but the exalted Teacher or an eschatological figure.

Permanent or temporary transformation

The *Self-Exaltation Hymn* is atypical of the Dead Sea Scrolls in many respects, but it is typical insofar as the exaltation of the speaker is discussed in a cultic context.⁵⁷ The question arises whether the experience of communion with the angels was limited to the context of cult. In her edition of the *Songs of the Sabbath Sacrifice*, Carol

---

⁵⁴ J. J. Collins, *The Scepter and the Star. Messianism in Light of the Dead Sea Scrolls* (New York: Doubleday, 1995) 149–64; Eshel, "The Identification of the Speaker," 635.

⁵⁵ Wise, "מי כמוני באלים," 216. So also Arnold, *The Social Role of Liturgy*, 221. Eileen Schuller, "*Hodayot*," in E. Chazon et al., *Qumran Cave 4. XX. Poetical and Liturgical Texts, Part 2* (DJD 29; Oxford: Clarendon, 1999) 102, writes, "Whoever the referent may be in 4Q491 11 I, in the recension of this psalm that is found in the *Hodayot* manuscripts, the 'I' is to be understood in relationship to the 'I' voice we hear speaking in the other psalms, particularly the other Hymns of the Community."

⁵⁶ Alexander, *The Mystical Texts*, 88.

⁵⁷ Fellowship with the angels is also attested in the War Rule, in the context of the final battle, but that is an exceptional circumstance, and so I leave it aside here. See Davidson, *Angels at Qumran*, 212–34; Frennesson, *"In a Common Rejoicing,"* 88–92.

Newsom suggested that the repetitive, hypnotic style of the *Songs* was meant to induce a sense of communion with the angels, and this suggestion has recently been revived by Alexander.[58] This sense was not necessarily present in all the worship of the community. Esther Chazon has argued that communion with the angelic host takes different forms; some prayers reflect a distinction between human and angelic worshippers.[59] But not all prayer texts found at Qumran were products of the *yahad*, or even of the broader movement of the "new covenant." Conversely, the word יחד occurs with remarkable frequency in connection with communion with the angels.[60] Moreover, as Alexander has noted, the members of the *yahad* lived in a permanent state of spiritual discipline and heightened religious susceptibility. They did not have to elevate themselves as far as would people living in the ordinary world, and struggling with the cares and distractions of ordinary life.[61] It remains true that the *Hodayot*, with the exception of the *Self-Exaltation Hymn*, retain a strong sense of the flesh-bound state of humanity. But the very fact that the members could enter into communion with the heavenly host, even if not yet on a permanent basis, meant that they had already been transformed to a considerable degree.

Resurrection and transformation

The reason that scholars have tended to speak of "realized eschatology" in the Scrolls, especially in the *Hodayot*, is not only that the hymnists speak of communion with the angels, but also the remarkable lack of any reflection on death as a problem in these texts. There has been extensive debate as to whether the *Hodayot*, and the sectarian scrolls more generally, express a hope for future resurrection. The authors of the Scrolls were certainly familiar with such a hope, from the books of Enoch and Daniel. They also use language that is consonant with such a belief, but this language is poetic and admits of more than one interpretation. 1QH^a 19, which we have already discussed in connection with communion with the angels, also expresses the transformation of the elect in another way: "to raise worms of the dead from the dust, to an everlasting council" (19:12). The phrase "worm of the dead," תולעת מתים, also occurs in 1QH^a 14:34 (a Teacher hymn): "Hoist a banner, you who lie in the dust; raise a standard, worm of dead ones." There is an allusion here to Isa 26:19, which refers to those who *dwell* in the dust. There is also an allusion to Isa 41:14: "do not fear, worm of Jacob, men of Israel." (The Hebrew for "men" here is

---

[58] Alexander, *The Mystical Texts*, 115–6.
[59] Esther Glickler Chazon, "Human and Angelic Prayer in the Light of the Dead Sea Scrolls," in eadem, ed., *Liturgical Perspectives. Prayer and Poetry in Light of the Dead Sea Scrolls* (Leiden: Brill, 2003) 35–48. See also eadem, "Liturgical Communion with the Angels at Qumran," in D. K. Falk, F. García Martínez and E. M. Schuller, eds., *Sapiential, Liturgical and Poetical Texts from Qumran* (Leiden: Brill, 2000) 95–105.
[60] Alexander, *The Mystical Texts*, 103.
[61] *Ibid.*, 116.

מתי, a rare word that occurs only in the construct plural in the Hebrew Bible, and which has the same consonants as the more familiar word for "dead ones.") In Isaiah 41, the addressees are in a lowly state, but they are not dead. Analogously, the phrase "worm of the dead" in the *Hodayot* may indicate metaphorically the abject state of unaided human nature. Just as the hymnist claims to be lifted up from Sheol or the Netherworld, he claims that the dead are raised from the dust to become members of the community and so enter into fellowship with the holy ones.[62] It is not necessary to suppose that the author has actual corpses in mind. It is possible that these passages have a future resurrection in mind, but the language is poetic and the reference uncertain.[63]

There are no unambiguous references to resurrection in the *Hodayot*, and even possible references are rare. This may be due in part to the genre of the hymns, but neither are there any unambiguous references to resurrection (as opposed to eternal life) in the rule books. The main eschatological focus of these hymns is on life with the angels, which is experienced to some degree as a present reality. It is remarkable that the sectarian scrolls contain no reflection on death as a problem. The emphasis is rather on continuity between the fellowship with the angels in the present and its fuller realization in the future.

In his contribution to the Festschrift for Émile Puech, George Brooke has tried to go beyond the impasse on the question of resurrection in the *Hodayot*. Brooke assumes that the authors were familiar with beliefs in resurrection, but "the question remains concerning what they might have done with their knowledge of these beliefs."[64] He goes on to argue, on the basis of an analysis of one Teacher hymn (1QH^a 12:5–13:4) that

It was on the basis of a belief in a future bodily resurrection that the poet ... was able to construct a literary entity that proclaimed precisely how he understood his present position as totally dependent on God. God had given him illumination, knowledge of the sort that seemed as if it had virtually transformed his physical body.[65]

Brooke argues that the motifs of illumination, both physical and mental, and "standing" in the presence of God "belong to the field of meaning associated with the afterlife, and with the afterlife in terms of physical, bodily resurrection."[66] As we have seen at the beginning of this article, the "physical, bodily" character of resurrection

---

[62] Hermann Lichtenberger, "Auferstehen in den Qumranfunden," in Friedrich Avemarie and Hermann Lichtenberger, eds., *Auferstehung/Resurrection* (WUNT 135; Tübingen: Mohr Siebeck, 2001) 82, states that 1QH^a 19 "mit grosster Gewissheit nicht im Sinne der Totenauferstehung zu interpreterieren."

[63] Puech, *La Croyance*, 413 finds another reference in 1QH 5:29 which seems to indicate a new creation, but not a resurrection of the dead.

[64] George J. Brooke, "The Structure of 1QH^ XII 5-XIII 4 and the Meaning of Resurrection," in F. García Martínez, A. Steudel and E. Tigchelaar, eds., *From 4QMMT to Resurrection. Mélanges qumraniens en homage à Émile Puech* (STDJ 61, Leiden: Brill, 2006) 15–33.

[65] Brooke, 33.

[66] *Ibid.*

in the traditions attested in the Scrolls is more complicated than Brooke allows. Enoch and Daniel seem to envision rather what might be called a spiritual body. But Brooke is right that the transformed, illuminated life "might be understood to represent the meaning of resurrection" for the poet.[67] Insofar as he speaks of resurrection, he uses it primarily as a metaphor for a transformed state in this life. How far the hymnist expected a further transformation after death is an open question. At least we should expect that the body would become more luminous in the hereafter, and freedom from irritation by the unredeemed world would presumably make some difference. But the Scrolls never clarify for us how the luminous body of the hereafter would be related to the bones that were neatly buried in single graves by the shore of the Dead Sea at Qumran. No significance is attached to the demise of flesh and blood. Since the well-attested ideal of the community was the angelic life, and angels were spirits, it is unlikely that the members had any desire to resume their bodily existence. The angelic life as experienced in the *yahad* may have been imperfect, but it was at least a foretaste of eternal life, and it was powerful enough that ordinary mortality was rendered insignificant.

There is an obvious analogy between the transformed life as we find it in the Dead Sea Scrolls and Christian monasticism, as Samuel Rubenson describes it on the basis of the letters of Ammonas.[68] There too the essential transformation takes place in the present. Revealed knowledge plays a crucial role in the transformation. The letters do not even refer to a future judgment, which appears occasionally in the scrolls, and unlike the scrolls they do not make an explicit contrast between "flesh" and "spirit." But the similarity is striking nonetheless. There is an interval of several hundred years between the demise of the Jewish sect and the rise of monasticism, and it is impossible to trace influence from the former to the latter. Rather, they shared the view that the goal of life was the presence of God in heaven, a view that was encouraged by various strands of thought, philosophical and mythical/apocalyptic, in late antiquity. In their eagerness to reach that goal, both the sectarians and the monks structured their lives so that they felt they could experience the heavenly life already in the present.

---

[67] *Ibid.*, 29. This reinterpretation of resurrection as a present experience is more explicit and emphatic in the later Gnostic texts. See the essay of Hugo Lundhaug, "'These are the Symbols and Likenesses of the Resurrection': Conceptualizations of Death and Transformation in the *Treatise on the Resurrection* (NHC 1.4)," in Turid Karlsen Seim and Jorunn Økland, eds., *Metamorphoses. Resurrection, Body and Transformative Practices in Early Christianity* (Ekstasis 1; Berlin: de Gruyter, 2009) 187–205.

[68] Samuel Rubenson, "As Already Translated to the Kingdom While Still in the Body," *ibid.*, 271–89.

CHAPTER FOURTEEN

The Essenes and the Afterlife

In his magisterial *magnum opus* on the belief of the Essenes in the afterlife, Émile Puech devotes a chapter to the testimonies of Josephus and Hippolytus.[1] The placement of that chapter at the end of his work reflects his belief that the primary Essene texts are actually the Hebrew and Aramaic texts found at Qumran. Yet it is only in the Greek and Latin authors that we find the name Essene. The focus of this essay is on the Greek accounts of Essene eschatology, their relation to each other and the ultimate source of their information. I will also address the question of their possible relations to the Dead Sea Scrolls.

Josephus and Hippolytus

Josephus addresses the subject twice. In his earliest work, on the *Jewish War*, he attributes to the Essenes

a firm belief ... that although bodies are corruptible and their matter unstable, souls are immortal and endure forever; that, come from subtlest ether, they are entwined with the bodies which serve them as prisons, drawn down as they are by some physical spell; but that when they are freed from the bonds of the flesh, liberated, so to speak, from long slavery, then they rejoice and rise up to the heavenly world. (*JW* 2.154–5)

He goes on to discuss their beliefs about reward and punishment after death. "An abode is reserved beyond the Ocean for the souls of the just," analogous to the Isles of the Blessed in Greek mythology, while "they relegate evil souls to a dark pit shaken by storms, full of unending chastisement." The latter state is compared to the punishment of Sisyphus and other condemned figures in Hades. In his later work, the *Antiquities,* he contents himself with a brief statement that "they also declare that souls are immortal" (*Ant* 18.18).[2]

The account of Hippolytus[3] is so close to that of Josephus in the order of topics, and sometimes even in literal wording, that some relationship between them must be

---

[1] Émile Puech, *La Croyance des Esséniens en la Vie Future: Immortalité, Résurrection, Vie Éternelle?* (Paris: Lecoffre, 1993) 703–87.

[2] For the texts see Geza Vermes and Martin D. Goodman, *The Essenes according to the Classical Sources* (Sheffield: Sheffield Academic Press, 1989) 46–7 (*JW* 2) and 54–5 (*Ant* 18).

[3] *Ibid.,* 72–3. The work in question (*Refutatio omnium haeresium*, books 4–10) was found in a

assumed.[4] On the topic of eschatology, however, Hippolytus differs from the Jewish historian:

> The doctrine of the resurrection has also derived support among them, for they acknowledge both that the flesh will rise again, and that it will be immortal, in the same manner as the soul is already imperishable. They maintain that when the soul has been separated from the body, it is now borne into one place, which is well ventilated and full of light, and there it rests until judgment. This locality the Greeks were acquainted with by hearsay, calling it Isles of the Blessed ... Among these, Pythagoras especially and the Stoics among the Egyptians derived their principles after becoming disciples of these men, for they affirm that there will be both a judgment and a conflagration of the universe, and that the wicked will be eternally punished. (Ref 9.27)

While this account parallels that of Josephus in correlating Essene beliefs with those of the Greeks, and specifically mentioning the Isles of the Blessed, it differs in claiming that they affirmed the resurrection of the flesh and expected a cosmic judgment and conflagration. While Josephus attributed to them a purely individual eschatology, Hippolytus describes an eschatology that is both individual and cosmic.

There is no doubt that Hippolytus used a source in composing his account. The Essenes had vanished from history by his time. It is disputed, however, whether he drew directly on Josephus or whether they drew on a common source. It is very likely that Josephus used a source for his account of the Essenes in *JW* 2.[5] It is disproportionately long in comparison to the treatment of the Pharisees and Sadducees. Even though the passage begins by stating that "there exist among the Jews three schools of philosophy," the next sentence informs us that the Essenes "are Jews by race." This statement would make more sense if the discussion of the Essenes were taken from a different source. The account of "marrying Essenes" in *JW* 2.160 seems extraneous to the main account, and to be appended as a correction. At the same time it is clear that Josephus put his own stamp on the material, so that it highlights themes that are prominent throughout *JW*.[6] Consequently, it is often difficult

---

manuscript on Mt. Athos in the 19th century and ascribed to Origen under the title *Philosophumena*, and is still sometimes referred to by that name. There is now a consensus, however, that it is the work of Hippolytus.

[4] The correspondences and differences are highlighted in a synopsis by Christoph Burchard, "Die Essener bei Hippolyt. Hippolyt, Ref. IX 18,2–28 und Josephus, Bell. 2,119–161," *JSJ* 8 (1977) 1–42. The synopsis is found on pp. 7–20.

[5] Roland Bergmeier, *Die Essener-Berichte des Flavius Josephus. Quellenstudien zu den Essenertexten im Werk des jüdischen Historiographen* (Kampen: Kok Pharos, 1993) 62–3. Josephus's reliance on sources for his account of the Essenes has been challenged by Steve Mason, "What Josephus says about the Essenes in his Judean War," http://orion.mscc.huji.ac.il/orion/programs/Mason00–1.shtml, and "Essenes and Lurking Spartans in Josephus' Judean War: From Story to History," in Zuleika Rodgers, ed., *Making History: Josephus and Historical Method* (JSJSup 110; Leiden: Brill, 2007) 219–61. I have discussed this issue in my essay "Josephus on the Essenes. The Sources of His Information," in Zuleika Rodgers et al., eds., *A Wandering Galilean. Essays in Honour of Sean Freyne* (JSJSup 132; Leiden: Brill, 2009) 51–72.

[6] This has been shown in detail by Mason. See also his essays, "What Josephus Says about the Essenes in His *Judean War*," in Stephen G. Wilson and Michel Desjardins, eds., *Text and Artifact*

to know when Josephus is following his source closely and when he is embellishing it.

Most scholars who have concerned themselves with the question, beginning with the first editor in 1851, have assumed that the author of the later passage drew directly on Josephus,[7] but the theory of a common source also has a long pedigree.[8] In recent years, two contributions have been especially influential.

First, in 1958 Morton Smith made the case for a common source.[9] Smith argued that the *Refutatio* usually quotes almost without alteration, but that its wording often differs from that of Josephus. Moreover, Hippolytus shows no certain knowledge of Josephus, and he contradicts Josephus in his *Chronicle*. Most importantly, each text contains extensive sections lacking in the other. There are three such sections in the accounts of the Essenes.

(i). *JW* 2.150–51, Josephus says that they are divided into four lots according to the duration of their discipline, and that the juniors are considered inferior to the elders. The corresponding passage in *Ref.* 26 says instead that they have been split up into four parties, one of which is called Zealots or Sicarii. Smith describes this passage in Hippolytus as "a mishmash of misinformation evidently concocted, from misunderstood reports, to explain the reference to four kinds, which was found in the text."[10] He argues, however, that this misunderstanding would be improbable if the author had the present text of Josephus before him.

(ii) In *JW* 2.151–53, Josephus offers a supposed personal reminiscence of the heroic endurance of the Essenes in the war against Rome, in the past tense. The corresponding passage, in *Ref.* 26, in the present tense, is a more general statement that they despise death, so long as they can die with a good conscience, and refuse to violate the law even under torture. Both passages are reminiscent of 2 Maccabees 7. Smith argues that Hippolytus would not have passed over the more specific language of Josephus, but would have copied it as an example for Christians of his own time.

(iii) The third major discrepancy occurs in the accounts of the afterlife in *JW* 2. 154–58. Here Smith supposed that Hippolytus was probably accurate, against Josephus, since his account of the resurrection and final judgment was more in accord-

---

in the *Religions of Mediterranean Antiquity: Essays in Honour of Peter Richardson* (Waterloo: Wilfrid Laurier University Press, 2000), 434–467 (= roughly the latter half of his internet essay) and his "Essenes and Lurking Spartans."

[7] E. Miller, *Origenis Philosophumena* (Oxford: Oxford University Press, 1851) 297, n.49.

[8] Beginning with L. Duncker and F. Schneidewin, *S. Hippolyti... Refutationis Omnium Haeresium* (10 vols.; Göttingen: Dieterich, 1859) 472.

[9] Morton Smith, "The Description of the Essenes in Josephus and the Philosophumena," *HUCA* 29 (1958) 273–313. Two years earlier, Matthew Black, "The Account of the Essenes in Hippolytus and Josephus," in W. D. Davies and D. Daube, eds., *The Background of the New Testament and Its Eschatology* (Cambridge: Cambridge University Press, 1956) 172–82, also argued for a common source, but in less detail. See also Black, *The Scrolls and Christian Origins* (New York: Scribners, 1961) 187–91.

[10] Smith, "The Account of the Essenes," 282–3.

ance with Palestinian Jewish beliefs. The common reference to the Isles of the Blessed showed that there was some common basis, which Hippolytus perhaps summarized and Josephus certainly developed.[11]

Smith's analysis was accepted by such scholars as George Nickelsburg[12] and Larry Schiffman.[13] He himself, however, subsequently changed his mind, and concluded that he was "probably mistaken in supposing Hippolytus independent of Josephus."[14] He was persuaded by Shaye Cohen's discussion of the way Josephus used his sources that if there was a common source there would not be so much verbal agreement between Josephus, who tended to paraphrase, and Hippolytus, who cited more faithfully.[15] Moreover, his analysis has been superseded in the minds of many by the second influential discussion of the issue, that of Christoph Burchard.[16]

Burchard rejected the broad arguments offered by some scholars that the account of Hippolytus is more authentically Semitic than that of the "hellenisierende Schönschreiber" Josephus. He disputed Smith's claim that Hippolytus always cited verbatim, and that he did not know Josephus, which seems *a priori* unlikely. Rather he looked to the style of the passage in the *Refutatio*, which he found to be consistent with that of Hippolytus. There are numerous parallels with early Christian literature. Moreover, Burchard claimed that Hippolytus sometimes agrees with Josephus where the latter appears to be editorializing, as in the reference to the Isles of the Blessed in the discussion of eschatology.

Burchard also considered the major discrepancies between the two accounts noted by Smith. The passage on four kinds of Essenes, which confuses the Essenes with the Zealots, appears to contain traditional material, but it is misplaced. It cannot have come from Josephus's source on the Essenes. In contrast to Smith, Burchard argues that the passage on Essene heroism in face of death can be plausibly understood as an adaptation of Josephus. Since the Jewish war was now ancient history, a more general statement was more appropriate. In the passage on eschatology, the distinctive elements in Hippolytus's account correspond almost exactly to what he says elsewhere about other groups. So he says about the Pharisees (*Ref.* 9.28.5): "they likewise acknowledge that there is a resurrection of flesh, and that soul is immortal, and that there will be a judgment and conflagration ..." His general summary of the Jewish religion concludes with a description of its eschatology (*Ref.* 9.30.8): after an eschatological battle in which the messiah would be killed, there would follow "the termination and conflagration of the universe, and in this way their opinions concerning the resurrection would receive completion, and a recom-

---

[11] *Ibid.*, 284.

[12] George W. E. Nickelsburg, *Resurrection, Immortality and Eternal Life in Intertestamental Judaism* (HTS 26; Cambridge, MA: Harvard, 1972) 168.

[13] L. H. Schiffman, "Essenes," *Encyclopedia of Religion* (1986) 5.163–66.

[14] M. Smith, "Helios in Palestine," *Eretz Israel* 16 (1982) 199*-214* (211*-12, n.24).

[15] S. J. D. Cohen, *Josephus in Galilee and Rome. His Vita and Development as a Historian* (Leiden: Brill, 1979) 24–47. Cohen does not discuss Hippolytus.

[16] Burchard, "Die Essener bei Hippolyt," 1–41.

pense be rendered to each man according to his works." Finally, in his concluding exhortation to his Christian readers in *Ref.* 10.34, he tells them that "by means of this knowledge you shall escape the approaching threat of the fire of judgment," and have "an immortal body and incorruptible, together with the soul." It seems most likely, then, that Hippolytus is correcting the eschatology described by Josephus to bring it into line with what he understood to be common Jewish, and also Christian, belief.

This latter point is especially telling. One could argue that the fact that this passage shows Hippolytus's style only means that he rewrote his source,[17] and that the alleged editorializing comments of Josephus were really part of the source. We could then suppose that both Josephus and Hippolytus embellished a common core in different ways, as Josephus surely embellished his source. But the major *Sondergut* of Hippolytus appears to be either drawn from a tradition not related to the Essenes in the case of the "Zealot" passage or from Hippolytus' own theology, in the case of the eschatology. If Hippolytus, then, does not preserve any significant information from the supposed common source that is not also found in Josephus, and if the whole passage is written in his own style, there is no reason to posit a common source. It seems easier to assume that he adapted Josephus directly.[18]

Burchard's analysis of this issue has been accepted as definitive by such different scholars as Mason[19] and Bergmeier.[20] Puech expresses appreciation for the detailed study, but claims that the conclusion goes beyond the evidence.[21] Why, he asks, would Hippolytus have adapted the elegant prose of Josephus when his own style is so laborious? His main objection, however, is methodological. For Puech, the way to determine whether the *Sondergut* of Hippolytus represents Essene tradition is to see whether it corresponds to what we find in the Dead Sea Scrolls, which he takes to be "internal" evidence for Essene eschatology.

Puech is by no means alone in his methodological assumption. Even Burchard occasionally appeals to the Scrolls as the criterion for what is genuinely Essene.[22] In my own judgment, the balance of evidence still favors the view that the "Essaeans"

---

[17] Cf. the comment of Puech, *La Croyance*, 722: "cela ne prouverait pas encore que le fond n'a rien d'historique et, dans ce cas, d'essénien."

[18] Compare the comment of Jan Bremmer, *The Rise and Fall of the Afterlife* (London: Routledge, 2001) 46, that Hippolytus "did not hesitate to doctor his documents whenever this suited his aims and did not shrink from ascribing to his sources views utterly alien to their argument."

[19] Mason, "What Josephus Says about the Essenes," internet version.

[20] Roland Bergmeier, "Die drei jüdischen Schulrichtungen nach Josephus und Hippolyt von Rom," *JSJ* 34 (2003) 443–70, especially 451–68. So also H. C. Cavallin, "Leben nach dem Tode im Spätjudentum und im frühjudentum und im frühen Christentum, I – Spätjudentum," *ANRW* II, 19/1 (Berlin: de Gruyter, 1979) 272–4.

[21] Albert Baumgarten, "Josephus and Hippolytus on the Pharisees," *HUCA* 55 (1984) 1–25, especially 6–7, is critical of Burchard on the grounds that Hippolytus usually quoted his sources accurately, and that the goals Burchard attributes to him are too subtle. Baumgarten argues that Hippolytus used a revision of Josephus that was sympathetic to the Pharisees.

[22] Burchard, "Die Essener bei Hippolyt," 32, 34; cf. Bergmeier, *Die Essener-Berichte*, 72–9; 94–107; Jörg Frey, "Zur historischen Auswertung der antiken Essenerberichte. Ein Beitrag zum Gespräch mit Roland Bergmeier," in Jörg Frey and Hartmut Stegemann, eds., *Qumran kontrovers*.

and "Essenes" of Philo, Josephus and Pliny referred to an actual Jewish sect, which is now known to us more accurately from the Dead Sea Scrolls. Nonetheless, it seems to me that the relationship between Hippolytus and Josephus is a literary question that should be settled by comparison of the two passages, with due attention to the different agendas of the two authors. Again, the provenance of material in Hippolytus that is not attested, or even is contradicted, in Josephus, should be considered first of all in terms of the nature of that material and its use in Hippolytus. Comparison of any of this material with the Dead Sea Scrolls is a secondary question. For while the identification of the *yahad* as Essene is probable, it is not certain, and it can only be maintained on the assumption that the Greek and Latin accounts are partial and distorted. If some elements in Hippolytus's description of Essene eschatology coincide with some passages in the Scrolls, we must still ask whether they were distinctive beliefs of the *yahad* or whether the resemblance is coincidental. Again, if the account in Hippolytus is judged to be his own invention, this does not necessarily authenticate that of Josephus. In each case we must begin by identifying the features of these accounts that seem to reflect the views and *Tendenz* of their authors, and keep these in mind when we compare them with what we find in the Scrolls.

Essene eschatology according to Josephus

In the case of Josephus, there is no doubt that the Essenes are portrayed in such a way as to maximize their affinities with Greek philosophy and mythology. Puech is quite right when he characterizes this account as "fundamentally Greek" and emphasizes its neo-Pythagorean character.[23] Moreover, the motif of death as the liberation of the soul from the body is one that occurs quite frequently in Josephus.[24] For example, in his deathbed speech, Aristobulus I says "how long, shameless body, wilt thou detain the soul that is sentenced to a brother's and a mother's vengeance?" (*JW* 1.84; cf. *Ant* 13.317). Again, in the climactic speech before the mass suicide on Masada, Eleazar tells his followers that

> Life, not death, is man's misfortune. For it is death which gives liberty to the soul and permits it to depart to its own pure abode, there to be free from all calamity; but so long as it is imprisoned in a mortal body and tainted with all its miseries, it is, in sober truth, dead ... it is not until, freed from the weight that drags it down to earth and clings about it, the soul is restored to its proper sphere, that it enjoys a blessed energy and a power untrammelled on every side, remaining, like God Himself, invisible to human eyes. (*JW* 7.343–46)

Beiträge zu den Textfunden vom Toten Meer (Paderborn: Bonifatius, 2003) 23–55, among many others.

[23] Puech, *La Croyance*, 732.

[24] Joseph Sievers, "Josephus and the Afterlife," in Steve Mason, ed., *Understanding Josephus. Seven Perspectives* (JSPSup 32; Sheffield: Sheffield Academic Press, 1998) 20–31.

In light of these parallels we might suspect that Josephus simply attributed to the Essenes his own beliefs about the afterlife.

Such an assumption would be too simple, however. In *JW* 3, Josephus attributes to himself a speech attempting to dissuade the defenders of Jotapata from committing suicide. In the course of this speech he reiterates some familiar themes: "All of us, it is true, have mortal bodies, composed of perishable matter, but the soul lives forever, immortal: it is a portion of the Deity housed in our bodies" (*JW* 3.372). Josephus does not argue that people should therefore liberate their souls from their bodies. Rather, those who depart this life in accordance with nature, when God recalls his loan, have a blessed afterlife: "their souls, remaining spotless and obedient, are allotted the most holy place in heaven, whence, in the revolution of the ages, they return to find in chaste bodies a new habitation." In contrast, those who commit suicide suffer a grim fate: "the darker regions of the netherworld receive their souls, and God, their father, visits upon their offspring the outrageous acts of the parents" (*JW* 3.374–5). The immortality of the soul, and the punishment of sinners in dark regions, parallel the account of the Essenes. But, remarkably, Josephus also expresses a belief in bodily resurrection: "in the revolution of the ages, they return to find in chaste bodies a new habitation." To be sure, his formulation of this belief is different from what we typically find in Jewish apocalypses, but it is unmistakable nonetheless. We might compare his slightly different formulation of Pharisaic belief in terms of metempsychosis: "every soul, they maintain, is imperishable, but the soul of the good alone passes into another body, while the souls of the wicked suffer eternal punishment" (*JW* 2.163). In neither case does he imagine resurrection simply as a return to earth in one's old body. Such an idea would have seemed absurd to any sophisticated Greek or Roman. But as Dale Martin has argued, "popular conceptions of the state of the dead were quite capable of portraying them as existing in some kind of embodied state."[25] Even astral immortality could be imagined as having a bodily form, although not a body of flesh and blood.[26] Josephus seems to envision resurrection as a return to earth in a new bodily form. He also seems to affirm a distinctively Jewish form of resurrection in his description of Jewish beliefs in *AgAp* 2.218: those who observe the laws and die for them if necessary are assured that "God has granted [them] a renewed existence and in the revolution of the ages the gift of a better life." Here, as in the Jotapata speech, he distinguishes between immortality of the soul, which follows immediately after death, and eventual resurrection on earth in bodily form. While the typical Jewish apocalyptic hope was for resurrection at the end of the ages, Josephus gives this a Stoic overtone by speaking of the revolution of the ages, or the periodic renewal of all things.[27]

---

[25] Dale B. Martin, *The Corinthian Body* (New Haven: Yale, 1995) 110.

[26] *Ibid.*, 118, on heavenly bodies, which were usually thought to be fiery.

[27] On the Stoic belief in cosmic renewal see A. A. Long and D. N. Sedley, *The Hellenistic Philosophers* (Cambridge: Cambridge University Press, 1987) 1. 274–79.

It is unlikely then that Josephus would have rejected a statement in his source about Essene belief in bodily resurrection. He would have presumably Hellenized it in some way, but as we see from his Jotapata speech he was quite capable of doing that, without embarrassment. As Nickelsburg observed: "although Josephus describes the eschatology of both Essenes and Pharisees in Hellenistic vocabulary, he does not attribute to the Essenes what he does attribute to the Pharisees, viz., a belief in a new bodily existence."[28] If he depicts the Essene belief as one in the immortality of the soul, this is presumably what he found in his source, even if he then embellishes it. This conclusion is supported by the fact that he also affirms their belief in the immortality of the soul, without reference to resurrection, and without further embellishment, in *Ant* 18.18, where he draws on a source, different from the one in *JW* 2, that is closely related to Philo's accounts of the Essaeans.[29]

Does Josephus reflect a Semitic belief?

The immortality of the soul, without further embellishment, is a distinctively Greek formulation of belief in the afterlife. But it is now widely recognized that the old assumption that Greeks believed in immortality of the soul, while Jews expected resurrection of the body, is far too simple.[30] As George Nickelsburg demonstrated, there is plenty of evidence for Jewish belief in forms of immortality that did not involve bodily resurrection, even in texts that were composed in Semitic languages in the land of Israel.[31] An obvious example is the formulation of Jubilees: "their bodies will rest in the earth, but their spirits will have much joy" (*Jub* 23:30–31). Even in the one clear biblical affirmation of resurrection in the Book of Daniel, the resurrected righteous are not said to return to earth, but to ascend to the stars. Their form is not discussed. It may be bodily, but it is scarcely a resurrection of the flesh. In fact, pre-Christian Jewish accounts of resurrection do not usually emphasize its bodily

---

[28] Nickelsburg, *Resurrection, Immortality and Eternal Life*, 168. Lester Grabbe, "Eschatology in Philo and Josephus," in Alan J. Avery-Peck and Jacob Neusner, eds., *Judaism in Late Antiquity. Part Four. Death, Life-After-Death, Resurrection and the World-to-Come in the Judaisms of Late Antiquity* (Handbuch der Orientalistik 1/49; Leiden: Brill, 2000) 176, seems to miss this crucial difference when he comments that the descriptions of Josephus's own views in the Jotapata speech and *AgAp* "look remarkably similar to the views ascribed by Josephus himself to both the Pharisees and the Essenes."

[29] For Philo's account, see *Quod omnis probus liber sit* 75–91, *Hypothetica* 11.1–8 (= *Apologia pro Judaeis*). Vermes and Goodman, *The Essenes*, 19–31.

[30] The classic expression of that assumption is that of Oscar Cullmann, "Immortality of the Soul or Resurrection of the Body," in Krister Stendhal, ed., *Immortality and Resurrection* (New York: Macmillan, 1965) 9–53.

[31] Nickelsburg, *Resurrection, Immortality and Eternal Life*, passim. See also his essay, "Judgment, Life-After-Death, and Resurrection in the Apocrypha and the Non-Apocalyptic Pseudepigrapha," in Avery-Peck and Neusner, eds., *Judaism in Late Antiquity*, 141–62, and my own essay, "The Afterlife in Apocalyptic Literature," *ibid.*, 119–39.

character. The account of the Maccabean martyrs in 2 Maccabees 7 is exceptional in this regard, and its emphasis on bodily resurrection is evidently evoked by the bodily sufferings of the martyrs. In light of the common assumption that the Essenes and the *yahad* of the Dead Sea Scrolls are one and the same, it is not only legitimate but necessary to ask how the depictions of Essene eschatology fit in the spectrum of Palestinian Jewish eschatology in this period, and specifically how they compare to the evidence of the Hebrew scrolls.[32]

This comparison is complicated by two considerations. First, not every text found at Qumran is a document of the *yahad*, and second, many of the texts found there are poetic in character, and are not necessarily to be read as doctrinal statements.

The evidence of the rule books

The obvious place to look for the doctrinal beliefs of the sect is the major sectarian rule books. These leave no doubt about the importance of reward and punishment after death in the ideology of the sect. In the *Instruction on the Two Spirits* in the *Community Rule*, the visitation of those who walk in the spirit of light "will be for healing, plentiful peace in a long life, fruitful offspring with all everlasting blessings, eternal enjoyment with endless life, and a crown of glory with majestic raiment in eternal light" (1QS 4:6–8). Some scholars have expressed doubts as to whether this passage refers to the afterlife, rather than to the blessings of this life.[33] The first three items (healing, peace in a long life, offspring) seem to envision an idealized earthly life, but the references to eternal life have a transcendent character. Moreover, the punishments of the damned are otherworldly. The visitation of those who walk in the spirit of darkness

> will be for a glut of punishments at the hands of all the angels of destruction, for eternal damnation, for the scorching wrath of the God of revenge, for permanent error and shame without end with the humiliation of destruction by the fire of the dark regions. And all the ages of their generations they shall spend in bitter weeping and harsh evils in the abysses of darkness until their destruction, without there being a remnant or a survivor among them.[34]

The punishments of the wicked in a place of darkness are quite reminiscent of Josephus's account of the eschatology of the Essenes, although as we have seen Josephus uses similar language elsewhere when the Essenes are not in view.

While some of the rewards of the righteous may be realized in this world, they also clearly include eternal life in glory.

The language of resurrection, however, is conspicuously absent.

---

[32] See already John J. Collins, *Apocalypticism in the Dead Sea Scrolls* (London: Routledge, 1997) 110–29.

[33] Jean Duhaime, "La Doctrine des Esséniens de Qumrân sur l'après-mort," in Guy Couturier et al., eds., *Essais sur la Mort* (Montreal: Fides, 1985) 99–121.

[34] 1QS 4:11–14; trans. García Martínez.

Puech argues that the term "visitation" refers to the final judgment, on the Day of the Lord.[35] The term is certainly used with reference to a final, global, judgment, even within the *Instruction on the Two Spirits* (1QS 3:18; 4:18–19). But the *Instruction* also speaks about the "visitation" of all who walk in each spirit, not of the visitation of God on these individuals or of what will happen to them on the day of visitation. Since the visitation of each spirit seems to follow automatically from their conduct, the passage lends itself more readily to the view that this "visitation" awaits each individual after death, in the sense of that which is appointed for them. There is still a final judgment by which God puts an end to wickedness, but neither the *Instruction* nor any of the clearly sectarian texts says that the dead are raised or brought back for that judgment. Rather, people seem to go directly to their rewards or punishments. Some of the rewards of the righteous would seem to require a corporeal state, but the body in question may be a spiritual rather than an earthly body, to use the distinction drawn by St. Paul. This conception is rather different from the Greek notion of immortality of the soul, and it is entirely in keeping with traditional Hebrew anthropology, whereby the *nephesh* survives the body in the Netherworld. Insofar as there is no mention of resurrection of the body, however, it is not difficult to see how this conception could be identified with immortality of the soul by a Hellenized observer.

The *Damascus Document*, CD 2:3–13 has several verbal parallels to the *Instruction on the Two Spirits*, although it lacks the underlying dualism of light and darkness.[36] The destiny of the wicked is described in terms that are very similar to 1QS 4:12: "great flaming wrath by the hand of all the Angels of Destruction ... without remnant or survivor." Like the *Community Rule*, CD teaches that those who hold fast to the covenant "are destined to live forever and all the glory of Adam shall be theirs" (CD 3:20; cf. 1QS 4:23). Both these rule books envisage a public, communal judgment when God will put an end to wickedness (1QS 4:18), and when the wicked "will have a visitation for destruction at the hand of Belial. This is the day when God will make a visitation" (CD 8:3–4). But they also specify the destiny entailed by the behavior of individuals, without any indication that all reward and punishment is deferred to the day of judgment, and rather implying that it is implemented immediately after the death of the individual.

The fact that the sectarian rule books present the beliefs of the group in this way is highly significant for our purpose. At least it shows that resurrection language was not essential to the eschatology of the sect. This does not mean that the members were not familiar with ideas of resurrection, or that some of them may not have held them. They were at least familiar with the Book of Daniel, and some texts expressing a belief in resurrection have been found at Qumran. But if resurrection language could be avoided in the rule books, which explicitly address the question

---

[35] Puech, *La Croyance*, 434.
[36] See Armin Lange, *Weisheit und Prädestination* (STDJ 18; Leiden: Brill, 1995) 242.

of afterlife, then it was not *de rigueur*. Neither Josephus nor his source is likely to have had an extensive knowledge of the sectarian literature. The closest parallels of Josephus's account of the Essenes in *JW* 2 are found precisely in the *Community Rule*. If his source was based on some form of that Rule, we can easily enough imagine how the hope for eternal life without resurrection would have been formulated for Greek readers as immortality of the soul. To be sure, the correspondence between Josephus and the *Community Rule* on the matter of eschatology is by no means complete. Josephus says nothing about spirits of light and darkness, or of a final judgment, or of messiahs. Not all copies of the *Community Rule* had the reference to the messiahs, but we would have to assume that some aspects of the *Instruction on the Two Spirits* were ignored or suppressed, if it were part of Josephus's source. But the belief in immortality of the soul seems to me to be a reasonable approximation of the Scroll's affirmation of eternal life, translated into Greek idiom.

Hippolytus and the Scrolls

The account of Hippolytus differs from that of Josephus in attributing to the Essenes belief in resurrection of the flesh and in a final conflagration.

The belief in resurrection is formulated as follows:

> They acknowledge both that the flesh will rise again and that it will be immortal, in the same manner as the soul is already imperishable. They maintain that when the soul has been separated from the body, it is now borne into one place, which is well ventilated and full of light, and there it rests until judgment.

The waiting place of the soul calls to mind one of the earliest Jewish passages about the afterlife, *1 Enoch* 22, which describes various chambers containing souls waiting for judgment, and says that the chamber of the righteous has a "bright fountain of water."[37] That passage, however, is exceptional in Jewish literature, and seems to have had little influence on the developing tradition. It is not reflected even indirectly in any of the other extant Dead Sea Scrolls. Neither do the Scrolls ever speak of resurrection of the flesh.

The idea of resurrection was certainly known to the members of the *yahad*. In addition to the Book of Daniel and the *Animal Apocalypse of Enoch* (*1 Enoch* 90:10), clear instances of resurrection are found in 4Q521 (the "Messianic Apocalypse")[38]

---

[37] See G. W. Nickelsburg, *1 Enoch 1. A Commentary on the Book of 1 Enoch, Chapters 1–36; 81–108* (Hermeneia; Minneapolis: Fortress, 2001) 300–09. The parallel is noted by Puech, *La Croyance*, 743–4. Also by Smith, "The Description of the Essenes," 284.

[38] Puech, *La Croyance*, 627–92; cf. J. J. Collins, "The Works of the Messiah," *DSD* 1 (1994) 98–112.

and 4Q385 (*Pseudo-Ezekiel*).[39] It is not clear whether either of these texts was sectarian, in the sense of being composed within the *yahad*.[40]

The strongest case for a belief in resurrection in the sectarian literature rests on a few passages in the *Hodayot*.

In 1QH[a] 19:10–14 (a hymn of the community) the hymnist thanks God

because you have done wonders with dust,
and have acted very mightily with a creature of clay.

The hymn goes on to say that

for your glory, you have purified man from sin
so that he can make himself holy for you
from every impure abomination and blameworthy iniquity,
to become united with the sons of your truth
and in a lot with your holy ones,
to raise from the dust the worm of the dead to an [everlasting] community,
and from a depraved spirit, to your knowledge,
so that he can take his place in your presence
with the perpetual host and the [everlasting] spirits,
to renew him with everything that will exist,
and with those who know in a community of jubilation.

The argument that this hymn implies bodily resurrection rests on the phrase "to raise the worm of the dead from the dust." The same phrase (תולעת מתים) occurs in 1QH[a] 14:34 (a Teacher hymn): "Hoist a banner, you who lie in the dust; raise a standard, worm of dead ones." There is an allusion here to Isa 26:19, which refers to those who *dwell* in the dust. There is also an allusion to Isa 41:14: "do not fear, worm of Jacob, men of Israel." (The Hebrew for "men" here is מתי, a rare word that occurs only in the construct plural in the Hebrew Bible, and which has the same consonants as the more familiar word for "dead ones.") In Isaiah 41, the addressees are in a lowly state, but they are not dead. Analogously, the phrase "worm of the dead" in the *Hodayot* may indicate metaphorically the abject state of unaided human nature. Just as the hymnist claims to be lifted up from Sheol or the Netherworld, he claims that the dead are raised from the dust to become members of the community and so enter into fellowship with the holy ones. It is not necessary to suppose that the author has actual corpses in mind. This is poetry, and its imagery should not be pressed for doctrinal teachings.

---

[39] Puech, *La Croyance*, 605–16; Collins, *Apocalypticism in the Dead Sea Scrolls*, 126–7.

[40] Puech also adduced 4Q245 (Pseudo-Daniel) and the *Words of the Heavenly Luminaries* (4Q504) as evidence for a belief in resurrection, but it is not apparent that these texts refer to resurrection at all. The *Testaments of Qahat* and *Amram* clearly envisage reward and punishment after death, but do not clearly use language of resurrection. See Collins, *Apocalypticism in the Dead Sea Scrolls*, 124–6.

The interpretation of these passages is not only a matter of deciding whether the language is literal or metaphorical. It also involves the contexts in which the passages occur. The passage in 1QH^a 14 is preceded by a passage describing the eschatological battle and judgment:

And then at the time of judgment the sword of God shall hasten, and all the sons of His truth shall awake to [overthrow] wickedness; all the sons of iniquity shall be no more. The Hero shall bend his bow; the fortress shall open on to endless space and the everlasting gates shall send out weapons of war. They shall be mighty from end to end [of the earth and there shall be no escape] for the guilty of heart [in their battle]; they shall be utterly trampled down without any [remnant. There shall be no] hope in the greatness [of their might], no refuge for the mighty warriors for [the battle shall be] to the Most High God ... Hoist a banner, you who lie in the dust; raise a standard, worm of dead ones (1QH^a 14: 29–33).

The call to those who lie in the dust, then, comes at the end of the eschatological battle, precisely where we should expect a reference to resurrection, by analogy with the apocalypses.[41]

The point is not conclusive, however. Those who lie in the dust could be those who are downcast during the dominion of Belial, or who have been defeated in one of the phases of the eschatological battle. A reference to resurrection is possible here, but it is not certain. The possibility is more remote in 1QH^a 19, where "the worm of the dead" is lifted up to commune with the children of truth. (The verb is *yahad.*) Even though this communion participates in the lot of the Holy Ones, it is most probably located in the *yahad* or community of the sect. Compare 1QS 11:8: "He has joined their assembly to the Sons of Heaven to be a Council of the Community."

The *Hodayot* frequently refer to the final cosmic war (see especially 1QH^a 11). It is not unreasonable to expect that this war would culminate in the resurrection of the dead, as it often does in apocalyptic texts of the time. Nonetheless there are no unambiguous references to resurrection in the *Hodayot*, and even possible references are rare.[42] The main eschatological focus of these hymns is on life with the angels, which is experienced as a present reality. This does not necessarily mean that there was no place for resurrection in the eschatology of the Dead Sea sect. But it does mean that resurrection language was not the primary vehicle of eschatological hope in the sect, nor even a necessary one. Rather, the focus was on sharing the angelic life within the community and thereby transcending death and continuing that life in heaven. The primary sectarian texts, such as the rule books and the *Hodayot*, then, provide no clear evidence, in support of the claim of Hippolytus that the Essenes believed in bodily resurrection. In view of the fact that Hippolytus attributes the same belief to Essenes and Pharisees, Jews and even Christians, his attribution of resurrection to the Essenes is unlikely to come from a reliable source.

---

[41] Puech, *La Croyance*, 361–63.
[42] Puech, *La Croyance*, 413, finds another reference in 1QH 5:29, which seems to indicate a new creation, but not a resurrection of the dead.

The case for reliable Essene tradition on the belief in a coming conflagration is also weak. Only one passage in the Scrolls suggests such a belief, and this is again a poetic passage in the *Hodayot* (col. 11:19–36). The language about a conflagration is introduced in the context of an extended metaphor, to illustrate how "the life of a poor person lives amongst great turmoil." The turmoil is illustrated by what appear to be eschatological upheavals:

Then the torrents of Belial will overflow their high banks,
like a devouring fire in all their watering channels,
destroying every tree green or dry, from their canals.
It roams with flames of fire until none of those who drink are left.
It consumes the foundations of clay and the tract of dry land.
It burns the bases of the mountains
and converts the roots of flint rock into streams of lava.
It consumes right to the great deep.
The torrents of Belial break into Abaddon.

The imagery of the poem draws on traditions about a final conflagration.

The idea that God would judge the world by fire had ample biblical precedent,[43] and the expectation of a conflagration leading to the renewal of the world was propagated by Stoicism.[44] Such traditions were widespread in the Hellenistic-Roman world,[45] including Hellenistic Jewish texts such as the Sibylline Oracles.[46] The motif of a river or flood of fire in the hymn from Qumran brings to mind the Persian *Bundahishn*, 30.19ff, which speaks of fire that melts the mountains and remains on the earth like a river. The same motif is found in a passage in Lactantius that is probably derived from the *Oracle of Hystaspes*.[47] Hippolytus attributes a belief in conflagration not only to Essenes, but also to Pharisees, Jews in general and even Christians. The fact that such imagery is used in one poem found at Qumran does not require that a belief in conflagration was a central tenet of the *yahad*, or make it likely that Hippolytus derived it from a source about the Essenes. Josephus claims, with apparent approval, that Adam had predicted "a destruction of the universe, at one time by fire, at another by a mighty deluge of water."[48] He would hardly have felt a need to censor a supposed Essene belief in conflagration if he had found it in his source.

---

[43] E.g. the coming Day of the Lord in Malachi 3.

[44] See Long and Sedley, *The Hellenistic Philosophers* 1. 274–79.

[45] E.g. Cicero, *Consolatio ad Marciam* 26.6; Seneca, *Nat Quaest* 3.29.1.

[46] Sib Or 4:171–78. See further John J. Collins, *The Sibylline Oracles of Egyptian Judaism* (SBLDS 13; Missoula, MT: Scholars Press, 1974) 101–10.

[47] Lactantius, *Div Inst* 7.21. Belief in the destruction of the world by fire is also attributed to the Oracle of Hystaspes by Justin, *Apol.* 20.1. See Hans Windisch, *Die Orakel des Hystaspes.* (Verhandelingen der Koninklijke Akademie van Wetenschappen te Amsterdam. Afdeeling Letterkunde, Nieuwe Reeks, Deel XXVIII no. 3; Amsterdam: Koninklijke Akademie van Wetenschappen, 1929) 29. On Persian ideas of conflagration see further Rudolf Mayer, *Die biblische Vorstellung vom Weltbrand* (Bonner Orientalische Studien, N. S. 4; Bonn: Selbstverlag des orientalischen Seminars, 1956).

[48] *Ant* 1.70.

Conclusion

The identification of the Essenes with the *yahad* of the Scrolls can neither be established nor disproved on the basis of the eschatological passages alone. We have argued, however, that Josephus's account of the Essene belief in immortality of the soul could be derived from something like the *Instruction on the Two Spirits* in the *Community Rule*, although it is translated into the imagery of Greek philosophy and mythology. In contrast, there is little basis for the view that the distinctive elements in Hippolytus' accounts derive from traditions about the *yahad*. Neither bodily resurrection nor conflagration is well attested in the Scrolls. There are of course many features of the Scrolls that are not attested in either Josephus or Hippolytus – messianic expectation, a final war, the dualism of light and darkness. Hippolytus knows no more of these than does Josephus. If indeed the *yahad* was Essene, we should have to conclude that the Greek accounts were not very well informed. Insofar as there is any reliable information in these accounts about an actual Jewish sect, however, it is more likely to be found in Josephus, despite his Hellenistic embellishments, than in the derivative and tendentious account of Hippolytus.

CHAPTER FIFTEEN

Prayer and the Meaning of Ritual in the Dead Sea Scrolls

The meaninglessness of ritual?

In a famous article published in 1979, the anthropologist Frits Staal argued for "The Meaninglessness of Ritual."[1] For Staal, ritual is activity governed by rules, and can be understood only as such. "What is essential in the ceremony is the precise and faultless execution, in accordance with rules, of numerous rites and recitations."[2] People may ascribe meaning to these actions from time to time, but these explanations are not a necessary part of ritual. A mantra is taken out of its ritual context and rendered as a series of stylized sounds, without regard for their meaning. Brahmin ritual experts are often ignorant of what the sounds they make actually mean, but they are skilled in rendering them correctly. "Like rocks or trees, ritual acts and sounds may be provided with meaning, but they do not require meanings and do not exist for meaning's sake."[3]

Staal's view of ritual contrasted sharply with other views that had been regnant in the twentieth century. In the *Encyclopedia of Religion*, edited by Mircea Eliade, ritual is defined as "those conscious and voluntary, repetitious and stylized symbolic bodily actions that are centered on cosmic structures and/or sacred presences," with the parenthetical addition that "verbal behaviors such as chant, song, and prayer are of course included in the category of bodily actions."[4] Eliade himself had regarded ritual as "a reenactment of a cosmogonic event or story recounted in myth."[5] There is a long history of scholarship on the relation of ritual to myth, dating back to the work of James G. Frazer in the early twentieth century.[6] Even without the appeal to myth, however, many scholars see ritual as a symbol system, and view rituals as "symbolic statements or encoded performances that act out or dramatize an already existing social message. Ritual symbols have a referential quality that

---

[1] Fritz Staal, "The Meaninglessness of Ritual," *Numen* 26 (1979) 2–22.
[2] *Ibid.*, 9.
[3] Staal, "The Sound of Religion: Parts IV-V," *Numen* 15/2 (1968) 218.
[4] Evan M. Zuesse, "Ritual [First Edition]" in Lindsay Jones, ed., *The Encyclopedia of Religion* (New York: Macmillan, 2005; first edition edited by Mircea Eliade, 1987) 7834.
[5] Catherine M. Bell, *Ritual. Perspectives and Dimensions* (New York: Oxford University Press, 1997) 11. See Eliade, *The Myth of the Eternal Return or, Cosmos and History* (trans. Willard R. Trask; Princeton: Princeton University Press, 1954).
[6] Bell, *Ritual*, 1–22.

points to a meaning that exists outside the rituals themselves."[7] So, for example, the anthropologist Edmund Leach wrote of "the material representation of abstract ideas" as "ritual condensation."[8]

Staal's formulation was undoubtedly extreme, but it has struck a chord with many theorists of religion, as a protest against the tendency of scholars to "regard rites as enactments of myths, theological ideas, or moral principles."[9] Consequently, there has been a tendency to insist "that ritual enactment refers to itself and not to a message that exists apart from, outside of, or above the ritual enactment proper."[10] Jonathan Z. Smith urged people to look at "the bare facts of ritual," although he was far from regarding it as meaningless.[11] Roy Rappaport defined ritual as "the performance of more or less invariant sequences of formal acts and utterances."[12] Other theorists emphasize ritual as action or practice.[13]

The emphasis on the practice of prescribed actions as distinct from the expression of symbolic meaning is not a modern conceit; in fact the reverse is more probably true. Talal Asad has argued that in medieval Christianity the goal of monastic life was "the disciplined formation of the Christian self."[14]

The ordered life of the monks was defined by various tasks, from working to praying, the most important being the singing of divine services ... The liturgy is not a species of enacted symbolism to be classified separately from activities defined as technical but is a practice among others essential to the acquisition of Christian virtues.[15]

One of the founders of modern anthropology, Marcel Mauss, proposed that human behavior should be conceptualized in terms of learned capabilities, for which he used the Latin word "habitus." "I believe precisely," he wrote,

---

[7] Frank H. Gorman Jr., "Ritual Studies and Biblical Studies: Assessment of the Past, Prospects for the Future," *Semeia* 67 (1994) 13–36, here 23. Gorman objects to this approach.

[8] Edmund Leach, *Culture and Communication. The Logic by Which Symbols Are Connected* (Cambridge: Cambridge University Press, 1976) 37.

[9] Ronald Grimes, *Beginnings in Ritual Studies* (Columbia, SC: University of South Carolina, 1995) 66.

[10] Gorman, "Ritual Studies and Biblical Studies," 23–4. Compare Roy Rappaport, *Ritual and Religion in the Making of Humanity* (Cambridge: Cambridge University Press, 1999); Richard E. DeMaris, *The New Testament in Its Ritual World* (London: Routledge, 2008) 7; Bruce Kapferer, "Ritual Dynamics and Virtual Practice: Beyond Representation and Meaning," in D. Handelman and Galina Lindquist, eds., *Ritual in Its Own Right: Exploring the Dimensions of Transformation* (New York: Berghahn, 2005) 35–54; Don Seeman, "Otherwise than Meaning: On the Generosity of Ritual," *ibid.*, 55–71.

[11] Jonathan Z. Smith, "The Bare Facts of Ritual," in idem., *Imagining Religion. From Babylon to Jonestown* (Chicago: The University of Chicago, 1982) 53–65.

[12] So Roy A. Rappaport, *Ecology, Meaning, and Religion* (Berkeley, CA: North Atlantic, 1979) 175.

[13] See Catherine M. Bell, "Ritual (Further Considerations)," in Lindsay Jones, ed., *The Encyclopedia of Religion* (2nd ed.; Detroit: Macmillan, 2005) vol. 11. 7848–7856, and eadem, *Ritual Theory, Ritual Practice* (New York: Oxford, 1992).

[14] Asad, *Genealogies of Religion* (Baltimore: Johns Hopkins, 1993) 62.

[15] *Ibid.*, 63.

that at the bottom of all our mystical states there are body techniques which we have not studied, but which were studied fully in China and India, even in very remote periods ... I think that there are necessarily biological means of entering into 'communion with God'.[16]

Asad comments: "thus, the possibility is opened up of inquiring into the ways in which embodied practices (including language in use) form a precondition for varieties of religious experience."[17] Mauss's approach may be reflected in the entry on ritual in the 1910 edition of the *Encyclopedia Britannica*:

> Ritual is to religion what habit is to life, and its rationale is similar, namely that by bringing subordinate functions under an effortless rule it permits undivided attention in regard to vital issues ... Just as the main business of habit is to secure bodily equilibrium ... so the chief task of routine in religion is to organize the activities necessary to its stability and continuance as a social institution.[18]

If we view rituals, including prayers, primarily as actions, then the fact that a ritual or prayer is performed in the prescribed manner is more important than its overt content. The daily recitation of prayers at fixed times constitutes a habitus, which itself implies a religious attitude regardless of the content of the prayers. This, of course, does not mean that rituals have no meaning at all. (Staal's provocative formulation was surely a deliberate overstatement.) But as Catherine Bell has argued, ritual often "works below the level of discourse.... Ritualized agents do not see themselves as projecting schemes; they see themselves only acting in a socially instinctive response to how things are ..."[19] Rituals are widely recognized as an effective way of creating solidarity and social cohesion through common action, on the basis of implicit assumptions about how things are.[20] Alternatively, the distinctive character of ritual action may be taken to reflect the contrast between the way things are and the way they ought to be, to represent the idealized way in which the world should be organized.[21]

It is perhaps a flaw in theoretical discussions that they tend to propose universal explanations for variable phenomena. Arguments for the "meaninglessness of ritual" are not without merit, as anyone who has experienced a routinized liturgy knows. In a religion oriented towards practice, as Judaism is, the observance of prescribed ritual is undoubtedly more important than the way it is understood. Moreover, the meanings of rituals may often be displaced, so that the official explanation is distinct either from the origin of the ritual (e.g. Passover) or from the associations that people now bring to it (Easter as a spring festival). But rituals are of different kinds,

[16] M. Mauss, "Body Techniques," in M. Mauss, *Sociology and Psychology: Essays* (ed. and trans. B. Brewster; London: Routledge and Kegan Paul, 1979) 122. The idea of "habitus" was popularized by Pierre Bourdieu, *Outline of a Theory of Practice* (Cambridge: Cambridge University Press, 1977).
[17] Asad, *Genealogies*, 76–7.
[18] Cited *ibid.*, 57.
[19] Catherine Bell, *Ritual Theory, Ritual Practice* (New York: Oxford, 1992) 206.
[20] See Bell, *Ritual Theory, Ritual Practice*, 171–2.
[21] Smith, "The Bare Facts of Ritual," 53–65. See also the summary by Bell, *Ritual*, 11–12.

and communities may differ in the importance they attach to meaning and interpretation. What is true of Brahmin rituals is not necessarily true of the Dead Sea Scrolls. The *yahad* was an unusually literate community, and it placed a high value on the intentions of its members. Moreover, it participated in a tradition that regarded study, especially of the Torah, as an act of piety, and that regarded psalms and traditional prayers as media of instruction.

Prayer in Dead Sea Scrolls

The Dead Sea Scrolls provide us with "the only written collections of established prayer texts from the period before the destruction of the Temple."[22] These include prayers for various occasions: for morning and evening of each day of the month, for festivals, for the Sabbath, and so forth.[23] They have been described, reasonably, as "the richest case study for prayer in ancient Judaism, and among the richest for any group in the ancient world."[24] Since many of these prayers are associated with rituals, they provide an opportunity to test the light that verbalized statements can shed on the meaning of rituals.

There has been a general tendency to assume that all these texts reflect the practice of prayer in the specific community at Qumran. As Daniel Falk puts it: "these were all found in the context of a community about which we have unprecedented information, from archaeology, texts preserved and composed by the group, and possible third-party descriptions."[25] There are problems with this assumption, however. Not only is it apparent that some of these texts were "non-sectarian" in origin, and are older than the settlement at Qumran, but it seems increasingly unlikely that all the scrolls hidden in the caves came from the library of one wilderness settlement. While it remains overwhelmingly probable that the entire collection has a sectarian character, the movement to which it testifies was itself widely dispersed.[26]

---

[22] Eileen M. Schuller, "Some Reflections on the Function and Use of Poetical Texts among the Dead Sea Scrolls," in Esther G. Chazon, ed., *Liturgical Perspectives: Prayer and Poetry in Light of the Dead Sea Scrolls. Proceedings of the Fifth International Symposium of the Orion Center for the Study of the Dead Sea Scrolls and Associated Literature, 19–23 January, 2000* (STDJ 48; Leiden: Brill, 2003) 173–89, here 174; Bilhah Nitzan, *Qumran Prayer and Religious Poetry* (STDJ 12; Leiden: Brill, 1994); James R. Davila, *Liturgical Works* (Eerdmans Commentaries on the Dead Sea Scrolls; Grand Rapids: Eerdmans, 2000).

[23] Daniel K. Falk, *Daily, Sabbath, and Festival Prayers in the Dead Sea Scrolls* (STDJ 27; Leiden: Brill, 1998).

[24] Daniel K. Falk, "The Contribution of the Qumran Scrolls to the Study of Ancient Jewish Liturgy," in Timothy H. Lim and John J. Collins, eds., *The Oxford Handbook of the Dead Sea Scrolls* (Oxford: Oxford University Press, 2010) 618.

[25] Falk, "The Contribution of the Qumran Scrolls," 618.

[26] See my book *Beyond the Qumran Community. The Sectarian Movement of the Dead Sea Scrolls* (Grand Rapids: Eerdmans, 2010); also Alison Schofield, *From Qumran to the Yahad: A New Paradigm of Textual Development for the Community Rule* (STDJ 77; Leiden: Brill, 2009).

The *Damascus Rule* speaks of "camps" in which married people lived (CD 7:6). Even the *yahad* cannot be equated with "the Qumran community," but allowed for multiple settlements with a quorum of ten (1QS 6:3–7). The scrolls, then, may have been brought to Qumran from many settlements, to be hidden in the wilderness in time of crisis. Whether all these settlements had a common liturgical practice, or whether all these scrolls pertain to one liturgical system, are open questions. As James Davila puts it, in the introduction to his translation of liturgical texts from Qumran, "it is perhaps more useful to think of a broad movement with different subgroups than of a well-defined sectarian community."[27]

That said, it is apparent that prayer played a prominent part in the daily life of the *yahad*, whether at Qumran or elsewhere. Much quoted in this regard is the so-called "Hymn of the Appointed Times" in 1QS 10:5–11:22:

At the commencement of the months in their seasons, and of the holy days in their sequence, as a reminder in their seasons, with the offering of lips I shall bless him, in accordance with the decree recorded forever ... At the onset of day and night I shall enter the covenant of God, and when evening and morning depart I shall repeat his precepts ... When I start to stretch out my hands and my feet I shall bless his name; when I start to go out and to come in, to sit and to stand up, and lying down in my bed I shall extol him; I shall bless him with the offering that issues from my lips in the row of men ...

As Schuller as observed, "there is an inherent problematic in attempting to make a poetic text function as a cultic calendar."[28] It represents an ideal, not necessarily a literal description of practice. The passage is part of a section relating to the *maskil* at the end of 1QS (but not found in all copies of the Community Rule). The *maskil*, in the words of Carol Newsom, "can be described not only as an apotheosis of sectarian selfhood but of the sect itself."[29] His ideals are the ideals of the sectarian movement. But since the *yahad* was a tightly organized association, it is safe to assume that these ideals were implemented. Some of the preserved liturgical texts are nicely compatible with the ideal of the *maskil* – e.g. the prayers for morning and evening in 4Q503.

We do not actually know the daily liturgical schedule in the *yahad*. Neither do we know exactly what texts were used, nor indeed whether all sectarian communities necessarily recited the same prayers at the same times. Both the passage in 1QS 10–11 and 4Q503 relate the schedule of blessing to the cycle of the sun and to the cosmic calendar, rather than to the times of sacrifices in the Jerusalem temple. It seems safe to infer that "the Qumran covenanters had fixed liturgical prayer rituals that were tied to their specific calendar, indeed which *enacted* that calendar."[30]

[27] Davila, *Liturgical Works*, 9.
[28] Schuller, "The Function and Use of Poetic Texts," 180.
[29] Carol A. Newsom, *The Self as Symbolic Space. Constructing Identity and Community at Qumran* (STDJ 52; Leiden: Brill, 2004) 189.
[30] Richard S. Sarason, "The Intersections of Qumran and Rabbinic Judaism: The Case of Prayer Texts and Liturgies," *DSD* 8 (2001) 179. See also Sarason, "Communal Prayer at Qumran and among the Rabbis," in Chazon, ed., *Liturgical Perspectives*, 151–72.

The very fact that written prayer texts are found at Qumran shows a tendency towards standardization and institutionalization.[31] As Shemaryahu Talmon has observed, "institutionalized prayer is a prayer in which the spontaneous, the individual, and the sporadic are replaced by the conventional, the universal and the periodic."[32] As such, institutionalized prayer must be seen as part of the ritual of the *yahad*.

The goal of the *yahad* is stated most explicitly in 1QS col. 8:

> When these things exist in Israel, the community council shall be founded on truth to be an everlasting plantation, a holy house for Israel and the foundation of the holy of holies for Aaron, true witnesses for the judgment and chosen by the will (of God) to atone for the land and to render the wicked their retribution. (1QS 8:4–7)

As is widely recognized, the *yahad* is hereby declared to be a substitute for the temple cult, which was rendered ineffectual in the eyes of the sectarians by incorrect halakhic observance and especially by the failure to observe the correct calendar.[33] Prayer, then, serves as a substitute for sacrifice in achieving atonement:[34]

> When these exist in Israel in accordance with these rules in order to establish the spirit of holiness in truth eternal, in order to atone for the guilt of iniquity and for the unfaithfulness of sin, and for approval for the earth, without the flesh of burnt offerings and without the fats of sacrifice – the offering of the lips in compliance with the decree will be like the pleasant aroma of justice and the perfectness of behavior will be acceptable like a freewill offering. (1QS 9:3–5)

The function of atonement, however, is not restricted to any one specific ritual. Rather, the entire life of the *yahad* was sanctified so that the community became "a holy house for Aaron," a "temple of men." As Rob Kugler has argued, "ritual at Qumran was hegemonic, making every aspect of their experience religious."[35] Prayer "in accordance with the decree recorded forever" was an integral part of that

---

[31] The increased use of Scripture in prayer is a related phenomenon. See Judith H. Newman, *Praying by the Book. The Scripturalization of Prayer in Second Temple Judaism* (SBLEJL 14; Atlanta: Scholars Press, 1999).

[32] Shemaryahu Talmon, "The Emergence of Institutionalized Prayer in Israel in Light of Qumran Literature," in idem, *The World of Qumran from Within* (Jerusalem: Magnes, 1989) 201.

[33] Sarason, "Communal Prayer at Qumran," 154. See however the reservations of Martin Goodman, "Constructing Ancient Judaism from the Scrolls," in Lim and Collins, eds., *The Oxford Handbook of the Dead Sea Scrolls*, 81–91, who questions the rejection of the temple, and Sacha Stern, "Qumran Calendars and Sectarianism," *ibid.*, 232–53, who questions the significance of the calendrical disputes.

[34] Daniel K. Falk, "Qumran Prayer Texts and the Temple," in Daniel K. Falk, Florentino García Martínez, Eileen M. Schuller, *Sapiential, Liturgical and Poetical Texts from Qumran* (STDJ 35; Leiden: Brill, 2000) 106–26, cautions that the situation of the *yahad* cannot explain the origin of institutionalized prayer in a text like the *Prayer of the Luminaries*, and suggests that elements of prayer already associated with the temple may have influenced the practices of the sect.

[35] Rob Kugler, "Making All Experience Religious: The Hegemony of Ritual at Qumran," *JSJ* 33 (2002) 131–52 (here, 152). Compare Russell C. D. Arnold, *The Social Role of Liturgy in the Religion of the Qumran Community* (STDJ 60; Leiden: Brill, 2006) 234: "The Qumran community developed an elaborate and extensive liturgical practice that encompassed all aspects of its communal life."

ritual, sanctifying life at key junctures during the day, year, and longer liturgical cycles. While the prayers certainly went beyond what was prescribed in the Torah, they were still "in accordance with the decree," insofar as they used traditional, biblical, language. More fundamentally, all prescriptions of the *yahad*, whether explicit in the Torah or not, were believed to be in accordance with divine decree. The ritualized life, then, was essentially a life of obedience.

Discourse and ritual in covenant renewal

An example of theologically meaningful discourse in a ritual context is provided by the covenant renewal ceremony in 1QS 1:16–3:12.

The ceremony as described in the *Serek* is essentially a series of blessings and curses, pronounced by priests and levites antiphonally, with affirming responses by those entering the covenant. It is obviously based on the covenant ceremony described in Deuteronomy 27, and the renewal of the covenant in Moab in Deuteronomy 29. There are also echoes of Nehemiah 8, Leviticus 16, and other passages.[36] As Carol Newsom has argued, "such evocations are part of the way the sect claims for itself the identity of Israel and contests the claims of others to that identity."[37] But as Newsom further notes, the ceremony is accented in ways that are distinctively sectarian. The sins confessed were committed "during the dominion of Belial" (1QS 1:23). In the biblical prototypes, both the blessings and the curses are addressed to those who enter the covenant. Here they distinguish between insiders and outsiders. The priests bless "all the men of God's lot who walk unblemished in all his paths," with a variant of the blessing of Aaron from Num 6:24–26: "May he illuminate our heart with the discernment of life and grace you with eternal knowledge. May he lift upon you the countenance of his favor for eternal peace" (1QS 2:3–4).[38] The Levites, in turn, curse all the men of the lot of Belial, who are condemned to the gloom of everlasting fire. The final curse, however, is reserved for "whoever enters this covenant, and places the obstacle of his iniquity in front of himself to fall over it." Such a person posed a threat to the community greater than that posed by outsiders, since he might undermine the community from within. The covenant here is not understood in terms of "a relationship between God and ethnic Israel," but as "a particularistic covenant relationship" between God and those who enter the new covenant voluntarily.[39] Despite all the continuity in language, the understanding of the covenant is transformed.

---

[36] See Newsom, *The Self as Symbolic Space*, 119–20.
[37] *Ibid.*, 120.
[38] Arnold, *The Social Role of Liturgy*, 67.
[39] Ellen Juhl Christiansen, *The Covenant in Judaism and Paul: A Study of Ritual Boundaries as Identity Markers* (AGJU 27; Leiden: Brill, 1995) 158.

Entry into the covenant, in principle, is a one-time event. In this case, however, we are told: "they shall act in this way year after year, all the days of Belial's dominion" (1QS 2:19). The terminology of "coming into" or "crossing over into" recalls the crossing of Israel into Canaan in the time of Joshua, but it also makes the ceremony into a rite of passage for the community, who have separated from the majority of the people, in the phrase of 4QMMT. The contingent and vulnerable nature of the community requires that its identity be reaffirmed, even reconstituted. The idea of renewing the covenant had good biblical precedents, and it dramatized nicely the elements of choice and separation.[40] In all of this, it is apparent that the language that accompanies the ritual is highly meaningful. Not only does it express the self-understanding of the covenanters by relating it to tradition and by articulating their distinction from the lot of Belial, but it also uses the occasion to instill the sectarian worldview into the participants.

The efficacy of the ritual, however, is not entirely dependent on the words of the curses and blessings. The ceremony has an extra-verbal component in the hierarchical order of the procession:

the priests shall enter in order foremost, one behind the other, according to their spirits. And the Levites shall enter after them. In the third place all the people shall enter in order, one after another, in thousands, hundreds, fifties and tens, so that each Israelite may know his standing in God's community, in conformity with an eternal plan (1QS 2:19–22).

The formation recalls Israel in the wilderness, but it also enacts the internal hierarchy of the community. The order reflects the ideal, of how power and precedence should be recognized, but it also acts it out in the present and thereby instills it in the participants more effectively than could any verbal formulation.

Confession and ablution

The covenant ceremony described in 1QS 1:16–3:12 departs from the model of Deuteronomy 27 by inserting a confession of sin:

All those who enter the covenant shall confess after them and they shall say: 'We have acted sinfully, we have [trans]gressed, we have [si]nned, we have committed evil, we and our fathers before us ...

Such confessions of sin are ubiquitous in Second Temple Judaism.[41] They are required in a covenantal context in Lev 26:40–2:

---

[40] On the biblical precedents for the idea of a new covenant, see Stephen Hultgren, *From the Damascus Covenant to the Covenant of the Community. Literary, Historical, and Theological Studies in the Dead Sea Scrolls* (STDJ 66; Leiden: Brill, 2007) 77–232; Michael Duggan, *Covenant Renewal in Ezra-Nehemiah (Neh 7:72b-10:40): An Exegetical, Literary, and Theological Study* (SBLDS 164; Atlanta: SBL, 2001).

[41] Rodney Alan Werline, *Penitential Prayer in Second Temple Judaism. The Development of a*

But if they confess their iniquity and the iniquity of their ancestors, in that they committed treachery against me and, moreover, that they continued hostile to me ... then I will remember my covenant with Jacob ... (and with Abraham and Isaac).

Public confession of sin precedes renewal of the covenant in 2 Kings 22:11, 19; 2 Chron 34:19, 27 and Nehemiah 9. Recognition, and presumably confession, of their sinful state is a crucial step in the formation of the group that enters into the "new covenant" in CD 1:8–9: "they realized their iniquity and knew that they were guilty." But one act of confession was not enough. The faithful are characterized in CD 20: 28–30 not only by listening to the voice of the Teacher but by confessing: "assuredly we have sinned, both we and our fathers, walking contrary to the ordinances of the covenant; justice and truth are your judgments against us."[42] Just as the renewal of the covenant required repetition, so did confession of sin. In this regard, the sectarians were not exceptional in the context of Second Temple Judaism, and it is likely that they continued to use prayers that were not of sectarian origin.[43]

According to the Priestly source in the Torah, the ritual for atoning for sin required both confession of sin and a sacrificial "sin offering."[44] The covenantal ceremony in 1QS does not call for such an offering. Instead, we read that

it is by the spirit of the true counsel of God that the paths of man are atoned ... and by the spirit of uprightness and of humility his sin is atoned. And by the compliance of his soul with all the laws of God his flesh is cleansed by being sprinkled with cleansing waters and being made holy with the waters of repentance (1QS 3:6–9).

Conversely, anyone who walks in stubbornness of heart

will not become clean by the acts of atonement, nor shall he be purified by the cleansing waters ... nor shall he be purified by all the water of ablution. Defiled, defiled shall he be ... (1QS 3: 4–5).

The practice of ritual washing prescribed in the Scrolls has long been a controversial topic, because of its relevance to the origin of Christian baptism. Frank Moore Cross was one of the more moderate and level-headed scholars in this regard, but even he wrote of "the central 'sacraments' of the Essene community," which he identified as "its baptism(s) and its communal meal."[45] (Cross was not the first to use

---

Religious Institution (SBLEJL 13; Atlanta: Scholars Press, 1998); Mark J. Boda, Daniel K. Falk, and Rodney A. Werline, eds., *Seeking the Favor of God* (3 vols.; SBLEJL 21–23; Atlanta: SBL/Leiden: Brill, 2006–2009). Note especially Eileen M. Schuller, "Penitential Prayer in Second Temple Judaism: A Research Survey," in vol. 2 (2007) 1–15, and Russell C. D. Arnold, "Repentance and the Qumran Covenant Ceremony," *ibid.*, 159–75.

[42] See further Bilhah Nitzan, "Repentance in the Dead Sea Scrolls," in Flint and VanderKam, eds., *The Dead Sea Scrolls after Fifty Years*, 2.156–7.

[43] Notably the *Words of the Luminaries*. See Esther G. Chazon, "The *Words of the Luminaries* and Penitential Prayer in Second Temple Times," in Boda, Falk, and Werline, eds., *Seeking the Favor of God*, 2.177–86; See Nitzan, "Repentance," 165–6.

[44] Lev 5:1–6, 16; Num 5:5–7.

[45] Cross, *The Ancient Library of Qumran* (3rd ed.; Sheffield: Sheffield Academic Press, 1995) 168.

such language. Long before the discovery of the Scrolls, Wilhelm Bousset had spoken of baptisms and communal meals of the Essenes as "sacraments.)[46] There is no doubt that ritual washing played an important part in the life of the sect, a point confirmed by the number of stepped pools, presumably used for immersion, at Qumran.[47] Whether ritual washing can be described as a "sacrament" is another matter. The differences over against early Christian practice are at least as important as the similarities.

Ritual bathing played a part in the process of admission to the *yahad*, but unlike Christian baptism it was not a unique performative act by which a person became a member of the community. The procedures for joining the sectarian community seem to have evolved over time. In CD 15, applicants are tested by the Inspector and then swear an oath to return to the Law of Moses. Again in 1QS 5:7–8 whoever enters the council of the community "shall swear a binding oath to revert to the Law of Moses ... in compliance with all that has been revealed of it to the sons of Zadok." In 1QS 6, however, a more elaborate, multi-year process is described. The postulant is not allowed to touch "the purity of the many" until he has completed a year in the community, and he may not touch the drink of the many until he has completed a second year. It is often assumed that "the purity of the many" refers to the common food, in contrast to the common drink, which is restricted for a further year.[48] According to Saul Lieberman: "The ritually clean articles (vessels, utensils, garments and particularly food) are generally called *tohoroth* and sometimes they are styled *tohorah* in rabbinic literature."[49] He further observed that "the rabbis of the first century attached a higher degree of ritual impurity to *Mashkin* (liquids) than to solid food."[50] The phrase, "purity of the Many," is unclear, however. Friedrich Avemarie concludes from a thorough study of the use of *tohorah* in the Scrolls that "it seems easier to understand *tohorah* as a quality proper to a person, as his state of purity, which the afflicted one must respect," and that

> although there is no definitive proof, we should face the possibility that *tohorath ha-rabbim* too is to be understood in such a broader sense. If a novice or a penitent during his first year is able to contaminate pure food, we may assume that he, by the same token, is able to contaminate vessels, clothing, and even other persons. If this is the case, the separation from *tohorath ha-rabbim* would be much more than some special kind of table taboo. In its practi-

---

[46] Wilhelm Bousset, *Die Religion des Judentums im späthellenistischen Zeitalter* (3rd ed.; Tübingen: Mohr, 1926) 461.

[47] Jonathan Lawrence, *Washing in Water. Trajectories of Ritual Bathing in the Hebrew Bible and Second Temple Literature* (Academia Biblica 23; Atlanta: Society of Biblical Literature, 2006) 173–83.

[48] This interpretation was argued by Saul Lieberman, "Discipline in the So-Called Dead Sea Manual of Discipline," *JBL* 71 (1952) 203 and Jacob Licht, *The Rule Scroll: A Scroll from the Wilderness of Judaea. 1QS, 1QSa, 1QSb. Text, Introduction and Commentary* (Jerusalem: Bialik, 1965) 294–303 (Heb.).

[49] Lieberman, "Discipline," 203.

[50] *Ibid.*

cal consequences, it would come close to a prevention of any personal contact with the full members of the community.[51]

Moreover, Russell Arnold has pointed out that in 1QS 6:24–25, one who lies about property is excluded from *tohorath ha-rabbim* for a year and fined one fourth of his food.[52] The "purity of the Many," then, cannot be simply identified with the community food. Rather it refers to the whole process of contact with objects (including food) and also with persons within the community.

"Purificatory baths" are not mentioned explicitly in 1QS 6, but the Rule makes clear elsewhere that they are necessary before one can fully participate in the community.[53] We are told, for instance, that a person who walks in the way of wickedness "should not go into the waters to share in the purity of the men of holiness" (1QS 5:13). They are mentioned as part of the initiation process in Josephus's account of the Essenes, which says that after a period of probation "he draws closer to the way of life and participates in the purificatory baths at a higher degree," although he still has to undergo two more years of probation.[54] Josephus further tells us that the Essenes "bathe their bodies in cold water" in preparation for their common meals. "After this purification they assemble in a private apartment which none of the uninitiated is permitted to enter; pure now themselves, they repair to the refectory, as to some sacred shrine" (*JW* 2.129). Even if we do not press the identification of the *yahad* as the Essenes, however, there can be little doubt about the importance of ritual ablutions as a pre-condition for participation in the life of the *yahad*. None of the wicked, we are told, may "enter the water in order to touch the purity of the men of holiness" (5:13). Purification liturgies (4Q512; 4Q414) preserved in Cave 4 specify various occasions for lustrations and also specify blessings to be associated with them. These specifications go beyond what is found in the laws of the Torah.

The idea that ritual washing was an appropriate way of expressing conversion from sin was not peculiar to the Scrolls. The proclamation of John the Baptist, as reported by the evangelists, was "repent, for the kingdom of heaven has come near" (Matt 3:2).[55] According to Mark, he proclaimed "a baptism of repentance for the forgiveness of sins" (Mark 1:4; cf. Luke 3:3). Josephus gives a more nuanced account. John

---

[51] Friedrich Avemarie, "'*Tohorath Ha-Rabbim*' and '*Mashqeh Ha-Rabbim*.' Jacob Licht Reconsidered," in M. Bernstein, F. García Martínez and J. Kampen, eds., *Legal Texts and Legal Issues* (STDJ 23; Leiden: Brill, 1997) 215–29 (227).

[52] Russell C. D. Arnold, *The Social Role of Liturgy in the Religion of the Qumran Community* (STDJ 60; Leiden: Brill, 2006) 91.

[53] Compare Lawrence, *Washing in Water*, 141.

[54] Josephus, *JW* 2.137–9.

[55] On John the Baptist see C. H. H. Scobie, *John the Baptist* (Philadelphia: Fortress, 1964); Robert L. Webb, *John the Baptizer and Prophet* (JSNTSup 62; Sheffield: Sheffield Academic Press, 1991); Joan E. Taylor, *The Immerser. John the Baptist within Second Temple Judaism* (Grand Rapids: Eerdmans, 1997).

exhorted the Jews to lead righteous lives, to practice justice towards their fellows and piety towards God, and in so doing to join in baptism. In his view this was a necessary preliminary if baptism was to be acceptable to God. They must not employ it to gain pardon for whatever sins they committed, but as a consecration of the body implying that the soul was already thoroughly cleansed by righteous behavior (*Ant* 18.116–9).

In John's case the urgency of baptism arose from the imminence of divine judgment, a point overlooked by Josephus.[56] We find an appeal for baptism in a similar context in Sib Or 4, where the Sibyl calls on "wretched mortals" to change their ways and abandon

daggers and groanings, murders and outrages, and wash your whole bodies in perennial rivers. Stretch out your hands to heaven and ask forgiveness for previous deeds and make propitiation for bitter impiety with words of praise (Sib Or 4:163–69).

If people fail to do this, God will destroy the world by fire. Despite repeated attempts to associate John the Baptist with the Essenes, there is really no basis for such an association.[57] John's baptism was a once and for all affair, laden with eschatological overtones, and was quite different from the constantly repeated ritual baths of the Essenes.

It is highly likely that ritual washing was a routinized part of the life of the *yahad*, at Qumran and elsewhere. It was certainly not meaningless, however. Joseph Baumgarten has argued that "the link between the purity of body and spirit is salient throughout the literature."[58] Indeed, in the passage quoted above from 1QS 3:7–9 acceptance of the holy spirit precedes sprinkling with water. Moreover, there are also multiple references to sprinkling the holy spirit, and the analogy is explicit in 1QS 4:20–21:

God will refine, with his truth, all man's deeds ... cleansing him with the spirit of holiness from every wicked deed. He will sprinkle over him the spirit of truth like lustral water ...

Moreover, one of the ways in which the practice of ritual washing in the Scrolls differs from that in the Bible is by the addition of blessings to be recited with the lustrations.[59]

The significance of the purificatory baths must be seen in the context of the priestly tradition in the Bible. As Jonathan Klawans has shown, impurity in the Hebrew Bible may be either ritual or moral. Ritual impurity results from contact with any of a number of natural sources, including childbirth, genital discharges, scale disease and contact with animal carcasses and corpses.[60] These sources are generally natural and more or less unavoidable. Ritual impurity is not sinful. It can be remedied by

---

[56] Scobie, *John the Baptist*, 111.
[57] So also Taylor, *The Immerser*, 48. See also Robert L. Webb, "John the Baptist," *ibid.*, 1.418–21.
[58] Baumgarten, "Purification Rituals," 207.
[59] Lawrence, *Washing in Water*, 145.
[60] Jonathan Klawans, *Impurity and Sin in Ancient Judaism* (New York: Oxford, 2000) 23.

ritual means, and washing figures prominently among the means prescribed.[61] Moral impurity, in contrast, arose from sinful behavior, specifically sexual sins, idolatry and bloodshed. According to Leviticus, these sins defiled the land of Israel and ultimately led to the exile.[62] Ritual washing is of no avail in these cases, but the prophets and psalms often speak metaphorically of washing as a way of purging iniquity nonetheless (e.g. Psalm 51:2, 7: "Wash me thoroughly from my iniquity and cleanse me from my sin ... Purge me with hyssop and I shall be clean, wash me and I shall be whiter than snow").[63] In the Scrolls, however, the distinction between ritual and moral purity is collapsed, and sin is held to be ritually defiling.[64] Consequently:

> repentance from sin and purification from defilement have become mutually dependent. According to the sectarians, moral repentance is not efficacious without ritual purification, and ritual purification without moral repentance is equally invalid.[65]

The requirement of ritual bathing in addition to confession of sin, then, is not merely complementary, but expresses the sectarian understanding of sin as defilement, and of the efficacy of ritual even in the case of moral transgression. Moreover, the repeated ritual of washing before significant community events dramatized the separation of the members from the outside world, which was viewed as defiled. The ritual is not efficacious on its own. Repentance, the intention of "turning back" from sin is presupposed – hence the designation of the members of the new covenant as "returnees of Israel" or "those who turn from sin" in the *Damascus Document*.[66] The verbal confession of sin provides a necessary context for the ritual of washing. Yet the meaning of the ritual is not exhausted by its verbal accompaniment. The act of washing dramatizes and enacts the process of cleansing, and thereby expresses an understanding of sin that is not explicit in the traditional, covenant-based, confession such as we find in 1QS 1:24–5.

Conclusion

The pronouncement of Frits Staal on the meaninglessness of ritual is clearly exaggerated, and indefensible in the case of the rituals described in the Dead Sea Scrolls.

---

[61] Lawrence, *Washing in Water*, 26–29.
[62] Klawans, *Sin and Impurity*, 26.
[63] Lawrence, *Washing in Water*, 35–38.
[64] Klawans, *Impurity and Sin*, 75–85. This aspect of sin is not treated by Gary A. Anderson, *Sin. A History* (New Haven: Yale, 2009).
[65] *Ibid.*, 85. Note, however, Klawans in Lim and Collins, eds., *The Oxford Handbook of the Dead Sea Scrolls*, 386, where he notes that the full-blown conflation of ritual impurity and moral impurity does not run through the entire corpus. He does not find the conflation in the Temple Scroll, 4QMMT or CD, but finds it especially in 1QS.
[66] CD 2:5; 4:2 etc. On the understanding of repentance in the Scrolls see David Lambert, "Was the Dead Sea Sect a Penitential Movement?" in Lim and Collins, eds., *The Oxford Handbook of the Dead Sea Scrolls*, 501–13.

Nonetheless, it has had, at least in part, a salutary impact on ritual studies, insofar as it has discouraged the tendency to explain rituals in terms of myths or theological ideas and focused attention on the actions themselves, which often work below the realm of discourse. The explicit theology expressed in prayers and treatises still provides a context for the ritual action, but it does not necessarily exhaust its meaning or fully articulate its effectiveness.

The significance of ritual in the Scrolls, however, cannot be properly appreciated by considering any one ritual on its own. Rob Kugler and Russell Arnold have drawn attention to the "ritual density" of life in the *yahad*. In Kugler's words, "ritual at Qumran was hegemonic, making every aspect of their experience religious."[67] It constituted a *habitus*, an enactment of the world as it ought to be, characterized by obedience to what was believed to be divine law, as interpreted and amplified by the priestly leaders of the community, and by purity, which entailed separation from the outside world. It ensured community cohesion, by requiring that members eat together, bless together and take counsel together.[68] At the same time, it implemented the hierarchical structure of the community. The common prayers, with texts standardized in writing, were part of this process, and articulate aspects of its meaning. They contributed to the sanctification of the whole life of the *yahad*, but it was that whole life, rather than any specific rituals or prayers, that was thought to be the effective replacement of the temple cult.

---

[67] Kugler, "Making All Experience Religious," 152.
[68] The much disputed issue of a "sacred meal" must also be viewed in this context. See Dennis E. Smith, "Meals," *EDSS*, 531, who describes the community meals as "a centerpiece for the elaborate purity rules specific to this community."

CHAPTER SIXTEEN

The Eschatologizing of Wisdom in the Dead Sea Scrolls

The phrase "the eschatologizing of wisdom," "*die Eschatologisierung der Weisheit*," is associated above all with Gerhard von Rad's celebrated thesis that the roots of *Apokalyptik* were to be sought in wisdom rather than in prophecy.[1] The problems with that thesis have often been rehearsed, and need not be repeated here.[2] Most fundamentally, von Rad did not pay sufficient attention to the range of materials that can be subsumed under the category wisdom. On the broadest level, any discourse that lays emphasis on knowledge and understanding can reasonably be called wisdom, but knowledge and understanding can be of many different kinds. In the context of biblical studies, wisdom literature is normally understood to refer to the books of Proverbs and Qoheleth and, with some qualification, the book of Job. These books derive from a tradition of instructional literature that was common to much of the ancient Near East, and exemplified especially in Egypt.[3] It is continued in the Book of Ben Sira, who expanded the tradition significantly by including the Torah and sacred writings of Israel in his curriculum.[4] In general, this tradition could be said to share a worldview that was this-worldly in focus and skeptical of claims of higher revelation. But there were other kinds of instruction available in ancient Judaism, including some that offered a higher, revealed, wisdom. The astronomical lore in *1 Enoch* 73–82 could reasonably be described as a kind of wisdom, even though it was supposedly revealed to the author by the angel Uriel and contained some restrained eschatological predictions at the end.[5] Von Rad rightly noted that the pseudonymous visionaries of the early apocalypses, Enoch and Daniel, were

---

[1] G. von Rad, *Theologie des Alten Testaments* (4th ed.; Munich: Kaiser, 1965) 2.315–30.

[2] P. von der Osten-Sacken, *Die Apokalyptik in ihrem Verhältnis zu Prophetie und Weisheit* (Theologische Existenz Heute 157; Munich: Kaiser, 1969); H. P. Müller, "Mantische Weisheit und Apokalyptik," *Congress Volume Uppsala* (VTSup 22; Leiden: Brill, 1972); J. J. Collins, "Cosmos and Salvation: Jewish Wisdom and Apocalypticism in the Hellenistic Age," *History of Religions* 17 (1977) 121–42 (= *Seers, Sibyls and Sages in Hellenistic-Roman Judaism* [JSJSup 54; Leiden: Brill, 1977] 317–38).

[3] See W. McKane, *Proverbs: A New Approach* (Philadelphia: Westminster, 1970) 51–150; G. E. Bryce, *A Legacy of Wisdom: The Egyptian Contribution to the Wisdom of Israel* (Lewisburg, Pa.: Bucknell, 1979); N. Shupak, *Where Can Wisdom Be Found? The Sage's Language in the Bible and in Ancient Egyptian Literature* (OBO 130; Fribourg: Fribourg University, 1993).

[4] J. J. Collins, *Jewish Wisdom in the Hellenistic Age* (Louisville: Westminster, 1997) 42–61.

[5] See M. Albani, *Astronomie und Schöpfungsglaube. Untersuchungen zum astronomischen Henochbuch* (Neukirchen-Vluyn: Neukirchener Verlag, 1994).

presented as wise men, and their teachings as wisdom.⁶ But this wisdom was very different in kind and worldview from the material that normally passed as wisdom in the biblical corpus.

With the publication of *4QInstruction*, however, we now have a *bona fide* example of a wisdom text of the traditional type in which eschatological expectations play a significant part.⁷ My purpose in this paper is to examine the kind of eschatology that we find in this document, its probable derivation, and its function in the sapiential text. I will conclude with some reflections on the relation of this text to the sectarian writings of the Scrolls and its relevance to the debate initiated by von Rad on the relation between sapiential and apocalyptic literature.

The eschatology of *4QInstruction*

4QInstruction is not a discourse on eschatology. Most of the references to a final judgment have the character of allusions, made in the context of a discourse on something else. So, for example, in 4Q417 1 i (formerly numbered 2 i) the addressee is told to meditate on the mystery that is to be, "and then thou shalt know truth and iniquity, wisdom [and foolish]ness thou shalt [recognize], every ac[t] in all their ways, together with their punishment(s) in all ages everlasting, and the punishment of eternity" (lines 6–8).⁸ The punishments are not described, as they often are in apocalypses. Or again in 4Q416 3, in a very fragmentary passage, we read "until wickedness comes to an end; for there will be wrath in every pe[riod] …"⁹ Here again there does not seem to be any description of how wickedness comes to an end, or of the wrath. This kind of allusive reference is typical of what we find in *4QInstruction*.¹⁰

The most extensive passage dealing with eschatology is found in 4Q416 1, a fragment which, in the judgment of the editors, came from the beginning of the work.¹¹

---

⁶ Von Rad, *Theologie*, 2.317.

⁷ J. Strugnell and D. J. Harrington, *Qumran Cave 4. XXIV. Sapiential Texts, Part 2. 4QInstruction (Musar le Mevin): 4Q405ff, with a re-edition of 1Q26; with an edition of 4Q423 by T. Elgvin* (DJD 34; Oxford: Clarendon, 1999).

⁸ Strugnell and Harrington, *4QInstruction*, 151, 154. Overlapping text is found in 4Q418 1–2, *ibid.*, 224–5. On the readings see now also E. J. C. Tigchelaar, *To Increase Learning for the Understanding Ones. Reading and Reconstructing the Fragmentary Early Jewish Sapiential Text in 4QInstruction* (STDJ 14; Leiden: Brill, 2001) 52–3.

⁹ *Ibid.*, 131.

¹⁰ The most substantial discussion to date of the eschatology of *4QInstruction* is found in the dissertation of Torleif Elgvin, "An Analysis of *4QInstruction*" (Diss. Hebrew University, 1997) 97–122. See also his article, "Early Essene Eschatology. Judgement and Salvation according to Sapiential Work A," in D. L. Perry and S. D. Ricks, eds., *Current Research and Technological Developments on the Dead Sea Scrolls* (STDJ 20; Leiden: Brill, 1996) 126–65.

¹¹ Strugnell and Harrington, *4QInstruction*, 79–80. They point to the wide margin, and the fact that the passage has no second person references. See also Tigchelaar, *To Increase Learning*, 43–44. On the reconstruction of this passage see further E. J. C. Tigchelaar, "Towards a Reconstruc-

The first nine lines or so are very fragmentary, and seem to deal with the order of nature. There are references to "season by season" and to "the host of heaven" and "for their portents," which suggests a discussion of heavenly bodies. But then verse 9 refers to "all their visitation" (כל פקודתמה). The word פקודה is a favorite term of *4QInstruction*, occurring 16 times.[12] It is not fully clear here whether the reference is to the visitation of the host of heaven (compare Isa 24:21: "on that day the Lord will punish the host of heaven in heaven," or the end of the *Astronomical Book of Enoch*) or whether it refers to the visitation of humanity in the following passage. The passage then continues, in the translation of Strugnell and Harrington:

From Heaven He shall pronounce judgement upon the work of wickedness, but all his faithful children will be accepted with favor by [Him] ... the end, and they shall feel dread, and all who defiled themselves in it (wickedness) shall cry out in distress. For the heavens shall fear ... The [se]as and the depths fear, and every spirit of flesh will be destroyed (?). But the sons of Heave[n] sh[all rejoice in the day when it (wickedness) is ju]dged, and (when) all iniquity shall come to an end, until the epoch of tru[th] will be perfected ... in all periods of eternity. For He is a God of fidelity, and from of old, (from) years of [eternity]... So that the righteous may distinguish (?)[13] between good and evil, so that ... every judgm[ent] ... [the in]clination of flesh is He(?), and from understanding ...[14]

This passage clearly implies a judgment scene in the tradition of the theophany of the divine warrior, where the appearance of the deity is greeted by convulsions of nature. Such theophanies are well known in biblical tradition (Judges 5:4–5; Ps 68:7–8; Habakkuk 3, etc.). Closer to the time of our text, it is of interest that the *Book of the Watchers* in *1 Enoch* begins with such a theophany (*1 Enoch* 1). In the biblical theophanies, God sometimes appears in defence of Israel, and sometimes in judgment on them. In *1 Enoch*, the judgment is on all flesh, but there is a distinction between the righteous, with whom God makes peace, and the impious whom he destroys.[15] There is a similar distinction in *4QInstruction*. Iniquity will come to an end, and "every spirit of flesh will be destroyed." In another passage of *4QInstruction*, 4Q417 1, the "spirit of flesh" is contrasted with "the people of spirit."[16] There is then an element of dualism here that goes beyond the usual sapiential antithesis of the

---

tion of the Beginning of *4QInstruction* (4Q416 Fragment 1 and Parallels)," in C. Hempel, A. Lange and H. Lichtenberger, eds., *The Wisdom Texts from Qumran and the Development of Sapiential Thought* (BETL 159; Leuven: Peeters, 2001).

[12] Strugnell and Harrington, *ibid.*, 28. On this term see further Tigchelaar, *To Increase Learning*, 240–2.

[13] So 4Q418 2. 4Q416 reads "to establish justice." See Elgvin, *An Analysis of 4QInstruction*, 98.

[14] 4Q416 1.10–16. See also the discussion of this passage in Tigchelaar, *To Increase Learning*, 175–93.

[15] See the analysis of this passage, and specifically of the Aramaic fragments from Qumran, by A. Bedenbender, *Der Gott der Welt tritt auf den Sinai. Entstehung, Entwicklung und Funktionsweise der frühjüdischen Apokalyptik* (Berlin: Institut Kirche und Judentum, 2000) 215–30.

[16] See further J. Frey, "The Notion of Flesh in *4QInstruction* and the Background of Pauline Usage," in D. K. Falk, F. García Martínez, E. M. Schuller, eds., *Sapiential, Liturgical and Poetical Texts from Qumran* (STDJ 35; Leiden: Brill, 2000) 197–226.

righteous and the wicked. The reference at the end of the passage to the "inclination of flesh" (יצר בשר) adds to the impression that the distinction between righteous and wicked is a permanent one. The righteous are also called "his faithful children" and are said to be accepted with favor. Elsewhere in *4QInstruction* they are called אנשי רצון "men of good pleasure" (4Q418 81 10, a passage that has been compared to Luke 2:14, "and on earth peace to men of good pleasure."

One other feature of this text requires comment: the use of the word קץ in the sense of "period." The word may be used in the sense of "end" in line 11 (קצה).[17] In line 13, however, קץ האמת means "the period of truth" which will be perfected forever. This is followed by a reference to כל קצי עד, all the periods of eternity. As Torleif Elgvin has noted, there is a parallel here to the *Apocalypse of Weeks* in *1 Enoch* 91:12, 17.[18] The eighth week in the apocalypse is the week of righteousness. After the tenth week "there will be many weeks without number forever." *4QInstruction* does not necessarily depend on the *Apocalypse of Weeks*, but at least it presupposes a similar division of history, and even of "eternity," into periods. Such an understanding of history is well attested in the Dead Sea Scrolls, e.g. in the *Pesher on the Periods* in 4Q180–81. The wisdom text, then, presupposes a fuller understanding of history and eschatology than it expounds explicitly.

Engraved is the ordinance

The terms קץ and פקודה also figure prominently in 4Q417 1 i.[19] There the addressee is told to gaze on the mystery that is to be, which evidently pertains to the deeds of old as well as that which is to come. By this study, the wise person is to know every deed "together with their punishment (פקודה) in all ages everlasting (קצי עולם) and everlasting punishment (פקודת עולם)." This passage does not go further in describing the punishment, but it puts it in a wider context:

> "Engraved is the ordinance, and ordained is all the punishment. For engraved is that which is ordained by God against all the ini[quities of] the children of Sheth, and written in his presence is a book of memorial of those who keep his word."

The book of memorial is an allusion to Mal 3:16, but the passage as a whole brings to mind the Mesopotamian tablets of destiny.[20] The idea that future events are written on tablets or in a book is an important motif in apocalyptic literature.[21] Compare

---

[17] The word קץ is used in both senses in 4Q416 3: there is wrath in every period, but there is no end to God's mercy.
[18] Elgvin, *An Analysis of 4QInstruction*, 103.
[19] Strugnell and Harrington, *4QInstruction*, 151–2; Tigchelaar, *To Increase Learning*, 52–54. The text is partially reconstructed with the aid of overlapping passages in 4Q418 43–45.
[20] S. M. Paul, "The Heavenly Tablets and the Book of Life," *JANES* 5 (1972) 345–53.
[21] A. Lange, *Weisheit und Prädestination. Weisheitliche Urordnung und Prädestination in den Textfunden von Qumran* (STDJ XVIII; Leiden: Brill, 1995) 69–79.

"the book of truth" in Dan 10:21, and the heavenly tablets in *1 Enoch* 93:2. I take "the sons of Sheth to be a reference to Balaam's Oracle in Num 24:17, which says that the scepter that rises from Jacob will crush the skulls of the sons of Sheth.²² The book of memorial, we are told, is the *Vision of the Hagu* (or meditation). A book of *Hagu* is mentioned three times in the *Damascus Document* (once restored) and once in the *Rule of the Congregation* (1QSa).²³ In each occurrence, it is an object of study. It has been variously identified as the Mosaic Torah or as some more esoteric document. In *4QInstruction*, at least, the latter alternative must be preferred. It is one of the distinctive characteristics of this text that it never thematizes, or explicitly discusses, the Torah. (It is possible, however, that the *Hagu* took on a new meaning in the sectarian texts.) The *Vision of the Hagu*, we are told, was given to אנוש with a spiritual people (עם רוח). I have argued elsewhere that אנוש in this passage should be read in the context of Genesis 1–3, as also in 1QS 3:17.²⁴ More precisely, the reference is to the Adam of Genesis 1, who was fashioned in the likeness of the holy ones (a paraphrase for "the image of God" in Gen 1:27), in contrast to the Adam of Genesis 2–3, who failed to distinguish between good and evil. Both Adams are understood typologically, one representing the עם רוח, or spiritual people, and the other the spirit of flesh that is doomed to destruction. The distinction comes close to the contrast of the spirits of light and darkness in 1QS 3, but does not yet have the developed dualistic terminology of light and darkness.²⁵ Note, however, that people are deemed wicked in accordance with their inheritance in the spirit of flesh (line 24; compare 1QS 4:24: "In agreement with man's inheritance in the truth, he shall be righteous ... and according to his share in the lot of injustice, he shall act wickedly ...").²⁶

This passage in 4Q417 goes some way towards filling out the theological presuppositions of *4QInstruction*. This instruction is not addressed to humanity at large, in the manner of Proverbs, or even to Judaism at large, like the book of Ben Sira. It is addressed to "the people of spirit," who are elect and enlightened. Their election is based on their יצר, the disposition given to them by their creator, which is in the likeness of the holy ones or angels. This elect status is affirmed very explicitly in 4Q418 69 10, where the elect are addressed as "you who are the truly chosen ones,"

---

[22] Strugnell and Harrington, *4QInstruction*, 163.

[23] See S. Fraade, "*Hagu*, Book of," in L. H. Schiffman and J. C. Vanderkam, eds., *Encyclopedia of the Dead Sea Scrolls* (New York: Oxford, 2000) 1.327. Fraade does not note the reference in *4QInstruction*.

[24] J. J. Collins, "In the Likeness of the Holy Ones: The Creation of Humankind in a Wisdom Text from Qumran," in D. W. Parry and E. Ulrich, eds., *The Provo International Conference on the Dead Sea Scrolls. Technological Innovations, New Texts, and Reformulated Issues* (STDJ XXX; Leiden: Brill, 1999) 609–18. On this passage see now C. Fletcher-Louis, *All the Glory of Adam. Liturgical Anthropology in the Dead Sea Scrolls* (STDJ 42; Leiden: Brill, 2002) 113–8.

[25] There are extensive terminological parallels between *4QInstruction* and the Instruction on the Two Spirits. See Tigchelaar, *To Increase Learning*, 196–203.

[26] Compare Frey, "The Notion of Flesh," 218–9.

and are urged to model themselves on "the sons of heaven" whose lot is eternal life.[27] Compare also 4Q418 81 1–2 which says "He separated thee from every fleshly spirit."[28] The elect have access to a revelation, known as the *Hagu* or Meditation, which is denied to those with spirit or inclination of flesh. This *Hagu* is evidently related to the "mystery that is to be." I am inclined, however, with Torleif Elgvin, to see the latter not as a specific writing but as a comprehensive term for the entire divine plan, embracing past, present and future.[29] The future aspects of this plan assure the elect that the wicked will be punished and destroyed in due course.

An inheritance of glory

The assurance given to the elect is not just that the wicked will be destroyed. By meditating on "the mystery that is to be" they can "comprehend the birth-times of salvation, and know who is to inherit glory and toil" (4Q417 2 i 11),[30] for joy has been appointed for those who mourn. 4Q416 2 iii 6–8 tells the addressee: "Let not thy spirit be corrupted by it (money?). And then thou shalt sleep in faithfulness, and at thy death thy memory will flow[er forev]er, and אחריתך will inherit joy." Strugnell and Harrington translate "your posterity,"[31] which might be taken to imply that the individual only enjoys immortality of remembrance. אחריתך, however, can be taken at least as well to mean "your hereafter," and this would fit better with the frequent comparisons with the immortal angels in this text.[32] 4Q418 126 ii 7–8 promises "to raise up the head of the poor . . . in glory everlasting and peace eternal." There seems little doubt that the elect are promised a blessed afterlife.

It is not apparent to me that there is any reference in this text to bodily resurrection. Elgvin finds such a reference in 4Q418 69 ii 7: דורשי אמת יעורו למשפטי, which he translates "the seekers of truth will wake up to the judgments [of God]."[33] The final *yod* of למשפטי is only a trace, and Strugnell and Harrington read a *kaph*.[34] They translate: "those who investigate the truth shall rouse themselves to judge y[ou," taking "those who investigate the truth" as some kind of angelic beings. The

---

[27] Strugnell and Harrington, *4QInstruction*, 283; compare also 4Q418 55, which also asks the addressees to consider the holy angels.
[28] Strugnell and Harrington, *4QInstruction*, 300, 302.
[29] Elgvin, "An Analysis of *4QInstruction*," 80. See also his essay, "The Mystery to Come: Early Essene Theology of Revelation," in T. L. Thompson and N. P. Lemche, eds., *Qumran between the Old and the New Testament* (Sheffield: Sheffield Academic Press, 1998) 113–150. See also D. J. Harrington, "The *Raz Nihyeh* in a Qumran Wisdom Text (1Q26, 4Q415–418, 4Q423)," *RevQ* 17 (1996) 549–53, who suggests that it is a body of teaching distinct from the Torah.
[30] Strugnell and Harrington, *4QInstruction*, 172, 176.
[31] *Ibid.*, 112.
[32] Elgvin, *An Analysis of 4QInstruction*, 113, translates "and in the end you will inherit joy."
[33] Elgvin, *An Analysis of 4QInstruction*, 113–7.
[34] So also Tigchelaar, *To Increase Learning*, 210. This is now accepted by Elgvin, who restores משפטך, your judgment (oral communication).

context favors the latter interpretation. The passage is addressed to people who are told "to the everlasting pit shall your return be. For it shall awaken (תקיץ) ... its dark places ... shall cry out against your pleading, and all those who will endure forever, those who investigate the truth, shall rouse themselves for judgment ..." The view of the afterlife here is similar to what we find in the second column of the *Damascus Document* or in the *Discourse on the Two Spirits* in the *Community Rule*. The wicked are damned to the dark places of the netherworld, and the righteous are promised eternal life.[35] The reward of the righteous is life with the angels, presumably in heaven, rather than bodily resurrection.[36] This is in fact the most common view of the afterlife in the early apocalyptic literature as well as in the sectarian scrolls.[37]

Elgvin has also argued that the perspective of "realized eschatology" can be found in *4QInstruction*.[38] By this he means the kind of present participation in glory with the angels that is widely acknowledged in the *Hodayot*.[39] The evidence for this in *4QInstruction*, however, now seems to me less than conclusive.[40] Most of the passages adduced as evidence can be read as anticipating future glory, rather than enjoying it in the present. So for example in 4Q418 81 3–5 we read:

And he made them to inherit each his own inheritance; but he is thy portion and thy inheritance among the children of mankind, [and over] his [in]heritance has he set them in authority. But thou, by (doing) this honor him, by consecrating thyself to him, just as he has appointed thee as a Holy of Holies [over all the] earth, and (just as) among all the [ ] has he cast thy lot, and has magnified thy glory greatly. He has appointed thee for Himself as a first-born among ...[41]

The phrase "thy portion and thy inheritance" is derived from Num 18:20, where Aaron is told that God is his portion and inheritance among the sons of Israel. The passage seems to imply that the person of understanding (מבין) is to humanity as Aaron was to Israel. Whether it implies actual priesthood is not clear; the priestly

---

[35] For the promise of "joy" compare also Jub 23:31: "their bodies will rest in the earth and their spirits will have much joy."

[36] Tigchelaar, *To Increase Learning*, 211, 213, also denies any reference to bodily resurrection in *4QInstruction*.

[37] See J. J. Collins, "Apocalyptic Eschatology as the Transcendence of Death," in *Seers, Sibyls and Sages*, 75–97; idem, "The Afterlife in Apocalyptic Literature," in A. J. Avery-Peck and J. Neusner, eds., *Judaism in Late Antiquity. Part Four. Death, Life-After-Death, Resurrection and the World-to-Come in the Judaisms of Antiquity* (Leiden: Brill, 2000) 119–39.

[38] Elgvin, *An Analysis of 4QInstruction*, 117.

[39] The classic discussion is that of H.-W. Kuhn, *Enderwartung und gegenwärtiges Heil* (SUNT 4; Göttingen: Vandenhoeck & Ruprecht, 1966).

[40] In *Jewish Wisdom in the Hellenistic Age*, 127, I wrote that "there is an element of realized eschatology in the Sapiential Work, insofar as the elect are granted in this life to share the knowledge of the angels and gaze at the mystery that is hidden from most of humanity." This is still true, but it falls short of the level of participation in the angelic life that we find in the *Hodayot*.

[41] Strugnell and Harrington, *4QInstruction*, 302.

role may be metaphorical.⁴² Neither is it clear whether the understanding person has already received the inheritance. Strugnell and Harrington restore "among all the [God]ly [Ones] has he cast thy lot," but even this may only mean that the person is destined for life among the angels, not that he already enjoys it, in the manner of the *Hodayot*. Another passage, in 4Q416 2 iii 11–12, seems to speak of present exaltation:

for out of poverty he has lifted up thy head, and with the nobles has he made thee to be seated, and over a glorious heritage he has placed thee in authority.⁴³

The context of this passage however is a hypothetical situation: "But if (men) restore thee to splendor (?) walk in it" (vs. 9). In light of this, it seems likely that the passage is giving advice for the eventuality that a person rise from poverty to wealth in this life, and has no bearing on eschatology at all. Nonetheless, it is true that the text expresses the certainty of future glory and it is a short step from there to the sense of present exaltation that we find in the *Hodayot*.

Wisdom and eschatology

Everything we have seen about *4QInstruction* up to this point suggests that this text has a view of the world that is very different from the wisdom of Proverbs or Ben Sira. It is surprising, then, that Strugnell and Harrington regard the text as "common Israelite wisdom" and place it typologically between Proverbs and Ben Sira.⁴⁴ Admittedly, we have only been looking at one aspect of the text. It also deals with traditional wisdom themes, such as poverty and marital relations. The question arises how these two aspects of the text, the practical and the speculative wisdom, are related to each other. There are, of course precedents for combining practical and speculative, or theological, wisdom in Proverbs and Ben Sira. The wisdom instructions in Proverbs 1–9 are quite different in character from Proverbs 10–31. In Ben Sira, poems on wisdom are interspersed with long sections of mundane advice. The speculative sections of *4QInstruction*, however, are of a different nature, and their role in the composition is partially obscured by the fragmentary character of the text.

Torleif Elgvin has argued that the presence of two kinds of material in the text should be explained by redaction criticism: "an editor has loosely bound together

---

⁴² A. Lange, "In Diskussion mit dem Tempel. Zur Auseinandersetzung zwischen Kohelet und weisheitlichen Kreisen am Jerusalemer Tempel," in A. Schoors, ed., *Qohelet in the Context of Wisdom* (BETL 136; Leuven: Leuven University Press, 1998) 131, argues that *4QInstruction* derives from Temple circles, because of several allusions to matters of priestly interest. It is not clear, however, that any of these allusions requires that the author be associated with the Temple. Fletcher-Louis, *All the Glory of Adam*, 178–85, takes the passage as describing the vocation of the priest.

⁴³ Strugnell and Harrington, *4QInstruction*, 113.

⁴⁴ *Ibid.*, 36.

older wisdom admonitions and texts which stress eschatology and revelation."[45] His argument is based on a perceived lack of coherence in some passages, and on theological tension in others. As an example of the lack of coherence, he cites 4Q417 2 i 9–19:

And not for thyself alone shalt thou increase [thy appetite ...]
For what is more insignificant than a poor man? And do not rejoice in thy mourning, lest thou have trouble in thy life. [Gaze upon the mystery] that is to come, and comprehend the birth-times of salvation. And know who is to inherit glory and toil. Has not [ ] and for those among them who mourn eternal joy. Be an advocate on behalf of thy own interests, and let not [ ] by every perversity of thine. Pronoun[ce] thy judgments like a righteous ruler ... and do not overlook thy own sins...[46]

Elgvin comments: "In this passage admonitions and eschatological statements follow closely upon another, but it is difficult to see any clear logical line between them."[47] But there is an obvious connection. The point is that the understanding person must do everything in light of "the mystery that is to be" and the expectation of a future judgment, that will determine who is to inherit glory or toil. In this case, the mystery provides a perspective on poverty. It relativizes the importance of wealth and reminds one of the importance of humility.

The perception of incoherence in a passage such as this may be due to the fact that the ethic of *4QInstruction* is not always different from the traditional ethic of Proverbs or Ben Sira. It is largely an ethic of caution. One should look out for one's own interests. One who borrows money should not rest until it is paid back, lest one fall into the power of the lender (4Q417 2 i 22–23). One should honor one's parents (4Q416 2 iii 15–17) and control the vows of one's wife (4Q416 2 iv 7–9). This is not the kind of "interim ethic" that one often associates with apocalyptic literature, where the time is supposed to be short.[48] But *4QInstruction* never indicates that the end is near, or that its admonitions are meant for a short time of crisis. The *eschaton* is not imminent, but it is assured. (In fact, while some apocalyptic literature is crisis literature, written in expectation of an imminent end, much of it is not.) One should live one's life *sub specie aeternitatis*. This does not mean that one should neglect this life, but that one should live it properly. Those who will inherit glory are those

---

[45] Elgvin, *An Analysis of 4QInstruction*, 53. See also his essay, "Wisdom and Apocalypticism in the Early Second Century BCE – The Evidence of *4QInstruction*," in L. H. Schiffman, E. Tov and J. C. VanderKam, eds., *The Dead Sea Scrolls Fifty Years after their Discovery* (Jerusalem: Israel Exploration Society in cooperation with the Shrine of the Book, Israel Museum, 2000) 226–47.

[46] I cite the translation of Strugnell and Harrington, which is different at some points from that of Elgvin. Elgvin cites it as 4Q417 III 9–19.

[47] Elgvin, *An Analysis of 4QInstruction*, 53.

[48] For a classic formulation see 1 Cor 7:29–31; "the appointed time has grown short; from now on, let even those who have wives be as though they had none, and those who mourn as though they were not mourning ... and those who deal with the world as though they had no dealings with it. For the present world is passing away."

who live life wisely, and that involves taking care of business and attending to family relations. Awareness of the mystery makes a difference on some issues. Poverty, for example, is seen to be inconsequential. But on many issues the only difference it makes is that it raises the stakes. What is at issue is not only one's prosperity in this life but also one's fate in the hereafter.

Elgvin has noted that *4QInstruction* appeals to two different kinds of authority.[49] The admonitions about business affairs are not incited by any expectation of the *eschaton*; they arise from the pragmatic tradition of old wisdom. In contrast, the mystery that is to be and the prospect of future glory are not things that can be learned from observing human experience. They presuppose revelation, over and above empirical wisdom. This is true, but the two sources of wisdom are complementary rather than opposed. The mystery does not require that one behave in a way that is counter to earthly wisdom. *4QInstruction* is not an ascetic document. Poverty is not an ideal. Knowledge of the mystery can help one endure it, but there is no virtue in remaining in poverty if one has any option about it.

I am skeptical, then, of Elgvin's argument that it is possible to separate the admonitions and the discourses into two distinct literary layers. It is true that there are different kinds of material in the text, and that only one of them is consistent with traditional wisdom. But whether an editor added the eschatological discourses to an older wisdom document or, as I think more likely, an author composed a wisdom text that embodied a new perspective, the presence of the eschatological material in a Hebrew wisdom text requires some explanation. How are we to account for the development of a new, eschatologically oriented perspective, in a wisdom text of the second century BCE?

The derivation of eschatological wisdom

Essentially, two kinds of answer have been offered for this question. Von Rad did not know *4QInstruction* but he argued that the apocalyptic view of history had its roots in the wisdom tradition itself. "Can we not interpret this interest in time and the secrets of the future shown by the apocalyptic writers," he asked, "in light of Wisdom teaching that everything has its times, and that it is the part of Wisdom to know about these times (Ecc. III.1ff)?"[50] Qoheleth chapter 3, to which he referred, is not a very good analogue for apocalyptic determinism, but there are some genuinely deterministic passages in Ben Sira.[51] God, we are told, did not make all days

---

[49] Elgvin, *An Analysis of 4QInstruction*, 55.
[50] Von Rad, *Old Testament Theology* (New York: Harper & Row, 1965) 2.307.
[51] See D. Winston, "Freedom and Determinism in Greek Philosophy and in Hellenistic Jewish Wisdom," in G. E. Sterling, ed., *The Ancestral Philosophy. Hellenistic Philosophy in Second Temple Judaism. Essays of David Winston* (BJS 331; Providence: Brown University, 2001) 44–56.

alike, but hallowed some and made some ordinary. Similarly, he blessed and exalted some people, while others he cursed and brought low (Sir 33:7–13). Moreover,

Good is the opposite of evil, and life is the opposite of death;
so the sinner is the opposite of the godly.
Look at all the works of the Most High;
They come in pairs, one the opposite of the other. (Sir 33:14–15)

One can trace a line of development from this kind of sapiential reflection, through *4QInstruction*, to the dualism of the two spirits at Qumran.[52] Armin Lange traces the continuity with respect to the *"Weisheitliche Urordnung*," entailing a concept of the totality of creation, which is a fundamental tenet of the biblical wisdom tradition, and here too there is genuine continuity that should not be denied.[53] One might add that it is not difficult to see how statements in the book of Proverbs that wisdom is "the tree of life" (Prov 3:18) could give rise to the hope for a blessed immortality. Yet the fact remains that no wisdom book down to Ben Sira uses "mystery" as a fundamental concept. It may well be that the רז נהיה is a reinterpretation of the figure of Wisdom in the older texts, as Elgvin has suggested,[54] but if so the reinterpretation is significant. Wisdom was in principle available to all, and it did not have the orientation to the future implied by "the mystery that is to be." Neither does any of the older wisdom texts have place for a judgment scene such as we find in 4Q416, nor do they promise an inheritance of glory to the elect.

A different kind of development is proposed by Elgvin. It is universally acknowledged that there are significant parallels between *4QInstruction* and the early apocalyptic literature, primarily with the Enoch literature, but the word *raz* is prominent in the book of Daniel. Elgvin argues that "*4QInstruction*'s understanding of the world and man is determined more by apocalypticism than by traditional wisdom" and notes that the text "shares what has been described as the core of the apocalyptic message: the unmasking of the otherwise unknown secrets of God."[55] The parallels with the *Epistle of Enoch* are especially important.[56] Here we find an explicit division into periods in the *Apocalypse of Weeks*. Moreover, the whole course of history is said to be engraved on the heavenly tablets. The *Epistle* promises the elect a blessed afterlife with the angels. Poverty is a prominent theme in both documents. The wisdom text does not exhibit as strong an animus against the rich as does Enoch, but

---

[52] See J. J. Collins, "Wisdom, Apocalypticism and the Dead Sea Scrolls," in *Seers, Sibyls and Sages*, 369–83.

[53] Lange, *Weisheit und Prädestination*. See also his essay, "Wisdom and Predestination in the Dead Sea Scrolls," *DSD* 2 (1995) 340–54. Continuities between the wisdom of Ben Sira and *4QInstruction* are explored by J. Aitken, "Apocalyptic, Revelation and Early Jewish Wisdom Literature," in P. J. Harland and C. T. R. Hayward, eds., *New Heaven and New Earth. Prophecy and the Millennium. Essays in Honour of Anthony Gelston* (Leiden: Brill, 1999) 181–93.

[54] Elgvin, "Wisdom and Apocalypticism," 235.

[55] *Ibid.*, 239.

[56] See also A. Caquot, "Les textes de sagesse de Qoumrân (Aperçu préliminaire)," *RHPhR* 76 (1996) 1–34, especially p. 22; Tigchelaar, *To Increase Learning*, 212–7.

it is clear that the addressees of both texts regarded themselves as poor. Even the motif of "planting," which appears in *4QInstruction* and again in several Qumran texts, can plausibly be traced to the *Apocalypse of Weeks*.[57] *4QInstruction* never refers to the Enochic books, as the *Damascus Document* refers to *Jubilees* (CD 16:3–4), nor does it mention unmistakable Enochic themes such as the story of the Watchers (as in CD 2:18). The evidence for literary dependence, then, is not fully conclusive.[58] But if the sapiential text was not influenced directly by the *Epistle of Enoch*, it must have had sources that were very similar to it. It is especially significant that both the *Epistle of Enoch* and *4QInstruction* are addressed to an elect group, not to Israel at large and certainly not to humanity at large in the manner of the older wisdom books. I do not suggest that the two groups should be identified, but there was surely some relationship between them.

It seems to me, however, that the whole debate about the origins of apocalypticism is misleading, insofar as it presupposes that there were pure streams of tradition and that a text must draw either from wisdom or from prophecy but not from both. All of this literature was an exercise in *bricolage*, that pieced together a new view of the world that drew motifs and ideas from many sources.[59] *4QInstruction* was certainly informed by the kind of traditional wisdom found in Proverbs and Ben Sira (without the latter's incorporation of the Torah as the prime exemplar of wisdom). It was also informed by apocalyptic traditions of the type reflected in the *Epistle of Enoch*. The manner in which *4QInstruction* alludes to the periods of history and the coming judgment shows that it presupposes an apocalyptic tradition that was already well developed. The author of *4QInstruction* was a wisdom teacher who found such ideas congenial, although the mode of discourse of the apocalypses was different from his own. Whether the apocalyptic tradition was itself indebted to wisdom traditions at an earlier stage is a question for another occasion. It seems to me that the earliest Enoch tradition, as found in the *Astronomical Book* and the *Book of the Watchers* has strong sapiential interests, but that these have little in common with the kind of wisdom found in Proverbs and Ben Sira.

4QInstruction and the Dead Sea sect

Finally, we must comment on the relation between *4QInstruction* and the sectarian writings from Qumran. The consensus that the wisdom text was not a product of the

---

[57] On the motif of planting, without reference to *4QInstruction*, see P. A. Tiller, "The 'Eternal Planting' in the Dead Sea Scrolls," *DSD* 4 (1997) 312–35.

[58] Tigchelaar, *To Increase Learning*, 216, asks whether the author of the Epistle knew *4QInstruction*. The possibility can not be excluded, in view of the uncertainty of the date of the Qumran work.

[59] See my comments in *The Apocalyptic Imagination* (revised ed.; Grand Rapids: Eerdmans, 1998) 1–42.

community described in *Serek Ha-Yahad* seems well founded. Not only does *4QInstruction* presuppose family life and make no mention of community structures, but it pays no *explicit* attention to the law of Moses, in sharp contrast to other wisdom texts of the period, such as Ben Sira and *4QBeatitudes* (4Q525). It alludes to the Torah many times, and evidently regards it as a source of wisdom.[60] When it touches on halakhic issues, however, such as the vows of women, it does not seem to share the understanding of these issues that we find in the sectarian scrolls.[61] For this reason, too, it seems unlikely to be a product of the "camps" of CD 7:6, or the "marrying Essenes" of Josephus, as these presumably shared the Torah-centered theology of the Teacher of Righteousness.[62] The use of the Torah in the wisdom literature, however, is a topic that requires further exploration.

The wisdom text has nonetheless significant points of comparison with some sectarian texts. Lange has demonstrated its affinities with the *Instruction on the Two Spirits*, the *Hodayot*, and the wisdom passage in CD 2.[63] We should not necessarily conclude that the people of the *yahad* came from "wisdom circles." There were evidently many groups in Judea in the early and middle second century BCE who considered themselves to enjoy special wisdom available only to the elect. Some of them may have come together in the Dead Sea sect, or perhaps we should only conclude that the leaders of the sect were well read, and cobbled together their theology from a range of sources. The community of the new covenant drew its ideas, and probably also its membership, from various sources. It was not outgrowth of any single stream of tradition.

Strugnell and Harrington described *4QInstruction* as "a veritable missing link" in the development of Jewish wisdom literature.[64] And so it is. Typologically, however, it does not belong between Proverbs and Ben Sira, but it represents a different line of development. Just as Ben Sira incorporated the Torah into his wisdom curriculum, so the authors of *4QInstruction* incorporated eschatology. The discovery of this wisdom text from Qumran shows that Jewish wisdom literature in the late Second Temple period was more diverse than we might infer from the book of Ben Sira.

---

[60] Some of these allusions are noted by Lange, "In Diskussion mit dem Tempel," 131.

[61] See Lawrence H. Schiffman, "Halakhic Elements in the Sapiential Texts from Qumran," in John J. Collins, Gregory E. Sterling and Ruth A. Clements, eds., *Sapiential Perspectives: Wisdom Literature in Light of the Dead Sea Scrolls* (STDJ 51; Leiden: Brill, 2004) 89–100.

[62] Elgvin, "Wisdom and Apocalypticism," 246, suggests that "the wisdom admonitions were probably used for didactic purposes in Essene 'camps' throughout Judea," but he seems to regard the camps as an early stage of the Essene movement, before the formation of the *Yahad*.

[63] Lange, *Weisheit und Prädestination*, 121–70; 195–270. He follows Hartmut Stegemann in regarding the *Instruction on the Two Spirits* as a pre-Qumran text. Compare Stegemann, *The Library of Qumran* (Grand Rapids: Eerdmans, 1998) 108–10.

[64] Strugnell and Harrington, *4QInstruction*, 36.

Epilogue

CHAPTER SEVENTEEN

The Dead Sea Scrolls and the New Testament. The Case of the Suffering Servant

The discovery of the Dead Sea Scrolls in 1947 and subsequent years in the caves near Qumran, south of Jericho, brought to light for the first time a corpus of writings from Judea, in their original languages, from New Testament times.[1] Before that, Judean writings from this time period were preserved mostly in translation (*1 Enoch, Psalms of Solomon, 4 Ezra* etc.), with the exception of the works of Josephus, which were composed in Rome, and not in the author's native language. The Scrolls, then, promised an unprecedented level of access to the religious and cultural environment in which Jesus lived. It was only natural that scholars would comb the newly discovered texts for parallels to the New Testament. In fact, scholarship on the Scrolls for the first decade or so after the discovery was preoccupied with their relevance to the New Testament.

That scholarship has vacillated between two poles. On the one hand, some scholars have posited very close continuity between the early Christians and the sectarian Judaism of the Scrolls. In extreme cases, a few scholars have even claimed that the Scrolls provide "nothing less than a picture of the movement from which Christianity sprang in Palestine," or rather "a picture of what Christianity actually *was* in Palestine."[2] At the other extreme, the views of many New Testament scholars were not substantially affected by the new discoveries at all. While the sweeping holistic comparisons between the early church and the so-called "Qumran Community" have certainly been exaggerated, however, the Scrolls can shed light on the New Testament in many matters of detail.[3]

---

[1] While Harry Attridge is not primarily known as a Scrolls specialist, it should be noted that he has contributed to the edition of the Cave 4 fragments by editing 4Q369, the *Prayer of Enoch*, with John Strugnell, in Attridge et al., *Qumran Cave 4. VIII. Parabiblical Texts. Part 1* (Oxford: Clarendon, 1994) 353–62.

[2] So Robert Eisenman in R. H. Eisenman and M. O. Wise, eds., *The Dead Sea Scrolls Uncovered. The First Complete Translation and Interpretation of 50 Key Documents Withheld for over 35 Years* (Rockport, MA: Element, 1992) 10.

[3] See the careful methodological study of Jörg Frey, "Critical Issues in the Investigation of the Scrolls and the New Testament," in Timothy H. Lim and John J. Collins, *The Oxford Handbook of the Dead Sea Scrolls* (Oxford: Oxford University Press, 2010) 517–45.

The Essenes and the New Testament

From the beginning, the relation between the Scrolls and Christianity was viewed through the lens of the Essenes. Almost immediately after the discovery of Scrolls, the religious association to which they refer was identified as the Essene sect. The identification was suggested independently by Millar Burrows of Yale, who was director of the American School of Oriental Research in Jerusalem, and by the Israeli scholar Eliezer Sukenik.[4] It was prompted by the location of the find, in the area west of the Dead Sea where Pliny had located the Essenes, by the similarity of the admissions procedures in the Community Rule to those of the Essenes as described by Josephus, and by other correspondences, such as the sharing of possessions. The Essenes had always been something of an enigma in ancient Judaism. They are known only from Greek and Latin sources, and their way of life is in striking contrast to that of rabbinic Judaism in some respects, such as the practice of celibacy.[5] For centuries, they and the Therapeutae, who were believed to be an Egyptian offshoot, were believed to be Christian ascetics, the first monks. This belief is found in Eusebius, and persisted down to the Reformation, and beyond in some circles.[6] At the time of the Enlightenment, Essenism was seen as an environment in which a pacifistic, non-materialist, spirituality might be nurtured. It exhibited an ideal of brotherhood and distrust of riches and the temple. A deist, Robert Taylor (1784–1844) declared that "in every rational sense that can be attached to the word, they [the Essenes] were the authors and real founders of Christianity."[7] Such views, of course, also encountered opposition. Taylor was imprisoned for heresy. But they were echoed at the end of the 19th century by no less a figure than Ernest Renan, who declared that "Christianity was an Essenism that survived" ("un essénisme qui a su durer").[8] Renan doubted that there was direct contact between the early Christians and the Essenes, but he thought the similarities were profound, noting the common meal, community of goods etc. Essenism represented an attempt to draw the moral consequences of Judaism and the preaching of the prophets. Essenism could not last,

---

[4] Weston W. Fields, *The Dead Sea Scrolls. A Full History* (Leiden: Brill, 2009) 58, 81, 87. According to Fields, the identification was first suggested by one Ibrahim Sowmy, whose brother was an assistant to the Syrian Metropolitan Mar Samuel.

[5] For the sources on the Essenes, see Geza Vermes and Martin D. Goodman, *The Essenes according to the Classical Sources* (Sheffield: Sheffield Academic Press, 1989), and the discussion by Joan E. Taylor, "The Classical Sources on the Essenes and the Scrolls," in Lim and Collins, eds., *The Oxford Handbook of the Dead Sea Scrolls*, 173–99.

[6] Eusebius, *Ecclesiastical History* 2.16. See Siegfried Wagner, *Die Essener in der Wissenschaftliche Diskussion vom Ausgang des 18. bis zum Beginn des 20. Jahrhunderts. Eine Wissenschaftsgeschichtliche Studie* (BZAW 79; Berlin: Töpelmann, 1960) 3.

[7] Robert Taylor, *The Diegesis, Being a Discovery of the Origin, Evidences, and Early History of Christianity* (Boston: Kneeland, 1834) 38.

[8] Ernest Renan, review of P. E. Lucius, *Der Essenismus in seinem Verhältnis zum Judenthum* (Strasbourg, 1881) in *Journal des Savants* (February, 1892) 91.

because of its extreme form of life, but it anticipated the Christian ideal of the meek who will inherit the earth.

Not all scholars shared this view of the Essenes. Another strand of scholarship saw the sect as "nur der Pharisaismus im Superlativ," in the words of Emil Schürer.[9] The place of the Essenes in Judaism was complicated by the discovery in the 19th century of *1 Enoch* and other apocalyptic writings. Inevitably, some scholars assigned this literature to the Essenes, on the grounds that they were the main representatives of a kind of Judaism different from that of the rabbis.[10] The likelihood that the Essenes were the carriers of apocalyptic traditions was affirmed by scholars of various persuasions, including Renan and Schuerer.

It should be noted that the links between the Essenes and early Christianity, and the identification of the community described in the Scrolls as Essene, were in place before the site of Qumran was excavated. Roland de Vaux and his collaborators have often been accused of imposing a monastic paradigm on the site. Be that as it may, neither the Essene identification of the sect nor the perceived analogies between the Essenes and early Christianity originated with the archeologist.

A foretaste of Christianity?

Renan's dictum was taken up in the earliest synthetic presentation of the Scrolls then available by André Dupont-Sommer.

> Already eminent historians have recognized in Essenism a 'foretaste of Christianity'. Everything in the Jewish New Covenant heralds and prepares the way for the Christian New Covenant. The Galilean Master, as He is presented to us in the writings of the New Testament, appears in many respects as an astonishing reincarnation of the Teacher of Righteousness.[11]

The Teacher, like Jesus, was the Messiah. He had been condemned and put to death, but he would return as the supreme judge. In the meantime, he too left a "church," supervised by an overseer or "bishop," whose essential rite was the sacred meal. Few scholars saw the similarities between Jesus and the Teacher as being as extensive as did Dupont-Sommer. His claim that the Teacher was condemned and put to death, or that he was expected to come again, was promptly and widely rejected. Dupont-Sommer himself toned down his views in his later publications. He contin-

---

[9] Emil Schürer, *Geschichte des Jüdischen Volkes im Zeitalter Jesu Christi* (3rd ed.; Leipzig: Hinrichs, 1898) 2.577. The affinity with Pharisaism had been argued by scholars of the *Wissenschaft des Judentums* movement, such as Solomon Rapoport and Zecharias Frankel.

[10] So especially Adolf Hilgenfeld, *Die jüdische Apokalyptik in ihrer geschichtlichen Entwicklung* (Jena: Mauke, 1857) 243.

[11] André Dupont-Sommer, *The Dead Sea Scrolls: a Preliminary Survey* (Oxford: Blackwell, 1952) 99–100, translated from his *Aperçus préliminaires sur les manuscripts de la mer morte* (Paris: Maisonneuve, 1950).

ued to argue, however, for a fundamental similarity between Jesus and the Teacher, mediated by the association of both with the figure of the Suffering Servant in Second Isaiah:

> Defining the mission of Jesus as prophet and saviour, the primitive Christian Church explicitly applied these Songs of the Servant of the Lord to him; about a century earlier, the Teacher of Righteousness applied them to himself.[12]

Dupont-Sommer's claims were endorsed and popularized in a much less critical manner by the literary critic Edmund Wilson, even though he was aware that the position of the French scholar was overstated. He wrote:

> If we look now at Jesus in the perspective supplied by the scrolls, we can trace a new continuity and, at last, get some sense of the drama that culminated in Christianity ... The monastery [of Qumran] ... is, perhaps, more than Bethlehem or Nazareth, the cradle of Christianity.[13]

Wilson suggested that the scholars working on the Scrolls were "somewhat inhibited in dealing with such questions by their various religious commitments."[14] The fire of this controversy was fanned by a radio broadcast in England by John Allegro, a member of the editorial team, who contended that "Dupont-Sommer was more right than he knew."[15] Allegro spun a scenario in which the Teacher was crucified and expected to rise again, which was promptly repudiated by Roland de Vaux on behalf of the rest of the editorial team. Thus was born the conspiracy theory, according to which the editorial team, led by a French Catholic priest (de Vaux) withheld or suppressed material that might be damaging to Christianity. This theory never gained wide currency, but it was aired periodically until the full corpus of the Scrolls was finally published in the 1990's.

The claims of Dupont-Sommer, popularized by Wilson and sensationalized by Allegro, provoked the first major debate about the significance of the Scrolls for early Christianity. As in the earlier debates about the Essenes, conflicting ideological agendas were at work. For Allegro and Wilson, similarity between the Teacher and Jesus, or between the Scrolls and Christianity, undercut the latter's claim to uniqueness and to divine revelation. For others, continuity with Judaism grounded Christianity in the tradition of biblical revelation. This was true for the Albright School in North America, and later for Martin Hengel and his pupils in Germany. For these scholars, the Scrolls served to counter the view of Christianity as a Hellenistic cult, associated with German scholarship of the Bultmannian school.

---

[12] Dupont-Sommer, *The Essene Writings from Qumran*, 361.
[13] Edward Wilson, *The Dead Sea Scrolls, 1947–1969* (New York: Oxford, 1969) 98. Wilson's original book appeared as *The Scrolls from the Dead Sea* (New York: Oxford University, 1955).
[14] *Ibid.*, 99.
[15] Michael Baigent and Richard Leigh, *The Dead Sea Scrolls Deception* (London: Jonathan Cape, 1991) 46.

Several scholars entered the lists to counter the exaggerated view of the affinities between the Scrolls and the early Church. In 1955, Millar Burrows wrote: "Direct influence of the Qumran sect on the early church may turn out to be less probable than parallel developments in the same general direction."[16] He was more impressed by the "basic contrasts" between Jesus and the Scrolls, especially with regard to ritual purity, than by the similarities.[17] For Krister Stendahl, "the issue between the Essenes and the early Christians was not one of 'originality,' but a searching question about who were the legitimate heirs to the prophetic promises and who could produce the most striking arguments for fulfillment."[18] Frank Cross also saw the significance of the Scrolls in the light they shed on the context of the New Testament rather than in specific points of influence. For Cross, "the Essenes prove to be the bearers, and in no small part the producers of the apocalyptic tradition of Judaism."[19] "In some sense," he wrote, "the primitive Church is the continuation of this communal and apocalyptic tradition."[20] Both were "apocalyptic communities." The various analogies between the Scrolls and the New Testament must be seen in the context of their common eschatological consciousness. Within this context, Cross could affirm the affinities of the Gospel of John with the Scrolls, in the symbolism of light and darkness, and the hope for eternal life: "the point is that John preserves authentic historical material which first took form in an Aramaic or Hebrew milieu where Essene currents still ran strong."[21] He also found continuity in messianic expectations, but he denied that the Teacher was either eschatological prophet or messiah, or that he was expected to return from the dead. He was similarly skeptical of attempts to make John the Baptist into an Essene. He was somewhat less guarded on some other issues, and spoke of "the central 'sacraments' of the Essene community," baptism and the communal meal, construing the latter as a messianic banquet. It is apparent that here Cross was using Christian analogies for heuristic purposes, to understand the new material of the Scrolls. This was an understandable move in the early years of Scrolls scholarship, but is increasingly viewed with caution in later years.

Debate renewed in the 1990's

Much of the debate about the Essenes and early Christianity was carried out on the basis of the seven scrolls that constituted the original find. The huge trove of texts

---

[16] Millar Burrows, *The Dead Sea Scrolls* (New York: Viking, 1955) 328.

[17] Millar Burrows, *More Light on the Dead Sea Scrolls* (New York: Viking, 1958) 39–132.

[18] Krister Stendahl, *The Scrolls and the New Testament* (New York: Harper, 1958), reprinted with a new introduction by J. H. Charlesworth (New York: Crossroad, 1992), 6.

[19] Frank M. Cross, *The Ancient Library of Qumran* (3rd ed.; Sheffield: Sheffield Academic Press, 1995), 144. Originally published by Doubleday in 1958.

[20] *Ibid.*, 145.

[21] Cross, *The Ancient Library*, 156.

from Cave 4 did not become fully available until the 1990's. By then, the general perception of the Scrolls had shifted. In the wake of the publication of the Temple Scroll, and especially of the presentation of 4QMMT at a conference in 1984, it became apparent that halakhic concerns, of the kind associated with rabbinic Judaism, were a much more important component of the Scrolls than had previously been realized.[22] The separation of the sect from the rest of Judaism was not occasioned by its messianic beliefs or apocalyptic expectations, but by disagreements about the minutiae of purity laws. Accordingly, it was not so obvious that the Scrolls reflected an "apocalyptic community" analogous to Christianity, or indeed that analogies with Christianity were important for understanding the Scrolls at all.

Nonetheless, when the fragmentary material from Cave 4 became generally available in the 1990's, many of the old issues from the 1950's were revived. Some writing on the subject, such as the book by the English journalists Baigent and Leigh, was blatantly sensational. Some, such as Robert Eisenman's claim that the Scrolls were the authentic writings of early Christianity, was merely idiosyncratic.[23] But there were also serious scholarly attempts, in the tradition of Dupont-Sommer, to argue that the Teacher and his movement anticipated Jesus and his followers in important ways.[24]

The context of the latter-day debate about the Scrolls and the New Testament, however, is significantly different from that of its earlier counterpart. It is complicated by the great wealth of Scrolls material now available, much of which is not clearly sectarian in provenance. While it still seems plausible that the Scrolls were a sectarian collection, from which certain kinds of material (Hasmonean, Pharisaic) were excluded, they can no longer be viewed as tightly coherent, or assumed to reflect a distinctively sectarian viewpoint in every case. Even within the clearly sectarian material, there is now a greater awareness of the differences between the Damascus Document, which provides for married life, and the Community Rule, which does not. In both cases, it is clear that the sectarian communities had their *raison d'être* in the precise observance of the Torah.[25] If the movement represented

---

[22] See e.g. L. H. Schiffman, *Reclaiming the Dead Sea Scrolls* (Philadelphia: Jewish Publication Society, 1994).

[23] Above, n. 2. See also Eisenman, *Maccabees, Zadokites, Christians and Qumran: A New Hypothesis of Qumran Origins* (Leiden: Brill, 1983); idem, *James the Brother of Jesus: The Key to Unlocking the Secrets of Early Christianity and the Dead Sea Scrolls* (New York: Viking, 1997). Even more fantastic is Barbara Thiering, *Jesus and the Riddle of the Dead Sea Scrolls: Unlocking the Secrets of His Life Story* (San Francisco, CA: Harper Collins, 1992), who identifies the Teacher as John the Baptist and the Wicked Priest and "Man of the Lie" as Jesus.

[24] Notably M. O. Wise, *The First Messiah: Investigating the Savior before Jesus* (San Francisco: Harper, 1999). Note also the controversial study of Israel Knohl, *The Messiah before Jesus: The Suffering Servant of the Dead Sea Scrolls* (Berkeley: University of California, 2000). See my discussion, "A Messiah before Jesus?" in John J. Collins and Craig A. Evans, eds., *Christian Beginnings and the Dead Sea Scrolls* (Grand Rapids: Baker, 2006) 15–35 and "An Essene Messiah? Comments on Israel Knohl, *The Messiah before Jesus*," ibid., 37–44.

[25] See my book, *Beyond the Qumran Community. The Sectarian Movement of the Dead Sea*

by the sectarian rule-books was Essene, then Christianity was not an Essenism in any meaningful sense. Suggestions that Jesus may have spent time at Qumran have long been dismissed as unfounded. Such suggestions are still occasionally made with regard to John the Baptist, but are equally baseless.[26] The kind of holistic comparison of the "Qumran community" and early Christianity that characterized the scholarship of the 1950's can no longer be sustained.

This does not, however, preclude the possibility that particular beliefs or customs in early Christianity can be illuminated if we view them in the context provided by the Scrolls. In fact, there have been many fine studies that have used the Scrolls responsibly in just this way, notably the essays of Joseph Fitzmyer on a range of topics,[27] or of George Brooke on shared exegetical traditions in the Scrolls and the New Testament.[28] The specific issue which I wish to discuss in the remainder of this essay concerns one of these shared exegetical traditions, regarding the "suffering servant" in Isaiah 53, which has figured prominently in arguments that Scrolls anticipated early Christianity in significant ways.

The "suffering servant"

Since the classic commentary of Bernhard Duhm in 1892,[29] it has been customary to identify four passages in Second Isaiah as "Servant Songs": Isa 42:1–4; 49:1–7; 50:4–9 and 52:13 to 53:12. The most famous of these passages is Isa 52:13–53:12, which describes a figure who is despised and afflicted but who is vindicated by God and makes many righteous by his suffering. These passages were not singled out in antiquity, and their distinctiveness has also been questioned in modern times.[30] Nonetheless, readers in antiquity might well have recognized the profile of an individual in the prophecies of the second half of the book of Isaiah. Joseph Blenkinsopp describes the profile as follows: "a prophetic individual acting as God's agent on

---

Scrolls (Grand Rapids: Eerdmans, 2010) 12–87, and my article, "Sectarian Communities in the Dead Sea Scrolls," in Lim and Collins, eds., *The Oxford Handbook of the Dead Sea Scrolls*, 151–72.

[26] See the concise discussion by Jörg Frey, "Critical Issues in the Investigation of the Scrolls and the New Testament," in Lim and Collins, eds., *The Oxford Handbook of the Dead Sea Scrolls*, 517–45, especially 528–30.

[27] Joseph A. Fitzmyer, *Essays on the Semitic Background of the New Testament* (London: Chapman, 1971); idem, *A Wandering Aramean: Collected Aramaic Essays* (Missoula, MT: Scholars Press, 1979); idem, *The Dead Sea Scrolls and Christian Origins* (Grand Rapids: Eerdmans, 2000).

[28] George J. Brooke, "Shared Exegetical Traditions between the Scrolls and the New Testament," in Lim and Collins, eds., *The Oxford Handbook of the Dead Sea Scrolls*, 565–91. See also Brooke, *The Dead Sea Scrolls and the New Testament* (Minneapolis: Fortress, 2005); Florentino García Martínez, ed., *Echoes from the Caves: Qumran and the New Testament* (STDJ 85; Leiden: Brill, 2009) and Craig A. Evans, "Jesus, John and the Dead Sea Scrolls: Assessing Typologies of Restoration," in Collins and Evans, *Christian Beginnings and the Dead Sea Scrolls*, 45–62.

[29] Bernhard Duhm, *Das Buch Jesaja* (Göttingen: Vandenhoeck & Ruprecht, 1892).

[30] Richard J. Clifford, *Fair Spoken and Persuading: An Interpretation of Second Isaiah* (New York: Paulist, 1984).

behalf of the people of Israel, an individual inspired and spirit-possessed (Isa 42:1; 50:4), the object of a special divine election (41:8–9, etc.) from the first moment of life (44:2; 50:4) and one whose mission led to opposition, abuse, violent death, and ultimate vindication (49:4–5; 50:5–9; 52:13–53:12) by the God whom he served."[31] As Blenkinsopp recognizes, this profile was not necessarily confined to the classic "Servant Songs." Other passages too seem to speak of a distinct individual. Isa 61:1–3 is a significant passage in this regard.

The servant in the *Hodayot*

We have already noted the claim of Dupont-Sommer that the Teacher of Righteousness had applied these songs to himself a century before the early Christians applied them to Jesus. He based this claim on the *Hodayot*, or Thanksgiving Hymns, which he took to be compositions of the Teacher. (No distinction between Hymns of the Teacher and Hymns of the Community had yet been drawn.) Citing such passages as 1QH^a 5:24; 6:25, 15:6–7, he wrote: "The expression 'thy servant' recurs in these passages with such insistence that one cannot fail to compare them with the celebrated poems known as the 'Songs of the Servant of the Lord' in the book of Isaiah."[32] This view received a surprisingly strong endorsement from William H. Brownlee, who regarded much of Dupont-Sommer's speculation as impossible but concluded: "Yet Professor Dupont-Sommer often has an uncanny knack for being ultimately right (or nearly so), even when his views are initially based on the wrong texts!"[33] He concluded: "Just as the Servant of the Lord of Second Isaiah is the most important single background element for the understanding and interpretation of the New Testament, so it is likely to prove for the Qumran Scrolls."[34]

Later scholarship became more skeptical. Jean Carmignac acknowledged allusions to only three "servant" passages in the *Hodayot*, Isa 49:4, 50:4 and 53:3.[35] After the work of Gert Jeremias in the early 1960's, it became customary to distinguish between Teacher Hymns and Hymns of the Community.[36] Many of the occurrences of "servant" on which Dupont-Sommer relied were now relegated to the Hymns of

---

[31] Joseph Blenkinsopp, *Opening the Sealed Book. Interpretations of the Book of Isaiah in Late Antiquity* (Grand Rapids: Eerdmans, 2006) 252.

[32] Dupont-Sommer, *The Essene Writings from Qumran*, 361. Dupont-Sommer cites these passages according to the older numbering of Sukenik's edition of the *Hodayot*.

[33] William H. Brownlee, "The Servant of the Lord in the Qumran Scrolls," *BASOR* 132 (December, 1953) 9.

[34] Brownlee, "The Servant of the Lord in the Qumran Scrolls II," *BASOR* 135 (October, 1954) 33.

[35] Jean Carmignac, "Les Citations de l'Ancien Testament, et spécialement des Poèmes du Serviteur," *RevQ* 3 (1960) 357–94, esp. 383–94. Not every use of the word "servant" could count as an allusion to Isaiah.

[36] Gert Jeremias, *Der Lehrer der Gerechtigkeit* (SUNT 2; Göttingen: Vandenhoeck & Ruprecht, 1963) 171–3.

the Community. Jeremias admitted only three cases in the Hymns of the Teacher where the speaker designated himself as "servant."[37] Martin Hengel felt that the idea that the servant was a model in the *Hodayot* had been so clearly refuted by Carmignac and Jeremias that it was unnecessary to discuss it further.[38]

The case for the servant paradigm in the *Hodayot* has been revived, however, by Michael Wise, in his book, *The First Messiah*. Wise accepts that a corpus of Teacher Hymns can be distinguished within the *Hodayot*. In this he follows the analysis of Michael Douglas, who refined the work of Jeremias,[39] but also finds support in the material evidence of the *Hodayot* scrolls from Qumran Cave 4, where these hymns seem to have constituted a distinct collection.[40] Whether this block of material should be attributed to the Teacher, or can be used for biographical purposes is still disputed. The argument for attribution to the Teacher rests on the forceful personality and claims made in these hymns. Jeremias argued that

> It is completely inconceivable that in [a single movement] within a short span of time there could have been two men, each of whom came before the group with revolutionary claims to bring about redemption through his teaching, and that both men were accepted by the community.[41]

Nonetheless, there has been a tendency in recent scholarship to avoid biographical claims and focus instead on the persona represented by the 'I' of these hymns. So Carol Newsom, who is critical of "a romantic model of authorship," acknowledges that "in a number of the compositions the persona of the speaker is that of a persecuted leader of the community, whether the Righteous Teacher or some other figure."[42] It may never be possible to prove that the leader in question is the Teacher (although we do not know of any other viable candidate). The question is whether the Suffering Servant served as an ideal in the Scrolls, whether that ideal was thought to be realized in the Teacher or not. For the convenience, we will follow

---

[37] *Ibid.*, 305.

[38] Martin Hengel, "The Effective History of Isaiah 53 in the Pre-Christian Period," in Bernd Janowski and Peter Stuhlmacher, eds., *The Suffering Servant. Isaiah 53 in Jewish and Christian Sources* (Grand Rapids: Eerdmans, 2004) 118.

[39] Michael C. Douglas, "Power and Praise in the *Hodayot*: A Literary Critical Study of 1QH 9:1–18:14," Ph. D. Diss, Chicago (1998); "The Techer Hymn Hypothesis Revisited: New Data for an Old Crux," *DSD* 6 (1999) 239–66.

[40] In the words of Eileen Schuller: "At least eight psalms of this [i.e. Teacher-hymn] type (some commentators would add a few more) are grouped together in cols. 10–17, that is, in the middle of the reconstructed 1QH^a scroll, and it is these same psalms that are found in 4QH^c and 4QH^f." Eileen Schuller, "*Hodayot* (1QH and Related Texts)," *DEJ* 747–9. Conversely, "all the material in 4QH^a that overlaps with material in 1QH^a is from the 'Hymns of the Community' type." See further Schuller, "427–432. 4Q*Hodayot*$^{a-e}$ and 4Qpap*Hodayot*^{f}: Introduction," in Esther Chazon et al., *Qumran Cave 4. XX. Poetical and Liturgical Texts, Part 2* (DJD 29; Oxford: Clarendon, 1999) 75.

[41] Jeremias, *Der Lehrer*, 176, trans. M. O. Wise, "The Origins and History of the Teacher's Movement," in Lim and Collins, eds., *The Oxford Handbook of the Dead Sea Scrolls*, 103.

[42] Carol A. Newsom, *The Self as Symbolic Space. Constructing Identity and Community at Qumran* (STDJ 53; Leiden: Brill, 2004) 197.

Wise in referring to the author of these hymns as the Teacher, while mindful that the historical identification is in dispute.

Wise builds his case, not on the use of the term "servant," which occurs in the Teacher Hymns, but not very frequently,[43] but on allusions to the servant poems. He claims that toward the end of the Teacher Hymns, the Teacher "came to speak of himself as the Servant of the Lord in concentrated fashion. He made allusion after allusion to the passages of Isaiah that modern scholars designate Servant Songs and others to portions that might easily be so construed."[44] 1QH^a 16 speaks of a shoot nourished by the streams; Isaiah speaks of the servant as a sapling and a root. The one who causes the shoot to grow is "without esteem" (בלוא נחשב) like the servant in Isa 53:3. The shoot in the hymn seems to be the community rather than the Teacher, but the Teacher is associated with the Servant by the lack of esteem. Again, 1QH^a 16:26–7 reads: "I sojourn with sickness and my heart is stricken with afflictions. I am like a man forsaken." Compare Isa 53:3: "He was despised and forsaken by men, a man of suffering and acquainted with sickness … We accounted him afflicted." Another clear allusion to Isa 53:3 is found in 1QH^a 12:8, where the author complains that "they do not esteem me," using the same verb, חשב, that is used with reference to the servant in the Isaianic passage: "despised, and we did not esteem him." The same allusion is found in 1QH^a 12:23. The claim of the hymnist in 12:27, "through me you have enlightened the face of the many," may also be taken as an allusion to Isa 53:11, which says that the servant will make many righteous. There are also clear allusions to other Isaianic passages that modern scholars identify as Servant Songs. 1QH^a 15:6–7, "I thank you, O Lord, for you have upheld me by your might and have poured out your holy spirit within me," echoes Isa 42:1: "Here is my Servant whom I uphold, my chosen, in whom my soul delights. I have put my spirit upon him." The gift of the spirit also recalls Isa 61:1, "the spirit of the Lord God is upon me, because the Lord has anointed me …" While Isaiah 61 is not regarded as a servant passage by modern scholars, it could reasonably have been taken to speak of the same figure. In 1QH^a 16:35–6, the hymnist says that God has made the tongue in his mouth strong "to sustain the weary with a word," echoing Isa 50:4b.

In all, Wise makes a persuasive case that the speaker in the Teacher Hymns applied to himself language used for the servant in the Book of Isaiah.[45] Like the servant, the Teacher claims to be endowed with the spirit and to have "a disciple's tongue" (1QH^a 15:10; cf. Isa 50:4), but is rejected and not esteemed, and afflicted with sickness. Nonetheless, his career benefits "the many." In some cases, the words of Isaiah are used. It is reasonable to conclude that the hymnist used the prophet's depiction of the servant to describe his own situation. He may even have regarded

---

[43] 1QH^a 13:15,28; 15:16; 17:11.
[44] Wise, *The First Messiah*, 290.
[45] So also Blenkinsopp, *Opening the Sealed Book*, 284–5.

himself as the one of whom Isaiah spoke, although that conclusion is not necessarily required by the correspondences.

The *Self-Exaltation Hymn*

It is of the essence of the servant poems that God exalts the servant in the end. This claim is muted in the *Hodayot*, presumably because the speaker has not yet been exalted, although his confidence is strong. Another text from Qumran speaks more clearly of exaltation, of a figure who is also reminiscent of the servant. This is the so-called *"Self-Exaltation Hymn,"* which is found in four fragmentary texts, one of which was part of the *Hodayot* Scroll from Cave 1 and another of which was part of the 4Q*Hodayot* fragments.[46] The speaker in this text makes several extraordinary claims: "No one can compare to my glory; no one is exalted except me . . . I am reckoned with the gods, and my dwelling is in the holy council." It refers to "a mighty throne in the council of the gods," and says: "I have taken my seat . . . in heaven." It even asks "who is like me among the gods?" Yet some other passages contain echoes of the Servant Songs: "who has been counted contemptible like me" uses language used of the Servant in Isaiah 53: "despised, and we did not esteem him" (the Hebrew verbs חשב and בוז are used in both cases). There are also possible allusions to taking away evil. While the text is fragmentary and difficult, it seems that a figure who was subjected to contempt is now enthroned in heaven, above the "gods" or angels. Scholars are divided as to whether the figure in question is the Teacher, an eschatological figure, or even an angel.[47] For our present purposes, it may suffice to say that here again the servant seems to serve as the paradigm for an ideal figure, who might then serve as a model for the sectarian reader. The hypothesis that this hymn was attributed to the Teacher after his death is attractive, but unverifiable.

4Q541

Another, even more obscure, example of a figure who undergoes adversity but is finally exalted is found in the fragmentary Aramaic text 4Q540–541. This refers to a figure who encounters opposition and falsehood, but who will shine like the sun and will atone for all the children of his generation.[48] The original editor, Jean

---

[46] The fullest edition is that of M. O. Wise, "מי כמוני באלים: A Study of 4Q491, 4Q471b, 4Q427 7 and 1QH^a 25:35–26:10," *DSD* 7 (2000) 173–219.

[47] See my discussion in *The Scepter and the Star. Messianism in Light of the Dead Sea Scrolls* (2nd ed.; Grand Rapids: Eerdmans, 2010) 149–64, and Philip Alexander, *The Mystical Texts* (London/New York: T. & T. Clark, 2006) 85–91.

[48] Émile Puech, "540. 4QApocryphe de Lévi^a ? ar," and "540. 4QApocryphe de Lévi^a ? ar," in Puech, *Qumrân Grotte 4. XXII. Textes Araméens. Première Partie. 4Q529–549* (DJD 31; Oxford: Clarendon, 2001) 217–56.

Starcky, suggested that it evoked "a suffering Messiah in the perspective opened up by the Servant Songs,"[49] while also suggesting that it referred to an eschatological High Priest. In this he was followed by the eventual editor, Émile Puech, and also by Martin Hengel.[50] In this case, however, there are no clear terminological echoes of the Servant Songs. When this figure is said to atone for the children of his generation, he presumably does so as a priest, by offering the appropriate sacrifices, not by his own suffering.[51]

Servant and messiah?

The Servant of Isaiah's poems is invoked a number of times in pre-Christian Judaism as a paradigm of humiliation and exaltation.[52] Examples can be found in Daniel 11–12 and Wis 2–5. He was not usually understood as a messiah. It has occasionally been suggested that the Servant was viewed as a messiah in the Scrolls. Besides the reference to anointing in Isaiah 61, there is a noteworthy reading in the great Isaiah Scroll from Qumran (1QIsa^a).[53] Where the Masoretic text reads "so his appearance was destroyed (משחת) beyond that of a man," the Qumran text reads "so I have anointed (משחתי) his appearance ..." The reading, which dates to the third century BCE, may have originated as a scribal mistake, but it lent itself inevitably to a messianic reading, especially if it was read in conjunction with Isa 61. The Teacher Hymns follow the readings of this scroll at several points, but not always, and do not actually cite this passage. Neither the *Hodayot* nor the *Self-Exhaltation Hymn* makes a specific messianic claim. Neither do they claim that the figure who was "not esteemed" and suffered contempt like the Servant suffered vicariously for others.[54]

How does this use of the Servant Poems in the Scrolls compare with what we find in the New Testament?

The Servant and Jesus

For Dupont-Sommer and Brownlee, writing in the 1950's, it was self-evident that the Suffering Servant provided the primary model for understanding the death of Jesus in the New Testament. The view that Jesus himself understood his death in terms of the Servant prophecies was expressed in classic form by Joachim Jeremias,

---

[49] Jean Starcky, "Les quatre étapes du messianisme à Qumrân," *RB* 481–705, here 492.
[50] Martin Hengel, "The Effective History of Isaiah 53," especially 106–18.
[51] See my discussion in *The Scepter and the Star*, 141–5.
[52] See Hengel, "The Effective History of Isaiah 53," 75–146.
[53] D. Barthélemy, "Le grand rouleau d'Isaïe trouvé près de la Mer Morte," *RB* 57 (1950) 530–49, especially 546–9.
[54] *Pace* Knohl, *The Messiah before Jesus*, 24.

even though he recognized that "the number of passages in which Jesus refers Is. 53 to Himself is not great."[55] This view was criticized sharply by C. K. Barrett[56] and Morna Hooker.[57] Hooker noted that most of the clear quotations of Isaiah 53 in the New Testament, such as the passage read by the Ethiopian eunuch in Acts 8:32–3, stop short of reference to the meaning of Jesus's death. Only in 1 Peter 2:22–25 is a quotation from Isaiah 53 associated with the atoning value of Jesus' death. There is also a clear allusion in Heb 9:28, as Harry Attridge has also recognized.[58] In her later work, Hooker recognized an allusion to the servant in Rom 4:25, "who was handed over to death for our trespasses and was raised for our justification."

The influence of the Servant paradigm, even on the thinking of Jesus, received strong affirmation from a group of scholars at the university of Tübingen in the 1990's.[59] For Peter Stuhlmacher, the understanding of Jesus' death in terms of the Suffering Servant

> was not first and foremost the fruit of post-Easter faith; its roots lie rather in Jesus' own understanding of his mission and death. He himself adopted the general messianic interpretation of Isaiah 53 current in early Judaism, but he understood his sufferings quite independently of the prevailing tradition in the light of the word of God given to him from Isaiah 53:3–4 and 53:11–12. After the completion of Jesus' mission in the cross and resurrection, the song of the Suffering Servant was applied in early Christianity consistently for the first time to a historical individual whose fate made the whole text transparent.[60]

For his claim that a general messianic interpretation of Isaiah 53 was current in early Judaism, Stuhlmacher relied on Émile Puech's interpretation of 4Q541, but in fact that text is not clearly an interpretation of the Servant at all.

Claims as to what the historical Jesus may have thought are at least as controversial as claims about what the Teacher may have written. In this case, we must be content to recognize the claims that were attributed to Jesus. Hooker's insistence on explicit citations is probably too restrictive. We must also recognize clear allusions. So, when Mark 9:31 says that the Son of Man will be *handed over* into the hands of human beings...(using the Greek verb *paradidomi*, also used in Rom 4:25), we must recognize an allusion to the LXX of Isa 53:12, which says that the Servant will be

---

[55] J. Jeremias, "*Pais Theou*," *TDNT* 5 (1967) 654–717 (here 716).

[56] "The Background of Mark 10:45," in A. J. B. Higgins, ed., *New Testament Essays. Studies in Memory of Thomas Walter Manson* (Manchester: Manchester University Press, 1959) 1–18.

[57] Hooker, *Jesus and the Servant. The Influence of the Servant Concept of Deutero-Isaiah in the New Testament* (London: SPCK, 1959). See also her later defence of her position, "Did the Use of Isaiah 53 to Interpret His Mission Begin with Jesus?" in William H. Bellinger and William R. Farmer, eds., *Jesus and the Suffering Servant* (Harrisburg, PA: Trinity Press International, 1998) 88–103. See also the comments of Sam K. Williams, *Jesus' Death as Saving Event. The Background and Origin of a Concept* (HDR 2; Missoula: Scholars Press, 1975) 224–9.

[58] Harold W. Attridge, *Hebrews* (Hermeneia; Minneapolis: Fortress, 1989) 266.

[59] Bernd Janowski and Peter Stuhlmacher, *The Suffering Servant* (Grand Rapids: Eerdmans, 2004).

[60] Peter Stuhlmacher, "Isaiah 53 in the Gospels and Acts," in Janowski and Stuhlmacher, *The Suffering Servant*, 149.

handed over to death and was reckoned among the lawless. The verb *paradidomi* is used ten times in Mark 14–15. As Adela Yarbro Collins has argued: "This frequent usage makes it into a kind of refrain and surely signifies its theological significance and its allusion to Isaiah 53."[61] Again, Mark 10:45, "For the Son of Man came not to be served but to serve, and to give his life as a ransom for many," has important similarities to Isaiah 53: 10b-12 LXX. In this case, however, the term "ransom" (*lutron*) is introduced, which brings to mind the Priestly writings in the Pentateuch, or Greek ideas of sacrifice, but not Isaiah.[62] In Mark 14:24, the description of Jesus' death as a "pouring out of his blood for many" seems to combine terminology of sacrifice with an allusion to Isaiah 53.[63]

As Hooker noted, allusions to Isaiah 53 are used in connection with Jesus in various ways. In Matt 8:17 ("he took our infirmities and bore our diseases"), Jesus is said to fulfill Isa 53:4 by casting out spirits and healing the sick. At Mark 15:28, a citation of Isa 53:12 LXX ("and he was considered to be among the lawless") is added to explain why Jesus was crucified between two thieves. In other cases, Isaiah is cited as prediction of Jesus' death (Acts 8:32–3) or Jesus is said to be "handed over," using the verb *paradidomi* that is used in Isa 53:12. When atoning significance is attached to the death of Jesus, this is usually brought out by additional sacrificial language beyond that of Isaiah 53.

A common scripture

If we compare this usage with that of the *Hodayot*, we find differences as well as similarities. The similarity is basic: Isaiah 53, and the other Servant passages, provide language that could be applied to the suffering of a righteous man. The particular aspects of Isaiah's prophecies that are highlighted, however, vary with the context. In the *Hodayot*, the main motif that is picked up is that the speaker suffers lack of esteem, but that God nonetheless upholds him. He is never said to be handed over to anyone, nor is he said to be put to death. The *Self-Exaltation Hymn* speaks of a Servant-like figure who is exalted, but nowhere in the Scrolls do we find a claim that he atoned for others by his suffering. Even if 4Q541 is taken to allude to the Servant, which is not at all clear, his atonement for the sins of his generation is presumably performed by ritual means, not by personal suffering. There is an obvious reason for this different appropriation of the servant figure. Jesus had been subjected to a

---

[61] Adela Yarbro Collins, *Mark* (Hermeneia; Minneapolis: Fortress, 2007) 441. She notes that the destiny of "being handed over" does not belong exclusively to Jesus, but also to John the Baptist and to the disciples. Stuhlmacher also finds an allusion to the *paradidomi* of Isa 53:12 in Luke 22:19, which adds "which is given for you" to the saying over the bread at the Last Supper.

[62] Adela Yarbro Collins, "The Signification of Mark 10:45 among Gentile Christians," *HTR* 90 (1997) 371–82.

[63] Yarbro Collins, *Mark*, 657.

shameful death, and this required explanation. Whatever trials he had to endure, the Teacher, or the figure envisioned in the *Hodayot*, suffered no such fate. Consequently, his death had no special significance.

What emerges from this comparison is that the main feature that the Scrolls share with the New Testament is a common reliance on a corpus of authoritative scriptures that could be used to contextualize and explain new experience. In many cases, there were also common exegetical traditions, as George Brooke and others have shown. In some cases, prophetic texts were believed to be fulfilled in different ways, as Stendhal observed, but prophetic texts could also be used allusively in ways that were not concerned with fulfillment. In the case of the Suffering Servant, however, we can only speak of the use of a common text, which was interpreted differently because of the different circumstances in which it was used.

Despite the long-standing attempts to make the Essenes into proto-Christians, the two movements were very different, and they applied their scriptures to different ends. Nonetheless, the different ways in which common traditions were used can still enrich our understanding of both movements.

Bibliography

Aitken, J. "Apocalyptic, Revelation and Early Jewish Wisdom Literature." Pages 181–93 in *New Heaven and New Earth. Prophecy and the Millennium. Essays in Honour of Anthony Gelston.* Edited by P.J. Harland and C.T.R. Hayward. Leiden: Brill, 1999.
Albani, M. *Astronomie und Schöpfungsglaube. Untersuchungen zum astronomischen Henochbuch.* Neukirchen-Vluyn: Neukirchener Verlag, 1994.
Alexander, Philip S. "Retelling the Old Testament." Pages 99–121 in *It Is Written. Scripture Citing Scripture.* Edited by D.A. Carson and H.G.M. Williamson. Cambridge: Cambridge University Press, 1988.
——. "The Redaction-History of *Serek ha-Yahad*: A Proposal." *RevQ* 17 (1996): 437–53.
——. "The Enochic Literature and the Bible." Pages 57–69 in *The Bible as Book. The Hebrew Bible and the Judaean Desert Discoveries.* Edited by Edward D. Herbert and Emanuel Tov. London: The British Library and Oak Knoll Press, 2002.
——. "Predestination and Free Will in the Theology of the Dead Sea Scrolls." Pages 27–46 in *Divine and Human Agency in Paul and His Cultural Environment.* Edited by John M.G. Barclay and Simon Gathercole. Library of New Testament Studies 335; London/New York: T&T Clark, 2006.
——. *The Mystical Texts. Songs of the Sabbath Sacrifice and Related Manuscripts.* Library of Second Temple Studies 61; London and New York: T. & T. Clark, 2006.
Alexander, Philip S., et al. *Qumran Cave 4. XXVI. Miscellanea, Part 1.* DJD 36; Oxford: Clarendon, 2000.
Allegro, J.M. "The Wiles of the Wicked Woman. A Sapiential Work from Qumran's Fourth Cave." *PEQ* 96 (1964): 53–55.
——. *Qumran Cave 4. I (4Q158–4Q186).* DJD 5; Oxford: Clarendon, 1968.
Anderson, Gary A. *The Genesis of Perfection. Adam and Eve in Jewish and Christian Imagination.* Louisville: Westminster John Knox, 2001.
——. *Sin. A History.* New Haven: Yale, 2009.
Angel, Joseph L. *Otherworldly and Eschatological Priesthood in the Dead Sea Scrolls.* STDJ 86; Leiden: Brill, 2010.
Arnold, Russell C.D. "Repentance and the Qumran Covenant Ceremony." Pages 159–75 in vol. 2 of *Seeking the Favor of God.* Edited by Mark J. Boda, Daniel K. Falk, and Rodney A. Werline. 3 vols.; SBLEJL 21–23; Atlanta: SBL/Leiden: Brill, 2006–2009.
——. *The Social Role of Liturgy in the Religion of the Qumran Community.* STDJ 60; Leiden: Brill, 2006.
Asad, Talal. *Genealogies of Religion. Discipline and Reasons of Power in Christianity and Islam.* Baltimore: Johns Hopkins, 1993.
Assmann, Jan. *Moses the Egyptian. The Memory of Egypt in Western Monotheism.* Cambridge, Mass.: Harvard, 1997.
Atkinson, Kenneth. *An Intertextual Study of the Psalms of Solomon Pseudepigrapha.* Lewiston, N.Y.: Mellen, 2001.

———. *I Cried to the Lord. A Study of the Psalms of Solomon's Historical Background and Social Setting.* JSJSup 84; Leiden: Brill, 2004.

———. "Representations of History in 4Q331 (4QPaphistorical Text C), 4Q332 (4QHistorical Text D), 4Q333 (4QHistorical Text E), and 4Q468E (4QHistorical Text F): An Annalistic Calendar Documenting Portentous Events?" *DSD* 12 (2007): 125–51.

Attridge, Harold W. *Hebrews. A Commentary on the Epistle to the Hebrews.* Hermeneia; Philadelphia: Fortress, 1989.

Attridge, Harold W., et al. *Qumran Cave 4. VIII. Parabiblical Texts. Part 1.* Oxford: Clarendon, 1994.

Avemarie, Friedrich. "'*Tohorath Ha-Rabbim*' and '*Mashqeh Ha-Rabbim.*' Jacob Licht Reconsidered." Pages 215–29 in *Legal Texts and Legal Issues.* Edited by M. Bernstein, F. García Martínez and J. Kampen. STDJ 23; Leiden: Brill, 1997.

Baigent, Michael, and Richard Leigh. *The Dead Sea Scrolls Deception.* London: Jonathan Cape, 1991.

Baillet, M. *Qumrân Grotte 4.III (4Q482–4Q520).* DJD 7; Oxford: Clarendon, 1982.

Baltzer, Klaus. *The Covenant Formulary.* Oxford: Blackwell, 1971.

Barr, James. *The Garden of Eden and the Hope of Immortality.* Minneapolis: Fortress, 1992.

Barrett, C. K. "The Background of Mark 10:45." Pages 1–18 in *New Testament Essays. Studies in Memory of Thomas Walter Manson.* Edited by A. J. B. Higgins. Manchester: Manchester University Press, 1959.

Barthélemy, D. "Le grand rouleau d'Isaïe trouvé près de la Mer Morte." *RB* 57 (1950): 530–49.

Barton, John. *Oracles of God. Perceptions of Prophecy in Ancient Israel after the Exile.* Revised ed.; Oxford: Oxford University Press, 1997.

Baumgarten, Albert I. "Josephus and Hippolytus on the Pharisees." *HUCA* 55 (1984): 1–25.

———. *The Flourishing of Jewish Sects in the Maccabean Era. An Interpretation.* JSJSup 55; Leiden: Brill, 1997.

———. "Seekers after Smooth Things." Pages 857–59 in vol. 2 of *The Encyclopedia of the Dead Sea Scrolls.* Edited by L. H. Schiffman and J. C. VanderKam. 2 vols.; New York: Oxford University Press, 2000.

———. "The Perception of the Past in the *Damascus Document.*" Pages 1–15 in *The Damascus Document. A Centennial of Discovery. Proceedings of the Third International Symposium of the Orion Center for the Study of the Dead Sea Scrolls and Associated Literature, 4–8 February, 1998.* Edited by J. M. Baumgarten, E. G. Chazon and A. Pinnick. STDJ 34; Leiden: Brill, 2000.

Baumgarten, Joseph M. "*Damascus Document.*" Pages 1–185 in *The Dead Sea Scrolls: Hebrew, Aramaic, and Greek Texts with English Translations, Vol. 3.* Edited by J. H. Charlesworth and H. W. M. Rietz. Louisville: Westminster/Tübingen: Mohr Siebeck, 2006.

Baumgarten, Joseph M., and Daniel R. Schwartz. "*Damascus Document.*" Pages 4–57 in *The Dead Sea Scrolls: Hebrew, Aramaic, and Greek Texts with English Translations, Vol. 2.* Edited by J. H. Charlesworth. Louisville: Westminster/Tübingen: Mohr Siebeck, 1995.

Beall, T. S. *Josephus' Description of the Essenes Illustrated by the Dead Sea Scrolls.* SNTSMS 58; Cambridge: Cambridge University Press, 1988.

Beckwith, Roger T. *The Old Testament Canon of the New Testament Church.* Grand Rapids: Eerdmans, 1985.

Bedenbender, Andreas. *Der Gott der Welt tritt auf den Sinai. Entstehung, Entwicklung und Funktionsweise der frühjüdischen Apokalyptik.* Berlin: Institut Kirche und Judentum, 2000.

———. "The Place of the Torah in the Early Enoch Literature." Pages 65–80 in *The Early*

Enoch Literature. Edited by Gabriele Boccaccini and John J. Collins. JSJSup 121; Leiden: Brill, 2007.
Bell, Catherine M. *Ritual Theory, Ritual Practice*. New York: Oxford University Press, 1992.
———. *Ritual. Perspectives and Dimensions*. New York: Oxford University Press, 1997.
———. "Ritual [Further Considerations]." Pages 7848–7856 in vol. 11 of *The Encyclopedia of Religion*. Edited by Lindsay Jones. 2nd ed.; Detroit: Macmillan, 2005.
Bengtsson, Håkan. *What's in a Name? A Study of Sobriquets in the Pesharim*. Uppsala: Uppsala University, 2000.
Bergmeier, Roland. *Die Essener-Berichte des Flavius Josephus. Quellenstudien zu den Essenertexten im Werk des jüdischen Historiographen*. Kampen: Kok Pharos, 1993.
———. "Die drei jüdischen Schulrichtungen nach Josephus und Hippolyt von Rom." *JSJ* 34 (2003): 443–70.
Bergsma, John S. "The Relationship between Jubilees and the Early Enochic Books." Pages 36–51 in *Enoch and the Mosaic Torah. The Evidence of Jubilees*. Edited by Gabriele Boccaccini and Giovanni Ibba. Grand Rapids: Eerdmans, 2009.
Bernstein, Moshe J. "Interpretation of Scriptures." Pages 376–83 in vol. 1 of *The Encyclopedia of the Dead Sea Scrolls*. Edited by L. H. Schiffman and J. C. VanderKam. 2 vols.; New York: Oxford University Press, 2000.
———. "'Rewritten Bible': A Generic Category Which Has Outlived Its Usefulness?" *Textus* 22 (2005): 169–96.
Berrin, Shani. *The Pesher Nahum Scroll from Qumran: An Exegetical Study of 4Q169*. STDJ 53; Leiden: Brill, 2004.
Berthelot, Katell, and Daniel Stökl Ben Ezra (eds.). *Aramaica Qumranica. Proceedings of the Conference on the Aramaic Texts from Qumran in Aix-en-Provence, 30 June – 2 July 2008*. STDJ 94; Leiden: Brill, 2010.
Beyer, K. *Die aramäischen Texte vom Toten Meer. Ergänzungsband*. Göttingen: Vandenhoeck & Ruprecht, 1994.
Bickerman, Elias J. *The God of the Maccabees. Studies on the Meaning and Origin of the Maccabean Revolt*. Leiden: Brill, 1979. Repr. pages 1025–1149 in vol. 2 of *Studies in Jewish and Christian History*. Leiden: Brill, 2011.
———. *Studies in Jewish and Christian History*. 3 vols.; Leiden: Brill, 2011.
Black, Matthew. "The Account of the Essenes in Hippolytus and Josephus." Pages 172–82 in *The Background of the New Testament and Its Eschatology*. Edited by W. D. Davies and D. Daube. Cambridge: Cambridge University Press, 1956.
———. *The Scrolls and Christian Origins*. New York: Scribners, 1961.
Blenkinsopp, Joseph. *Opening the Sealed Book. Interpretations of the Book of Isaiah in Late Antiquity*. Grand Rapids: Eerdmans, 2006.
Boccaccini, Gabriele. *Beyond the Essene Hypothesis. The Parting of the Ways between Qumran and Enochic Judaism*. Grand Rapids: Eerdmans, 1998.
———. "From a Movement of Dissent to a Distinct Form of Judaism: The Heavenly Tablets in *Jubilees* as the Foundation of a Competing Halakah." Pages 193–210 in *Enoch and the Mosaic Torah. The Evidence of Jubilees*. Edited by Gabriele Boccaccini and Giovanni Ibba. Grand Rapids: Eerdmans, 2009.
Boccaccini, Gabriele, and Giovanni Ibba (eds.). *Enoch and the Mosaic Torah. The Evidence of Jubilees*. Grand Rapids: Eerdmans, 2009.
Boda, Mark J., Daniel K. Falk, and Rodney A. Werline (eds.). *Seeking the Favor of God*. 3 vols.; SBLEJL 21–23; Atlanta: SBL/Leiden: Brill, 2006–2009.
Böttrich, Christoph. "Konturen des 'Menschensohnes in äthHen 37–71.'" Pages 53–90 in

Gottessohn und Menschensohn. Exegetische Paradigmen biblischer Intertextualität. Edited by Dieter Sänger. Neukirchen-Vluyn: Neukirchener Verlag, 2004.

Bourdieu, Pierre. *Outline of a Theory of Practice.* Cambridge: Cambridge University Press, 1977.

Bousset, Wilhelm. *Volksfrömmigkeit und Schriftgelehrtentum. Antwort auf Herrn Perles' Kritik meiner 'Religion des Judentums im N.T. Zeitalter.'* Berlin: Reuther und Reichard, 1903.

———. *Die Religion des Judentums im späthellenistischen Zeitalter.* 3rd ed.; Tübingen: Mohr, 1926.

Bremmer, Jan. *The Rise and Fall of the Afterlife.* London: Routledge, 2001.

Brooke, George J. *Exegesis at Qumran. 4QFlorilegium in Its Jewish Context.* JSOTSup 29; Sheffield: JSOT Press, 1985.

———. "Isaiah 40:3 and the Wilderness Community." Pages 117–32 in *New Qumran Texts and Studies.* Edited by G.J. Brooke and F. García Martínez. Leiden: Brill, 1994.

———. "The *Pesharim* and the Origin of the Dead Sea Scrolls." Pages 339–52 in *Methods of Investigation of the Dead Sea Scrolls and the Khirbet Qumran Site: Present Realities and Future Prospects.* Edited by M.O. Wise et al. Annals of the New York Academy of Sciences 722; New York: The New York Academy of Sciences, 1994.

———. "Miqdash Adam, Eden, and the Qumran Community." Pages 285–301 in *Gemeinde ohne Tempel = Community without Temple. Zur Substituierung und Transformation des Jerusalemer Tempels und seines Kults im Alten Testament, antiken Judentum und frühen Christentum.* Edited by Beate Ego, Armin Lange, and Peter Pilhofer with Kathrin Ehlers. Tübingen: Mohr Siebeck, 1999.

———. "*Florilegium*," "Rewritten Bible." Pages 297–98 in vol. 1 and 777–81 in vol. 2 of *The Encyclopedia of the Dead Sea Scrolls.* Edited by L.H. Schiffman and J.C. VanderKam. 2 vols.; New York: Oxford University Press, 2000.

———. "4Q158: Reworked Pentateuch^a or Reworked Pentateuch A?" *DSD* 8 (2001): 219–41.

———. "Biblical Interpretation in the Wisdom Texts from Qumran." Pages 201–20 in *The Wisdom Texts from Qumran and the Development of Sapiential Thought.* Edited by C. Hempel et al. Leuven: Peeters, 2002.

———. "The Rewritten Law, Prophets and Psalms: Issues for Understanding the Text of the Bible." Pages 31–40 in *The Bible as Book: The Hebrew Bible and the Judaean Desert Discoveries.* Edited by E.D. Herbert and Emanuel Tov. London: British Library, 2002.

———. "Shared Intertextual Interpretations in the Dead Sea Scrolls and the New Testament." Pages 35–57 in *Biblical Perspectives. Early Use and Interpretation of the Bible in Light of the Dead Sea Scrolls.* Edited by M.E. Stone and E.G. Chazon. STDJ 28; Leiden: Brill, 1998. Repr. pages 70–94 in Brooke, *The Dead Sea Scrolls and the New Testament.* Minneapolis: Fortress, 2005.

———. *The Dead Sea Scrolls and the New Testament.* Minneapolis: Fortress, 2005.

———. "The Formation and Renewal of Scriptural Tradition." Pages 39–59 in *Biblical Traditions in Transmission. Essays in Honour of Michael A. Knibb.* Edited by Charlotte Hempel and Judith M. Lieu. JSJSup 111; Leiden: Brill, 2006.

———. "The Structure of 1QH^A XII 5–XIII 4 and the Meaning of Resurrection." Pages 15–33 in *From 4QMMT to Resurrection. Mélanges qumraniens en homage à Émile Puech.* Edited by F. García Martínez, A. Steudel and E. Tigchelaar. STDJ 61, Leiden: Brill, 2006.

———. "Types of Historiography in the Dead Sea Scrolls." Pages 211–30 in *Ancient and Modern Scriptural Historiography. L'Historiographie Biblique, Ancienne et Moderne.* Edited by George J. Brooke and Thomas Römer. BETL 207; Leuven: Leuven University, 2007.

———. "Shared Exegetical Traditions between the Scrolls and the New Testament." Pages

565–91 in *The Oxford Handbook of the Dead Sea Scrolls*. Edited by T.H. Lim and J.J. Collins. Oxford: Oxford University Press, 2010.
Broshi, M., and A. Yardeni. "4Q List of False Prophets ar." Pages 77–79 in M. Broshi et al., *Qumran Cave 4. XIV. Parabiblical Texts Part 2*. DJD 19; Oxford: Clarendon, 1995.
———. "4Q List of Netinim." Pages 81–4 in M. Broshi et al., *Qumran Cave 4. XIV. Parabiblical Texts Part 2*. DJD 19; Oxford: Clarendon, 1995.
Broshi, M., and E. Eshel. "The Greek King is Antiochus IV (4Qhistorical Text – 4Q248)." *JJS* 48 (1997): 120–9.
Brown, Judith Ann. *John Marco Allegro. The Maverick of the Dead Sea Scrolls*. Grand Rapids: Eerdmans, 2005.
Brownlee, William H. "Biblical Interpretation among the Sectaries of the Dead Sea Scrolls." *BA* 14 (1951): 54–76.
———. "The Servant of the Lord in the Qumran Scrolls." *BASOR* 132 (December, 1953): 8–15.
———. "The Servant of the Lord in the Qumran Scrolls II." *BASOR* 135 (October, 1954): 33–38.
Bruce, Frederick F. *Biblical Exegesis in the Qumran Texts*. Grand Rapids: Eerdmans, 1959.
———. "The Book of Daniel and the Qumran Community." Pages 221–35 in *Neotestamentica et Semitica: Studies in Honour of Matthew Black*. Edited by E. Earle Ellis and M. Wilcox. Edinburgh: Clark, 1969.
Bruns, Gerald L. *Hermeneutics Ancient and Modern*. New Haven: Yale, 1992.
Bryce, G.E. *A Legacy of Wisdom. The Egyptian Contribution to the Wisdom of Israel*. Lewisburg, Pa.: Bucknell, 1979.
Burchard, Christoph. "Die Essener bei Hippolyt. Hippolyt, Ref. IX 18,2–28 und Josephus, Bell. 2,119–161." *JSJ* 8 (1977): 1–42.
Burrows, Millar. *The Dead Sea Scrolls*. New York: Viking, 1955.
———. *More Light on the Dead Sea Scrolls*. New York: Viking, 1958.
Byrskog, Samuel. *Jesus the Only Teacher. Didactic Authority and Transmission in Ancient Israel, Ancient Judaism and the Matthean Community*. Con Bib, NT series 24; Stockholm: Almqvist & Wiksell, 1994.
Callaway, Philip R. *The History of the Qumran Community. An Investigation*. Sheffield: JSOT Press, 1988.
Campbell, Jonathan G. *The Use of Scripture in the Damascus Document 1–8, 19–20*. Berlin: de Gruyter, 1995.
———. "'Rewritten Bible' and 'Parabiblical Texts': A Terminological and Ideological critique." Pages 43–68 in *New Directions in Qumran Studies: Proceedings of the Bristol Colloquium on the Dead Sea Scrolls, 8–10 September 2003*. Edited by J.G. Campbell, et al. London: T&T Clark, 2005.
Caquot, A. "Les textes de sagesse de Qoumrân (Aperçu préliminaire)." *RHPhR* 76 (1996): 1–34.
Carmignac, Jean. "Le retour du docteur de Justice à la fin des jours?" *RevQ* 1 (1958–59): 235–48.
———. "Les Citations de l'Ancien Testament, et spécialement des Poèmes du Serviteur." *RevQ* 3 (1960): 357–94.
Carr, David M. *Writing on the Tablets of the Heart*. New York: Oxford University Press, 2005.
Cavallin, H.C. "Leben nach dem Tode im Spätjudentum und im frühjudentum und im frühen Christentum, I – Spätjudentum." Pages 240–345 in *Aufstieg und Niedergang der Römischen Welt* II, 19/1. Edited by W. Haase and H. Temporini. Berlin: de Gruyter, 1979.

Chancey, Mark A. "Stone Vessels." Pages 1256–7 in *The Eerdmans Dictionary of Early Judaism*. Edited by J.J. Collins and D. Harlow. Grand Rapids: Eerdmans, 2010.

Charlesworth, James H. *The Pesharim and Qumran History. Chaos or Consensus?* Grand Rapids: Eerdmans, 2002.

Charlesworth, James H., and Andrew de la Ronde van Kirk. "Temple Scroll Source or Earlier Edition (4Q524[4QT^b])." Pages 247–65 in *Temple Scroll and Related Documents*. Edited by Lawrence H. Schiffman, Andrew D. Gross, and Michael C. Rand. The Dead Sea Scrolls. Hebrew, Aramaic, and Greek Texts with English Translations 7; Tübingen: Mohr Siebeck/Louisville: Westminster, 2011.

Chazon, Esther Glickler. "The Creation and Fall of Adam in the Dead Sea Scrolls." Pages 13–23 in *The Book of Genesis in Jewish and Oriental Christian Interpretation*. Edited by J. Frishman and L. van Rampay. Leuven: Peeters, 1997.

———. "Liturgical Communion with the Angels at Qumran." Pages 95–105 in *Sapiential, Liturgical and Poetical Texts from Qumran*. Edited by D.K. Falk, F. García Martínez and E.M. Schuller. Leiden: Brill, 2000.

———. "Human and Angelic Prayer in the Light of the Dead Sea Scrolls." Pages 35–48 in *Liturgical Perspectives. Prayer and Poetry in Light of the Dead Sea Scrolls*. Edited by E. Chazon. Leiden: Brill, 2003.

———. "The *Words of the Luminaries* and Penitential Prayer in Second Temple Times." Pages 177–86 in vol. 2 of *Seeking the Favor of God*. Edited by Mark J. Boda, Daniel K. Falk, and Rodney A. Werline. 3 vols.; SBLEJL 21–23; Atlanta: SBL/Leiden: Brill, 2006–2009.

Childs, B.S. *Introduction to the Old Testament as Scripture*. Philadelphia: Fortress, 1979.

Christiansen, Ellen Juhl. *The Covenant in Judaism and Paul. A Study of Ritual Boundaries as Identity Markers*. AGJU 27; Leiden: Brill, 1995.

———. "The Consciousness of Belonging to God's Covenant and What It Entails, according to the *Damascus Document* and the *Community Rule*." Pages 69–97 in *Qumran between the Old and New Testaments*. Edited by F.H. Cryer and T.L. Thompson. Sheffield: Sheffield Academic Press, 1998.

Clifford, Richard J. *Fair Spoken and Persuading. An Interpretation of Second Isaiah*. New York: Paulist, 1984.

Cohen, Shaye J.D. *Josephus in Galilee and Rome. His Vita and Development as a Historian*. Leiden: Brill, 1979.

———. "Hellenism in Unexpected Places." Pages 218–43 in *Hellenism in the Land of Israel*. Edited by John J. Collins and Gregory E. Sterling. Notre Dame, Ind.: Notre Dame University, 2001.

Cohen Stuart, G.H. *The Struggle in Man between Good and Evil. An Inquiry into the Origin of the Rabbinic Concept of Yeser HaRa^c*. Kampen: Kok, 1984.

Collins, Adela Yarbro. *Cosmology and Eschatology in Jewish and Christian Apocalypticism*. JSJSup 50; Leiden: Brill, 1996.

———. "The Signification of Mark 10:45 among Gentile Christians." *HTR* 90 (1997): 371–82.

———. *Mark*. Hermeneia; Minneapolis: Fortress, 2007.

Collins, Adela Yarbro, and John J. Collins. *King and Messiah as Son of God*. Grand Rapids: Eerdmans, 2008.

Collins, John J. *The Sibylline Oracles of Egyptian Judaism*. SBLDS 13; Missoula, Mont.: Scholars Press, 1974.

———. *The Apocalyptic Vision of the Book of Daniel*. HSM 16; Missoula: Scholars Press, 1977.

———. "Cosmos and Salvation: Jewish Wisdom and Apocalypticism in the Hellenistic Age." *History of Religions* 17 (1977): 121–42. Repr. pages 317–38 in *Seers, Sibyls and Sages in Hellenistic-Roman Judaism*. JSJSup 54; Leiden: Brill, 1977.

―――. "Was the Dead Sea Sect an Apocalyptic Movement?" Pages 25–51 in *Archaeology and History in the Dead Sea Scrolls*. Edited by L. H. Schiffman. JSPSup 8; Sheffield: Sheffield Academic Press, 1990.

―――. "Essenes." Pages 619–26 in vol. 2 of *Anchor Bible Dictionary*. Edited by D. N. Freedman. 6 vols.; New York: Doubleday, 1992.

―――. "The Son of Man in First Century Judaism." *New Testament Studies* 38 (1992): 448–66.

―――. *Daniel. A Commentary on the Book of Daniel*. Hermeneia; Minneapolis: Fortress, 1993.

―――. "The *Son of God* Text from Qumran." Pages 65–82 in *From Jesus to John. Essays on Jesus and New Testament Christology in Honour of Marinus de Jonge*. Edited by M. de Boer. JSNT 84; Sheffield: JSOT Press, 1993.

―――. "Teacher and Messiah? The One Who Will Teach Righteousness at the End of Days." Pages 193–210 in *The Community of the Renewed Covenant*. Edited by Eugene Ulrich and James VanderKam. Notre Dame, Ind.: University of Notre Dame, 1994.

―――. "The Works of the Messiah." *DSD* 1 (1994): 98–112.

―――. "242. 4Q*Prayer of Nabonidus* ar." Pages 83–93 in George Brooke et al., *Qumran Cave IV. XVII. Parabiblical Texts, Part 3*. DJD 22; Oxford: Clarendon, 1996.

―――. "Pseudo-Daniel Revisited." *RevQ* 17 (1996): 111–35.

―――. *Apocalypticism in the Dead Sea Scrolls*. London: Routledge, 1997.

―――. *Jewish Wisdom in the Hellenistic Age*. Louisville: Westminster, 1997.

―――. *Seers, Sibyls and Sages in Hellenistic-Roman Judaism*. JSJSup 54; Leiden: Brill, 1997.

―――. "The Background of the 'Son of God' Text." *Bulletin for Biblical Research* 7 (1997): 1–12.

―――. *The Apocalyptic Imagination*. Revised ed.; Grand Rapids: Eerdmans, 1998.

―――. "New Light on the Book of Daniel from the Dead Sea Scrolls." Pages 180–96 in *Perspectives in the Study of the Old Testament and Early Judaism*. Edited by F. García Martínez and E. Noort. VTSup 73; Leiden: Brill, 1998.

―――. "In the Likeness of the Holy Ones: The Creation of Humankind in a Wisdom Text from Qumran." Pages 595–618 in *The Provo International Conference on the Dead Sea Scrolls. Technological Innovations, New Texts, and Reformulated Issues*. Edited by D. W. Parry and E. C. Ulrich. STDJ 30; Leiden: Brill, 1999.

―――. "Pseudepigraphy and Group Formation in Second Temple Judaism." Pages 43–58 in *Pseudepigraphic Perspectives: The Apocrypha and Pseudepigrapha in Light of the Dead Sea Scrolls*. Edited by E. G. Chazon and M. E. Stone. STDJ 31; Leiden: Brill, 1999.

―――. *Between Athens and Jerusalem. Jewish Identity in the Hellenistic Diaspora*. 2nd ed.; Grand Rapids: Eerdmans, 2000.

―――. "The Afterlife in Apocalyptic Literature." Pages 119–39 in *Judaism in Late Antiquity. Part Four. Death, Life-After-Death, Resurrection and the World-to-Come in the Judaisms of Late Antiquity*. Edited by Alan J. Avery-Peck and Jacob Neusner. Handbuch der Orientalistik; First Series 49; Leiden: Brill, 2000.

―――. "The Construction of Israel in the Sectarian Rule Books." Pages 25–42 in *Judaism in Late Antiquity. Part 5, Volume 1; The Judaism of Qumran. A Systemic Reading of the Dead Sea Scrolls*. Edited by Alan J. Avery-Peck, Jacob Neusner and Bruce Chilton. Leiden: Brill, 2001.

―――. "Forms of Community in the Dead Sea Scrolls." Pages 97–111 in *Emanuel. Studies in Hebrew Bible, Septuagint and Dead Sea Scrolls in honor of Emanuel Tov*. Edited by S. M. Paul, R. A. Kraft, L. H. Schiffman, and W. W. Fields. VTSup 94; Leiden: Brill, 2003.

―――. "Before the Fall: The Earliest Interpretations of Adam and Eve." Pages 293–308 in *The*

———. *Idea of Biblical Interpretation. Essays in Honor of James L. Kugel.* Edited by H. Najman and J.H. Newman. JSJSup 83; Leiden: Brill, 2004.

———. *Introduction to the Hebrew Bible.* Minneapolis: Fortress, 2004.

———. *Jewish Cult and Hellenistic Culture.* JSJSup 100; Leiden: Brill, 2005.

———. *The Bible after Babel. Historical Criticism in a Postmodern Age.* Grand Rapids: Eerdmans, 2005.

———. "The Judaism of the Book of Tobit." Pages 23–40 in *The Book of Tobit. Text, Tradition, Theology.* Edited by Géza G. Xeravits and József Zsengellér. JSJSup 98; Leiden: Brill, 2005.

———. "A Messiah before Jesus?" Pages 15–35 in *Christian Beginnings and the Dead Sea Scrolls.* Edited by John J. Collins and Craig A. Evans. Grand Rapids: Baker, 2006.

———. "An Essene Messiah? Comments on Israel Knohl, *The Messiah before Jesus.*" Pages 37–44 in *Christian Beginnings and the Dead Sea Scrolls.* Edited by John J. Collins and Craig A. Evans. Grand Rapids: Baker, 2006.

———. "The *Yahad* and the Qumran Community." Pages 81–96 in *Biblical Traditions in Transmission. Essays in Honour of Michael A. Knibb.* Edited by C. Hempel and J.M. Lieu. Leiden: Brill, 2006.

———. "Beyond the Qumran Community: Social Organization in the Dead Sea Scrolls." *DSD* 16 (2009): 351–69.

———. "Josephus on the Essenes. The Sources of His Information." Pages 51–72 in *A Wandering Galilean. Essays in Honour of Sean Freyne.* Edited by Zuleika Rodgers et al. JSJSup 132; Leiden: Brill, 2009.

———. *Beyond the Qumran Community. The Sectarian Movement of the Dead Sea Scrolls.* Grand Rapids: Eerdmans, 2010.

———. "Prophecy and History in the *Pesharim*." Pages 209–26 in *Authoritative Scriptures in Ancient Judaism.* Edited by M. Popović. JSJSup 141; Leiden: Brill, 2010.

———. "Sectarian Communities in the Dead Sea Scrolls." Pages 151–72 in *The Oxford Handbook of the Dead Sea Scrolls.* Edited by T.H. Lim and J.J. Collins. Oxford: Oxford University Press, 2010.

———. *The Scepter and the Star. Messianism in Light of the Dead Sea Scrolls.* 2nd ed.; Grand Rapids: Eerdmans, 2010.

———. "Enochic Judaism. An Assessment." Pages 219–34 in *The Dead Sea Scrolls and Contemporary Culture. Proceedings of the International Conference held at the Israel Museum, Jerusalem (July 6–8, 2008).* Edited by Adolfo D. Roitman, Lawrence H. Schiffman and Shani Tzoref. STDJ 93; Leiden: Brill, 2011.

———. "Early Judaism in Modern Scholarship." Pages 1–29 in *Early Judaism. A Comprehensive Overview.* Edited by John J. Collins and Daniel C. Harlow. Grand Rapids: Eerdmans, 2012.

———. *The Dead Sea Scrolls. A Biography.* Princeton: Princeton University Press, 2012.

———. "The Interpretation of Genesis in the Dead Sea Scrolls." Pages 157–75 in *Pentateuchal Traditions in the Late Second Temple Period. Proceedings of the International Workshop in Tokyo (August 28–31, 2007).* Edited by Akio Moriya and Gohei Hata. JSJSup 158; Leiden: Brill, 2012.

Collins, John J., and P.W. Flint. "243–245. 4Qpseudo-Daniel[a–c]." Pages 95–164 in George Brooke et al., *Qumran Cave IV. XVII. Parabiblical Texts, Part 3.* DJD 22; Oxford: Clarendon, 1996.

Collins, John J., and D. Harlow (eds.). *The Eerdmans Dictionary of Early Judaism.* Grand Rapids: Eerdmans, 2010.

Collins, John J., G. E. Sterling, and R. A. Clements (eds.). *Sapiential Perspectives. Wisdom Literature in Light of the Dead Sea Scrolls*. STDJ 51; Leiden: Brill, 2004.
Collins, Matthew A. *The Use of Sobriquets in the Qumran Dead Sea Scrolls*. Library of Second Temple Studies 67; London: T&T Clark, 2009.
Cook, E. "4Q246." *Bulletin for Biblical Research* 5 (1995): 43–66.
Crawford, Sidnie White. *The Temple Scroll and Related Texts*. Sheffield: Sheffield Academic Press, 2000.
———. *Rewriting Scripture in Second Temple Times*. Grand Rapids: Eerdmans, 2008.
Cross, Frank Moore. *The Ancient Library of Qumran and Modern Biblical Studies*. Garden City, N.Y.: Doubleday, 1958. 3rd ed., Sheffield: Sheffield Academic Press, 1995.
———. *Canaanite Myth and Hebrew Epic. Essays in the History of the Religion of Israel*. Cambridge, Mass.: Harvard University Press, 1973.
———. "Fragments of the *Prayer of Nabonidus*." *IEJ* 34 (1984): 260–4.
Cullmann, Oscar. "Immortality of the Soul or Resurrection of the Body." Pages 9–53 in *Immortality and Resurrection*. Edited by Krister Stendhal. New York: Macmillan, 1965.
Davenport, Gene. "The 'Anointed of the Lord' in *Psalms of Solomon* 17." Pages 67–92 in *Ideal Figures in Ancient Judaism*. Edited by G. W. E. Nickelsburg and J. J. Collins. SBLSCS 12; Chico, Calif.: Scholars Press, 1980.
Davidson, Donald. *Inquiries into Truth and Interpretation*. Oxford: Clarendon, 1984.
Davidson, Maxwell J. *Angels at Qumran*. JSPSup 11; Sheffield; Sheffield Academic Press, 1992.
Davies, Philip R. "Hasidim in the Maccabean Period." *JJS* 28 (1977): 127–40.
———. *The Damascus Covenant. An Interpretation of the "Damascus Document."* JSOTSup 25; Sheffield: JSOT Press, 1983.
———. "History and Hagiography." Pages 87–106 in *Behind the Essenes: History and Ideology in the Dead Sea Scrolls*. BJS 94; Atlanta: Scholars Press, 1987.
———. "Three Essene Texts." Pages 107–34 in *Behind the Essenes. History and Ideology in the Dead Sea Scrolls*. BJS 94; Atlanta: Scholars Press, 1987.
———. "The Teacher of Righteousness at the End of Days." *RevQ* 13 (1988): 313–7.
———. "The Prehistory of the Qumran Community." Pages 116–25 in *The Dead Sea Scrolls. Forty Years of Research*. Edited by D. Dimant and U. Rappaport. Leiden: Brill, 1992.
———. "The Judaism(s) of the *Damascus Document*." Pages 27–43 in *The Damascus Document. A Centennial of Discovery*. Edited by J. M. Baumgarten, E. G. Chazon, and A. Pinnick. Leiden: Brill, 2000.
———. "Spurious Attribution in the Hebrew Bible." Pages 258–75 in *The Invention of Sacred Tradition*. Edited by James R. Lewis and Olav Hammer. Cambridge: Cambridge University Press, 2007.
———. "What History Can We Get from the Scrolls, and How." Pages 31–46 in *The Dead Sea Scrolls. Texts and Context*. Edited by C. Hempel. STDJ 90; Leiden: Brill, 2010.
Davila, James R. *Liturgical Works*. Eerdmans Commentaries on the Dead Sea Scrolls; Grand Rapids: Eerdmans, 2000.
Dawson, L. L. "Creating 'Cult' Typologies: Some Strategic Considerations." *Journal of Contemporary Religion* 12 (1997): 363–81.
Day, John. "The Canaanite Inheritance of the Israelite Monarchy." Pages 72–90 in *King and Messiah in Israel and the Ancient Near East*. Edited by J. Day. JSOTSup 270; Sheffield: Sheffield Academic Press, 1998.
Delcor, M. "Le milieu d'origine et le développement de l'apocalyptique juive." Pages 101–17 in *La Littérature Juive entre Tenach et Mischna*. Edited by W. C. van Unnik. Leiden: Brill, 1974.

DeMaris, Richard E. *The New Testament in Its Ritual World.* London: Routledge, 2008.

Dimant, Devorah. "Qumran Sectarian Literature." Pages 483–550 in *Jewish Writings of the Second Temple Period.* Edited by M.E. Stone. CRINT; Second Series 2; Philadelphia: Fortress, 1984.

———. "Men as Angels: The Self-Image of the Qumran Community." Pages 93–103 in *Religion and Politics in the Ancient Near East.* Edited by A. Berlin. Bethesda, Md.: University of Maryland, 1996.

———. *Qumran Cave 4, XXI, Parabiblical Texts, IV.* DJD 30; Oxford: Clarendon, 2001.

———. "Themes and Genres in the Aramaic Texts from Qumran." Pages 15–45 in *Aramaic Qumranica Proceedings of the Conference on the Aramaic Texts from Qumran in Aix-en-Provence, 30 June – 2 July 2008.* Edited by Katell Berthelot and Daniel Stökl Ben Ezra. STDJ 94; Leiden: Brill, 2010.

DiTommaso, L. "4Qpseudo-Daniel[a–b] (4Q243–4Q244) and the Book of Daniel." *DSD* 12 (2005): 101–33.

Doran, Robert. "The Non-dating of Jubilees. Jub 34–38; 23:14–32 in Narrative Context." *JSJ* 20 (1989): 1–11.

———. "The Persecution of Judeans by Antiochus Epiphanes. The Significance of 'Ancestral Laws.'" Page 423–33 in *The 'Other' in Second Temple Judaism.* Edited by Daniel C. Harlow, Karina Martin Hogan, Matthew Goff and Joel Kaminsky. Grand Rapids: Eerdmans, 2011.

Doudna, Gregory L. *4Q Pesher Nahum: A Critical Edition.* London: Sheffield Academic Press, 2001.

Douglas, Michael C. "*11QMelchizedek* and a Dying Eschatological Figure." Paper presented at the annual meeting of the Society of Biblical Literature, Washington, D.C., 1993.

———. "Power and Praise in the Hodayot: A Literary Critical Study of 1QH 9:1–18:14." Ph.D. diss., University of Chicago, 1998.

———. "The Teacher Hymn Hypothesis Revisited: New Data for an Old Crux." *DSD* 6 (1999): 239–66.

Dozeman, T.B., and K. Schmid. *A Farewell to the Yahwist? The Composition of the Pentateuch in Recent European Interpretation.* SBLSymS 34; Atlanta: Society of Biblical Literature, 2006.

Duggan, Michael. *Covenant Renewal in Ezra-Nehemiah (Neh 7:72b-10:40). An Exegetical, Literary, and Theological Study.* SBLDS 164; Atlanta: SBL, 2001.

Duhaime, Jean. "La Doctrine des Esséniens de Qumrân sur l'après-mort." Pages 99–121 in *Essais sur la Mort.* Edited by Guy Couturier et al. Montreal: Fides, 1985.

———. "Dualistic Reworking in the Scrolls from Qumran." *CBQ* 49 (1987): 32–56.

Duhm, Bernhard. *Das Buch Jesaja.* Göttingen: Vandenhoeck & Ruprecht, 1892.

Duncker, L., and F. Schneidewin. *S. Hippolyti . . . Refutationis Omnium Haeresium.* 10 vols.; Göttingen: Dieterich, 1859.

Dupont-Sommer, André. *The Dead Sea Scrolls: a Preliminary Survey.* Oxford: Blackwell, 1952. Translation of *Aperçus préliminaires sur les manuscrits de la mer morte.* Paris: Maisonneuve, 1950.

———. "Exorcismes et guérisons dans les écrits de Qoumrân." Pages 246–62 in *Oxford Congress Volume.* Edited by J.A. Emerton. VTSup 7; Leiden: Brill, 1960.

———. *The Essene Writings from Qumran.* Translated by G. Vermes. Gloucester, Mass.: Peter Smith, 1973.

Eisenman, R.H. *Maccabees, Zadokites, Christians and Qumran. A New Hypothesis of Qumran Origins.* Leiden: Brill, 1983.

———. *James the Brother of Jesus. The Key to Unlocking the Secrets of Early Christianity and the Dead Sea Scrolls*. New York: Viking, 1997.
Eisenman R. H., and M. O. Wise (eds.). *The Dead Sea Scrolls Uncovered. The First Complete Translation and Interpretation of 50 Key Documents Withheld for over 35 Years*. Rockport, Mass.: Element, 1992.
Elgvin, Torleif, "The Genesis Section of 4Q422 (4QparaGenExod)." *DSD* 1 (1994): 180–96.
———. "Early Essene Eschatology. Judgement and Salvation according to Sapiential Work A." Pages 126–65 in *Current Research and Technological Developments on the Dead Sea Scrolls*. Edited by D. L. Perry and S. D. Ricks. STDJ 20; Leiden: Brill, 1996.
———. "An Analysis of *4QInstruction*." Ph. D. diss. Hebrew University, 1997.
———. "The Mystery to Come: Early Essene Theology of Revelation." Pages 113–150 in *Qumran between the Old and the New Testament*. Edited by T. L. Thompson and N. P. Lemche. Sheffield: Sheffield Academic Press, 1998.
———. "423. 4QInstruction^g (*Musar l^e Mevin^g*)." Pages 505–533 in John Strugnell, Daniel Harrington and Torleif Elgvin, *Qumran Cave 4. XXIV. Sapiential Texts, Part 2*. DJD 34; Oxford: Clarendon, 1999.
———. "Wisdom and Apocalypticism in the Early Second Century BCE – The Evidence of *4QInstruction*." Pages 226–47 in *The Dead Sea Scrolls Fifty Years after Their Discovery*. Edited by L. H. Schiffman, E. Tov and J. C. VanderKam. Jerusalem: Israel Exploration Society in cooperation with the Shrine of the Book, Israel Museum, 2000.
———. "Priestly Sages? The Milieus of Origin of *4QMysteries* and *4QInstruction*." Pages 67–87 in *Sapiential Perspectives. Wisdom Literature in Light of the Dead Sea Scrolls. Proceedings of the Sixth International Symposium of the Orion Center, 20–22 May, 2001*. Edited by J. J. Collins, G. E. Sterling and Ruth A. Clements. STDJ 51; Leiden: Brill, 2004.
Elgvin, Torleif, and E. Tov, "422. 4QParaphrase of Genesis and Exodus." Pages 417–41 in H. W. Attridge et al., *Qumran Cave 4. VIII: Parabiblical Texts, Part I*. DJD 13; Oxford: Clarendon, 1994.
Eliade, Mircea. *The Myth of the Eternal Return or, Cosmos and History*. Translated by Willard R. Trask; Princeton: Princeton University Press, 1954.
Elior, R. *The Three Temples. On the Emergence of Jewish Mysticism*. Oxford/Portland, Oregon: Littmann, 2004.
Elliger, Karl. *Studien zum Habakkuk Kommentar vom Toten Meer*. Tübingen: Mohr, 1953.
Engberg-Pedersen, Troels. "Total Transformation in 1 Corinthians 15 – a Philosophical Reading of Paul on Body and Spirit." Pages 123–46 in *Metamorphoses. Resurrection, Body and Transformative Practices in Early Christianity*. Edited by Turid Karlsen Seim and Jorunn Økland. Ekstasis 1; Berlin: de Gruyter, 2009.
Eshel, E. "The Identification of the 'Speaker' of the Self-Glorification Hymn." Pages 619–35 in *The Provo International Conference on the Dead Sea Scrolls. Technological Innovations, New Texts, and Reformulated Issues*. Edited by D. W. Parry and E. Ulrich. STDJ 30; Leiden: Brill, 1999.
Eshel, Hanan. "4QMMT and the History of the Hasmonean Period." Pages 53–65 in *Reading 4QMMT. New Perspectives on Qumran Law and History*. Edited by J. Kampen and M. J. Bernstein. SBLSymS 2; Atlanta: Society of Biblical Literature, 1996.
———. *The Dead Sea Scrolls and the Hasmonean State*. Grand Rapids: Eerdmans, 2008.
Evans, Craig A. "Jesus, John and the Dead Sea Scrolls: Assessing Typologies of Restoration." Pages 45–62 in *Christian Beginnings and the Dead Sea Scrolls*. Edited by John J. Collins and Craig A. Evans. Grand Rapids: Baker, 2006.
Falk, Daniel K. *Daily, Sabbath, and Festival Prayers in the Dead Sea Scrolls*. STDJ 27; Leiden: Brill, 1998.

———. "Qumran Prayer Texts and the Temple." Pages 106–26 in *Sapiential, Liturgical and Poetical Texts from Qumran*. Edited by Daniel K. Falk, Florentino García Martínez, Eileen M. Schuller. STDJ 35; Leiden: Brill, 2000.

———. *The Parabiblical Texts. Strategies for Extending the Scriptures*. London and New York: Clark, 2007.

———. "The Contribution of the Qumran Scrolls to the Study of Ancient Jewish Liturgy." Pages 617–51 in *The Oxford Handbook of the Dead Sea Scrolls*. Edited by T. H. Lim and J. J. Collins. Oxford: Oxford University Press, 2010.

Fields, Weston W. *The Dead Sea Scrolls. A Full History*. Leiden: Brill, 2009.

Fishbane, Michael. *Biblical Interpretation in Ancient Israel*. Oxford: Clarendon, 1985.

———. "From Scribalism to Rabbinism." Pages 439–56 in *The Sage in Israel and the Ancient Near East*. Edited by John G. Gammie. Winona Lake, Ind.: Eisenbrauns, 1990.

Fitzmyer, Joseph A., S. J. *Essays on the Semitic Background of the New Testament*. London: Chapman, 1971.

———. *A Wandering Aramean. Collected Aramaic Essays*. Missoula, Mont.: Scholars Press, 1979.

———. "A Feature of Qumran Angelology and the Angels of 1 Cor 11:10." Pages 31–47 in *Paul and the Dead Sea Scrolls*. Edited by J. Murphy-O'Connor and J. H. Charlesworth. New York: Crossroad, 1990.

———. *Romans*. AB 33; New York: Doubleday, 1992.

———. *The Acts of the Apostles*. AB 31; New York: Doubleday, 1998.

———. "331. 4QpapHistorical Text C." Pages 275–80 in J. C. VanderKam and M. Brady, *Qumran Cave 4.XXVI: Cryptic Texts and Miscellanea, Part I*. DJD 36; Oxford: Clarendon, 2000.

———. *The Dead Sea Scrolls and Christian Origins*. Grand Rapids: Eerdmans, 2000.

———. *The One Who Is to Come*. Grand Rapids: Eerdmans, 2007.

Fitzpatrick McKinley, Anne. *The Transformation of Torah from Scribal Advice to Law*. JSOTSup 287; Sheffield: Sheffield Academic Press, 1999.

Fletcher-Louis, C. H. T. *All the Glory of Adam. Liturgical Anthropology in the Dead Sea Scrolls*. STDJ 42; Leiden: Brill, 2002.

Flint, P. W. "4Qpseudo-Daniel ar^c (4Q245) and the Restoration of the Priesthood." *RevQ* 17 (1996): 137–50.

———. "The Daniel Tradition at Qumran." Pages 329–67 in *The Book of Daniel. Composition and Reception*. Edited by J. J. Collins and P. W. Flint. VTSup 83.2; Leiden: Brill, 2001.

Flusser, D. *Judaism of the Second Temple Period. Vol. 1. Qumran and Apocalypticism*. Translated by Azzan Yadin. Grand Rapids: Eerdmans, 2007.

Fraade, Steven D. *Enosh and His Generation. Pre-Israelite Hero and History in Postbiblical Interpretation*. SBLMS 30; Chico, Calif.: Scholars Press, 1984.

———. "Interpretive Authority at Qumran." *JJS* 44 (1993): 46–69.

———. "Hagu, Book of." Page 327 in vol. 1 of *The Encyclopedia of the Dead Sea Scrolls*. Edited by L. H. Schiffman and J. C. VanderKam. 2 vols.; New York: Oxford University Press, 2000.

Freedman, H., and M. Simon. *Midrash Rabbah*. New York: Soncino, 1983.

Frei, Peter. "Persian Imperial Authorization: A Summary." Pages 5–40 in *Persia and Torah. The Theory of Imperial Authorization of the Pentateuch*. Edited by James W. Watts. SBLSymS 17; Atlanta: SBL, 2001.

Frei, Peter, and Klaus Koch. *Reichsidee und Reichsorganisation im Perserreich*. OBO 55; Fribourg: Universitätsverlag, 1984.

Frennesson, Bjorn. *"In a Common Rejoicing." Liturgical Communion with Angels in Qum-*

ran. Acta Universitatis Upsaliensis. Studia Semitica Upsaliensia 14; Uppsala: Uppsala University, 1999.

Frey, Jörg. "Different Patterns of Dualistic Thought in the Qumran Library." Pages 275–335 in *Legal Texts and Legal Issues.* Edited by Moshe Bernstein, Florentino García Martínez and John Kampen. Leiden: Brill, 1997.

———. "The Notion of 'Flesh' in *4QInstruction* and the Background of Pauline Usage." Pages 197–226 in *Sapiential, Liturgical and Poetical Texts from Qumran. Proceedings of the Third Meeting of the International Organization for Qumran Studies, Oslo 1998.* Edited by D. K. Falk, F. García Martínez, E. M. Schuller. Leiden: Brill, 2000.

———. "Flesh and Spirit in the Palestinian Jewish Sapiential Tradition and in the Qumran Texts: An Inquiry into the Background of Pauline Usage." Pages 367–404 in *The Wisdom Texts from Qumran and the Development of Sapiential Thought.* Edited by C. Hempel, A. Lange and H. Lichtenberger. BETL CLIX; Leuven: Peeters, 2002.

———. "Zur historischen Auswertung der antiken Essenerberichte. Ein Beitrag zum Gespräch mit Roland Bergmeier." Pages 23–55 in *Qumran kontrovers. Beiträge zu den Textfunden vom Toten Meer.* Edited by Jörg Frey and Hartmut Stegemann. Paderborn: Bonifatius, 2003.

———. "Critical Issues in the Investigation of the Scrolls and the New Testament." Pages 517–45 in *The Oxford Handbook of the Dead Sea Scrolls.* Edited by T. H. Lim and J. J. Collins. Oxford: Oxford University Press, 2010.

———. "Apocalyptic Dualism." Chapter 16 in *The Oxford Handbook of Apocalyptic Literature.* Edited by J. J. Collins. New York: Oxford University Press, 2014.

Frey, Jörg, Jens Herzer, Martina Janssen and Clare K. Rothschild. *Pseudepigraphie und Verfasserfiktion in frühchristlichen Briefen.* WUNT 246; Tübingen: Mohr Siebeck, 2009.

Fuks, Alexander. *The Ancestral Constitution. Four Studies in Athenian Party Politics at the End of the Fifth Century B. C.* London: Routledge and Kegan Paul, 1953.

Gager, John G. *Moses in Greco-Roman Paganism.* SBLMS 16; Nashville: Abingdon, 1972.

García Martínez, Florentino. "Qumran Origins and Early History: A Groningen Hypothesis." *Folia Orientalia* 25 (1988): 113–36.

———. *Qumran and Apocalyptic.* Leiden: Brill, 1992.

———. "The Heavenly Tablets in the Book of Jubilees." Pages 116–36 in *Studies in the Book of Jubilees.* Edited by M. Albani, J. Frey and A. Lange. Tübingen: Mohr Siebeck, 1997.

———. "Man and Woman: Halakhah Based upon Eden in the Dead Sea Scrolls." Pages 95–115 in *Paradise Interpreted.* Edited by G. P. Luttikhuizen. Leiden: Brill, 1999.

———. "Temple Scroll." Pages 926–33 in vol. 2 of *The Encyclopedia of the Dead Sea Scrolls.* Edited by L. H. Schiffman and J. C. VanderKam. 2 vols.; New York: Oxford University Press, 2000.

———. "Angel, Hombre, Mesías, Maestro de Justicia? El Problemático 'Yo' de un Poema Qumránico." Pages 103–31 in *Plenitudo Temporis. Miscelánea Homenaje al Prof. Dr. Ramón Trevijano Etcheverría.* Edited by J. J. Fernández Sangrador and S. Guijarro Oporto. Bibliotheca Salmanticensis, Estudios 249; Salamanca: Universidad Pontificia, 2002.

———. *Qumranica Minora I. Qumran Origins and Apocalypticism.* STDJ 63; Leiden: Brill, 2007.

———. *Qumranica Minora II. Thematic Studies on the Dead Sea Scrolls.* STDJ 64; Leiden: Brill, 2007.

———. (ed.). *Echoes from the Caves. Qumran and the New Testament.* STDJ 85; Leiden: Brill, 2009.

García Martínez, Florentino, and E. J. C. Tigchelaar. *The Dead Sea Scrolls Study Edition.* Leiden: Brill, 1998.

García Martínez, Florentino, and A. S. van der Woude. "A Groningen Hypothesis of Qumran Origins." *RevQ* 14 (1990): 521–41.
Gerstenberger, Erhard S. *Psalms. Part One, with an Introduction to Cultic Poetry.* FOTL XIV; Grand Rapids: Eerdmans, 1988.
Gillingham, S. E. "The Messiah in the Psalms." Pages 209–37 in *King and Messiah in Israel and the Ancient Near East.* Edited by John Day. JSOTSup 270; Sheffield: Sheffield Academic Press, 1998.
Goff, Matthew J. *The Worldly and Heavenly Wisdom of 4QInstruction.* STDJ 50; Leiden: Brill, 2003.
———. *Discerning Wisdom. The Sapiential Literature of the Dead Sea Scrolls.* VTSup 116; Leiden: Brill, 2007.
———. "Recent Trends in the Study of Early Jewish Wisdom Literature: The Contribution of *4QInstruction* and Other Qumran Texts." *Currents in Biblical Research* 7 (2009): 377–416.
Golb, Norman. *Who Wrote the Dead Scrolls? The Search for the Secret of Qumran.* New York: Scribner, 1995.
Goldman, Liora. "Dualism in the Visions of Amram." *RevQ* 95 (2010): 421–32.
Goodman, Martin. "Jewish Literature Composed in Greek." Pages 509–66 in vol. 3 part 1 of Emil Schürer, *The History of the Jewish People in the Age of Jesus Christ.* Edited by Geza Vermes, Fergus Millar, and Martin Goodman. 3 vols.; Edinburgh: Clark, 1986.
———. "Constructing Ancient Judaism from the Scrolls." Pages 81–91 in *The Oxford Handbook of the Dead Sea Scrolls.* Edited by T. H. Lim and J. J. Collins. Oxford: Oxford University Press, 2010.
Gorman, Frank H., Jr. "Ritual Studies and Biblical Studies: Assessment of the Past, Prospects for the Future." *Semeia* 67 (1994): 13–36.
Grabbe, Lester L. *Ezra-Nehemiah.* London: Routledge, 1998.
———. "Eschatology in Philo and Josephus." Pages 163–85 in *Judaism in Late Antiquity. Part Four. Death, Life-After-Death, Resurrection and the World-to-Come in the Judaisms of Late Antiquity.* Edited by Alan J. Avery-Peck and Jacob Neusner. Handbuch der Orientalistik; Series One 49; Leiden: Brill, 2000.
———. *A History of Jews and Judaism in the Second Temple Period. Vol. 1. Yehud. A History of the Persian Province of Judah.* New York and London: T&T Clark, 2004.
Greenberg, M. *Ezekiel 21–37.* AB 22A; New York: Doubleday, 1997.
Grelot, P. "L'eschatologie des Esséniens et le livre d'Hénoch." *RevQ* 1 (1958): 113–31.
———. "La Prière de Nabonide (4Q Or Nab). Nouvelle Essai de Restauration." *RevQ* 9 (1978): 483–95.
Griffiths, J. Gwyn. *Plutarch's De Iside et Osiride.* Cardiff: University of Wales, 1970.
Grimes, Ronald. *Beginnings in Ritual Studies.* Columbia, S. C.: University of South Carolina, 1995.
Grossman, Maxine L. *Reading for History in the Damascus Document. A Methodological Study.* STDJ 45; Leiden: Brill, 2002.
———. "Cultivating Identity: Textual Virtuosity and 'Insider' Status." Pages 1–11 in *Defining Identities. We, You, and the Other in the Dead Sea Scrolls.* Edited by Florentino García Martínez and Mladen Popović. STDJ 70; Leiden: Brill, 2008.
Gruen, Erich. *Heritage and Hellenism. The Reinvention of Jewish Tradition.* Cambridge, Mass.: Harvard, 1998.
Gzella, Holger. *Lebenszeit und Ewigkeit. Studien zur Eschatologie und Anthropologie des Septuaginta-Psalters.* BBB 134; Berlin: Philo, 2002.
Halbwachs, Maurice. *The Collective Memory.* New York: Harper Colophon, 1980.

—. *On Collective Memory*. Edited and translated by L. A. Coser; Chicago: University of Chicago, 1992.
Halpern, Baruch. *The First Historians: The Hebrew Bible and History*. San Francisco: Harper & Row, 1988.
Hamilton, Mark W. *The Body Royal. The Social Implications of Kingship in Ancient Israel*. Leiden: Brill, 2005.
Harrington, D. J. "The *Raz Nihyeh* in a Qumran Wisdom Text (1Q26, 4Q415–418, 4Q423)." *RevQ* 17 (1996): 549–53.
—. *Wisdom Texts from Qumran*. London: Routledge, 1996.
—. "Holy War Texts Among the Qumran Scrolls." Pages 175–83 in *Studies in the Hebrew Bible, Qumran, and the Septuagint presented to Eugene Ulrich*. Edited by P. W. Flint, E. Tov and J. C. VanderKam. VTSup 101; Leiden: Brill, 2006.
Hartenstein, Friedhelm. "'Der im Himmel thront, lacht' (Ps 2,4)." Pages 158–88 in *Gottessohn und Menschensohn. Exegetische Paradigmen biblischer Intertextualität*. Edited by Dieter Sänger. Neukirchen-Vluyn: Neukirchener Verlag, 2004.
Healey, John. "The Immortality of the King: Ugarit and the Psalms." *Or* 53 (1984): 245–54.
Heger, Paul. "Another Look at Dualism in Qumran Writings." Pages 39–101 in *Dualism in Qumran*. Edited by Geza G. Xeravits. Library of Second Temple Studies (JSPSup) 76; London and New York, 2010. Repr. pages 227–310 in idem, *Challenges to Conventional Opinions on Qumran and Enoch Issues*. STDJ 100; Leiden: Brill, 2012.
Hempel, Charlotte. *The Laws of the Damascus Document. Sources, Traditions and Redaction*. Leiden: Brill, 1998.
—. "Community Origins in the *Damascus Document* in the Light of Recent Scholarship." Pages 316–29 in *The Provo International Conference on the Dead Sea Scrolls. Technological Innovations, New Texts, and Reformulated Issues*. Edited by D. W. Parry and E. Ulrich. STDJ 30; Leiden: Brill, 1999.
—. "Community Structures in the Dead Sea Scrolls: Admission, Organization, Disciplinary Procedures." Pages 67–92 in vol. 2 of *The Dead Sea Scrolls after Fifty Years. A Comprehensive Assessment*. Edited by P. W. Flint and J. C. VanderKam. 2 vols.; Leiden: Brill, 1999.
—. *The Damascus Texts*. Sheffield: Sheffield Academic Press, 2000.
—. "The Qumran Sapiential Texts and the Rule Books." Pages 277–95 in *The Wisdom Texts from Qumran and the Development of Sapiential Thought*. Edited by C. Hempel, A. Lange and H. Lichtenberger. BETL CLIX; Leuven: Peeters, 2002.
—. "Interpretative Authority in the Community Rule Tradition." *DSD* 10 (2003): 59–80.
—. "The Context of 4QMMT and Comfortable Theories." Pages 275–92 in *The Dead Sea Scrolls: Texts and Context*. Edited by C. Hempel. STDJ 90; Leiden: Brill, 2010.
—. "The *Instruction on the Two Spirits* and the Literary History of the Rule of the Community." Pages 102–20 in *Dualism in Qumran*. Edited by Geza G. Xeravits. LSTS (JSPSup) 76; New York/London: T. & T. Clark, 2010.
Hengel, Martin. *Judaism and Hellenism*. Philadelphia: Fortress, 1974.
—. "The Effective History of Isaiah 53 in the Pre-Christian Period." Pages 75–146 in *The Suffering Servant. Isaiah 53 in Jewish and Christian Sources*. Edited by Bernd Janowski and Peter Stuhlmacher. Grand Rapids: Eerdmans, 2004.
Henten, J. W. van. "The Hasmonean Period." Pages 15–28 in *Redemption and Resistance.The Messianic Hopes of Jews and Christians in Antiquity*. Edited by M. Bockmuehl and J. C. Paget. New York/London: T. & T. Clark, 2007.
Henze, Matthias (ed.). *Hazon Gabriel. New Readings of the Gabriel Revelation*. Atlanta: SBL, 2011.

Hilgenfeld, Adolf. *Die jüdische Apokalyptik in ihrer geschichtlichen Entwicklung.* Jena: Mauke, 1857.

Himmelfarb, Martha. *Ascent to Heaven in Jewish and Christian Apocalypses.* New York: Oxford University Press, 1993.

———. "Torah, Testimony, and Heavenly Tablets: The Claim to Authority in the *Book of Jubilees.*" Pages 22–8 in *A Multiform Heritage. Studies on Early Judaism and Christianity in Honor of Robert A. Kraft.* Edited by Benjamin G. Wright. Atlanta: Scholars Press, 1999.

———. *A Kingdom of Priests. Ancestry and Merit in Ancient Judaism.* Philadelphia: University of Pennsylvania, 2006.

Hirschfeld, Y. "Early Roman Manor Houses in Judea and the Site of Khirbet Qumran." *JNES* 57 (1998): 161–89.

———. "The Architectural Context of Qumran." Pages 673–83 in *The Dead Sea Scrolls Fifty Years after Their Discovery.* Edited by L. H. Schiffman, E. Tov, and J. C. VanderKam. Jerusalem: Israel Exploration Society in cooperation with The Shrine of the Book, Israel Museum, 2000.

Hobsbawm, Eric. "Introduction: Inventing Traditions." Pages 1–14 in *The Invention of Tradition.* Edited by Eric Hobsbawm and Terence Ranger. Cambridge: Cambridge University Press, 1983.

Hogeterp, A. L. A. "Daniel and the Qumran Daniel Cycle: Observations on 4QFour Kingdoms^{a-b} (4Q552–553)." Pages 173–91 in *Authoritative Scriptures in Ancient Judaism.* Edited by M. Popović. JSJSup 141; Leiden: Brill, 2010.

Holladay, Carl R. *Fragments from Hellenistic Jewish Authors, Volume 1. Historians.* Chico, Calif.: Scholars Press, 1983.

Holladay, William L. *Jeremiah 1.* Hermeneia; Philadelphia: Fortress, 1986.

Holm-Nielsen, Svend. *Hodayot. Psalms from Qumran.* Acta Theologica Danica 2; Aarhus: Universitetsvorlaget, 1960.

Hooker, Morna D. *Jesus and the Servant. The Influence of the Servant Concept of Deutero-Isaiah in the New Testament.* London: SPCK, 1959.

———. "Did the Use of Isaiah 53 to Interpret His Mission Begin with Jesus?" Pages 88–103 in *Jesus and the Suffering Servant.* Edited by William H. Bellinger and William R. Farmer. Harrisburg, PA: Trinity Press International, 1998.

Horgan, Maurya P. "Nahum *Pesher.*" Pages 1–247 in *The Dead Sea Scrolls: Hebrew, Aramaic, and Greek Texts with English Translations, 6B. Pesharim, Other Commentaries and Related Documents.* Edited by J. H. Charlesworth et al. Louisville: Westminster/Tübingen: Mohr Siebeck, 2002.

Hultgård, Anders. "Persian Apocalypticism." Pages 39–83 in *The Encyclopedia of Apocalypticism. Vol. 1. The Origins of Apocalypticism in Judaism and Christianity.* Edited by J. J. Collins. New York: Continuum, 1998.

Hultgren, Stephen. *From the Damascus Covenant to the Covenant of the Community. Literary, Historical, and Theological Studies in the Dead Sea Scrolls.* STDJ 66; Leiden: Brill, 2007.

Jackson, B. S. *Studies in the Semiotics of Biblical Law.* JSOTSup 314; Sheffield: Sheffield Academic Press, 2000.

Jaffee, Martin. *Torah in the Mouth. Writing and Oral Tradition in Palestinian Judaism, 200 BCE – 400 CE.* New York: Oxford University Press, 1991.

Jeremias, Gert. *Der Lehrer der Gerechtigkeit.* SUNT 2; Göttingen: Vandenhoeck & Ruprecht, 1963.

Jeremias, J. "*Pais Theou.*" Pages 654–717 in vol. 5 of *Theological Dictionary of the New*

Testament. Edited by G. Kittel and G. Friedrich. Translated by G. W. Bromiley. 10 vols.; Grand Rapids: Eerdmans, 1967.

Jokiranta, Jutta. "'Sectarianism' of the Qumran 'Sect': Sociological Notes." *RevQ* 20 (2001): 223–40.

———. "Pesharim: A Mirror of Self-Understanding." Pages 23–34 in *Reading the Present in the Qumran Library. The Perception of the Contemporary by Means of Scriptural Interpretations.* Edited by Kristin de Troyer and Armin Lange. SBLSymS 30; Atlanta: Society of Biblical Literature, 2005.

———. "Social Identity Approach: Identity-Constructing Elements in the Psalms Pesher." Pages 85–109 in *Defining Identities: We, You, and the Other in the Dead Sea Scrolls.* Edited by Florentino García Martínez and Mladen Popović. STDJ 70; Leiden: Brill, 2008.

Jong, Albert de. *Traditions of the Magi. Zoroastrianism in Greek and Latin Literature.* Leiden: Brill, 1997.

———. "Iranian Connections in the Dead Sea Scrolls." Pages 479–500 in *The Oxford Handbook of the Dead Sea Scrolls.* Edited by T. H. Lim and J. J. Collins. Oxford: Oxford University Press, 2010.

Jonnes, L. *The Inscriptions of the Sultan Dagi, I.* Inschriften griechischer Städter aus Kleinasien 62; Bonn: Habelt, 2002.

Kampen, J. *The Hasideans and the Origin of Pharisaism.* SCS 24; Atlanta: Scholars Press, 1988.

———. "Hasidim." Pages 66–67 in vol. 3 of *Anchor Bible Dictionary.* Edited by D. N. Freedman. 6 vols.; New York: Doubleday, 1992.

Kapferer, Bruce. "Ritual Dynamics and Virtual Practice: Beyond Representation and Meaning." Pages 35–54 in *Ritual in Its Own Right. Exploring the Dimensions of Transformation.* Edited by D. Handelman and Galina Lindquist. New York: Berghahn, 2005.

Kartveit, Magnar. *The Origin of the Samaritans.* VTSup 128; Leiden: Brill, 2009.

Kellens, Jean, and Eric Pirart. "La strophe des jumeaux: stagnation, extravagance et autres methods d'approche." *JA* 285 (1997): 31–72.

Kim, Dong-Hyuk. "Free Orthography in a Strict Society: Reconsidering Tov's 'Qumran Orthography'." *DSD* 11 (2004): 72–81.

Kister, Menahem. "Concerning the History of the Essenes: A Study of the *Animal Apocalypse*, the *Book of Jubilees*, and the Damascus Covenant." *Tarbiz* 56 (1986): 1–18 [Heb].

Klawans, Jonathan. *Impurity and Sin in Ancient Judaism.* New York: Oxford University Press, 2000.

———. "Purity in the Dead Sea Scrolls." Pages 377–402 in *The Oxford Handbook of the Dead Sea Scrolls.* Edited by T. H. Lim and J. J. Collins. Oxford: Oxford University Press, 2010.

———. *Josephus and the Theologies of Ancient Judaism.* New York: Oxford University Press, 2012.

Klinghardt, M. "The Manual of Discipline in the Light of Statutes of Hellenistic Associations." Pages 251–70 in *Methods of Investigation of the Dead Sea Scrolls and the Khirbet Qumran Site. Present Realities and Future Prospects.* Edited by M. O. Wise et al. Annals of the New York Academy of Sciences 722; New York: The New York Academy of Sciences, 1994.

Klinzing, Georg. *Die Umdeutung des Kultus in der Qumrangemeinde und im Neuen Testament.* SUNT 7; Göttingen: Vandenhoeck & Ruprecht, 1971.

Knibb, Michael A., and R. J. Coggins. *The First and Second Books of Esdras.* Cambridge Bible Commentary; Cambridge: Cambridge University, 1979.

———. "The Teacher of Righteousness – A Messianic Title?" Pages 51–65 in *A Tribute to Geza*

Vermes. *Essays on Jewish and Christian Literature and History.* Edited by P. R. Davies and R. T. White. JSOTSup 100; Sheffield: Sheffield Academic Press, 1990.

———. "The Structure and Composition of the Book of Parables." Pages 48–64 in *Enoch and the Messiah Son of Man*. Edited by Gabriele Boccaccini. Grand Rapids: Eerdmans, 2007.

Knohl, Israel M. *The Messiah before Jesus. The Suffering Servant of the Dead Sea Scrolls.* Berkeley, Calif.: University of California Press, 2000.

Kobelski, Paul J. *Melchizedek and Melchireshaʻ.* CBQMS 10; Washington, D.C.: Catholic Biblical Association, 1981.

Koch, Klaus. "Is Daniel Also among the Prophets?" *Interpretation* 39 (1985): 117–30.

———. "Gottes Herrschaft über das Reich des Menschen. Daniel 4 im Licht neuer Funde." Pages 77–119 in *The Book of Daniel in the Light of New Findings*. Edited by A. S. van der Woude. BETL 106; Leuven: Leuven University Press, 1993.

———. "Der König als Sohn Gottes in Ägypten und Israel." Pages 1–32 in *'Mein Sohn bist du,' (Ps 2,7). Studien zu den Königspsalmen*. Edited by E. Otto and E. Zenger. Stuttgarter Bibelstudien 192; Stuttgart: Verlag Katholisches Bibelwerk, 2002.

Kraus, Hans-Joachim. *Psalms 1–59. A Continental Commentary.* Minneapolis: Fortress, 1993. Translation of *Psalmen 1. Teilband, Psalmen 1–59.* 5th ed.; BK; Neukirchen-Vluyn: Neukirchener Verlag, 1978.

Kugel, James L. *The Bible as It Was.* Cambridge, Mass.: Harvard, 1997.

———. *The Traditions of the Bible.* Cambridge, Mass.: Harvard, 1998.

———. "On the Interpolations in the Book of Jubilees." *RevQ* 24 (2009): 215–72.

———. *A Walk through Jubilees. Studies in the Book of Jubilees and the World of Its Creation.* JSJSup 156; Leiden: Brill, 2012.

Kugler, Rob. "Making All Experience Religious: The Hegemony of Ritual at Qumran," *JSJ* 33 (2002): 131–52.

Kuhn, H. W. *Enderwartung und gegenwärtiges Heil.* SUNT 4; Göttingen: Vandenhoeck & Ruprecht, 1966.

Kuhn, K. G. "Die Sektenschrift und die iranische Religion." *ZTK* 49 (1952): 296–316.

Kvanvig, H. S. "The Son of Man in the Parables." Pages 179–215 in *Enoch and the Messiah Son of Man*. Edited by Gabriele Boccaccini. Grand Rapids: Eerdmans, 2007.

Laato, Antti, and Jacques van Ruiten (eds.). *Rewritten Bible Reconsidered.* Winona Lake, Ind.: Eisenbrauns, 2008.

Lambert, David. "Was the Dead Sea Sect a Penitential Movement?" Pages 501–31 in *The Oxford Handbook of the Dead Sea Scrolls*. Edited by T. H. Lim and J. J. Collins. Oxford: Oxford University Press, 2010.

Lane, W. R. "A New Commentary Structure in 4Q*Florilegium*." *JBL* 78 (1959): 343–6.

Lange, Armin. *Weisheit und Prädestination. Weisheitliche Urordnung und Prädestination in den Textfunden von Qumran.* STDJ 18; Leiden: Brill, 1995.

———. "Wisdom and Predestination in the Dead Sea Scrolls." *DSD* 2 (1995): 340–54.

———. "In Diskussion mit dem Tempel. Zur Auseinandersetzung zwischen Kohelet und weisheitlichen Kreisen am Jerusalemer Tempel." Pages 113–59 in *Qohelet in the Context of Wisdom*. Edited by A. Schoors. BETL 136; Leuven: Leuven University Press, 1998.

———. "Die Weisheitstexte aus Qumran: Eine Einleitung." Pages 3–30 in *The Wisdom Texts from Qumran and the Development of Sapiential Thought*. Edited by C. Hempel, A. Lange, and H. Lichtenberger. BETL 159; Leuven: Peeters, 2002.

———. "2 Maccabees 2:13–15: Library or Canon?" Pages 156–64 in *The Books of the Maccabees. History, Theology, Ideology*. Edited by Géza G. Xeravits and József Zsengellér. JSJSup 118; Leiden: Brill, 2007.

———. "'Nobody dared to add to them, to take from them, or to make changes' (Josephus,

*Ag.Ap.*1.42. The Textual Standardization of Jewish Scriptures in Light of the Dead Sea Scrolls." Pages 105–26 in *Flores Florentino. Dead Sea Scrolls and Other Early Jewish Studies in Honour of Florentino García Martínez.* Edited by Anthony Hilhorst, Émile Puech and Eibert Tigchelaar. JSJSup 122; Leiden: Brill, 2007.

———. "Sages and Scribes in Qumran Literature." Pages 271–93 in *Scribes, Sages and Seers. The Sage in the Eastern Mediterranean World.* Edited by L.G. Perdue. FRLANT 219; Göttingen: Vandenhoeck & Ruprecht, 2008.

———. *Handbuch der Textfunde vom Toten Meer. Bd. 1: Die Handschriften biblischer Bücher von Qumran und den anderen Fundorten.* Tübingen: Mohr Siebeck, 2009.

Lange, Armin, with U. Mittmann-Richert. "Annotated List of the Texts from the Judaean Desert Classified by Content and Genre." Pages 114–64 in Emanuel Tov et al., *The Texts from the Judaean Desert. Indices and an Introduction to the Discoveries in the Judaean Desert Series.* DJD 39; Oxford: Clarendon, 2002.

Lawrence, Jonathan. *Washing in Water. Trajectories of Ritual Bathing in the Hebrew Bible and Second Temple Literature.* Academia Biblica 23; Atlanta: Society of Biblical Literature, 2006.

Leach, Edmund. *Culture and Communication. The Logic by Which Symbols Are Connected.* Cambridge: Cambridge University Press, 1976.

Leaney, A.R.C. *The Rule of Qumran and Its Meaning.* London: SCM/Philadelphia: Westminster, 1966.

Lee, Kyong-Jin. *The Authority and Authorization of Torah in the Persian Period.* Leuven: Peeters, 2011.

LeFebvre, Michael. *Collections, Codes, and Torah. The Re-Characterization of Israel's Written Law.* New York/London: T&T Clark, 2006.

Leonhardt-Baltzer, Jutta. "Evil, Dualism and Community: Who/What Did the Yahad Not Want to Be." Pages 121–47 in *Dualism in Qumran.* Edited by Geza G. Xeravits. Library of Second Temple Studies (JSPSup) 76; New York/London, 2010.

Levenson, Jon D. *Sinai and Zion. An Entry into the Jewish Bible.* San Francisco: Harper, 1987.

Levine, Baruch A. "The Temple Scroll: Aspects of Its Historical Provenance and Literary Character." *BASOR* 232 (1978): 5–23.

Levinson, Bernard M. *Deuteronomy and the Hermeneutics of Legal Innovation.* New York: Oxford University Press, 1997.

———. *A More Perfect Torah. At the Intersection of Philology and Hermeneutics in Deuteronomy and the Temple Scroll.* Winona Lake, Ind.: Eisenbrauns, 2013.

Levison, J.R. "Is Eve to Blame? A Contextual Analysis of Sirach 25:24." *CBQ* 47 (1985): 617–23.

Licht, Jacob. *The Rule Scroll. A Scroll from the Wilderness of Judaea. 1QS, 1QSa, 1QSb. Text, Introduction and Commentary.* [Heb.] Jerusalem: Bialik, 1965.

Lichtenberger, Hermann. "Auferstehen in den Qumranfunden." Pages 79–91 in *Auferstehung/Resurrection.* Edited by Friedrich Avemarie and Hermann Lichtenberger. WUNT 135; Tübingen: Mohr Siebeck, 2001.

Lichtheim, Miriam. *Ancient Egyptian Literature. Volume III. The Late Period.* Berkeley, Calif.: University of California, 1980.

Lieberman, Saul. "Discipline in the So-Called Dead Sea Manual of Discipline." *JBL* 71 (1952): 199–206.

Lied, Liv Ingeborg. "Recognizing the Righteous Remnant? Resurrection, Recognition, and Eschatological Reversals in 2 Baruch 49–51." Pages 311–35 in *Metamorphoses. Resurrec-*

tion, Body and Transformative Practices in Early Christianity. Edited by Turid Karlsen Seim and Jorunn Økland. Ekstasis 1; Berlin: de Gruyter, 2009.

Lim, Timothy H. "The Wicked Priests of the Groningen Hypothesis." *JBL* 112 (1993): 415–25.

———. "303. Meditation on Creation A." Pages 151–3 in T. Elgvin et al., *Qumran Cave 4. XV. Sapiential Texts, Part 1.* DJD 20; Oxford: Clarendon, 1997.

———. "Wicked Priest." Pages 973–76 in vol. 2 of *The Encyclopedia of the Dead Sea Scrolls*. Edited by L.H. Schiffman and J.C. VanderKam. 2 vols.; New York: Oxford University Press, 2000.

———. *Pesharim*. London: Continuum, 2002.

———. "Authoritative Scriptures in the Dead Sea Scrolls." Pages 303–22 in *The Oxford Handbook of the Dead Sea Scrolls*. Edited by T.H. Lim and J.J. Collins. Oxford: Oxford University Press, 2010.

———. *The Formation of the Jewish Canon*. Anchor Yale Bible Reference Library; New Haven: Yale, 2013.

Lim, Timothy H., and J.J. Collins (eds.). *The Oxford Handbook of the Dead Sea Scrolls*. Oxford: Oxford University Press, 2010.

Long, A.A., and D.N. Sedley. *The Hellenistic Philosophers*. Cambridge: Cambridge University Press, 1987.

Lundhaug, Hugo. "'These are the Symbols and Likenesses of the Resurrection': Conceptualizations of Death and Transformation in the *Treatise on the Resurrection* (NHC 1.4)." Pages 187–205 in *Metamorphoses. Resurrection, Body and Transformative Practices in Early Christianity*. Edited by Turid Karlsen Seim and Jorunn Økland. Ekstasis 1; Berlin: de Gruyter, 2009.

Ma, John. *Antiochus III and the Cities of Western Asia Minor*. Oxford: Oxford University Press, 2000.

Mach, Michael. *Entwicklungsstudien des jüdischen Engelglaubens in vorrabbinischer Zeit*. TSAJ 34; Tübingen: Mohr Siebeck, 1992.

Magness, Jodi. *The Archaeology of Qumran and the Dead Sea Scrolls*. Grand Rapids: Eerdmans, 2002.

Maiberger, Paul. "Das Verständnis von Psalm 2 in der Septuaginta, im Targum, in Qumran, im frühen Judentum und im Neuen Testament." Pages 85–151 in *Beiträge zur Psalmenforschung. Psalm 2 und 22*. Edited by Josef Schreiner. Forschung zur Bibel; Würzburg: Echter, 1988.

Maier, Christl. *Jeremia als Lehrer der Tora. Soziale Gebote des Deuteronomiums in Fortschreibungen des Jeremiabuches*. Göttingen: Vandenhoeck & Ruprecht, 2002.

Maier, J. "Early Jewish Biblical Interpretation in the Qumran Literature." Pages 108–29 in *Hebrew Bible/Old Testament. The History of Its Interpretation, vol. 1. From the Beginnings to the Middle Ages (until 1300)*. Edited by M. Saebø. Göttingen: Vandenhoeck & Ruprecht, 1996.

Martin, Dale B. *The Corinthian Body*. New Haven: Yale, 1995.

Mason, Steve. "What Josephus Says about the Essenes in His *Judean War*." Pages 434–67 in *Text and Artifact in the Religions of Mediterranean Antiquity. Essays in Honour of Peter Richardson*. Edited by Stephen G. Wilson and Michel Desjardins. Waterloo: Wilfrid Laurier University Press, 2000.

———. "Essenes and Lurking Spartans in Josephus' Judean War: From Story to History." Pages 219–61 in *Making History. Josephus and Historical Method*. Edited by Zuleika Rodgers. JSJSup 110; Leiden: Brill, 2007.

———. "What Josephus says about the Essenes in his Judean War." Online: http://orion.mscc.huji.ac.il/orion/programs/Mason00-1.shtml

Mauss, M. *Sociology and Psychology. Essays.* Edited and translated by B. Brewster. London: Routledge and Kegan Paul, 1979.

Mayer, Rudolf. *Die biblische Vorstellung vom Weltbrand.* Bonner Orientalische Studien, N.S. 4; Bonn: Selbstverlag des orientalischen Seminars, 1956.

McCane, Byron. "Miqva'ot." Pages 954–6 in *The Eerdmans Dictionary of Early Judaism.* Edited by J.J. Collins and D. Harlow. Grand Rapids: Eerdmans, 2010.

McCann, J. Clinton. "Books I-III and the Editorial Purpose of the Hebrew Psalter." Pages 93–107 in *The Shape and Shaping of the Psalter.* Edited by J.C. McCann. JSOTSup 159; Sheffield: JSOT Press, 1993.

McConville, J.G. *Deuteronomy.* Leicester: Apollos, 2002.

McKane, W. *Proverbs: A New Approach.* Philadelphia: Westminster, 1970.

Mendels, Doron. *The Land of Israel as a Political Concept in Hasmonean Literature.* Tübingen: Mohr Siebeck, 1987.

Mertens, A. *Das Buch Daniel im Lichte der Texte vom Toten Meer.* Würzburg: Echter, 1971.

Metso, Sarianna. *The Textual Development of the Qumran Community Rule.* STDJ 21; Leiden: Brill, 1997.

———. "In Search of the *Sitz im Leben* of the *Community Rule.*" Pages 306–15 in *The Provo International Conference on the Dead Sea Scrolls. Technological Innovations, New Texts, and Reformulated Issues.* Edited by D.W. Parry and E. Ulrich. STDJ 30; Leiden: Brill, 1999.

———. "The Relationship between the *Damascus Document* and the *Community Rule.*" Pages 85–93 in *The Damascus Document. A Centennial of Discovery.* Edited by J.M. Baumgarten, E.G. Chazon and A. Pinnick. Leiden: Brill, 2000.

Metzger, Bruce M. "Literary Forgeries and Canonical Pseudepigrapha." *JBL* 91 (1972): 3–24.

Meyer, R. *Das Gebet des Nabonid. Eine in den Qumran-Handschriften wiederentdeckte Weisheitserzählung.* Berlin: Akademie Verlag, 1962.

Meyers, Carol. *Discovering Eve. Ancient Israelite Women in Context.* New York: Oxford University Press, 1988.

Meyers, Eric M., and Mark A. Chancey. *Archaeology of the Land of the Bible. From Cyrus to Constantine.* YABRL; New Haven: Yale, 2013.

Milik, J.T. "'Prière de Nabonide' et autres écrits d'un cycle de Daniel." *RB* 63 (1956): 407–15.

———. *Ten Years of Discovery in the Wilderness of Judaea.* London: SCM, 1959.

———. *The Books of Enoch. Aramaic Fragments from Qumran Cave 4.* Oxford: Clarendon, 1976.

———. "Daniel et Susanne à Qumrân?" Pages 337–59 in *De la Tôrah au Messie.* Edited by J. Doré et al. Paris: Desclée, 1981.

Miller, E. *Origenis Philosophumena.* Oxford: Oxford University Press, 1851.

Mittag, Peter Franz. *Antiochos IV. Epiphanes. Eine politische Biographie.* Klio NF 11; Berlin: Akademie Verlag, 2006.

Moore, George Foot. "Christian Writers on Judaism." *HTR* 14 (1921): 197–254.

———. *Judaism in the First Centuries of the Christian Era.* New York: Schocken, 1975.

Müller, H.P. "Mantische Weisheit und Apokalyptik." Pages 268–93 in *Congress Volume Uppsala 1971.* VTSupp 22; Leiden: Brill, 1972.

Murphy, C.M. *Wealth in the Dead Sea Scrolls and in the Qumran Community.* STDJ 40; Leiden: Brill, 2002.

Murphy-O'Connor, Jerome. "La genèse littéraire de la Règle de la Communauté." *RB* 76 (1969): 528–49.

———. "The Essenes and Their History." *RB* 81 (1974): 215–44.
———. "Judah the Essene and the Teacher of Righteousness." *RevQ* 10 (1981): 579–86.
Najman, Hindy. *Seconding Sinai. The Development of Mosaic Discourse in Second Temple Judaism*. JSJSup 77; Leiden: Brill, 2004.
———. "Interpretation as Primordial Writing: *Jubilees* and Its Authority Conferring Strategies." *JSJ* 30 (1999): 379–410. Repr. pages 39–71 in eadem, *Past Renewals. Interpretative Authority, Renewed Revelation and the Quest for Perfection in Jewish Antiquity*. JSJSup 53; Leiden: Brill, 2010.
Neusner, Jacob. *Method and Meaning*. BJS 10; Atlanta: Scholars Press, 1979.
Newman, Judith H. *Praying by the Book. The Scripturalization of Prayer in Second Temple Judaism*. SBLEJL 14; Atlanta: Scholars Press, 1999.
Newsom, Carol A. *Songs of the Sabbath Sacrifice. A Critical Edition*. HSS 27; Atlanta: Scholars Press, 1985.
———. "'Sectually Explicit' Literature from Qumran." Pages 167–87 in *The Hebrew Bible and Its Interpreters*. Edited by W. H. Propp, B. Halpern and D. N. Freedman. Winona Lake, Ind.: Eisenbrauns, 1990.
———. "The Sage in the Literature of Qumran: The Function of the Maskil." Pages 373–82 in *The Sage in Israel and the Ancient Near East*. Edited by J. G. Gammie and L. G. Perdue. Winona Lake, Ind.: Eisenbrauns, 1990.
———. "4QShirot 'Olat HaShabbat[a]." Pages 173–401 in E. Eshel et al., *Qumran Cave 4. VI. Poetical and Liturgical Texts, Part 1*. DJD 11; Oxford: Clarendon, 1998.
———. *Angelic Liturgy. Songs of the Sabbath Sacrifice*. Louisville: WestminsterJohnKnox/ Tübingen: Mohr Siebeck, 1999.
———. *The Self as Symbolic Space. Constructing Identity and Community at Qumran*. STDJ 52; Leiden: Brill, 2004.
Nickelsburg, George W. E. *Resurrection, Immortality and Eternal Life in Intertestamental Judaism*. HTS 26; Cambridge, Mass.: Harvard, 1972.
———. "Social Aspects of Palestinian Jewish Apocalypticism." Pages 641–54 in *Apocalypticism in the Mediterranean World and the Near East*. Edited by D. Hellholm. Tübingen: Mohr Siebeck, 1983.
———. "The Bible Rewritten and Expanded." Pages 89–156 in *Jewish Writings of the Second Temple Period*. Edited by Michael E. Stone. CRINT; Second Series 2; Philadelphia: Fortress/Assen: van Gorcum, 1984.
———. "Enochic Wisdom: An Alternative to the Mosaic Torah?" Pages 123–32 in *Hesed Ve-Emet. Studies in Honor of Ernest S. Frerichs*. Edited by Jodi Magness and Seymour Gitin. BJS 320; Atlanta: Scholars Press, 1998.
———. "Judgment, Life-After-Death, and Resurrection in the Apocrypha and the Non-Apocalyptic Pseudepigrapha." Pages 141–62 in *Judaism in Late Antiquity. Part Four. Death, Life-After-Death, Resurrection and the World-to-Come in the Judaisms of Late Antiquity*. Edited by Alan J. Avery-Peck and Jacob Neusner. Handbuch der Orientalistik; Series One 49; Leiden: Brill, 2000.
———. *1 Enoch 1. A Commentary on the Book of 1 Enoch, Chapters 1–36; 81–108*. Hermeneia; Minneapolis: Fortress, 2001.
———. *Jewish Literature between the Bible and the Mishnah*. Revised ed.; Minneapolis: Fortress, 2005.
———. "Discerning the Structure(s) of the Enochic Book of Parables." Pages 23–47 in *Enoch and the Messiah Son of Man*. Edited by Gabriele Boccaccini. Grand Rapids: Eerdmans, 2007.
———. "Enochic Wisdom and Its Relationship to the Mosaic Torah." Pages 81–94 in *The Early*

Enoch Literature. Edited by Gabriele Boccaccini and John J. Collins. JSJSup 121; Leiden: Brill, 2007.
——. "Polarized Self-Identification in the Qumran Texts." Pages 85–109 in *Defining Identities: We, You, and the Other in the Dead Sea Scrolls*. Edited by Florentino García Martínez and Mladen Popović. STDJ 70; Leiden: Brill, 2008.
Nickelsburg, George W. E., and James C. VanderKam. *1 Enoch. A New Translation*. Minneapolis: Fortress, 2004.
Nitzan, Bilhah. *Qumran Prayer and Religious Poetry*. STDJ 12; Leiden: Brill, 1994.
——. "Repentance in the Dead Sea Scrolls." Pages 145–70 in vol. 2 of *The Dead Sea Scrolls after Fifty Years. A Comprehensive Assessment*. Edited by P. W. Flint and J. C. VanderKam. 2 vols.; Leiden: Brill, 1999.
Noam, Vered. *Megillat Taʿanit. Versions, Interpretation, History*. [Heb.] Jerusalem: Yad Ben-Zvi, 2003.
Osten-Sacken, Peter von der. *Die Apokalyptik in ihrem Verhältnis zu Prophetie und Weisheit*. Theologische Existenz Heute 157; Munich: Kaiser, 1969.
——. *Gott und Belial. Traditionsgeschichtliche Untersuchungen zum Dualismus in den Texten aus Qumran*. SUNT 6; Göttingen: Vandenhoeck & Ruprecht, 1969.
Otto, Eckart. "Politische Theologie in den Königspsalmen zwischen Ägypten und Assyrien. Die Herrscherlegitimation in den Psalmen 2 und 18 in ihrem altorientalischen Kontexten." Pages 33–65 in *'Mein Sohn bist du,' (Ps 2,7). Studien zu den Königspsalmen*. Edited by E. Otto and E. Zenger. Stuttgarter Bibelstudien 192; Stuttgart: Verlag Katholisches Bibelwerk, 2002.
——. "Psalm 2 in neuassyrischer Zeit. Assyrische Motive in der judäischen Königsideologie." Pages 335–49 in *Textarbeit. Studien zu Texten und ihrer Rezeption aus dem Alten Testament und der Umwelt Israels. Festschrift für Peter Weimar*. Edited by Klaus Kiesow and Thomas Meurer. AOAT 294; Münster: Ugarit-Verlag, 2003.
Parry, Donald W., and Emanuel Tov. *Calendrical and Sapiential Texts*. The Dead Sea Scrolls Reader 4; Leiden: Brill, 2004.
Patrick, Dale. *Old Testament Law*. London: SCM, 1986.
Paul, S. M. "The Heavenly Tablets and the Book of Life." *JANES* 5 (1972): 345–53.
Pedersén, Olof. *Archives and Libraries in the Ancient Near East 1500–300 B. C.* Bethesda, Md.: CDL Press, 1998.
Perdue, Leo G. "Pseudonymity and Graeco-Roman Rhetoric." Pages 27–59 in *Pseudepigraphie und Verfasserfiktion in frühchristlichen Briefen*. Edited by Jörg Frey, Jens Herzer, Martina Janssen and Clare K. Rothschild. WUNT 246; Tübingen: Mohr Siebeck, 2009.
Petersen, Anders Klostergaard. "Rewritten Bible as a Borderline Phenomenon – Genre, Textual Strategy or Canonical Anachronism?" Pages 284–306 in *Flores Florentino. Dead Sea Scrolls and Other Early Jewish Studies in Honour of Florentino García Martínez*. Edited by Anthony Hilhorst, Émile Puech and Eibert Tigchelaar. JSJSup 122; Leiden: Brill, 2007.
Philonenko, M. "La Doctrine Qoumrânienne de Deux Esprits." Pages 163–211 in *Apocalyptique Iranienne et Dualisme Qoumrânien*. Edited by G. Widengren, A. Hultgård, M. Philonenko. Paris: Maisonneuve, 1995.
Pietersen, Lloyd K. "'False Teaching, Lying Tongues and Deceitful Lips' (4Q169 FRGS 3–4 2.8): The *Pesharim* and the Sociology of Deviance." Pages 166–81 in *New Directions in Qumran Studies. Proceedings of the Bristol Colloquium on the Dead Sea Scrolls, 8–10 September 2003*. Edited by Jonathan G. Campbell et al. London: T&T Clark, 2005.
Plöger, O. *Theocracy and Eschatology*. Richmond: Knox, 1968.
Popović, Mladen. *Reading the Human Body. Physiognomics and Astrology in the Dead Sea Scrolls and Hellenistic–Early Roman Period Judaism*. STDJ 67; Leiden: Brill, 2007.

———. "Apocalyptic Determinism." Chapter 15 in *The Oxford Handbook of Apocalyptic Literature*. Edited by J.J. Collins. New York: Oxford University Press, 2014.
Popper, Karl. "Towards a Rational Theory of Tradition." *The Rationalist Annual* 66 (1949): 36–55. Repr. pages 120–35 in *Conjectures and Refutations. The Growth of Scientific Knowledge*. 3rd ed.; London: Routledge and Kegan Paul, 1972.
Portier-Young, Anathea. *Apocalypse Against Empire. Theologies of Resistance in Early Judaism*. Grand Rapids: Eerdmans, 2011.
Puech, Émile. "Notes sur le manuscript de XIQ Melkîsédeq." *RevQ* 12 (1985–1987): 483–513.
———. "Fragment d'une apocalypse en araméen (4Q246=pseudo-Dan^d) et le 'royaume de Dieu'." *RB* 99 (1992): 98–131.
———. *La Croyance des Esséniens en la Vie Future. Immortalité, Resurrection, Vie Éternelle*. Paris: Gabalda, 1993.
———. "Préséance sacerdotale et messie-roi dans la Règle de la Congrégation (1QSa ii 11–22)." *RevQ* 16 (1993–1995): 351–65.
———. "246. 4QApocryphe de Daniel ar." Pages 165–84 in G. Brooke et al., *Qumran Cave IV. XVII*. DJD 22; Oxford: Clarendon, 1996.
———. "La prière de Nabonide (4Q242)." Pages 208–28 in *Targumic and Cognate Studies: Essays in Honour of Martin McNamara*. Edited by K.J. Cathcart and M. Maher. JSOTSup 230; Sheffield: Sheffield Academic Press, 1996.
———. "4QRouleau du Temple." Pages 85–114 in idem, *Qumrân Grotte 4, XVIII: Textes hébreux (4Q521–528, 4Q576–579)*. DJD 25; Oxford: Clarendon, 1998.
———. *Qumrân Grotte 4. XVIII. Textes Hébreux (4Q521– 4Q528, 4Q576–4Q579)*. DJD 25; Oxford: Clarendon, 1998.
———. "4Q543–4Q549. 4QVisions de ᶜAmram^{a–g} ar: Introduction." Pages 283–405 in idem, *Qumrân Grotte IV.22. Textes Araméens. Première Partie 4Q529–549*. DJD 31; Oxford: Clarendon, 2001.
———. *Qumrân Grotte 4. XXII. Textes Araméens, Première Partie, 4Q529–549*. DJD 31; Oxford: Clarendon, 2001.
———. "540. 4QApocryphe de Lévi^a? ar," and "540. 4QApocryphe de Lévi^b? ar." Pages 217–56 in idem, *Qumrân Grotte 4. XXII. Textes Araméens. Première Partie. 4Q529–549*. DJD 31; Oxford: Clarendon, 2001.
———. *Qumrân Grotte 4. XXVII. Textes Araméens, Deuxième Partie (4Q550–4Q575a, 4Q580–4Q587)*. DJD 37; Oxford: Clarendon, 2009.
Qimron, Elisha, and John Strugnell. *Qumran Cave 4. V. Miqsat Maʻase Ha-Torah*. DJD 10; Oxford: Clarendon, 1994.
Rad, Gerhard von. *Old Testament Theology*. 2 vols.; New York: Harper & Row, 1965. Translation of *Theologie des Alten Testaments*. 4th ed.; Munich: Kaiser, 1965.
Rappaport, Roy A. *Ecology, Meaning, and Religion*. Berkeley, Calif.: North Atlantic, 1979.
———. *Ritual and Religion in the Making of Humanity*. Cambridge: Cambridge University Press, 1999.
Regev, Eyal. *Sectarianism in Qumran. A Cross-Cultural Perspective*. Berlin: de Gruyter, 2007.
Renan, Ernest. Review of P.E. Lucius, *Der Essenismus in seinem Verhältnis zum Judenthum* (Strasbourg, 1881). *Journal des Savants* (February, 1892): 91.
Rengstorff, K.H. *Ḥirbet Qumran and the Problem of the Dead Sea Cave Scrolls*. Leiden: Brill, 1963.
Rösel, Christoph. *Die messianische Redaktion des Psalters. Studien zu Entstehung und Theologie der Sammlung Psalm 2–89**. Stuttgart: Calwer, 1999.

Rosen-Zvi, Ishay. "Two Rabbinic Inclinations? Rethinking a Scholarly Dogma." *JSJ* 39 (2008): 513–39.
Rubenson, Samuel. "As Already Translated to the Kingdom While Still in the Body." Pages 271–89 in *Metamorphoses. Resurrection, Body and Transformative Practices in Early Christianity*. Edited by Turid Karlsen Seim and Jorunn Økland. Ekstasis 1; Berlin: de Gruyter, 2009.
Ruiten, J. T. A. G. M. van. "Eden and the Temple: The Rewriting of Genesis 2:4–3:24 in the Book of *Jubilees*." Pages 63–94 in *Paradise Interpreted. Representations of Biblical Paradise in Judaism and Christianity*. Edited by G. P. Luttikhuizen. Leiden: Brill, 1999.
———. *Primaeval History Interpreted. The Rewriting of Genesis 1–11 in the book of Jubilees*. JSJSup 66; Leiden: Brill, 2000.
———. "The Creation of Man and Woman in Early Jewish Literature." Pages 34–62 in *The Creation of Man and Woman. Interpretations of the Biblical Narratives in Jewish and Christian Traditions*. Edited by G. P. Luttikhuizen. Themes in Biblical Narrative 3; Leiden: Brill, 2000.
Ryle, H. E., and M. R. James. *Psalms of the Pharisees. Commonly Called the Psalms of Solomon*. Cambridge: Cambridge University Press, 1891.
Sacchi, P. *Jewish Apocalyptic and Its History*. JSPSup 20; Sheffield: Sheffield Academic Press, 1997.
Sanders, E. P. *Paul and Palestinian Judaism. A Comparison of Patterns of Religion*. Philadelphia: Fortress, 1977.
Sarason, Richard S. "The Intersections of Qumran and Rabbinic Judaism: The Case of Prayer Texts and Liturgies." *DSD* 8 (2001): 169–81.
———. "Communal Prayer at Qumran and among the Rabbis." Pages 151–72 in *Liturgical Perspectives. Prayer and Poetry in Light of the Dead Sea Scrolls. Proceedings of the Fifth International Symposium of the Orion Center for the Study of the Dead Sea Scrolls and Associated Literature, 19–23 January, 2000*. Edited by Esther G. Chazon. STDJ 48; Leiden: Brill, 2003.
Sarot, Marcel. "Counterfactuals and the Invention of Religious Tradition." Pages 21–40 in *Religious Identity and the Invention of Tradition*. Edited by Jan Willem van Henten and Anton Houtepen. Assen: van Gorcum, 2001.
Schäfer, P. *Studien zur Geschichte und Theologie des Rabbinischen Judentums*. Leiden: Brill, 1978.
Schaper, Joachim. "Der Septuaginta-Psalter als Dokument jüdischer Eschatologie." Pages 38–61 in *Die Septuaginta zwischen Judentum und Christentum*. Edited by Martin Hengel and Anna Maria Schwemer. Tübingen: Mohr Siebeck, 1994.
———. *Eschatology in the Greek Psalter*. WUNT; Second Series 76; Tübingen: Mohr Siebeck, 1995.
Schiffman, Lawrence H. "Essenes." Pages 163-66 in vol. 5 of *The Encyclopedia of Religion*. Edited by Lindsay Jones. Detroit: Macmillan, 1986.
———. *The Eschatological Community of the Dead Sea Scrolls*. SBLMS 38; Atlanta: Scholars Press, 1989.
———. *Reclaiming the Dead Sea Scrolls*. Philadelphia: Jewish Publication Society, 1994.
———. "Community without Temple: The Qumran Community's Withdrawal from the Jerusalem Temple." Pages 267–84 in *Gemeinde ohne Tempel = Community without Temple. Zur Substituierung und Transformation des Jerusalemer Tempels und seines Kults im Alten Testament, antiken Judentum und frühen Christentum*. Edited by Beate Ego, Armin Lange, and Peter Pilhofer with Kathrin Ehlers. Tübingen: Mohr Siebeck, 1999.
———. "The Temple Scroll and the Halakhic Pseudepigrapha of the Second Temple Period."

Pages 121–31 in *Pseudepigraphic Perspectives. The Apocrypha and Pseudepigrapha in Light of the Dead Sea Scrolls*. Edited by E. Chazon and M.E. Stone. STDJ 31; Leiden: Brill, 1999.

———. "Halakhic Elements in the Sapiential Texts from Qumran." Pages 89–100 in *Sapiential Perspectives: Wisdom Literature in Light of the Dead Sea Scrolls. Proceedings of the Sixth International Symposium of the Orion Center, 20–22 May, 2001.* Edited by J.J. Collins, G.E. Sterling and Ruth A. Clements. STDJ 51; Leiden: Brill, 2004.

———. "The *Book of Jubilees* and the *Temple Scroll*." Pages 99–115 in *Enoch and the Mosaic Torah. The Evidence of Jubilees*. Edited by Gabriele Boccaccini and Giovanni Ibba. Grand Rapids: Eerdmans, 2009.

Schimanowski, Gottfried. *Weisheit und Messias. Die jüdischen Voraussetzungen der urchristlichen Präexistenzchristologie*. Tübingen: Mohr Siebeck, 1985.

Schniedewind, William M. *How the Bible Became a Book. The Textualization of Ancient Israel*. Cambridge: Cambridge University Press, 2004.

Schofield, Alison. *From Qumran to the Yahad. A New Paradigm of Textual Development for the Community Rule*. STDJ 77; Leiden: Brill, 2009.

Schreiber, Stefan. *Gesalbter und König. Titel und Konzeptionen der königlichen Gesalbtenerwartung in frühjudischen und urchristlichen Schriften*. BZNW 105; Berlin: de Gruyter, 2000.

Schuller, Eileen M. "*Hodayot*." Pages 69–254 in *Qumran Cave 4. XX. Poetical and Liturgical Texts, Part 2*. Edited by Esther Chazon et al. DJD 29; Oxford: Clarendon, 1999.

———. "Petitionary Prayer and the Religion of Qumran." Pages 29–45 in *Religion in the Dead Sea Scrolls*. Edited by J.J. Collins and R.A. Kugler. Grand Rapids: Eerdmans, 2000.

———. "Some Reflections on the Function and Use of Poetical Texts among the Dead Sea Scrolls." Pages 173–89 in *Liturgical Perspectives: Prayer and Poetry in Light of the Dead Sea Scrolls. Proceedings of the Fifth International Symposium of the Orion Center for the Study of the Dead Sea Scrolls and Associated Literature, 19–23 January, 2000*. Edited by Esther G. Chazon. STDJ 48; Leiden: Brill, 2003.

———. "Penitential Prayer in Second Temple Judaism: A Research Survey." Pages 1–15 in vol. 1 of *Seeking the Favor of God*. Edited by Mark J. Boda, Daniel K. Falk, and Rodney A. Werline. 3 vols.; SBLEJL 21–23; Atlanta: SBL/Leiden: Brill, 2006–2009.

———. "*Hodayot* (1QH and Related Texts)." Pages 747–9 in *The Eerdmans Dictionary of Early Judaism*. Edited by J.J. Collins and D. Harlow. Grand Rapids: Eerdmans, 2010.

Schultz, B. *Conquering the World. The War Scroll (1QM) Reconsidered*. STDJ 76; Leiden: Brill, 2009.

Schürer, Emil. *History of the Jewish People in the Age of Jesus Christ*, revised and edited by Geza Vermes et al. 3 vols.; Edinburgh: Clark, 1973–1987. Translation of *Geschichte des Jüdischen Volkes im Zeitalter Jesu Christi*. 3rd ed. Leipzig: Hinrichs, 1898.

Schwartz, Daniel R. *2 Maccabees*. CEJL; Berlin: de Gruyter, 2008.

Schwartz, Seth. *Imperialism and Jewish Society, 200 B.C.E to 640 C.E.* Princeton: Princeton University Press, 2001.

Scobie, C.H.H. *John the Baptist*. Philadelphia: Fortress, 1964.

Seeman, Don. "Otherwise than Meaning: On the Generosity of Ritual." Pages 55–71 in *Ritual in Its Own Right: Exploring the Dimensions of Transformation*. Edited by D. Handelman and Galina Lindquist. New York: Berghahn, 2005.

Segal, Michael. "4QReworked Pentateuch or 4QPentateuch?" Pages 391–99 in *The Dead Sea Scrolls: Fifty Years after Their Discovery*. Edited by L. Schiffman, E. Tov, and J. VanderKam. Jerusalem: Israel Exploration Society/Shrine of the Book, Israel Museum, 2000.

———. "Between Bible and Rewritten Bible." Pages 10–28 in *Biblical Interpretation at Qumran*. Edited by Matthias Henze. Grand Rapids: Eerdmans, 2005.
———. *The Book of Jubilees. Rewritten Bible, Redaction, Ideology and Theology*. JSJSup 117; Leiden: Brill, 2007.
Sharp, Carolyn. *Prophecy and Ideology in Jeremiah. Struggles for Authority in Deutero-Jeremianic Prose*. London/New York: T&T Clark, 2003.
Shaver, Judson R. *Torah and the Chronicler's History Work. An Inquiry into the Chronicler's References to Laws, Festivals, and Cultic Institutions in Relationship to Pentateuchal Legislation*. BJS 196; Atlanta: Scholars Press, 1989.
Shavit, Yaacov. "The 'Qumran Library' in the Light of the Attitude towards Books and Libraries in the Second Temple Period." Pages 299–315 in *Methods of Investigation of the Dead Sea Scrolls and the Khirbet Qumran Site. Present Realities and Future Prospects*. Edited by Michael O. Wise et al. Annals of the New York Academy of Sciences 722; New York: The New York Academy of Sciences, 1994.
Sherwood, Yvonne. *A Biblical Text and Its Afterlives. The Survival of Jonah in Western Culture*. Cambridge: Cambridge University Press, 2000.
Shupak, N. *Where Can Wisdom be Found? The Sage's Language in the Bible and in Ancient Egyptian Literature*. OBO 130; Fribourg: Fribourg University, 1993.
Sievers, Joseph. "Josephus and the Afterlife." Pages 20–31 in *Understanding Josephus. Seven Perspectives*. Edited by Steve Mason. JSPSup 32; Sheffield: Sheffield Academic Press, 1998.
Silberman, Lou H. "Unriddling the Riddle." *RevQ* 3 (1961): 323–64.
Sivertsev, Alexei. *Households, Sects, and the Origins of Rabbinic Judaism*. JSJSup 102; Leiden: Brill, 2005.
———. "Sects and Households: Social Structure of the Proto-Sectarian Movement of Nehemiah 10 and the Dead Sea Sect." *CBQ* 67 (2005): 59–78.
Skehan, P. W. "Two Books on Qumran Studies." *CBQ* 21 (1959): 53–90.
Skjaervø, Prods Oktor. "Zoroastrian Dualism." Pages 55–91 in *Light against Darkness*. Edited by Armin Lange, Eric M. Meyers, Bennie H. Reynolds III, Randall Styers. JAJSup 2; Göttingen: Vandenhoeck & Ruprecht, 2011.
Smith, Dennis E. "Meals." Pages 530–532 in vol. 1 of *The Encyclopedia of the Dead Sea Scrolls*. Edited by L.H. Schiffman and J.C. VanderKam. 2 vols.; New York: Oxford University Press, 2000.
Smith, Jonathan Z. *Imagining Religion. From Babylon to Jonestown*. Chicago: The University of Chicago, 1982.
Smith, Morton. "The Description of the Essenes in Josephus and the Philosophumena." *HUCA* 29 (1958): 273–313.
———. "The Dead Sea Sect in Relation to Ancient Judaism." *NTS* 7 (1961): 347–60.
———. "Helios in Palestine." *Eretz Israel* 16 (1982): 199*–214*.
Speyer, Wolfgang. *Die literarische Fälschung im Altertum*. Munich: Beck, 1971.
Staal, Fritz. "The Sound of Religion: Parts IV-V." *Numen* 33 (1968): 184–224.
———. "The Meaninglessness of Ritual." *Numen* 26 (1979): 2–22.
Starcky, Jean. "Les quatre étapes du messianisme à Qumrân." *RB* 70 (1963): 481–505.
Stark, R., and W.S. Bainbridge. *The Future of Religion. Secularization, Revival and Cult Formation*. Berkeley: University of California Press, 1985.
Stegemann, Hartmut. *Die Entstehung der Qumran Gemeinde*. Bonn: published privately, 1971.
———. "The Qumran Essenes – Local Members of the Main Jewish Union in Late Second Temple Times." Pages 83–166 in vol. 1 of *The Madrid Qumran Congress: Proceedings of*

the International Congress on the Dead Sea Scrolls, Madrid, 18–21 March 1991. Edited by J. Trebolle Barrera and L. Vegas Montaner. 2 vols.; STDJ 11; Leiden: Brill, 1992.

———. *The Library of Qumran. On the Essenes, Qumran, John the Baptist and Jesus*. Grand Rapids: Eerdmans, 1998. Translation of *Die Essener, Qumran, Johannes der Täufer und Jesus*. Freiburg: Herder, 1993.

Stendahl, Krister. *The Scrolls and the New Testament*. New York: Harper, 1958. Reprinted with a new introduction by J. H. Charlesworth. New York: Crossroad, 1992.

Stern, Menahem. *Greek and Latin Authors on Jews and Judaism. I. From Herodotus to Plutarch*. Jerusalem: Israel Academy of Sciences, 1976.

Stern, Sacha. Review of Vered Noam, *Megillat Ta'anit: Versions, Interpretation, History. JJS* 57 (2006): 184–6.

———. "Qumran Calendars and Sectarianism." Pages 232–53 in *The Oxford Handbook of the Dead Sea Scrolls*. Edited by T. H. Lim and J. J. Collins. Oxford: Oxford University Press, 2010.

Steudel, Annette. *Der Midrasch zur Eschatologie aus der Qumrangemeinde (4QMidrEschat$^{a.b}$)*. STDJ 13; Leiden: Brill, 1994.

———. "The Eternal Reign of the People of God – Collective Expectations in Qumranic Texts." *RevQ* 17 (1996): 507–25.

———. "Psalm 2 im antiken Judentum." Pages 189–97 in *Gottessohn und Menschensohn. Exegetische Paradigmen biblischer Intertextualität*. Edited by Dieter Sänger. Neukirchen-Vluyn: Neukirchener Verlag, 2004.

Stökl Ben Ezra, Daniel. "Old Caves and Young Caves: A Statistical Reevaluation of a Qumran Consensus." *DSD* 14 (2007): 313–33.

Stone, Michael E. "The Question of the Messiah in *4 Ezra*." Pages 209–24 in *Judaisms and Their Messiahs*. Edited by J. Neusner, W. S. Green and E. Frerichs. Cambridge: Cambridge University Press, 1987.

———. *Features of the Eschatology of Fourth Ezra*. Atlanta: Scholars Press, 1989.

———. *Fourth Ezra. A Commentary on the Book of Fourth Ezra*. Hermeneia; Minneapolis: Fortress, 1990.

———. *Ancient Judaism. New Visions and Views*. Grand Rapids: Eerdmans, 2011.

Strack, H. L., and P. Billerbeck. *Kommentar zum Neuen Testament aus Talmud und Midrasch*. München: Beck, 1924, 1989.

Strawson, P. F. *Freedom and Resentment, and Other Essays*. London: Methuen, 1974.

Strugnell, John. "Notes en marge du volume V des 'Discoveries in the Judaean Desert of Jordan.'" *RevQ* 7 (1970): 263–8.

Strugnell, John, and Daniel J. Harrington. "*Instruction*." Pages 1–503 in J. Strugnell, D. J. Harrington, and T. Elgvin, *Qumran Cave 4. XXIV. Sapiential Texts, Part 2*. DJD 34; Oxford: Clarendon, 1999.

———. *Qumran Cave 4. XXIV. Sapiential Texts, Part 2*. DJD 34; Oxford: Clarendon, 1999.

Stuckenbruck, L. T. *The Book of Giants from Qumran. Text, Translation, and Commentary*. Tübingen: Mohr Siebeck, 1997.

———. "The Throne-Theophany of the Book of Giants: Some New Light on the Background of Daniel 7." Pages 211–20 in *The Scrolls and the Scriptures. Qumran Fifty Years After*. Edited by S. E. Porter and C. A. Evans. JSPSup 26; Sheffield: Sheffield Academic Press, 1997.

———. "The Formation and Re-Formation of Daniel in the Dead Sea Scrolls." Pages 101–30 in *The Bible and the Dead Sea Scrolls. The Princeton Symposium on the Dead Sea Scrolls*. Edited by J. H. Charlesworth. Waco, Tex.: Baylor University Press, 2006.

Stuhlmacher, Peter. "Isaiah 53 in the Gospels and Acts." Pages 147–62 in *The Suffering Serv-

ant. Isaiah 53 in Jewish and Christian Sources. Edited by Bernd Janowski and Peter Stuhlmacher. Grand Rapids: Eerdmans, 2004.
Sussmann, Y. "Appendix 1: The History of the Halakha and the Dead Sea Scrolls." Pages 179–200 in E. Qimron and J. Strugnell, *Qumran Cave 4. V. Miqsat Ma'ase Ha-Torah.* DJD 10; Oxford: Clarendon, 1994.
Sutcliffe, E. F. "The First Fifteen Members of the Qumran Community." *JSS* 4 (1959): 134–8.
Talmon, Shemaryahu. *The World of Qumran from Within.* Jerusalem: Magnes, 1989.
———. "Oral and Written Transmission in Judaism." Pages 121–58 in *Jesus and the Oral Gospel Tradition.* Edited by Henry Wansbrough. JSNTSup 64; Sheffield: Sheffield Academic Press, 1991.
Talmon, Shemaryahu, and Jonathan Ben-Dov. *Qumran Cave 4. XVI: Calendrical Texts.* DJD 21; Oxford: Clarendon, 2001.
Taylor, Joan E. *The Immerser. John the Baptist within Second Temple Judaism.* Grand Rapids: Eerdmans, 1997.
———. "The Classical Sources on the Essenes and the Scrolls." Pages 173–99 in *The Oxford Handbook of the Dead Sea Scrolls.* Edited by T. H. Lim and J. J. Collins. Oxford: Oxford University Press, 2010.
Taylor, Robert. *The Diegesis, Being a Discovery of the Origin, Evidences, and Early History of Christianity.* Boston: Kneeland, 1834.
Tcherikover, Victor. *Hellenistic Civilization and the Jews.* Peabody, Mass.: Hendrickson, 1999. Originally published by the Jewish Publication Society in 1959.
Theisohn, Johannes. *Der auserwählte Richter.* SUNT 12; Göttingen: Vandenhoeck & Ruprecht, 1975.
Thiering, Barbara. *Jesus and the Riddle of the Dead Sea Scrolls. Unlocking the Secrets of His Life Story.* San Francisco: Harper Collins, 1992.
Tigchelaar, Eibert J. C. "The Addressees of *4QInstruction*." Pages 62–75 in *Sapiential, Liturgical and Poetical Texts from Qumran. Proceedings of the Third Meeting of the International Organization for Qumran Studies, Oslo 1998.* Edited by D. K. Falk et al. Leiden: Brill, 2000.
———. "322a. 4QHistorical Text H?" Pages 125–8 in *Qumran Cave 4. XXVIII. Miscellanea, Part 2.* M. Bernstein et al. 28; Oxford: Clarendon, 2001.
———. *To Increase Learning for the Understanding Ones. Reading and Reconstructing the Fragmentary Early Jewish Sapiential Text in 4QInstruction.* STDJ 44; Leiden: Brill, 2001.
———. "Towards a Reconstruction of the Beginning of *4QInstruction* (4Q416 Fragment 1 and Parallels)." Pages 99–126 in *The Wisdom Texts from Qumran and the Development of Sapiential Thought.* Edited by C. Hempel, A. Lange and H. Lichtenberger. BETL 159; Leuven: Peeters, 2001.
Tiller, P. A. "The 'Eternal Planting' in the Dead Sea Scrolls." *DSD* 4 (1997): 312–35.
Tobin, T. H. *The Creation of Man: Philo and the History of Interpretation.* Washington, D. C.: Catholic Biblical Association, 1983.
Toorn, Karel van der. *Scribal Culture and the Making of the Hebrew Bible.* Cambridge, Mass.: Harvard University Press, 2007.
Tov, Emanuel. "Reply to Dong-Hyuk Kim's Paper on 'Tov's Qumran Orthography'." *DSD* 11 (2004): 359–60.
———. *Scribal Practices and Approaches Reflected in the Texts Found in the Judean Desert.* STDJ 54; Leiden: Brill, 2004.
Tov, Emanuel, et al. *The Texts from the Judaean Desert. Indices and An Introduction to the Discoveries in the Judaean Desert Series.* DJD 39; Oxford: Clarendon, 2002.

Tov, Emanuel, and Sidnie White Crawford. "Reworked Pentateuch." Pages 187–351 in H. W. Attridge et al., *Qumran Cave 4, VIII*. DJD 13. Oxford: Clarendon, 1994.
Ulrich, Eugene C. *The Dead Sea Scrolls and the Origin of the Bible*. Grand Rapids: Eerdmans, 1999.
———. "The Text of Daniel in the Dead Sea Scrolls." Pages 573–85 in *The Book of Daniel. Composition and Reception*. Edited by J. J. Collins and P. W. Flint. VTSup 83.2; Leiden: Brill, 2001.
———. "From Literature to Scripture: Reflections on the Growth of a Text's Authoritativeness." *DSD* 10 (2003): 3–25.
———. "The Non-Attestation of a Tri-Partite Canon in 4QMMT." *CBQ* 65 (2003): 202–14.
Urbach, Ephraim. *The Sages. Their Concepts and Beliefs*. Jerusalem: Magnes, 1975.
VanderKam, James C. *Textual and Historical Studies on the Book of Jubilees*. HSM 14; Missoula: Scholars Press, 1977.
———. "The Origin, Character, and Early History of the 364-Day Calendar: A Reassessment of Jaubert's Hypotheses." *CBQ* 41 (1979): 390–411.
———. "2 Maccabees 6,7a and Calendrical Change in Jerusalem." *JSJ* 12 (1981): 1–23.
———. "The *Temple Scroll* and the *Book of Jubilees*." Pages 211–36 in *Temple Scroll Studies*. Edited by George J. Brooke. JSPSup 7; Sheffield: Sheffield Academic Press, 1989.
———. "Righteous One, Messiah, Chosen One, and Son of Man in *1 Enoch* 37–71." Pages 169–91 in *The Messiah*. Edited by J. H. Charlesworth. Minneapolis: Fortress, 1992.
———. *Calendars in the Dead Sea Scrolls. Measuring Time*. London: Routledge, 1998.
———. "Identity and History of the Community." Pages 487–533 in vol. 2 of *The Dead Sea Scrolls after Fifty Years: A Comprehensive Assessment*. Edited by P. W. Flint and J. C. VanderKam. 2 vols.; Leiden: Brill, 1999.
———. *The Book of Jubilees*. Sheffield: Sheffield Academic Press, 2001.
———. "Questions of Canon Viewed through the Dead Sea Scrolls." Pages 91–109 in *The Canon Debate*. Edited by Lee Martin McDonald and James A. Sanders. Peabody, Mass.: Hendrickson, 2002.
———. "Those Who Look for Smooth Things, Pharisees, and Oral Law." Pages 464–77 in *Emanuel. Studies in Hebrew Bible, Septuagint and Dead Sea Scrolls in Honor of Emanuel Tov*. Edited by S. M. Paul, R. A. Kraft, L. H. Schiffman, and W. W. Fields. VTSup 94; Leiden: Brill, 2003.
———. "Mapping Second Temple Judaism." Pages 1–20 in *The Early Enoch Literature*. Edited by Gabriele Boccaccini and John J. Collins. JSJSup 121; Leiden: Brill, 2007.
———. "Moses Trumping Moses: Making the Book of Jubilees." Pages 25–44 in *The Dead Sea Scrolls. Transmission of Traditions and Production of Texts*. Edited by S. Metso, H. Najman and E. Schuller. STDJ 92; Leiden: Brill, 2010.
———. *The Dead Sea Scrolls Today*. 2nd ed.; Grand Rapids: Eerdmans, 2010.
———. *The Dead Sea Scrolls and the Bible*. Grand Rapids: Eerdmans, 2012.
VanderKam, James C., and P. W. Flint. *The Meaning of the Dead Sea Scrolls. Their Significance for Understanding the Bible, Judaism, Jesus, and Christianity*. San Francisco: HarperSanFrancisco, 2002.
Vaux, Roland de. *Archaeology and the Dead Sea Scrolls*. The Schweich Lectures; London: Oxford University Press, 1973.
Vermes, Geza. *Scripture and Tradition in Judaism. Haggadic Studies*. SPB 4; Leiden: Brill, 1973, first edition 1961.
———. "Eschatological World View in the Scrolls and in the New Testament." Pages 479–94 in *Emanuel: Studies in the Hebrew Bible, Septuagint, and Dead Sea Scrolls in Honor of Emanuel Tov*. Edited by S. M. Paul et al. VTSup 94; Leiden: Brill, 2003.

———. *The Complete Dead Sea Scrolls in English*. Revised ed.; London: Penguin, 2004.
———. "Historiographical Elements in the Qumran Writings: A Synopsis of the Textual Evidence." *JJS* 58 (2007): 121–39.
Vermes, Geza, and Martin D. Goodman. *The Essenes. According to the Classical Sources*. Sheffield: Sheffield Academic Press, 1989.
Wacholder, Ben Zion. "The Relationship between 11Q Torah (the Temple Scroll) and the Book of Jubilees, One Single or Two Independent Compositions." Pages 205–16 in *Society of Biblical Literature Seminar Papers*. Edited by K. H. Richards. Atlanta: Scholars Press, 1985.
———. "Jubilees as the Super Canon." Pages 195–211 in *Legal Texts and Legal Issues*. Edited by M. Bernstein, F. García Martínez and J. Kampen. STDJ 23; Leiden: Brill, 1997.
Wacholder, Ben Zion, and M. G. Abegg. *A Preliminary Edition of the Unpublished Dead Sea Scrolls*. Washington: Biblical Archeology Society, 1995.
Wagner, Siegfried. *Die Essener in der Wissenschaftliche Diskussion vom Ausgang des 18. bis zum Beginn des 20. Jahrhunderts. Eine Wissenschaftsgeschichtliche Studie*. BZAW 79; Berlin: Töpelmann, 1960.
Wallis, R. (ed.). *Sectarianism. Analyses of Religious and Non-Religious Sects*. London: Owen, 1975.
Webb, Robert L. *John the Baptizer and Prophet*. JSNTSup 62; Sheffield: Sheffield Academic Press, 1991.
———. "John the Baptist." Pages 418–21 in vol. 1 of *The Encyclopedia of the Dead Sea Scrolls*. Edited by L. H. Schiffman and J. C. VanderKam. 2 vols.; New York: Oxford University Press, 2000.
Weinfeld, M. *The Organizational Pattern and the Penal Code of the Qumran Sect. A Comparison with Guilds and Religious Associations of the Hellenistic-Roman Period*. Göttingen: Vandenhoeck & Ruprecht, 1986.
Weissenberg, Hanne von. *4QMMT. Reevaluating the Text, the Function and the Meaning of the Epilogue*. STDJ 82; Leiden: Brill, 2009.
Werline, Rodney Alan. *Penitential Prayer in Second Temple Judaism. The Development of a Religious Institution*. SBLEJL 13; Atlanta: Scholars Press, 1998.
Werman, Cana. "The תורה and the תעודה Engraved on the Tablets." *DSD* 9 (2002): 75–103.
Wernberg-Møeller, P. *The Manual of Discipline. Translated and Annotated with an Introduction*. STDJ 1; Leiden: Brill, 1957.
———. "A Reconsideration of the Two Spirits in the Rule of the Community (1Q Serek III,13 – IV,26)." *RevQ* 3 (1961): 413–41.
Wessetzky, Vilmos. "Die Bücherliste des Tempels von Edfu und Imhotep." *Göttinger Miszellen* 83 (1984): 85–9.
Westbrook, Raymond. "Cuneiform Law Codes and the Origins of Legislation." *ZA* 79 (1989): 201–22.
———. "The Character of Ancient Near Eastern Law." Pages 12–24 in vol. 1 of *A History of Ancient Near Eastern Law*. Edited by R. Westbrook. 2 vols.; Leiden: Brill, 2003.
Widengren, Geo, Anders Hultgård, and Marc Philonenko. *Apocalyptique Iranienne et Dualisme Qoumrânien*. Paris: Maisonneuve, 1995.
Williams, Sam K. *Jesus' Death as Saving Event. The Background and Origin of a Concept*. HDR 2; Missoula: Scholars Press, 1975.
Wilson, B. R. *Magic and the Millennium. A Sociological Study of Religious Movements of Protest among Tribal and Third-World Peoples*. London: Heinemann, 1973.
———. *The Social Dimensions of Sectarianism*. Oxford: Clarendon, 1990.

Wilson, Edward. *The Dead Sea Scrolls, 1947–1969.* New York: Oxford University Press, 1969. Reprint of *The Scrolls from the Dead Sea.* New York: Oxford University, 1955.
Windisch, Hans. *Die Orakel des Hystaspes.* Verhandelingen der Koninklijke Akademie van Wetenschappen te Amsterdam. Afdeeling Letterkunde, Nieuwe Reeks, Deel XXVIII no. 3; Amsterdam: Koninklijke Akademie van Wetenschappen, 1929.
Winston, David. "Freedom and Determinism in Greek Philosophy and in Hellenistic Jewish Wisdom." Pages 44–56 in *The Ancestral Philosophy. Hellenistic Philosophy in Second Temple Judaism. Essays of David Winston.* Edited by G. E. Sterling. BJS 331; Providence: Brown University, 2001.
Wise, Michael O. "The Teacher of Righteousness and the High Priest of the Intersacerdotium: Two Approaches." *RevQ* 14 (1989–1990): 587–613.
——. *A Critical Study of the Temple Scroll from Qumran Cave 11.* Studies in Ancient Oriental Civilization 49; Chicago: Oriental Institute, 1990.
——. "Accidents and Accidence: A Scribal View of Linguistic Dating of the Aramaic Scrolls from Qumran." Pages 103–52 in *Thunder in Gemini and Other Essays on the History, Language and Literature of Second Temple Palestine.* JSPSup 15; Sheffield: Sheffield Academic Press, 1994.
——. "An Annalistic Calendar from Qumran." Pages 389–408 in *Methods of Investigation of the Dead Sea Scrolls and the Khirbet Qumran Site. Present Realities and Future Prospects.* Edited by M. O. Wise et al. Annals of the New York Academy of Sciences 722; New York; The New York Academy of Sciences, 1994.
——. "*Primo Annales Fuere*: An Annalistic Calendar from Qumran." Pages 186–221 in *Thunder in Gemini and Other Essays on the History, Language and Literature of Second Temple Palestine.* JSPSup 15; Sheffield: Sheffield Academic Press, 1994.
——. *The First Messiah. Investigating the Savior before Jesus.* San Francisco: Harper, 1999.
——. מי כמוני באלים: A Study of 4Q491c, 4Q471b, 4Q427 7 and 1QH^a 25:35–26:10." *DSD* 7 (2000): 173–219.
——. "Dating the Teacher of Righteousness and the *Floruit* of His Movement." *JBL* 122 (2003): 53–87.
——. "4Q245 and the High Priesthood of Judas Maccabaeus." *DSD* 12 (2005): 313–62.
——. "The Origins and History of the Teacher's Movement." Pages 92–122 in *The Oxford Handbook of the Dead Sea Scrolls.* Edited by T. H. Lim and J. J. Collins. Oxford: Oxford University Press, 2010.
Wise, Michael O., M. Abegg, Jr., and E. Cook. *The Dead Sea Scrolls. A New Translation.* San Francisco: HarperSanFrancisco, 1996.
Woude, Adam S. van der. "Wicked Priest or Wicked Priests? Reflections on the Identification of the Wicked Priest in the Habakkuk Commentary." *JJS* 33 (1982): 349–59.
Wright, David. *Inventing God's Law. How the Covenant Code of the Bible Used and Revised the Laws of Hammurabi.* New York: Oxford University Press, 2009.
Wyrick, Jed. *The Ascension of Authorship. Attribution and Canon Formation in Jewish, Hellenistic, and Christian Traditions.* Cambridge, Mass.: Harvard University Press, 2004.
Yuval, Israel J. "All Israel Have a Portion in the World to Come." Pages 114–38 in *Redefining First-Century Jewish and Christian Identities. Essays in Honor of Ed Parish Sanders.* Edited by Fabian Udoh, with Susannah Heschel, Mark Chancey, and Gregory Tatum. Notre Dame, Ind.: University of Notre Dame Press, 2008.
Zaehner, R. C. *The Dawn and Twilight of Zoroastrianism.* London: Weidenfeld & Nicolson, 1961.
Zahn, Molly M. "The Problem of Characterizing the 4QReworked Pentateuch Manuscripts: Bible, Rewritten Bible, or None of the Above?" *DSD* 15 (2008): 315–39.

———. "Rewritten Scripture." Pages 323–36 in *The Oxford Handbook of the Dead Sea Scrolls*. Edited by T. H. Lim and J. J. Collins. Oxford: Oxford University Press, 2010.

———. *Rethinking Rewritten Scripture. Composition and Exegesis in the 4Q Reworked Pentateuch Manuscripts*. Leiden: Brill, 2011.

Zimmermann, Johannes. *Messianische Texte aus Qumran*. WUNT; Second Series 104; Tübingen: Mohr Siebeck, 1998.

Zuesse, Evan M. "Ritual [First Edition]." Page 7834 in *The Encyclopedia of Religion*. Edited by Lindsay Jones. New York: Macmillan, 2005. First edition edited by Mircea Eliade, 1987.

Index of Ancient Names and Sobriquets

Alcimus, 153
Alexander, son of Aristobulus, 131
Alexander Balas, 14
Alexander Jannaeus, 2, 11, 30, 106, 122, 125–126, 129, 142, 145, 147–148
Antiochus III, 25, 27, 29, 55
Antiochus IV Epiphanes, 28–30, 34, 100, 120, 126–128, 130, 161
Antiochus Sidetes, 30
Aristobulus I, 30, 57, 122, 129–131
Asshurbanipal, 2, 52

Balacros, 126
Belial, 189, 191, 221, 224, 233–234

Cambyses, 26

Demetrius III Akairos, 125, 142
Demetrius the Chronographer, 137

Eumenes II, 28
Ezra, 22, 23, 24, 27, 55

Gabinius, 131
Geron the Athenian, 28

Hasidim, 152–154, 156
Herod, 3n.8, 148

Interpreter of the Law, 19, 61, 64, 87, 138–139, 158

Jason, 28, 67
Jesus, 12–16, 65, 89, 193, 204, 257, 259–264, 268–270
John Hyrcanus I, 11, 30, 33, 43, 122–123, 129
John Hyrcanus II, 11, 130, 146–148
John the Baptist, 237–238, 261, 263

Jonathan Maccabee, 12, 122, 136, 146–147, 153–155
Josephus, 4
Josiah, 21, 22
Judas Maccabee, 52, 153n.14

Lion of Wrath, 67

Man of the Lie, 50, 137–139, 144, 147–148, 154–155, 161, 262n.23
Marcus Aemilius Scaurus, 130
Men of Deceit, 143
Menelaus, 28

Nabonidus, 109
Naram-Sin, 57
Nehemiah, 23, 24, 52, 55

Onias III, 103

Peitholaus, 131
Philip V of Macedon, 25
Pompey, 67, 128, 142
Popilius Laenas, 28
Ptolemy I Soter, 127
Ptolemy II, 27
Ptolemy IV, 137

Salome Alexandra, 11, 129, 147–148
Sargon, 57
Scoffer, 170
Seekers After Smooth Things, 10, 105, 125, 141–143, 147
Simon (High Priest), 33, 57, 122
Simon Maccabee, 146
Sons of Zadok, 153, 167, 181, 204
Sosius, 148

Teacher of Righteousness, 2, 9, 11, 12, 16, 50, 61, 64–65, 67–68, 104, 119, 124, 131,

136–141, 143–148, 150, 154–162, 166, 170, 176, 181, 205, 207, 235, 253, 259–262, 264–267, 269, 271
Titus, 53
Tobias the Ammonite, 27
Trypho, 146

Udjahoresnet, 26

Wicked Priest, 2, 9, 11, 12, 67–68, 131, 136, 139, 143–148, 154, 262n.23

Index of Modern Authors

Abegg, M., Jr., 103n.12, 127n.26
Aitken, J., 251n.53
Albani, M., 241n.5
Albright, William F., 4
Alexander, Philip S., 42n.45, 58n.38, 167n.12, 182, 182n.13, 183, 183n.18, 183n.20, 188n.41, 188n.42, 190, 190n.51, 191n.54, 192, 192n.61, 193nn.67–68, 202, 202n.24, 202n.27, 203n.28, 203nn.31–33, 208, 208n.56, 209, 209n.58, 209nn.60–61, 267n.47
Allegro, John, 12, 12n.28, 13, 74, 74n.21, 260
Anderson, Gary, 71n.8, 74n.22, 199n.16, 239n.64
Angel, Joseph, 134n.9, 139n.33
Arnold, Russell C. D., 206nn.44–45, 208n.55, 232n.35, 233n.38, 234n.41, 237, 237n.52, 240
Asad, Talal, 228, 228nn.14–15, 229, 229n.17
Assmann, Jan, 135, 135n.14
Atkinson, Kenneth, 93n.40, 94n.42, 128n.32, 130, 131, 131n.44
Attridge, Harold, 41n.33, 87, 87nn.2–3, 257n.1, 269, 269n.58
Avemarie, Friedrich, 236, 237n.51

Baigent, Michael, 12, 12n.29, 260n.15, 262
Baillet, M., 114, 114n.68, 208
Bainbridge, W. S., 164n.1
Baltzer, Klaus, 189, 189n.46
Barr, James, 70n.2
Barrett, C. K., 269, 269n.56
Barthélemy, D., 268n.53
Barton, J., 103n.7
Baumgarten, Albert, 34, 34n.79, 34n.80, 105n.19, 120n.5, 134n.5, 137n.26, 164n.2, 176, 176n.54, 216n.21
Baumgarten, Joseph M., 137n.24, 139n.35, 238, 238n.58

Beall, T. S., 151n.6
Beckwith, Roger T., 52n.10
Bedenbender, Andreas, 20n.5, 72n.14, 162n.57, 243n.15
Bell, Catherine M., 227nn.5–6, 228n.13, 229, 229nn.19–20
Ben-Dov, Jonathan, 130, 130n.38
Bengtsson, Hakan, 142n.53
Bergmeier, R., 152n.10, 213n.5, 216, 216n.20, 216n.22
Bergsma, John S., 46n.58
Bernstein, Moshe, 42n.44, 46n.60, 85n.54
Berrin, Shani, 125n.20, 125n.23, 141n.48, 142n.52
Berthelot, Katell, 19n.3, 56n.30
Beyer, K., 112, 113n.56
Bickerman, Elias, 25, 25n.36, 25n.37, 26, 26n.39, 26n.43, 27, 27n.44, 27n.45, 27n.47, 28, 28n.49
Billerbeck, P., 88n.10
Black, Matthew, 214n.9
Blenkinsopp, Joseph, 263–264, 264n.31, 266n.45
Boccaccini, Gabriele, 20n.5, 32n.65, 34n.78, 46n.58, 47n.65, 150n.1, 151, 151n.2, 156, 156nn.37–38, 157, 157nn.40–45, 159n.52, 160, 160n.53, 161, 161n.54, 162, 162nn.59–61
Boda, Mark J., 234n.41
Böttrich, Christoph, 95n.49
Bourdieu, Pierre, 229n.16
Bousset, Wilhelm, 8, 8n.20, 236, 236n.46
Bremmer, Jan, 216n.18
Brooke, George, 34n.78, 41n.34, 42n.44, 42n.45, 51, 52n.4, 57n.34, 66, 66nn.71–72, 87n.4, 88, 88nn.7–8, 89, 89n.17, 89n.19, 90, 90n.22, 90nn.24–25, 101, 101n.77, 119n.3, 123, 123nn.12–13, 124, 124n.14, 130, 130n.37, 131, 131n.43, 133, 133n.4, 134n.6, 134n.9, 135, 141n.46,

158n.50, 171n.30, 173n.39, 201n.22, 210, 210nn.64–66, 211, 211n.67, 263, 263n.28, 271
Broshi, M., 106n.28, 123, 123nn.8–10, 126, 126n.25, 127
Brown, Judith Ann, 12n.28
Brownlee, William, 124, 124n.15, 264, 264nn.33–34, 268
Bruce, F.F., 104, 104n.16, 136n.19
Bruns, Gerald, 85, 85n.55
Bryce, G.E., 241n.3
Burchard, Christoph, 213n.4, 215, 215n.16, 216, 216n.22
Burrows, Millar, 151, 258, 261, 261nn.16–17
Byrskog, Samuel, 62, 62n.50

Callaway, Philip R., 142n.53
Campbell, Jonathan G., 42n.41, 50n.76, 66n.68
Caquot, A., 251n.56
Carmignac, Jean, 138n.31, 264, 264n.35, 265
Carr, David M., 35n.3, 53n.13
Carson, D.A., 42n.45
Cavallin, H.C., 216n.20
Chancey, Mark A., 30n.57, 30n.58
Charles, R.H., 8
Charlesworth, James H., 32n.67, 134n.8
Chazon, E., 48n.70, 77, 77n.26, 77n.28, 77n.30, 209, 209n.59, 235n.43
Childs, Brevard, 91, 91n.33
Christiansen, Ellen Juhl, 181n.11, 233n.39
Clements, Ruth A., 21n.9, 162n.62
Clifford, Richard J., 263n.30
Coggins, R.J., 98n.62
Cohen, Shaye, 123, 123n.11, 215, 215n.15
Collins, Adela Yarbro, 91n.32, 95n.50, 97n.56, 100n.71, 100n.73, 111n.50, 202n.26, 270, 270n.61–63
Collins, John J., 1n.1, 3n.6, 5n.13, 8n.20, 9n.21, 11n.24, 13n.32, 13n.33, 14n.34, 14n.35, 20n.5, 20n.6, 20n.7, 21n.9, 29n.54, 41n.36, 43n.47, 54n.22, 58n.36, 58n.39, 61n.45, 62n.48, 64n.60, 70n.3, 71n.6, 72nn.12–13, 73n.19, 78nn.33–34, 83n.49, 91n.32, 94n.45, 95n.50, 97nn.56–57, 98n.59, 99n.65, 100, 100n.71, 100nn.73–74, 102n.3, 103nn.9–10, 104n.16, 105n.20, 106n.25, 106nn.27–28, 107, 107n.32, 109n.40, 109n.43, 110n.44, 111, 111n.50, 112nn.53–54, 113n.61, 121n.6, 124n.18, 127n.28, 133n.1, 136n.17, 136n.19, 139n.33, 141n.47, 143n.58, 146n.74, 150n.1, 151n.6, 153n.16, 154n.20, 155n.30, 158n.46, 158n.51, 162n.58, 162n.62, 165n.5, 167n.11, 167n.14, 173n.38, 179n.2, 180n.8, 183n.21, 184n.23, 185n.26, 187n.37, 191n.55, 195nn.1–2, 199n.17, 208n.54, 213n.5, 220n.32, 222n.38, 223nn.39–40, 225n.46, 230n.26, 241n.2, 241n.4, 245n.24, 247n.37, 247n.40, 251n.52, 252n.59, 262nn.24–25, 267n.47, 268n.51
Collins, Matthew, 135n.9, 138n.32, 139n.34, 142n.53, 144n.62
Cook, E., 103n.12, 111n.49
Crawford, Sidnie White, 5n.13, 41, 41nn.33–39, 42n.42, 44n.49, 48n.67, 49nn.72–73, 49n.75
Cross, Frank Moore, 2, 2n.3, 4, 4n.11, 9, 99, 99n.68, 107, 107n.31, 108–109, 111, 111n.50, 143n.59, 152n.12, 154, 235, 235n.45, 261, 261nn.19–21
Cullmann, Oscar, 219n.30

Davidson, Donald, 85n.55
Davidson, Maxwell J., 203n.29, 208n.57
Davies, Philip R., 36n.10, 61n.45, 64n.62, 135, 135n.10, 135nn.14–16, 136n.18, 138, 138nn.28–30, 138n.32, 139nn.33–34, 142n.53, 143, 143nn.55–58, 144, 144nn.61–64, 145, 145n.67, 150n.1, 153, 153nn.16–17, 155, 155n.30, 156, 156nn.31–34, 169n.18
Dawson, L.L., 164n.1
Davila, James R., 230n.22, 231, 231n.27
Day, John, 91n.30, 198n.13
de Jong, Albert, 186nn.32–33, 187, 187n.36, 187nn.38–39
de la Ronde van Kirk, Andrew, 32n.67
de Vaux, Roland, 53, 53n.15, 151, 151n.5, 259–260
Delcor, M., 153n.15
DeMaris, Richard E., 228n.10
Dimant, Devorah, 19n.3, 128nn.29–30, 150n.1, 171n.24, 199n.17
DiTommaso, Lorenzo, 111, 111n.46

Index of Modern Authors

Doran, Robert, 25n.34, 25n.37, 28, 29, 29n.53, 29n.55, 33n.77
Doudna, Gregory L., 125n.23, 142n.52
Douglas, Michael, 103, 103n.13, 140n.39, 205n.40, 265, 265n.39
Dozeman, T. B., 71n.9
Duggan, Michael, 55n.24, 234n.40
Duhaime, Jean, 183, 183n.17, 191, 192n.60, 197n.8, 220n.33
Duhm, Bernhard, 263, 263n.29
Duncker, L., 214n.8
Dupont-Sommer, André, 12, 12n.27, 108, 108nn.38–39, 138n.31, 151, 151n.3, 259–260, 259n.11, 260n.12, 262, 264, 264n.32, 268

Eisenman, R., 112, 112n.55, 257n.2, 262, 262n.23
Elgvin, Torleif, 77n.29, 81nn.44–45, 171n.28, 172n.35, 174n.48, 175, 175n.50, 175n.52, 176n.53, 242n.10, 243n.13, 244, 244n.18, 246, 246n.29, 246nn.32–34, 247, 247n.38, 248, 249nn.45–47, 250, 250n.49, 251, 251nn.54–55, 253n.62
Eliade, Mircea, 227, 227n.5
Elior, R., 202n.25
Elliger, Karl, 124, 124n.16
Engberg-Pedersen, Troels, 196n.5
Eshel, E., 106n.28, 126, 126n.25, 127, 207n.50, 208n.54
Eshel, Hanan, 12n.26, 68, 68n.79, 128, 128nn.31–32, 129, 129n.34, 130n.40, 131, 131n.42, 131n.45, 133, 133nn.1–3, 134–135, 136nn.19–20, 137n.21, 145n.69, 146, 146n.75, 149
Evans, Craig A., 13n.32, 263n.28

Falk, Daniel L., 5n.13, 205, 205n.41, 206nn.43–44, 230, 230nn.23–25, 232n.34, 234n.41
Fields, Weston W., 258n.4
Fishbane, Michael, 21n.8, 23, 23n.25, 23n.27, 24, 24n.28, 35, 36n.4
Fitzmyer, J. A., 88n.10, 91n.28, 101, 101n.76, 103n.9, 128n.33, 129–130, 193, 193n.66, 204n.35, 263, 263n.27
Fletcher-Louis, C. H. T., 79n.34, 174, 174n.46, 198, 198n.15, 200n.19, 202n.27, 245n.24, 248n.42

Flint, P. W., 102nn.5–6, 106n.28, 109n.43, 113n.60, 113n.62, 114n.69, 119n.4, 121n.6
Flusser, D., 105, 105nn.20–22
Fraade, Steven, 62, 62n.49, 64, 64n.61, 65, 65n.64, 80, 80nn.37–38, 81n.42, 170n.21, 245n.23
Frazer, James G., 227
Frei, Peter, 22, 22n.19
Frennesson, Bjorn, 201n.23, 203nn.33–34, 208n.57
Frey, Jörg, 36n.9, 37n.12, 79, 79n.36, 80, 80n.39, 81n.43, 173n.41, 182n.14, 183, 183n.18, 185, 185n.25, 185n.27, 189, 189n.45, 190, 190n.47, 203n.30, 216n.22, 243n.16, 245n.26, 257n.3, 263n.26
Fuks, Alexander, 25n.38

Gager, John G., 26n.40
Gammie, John G., 23n.27
García Martínez, Florentino, 31n.59, 32, 32n.70, 32n.71, 46n.60, 59n.41, 84n.52, 101, 101n.75, 107n.34, 110n.44, 150n.1, 156, 156nn.35–36, 199n.16, 207n.51, 208, 263n.28
Gaster, Theodore, 99n.68
Gerstenberger, Erhard S., 91n.31
Gillingham, S. E., 91, 91n.28, 92nn.35–36
Gitin, Seymour, 58n.37
Goff, Matthew, 25n.34, 56n.29, 74n.21, 77n.27, 79n.34, 174nn.43–44, 176n.53, 205n.38
Golb, Norman, 1, 2, 2n.5, 166n.9
Goldman, Liora, 186n.30
Goodman, Martin, 43n.47, 151n.4, 202nn.2–3, 219n.29, 232n.33, 258n.5
Gorman, Frank H., Jr., 228n.7, 229n.10
Grabbe, Lester, 219n.28
Greenberg, M., 72nn.10–11
Grelot, Pierre, 108, 108n.37, 150n.1
Griffiths, J. Gwyn, 187n.35
Grimes, Ronald, 228n.9
Gropp, Douglas, 107
Gross, Andrew D., 32n.67
Grossman, Maxine, 67, 67n.75, 135, 135nn.11–12
Gruen, Erich, 25, 25n.33
Gzella, Holger, 92n.39

Halbwachs, Maurice, 135, 135n.13

Halpern, Baruch, 143n.60
Hamilton, Mark W., 90n.27
Hammer, Olav, 36n.10
Harlow, Daniel C., 8n.20, 25n.34, 133n.1
Harrington, D.J., 74n.21, 78n.31, 79n.34, 171n.28, 173n.40, 185n.24, 242nn.7–8, 242n.11, 243, 243n.12, 244n.19, 245n.22, 246nn.27–31, 247n.41, 248, 248nn.43–44, 249n.46, 253, 253n.64
Hartenstein, Friedhelm, 91n.31
Hata, Gohei, 20n.7
Healey, John, 198n.13
Heger, Paul, 188, 188n.40
Hempel, Charlotte, 52n.4, 63n.57, 64, 64n.60, 147n.83, 155n.28, 165n.6, 168nn.15–17, 169nn.18–19, 176, 176n.53, 183n.15, 188n.41
Hengel, Martin, 121, 150n.1, 152n.12, 153n.15, 260, 265, 265n.38, 268, 268n.50, 268n.52
Henze, Matthias, 13n.31, 40n.32
Herbert, E.D., 42n.44, 58n.38
Herzer, Jens, 36n.9
Hilgenfeld, Adolf, 259n.10
Hilhorst, Anthony, 40n.30, 42n.41
Himmelfarb, Martha, 45n.57, 47, 47nn.64–65, 196, 196n.6
Hirschfeld, Y., 166n.9
Hobsbawm, Eric, 51, 51n.1, 57
Hogan, Karina Martin, 25n.34
Hogeterp, A.L.A., 113, 113n.60, 113n.62, 113nn.64–65
Holladay, Carl R., 137n.23
Holladay, William L., 35n.1
Holm-Nielsen, Svend, 205n.41
Hooker, Morna, 269, 269n.57
Horbury, William, 131n.45
Horgan, Maurya P., 142n.51, 146nn.76–77
Houtepen, Anton, 51n.2
Hultgård, Anders, 186n.31
Hultgren, Stephen, 137n.25, 179n.1, 180n.8, 234n.40

Ibba, Giovanni, 32n.65, 34n.78, 46n.58

Jackson, B.S., 21n.12, 22, 22n.18
Jaffee, Martin, 63n.57, 65nn.65–66
James, M.R., 94n.41
Janowski, Bernd, 269n.59

Janssen, Martina, 36n.9
Jeremias, Gert, 140n.40, 154, 154n.18, 205n.40, 264, 264n.36, 265, 265n.37, 265n.41
Jeremias, Joachim, 269, 269n.55
Jokiranta, Jutta, 66, 67nn.73–74, 141n.45, 164n.1, 164n.3
Jonnes, L., 28n.50

Kaminsky, Joel, 25n.34
Kampen, J., 46n.60, 153n.14
Kapferer, Bruce, 228n.10
Kartveit, Magnar, 40n.32
Kellens, Jean, 187n.36
Kim, Dong-Hyuk, 53n.18
Kister, Menahem, 33, 33n.75
Klawans, Jonathan, 191n.59, 238, 238n.60, 239n.62, 239nn.64–65
Klinghardt, M., 167n.13
Klinzing, Georg, 201n.21
Knibb, Michael, 61n.45, 95n.47, 98n.62, 139n.33, 155n.30
Knohl, Israel, 13, 13n.30, 207n.53, 262n.24, 268n.54
Kobelski, P.J., 103n.11, 186n.29
Koch, Klaus, 22n.19, 91n.29, 103n.8, 109n.40
Kraus, Hans-Joachim, 90n.27
Kugel, James L., 31n.62, 31n.63, 33, 46, 47, 47n.62, 59n.41, 70, 70n.1, 74n.22, 86, 86n.56
Kugler, Rob, 232, 232n.35, 240, 240n.67
Kuhn, H.W., 199n.17, 200n.18, 206nn.47–49, 247n.39
Kuhn, K.G., 187, 187n.37
Kvanvig, H.S., 95n.49

Laato, Antti, 42n.44
Lambert, David, 181n.12, 239n.66
Lange, Armin, 40n.30, 52n.6, 53n.13, 57, 57n.35, 66n.70, 67, 67n.76, 68, 79, 79n.36, 80, 85n.53, 104n.17, 119, 119n.1, 134n.7, 170n.23, 171, 171n.26, 172, 172n.37, 173n.39, 174, 174n.47, 185, 185n.27, 189, 189n.44, 191n.54, 221n.36, 244n.21, 248n.42, 251, 251n.53, 253, 253n.60, 253n.63
Lawrence, Jonathan, 236n.47, 237n.53, 238n.59, 239n.61, 239n.63

Leach, Edmund, 228, 228n.8
Leaney, A.R.C., 63, 63n.58, 197n.8
Lee, Kyong-Jin, 23, 23n.21, 24, 24n.29
LeFebvre, Michael, 21n.10, 21n.12, 22, 22n.14, 23, 23n.20, 23n.24, 23n.26, 24, 24n.31, 27, 27n.48, 39, 39n.24, 39n.27
Lehtipou, Outi, 196n.5
Leigh, Richard, 12, 12n.29, 260n.15, 262
Leonhardt-Baltzer, Jutta, 182n.14, 187n.35
Levenson, Jon D., 179n.4
Levine, Baruch A., 48n.70
Levinson, Bernard M., 5n.15, 36, 36n.5, 36n.6, 36n.7, 37, 38n.18, 38n.21
Levison, J.R., 74n.20
Lewis, James R., 36n.10
Licht, Jacob, 99n.68, 236n.48
Lichtenberger, Hermann, 210n.62
Lichtheim, Miriam, 26n.42
Lieberman, Saul, 236, 236nn.48–50
Lied, Liv Ingeborg, 198n.11
Lieu, Judith M., 52n.4
Lim, Timothy H., 5n.13, 6n.17, 7n.19, 41n.36, 77n.27, 125, 125n.22, 133n.1, 142, 142n.50, 145n.66, 146n.73
Long, A.A., 218n.27, 225n.44
Lundhaug, Hugo, 196n.5, 211n.67

Ma, John, 25n.36
Mach, Michael, 201n.23, 205n.37
Magness, Jodi, 30n.58, 58n.37, 148, 148n.86, 151n.8, 154n.22, 166n.9
Maiberger, Paul, 88n.10, 89n.14, 89n.18, 90n.24, 92n.39, 99n.67
Maier, Christl, 35n.2
Maier, J., 64n.63
Martin, Dale, 195, 196nn.3–5, 218, 218nn.25–26
Mason, Steve, 213n.5, 213n.6, 216, 216n.19
Mauss, Marcel, 228, 229, 229n.16
Mayer, Rudolf, 225n.47
McCane, Byron, 30n.58
McCann, J. Clinton, 92, 92n.36
McConville, J.G., 22, 22n.15
McKane, W., 241n.3
McKinley, Anne Fitzpatrick, 21n.11, 39n.26
Mendels, Doron, 33, 33n.76
Mertens, A., 104n.16, 104n.18, 105n.20, 110n.44

Metso, Sarianna, 5n.14, 31n.61, 44n.53, 63, 64n.59, 165n.7, 167n.12, 188, 188n.42
Metzger, Bruce M., 37n.12
Meyer, Rudolf, 107, 107n.30, 107nn.34–35, 109, 109n.41
Meyers, Carol, 70n.4
Meyers, Eric M., 30n.57
Milik, J.T., 14, 99–100, 107, 107n.29, 108–109, 109n.42, 110, 110n.44, 111, 113, 114, 114n.66, 114n.70, 127–128, 130, 130n.39, 146, 146n.72, 146n.79, 152n.12, 154
Millar, Fergus, 43n.47
Miller, E., 214n.7
Mittag, Peter Franz, 29n.54, 29n.56
Mittmann-Richert, U., 119n.1, 134n.7
Moore, George Foot, 8, 8n.20, 76n.23
Moriya, Akio, 20n.7
Müller, H.P., 241n.2
Murphy, C.M., 171n.29
Murphy-O'Connor, Jerome, 137, 138n.27, 154, 154nn.23–24, 155, 155nn.25–27, 156, 156n.34, 158n.49

Najman, Hindy, 5n.14, 31n.61, 36, 36n.8, 37, 37n.15, 37n.17, 38, 38n.19, 38n.20, 39, 44, 44nn.50–52, 45n.54, 46n.59, 47n.65, 48, 48nn.68–69, 48n.71, 50, 59, 59nn.40–41, 60n.42
Neusner, Jacob, 65n.65
Newman, Judith H., 232n.31
Newsom, Carol, 3, 3n.9, 104n.17, 140, 140n.41, 164, 165, 165n.4, 166, 166n.8, 170, 191n.52, 202n.24, 202n.27, 204n.36, 205, 205n.39, 209, 231, 231n.29, 233, 233nn.36–37, 265, 265n.42
Nickelsburg, George W.E., 20, 20n.4, 20n.5, 33, 33n.74, 58, 58n.37, 67n.74, 72n.14, 94n.44, 95n.47, 153n.16, 161, 171n.56, 199n.17, 215, 215n.12, 219, 219n.28, 219n.31, 222n.37
Nitzan, Bilhah, 205n.42, 230n.22, 235n.42
Noam, Vered, 130n.41

Økland, Jorunn, 196n.5
Otto, Eckart, 90n.27, 91n.29

Parry, Donald W., 128n.33
Patrick, Dale, 21, 22n.13, 39n.25

Paul, S. M., 244n.20
Pedersén, Olof, 52n.7
Perdue, Leo G., 36n.9, 36n.10
Petersen, Anders Klostergaard, 42n.41
Philonenko, M., 83n.49, 186n.31
Pietersen, Lloyd K., 50n.76
Pirart, Eric, 187n.36
Plöger, O., 153n.15
Popović, Mladen, 183n.19, 190n.50
Popper, Karl, 51, 51nn.2–3, 69n.80
Portier-Young, Anathea, 29n.56
Puech, Émile, 32n.68, 40n.30, 49n.74, 56, 56n.31, 90n.21, 99n.68, 103n.11, 103n.14, 107, 107n.33, 107n.36, 110n.45, 111nn.47–48, 112, 112n.52, 113, 113nn.57–59, 114n.67, 114n.71, 185n.28, 197n.7, 197n.9, 199, 200n.18, 206nn.46–47, 210, 210n.63, 212, 212n.1, 215n.17, 216, 217, 217n.23, 221, 221n.35, 222nn.37–38, 223nn.39–40, 224nn.41–42, 267n.48, 268, 269

Qimron, Elisha, 7n.18, 9, 19n.1, 27n.46, 55n.27, 68, 68n.78, 123, 145n.68, 170n.20

Rand, Michael C., 32n.67
Ranger, Terence, 51n.1
Rappaport, Roy, 228, 228n.10, 228n.12
Regev, Eyal, 55n.28
Reich, Ronny, 30n.58
Renan, Ernest, 258, 258n.8, 259
Rengstorff, Karl-Heinrich, 2, 2n.4
Richards, K. H., 44n.48
Rofé, Alexander, 123
Roitman, Adolfo D., 20n.5
Rösel, Christoph, 91, 91n.34
Rosen-Zvi, Ishay, 191n.56
Rothschild, Clare K., 36n.9
Rubenson, Samuel, 211, 211n.68
Ryle, H. E., 94n.41

Sacchi, Paolo, 157, 157n.39
Sanders, E. P., 179, 179n.3, 179n.5, 180, 180n.6, 181, 181nn.9–10
Sarason, Richard S., 231n.30, 232n.33
Sarot, Marcel, 51n.2
Schäfer, Peter, 80n.38
Schaper, Joachim, 92, 92nn.37–38
Schiffman, Lawrence H., 9n.21, 20n.5, 21n.9, 31n.60, 32n.67, 32n.69, 33, 33n.72, 34n.78, 41n.34, 42n.44, 48, 48n.70, 56n.29, 60, 60n.44, 99n.68, 172, 172nn.31–32, 201n.21, 215n.13, 253n.61, 262n.22
Schimanowksi, Gottfried, 96n.51
Schmid, K., 71n.9
Schniedewin, F., 214n.8
Schniedewind, William M., 35n.3
Schofield, Alison, 54n.23, 230n.26
Schreiber, Stefan, 96n.53, 97n.55, 98n.60, 98n.63
Schuller, Eileen, 5n.14, 31n.61, 190n.49, 208n.55, 230n.22, 231, 231n.28, 234n.41, 265
Schultz, B., 105, 105n.20, 105nn.22–24, 106n.26
Schürer, Emil, 38n.22, 259, 259n.9
Schwartz, Daniel R., 28, 28n.50, 28n.51, 28n.52, 131n.45, 137n.24
Schwartz, Seth, 192, 192nn.62–63, 193, 193n.69
Scobie, C. H. H., 237n.55, 238n.56
Sedley, D. N., 218n.27, 225n.44
Seeman, Don, 228n.10
Segal, Michael, 31, 31n.63, 32, 32n.64, 33, 33n.75, 40n.32, 41n.34, 42, 42n.43, 46n.58, 47n.62, 60n.43, 73, 73n.16, 73n.18
Sharp, Carolyn, 35n.2
Shaver, Judson R., 23n.24
Shavit, Yaacov, 52n.9
Sherwood, Yvonne, 71n.7
Shupak, N., 241n.3
Sievers, Joseph, 217n.24
Silberman, Lou, 124, 124n.17
Sivertsev, Alexei, 200n.20
Skehan, P. W., 99n.68
Skjaervo, Prods Oktor, 186n.31
Smith, Dennis E., 240n.68
Smith, Jonathan Z., 228n.11, 229n.21
Smith, Morton, 34, 34n.80, 152n.10, 200n.20, 214, 214nn.9–10, 215n.11, 222n.37
Speyer, Wolfgang, 37n.12
Staal, Frits, 227, 227nn.1–3, 228–229, 239
Stark, R., 164n.1
Starky, Jean, 268, 268n.49
Stegemann, Hartmut, 32, 52, 52n.5, 85n.53, 137, 137n.23, 137n.25, 152n.12, 154,

Index of Modern Authors

154n.19, 154n.21, 158, 158nn.47–48, 170, 171n.25, 188, 188n.43, 253n.63
Stendahl, Krister, 261, 261n.18, 271
Sterling, Gregory E., 21n.9, 162n.62
Stern, Menahem, 26n.41, 55n.25
Stern, Sacha, 130n.41, 232n.33
Steudel, Annette, 87nn.4–6, 88, 88n.11, 89, 89nn.15–16, 89n.20, 90, 90nn.21–23, 90n.26, 92, 94, 94n.46, 99, 99n.64, 99n.66, 100, 100n.72, 101
Stökl Ben Ezra, Daniel, 3n.8, 19n.3, 54, 54n.21, 56n.30
Stone, Michael E., 33n.74, 48n.70, 97nn.57–58, 98, 98n.61, 98n.63, 119n.2
Strack, H. L., 88n.10
Strawson, P. F., 192, 192n.61
Strugnell, John, 7n.18, 9, 19n.1, 27n.46, 55n.27, 68, 68n.78, 74n.21, 78n.31, 79n.34, 131n.45, 145n.68, 170n.20, 171n.28, 173n.40, 185n.24, 242nn.7–8, 242n.11, 243, 243n.12, 244n.19, 245n.22, 246nn.27–28, 246nn.30–31, 247n.41, 248, 248nn.43–44, 249n.46, 253, 253n.64, 257n.1
Stuart, G. H. Cohen, 76n.23
Stuckenbruck, L. T., 102n.6, 106nn.27–28, 112n.51, 113n.60, 113nn.62–63, 114, 114nn.71–72
Stuhlmacher, Peter, 269, 269nn.59–60, 270n.61
Sukenik, E. L., 151, 258
Sussman, Y., 10n.23
Sutcliffe, E. F., 158n.49, 166, 166n.10

Talmon, Shemaryahu, 63, 63nn.55–56, 130, 130n.38, 232, 232n.32
Taylor, Joan E., 237n.55, 238n.57, 258n.5
Taylor, Robert, 258, 258n.7
Tcherikover, Victor, 55n.26
Theisohn, Johannes, 96, 96n.52, 96n.54, 97n.55
Thiering, Barbara, 262n.23
Tigchelaar, Eibert, 40n.30, 78n.31, 131, 131n.46, 172, 172n.33, 172nn.35–36, 173, 173n.42, 174, 174n.45, 175n.49, 183n.17, 199n.16, 242nn.8–9, 242n.11, 243n.12, 243n.14, 244n.19, 245n.25, 246n.34, 246n.36, 251n.56, 252n.58
Tiller, P. A., 252n.57

Tobin, T. H., 82n.46
Tov, Emanuel, 1n.2, 41n.33, 41n.34, 41n.36, 42n.44, 53, 53n.14, 53nn.16–20, 58n.38, 77n.29, 128n.33
Tzoref, Shani, 20n.5

Ulrich, Eugene C., 4n.12, 40n.31, 55n.27, 57n.35, 102nn.1–2, 102n.4, 170n.20
Urbach, E. E., 76n.23

van der Toorn, Karel, 35n.3, 36, 36n.9, 37n.11, 52nn.7–8, 57n.33
van der Woude, A. S., 146n.73, 156, 156nn.35–36
van Henten, Jan Willem, 51n.2, 99, 99n.70
van Ruiten, Jacques, 42n.44, 71n.8, 73nn.15–16
VanderKam, James C., 4n.10, 5n.14, 12n.26, 31n.61, 33, 33n.73, 34n.78, 41n.34, 42n.44, 44n.49, 44n.53, 45, 45nn.55–56, 46, 46n.61, 47, 47n.66, 60n.43, 66n.67, 68n.77, 95nn.47–48, 96n.52, 119n.4, 137n.26, 139n.36, 161, 161n.55, 163, 163n.63
Vermes, Geza, 38n.22, 42n.40, 42n.45, 43, 43n.47, 99, 99n.69, 133n.3, 137n.22, 151n.4, 152n.9, 172, 172n.34, 212nn.2–3, 219n.29, 258n.5
von der Osten-Sacken, Peter, 183, 183n.16, 241n.2
von Rad, Gerhard, 241, 241n.1, 242, 242n.6, 250, 250n.50
von Weissenberg, Hanne, 55n.27

Wacholder, Ben Zion, 44, 44n.48, 46n.60, 127n.26
Wagner, Siegfried, 258n.6
Wallis, R., 164n.1
Watts, James W., 22n.19, 23, 23n.22
Webb, Robert L., 237n.55, 238n.57
Weinfeld, M., 167n.13
Werline, Rodney Alan, 234n.41
Werman, Cana, 45n.55, 45n.57
Wernberg,-Moeller, P., 83–84, 84n.51, 198, 198n.12
Wessetzky, Vilmos, 52n.8
Westbrook, Raymond, 21n.10, 22n.17, 39n.25
Widengren, Geo, 186n.31

Williams, Sam K., 269n.57
Williamson, H.G.M., 42n.45
Wilson, B.R., 164n.1
Wilson, Edmund, 260, 260nn.13–14
Windisch, Hans, 225n.47
Winston, D., 250n.51
Wise, Michael O., 11n.25, 12, 13, 13n.30, 32n.66, 52n.9, 53n.14, 57n.32, 68, 68n.79, 103, 103nn.12–13, 104, 104n.15, 112, 112n.55, 122, 122n.7, 125n.19, 127, 127n.27, 129, 129n.35, 130, 130n.40, 132, 132n.47, 133n.3, 134, 134n.8, 140, 140nn.37–39, 140nn.42–43, 141, 145n.69, 147n.82, 148, 148nn.84–85, 154n.20, 168n.17, 207n.50, 207n.52, 208, 208n.55, 257n.2, 262n.24, 265, 266, 266n.44, 267n.46

Wright, Benjamin G., 45n.57
Wright, David, 38n.23, 39n.28
Wyrick, Jed, 36n.9

Xeravitz, Géza G., 52n.6

Yardeni, A., 123, 123nn.8–10
Yuval, Israel J., 180n.7, 193, 193nn.64–65

Zaehner, R.C., 187n.34
Zahn, Molly M., 5n.13, 6n.16, 41n.34, 41n.36
Zimmermann, Johannes, 90n.22, 100n.71
Zsengellér, József, 52n.6
Zuesse, Evan M., 227n.4

Index of Scripture and Other Ancient Sources

ANCIENT NEAR EASTERN LITERATURE

Epic of Gilgamesh 57

HEBREW BIBLE

Genesis	31, 40, 43, 57, 59, 75–76, 83–86, 173, 184
1	71, 75, 77, 81, 182, 245
1–3	83, 85, 183
1–11	71
1:26	83, 185
1:27	81, 173, 245
1:27–28	80
1:28	183
2	77
2–3	71, 73, 75–76, 81, 85, 173, 185, 245
2:7	76, 81, 83
2:9	78
3:6	78
3:21	199
3:22	70
4:26	79–80
5:6–7	79
5:9–11	79
6	20, 72
6:3	77
6:5	76–77
8:21	76–77
19:4–7	114
49	99
Exodus	5, 31, 38, 39, 40, 43, 59
14	143
15	143
15:17	87
19	31
24:12–18	44
30:20	27
34	31
34:29	90
Leviticus	32, 48, 239
5:1–6	235n.44
5:16	235n.44
5:21	235n.44
11	27
16	233
26:40–42	234
Numbers	175
5:5–7	235n.44
6:24–26	233
8:14	174
16:9	174
18:20	174, 247
21	168
21:18	61, 64
24:17	80, 245
Deuteronomy	32, 36–40, 43–45, 48, 55, 75, 179–180, 192
12–23	31
13:1	39, 48
17	31, 94
23:3–4	87
24	49
27	233–234
29	233
29:18	146
32:43 (LXX)	87n.1
33	87
33:5	200n.19
Judges	
4	143
5	143
5:4–5	243
19:15–23	114

1 Samuel
19:9	76

2 Samuel
7	87–90, 93, 98–99, 101
7:10–14	87
7:14	87–89

1 Kings
	119, 133
22:8	24
22:11	235
22:19	235

2 Kings
	119, 133

Isaiah
	132, 264, 266
8:11	88
9	97, 99
11	96, 99
11:1–5	94
11:4	98
24:21	243
26:3	76
26:19	209, 223
40:3	62
41	210
41:8–9	264
41:14	209, 223
42:1	264, 266
42:1–4	263
43:33–34	269
44:2	264
45:7	186, 188
49:1–7	263
49:4	264
49:4–5	264
50:4	264, 266
50:4–9	263
50:5–9	264
52:7	103
52:13–53:12	263–264
53	263, 267, 269
53:3	264, 266
53:4	270
53:10–12 (LXX)	270
53:11	266
53:11–12	269
53:12 (LXX)	269–270
55:3	88
61	14, 268
61:1	14, 266
61:1–3	264

Jeremiah
	4, 40, 124
8:8	35
31:31	169
31:33	192

Ezekiel
	58, 195
4:5	104, 120, 136
17:1–24	113
28:13–16	72
31:1–14	113
37:23	88
40–48	202
44:9	27

Hosea
9:6	128

Amos
9:11	87

Micah
1:4	97

Nahum
2:12–14	125n.20, 141n.48
2:13	125, 142

Habakkuk
1:13	143
3	243

Malachi
3	225n.43
3:16	244

Psalms
	7, 40, 105, 144
1	20, 87, 89
1–2	101
1:1	88
2	87–95, 98–101
2:1–2	88, 89
2:1–9	90
2:2	88, 90, 92, 94, 97
2:6	88, 98
2:7	87–89
2:8–9	93
2:9	89n.14
5	87
8:5	197
21	198
45:6–7	87n.1

Index of Scripture and Other Ancient Sources

48	94	9:24–27	103
51:2	239	9:25	103
51:7	239	9:26	103–104
68:7–8	243	10:21	245
72	92	11	121, 126–127
73:21	107	11–12	105, 127, 268
89	91–92	11:33	104
89:26–27	91	11:39	127
102:25–27	87n.1	11:42	105
104:4	87n.1	11:45	105
110	91n.30, 92, 96–97	12	100, 102, 110, 195, 206
110:1	87n.1	12:1	105
119	20	12:2	197
119:27	20	12:7	106n.28, 127
		12:10	102
Proverbs	8, 56, 173, 241, 245, 248, 249, 251–253	**Ezra**	
1–9	248	1	66n.69
3:18	251	2:43–54	123
7	74	7:6	24
10–31	248	7:10	24
		7:26	22
Job	241	9	24
17:16	196	10:3	24
Ecclesiastes	8, 56, 241	**Nehemiah**	
3:1	250	5	23
		7:46–56	123
Esther	1, 7	8	23, 24, 233
Daniel	15, 56–57, 96, 100, 102–107, 111–115, 121, 127, 153, 157, 160–161, 195–197, 199, 209, 211, 219, 221–222, 241, 251	8:1–8	22
		8:13–18	23
		9	235
		10	23
		10:13	24
1–11	102	10:29	200
2	97, 115	10:31–32	23
4	107, 109, 113–114	**1 Chronicles**	7, 8, 31, 119–120, 122, 133
4:3	112		
4:30	107	5:27–41	122
4:31	112	29:18	76
5:21	107	**2 Chronicles**	7, 8, 31, 119–120, 122, 133
7	95, 97, 100–101, 112, 114–115		
		28:27–29:3	119
7–12	104	34:19	235
7:9–10	114	34:27	235
7:14	112		
7:25	161n.55		
7:27	112		
9	66, 102, 110, 124, 136		

APOCRYPHA

1 Maccabees	120, 133, 152–153
1:20–28	127
1:56	29
2:21	58
2:27	29
2:40–41	29
2:42	153
2:44–47	30
7:12–13	153
16:16	146n.71, 146n.78
2 Maccabees	133, 152–153
2:13–16	52
4:9–11	28
4:33–38	103n.10
5:11	28
6:1	28
6:7	161n.55
7	196, 214, 220
14:6	153n.14
Ben Sira	7, 56, 58, 71n.8, 73–76, 81, 83–84, 170–171, 173, 191, 241, 245, 248–253
Prologue	7
15:11–20	75
15:14	76n.25, 191n.55
17	77
17:1–7	184
17:1–12	74–75
24:23	20
25:24	73
33:7–13	251
33:10–13	76, 170n.22, 184
33:12	85
33:14–15	251
33:15	85
39:27	78
41:4	75
49:14	75
49:16	80
Tobit	58
Wisdom of Solomon	
2–5	268
2:13	98
2:16	98
2:24	70n.5
5:15–16	197

NEW TESTAMENT

Matthew	
3:2	237
3:16–17	89
5:5	193
8:17	270
11	14
Mark	37
1:4	237
1:10–11	89n.12
2:7	108
7:5	65
9:31	269
10:45	270
12:25	204
14–15	270
14:24	270
15:28	270
Luke	13, 14, 37
1:32	100
1:35	100
2:14	244
3:3	237
3:21–22	89n.12
4:18	14
5:21	108
22:19	270n.61
Acts	
8:32–33	269–270
13:33–34	88, 89n.13
Romans	
4:25	269
8:29	95
11:25	193
11:26	193
1 Corinthians	
7:29–31	249
2 Corinthians	
5:4	197
1 Timothy	
2:13–14	73

Index of Scripture and Other Ancient Sources

Hebrews	15, 87, 89	12:23	266
1	88	12:24–25	206
9:28	269	12:27	266
		13:15	266
1 Peter		13:28	266
2:22–25	269	14	224
5:4		14:29–33	224
		14:34	209, 223
Revelation	157	15:6–7	264, 266
2:10	197	15:10	266
3:5	197	15:16	266
3:11	197n.10	16	266
12:5	89n.14	16:26–27	266
12:9	70n.5	16:35–36	266
19:15	89n.14	17:11	266
		19	209, 210n.62, 224
DEAD SEA SCROLLS		19:3–14	206
1QH	13, 50, 134–136,	19:10–14	223
	140–141, 143–145,	19:12	209
	148–149, 172, 180,	25:35–26:10	207n.50, 266n.46
	203, 205–209,	27:25	197
	223–224, 247–248,		
	253, 264–268, 270	**1QIsa**[a]	268
4:14–15	198	**1QM (War Scroll)**	9, 15, 105–106, 150,
4:25	81		180–181, 183, 190,
5	172		192, 203, 208
5:19–20	81	1:2	105
5:23	197n.9	1:4	105
5:24	264	1:6	105
5:29	210n.63, 224n.42	1:11–12	105
6:25	264	11:6	80
7:7	207	17:7	100, 105
9:1–18:14	140		
9:25	79	**1QMysteries**	185, 205
10–17	105	**1QpHab**	9, 123, 143–144,
10:15–16	143		146n.73, 147–148
10:31	143	2:1–6	144n.65
10:31–32	143	2:3	180
11	99, 201, 224	2:7–10	62
11:19–21	199, 206	6:12–7:8	123
11:19–36	224	7:1–5	61
11:23–25	206	7:3–5	124
12:5–13:4	210	7:7	147
12:8	266	8:10	147
12:9–10	143	8:16	145
12:10	143	9:2	146n.76
12:11–12	140	9:4–7	148
12:18	50	9:10	146
12:22–23	198	9:10–11	146n.77

11:5	143	4:20–21	238
11:12–15	145	4:22–23	198
		4:23	84, 184, 221

1QS (Manual of Discipline)

	2, 3, 9, 53, 55, 65, 80,	4:23–26	183
	104, 132, 150–152,	4:24	190n.48, 245
	155, 158–159, 161,	4:26	184n.22
	164–172, 179–183,	5	167, 188
	186n.30, 187–189,	5:1–3	167n.12
	192–193, 200–201,	5:5	83
	203–205, 220–222,	5:7–8	236
	226, 231, 235, 239,	5:7–9	55
	247, 252, 258	5:8–9	181
		5:13	237
1:16–3:12	233–234	5:22	167, 181
1:16–3:13	190	6	65, 235, 237
1:23	233	6:2	158
1:24–25	239	6:3	3, 158
2:3–4	233	6:3–7	231
2:11–17	190	6:6	3
2:19	234	6:6–7	2, 63
2:19–22	234	6:13–15	63
3	245	6:24–25	237
3–4	170	8	159, 166, 175, 201
3:4–5	235	8:3	83
3:6–9	235	8:4–7	232
3:7–9	238	8:5–6	201
3:13–15	182	8:11–12	158
3:13–18	172	8:12–16	62
3:13–4:26	83–86	8:13–14	158
3:15	205	8:15	19
3:15–18	182	9:3–5	201, 232
3:15–21	83	9:3–6	201
3:15–23	182	10–11	231
3:17	245	10:5–11:22	231
3:18	221	11:2–7	204
3:18–25	183	11:3	197
3:18–4:1	182	11:7–8	199–200
4	199	11:8	224
4:2–14	182		
4:4–6	190	**1QSa**	203, 245
4:5	83	1:1–2	180
4:6–8	197, 220	1:6–8	79
4:11–14	220	2:3–9	204
4:12	221	2:11–12	99
4:15–16	190n.48		
4:15–23	183	**1QSb**	104, 203
4:15–26	172, 182		
4:18	221	**1Q27**	
4:18–19	221	See *1QMysteries*	

Index of Scripture and Other Ancient Sources

4QD[a]	
See 4Q266	
4QDan[a]	102
4QDan[b]	102
4QDan[c]	102
4QDan[e]	102
4QFlorilegium	
See 4Q174	
4QInstruction	20, 56, 78, 80–81, 84–85, 162, 166, 171–176, 183n.17, 184–185, 205, 242–253
See also 4Q416–418	
4QJer[a]	4
4QJer[b]	4
4QJer[d]	4
4QMMT	2, 6, 9–11, 15, 19, 33, 34, 43, 53, 55, 68, 145, 147, 164, 166, 169, 180, 194, 234, 239n.65, 262
B 21–22	27
B 58	27
C 10	7n.18, 19n.2, 55n.27, 170n.20
C 27–28	145
C 27	145
4QNum[b]	4
4QpaleoExod[m]	4
4QpHos[b]	
2 2–4	125n.23, 142n.52
4QpNah	105n.19, 125, 141
4QpPs[a]	11, 68, 144
3:1–2	198
3:15	154
1–10 4:8–9	68
3–10 2	147
3–10 4:8–9	145
3–10 4:10	146

4QQoh[a]	53
4QReworked Pentateuch	6, 40, 42, 43
4QS[c]	188
4QS[d]	188
4QS[e]	188
4QSam[a]	4
4QTestimonia	87n.2
4Q114	
See 4QDan[c]	
4Q116	
See 4QDan[e]	
4Q118	119
4Q158	40, 41n.34
4Q169	
3–4 i 1–2	125n.20, 141n.48
3–4 i 3	125, 142
3–4 i 5	125, 142
4Q171	
See 4QpPs[a]	
4Q174	87–90, 100–102, 104
1:6	201
1–2 i 11–12	138
4	90
4Q175	
13	80
4Q180	244
4Q181	244
4Q184	74
4Q186	183, 190
4Q199	
1	171n.29
4Q216	33, 44
4Q242	
See Prayer of Nabonidus	

4Q243	106, 109–111, 114, 121, 134	4Q390	110, 121, 134
2	111	4Q400	
16	110	See also Songs of the Sabbath Sacrifice	
4Q244	106, 109–111, 114, 121, 134	1	202
		4Q402	
4Q245	57, 106, 109–111, 114, 121–123, 134, 223n.40	4 12–15	191n.52
		4Q406	
4Q246	13, 57n.32, 100–101, 106, 111–112, 115	1 1–2	191n.52
		4Q414	237
1	112	4Q416	243, 251
2:3	112	1	242
2:5	112	1 10–13	81
2:9	112	1 10–16	243n.14
		1 i 15–16	79
4Q248	106n.28, 126, 134	2 iii 6–8	246
4Q252	99	2 iii 11–12	248
4Q266	191n.53, 192	2 iii 15–17	249
		2 iv 7–9	249
		3	242, 244n.17
4Q303	77		
		4Q417	175, 245
4Q322a	131, 134	See also 4QInstruction	
4Q329		1	172–174, 243
8:9	129	1 i	244
		1 i 6–8	242
4Q331	128–129, 131, 134	1 i 11	79
1 i	129	1 i 14–18	185
1 ii	129	1 i 16–18	79
		2 i 9–19	249
4Q332	119, 128–129, 131, 134	2 i 11	246
4Q333	119, 128–129, 131, 134	2 i 17	171n.29
		2 i 22–23	249
4Q339	122	2 ii 12–13	78
4Q340	123	4Q418	
4Q364	40, 41	See also 4QInstruction	
4Q365	40, 41	2	243n.13
		43–45	244n.19
4Q366	40	43–45 6	80n.41
4Q367	40	55	246n.27
		69 ii	174
4Q369	257n.1	69 ii 7	246
		69 10	245
4Q385	223	81	174, 176
4Q386	128	81 1–2	80n.41, 81, 246
2	128	81 3–5	247
		81 4	175

Index of Scripture and Other Ancient Sources 325

81 10	175n.51, 244	35	49
81 13	175	44:5	47
126 ii 7–8	246	50–66	49
4Q422	77	50:5–9	48
		50:17	48
4Q423	78	51:6	47
4Q427		54:5–7	48
7	207	56:20–21	47
		57:1	47
4Q448	2	59–66	32
4Q453–459	185	59:7–10	47
4Q468e	119, 131, 134	**11QMelchizedek**	
		See 11Q13	
4Q468f	134	**Aramaic Levi Document**	43, 56
4Q471b	207	**Book of Giants**	56–57, 114
4Q489	114	**Damascus Document (CD)**	
4Q491c	207–208		2, 3, 5, 10, 33, 55, 61,
2	208		62, 110, 120, 134–141,
4Q502	190		144–145, 148, 150, 152–161, 163–165,
4Q503	231		168–172, 176, 179, 181,
4Q504	77, 223n.40		191–192, 200–201,
8 4–6	198		204, 221, 231, 239n.65, 245, 247, 252
4Q512	237	1	61, 137, 146–147, 153, 160, 168, 170, 176
4Q521	14, 222	1–6	145
4Q524	32	1:1–6:7	136
4Q525	20, 253	1:3–11	120
		1:5–6	104
4Q540	57n.32, 267	1:8–9	181, 235
4Q541	57n.32, 267, 269–270	1:10	104
4Q544		1:14–15	137
2 13	186	1:15	50, 138
		1:18	137
4Q548	186n.30	2	170, 253
4Q551	113	2:2–13	191
		2:3–13	221
4Q552–553	106, 112, 115	2:5	239
4Q578	134	2:7–8	170
		2:18	252
11Q13	101–104, 134, 186	3:12–13	168
2:18	103	3:12–15	60, 180–181
11Q19 (Temple Scroll)		3:12–16	19
	5, 8, 10, 31–34, 41–44, 47–50, 59–60, 262	3:20	198, 221
		4	10
		4:2	239

4:3–4	64n.60	**Hodayot**	
4:10–11	169	*See 1QH*	
4:18	201		
5:17–19	191	**Mas1k**	
6	10, 64, 139n.33, 168	i 1–7	191n.52
6:3–10	61	**Pesher Nahum**	
6:4	19	*See 4Q169*	
6:7	138–139		
6:10–11	155	**Prayer of Nabonidus**	
6:11	61n.45, 65		106–109, 114
6:19	169, 180	1:3	109
7:4–8	160	1:3–4	107–108
7:5–6	198n.14, 204	1:7	108
7:5–8	159	1:8	108
7:6	3, 231, 253	**Pseudo-Daniel**	8, 106, 109–111, 114,
7:18	138		121–122, 126–127
7:21	80	*See also 4Q243–245*	
8:3–4	221		
8:16	169	**Pseudo-Ezekiel**	9, 128
8:21	169, 180	*See also 4Q385 & 4Q386*	
10:6	79		
13:2	79	**Pseudo-Jeremiah**	9, 121
13:2–3	64	**Pseudo-Moses**	
13:10	108n.39	*See 4Q390*	
14:13	200		
15	235	**Songs of the Sabbath Sacrifice**	
15:5	180		190, 202–204,
15:5–6	55, 169		208–209
15:8–9	180	**Testament of Amram**	
15:12	55, 200		56, 173, 185–187,
16:3–4	252		223n.40
19:33–34	169	*See also 4Q453–459*	
20:6–7	63		
20:11	138	**Testament of Qahat**	
20:12	180		223n.40
20:14	136n.19, 147	**Community Rule**	
20:14–15	104, 137	*See 1QS*	
20:15	50, 138		
20:28–30	235	**Damascus Rule**	
20:31–32	61	*See Damascus Document (CD)*	

Florilegium
See 4Q174

Four Kingdoms Text
See 4Q552–553

Genesis Apocryphon
    5, 42–43, 57

GREEK AND LATIN TEXTS

Andokides
1.83   25

Cicero
Consolatio ad Marciam
26.6   225n.45

Index of Scripture and Other Ancient Sources

Diodorus Siculus
Bibliotheca Historica
40.3 (6)   26n.41, 55n.25

Eusebius   258
Ecc. Hist.
2.16   258
Praep. Ev.
8.6–7   3n.7

Hippolytus   212–217, 222, 224–226
Chronicle   214
Refutatio Omnium Haeresium
    215
9.27   213
9.28.5   215
9.30.8   215
10.34   216
26   214

Iamblichus
De Vita Pythagorica
198   37

Josephus   8, 151–152, 155, 157,
    159–160, 201,
    212–220, 222,
    225–226, 237,
    257–258

Against Apion
1.29   52n.11
1.31   53n.12
1.39   8
2.218   218
Antiquities   42, 43
1.70   225n.48
3.1.7 (38)   52n.10
5.1.7 (61)   52n.10
5.361–362   122n.7
6.68–9   4
11.338   25n.32
12.142   25, 55n.26
12.145–6   26
12.278   30
13.228   146n.78
13.245   30
13.257–8   30
13.297–8   65n.66
13.317   217
13.318–9   30
13.372–416   125n.21, 142n.49
13.379–383   126, 142n.54
13.398   146
13.400   30
13.405–432   146n.80
13.408–409   11, 30, 147
18.13   191n.57
18.18   212, 219
18.116–119   238
Jewish War   213
1.84   217
1.107–119   146n.80
2   213, 219, 222
2.124   3
2.129   237
2.150–151   214
2.151–153   214
2.154–155   212
2.154–158   214
2.160   151n.7, 155n.29, 213
2.163   191n.57, 218
3   218
3.372   218
3.374–375   218
7.150   53
7.162   53
7.343–346   217
Life of Flavius Josephus
9–11   152n.11
418   53

Justin
Apol.
20.1   225n.47

Lactantius
Div. Inst.
7.21   225n.47

Philo   151–152, 155, 157, 159,
    201, 217, 219
Allegorical Interpretation
31   82n.46
De Opificio Mundi
134–135   82n.46
Questions on Genesis
1:8   82n.47
Quod Omnis Probus Liber Sit
75–76   3n.7
75–91   219n.29

Hypothetica		48:10	93, 96
1–2	3n.7	49:1–4	96
11.1–8	219n.29	51:3	96
Pliny the Elder	151, 157, 201, 217, 258	53:4	97
		55:4	96
Plutarch	186–187	60:4–5	95
Isis and Osiris		61:8	96
47	187	62:2	96
		62:7	96
Porphyry		62:15–16	197
De Abstinentia 4.6	26n.43	69:14	95
Pseudo-Philo		69:29	96
Biblical Antiquities	42	70–72	95
		71:3	95
Seneca		71:8	95
Nat Quaest		71:9	95
3.29.1	225n.45	71:13	95
		71:14	95
Tertullian		73–82	241
Adversus Marcionem		90:10	222
6.5	37n.14	91:12	244
De Baptismo		91:17	244
17	37n.13	93:2	245
		104:2–6	195
Thucydides			
8.76.6	25	**2 Enoch**	196
		22:8	196
PSEUDEPIGRAPHA			
		2 Baruch	
1 Enoch	7, 8, 15, 20, 32, 56–59,	48:42	85
	71n.8, 72–73, 84–85,	51:3	198
	98, 101, 106, 110, 112,		
	121, 150, 152–153,	**3 Baruch**	
	156, 159–163,	4:16	199n.16
	175–176, 195–197,		
	199, 204, 209, 211,	**4 Ezra**	8, 76, 97–98, 101, 157,
	241, 243–244,		257
	251–252, 257, 259	7:28	98
1	243	7:29	98
1–5	162n.57	12	97
1–36	72	12:11	97
15–16	160	12:32	98
22	222	13	93, 97–98, 112
25:3–6	72	13:32	98
32	72	13:37	98
37	95		
38–69	95	**Apocalypse of Abraham**	
46	95	13:14	196
46:1	95		
48:2–3	96	**Jubilees**	5, 8, 10, 20, 31–34,
48:6	96		40–50, 56, 59–62, 68,
			72–73, 80, 152,

Index of Scripture and Other Ancient Sources 329

	156–157, 159, 162, 196, 252	**Testaments of the Twelve Patriarchs**	157
1:26	45	**Testament of Levi**	
1:27	59	4:2	93
2:1	59		
2:17–21	73	**Testament of Moses**	45
4:19	47	**Vision of Gabriel**	13
6:20–22	31, 45		
8:11	47n.64	**RABBINIC TEXTS**	
10:7–11	73n.17	**m. Aboth**	
10:13	47n.64	1:1	65
21:10	47n.64	3:16	191n.58
23:9–32	33		
23:30–31	219	**m. Qidd.**	
23:31	196, 247n.35	4:1	123
30:12	31, 45		
48–49	47n.63	**m. Sanhedrin**	
		10:1	180
Psalms of Solomon	93–95, 257	**b. Berakot**	
2	128	9b	88n.10
7:5–7	93		
7:32	94	**Genesis Rabbah**	
17	93–94, 98, 101	14:3	82n.48
17:11	93	14:4	76n.24
17:21	93	20:12	199
17:27	94	23:6	81
17:33	94		
17:34	94	**Deuteronomy Rabbah**	
18:7	94n.41	11:3	199n.16
Pseudo-Aristeas		**PERSIAN SOURCES**	
30	26	**Bundahishn**	
Sibylline Oracles	225	30.19	225
3:664–668	93	**Yasna**	
4:163–169	238	30	187n.34
4:171–178	225n.46		

www.ingramcontent.com/pod-product-compliance
Lightning Source LLC
Chambersburg PA
CBHW020752020526
44116CB00028B/119